STANDARD HISTORICAL WORKS.

By JAMES A. FROUDE.

THE HISTORY OF ENGLAND, from the Fall of Wolsey to the Defeat of the Spanish Armada. 12 vols. Crown 8vo, 3s. 6d. each.

THE DIVORCE OF CATHERINE OF ARAGON. Crown 8vo, 3s. 6d.

THE SPANISH STORY OF THE ARMADA, and other Essays. Crown 8vo, 3s. 6d.

ENGLISH SEAMEN IN THE SIXTEENTH CENTURY. Crown 8vo, 3s. 6d. Illustrated Edition. With 5 Photogravures and 16 other Illustrations. Large crown 8vo, 6s. net.

THE ENGLISH IN IRELAND IN THE EIGHTEENTH CENTURY. 3 vols. Crown 8vo, 10s. 6d.

SHORT STUDIES ON GREAT SUBJECTS. 4 vols. Crown 8vo, 3s. 6d. each. Pocket Edition. 5 vols. Fcp. 8vo, cloth, 2s. net each; leather, 3s. net each.

THE COUNCIL OF TRENT. Crown 8vo, 3s. 6d.

LIFE AND LETTERS OF ERASMUS. Crown 8vo, 3s. 6d.

CÆSAR: a Sketch. Crown 8vo, 3s. 6d.

By WILLIAM EDWARD HARTPOLE LECKY.

HISTORY OF ENGLAND IN THE EIGHTEENTH CENTURY.
Library Edition. 8 vols. 8vo. Vols. I. and II., 36s. Vols. III. and IV., 36s. Vols. V. and VI., 36s. Vols. VII. and VIII., 36s.
Cabinet Edition. ENGLAND. 7 vols. Crown 8vo, 5s. net each. IRELAND. 5 vols. Crown 8vo, 5s. net each.

LEADERS OF PUBLIC OPINION IN IRELAND: FLOOD, GRATTAN, O'CONNELL. 2 vols. 8vo, 25s. net.

HISTORY OF EUROPEAN MORALS FROM AUGUSTUS TO CHARLEMAGNE. 2 vols. Crown 8vo, 10s. net.

HISTORY OF THE RISE AND INFLUENCE OF THE SPIRIT OF RATIONALISM IN EUROPE. 2 vols. Crown 8vo, 10s. net. *Popular Edition. In One Volume.* Crown 8vo, 2s. 6d. net.

DEMOCRACY AND LIBERTY.
Library Edition. 2 vols. 8vo, 36s. | Cabinet Edition. 2 vols. Crown 8vo, 10s. net.

HISTORICAL AND POLITICAL ESSAYS. 8vo, 10s. 6d. net.

By MANDELL CREIGHTON, D.D., LL.D.

HISTORY OF THE PAPACY FROM THE GREAT SCHISM TO THE SACK OF ROME (1378-1527). 6 vols. Crown 8vo, 5s. net each.

HISTORICAL ESSAYS AND REVIEWS. Crown 8vo, 5s. net.

HISTORICAL LECTURES AND ADDRESSES. Crown 8vo, 5s. net.

QUEEN ELIZABETH. With Portrait. Crown 8vo, 5s. net.

A HISTORY OF ENGLAND. By J. FRANCK BRIGHT, D.D. Crown 8vo.
Period I.—MEDIÆVAL MONARCHY: the Departure of the Romans to Richard III. From A.D. 449 to 1485. 4s. 6d.
Period II.—PERSONAL MONARCHY: Henry VII. to James II. From 1485 to 1688. 5s.
Period III.—CONSTITUTIONAL MONARCHY: William and Mary to William IV. From 1689 to 1837. 7s. 6d.
Period IV—THE GROWTH OF DEMOCRACY: Victoria. From 1837 to 1880. 6s.
Period V.—IMPERIAL REACTION: Victoria. From 1880 to 1901. 4s. 6d.

HISTORY OF CIVILISATION IN ENGLAND AND FRANCE, SPAIN AND SCOTLAND. By HENRY THOMAS BUCKLE. 3 vols. Crown 8vo, 10s. 6d.

THE HISTORICAL GEOGRAPHY OF EUROPE. By EDWARD A. FREEMAN, D.C.L., LL.D. 8vo, 12s. 6d.
ATLAS to the above. With 65 Maps in Colour. 8vo, 6s. 6d.

LONGMANS, GREEN, AND CO., 39 Paternoster Row, London, E.C.;
New York, Bombay, and Calcutta.

STANDARD HISTORICAL WORKS.

By LORD MACAULAY.

COMPLETE WORKS OF LORD MACAULAY.
Cabinet Edition. 16 vols. Post 8vo, £4 16s.
"Albany" Edition. 12 vols. With 12 Portraits. Large crown 8vo, 3s. 6d. each.
"Edinburgh" Edition. 8 vols. 8vo, 6s. each.

HISTORY OF ENGLAND FROM THE ACCESSION OF JAMES THE SECOND.
Popular Edition. 2 vols. Crown 8vo, 5s. | "Albany" Edition. 6 vols. Large crown
Student's Edition. 2 vols. Crown 8vo, | 8vo, 3s. 6d. each.
12s. | "Edinburgh" Edition. 4 vols. 8vo, 6s. each.
Cabinet Edition. 8 vols. Post 8vo, 48s. | Library Edition. 5 vols. 8vo, £4.

CRITICAL AND HISTORICAL ESSAYS, with LAYS OF ANCIENT ROME. In 1 volume.
Popular Edition. Crown 8vo, 2s. 6d. | "Silver Library" Edition. Cr. 8vo, 3s. 6d.

CRITICAL AND HISTORICAL ESSAYS.
Student's Edition. 1 vol. Crown 8vo, 6s. | "Edinburgh" Edition. 3 vols. 8vo, 6s. each.
"Trevelyan" Edition. 2 vols. Cr. 8vo, 9s. | Cabinet Edition. 4 vols. Post 8vo, 24s.
Library Edition. 3 vols. 8vo, 36s.

THE AMERICAN REVOLUTION. By the Right Hon. Sir G. O. TREVELYAN, Bart. Vols.
I., II., III. Crown 8vo, 5s. net each.

By GEORGE MACAULAY TREVELYAN.

ENGLAND IN THE AGE OF WYCLIFFE. Crown 8vo, 6s. net.
GARIBALDI'S DEFENCE OF THE ROMAN REPUBLIC. With 7 Maps and 35 Illustrations. 8vo, 6s. 6d. net.
GARIBALDI AND THE THOUSAND. With 5 Maps and numerous Illustrations. 8vo, 7s. 6d. net.

By SAMUEL RAWSON GARDINER, D.C.L.

HISTORY OF ENGLAND, from the Accession of James I. to the Outbreak of the Civil War, 1603-1642. 10 vols. Crown 8vo, 5s. net each.
HISTORY OF THE GREAT CIVIL WAR, 1642-1649. 4 vols. Crown 8vo, 5s. net each.
HISTORY OF THE COMMONWEALTH AND PROTECTORATE, 1649-1656. 4 vols. Crown 8vo, 5s. net each.
THE STUDENT'S HISTORY OF ENGLAND. 378 Illustrations. Crown 8vo, 12s.
CROMWELL'S PLACE IN HISTORY. Crown 8vo, 3s. 6d.
OLIVER CROMWELL. With Frontispiece. Crown 8vo, 5s. net.

THE LAST YEARS OF THE PROTECTORATE. By C. H. FIRTH, M.A., LL.D. Vols.
I. and II., 1656-1658. With Plans. 8vo, 24s. net.
This work is a continuation of the "History of the Commonwealth and Protectorate," undertaken and left unfinished by Dr. S. R. Gardiner.

By W. STUBBS, D.D., LATE BISHOP OF OXFORD.

HISTORICAL INTRODUCTIONS TO THE ROLLS SERIES. 8vo, 12s. 6d. net.
LECTURES ON EUROPEAN HISTORY. 8vo, 12s. 6d. net.
LECTURES ON EARLY ENGLISH HISTORY. 8vo, 12s. 6d. net.
GERMANY IN THE EARLY MIDDLE AGES, 476-1250. With 2 Maps. 8vo, 6s. net.
GERMANY IN THE LATER MIDDLE AGES, 1200-1500. With 2 Maps. 8vo, 7s. 6d. net.

LONGMANS, GREEN, AND CO., 39 Paternoster Row, London, E.C.;
New York, Bombay, and Calcutta.

THE POLITICAL HISTORY OF ENGLAND

Seventy-five years have passed since Lingard completed his HISTORY OF ENGLAND, which ends with the Revolution of 1688. During that period historical study has made a great advance. Year after year the mass of materials for a new History of England has increased; new lights have been thrown on events and characters, and old errors have been corrected. Many notable works have been written on various periods of our history; some of them at such length as to appeal almost exclusively to professed historical students. It is believed that the time has come when the advance which has been made in the knowledge of English history as a whole should be laid before the public in a single work of fairly adequate size. Such a book should be founded on independent thought and research, but should at the same time be written with a full knowledge of the works of the best modern historians and with a desire to take advantage of their teaching wherever it appears sound.

The vast number of authorities, printed and in manuscript, on which a History of England should be based, if it is to represent the existing state of knowledge, renders co-operation almost necessary and certainly advisable. The History, of which this volume is an instalment, is an attempt to set forth in a readable form the results at present attained by research. It will consist of twelve volumes by twelve different writers, each *of them chosen as being specially capable of dealing with the period which he undertakes, and the editors, while leaving to each author as free a hand as possible, hope to insure a general similarity in method of treatment, so that the twelve volumes may in their contents, as well as in their outward appearance, form one History.*

As its title imports, this History will primarily deal with politics, with the History of England and, after the date of the union with Scotland, Great Britain, as a state or body politic; but as the life of a nation is complex, and its condition at any given time cannot be understood without taking into account the various forces acting upon it, notices of religious matters and of intellectual, social, and economic progress will also find place in these volumes. The footnotes will, so far as is possible, be confined to references to authorities, and references will not be appended to statements which appear to be matters of common knowledge and do not call for support. Each volume will have an Appendix giving some account of the chief authorities, original and secondary, which the author has used. This account will be compiled with a view of helping students rather than of making long lists of books without any notes as to their contents or value. That the History will have faults both of its own and such as will always in some measure attend co-operative work, must be expected, but no pains have been spared to make it, so far as may be, not wholly unworthy of the greatness of its subject.

Each volume, while forming part of a complete History, will also in itself be a separate and complete book, will be sold separately, and will have its own index, and two or more maps.

The History is divided as follows:—

Vol. I. FROM THE EARLIEST TIMES TO THE NORMAN CONQUEST (to 1066). By Thomas Hodgkin, D.C.L., Litt.D., Fellow of University College, London; Fellow of the British Academy. With 2 Maps.

Vol. II. FROM THE NORMAN CONQUEST TO THE DEATH OF JOHN (1066-1216). By George Burton Adams, Professor of History in Yale University. With 2 Maps.

Vol. III. FROM THE ACCESSION OF HENRY III. TO THE DEATH OF EDWARD III. (1216-1377). By T. F. Tout, M.A., Professor of Mediæval and Modern History in the University of Manchester; formerly Fellow of Pembroke College, Oxford. With 3 Maps.

Vol. IV. FROM THE ACCESSION OF RICHARD II. TO THE DEATH OF RICHARD III. (1377-1485). By C. Oman, M.A., Chichele Professor of Modern History in the University of Oxford; Fellow of the British Academy. With 3 Maps.

Vol. V. FROM THE ACCESSION OF HENRY VII. TO THE DEATH OF HENRY VIII. (1485-1547). By H. A. L. Fisher, M.A., Fellow and Tutor of New College, Oxford; Fellow of the British Academy. With 2 Maps.

Vol. VI. FROM THE ACCESSION OF EDWARD VI. TO THE DEATH OF ELIZABETH (1547-1603). By A. F. Pollard, M.A., Fellow of All Souls' College, Oxford, and Professor of English History in the University of London. With 2 Maps.

Vol. VII. FROM THE ACCESSION OF JAMES I. TO THE RESTORATION (1603-1660). By F. C. Montague, M.A., Astor Professor of History in University College, London; formerly Fellow of Oriel College, Oxford. With 3 Maps.

[Continued on next page.

The Political History of England

IN TWELVE VOLUMES

EDITED BY WILLIAM HUNT, D.LITT., AND
REGINALD L. POOLE, M.A., LL.D.

VI.

THE HISTORY OF ENGLAND

FROM THE ACCESSION OF EDWARD VI.

TO THE DEATH OF ELIZABETH

(1547-1603)

THE

HISTORY OF ENGLAND

FROM THE ACCESSION OF EDWARD VI.
TO THE DEATH OF ELIZABETH

(1547-1603)

BY

A. F. POLLARD, M.A.

FELLOW OF ALL SOULS' COLLEGE, OXFORD
PROFESSOR OF ENGLISH HISTORY IN THE UNIVERSITY OF LONDON

LONGMANS, GREEN, AND CO.
39 PATERNOSTER ROW, LONDON
NEW YORK, BOMBAY, AND CALCUTTA
1910

CONTENTS.

CHAPTER I.

THE PROTECTORATE.

CHAPTER II.

A YEAR OF TROUBLES.

CHAPTER III.

SOMERSET AND WARWICK.

CHAPTER IV.

THE PROTESTANT REFORMATION.

CHAPTER VII.

The Restoration of the Church.

CHAPTER VIII.

THE PROTESTANT MARTYRS.

CHAPTER IX.

PHILIP AND MARY.

CHAPTER XII.

ENGLAND AND SCOTLAND.

CHAPTER XIII.

THE RIVAL QUEENS.

CHAPTER XIV.

THE FALL OF MARY.

CHAPTER XV.

THE CRISIS OF ELIZABETH'S REIGN.

CHAPTER XVI.

THE EXPANSION OF ENGLAND.

CHAPTER XIX.

CHURCH AND STATE.

CHAPTER XX.

PLOT AND COUNTERPLOT.

CHAPTER XXI.

THE ARBITRAMENT OF WAR.

CHAPTER XXII.

The Conquest of Ireland.

CHAPTER XXIII.

THE AGE OF SHAKESPEARE.

CHAPTER XXIV.

THE LAST YEARS OF ELIZABETH.

APPENDIX I.—ON AUTHORITIES.

APPENDIX II.—GENEALOGIES.

(i.) The Tudors and their Rivals.
(ii.) Queen Elizabeth's kinsfolk.
(iii.) The Stuart and Suffolk lines.

MAPS.

(AT THE END OF THE VOLUME.)

1. The war with Spain, 1587-1603.
2. The principal navigations of Elizabethan seamen.

ERRATUM.

Page 252, 8 lines from foot of text, *for* " Paul V. " *read* " Pius V.".

CHAPTER I.

THE PROTECTORATE.

THE death of Henry VIII. put the Tudor despotism to its severest test, a royal minority. Active control of the work of government by the sovereign was the essence of the English constitution throughout the middle ages; and the absence of this control during the early years of Henry III., Richard II., Henry VI., and Edward V. had in each case led to faction, lack of governance, and civil strife. Sixty-two years of Tudor monarchy had not impaired the constitutional importance of the monarch, and the privy council without the king was as unfinished an administrative machine as a modern cabinet without a premier; without the keystone of the arch stability was impossible. The troubles of the reign of Edward VI. must therefore be ascribed in the first place not to the feebleness or folly of this or that statesman, nor to the policy which he adopted, but to a constitutional system that required a ruler, crowned and actual, to make it work.

Both the policy and the *personnel* of the new government had been foreshadowed during the closing months of the preceding reign. In June, 1546, while the Earl of Hertford and Viscount Lisle were absent in France, the catholic party struck its last blow in Henry's lifetime at reform. But its efforts to implicate the queen, Hertford, and others in Anne Askew's fate were foiled; and the return of Hertford and Lisle to England was followed by the overthrow of the conservatives and the initiation of various schemes for further change. We have Cranmer's word for it that Henry VIII., in September, 1546, was meditating the transformation of the mass into a communion; and in December, Hooper was rejoicing at Strassburg over the news that, if Charles V. were defeated by the Lutherans, there would "be a change of religion in England,

I

and the king would take up the gospel of Christ". The imperial ambassador in London, Van der Delft, noted the symptoms with alarm. The people at large were, he thought, to
a great extent in favour of Hertford's and Lisle's religious
views, and the majority wanted to get rid of the bishops. The
heresy prosecutions had ceased ; some "strange acts and constitutions" would probably be passed in the approaching parliament ; and the understanding between England and Charles
V. was in danger. The French ambassador wrote in January,
1547, that while many councillors were opposed to it, Henry
VIII. himself was inclined to a French alliance.

The experienced Chapuys was consulted as to the possibility of averting these evils. Before his report, which is dated
from Louvain, January 29, 1547, was written, Van der Delft
had to record the fall of the Howards and the desertion of
other conservatives, probably Wriothesley, St. John, and Paget,
to the side of Hertford and Lisle. Nor could Chapuys give
the emperor much comfort : the queen, he thought, would not
have declared so openly in favour of the reformers unless she
had been sure of the king ; no exhortations would have any
effect on Henry VIII. ; none of the councillors would be likely
to attempt anything against Hertford and Lisle ; even Gardiner
in 1545 had only been saved from the Tower by Norfolk's
intervention ; and there was no counteracting influence amongst
the secular nobility. "It is therefore to be feared that in this
coming parliament the bishops will be divested of their property and authority, and will henceforward receive nothing but
certain pensions from the king's coffers. . . . Hertford and Lisle
will probably have the management of affairs, because, apart
from the king's affection for them, there are no other nobles of
a fit age and ability for the task. . . . The best and quickest
cure that can be adopted is to leave the evil untouched to
avoid irritating it further." [1]

The domestic rivals of Hertford and Lisle lost the patience
which Chapuys successfully impressed upon Charles V. ; and
the swelling triumph of the new men with the New Learning
hurried the hasty Surrey into resentment, which involved himself and his more cautious father Norfolk in ruin. "Nor,"

---

[1] *Calendar of State Papers, Spanish*, 1545-46, pp. 555-58; *cf.* Bergenroth's
transcripts in Brit. Mus., Add. MSS., 28595-7.

wrote a protestant to Bullinger from Strassburg on the last
day of 1546, "is any one wanting, but [the bishop of] Winchester alone; and unless he also be caught, the evangelical
truth cannot be restored." Gardiner himself had in November
come into violent conflict with Lisle; and although he continued to attend the privy council to the end of Henry's reign,
he was not included in the list of executors of his will and
councillors to his son which the old king revised at Christmas.
The equilibrium between conservatives and reformers, which
Henry is thought to have contemplated, had no real existence ;
and while he may have recommended Hertford, as the earl told
the French ambassador, to leave things as they were during
Edward's minority, he can hardly have wished to saddle his
son with a council divided equally against itself.

That his own mind was moving in the direction of further
change is clear. It is difficult to account in any other way for the
facts that he selected three such reformers as Sir John Cheke, Sir
Anthony Cooke, and Dr. Richard Coxe as tutors for his son, and
that no catholic capable of stemming the tide was found in the
new government. The lord chancellor, Wriothesley, originally
one of Cromwell's creatures, had latterly signalised himself by
zeal against heretics ; but his past was against him, and, though
capable enough, he was not really trusted by any one. Tunstall
was a sincere and respected conservative, but he lacked vigour
and force. St. John, afterwards Earl of Wiltshire and Marquis
of Winchester, was, as he explained himself, sprung from the
willow and not from the oak ; and, though his bent was towards
catholicism, he always bowed to the national religion. Paget
and Dr. Nicholas Wotton were of the same pliant disposition ;
Thirlby, Bishop of Westminster, who was Gardiner's henchman,
shared his exclusion ; while Bonner had not been a member of
Henry's privy council. Nine others disappeared from the list
of executors nominated in his will, and were reduced to the rank
of assistants, who were only to be consulted when their superiors
chose.

The rest of the council were committed by inclination or
by interest to the New Learning. Cranmer and Hertford were
honest enough, and both had run risks for their opinions in
Henry's reign. Lisle would have passed into history as a genuine
protestant but for his recantation in Mary's reign. Russell,

Herbert, and North were, like St. John, servants of the state rather than partisans of a creed, but their leanings were protestant. Sir Anthony Denny and Sir Edward Wotton may perhaps be credited with a little more constancy; but the two judges, Bromley and Montague, were not expected to express other than legal convictions. Nor is it possible to divide Edward's privy council into sharply defined protestant and catholic parties. Even for churchmen the lines had not yet been clearly drawn; the council of Trent had begun, but it was still sixteen years from its finish; there were as yet no Thirty-nine Articles and no Books of Common Prayer.

Moreover, the first business of the privy council was to rule, and not to define theological dogmas. It had not even been accustomed to determine questions of temporal policy; for sixty years its work had been to advise and to administer; and its members were permanent civil servants trained to execute the king's decisions. They enjoyed no independent authority; they derived no powers from parliament; and they depended solely on the crown, by which they were chosen and removed at will. Exceptional ministers, such as Wolsey and Cromwell, had been enabled by royal favour to carry out a policy of their own; but from the date of Cromwell's fall the responsibility had been exclusively Henry's, and the executors of his will were unused to the burden of decision and command. Nor was this the worst of their difficulties. In more recent times, as in 1788, inconveniences have arisen from royal incapacity, but they have been minimised by the differentiation of the sovereignty of the state from the authority of the king. In 1547 such a distinction was not comprehended; sovereignty was personal, and it was vested in a child nine years of age. A constitutional fiction was indispensable; it was necessary to identify the will of the king with that of his council, and to pretend that the child's authority was a man's.

The fiction, inevitable though it was under a personal hereditary monarchy, was too patent for acceptance by those who wished to dispute the regents' authority. Especially violent did the assumption appear in the ecclesiastical sphere. Fortune had played a strange trick with the headship of the church when, thirteen years after its transference from pope to king, it passed to a child. The papal monarchy had derived at least one advantage from its electoral system, and popes were seldom too young at election. They had, it is true, often made cardinals and archbishops of nephews and children; but the minors had enjoyed the emoluments, without being expected to perform the duties, of their office. How could a child exercise supreme jurisdiction in the church? Regents had often wielded royal power in the state, but the council of Edward VI. were not the Lord's anointed, and did not share the semi-ecclesiastical character which had long attached to kings. Henry VIII. himself and his parliament, which trusted the council far less than it did the king, had given colour to these doubts by passing an act that Edward might of his own authority on coming of age repeal any measure enacted during his minority. Rival monarchs were not slow to take advantage of the new government by professing doubts of the validity of its commissions and of the value of its concessions; and conservatives, when other arguments failed, could always plead the inadvisability of action till the king came of age.

Finally there was a threefold suspicion about Henry's will itself. Was it really his or the fabrication of his successors? If it were his, was it not void by reason of a technical informality? And thirdly, what was the precise value of a dead king's authority? The first doubts may be dismissed in a few words; they were only raised by interested partisans of the Scottish claim to the throne, and only entertained by serious historians when personal testimony was no longer available and before the study of documents had taken its place. There is ample evidence that the will was drawn up, and finally revised at Christmas, 1546, under Henry's personal instructions. Hertford was entrusted with its custody, and his enemies, who brought every plausible accusation against him in 1549, did not charge him with its forgery. Nor would he in any case have been likely to concoct a document which placed him only fifth in order of precedence in the new government, and was the chief obstacle to be swept away in his pursuit of power. The technical invalidity of the will is inferred from the fact that it appears, together with the commission for giving the royal assent to the act for Norfolk's attainder, in a list of documents to which the king's clerk of the signet stated that he had affixed the royal stamp. Both documents required

the king's personal signature to render them valid, and on this
ground Norfolk's attainder was in Mary's reign annulled by a
declaratory act.[1] This would be conclusive were it not that a
minute examination of the will now in the Record Office
reveals a signature at both the head and foot of the document,
written in a tremulous hand with none of the regularity or
marks of indenture which characterise the king's stamp.

It was the third question which troubled the council most.
The custom of the constitution only recognised a living sovereign; it is true that the law of the constitution included an act
giving statutory force to Henry's will, but only for certain purposes, and in certain remote contingencies. He was empowered,
in case the young king died without legitimate issue, to determine
the conditions upon which Mary and Elizabeth should succeed,
and who should be their successors;[2] and another act had
authorised him to nominate a council for his son in case he
were a minor.[3] Here his power ended; he might select the
council, but the council could only exercise the authority of
a living king, and the commission of a living king alone could
authorise that exercise. All commissions and all delegations
of royal authority determined with the royal demise; parliament itself became an empty show, and the privy council had
to seek a new commission from the boy of nine.

The possession of his person was the first requisite of
government; and Hertford, who had spent Henry's dying
hours on the early morning of January 28, 1547, in consultation with Sir William Paget, hurried off to Hatfield to bring
the young king to the Tower. Henry's death was kept secret,
and on Saturday the 29th parliament transacted business as if
nothing had happened. But when it met on Monday morning,
Lord Chancellor Wriothesley announced Henry's death, and
Edward VI. was proclaimed. He reached London that afternoon, and a few hours later the privy council chose Hertford
to be protector of the realm and governor of the king's person.
Paget is said to have made, and Wriothesley to have resisted,
the proposal; but there was no other opposition. Sir Anthony

---

[1] Paget is reported (*e.g.*, in *Spanish Cal.*, Eliz., i., 601-2) to have testified to
the invalidity of the commission during the debate in the lords on the bill for
Norfolk's restitution. The Lords' Journals for that session (1553) are now missing.

[2] 35 H. VIII., c. 1.   [3] 28 H. VIII., c. 7.

Browne, a better catholic than the lord chancellor, had already CHAP. I. expressed his approval; such a step was not forbidden in Henry's will, and there were many precedents in its favour. Chapuys had in the last reign designated Hertford and Lisle as the only noblemen fit to rule after Henry's death, and Hertford had over Lisle the advantages of precedence, seniority, and blood-relationship to the king. He was also the senior peer among the executors, having been created Viscount Beauchamp in 1536, while St. John's and Russell's peerages dated from 1539 and Lisle's from 1542; and he could boast descent from Edward I.[1] He had served Henry well in various diplomatic and administrative posts, had succeeded in all the military operations with which he had been entrusted, and had been named lieutenant to Catherine Parr when she was regent during Henry's absence in 1544.

Hertford's appointment having been decided, the council resolved that the lord chancellor should surrender the great seal to Edward VI. and receive it back from him, and that the executors should take the oath to Edward before they took their oath to execute Henry's will. Both decisions indicated a preference of the new to the old authority. Wriothesley was required to make out new patents for the judges and other crown officials; and after a few days' deliberation the same measure was meted out to the bishops. Whereas they exercised their jurisdiction by instruments under the king's seal *ad res ecclesiasticas*, that jurisdiction had determined by the king's decease; and Paget, the keeper of that seal, was directed to seal fresh commissions *durante bene placito* and *quam diu se bene gesserint*. On the same day Paget produced a list of promotions in the peerage intended, he alleged, by Henry. Hertford became Duke of Somerset as well as lord high treasurer and earl marshal in Norfolk's place; Lisle was made Earl of Warwick, and Wriothesley, Earl of Southampton; Parr, Earl of Essex, was raised to the marquisate of Northampton, and baronies were conferred on Sir Thomas Seymour, Rich, and Sheffield. But Russell and St. John had to wait for their promised earldoms, and seven others for their baronies; while their more fortunate colleagues disclaimed the revenues intended as supports for their new dignities.

---

[1] Jane Seymour, like all Henry VIII.'s wives, was descended from Edward I.

On February 20, Edward VI. was crowned by Cranmer, who employed the occasion to assert the divine right of kings, and to repudiate alike the pretence of popular election and the ecclesiastical claim to deprive. Edward had the best of all titles, a parliamentary statute reinforcing hereditary right. The coronation was followed by the fall of the last formidable catholic and by the emancipation of the protector from all restraints. Wriothesley had been closely identified with the reactionary measures of Henry's closing years, and the lord chancellor, who had racked Anne Askew with his own hands, was not in congenial company. "I was afraid," wrote a Protestant, "of a tempest all the while that Wriothesley was able to raise any. I knew he was an earnest follower of whatsoever he took in hand, and did very seldom miss where either wit or travail were able to bring his purposes to pass."[1] To secure more leisure for politics, he had on February 18 issued a commission to four masters in chancery to act as his deputies; and he had neglected to obtain a warrant from the council. The common lawyers, ever jealous of the chancery side, needed little prompting to lodge a complaint; and the judges declared that Wriothesley had forfeited his office and incurred liability to fine and imprisonment during the king's pleasure. The great seal was entrusted to St. John till October, when Rich became chancellor; and on March 5 Wriothesley was removed from the council.

The French king meanwhile had suggested a doubt whether the council was really empowered to sign a treaty on Edward's behalf. It had no commission from him, but only from Henry VIII.; and the council itself professed doubts as to whether it could authorise St. John to use the great seal. It determined therefore to seek a new commission, signed with Edward's hand. This commission was granted on the 13th, and it released the government from Henry's mortmain. Somerset was appointed protector by letters patent with none of the limitations imposed by the council six weeks before; he was not bound by their consent, and he became king in all but name. The executors and assistant-executors were merged in one privy council appointed by Edward. The protector need

---

[1] *Calendar of State Papers, Foreign,* 1547-53, p. 196.

consult only such and so many as from time to time he should CHAP.
think convenient, and he could add new members at will.

The task to which Somerset thought he had been divinely
called was by no means light. Henry's last war had been
successful in that the French invasion had ignominiously failed
and that he had retained his conquest of Boulogne. But the
cost had only been met by the debasement of the coinage;
and in 1547 the gold currency contained one-fifth, and the
silver currency two-thirds, alloy. Boulogne itself was a doubtful gain, and most of Henry's council had been opposed to
its retention, which strained alike the resources of England
and its relations with France. From Boulogne Lord Grey
reported in February a lack of money, victuals, and labourers;
and its outlying forts, the Old Man, the Young Man, and
Boulogneberg, needed strengthening. It was particularly exposed to attack because its loss rankled in the French mind,
and it was not covered by the defensive treaties between England and the emperor. The dauphin had expressed his determination to regain it at all costs; and before Henry's death
there were rumours of a renewal of war between England and
France. Advices, too, came from Rome that the pope and
Cardinal Pole were practising with the French king and impressing their views on Charles V. Venetian aid was requested for the reduction of England to papal obedience; and
Pole wrote that Edward VI., being born of a schismatic and
heretical king, had at best but a doubtful claim to the throne,
and that it was the emperor's duty to provide for the common
weal of all kingdoms and countries.

Charles, however, had no love for the temporal claims of
the papacy; and now that Paul III. was recalling his troops from
the emperor's camp and the council from Trent, Charles was
less likely than ever to lead a papal crusade against England.
Nor was Francis I. in a belligerent mood; worn out by disease
and debauch, he commissioned the Baron de la Garde and
Odet de Selve, his resident ambassador in London, to conclude
a defensive league with England and an agreement for the
delimitation of the English frontiers in France. On March
12 the council notified to Wotton in Paris the conclusion of
the alliance; but before it was ratified Francis died on the 31st,
and his successor Henry II. reversed his policy. De la Garde

was recalled and disgraced; neither the league nor the frontier-agreement was confirmed; and at the instigation of Diana of Poitiers and of the Guises, Henry adopted that skilful and aggressive policy which recovered the prestige lost by Francis I. The emperor's victory at Mühlberg in April warned the French king to leave Charles alone for the present. He therefore turned to Boulogne and to Scotland, the ancient ties with which had been strengthened by the kinship between the Queen of Scots and the Guises.

Henry VIII.'s Scottish policy had combined right aims with wrong methods. The union of the two realms had been in the mind of Henry VII.; but the marriage bond which he forged had proved weaker than the Franco-Scottish alliance; and after James IV.'s aggression at Flodden, force again became the order of the day. As early as 1527 the old claim of suzerainty was revived, and it was re-asserted with special emphasis after Solway Moss. For a moment in 1543 diplomacy seemed triumphant, and the Scots parliament committed itself to a treaty of marriage between Mary and Edward. But the French persuasions of Mary of Guise and the Roman inducements of Cardinal Beaton once more prevailed against Arran's English leanings; the treaty was torn up, and the "auld enemy" laid revengeful hands upon the Scottish capital and the papist abbeys. The campaign was an action for breach of promise, and not a conquest of Scotland. Such conquests were beyond the military capacity of the sixteenth century; popular indifference to foreign masters, which had facilitated the continental exploits of Edward III. and Henry V. had passed away; and the growth of national feeling imposed on invaders tasks with which they were as yet ill-equipped to deal. Wars were border affairs and were never fought to a finish; few capitals saw a foreign army except Edinburgh and Rome; and Italy invited the invader, while Hertford went by sea to Edinburgh. All that Henry VIII. sought to do in Scotland was to make himself so unpleasant that the Scots must needs prefer his friendship to that of the French. Hence his burnings and slayings, which might have succeeded but for Francis I. and Cardinal Beaton. Both were disposed of in 1546, Francis by peace and Beaton by murder; and the last few months of Henry's reign were spent preparing for a fresh attempt on Scotland.

This task is said to have been urged upon Somerset with Henry's last breath; and the protector put Scotland in the forefront of his programme. In some ways his ideas were larger than Henry's; he saw visions and dreamt dreams of an empire of Great Britain, under Edward VI. as emperor, "having the sea for a wall and mutual love for its garrison," a monarchy which "should neither in peace be ashamed nor in war afraid of any worldly or foreign power". And he desired a union by consent; he prayed that all war and hostility might be put from English and Scots; and he offered liberal terms for Scotland's acceptance, the maintenance of her own laws and customs—"for policy," he wrote, "must in sundry places of necessity require sundry laws"—freedom of trade, and equal protection. He repudiated the idea of conquest, and was by nature averse from coercion; he had protested against his orders to burn Edinburgh in 1544; and now he abandoned the claim to suzerainty. But his end was clearer to him than his means; union there must be, if not by consent, then by compulsion. He had a good legal case; Scotland had bound herself under her great seal to the treaty of marriage; and obstinate breach of that contract justified war. He would fight "to make an end of all wars, to conclude an eternal and perpetual peace"; he would force the Scots to be free of French and papal bonds.

Scottish pride would not consent under threat of coercion. "What would you say," asked a Scot, "if your lad were a lass, and our lass were a lad?"[1] Mary's sex was beyond repair, and there was danger to Scots independence wherever she married. It was in fact a question between English and French domination. "Let the Scots be Scots till the king come of age," wrote Gardiner to the protector; but the problem was to prevent their becoming French. French forces were already besieging St. Andrews and thronging the streets of Edinburgh; and early in March it was reported that twelve French galleys were sailing to Scotland to fetch the young queen. Encouraged by French gold, French troops, and French munitions of war, the Scots turned a deaf ear to Somerset's offers, captured Langholm, and made raids into England. Sir Andrew Dudley failed to stop Strozzi's fleet; St. Andrews surrendered on July 31; and among

[1] Sadler, *State Papers*, ii., 560.

the prisoners carried off to the French galleys was John Knox. No answer was given to the protector's request that commissioners should be sent to Berwick to discuss an agreement; and on August 22 he started from London to conduct yet another Scottish campaign.

On Sunday, September 4, he crossed the border, and, supported by the fleet under Clinton, marched along the coast. On the 9th he came in sight of the Scottish army encamped behind the Esk, with the sea on their left and a marsh covering their right. The fiery cross had sped throughout Scotland, but the response had not been unanimous. Lennox, Bothwell, and Glencairn were in correspondence with Somerset; Arran and Mary of Guise were at variance; and not a few of the 23,000 men who faced the protector's 12,000 foot and 4,000 horse at Pinkie were raw Irish levies brought up by Argyll. But numbers inspired the Scots with confidence; at night they gambled with the ransoms of their prospective captives, and in the morning they threw away their best chance of success. As at Dunbar in 1650, they abandoned their strong position, and crossed the Esk to seize the hills above the English left. Grey's cavalry charged the lowland pikemen, but broke against their wall of steel, and fled. The Scots pursued with fatal effect to themselves. Their ranks grew ragged in face of the English men-at-arms and the Italian musketeers. Grey re-formed his cavalry and charged the Scots in their confusion; a panic seized the ill-disciplined troops, and the battle became a rout and then a massacre. The memory of Ancrum Moor and their initial check at Pinkie inflamed the English blood: little quarter was given; hundreds, multiplied by rumour into thousands, of priests lay dead on the field; and the lowest estimate of the slain was six thousand, while the English lost not so many hundreds.

Pinkie was the last and the bloodiest of the battles between the independent kingdoms. Yet no conquest was intended because no permanent occupation was possible. Somerset's army had come provisioned only for a month, and it was not composed of professional soldiers. The campaign was only a demonstration in force, a sanguinary proclamation *quoad terrorem populi.* But the terror that is to tell must be systematic and insistent; men cannot govern by battles, and fear does not

make friends. It reduced, however, many to subjection, and
numbers of Scots gave in their adhesion. Leith was fired without the protector's leave, while Edinburgh was spared. Inch-
colm and Blackness were seized to command the Forth, and
Broughty Castle to control the Tay; and Arbroath and Dun-
dee were occupied in December. In the lowlands, Dunglas,
Roxburgh, and Home Castle were fortified; while in the west,
Lennox, Wharton, and Grey captured Dumfries, Hailes, Yester,
and Waughton; and in 1548 the occupation of Haddington
made the English masters of the country almost up to the
gates of Edinburgh. It was on the possession of these strongholds, on his proposals for union, and on the missionary efforts
of his lieutenants, who imported cartloads of Bibles into Scotland, that the protector relied to confirm the results of Pinkie.

He returned south in October, 1547, surrounded by a halo
of military glory and popular favour to open his first parliament. But the Tudor dictatorship did not exist for nought,
and much had been done since Henry's death without parliamentary authorisation. Rarely have dictatorial powers been
put to such singular uses as under Protector Somerset. "What
is the matter then?" wrote Paget to Somerset on the rising of
the commons in July, 1549, "Liberty, liberty! And your grace
would have too much gentleness."[1] One of the most obstinate
optimists in English history, he believed that he could almost
dispense with the axe and the gallows; and the whole appa-
ratus of despotism, with which Henry VIII. and Cromwell
had furnished the monarchy, was laid aside in 1547. The
winter of discontent had passed, and lighter garments, as parliament expressed it, might be used. The engines of terror
were brought to a sudden standstill, and the treason and heresy
laws of Henry VIII. were quietly ignored.[2] The result of
this liberty was a popular licence which, as in the cities of
Germany, took the forms of image-breaking and of scurrilous
ballads and tracts against the mass. Even before Henry's
death the curate and churchwardens of St. Martin's, Iron-
monger Lane, had set up the royal arms in place of the crucifix, and had covered the walls with texts from Scripture; and

---

[1] Strype, *Ecclesiastical Memorials*, II., ii., 429-36.
[2] Two priests were condemned for treason under Henry's laws in May, 1547
(Wriothesley, *Chron.*, i., 184), but they do not seem to have been executed.

in May Gardiner complained to the protector of iconoclasm at Portsmouth. The council compelled the restoration of the crucifix in St. Martin's, but were not earnest in the defence of images. Henry VIII. had set them a bad example; and Bishop Barlow of St. David's, Nicholas Ridley, and Cranmer's commissary were allowed to preach at St. Paul's Cross in Lent against the veneration of images and other catholic customs.

The official attitude was indicated by the publication of Nicholas Udall's edition of Erasmus' *Paraphrases*, of Cranmer's *Book of Homilies*, and of a number of *Injunctions* to be enforced in a general visitation of the realm. These were measures of moderation; Erasmus' *Paraphrases* were as far removed from the popular versions of the protestants as from the Vulgate of the catholics, and the Lady Mary had taken part in the translation. The *Homilies* were mainly wholesome practical exhortations; but that on salvation, which excluded charity from the work of justification, incurred Gardiner's censure and Bucer's praise; and only those which excited controversy were thought worthy of attention. The *Injunctions* repeated those issued by Cromwell in 1536 for preaching at least one sermon a quarter in every parish church, for keeping parish registers, for teaching the Creed and the Ten Commandments, for the relief of the poor, and against the sale of livings; substituted Cranmer's English litany, with its modern procedure, for the old "processions" round the churchyard and the church; and required the use of English for the gospel and epistle.

These were not the cause of strife. The really irritating change was that men who had been regarded as heretics were now allowed to teach and to preach instead of being burnt or having to carry a faggot; and their doctrine went a great deal further than the government's *Homilies* and *Injunctions*. The spirit of resistance was provoked not so much by what the government did itself, as by what it refrained from doing to others. But resistance itself could only be offered to positive acts, and Bonner and Gardiner began by opposing the visitation. The growing breach between the two sections, which had formed a common government under Henry VIII., was due as much to the reaction of the catholics as to the advance of the protestants. Gardiner admitted that he had favoured Erasmus, but now he could only see in him the man who laid

the egg which Luther hatched;[1] and he denounced the injunction for the purchase of his *Paraphrases.* He objected to
the whole ecclesiastical policy of the government, and the
stress of controversy drove him into the liberal contention—
alien both from the papacy and from the act of supremacy—
that the royal authority in the church was, or should be,
limited by the same statutory and common-law restrictions
as in the state. The *Injunctions,* he said, had not received
parliamentary authorisation, and were therefore illegal. The
same might have been said of Cromwell's *Injunctions ;* but the
act of supremacy covered both cases, unless Gardiner's further
contention held good that the royal supremacy was in abey-
ance during the royal minority. But if that were so, he should
have refused to take out a new licence for the exercise of his
episcopal jurisdiction ; if Edward VI. was old enough to authorise jurisdiction, he was not too young to issue injunctions ;
and Gardiner's real objections were not to the powers of the
supreme head, but to the uses to which they were put and to
the persons by whom they were wielded. Both he and Bonner
were sent to the Fleet prison ; Gardiner was not released till
the general pardon in January, 1548 ; but Bonner made a
complete submission, and was free to take part in the parliamentary session which began in November, 1547.

The general election, which took place during the Protector's absence in Scotland, was spread over nearly two
months, the earliest return being dated September 5, and the
latest November 1. As was usual in Tudor parliaments, few
old members were returned, not more than a third seeking or
finding seats.[2] There is even less evidence than usual of
government interference in the elections, the only known instance being the council's recommendation of Sir John Baker
to the electors of Kent, who resented the attempt and in spite
of the council's apology compelled Baker to find another seat.
The measures passed by this parliament were, as is always the
case except in disorderly times, mainly government bills ; and
the great act repealing Henry's treason and heresy laws was

---

[1] Gardiner to Somerset, Foxe, *Acts and Monuments,* ed. Townsend, vi., 47.

[2] Only about half the returns are extant for 1547, and three-fifths for 1545 ;
and when the returns for a shire are extant for 1545 they are in many cases
wanting for 1547. Comparison is only possible in about one-third of the constituencies, and of this third about two-thirds returned new members,

probably drafted by the protector himself.   This act[1] removed
almost all the accretions on the treason law of Edward III. ;
but it was still to be treason to attempt to alter the succession
to the crown as regulated by statute and by Henry's will ; and
although it was no longer treason to deny the royal supremacy
over the church by " open preaching, express words or sayings,"
that penalty was still attached to denial " by writing, printing,
overt deed or act ".   The amelioration was, however, considerable ; and a conservative politician, Sir John Mason, described
this repeal of the " act of words " as the worst deed done in
that generation.[2]   It was further provided that accusations of
treason must be made within thirty days of the offence, and be
supported by two witnesses unless the accused " willingly,
without violence " confessed.   The same act repealed all the
statutes *de haeretico comburendo*, the Act of Six Articles—which
Cardinal Pole considered " the best thing Henry VIII. ever did
in this world "[3]—all restrictions on printing, reading, teaching,
or expounding the Scriptures, " and all and every other act or
acts of parliament touching doctrine or matters of religion ".
It also repealed the act of 1540 giving royal proclamations
the force of law ; and another bill annulled Henry's statute
enabling Edward VI. on coming of age to repudiate all legislation passed in his minority.

This self-denying orgy on the part of the government seems
to have suggested hopes to the clergy that they might come
by their own again ; and among the petitions sent up by the
lower house of convocation was one that the clergy might sit
in the house of commons, or have bills affecting the church
submitted for their approval.   It was too late in the day to
repair the constitutional isolation which the clergy had imposed
on themselves in the fourteenth century ; and Somerset was
not likely to remove the clerical disability.   Nevertheless, there
seems to have been a singular harmony between convocation
and parliament.   The measures of that session at least were
not thrust by the laity upon a recalcitrant church ; and a
majority of the bishops themselves voted for all the protector's
ecclesiastical bills.   The lower house of convocation unanimously petitioned for the administration of the communion in

[1] 1 Edw. VI., c. 12.   [2] *Foreign Cal.*, 1553-58, p. 119.
[3] *Calendar of State Papers, Venetian*, v., 249.

both elements; and by a majority of 53 to 22 votes requested
the removal of positive laws against the marriage of the clergy.
The former petition was combined with a bill against irreverence
towards the sacrament of the altar; but it was not till the following session that a grudging assent was given to clerical
marriage.   Henry VIII.'s fear, that priests would, like Albert
of Prussia, convert benefices into hereditary fiefs and revive the
forces of feudalism, still counted for something.

Two more ecclesiastical measures, one simple and the other
complex, completed the important work of the session.   Episcopal elections had already been reduced to a mere formality.
Chapters were first given leave to elect by the *congé d'élire;*
letters missive were then sent in which the person to be elected
was nominated by the crown; and omission to elect this
nominee within twelve days was punishable, under the act of
appeals, with forfeiture of goods and lifelong imprisonment.
This elaborate ritual was now swept away, and bishops were
henceforth to be appointed by letters patent.[1]

The other measure was the chantries act.   The policy of
the government since 1529 had been to make the church a
national institution subject to the crown; and its financial aspect
was the confiscation or control of all religious endowments.
Bishops were regarded as necessary and, being nominated by
the crown, as comparatively harmless; their revenues were to
be controlled by substituting for episcopal lands fixed stipends
payable by the crown.   But monastic life, the worship of saints,
and prayers for the dead, were not considered such necessary
parts of religion as to justify endowment; and the revenues
previously devoted to those purposes were one by one appropriated by the crown or local magnates.   Even after the destruction of the monasteries there remained considerable foundations
designed for what were now regarded as superstitious uses.
Every association in the middle ages tended to adopt religious
forms; the patronage of a saint was thought helpful in the most
mundane concerns; and organisations formed for the purpose of
religious celebrations or charitable objects were often used to
secure the civil and political enfranchisement of their members,
and to regulate their trades and crafts.   On the other hand,

---

[1] By 31 Henry VIII., c. 9, the king had been empowered to make new
bishops and bishoprics by letters patent.

CHAP.
I.

associations primarily secular received endowments for religious or educational purposes, such as maintaining perpetual masses for the founder or providing education for the poor ; and the chantry-priest sometimes also kept a school. As the religious impulse weakened and secular interests grew with the expansion of trade and development of industry, there would be strong temptation to divert religious funds to secular objects. Guilds like that of the Holy Trinity at Lynn used some of its endowments for keeping up a pier and keeping out the sea ; the famous Trinity House was something of a guild ; and ships were long named after saints, and still continue to be christened. There were few associations without some religious use ; and it was the purpose of the chantries acts to differentiate between their secular and superstitious objects, to confiscate the revenues devoted to the latter, and to abolish altogether the "colleges" of singing men and chantries. There may have been a further motive. "There is no one thing," wrote Sir John Mason, "that more continueth a daily hurt to the realm than corporations ;"[1] and the civilians of the sixteenth century, bred up on Roman law, had as rooted an objection as any Frenchman of the twentieth century to all associations which might impair the sovereignty of the state.

The reason for confiscation stated in Henry's act of 1545 was that many of these colleges, chantries, fraternities, and so forth, had already been secularised by founders' representatives and others without the royal licence. Such secularised chantries and colleges were summarily annexed to the crown. The act then proceeded to state that even the colleges and chantries which had survived were not put to their original or proper uses ; and on this ground the king was empowered to appoint commissioners from time to time "during his natural life" to appropriate them to the royal necessities. In pursuance of this act commissions were appointed in February, 1546, but only to survey and not to seize the chantries and the colleges ; and very few had been dissolved when Henry's death put an end to the operation of the act.

The new government had no motives for letting the matter rest. Financial needs were pressing ; the doctrine of purgatory, on which chantries depended, lost its legal protection with the

[1] Tytler, i., 162 ; *Foreign Cal.*, 1547-53, p. 90.

repeal of the Six Articles ; even those who believed in the effi-
cacy of prayers for the dead doubted the value of hired prayers,
and Gardiner expressed his concurrence in the abolition of
chantries.   But the complicated measure introduced in 1547
provoked debate and obstruction which almost proved fatal ;
and it was only by concessions to the members for Lynn and
Coventry that the government saved its bill.   The preamble
alleged religious grounds, and spoke of educational needs.   The
two chief clauses of Henry's act were re-enacted ; but to them
were added sections conferring on the crown all lands set apart
for the keeping of anniversaries, obits, lights or lamps, and all
payments made by guilds, corporations, companies or fellow-
ships of mysteries or crafts for similar purposes.   The act is
obscurely worded, but it was not its intention or effect to confiscate the general revenues of the secular guilds and corporations ;[1] the payments previously made for superstitious
objects were merely now converted into a rent-charge payable
to the crown.   There were also numerous exemptions of religious foundations, the colleges, hostels, and halls of Oxford
and of Cambridge and their chantries, St. George's Chapel,
Windsor, Winchester, Eton, all cathedral churches, and chapels
of ease.   Certain funds were to be applied to such religious objects as preaching and the support of vicars ; charitable and
educational endowments were to be maintained, ; and adequate
pensions were provided for those whose office was abolished.

The act has been described as " a far more statesmanlike
act than that of Henry " ;[2] but its execution did not come up
to its intentions, and its definitions were at fault.   All religious
associations, with the specified exceptions, were dissolved ; but
many of them fulfilled useful secular purposes, and while the
burgesses of Lynn saved the funds of their Holy Trinity guild,
which were spent on piers and sea-walls, others were not so
fortunate, and had to redeem from the crown endowments used
for poor-relief, bridge-building, and clockmaking.   Many guilds

[1] In March, 1553, Abingdon received back " such lands as, having been appointed for the maintenance of two bridges and the sustentation of certain poor
men, were lately taken from them to the King's Majesty's behoof upon colour
that the same were within the compass of the Act of Chantries " (*Acts of the Privy
Council*, 1552-54, p. 227).

[2] Leach, *English Schools at the Reformation*, p. 68; compare Ashley,
Economic History, I., ii., 135-69, and his references, pp. 183-89.

2 *

were too small and too poor to purchase even this amount of
favour; the confiscation of their property cannot have improved
the conditions of life among the lower classes; and popular
religion—or superstition—suffered a heavy blow. This grievance does not, however, figure prominently in the complaints
of the insurgents of 1549; and in any case it was not the
crown which profited from the change. Its feeble control over
wealthy landlords left the proceeds of the revolution at their
mercy.

The greatest damage was done to the cause of education.
Edward VI.'s grammar schools have earned him a reputation
as a founder beyond that of any other sovereign, and far beyond
his own or his advisers' merits. These schools had really been
founded long before his time; his government merely refrained
from destroying them. Schools kept by chantry-priests and
maintained out of funds confiscated by this act were continued
by the commissioners appointed for its execution. But the
endowments they received were fixed stipends in a rapidly de-
preciating currency; the endowments they lost were in lands
of vast potential value. A few schools were founded by private
benefactions, but the funds came mostly from the sale of chantry
lands or plate; and Christ's Hospital, with which Edward's
name is closely associated, was founded not as a grammar
school but as a foundling hospital. In most cases the temporary shift, by which a mere annual payment was continued to
schoolmasters, took the place of a proper re-foundation. Even
this was sometimes neglected, and a bill "for the making of
schools," which was carried through the commons in 1549,
failed to pass the house of lords. The greatest educational
opportunity in English history was lost, and the interests of
the nation were sacrificed to those of its aristocracy; between
the endowment of Seymours and of "superstition" there was
not very much to choose.

The formal abandonment of coercion in the parliament of
1547 must be taken as some indication of the protector's belief
that the nation, if left to itself, would go in the direction he
wished; and the grand national debate which lasted through
1548 was the prelude to the decision of 1549. It was not an
orderly proceeding; the rules were laxly observed and not
impartially administered; and the licence was shocking at

least to conservatives. Every parish church became the scene of religious experiment and theological argument. Some observed holy-days, some kept none; here images were revered, there abused, and elsewhere broken in pieces; a priest bearing the sacrament of the altar to a parishioner's house might be greeted in one street with adoration, in another with cries of *hocus pocus;* one faction used ashes, palms, and candles, while another looked on and jeered. As in Germany between 1521 and 1525, the press teemed with libels and satires, mostly of a protestant character, while the voice of command was mute or half-hearted, in England from deliberate choice, in Germany from helplessness; and in both the religious din was accompanied by the ominous rumble of social revolution. Strangers flocked from abroad with their torches of learning and strife. Germans like Bucer and Fagius, Jews like Tremellius, Italians like Peter Martyr and Bernardino Ochino, Poles like John à Lasco, Spaniards like Francis Dryander, Flemings like Uitenhove, and Frenchmen like Véron and Poullain, fleeing from the *Interim* or the inquisition, found an unwonted welcome in England, and made it the "harbour of all infidelity".

But their influence was not equal to the stir they made; and the English reformation maintained its insular course in spite of all distractions from Augsburg, Zürich, or Geneva. Cranmer, indeed, passed through a Lutheran phase; but Lutheranism in England never recovered from the blow dealt by Henry VIII. in 1538, when he categorically refused the three demands which the Lutheran envoys laid down as preliminaries to a political and theological understanding. Calvinism proved more formidable, but its day was not yet: the protestant influence which came from abroad in the reign of Edward VI. flowed from Zürich; and the oracle was not Calvin nor Melanchthon, but Zwingli's successor Bullinger. Even he spoke to ears that were for the most part deaf; Hooper listened and obeyed, but as late as 1552 he could not charm his brethren on the bench; and at no time in its history could the English church be properly described as Zwinglian. England had not rejected Rome to submit to Zürich; national feeling fired the movement, and independence was its aim. Indigenous heresy, kindled by Wycliffe, was still smouldering in spite of a century of repression, when blasts from the foreign

CHAP.
I.

furnaces of renaissance and reformation fanned its embers into freshening flames. Wycliffe had outlined the principal features of the Anglican reformation, its appeal from the pope to the Scriptures, its call to the state to reform a corrupted church, its revolt against clerical wealth and privilege, its rejection of the mass. The difference between his design and the Anglican realisation is the limitation of the latter ; and the painted glass of the Anglican church intercepted some of the puritan rays of the morning star of the reformation.

Compromise and caution were still in vogue in the spring of 1548. The acts of the late session had conceded less than the German catholics granted at the colloquy of Ratisbon in 1541 ; and the new Order of the Communion, dated March 8, forbade the celebrating priest to vary the old rites and ceremonies of the mass. It was still to be said in Latin, but after the old private priestly sacrifice was now inserted a communion service in English for the people. The sacrament was to be administered to them in both kinds, as parliament had ordained ; and a general public confession was required, private auricular confession being no longer compulsory since the repeal of the Six Articles. The same idea of calling in the laity to participate in religious services, which suggested the Order of the Communion, dictated the substitution of a tongue common to the English people for a language common only to the specialised clerical order. An English litany had been authorised by Henry VIII., and Edward VI.'s royal chapel gradually set the example for further use of the vernacular. Compline had been sung in English at Easter, 1547, the " Te Deum" for Pinkie in September, and the " Gloria in Excelsis," the Creed, and the " Agnus" at the opening of parliament in November ; while Thomas Sternhold was engaged on his metrical version of the English psalms, the vogue of which made " psalm-singing" a puritan characteristic. More distinctive of protestant bias were the proclamations of 1548, ordering the removal of all images and the disuse of candles, ashes, palms, holy bread and holy water, and creeping to the Cross; but respect was still proclaimed for Lent and fast-days, and private innovations were condemned. It was the prerogative of the government to lead ; and in May Latin was excluded from the services in St. Paul's and in the royal chapel, while

Latimer—who still believed in a Real Presence—lashed the CHAP.
" unpreaching prelates" of the old learning and the "butter-   I.
flies" of the capital.[1]

Proclamations seem, however, to have lost some of their
terror since the repeal of Henry's act, and the compromising
combination of the mass and the communion service only
raised contention as to which was really meant. The mass
was the material point, and the French ambassador affirms
that there were daily fights upon the question. So embittered
grew the strife that the council was constrained to impose
silence even upon its own licensed preachers; and Gardiner,
who neglected the injunction, was committed to the Tower.
Liberty was very well, but licence like that of 1548 threatened
England with religious war, and forced the government to
prescribe some sort of rule. Freedom of worship was not
permissible to those who could not agree to differ ; and where
differences were dangerous to peace the interests of order
required uniformity. To that end the church in England had
been tending since its breach with Rome ; and the Ten Articles,
the Six Articles, the Bishops' Book, and King's Book had
represented various phases of Anglican effort at uniformity
in discipline and doctrine.

In 1543 convocation had recommended the general adoption of the Sarum use, but reform no less than uniformity was
wanted, and Cranmer had been busy with liturgical experiments
for years before the death of Henry. The time had come for
the production of his labours ; and in the autumn of 1548 they
were submitted to an informal body of bishops and divines who
sat at Windsor and at Chertsey. Bishop Day of Chichester refused subscription, and others who consented did so with mental
reservations. The draft Book of Common Prayer which was
laid before parliament in the ensuing session was to all intents
and purposes the work of Cranmer, and little in it seems to have
challenged opposition except its treatment of the mass. But
here it struck at the heart of the catholic position. Persuaded,
as he himself said, by Ridley, or, as another contemporary writes,
by John à Lasco, Cranmer had abandoned not only transubstantiation, but also the Lutheran point of view, and with Latimer had gone over to Zwinglianism. The elevation and adora-

---

[1] Latimer, *Sermons* (Parker Soc.), p. 64.

tion of the sacrament were left out, the word *oblation* was studiously avoided, and the elements were still described as bread and wine after the completion of those rites which to a catholic implied their transubstantiation. There was "heresy in the book," declared Bonner in the house of lords, where it was debated for three whole days. "It is all over with Lutheranism," wrote a triumphant Zwinglian to Bullinger. His pæan was premature, for Cranmer's draft succumbed to catholic criticism. It was a month after this debate before the act of uniformity, of which the Book of Common Prayer was a schedule, was passed; and in the interval the book was so modified as to secure the assent of a majority of the bishops. Eight spiritual and three temporal peers voted against the third reading of the bill, but twelve bishops and all the other lay peers present voted in its favour. There is no evidence that it was ever submitted to convocation, but the government could maintain that its ecclesiastical policy had the approval of both church and state.

The Zwinglians were sadly disappointed: "the foolish bishops," wrote one, "have made a marvellous recantation," and Hooper thought the book defective, doubtful in construction, and in some points manifestly impious. Concessions, wrote Bucer, had been made both to respect for antiquity and to the infirmity of the age. Dryander was struck by its obscurity, and Cranmer and Gardiner were soon engaged in drawing opposite conclusions from its language. It was intended as a manual of devotion and not of Roman, Zwinglian, or any other doctrine. The influence of the *Pia Consultatio* of Hermann von Wied, the deprived Archbishop of Cologne, is patent in its pages, but its chief resemblance to Lutheranism arises from the common conservatism of the Anglican and Lutheran compared with the "reformed" churches. Cranmer accomplished two great things, the prayer book and his final recantation; many of his prayers and collects are translations, but they achieve the rare distinction of being superior to the originals. As a vehicle of devotion the English language reached its climax in the Book of Common Prayer; and three and a half centuries after its composition the rhythmic cadence of its phrases charms a wider circle than the communion of the English church.

CHAPTER II.

A YEAR OF TROUBLES.

THE Act of Uniformity, by which the first Book of Common
Prayer was enforced, was the mildest act which ever bore that
unhappy name. It imposed no penalties on laymen who
merely refused to attend the new service; but those who disturbed its celebration or abetted priests in using any other were
liable to a fine of ten pounds on a first conviction, twenty
pounds on a second, and total forfeiture of goods and life-
long imprisonment on the third. For using any other service
priests were liable to the loss of one year's profit from one bene-
fice and six months' imprisonment on the first conviction, to
the forfeiture of all benefices and a year's imprisonment on the
second, and to life-long incarceration on the third. In universities and in private the service might be celebrated in Greek,
Latin, Hebrew, "or any other strange tongue," and any one
might use psalms or prayers taken from the Bible. Nor did
the act attempt to set up any standard of doctrinal uniformity,
except such as was implied in the ritual and forms of prayer
adopted; there were as yet no Articles in the Book of Common
Prayer, and the implications in the new communion service
were capable of various constructions.

National uniformity was the consequence of separation from
the church of Rome, but its achievement was beyond the power
of even Tudor despotism. Englishmen almost worshipped the
state, but there was enough catholicism left and enough protestantism in ferment to resist the pressure of the Procrustean
bed; and catholics lost no time in showing their repugnance to
a uniformity that was not their own. Gardiner was in the
Tower, Bonner merely refrained from enforcing the act, which
was not a breach of its letter, and the Lady Mary was allowed
to have mass in her household because the government wanted

the emperor's aid. In the west of England, however, the
peasantry rose in revolt not only against the new service, but
against all the principles of the reformation. Indeed there had
been a slight rising in Cornwall in the previous year;[1] but the
signal for a more formidable rebellion was given, when on
Whit-Sunday, June 9, 1549, every parish priest was to adopt
the Book of Common Prayer.

Next day the parishioners of Sampford Courtenay, led by
the village tailor, compelled their priest to resume the ancient
use. They had been tenants of the Marquis of Exeter,[2] who
was executed in 1539, and whose son Edward Courtenay was
now a prisoner in the Tower; and a chaplain of his cousin, the
Lady Mary, was busy in the parish,[3] while the old bishop of
Exeter, Veysey, was anything but a friend of change. The
example of Sampford Courtenay proved contagious, and the
rebels marched on Crediton which they rudely fortified. A
simultaneous movement broke out in Cornwall: some of the
leaders were country gentry like the Arundells; others were
influential townsmen, such as Henry Braye, mayor of Bod-
min, and Henry Lee, mayor of Torrington. But for the
most part the rising was one of priests and peasants; priests
drew up the peasants' articles, organised their camps, and
administered martial law. The sea-faring folk fought for the
new religion, and Sir Walter Raleigh's father was rescued from
the peasants by some mariners. On the same side were the
trading classes in the towns, and Exeter, in spite of a catholic
party within, stood a six weeks' siege with no resources to rely
on but its own. The old forces were ranged against the
new, and the rebels' demands[4] were a forecast of Mary's
reign. They would have the Six Articles restored and the
old Latin mass celebrated by the priest "without any man or
woman communicating with him"; the sacrament was to be
hung over the altar and worshipped as of old, and those who
would not were to die as heretics; and it was to be administered

---

[1] *Acts of the P.C.*, 1547-50, p. 554.
[2] *Letters and Papers of Hen. VIII.*, 1541, p. 241.
[3] State Papers, Dom., Edw. VI., vol. viii., No. 30.
[4] There are three versions extant; see Pocock, *Troubles connected with the
First Book of Common Prayer* (Camden Society); Holinshed, p. 1009; Dixon,
iii., 57, etc. Four answers were written, two by Somerset, one by Cranmer, and
one by Nicholas Udall.

to the laity only at Easter and in one kind. Baptism should CHAP.
II. be administered at all times and on all days ; holy bread and holy water were to be made on every Sunday ; and palms, ashes, and images were to be restored. The new service was " like a Christmas game," and, as certain of the Cornishmen understood no English, they would have the old service in Latin ; and priests should pray, " specially by name," for souls in purgatory. The Bible in English was to be called in again, for otherwise the clergy could not confound the heretics ; and Cardinal Pole was to be summoned from Rome and " promoted to be first or second of the king's council ".

The soft answer, which the protector returned by the mouth of Sir Peter and Gawain Carew, was accompanied by wrathful instructions from the council, of which Somerset was kept in ignorance. The rebels refused a conference and forfeited the proffered pardon ; and their position was taken by the burning of the barns at Crediton. This added fuel to the flames ; Russell, the commander-in-chief, soon lay helpless at Honiton, and the rebels laid siege to Exeter. It was well for the government that the insurgents thus locked up their forces, for there was little to stop their progress. In Oxford the disputations of Peter Martyr had angered the neighbouring clergy, who roused the adjoining shires ; and orders were even sent for the destruction of Staines bridge to check a march on the capital. But prompt measures were taken by Lord Grey ; the Oxfordshire rising was quelled with ruthless severity, scores of priests were hanged from their own church-steeples, and Grey went on to Russell's support, while Herbert collected the archers of Wales. At length, towards the end of July, Russell had received enough reinforcements, largely German and Italian mercenaries, to advance to the relief of Exeter. After some skirmishes and a stubborn fight at St. Mary Clyst, the siege was raised on August 6 ; the rebels rallied at Sampford Courtenay, but on the 17th they were completely routed by the artillery and discipline of the mercenaries, and Russell had an easy task in dealing with Cornwall.

The real peril of the situation did not consist in local resistance to the religious policy of the government, but in the social unrest which agitated most parts of the realm and portended in the minds of intelligent observers a crisis hardly less serious than that of the Peasants' Revolt in Germany. A "revolution of the rich against the poor" is not a fair description of the Reformation. But it indicates with some approach to accuracy the economic development which preceded and accompanied religious change; and it is easier to see in the Reformation an outcome of social revolution than to discern in the social revolution an outcome of religious reformation. In 1517, the year of Luther's theses, Sir Thomas More regarded the existing social organism as "a conspiracy of the richer sort, who, on pretence of managing the public, do only pursue their private ends"; and no economic system has yet been devised which will increase wealth without increasing the distance between wealth and poverty. The expansion of trade expands the scope of the expert in accumulation, and the more complex the industrial organisation, the greater the number of grades which compose it. The ends of the economic scale are further apart than they were in the middle ages, and further from the golden mean; the dark ages produced no vast fortunes, but neither did they need a poor law or a workhouse system. Destitution was then the occasional result of war or pestilence and not the persistent concomitant of normal economic conditions; and the moral force of custom checked the lawless tendencies of competition. But the statics of the old had yielded to the dynamics of the new order; the town-market was expanding into the world-market; the mobilisation of labour, due to the break-up of the manor, to the emancipation of the villein, and to the growth of capital, led to the substitution of factories, like those of Jack of Newbury,[1] for domestic craftsmanship, and of cultivation on a large, for cultivation on a small, scale. The production of wealth, instead of being merely a means of subsistence, became an end in itself or a means to political influence; the power of the purse behind the throne, in parliament, in the courts of law, and in local affairs was a constant theme for denunciation by penniless pamphleteers; and all the great Tudor ministers sprang from families newly enriched by novel methods.

The increased rewards attaching to wealth stimulated greater efficiency in the means employed for its production; and large inroads were made on the older, uneconomical sys-

[1] See *Dict. of Nat. Biogr.*, s.v. Winchcombe, John,

tem of common cultivation and small individual tenements. The acreage inclosed or "ingrossed"[1] was small compared with the total acreage of the land, but the comparison is irrelevant; for inaccessible land is valueless and the greater part of England was still inaccessible for the practical purposes of agricultural life. Ten or twenty thousand acres inclosed in a single county might be a small proportion of its total area, but it might be a serious percentage of the acreage from which the peasants had derived subsistence; and the only useful comparison would be between the acreage inclosed and the acreage of land capable of occupation under the existing conditions. For this comparison materials are not now available, and we have to fall back upon the few doubtful figures and many wild denunciations of contemporary literature. Bishop Scory wrote to Edward VI. in 1551: "there are not at this day ten ploughs whereas were wont to be forty or fifty"; and he went on to complain that owing to the "great sheepmasters" the rural population had "become more like the slavery and peasantry of France than the ancient and godly yeomanry of England".[2] A "Supplication of the Commons" in 1548 estimated that one plough in each of the 50,000 townships and villages in the country had been "decayed," and that some 300,000 persons had thus been thrown out of work;[3] and Somerset's proclamation of June 1, 1548, asserts that "in divers and sundry places of the realm . . . whereas in times past ten, twenty, yea and in some place a hundred or two hundred Christian people have been inhabiting and kept household . . . now there is nothing kept but sheep or bullocks". The people thus evicted were driven, as a "Supplication" puts it, "some of them to beg and some to steal"; and a long series of vagrant acts culminated in 1549 in the provision that confirmed vagabonds might be sold into slavery and branded.

Vagabondage produced not a little of the raw material out of which revolts in Tudor times were made; but the position of

---

[1] "Inclosure" is a generic term used to designate three different processes : (a) the substitution of large holdings for small ones by the ejection of tenants and "decay" of their tenements; (b) the conversion of arable land or grazing land into sheep-runs, the sheep being kept for their wool and not their meat; and (c) the inclosure of common lands and wastes.

[2] Strype, *Eccl. Mem.*, II., ii., 482.

[3] *Four Supplications* (Early English Text Society).

CHAP.
II.

hired labourer, into which many of the smaller copy-holders and customary tenants sank, was little better than vagrancy. When the price of wheat could rise from four shillings a quarter in 1547 to eight in 1548, and sixteen in 1549, the price of barley from three shillings and four pence to four shillings, and then to eleven in the same period ; oats from three to six shillings, and oxen from thirty-nine to seventy ; while the wages for unskilled labour only rose from four pence half-penny to five pence, the ebullitions of the peasantry of nearly every shire in 1549 can hardly cause surprise.[1] Even those who still retained their holdings had cause for discontent in the inclosure of common lands and wastes, in the " forestalling " and " ingrossing " operations of capitalists, and in the debasement of the currency, which Somerset made but feeble efforts to reform. The poorer classes in the towns, though they did not labour under the purely agrarian hardship of inclosures, were even more affected by the rise in prices, by fraudulent manufactures, against which scores of acts were passed in vain, and by the condition of the coinage.   They bitterly complained of the employers who sought labour in the cheapest market and preferred apprentices to the married journeymen because their wages would be less.[2] Rents, too, were rising almost as fast as prices ; men speculated in house property, " buying up whole rows and alleys of houses ; yea, whole streets and lanes, and raising the rents double, triple, or even fourfold what they were twelve years past ".[3] Nine-tenths of the houses in London were already let by middlemen ; and Latimer said that there was more pride, covetousness, cruelty, and oppression in London than in Nebo.[4] If the poorer classes in the cities and boroughs had ever shared in those rights of jurisdiction and municipal government which their wealthier fellows had purchased from the crown, they had lost that

---

[1] Thorold Rogers, *History of Agriculture and Prices*, iv., 282-292. On the other hand wheat had been 12s. 11d. in 1527, 10s. 7d. in 1536, 15s. 7d. in 1545, and it rose to 28s. 6d. in 1556; but all these years, except 1545, were marked by risings more or less serious. The effect should be discounted by the fact that labourers were often paid in kind, and must have benefited to some extent by the high prices obtained by their employers. It may be observed that all the inclosures, debasement of the coinage, and influx of precious metals did not prevent the price of wheat from sinking in 1547, to two-thirds of the average price between 1401 and 1540. The first year of the protectorate must have seen a marvellous harvest.

[2] Miss Lamond, *Discourse of the Common Weal of England*, 1893, p. lxvi.

[3] Crowley, *Works*, p. 133.   [4] Latimer, *Sermons*, p. 63.

share before the sixteenth century; and everywhere the municipal and parliamentary franchise and the wealth of the guilds
were monopolised and exploited by the few.

The antagonism between peasant and lord, artisan and
capitalist, never attained in England the dangerous propor-
tions which it did in Germany during the sixteenth century,
because the central government exerted greater control over
local affairs, and the grievances of the commons enlisted more
active support among the governing classes. The Cæsarism
of the new monarchy made it no friend of aristocratic privilege and inclined its ear to popular complaints; but its
demagogic tendencies were controlled by a lively appreciation
of the influence of wealth, and Somerset found to his cost
that the favour of the masses counted for little against the
serried ranks of property. Wolsey might issue decrees for
the demolition of inclosures made since 1485, and laws might
be passed with the same intention; but, as John Hales[1] remarked in 1549, the inclosers did not mind how many laws
were passed, provided none were put into execution; and the
opposition to the spoliation of the poor was left to men of
letters like Sir Thomas More, or radical pamphleteers like
Simon Fish, Henry Brynkelow, and Robert Crowley, who not
only wished to stop inclosures but to reform the house of
commons and restrict the powers of the house of lords. Their
views on social questions became important after 1547 through
the patronage of the protector; and staid officials wrote in
alarm about the new commonwealth's party, which laid more
stress on the duties than on the rights of property and wished
to check individualist exploitation of the community. Latimer
lent his powerful invective to the cause, Cranmer gave his
sympathy, and the protector erected an illegal "court of poor
men's causes" in Somerset House, and obtained a private act
of parliament giving his customary tenants special protection
against eviction by himself.[2]

But the most active instrument of this policy was John
Hales, to whom the whole movement against inclosures has
been erroneously ascribed. Hales was member for Preston, and

---

[1] Trans. of the Royal Hist. Soc., N.S., xi., 116-18.
[2] 2 and 3 Edw. VI., c. 12; Leadam, Select Cases in the Court of Requests
(Selden Soc.), p. xvii.

may have introduced the first bill of Edward VI.'s reign, which apparently embodied a suggestion by Brynkelow that a certain number of poor men's children should be educated at the public expense. This and other measures introduced by Hales during the sessions of 1547-48 and 1548-49 for the maintenance of tillage and husbandry, putting down parks, restraining combinations and regulating sheep pastures were rejected after acrimonious debates and close divisions either in the upper or lower house; and the parliamentary campaign of the commonwealth's party proved a failure. But petitions poured in upon the protector; Latimer, in his sermon, " Of the Plough," in January, 1548, denounced inclosures, and a few weeks later the peasants in Hertfordshire rose against them. On June 1 Somerset issued his indignant proclamation, and appointed a commission to make a return of inclosures. It met with determined opposition; the juries empanelled to make the returns were packed by the neighbouring gentry, and browbeaten when packing failed. Fraud was employed to supplement intimidation;[1] a single furrow would be ploughed across a pasture and the land returned as tillage; or a solitary ox would be turned loose on a sheep-run to make it appear land devoted to fatting cattle.[2] A general pardon was granted to all offenders presented by the commission, but this weakness encouraged contempt. They returned, writes Hales, "to their old vomit, began immediately to inclose, to take away the poor men's commons, and were more greedy than ever they were before". The commission secured one fatal success, and ploughed up a park belonging to the Earl of Warwick.

Mutual exasperation of landlord and tenant was the result of the failure. "We must needs fight it out," cried the peasants, " or else be brought to the like slavery that the Frenchmen are in"; and in the early summer of 1549 risings began in Somerset, spreading thence to Gloucestershire, Wiltshire, Dorset, Hampshire, Oxfordshire, Buckinghamshire, Surrey, Sussex, and Kent. There was not a county in the south of England that remained undisturbed, and even in Yorkshire the fate of the Pilgrimage of Grace did not prevent a peasants' rising in September; but these insurrections did not gather head, and were soon overshadowed by the greater

[1] Latimer, *Sermons*, p. 247.   [2] Brit. Mus., Lansdowne MS., 238.

revolts in the west and East Anglia. The county of Norfolk CHAP.
is given [1] as one of those in which inclosures were only sporadic; II.
but all inclosures were sporadic, and those in Norfolk provoked
a fiercer resistance than elsewhere, because the soil was richer,
its cultivators were more prosperous and independent, and so
had more to lose. On June 20 a riot broke out at Attleborough,
and fences were demolished. On July 7 the rustics of Wymondham, a manor granted to Warwick in 1544, turned from
celebrating the festivities of that day [2] to tearing down the
fences of the neighbouring gentry, and among them those of
one Serjeant Flowerdew who was already engaged in a local
quarrel with Robert and William Kett. Flowerdew ascribed
the injury to Robert Kett's malevolence, and bribed some
peasants to retaliate; for Kett, albeit a tanner, had prospered
in his trade and purchased several manors; indeed, the chronicler remarks with some disgust that he could dispend £50 a
year in lands and had 1,000 marks in movables.[3] Either
Kett's sympathies were still with the commons, or his enmity
to Flowerdew was stronger than his liking for the landed
gentry whose ranks he had but lately joined; and he threw
himself into the movement against inclosures. He assisted
Flowerdew's hirelings to destroy his own inclosures, and then
with their help made a clean sweep of Flowerdew's. The
same was done at Cringleford and Bowthorpe, and the
rustics marched on Norwich. Their numbers rose to 16,000
men, and from their camp at Mousehold Hill, within a mile
of the city, they dictated communistic law to the greater portion
of East Anglia.

The fear lest the Lady Mary should be at the rebels' back
gave members of the council sleepless nights, but the religion
of these peasants was revolutionary rather than reactionary.
The German insurgents of 1525 had sung "Dan Christus hat
uns all befreit" ("For Christ has freed us all"), and the Norfolk
rustics echoed the refrain, demanding the enfranchisement of
all bondmen on the ground that God had by His bloodshed
made all men free. Apart from this theological proposition

---

[1] Ashley, *Economic History*, I., ii., 304.

[2] It was the Translation of St. Thomas of Canterbury. Henry VIII.'s crusade
against the memory of that "traitor" had not eradicated his feasts.

[3] Wriothesley, *Chron.*, ii., 21-2.

and a request that the clergy should reside on their benefices and be diligent in teaching, their demands were purely agrarian, and might have been transcribed from the German twelve articles of 1525. They regarded the inclosure of common lands, the enforcement of private property in the fish of running water and fowl of the air as theft from the community, and innocently thought that the gifts of God in Nature were made to man and not to landlords only. They took a singular pleasure in slaughtering the sheep, which pastured on their whilom commons and, in the words of the protector's proclamation, ate them out of house and home; 20,000 were consumed on Mousehold Heath, and one Norfolk squire alone, Thomas Wodehouse, lost 2,000, besides his horses, corn, and cattle. But apart from this recovery of what the peasants thought was stolen property, their conduct was restrained and almost orderly. Rude courts were held by Kett and his reluctant assessor, the mayor of Norwich, in the rebels' camp; and if the justice they administered was rough, it was probably as fair as that obtainable in the king's courts where, according to the proverb of that day, the law was ended as a man was friended. Landlords were detained as prisoners, but only put in irons when they attempted to escape. Murder there was none, and of sacrilege but little. The new morning and evening services were daily read in the camp by a Norwich vicar; and a future archbishop, Matthew Parker—himself the son of a Norwich citizen and the son-in-law of a Norfolk squire—was allowed to discourse from the "oak of reformation" to the rebels on the evil of their ways. Seldom was a mob so orderly with so little police assistance.[1]

The Norfolk peasants seemed quite content with their commonwealth and community of goods, so long as there was plenty; and they showed no desire to march on London or disturb the other shires. Their example might by itself suffice, and it was a perilous precedent for any government to tolerate. The protector would have been content with a very shadowy

---

[1] Most available information on this subject is collected in F. W. Russell's *Kett's Rebellion*, 1859, which does not appear to have been used either by Froude or Dixon. Parker inspired and rewarded Alexander Neville's *De Furoribus Norfolcensium Ketto duce*, which was published in 1575. Blomefield's *Hist. of Norfolk* (ii,, 160-83) contains some interesting particulars from the Norwich archives,

submission; he was credited with evil designs against landlords CHAP.
and with a desire to pardon peasants. But no man of influ- II.
ence, save Latimer, supported his policy. Paget denounced
the peasants for resisting inclosures which their elders had
suffered for sixty years. Cranmer preached an impartial
sermon against the avarice of the gentry, the turbulence of
the commons, and the weakness of the government; and even
Sir Thomas Smith lamented the lack of decisive measures.
Somerset was distracted between his sympathy for the peasants
and his duty to keep order. It was not till the end of July
that a herald was sent to Norwich with a pardon for all the
insurgents who would disperse. Kett took offence at the word,
and said he had done no wrong; the herald declared him a
traitor, and withdrew with some of the moderates, including
the mayor, into Norwich. The gates of the city were shut
against the peasants, but in a few days they recovered possession. The council now took stronger measures; the Marquis of
Northampton advanced with some Italian mercenaries and a
body of retainers, and Norwich opened its gates to the royal
forces. But the marquis was no soldier; the Italians were
overpowered by numbers, and their leader was taken and
hanged. Lord Sheffield was killed, the rest fled for their lives,
and Norwich fell again into the rebels' hands.

The protector then meditated taking command in person;
but on second thoughts, which were unfortunate for him, the
work was given to Warwick, who rallied Northampton's de-
jected troops, and on August 22 appeared before Norwich. A
herald was once more sent with a pardon, and Kett was inclined to parley; but during the herald's oration a youth was
shot by one of the herald's suite for an indecent insult, and the
prospect of conciliation vanished. The peasants again forced
their way into Norwich, but could not dislodge Warwick, who
remained in great peril until the 26th, when the arrival of
eleven hundred *landsknechts*, originally intended for Scotland,
enabled him to take the offensive against the camp on Mousehold Heath. Encouraged by an old rhyme foretelling that
the " country gnuffes,"

> " With clubs and clouted shoon
> Shall fill the vale of Dussindale
> With slaughtered bodies soon," [1]

[1] Russell, p. 142,

3 *

Kett moved down into the valley where the fire of the *lands-knechts* and a charge by Drury's pikemen soon broke the rebel ranks; and the slaughter of some 3,000 peasants fulfilled the dubious prophecy.[1] Hundreds were taken prisoners; and while Warwick was "doing execution on many men" at Norwich,[2] another commission of oyer and terminer set to work at Yarmouth. The two ringleaders were sent up to the Tower, and three months later, after the protector's fall, they were hanged, Robert Kett in Norwich Castle and William from Wymondham steeple.

So ended the Norfolk rising, like every other peasants' revolt, in disillusion and defeat. The stars in their courses fought against them : it was not possible to restore an agricultural system which was economically wasteful and effete, and it is always hard to restrain the greed of those who control the government. The removal of medieval shackles let loose forces good and evil; it meant more chances for the strong and less protection for the weak; and liberty has often been the privilege of those who can do as they like with whatsoever they are pleased to call their own. The peasants' revolts in England and abroad involved at once both revolution and reaction; they heralded the coming of the "common man," but advocated a return from individual licence to collectivist control. Their immediate object was a total failure, but in England alone of the countries of Europe was the peasant entirely divorced from the ownership of the soil he tilled. The consequent mobility of labour facilitated the development of industry and manufactures, and the modern preponderance of English commerce over English agriculture has its origin in the social revolution of the sixteenth century. That was not made with rosewater any more than other revolutions, and even at the end of Elizabeth's reign sympathetic souls lamented the passing of "merry England". Formal slavery, however,

---

[1] In a letter from the protector, and another from the council, the number is put at 1,000, Strype, *Eccl. Mem.*, II., ii., 427; *Foreign Cal.*, 1547-1553, p. 46. Holinshed, who made particular inquiries, says 3,500, and the contemporary Wriothesley gives 5,000.

[2] T. Wodehouse to Sir W. Wodehouse, Sept. 3, 1549, State Papers, Dom., viii., 55; Tytler, i., 195. Froude thinks the executions were not numerous considering the circumstances, and Dixon says they took place after Warwick's return to London, *History*, iii., 93. Blomefield, *History of Norfolk*, ii., 181, puts the number of executions at about 300.

died out, and the prayer of the Norfolk insurgents "that all bondmen may be made free" was gradually realised during the latter half of the century.

It would be as absurd to attribute Somerset's agrarian policy to intelligent anticipation of the far-off consequences of inclosures as to deny his real sympathy with the living victims of the movement. He took his office seriously and himself too seriously; regarding himself as called by Providence to rule, he held it to be his duty to hear poor men's complaints and redress their grievances. No attitude could have been more irritating to his colleagues on the council who felt no call in that direction; and the protector's assumption of moral superiority angered them more than his assertion of political pre-eminence. The moral claim was confronted with Somerset House which arose on the ruins of chapels and chantries; and his title to rule was impugned by the ill-success of his government. It was no easy task to wield a royal autocracy without a royal immunity; no divinity hedged a protector's person, and misfortune enhanced the protector's faults.

Somerset was not responsible for his brother Thomas, Lord Seymour of Sudeley, who did not a little to ruin the family. Not content with the privy councillorship which he received a few days before Henry's death, with the barony which he was granted in March, 1547, and with the office of lord high admiral in which he succeeded Warwick, and regarding public life as merely a field for private adventure, Thomas Seymour had at once set to work to exploit the family fortune. He sought in succession the hands of Anne of Cleves, of Mary, and of Elizabeth. The council was not likely to assent to either of the latter matches, and neither princess would have cared to risk her title to the succession by marrying without the council's leave. Eventually Seymour wedded surreptitiously before the end of May, 1547, his old love, Catherine Parr. The step was indiscreet, almost indecent in its haste and secrecy; the two brothers quarrelled over the question whether Catherine's jewels were crown or personal property, and their two wives disputed each other's precedence. Seymour asserted that he had as much right to be governor of the king's person as his brother had to be protector; he bribed Edward's attendants, gave pocket-money to the boy himself, and incited him to assert his claim to rule.   He sulked at home instead of commanding the fleet against Scotland in 1547 and 1548, voted steadily against government measures in the house of lords, and was publicly noted for " his slothfulness to serve and greediness to get ".[1]   As lord high admiral he connived at piracy, received a share in the spoils, and perverted justice in the admiralty courts.   When Catherine Parr died in September, 1548, he paid court to Elizabeth, whom he had treated with gross familiarity, and planned a marriage between Edward VI. and Lady Jane Grey, whose father Dorset had been wheedled into acquiescence in his schemes.   He induced Sir William Sharington to tamper with the mint at Bristol and supply him with the proceeds, in order to gather arms and swell the ranks of his dependants.

Sharington's practices became known in January, 1549, and his examination brought Seymour's intrigues to light. Less evidence sent many a better man and woman to the block in Tudor times ; but the impression that Seymour's bark was worse than his bite, and the fact that his brother was at the head of the government which condemned him gave an appearance of cruelty to his execution.   That his conduct had been factious, unprincipled, and mischievous in the last degree, and that his character was vicious hardly admit of doubt ; but it is questionable whether his proceedings were sufficiently dangerous to the state to justify his execution, and he might well have been left in the Tower like Norfolk.   It was not vindictiveness on the protector's part that excluded mercy from the case, but the calculations of those who hoped to profit by the odium in which a plausible charge of fratricide would involve the protector.   The principal share in the proceedings against the lord high admiral was taken by Wriothesley, Warwick, and Rich, while Somerset was excused participation in the deliberations of the council and in the voting on the bill of attainder. It passed without contradiction in the house of lords, Northampton and Dorset not being the men to help a falling friend.   The commons tried to assert a claim to share in the judicial functions of the lords, and desired to hear the witnesses for the prosecution and the lord admiral in his defence ; but the government would only permit the lords to repeat in the presence of the commons the evidence they had heard in their own house.

[1] *Hatfield MSS.*, i., 61 ; Haynes, p. 68.

The lower house had to content itself with a spirited debate and a division in which a dozen members voted against the bill; and on March 20 Seymour was beheaded on Tower Hill. His fate provoked much adverse comment which Latimer sought to meet in a sermon on the 29th, denouncing Seymour's private character and asserting that his last act was an attempt to instigate Mary and Elizabeth to sedition. But all Latimer's eloquence could not relieve the protector of the consequences of his consent to his brother's death. Later on, he lamented his weakness, and declared that he had been misled by others who persuaded him that his own life was not safe so long as the admiral lived. This miserable compliance played into the hands of those who, in the words of Bishop Ponet, "conspired the death of the two brethren . . . so as they might rob the king and spoil the realm at their pleasure".

Another foe was fishing in the troubled waters. Henry II. of France hoped to find in the affair the means of embroiling England in civil war: he instructed his ambassador, Odet de Selve, to take what measures he could to foster the admiral's faction;[1] and a secret French agent was busy in England during the commotions of the following summer.[2] Relations between England and France had been going from bad to worse since the death of Francis I. The new French king was equally determined to save Scotland and to recover Boulogne. Bickerings about the fortifications of Boulogne and the frontiers of the Boulonnais had been exasperating and incessant, but the battle of Pinkie had inspired a temporary respect for English arms. French men and money, however, flowed in a steady stream towards Scotland, where the English hold on the Lowlands could not prevent Queen Mary's transference from Stirling to Dumbarton, and thence in August, 1548, to Brittany. To meet the threat of her marriage with the dauphin, Somerset in September revived the English claim to suzerainty over Scotland which he had dropped in 1547. But the claim was futile without a heavy arm and a long purse to support it. England's resources were not equal to the double burden of Boulogne and Scotland; and a revolt in

[1] *Hatfield MSS.*, i., 63-64.
[2] *Ibid.*, i., 85, 102; *Foreign Cal.*, 1547-53, pp. 72, 78; *Lit. Remains of Edward VI.* (Roxburghe Club), p. 472; *Troubles* (Camden Soc.), pref. pp. xviii-xx.

Guienne against the *gabelle*, on which the protector set some
hope, proved little help.[1] It was a happier inspiration to offer
the immediate retrocession of Boulogne if France would support
the Anglo-Scottish marriage; but Henry II. wanted Calais as
well, a surrender which no English statesman could then have
ventured to make.

Boulogne was in fact a fatal entanglement; the English
government could not afford to surrender Henry VIII.'s conquest except at a price which France was not prepared to pay.
Charles V. had persistently refused to include it in his treaty
liabilities for the defence of English dominions; and he repeated
the refusal when Paget was sent in July, 1549, to press for its
inclusion. Boulogne was therefore a vulnerable point, for the
defence of which England had to rely on her own resources;
and the strain reached the breaking-point when rebellions broke
out in the west and the east. Troops destined for the defence
of English strongholds in Scotland and the Boulonnais had to
be diverted to Devon and Norfolk; and the temptation for
France to declare war was irresistible. The gage was thrown
down by Odet de Selve on August 8; French forces surged into
the Boulonnais, and aided by treachery made themselves masters
of Ambleteuse, Boulogneberg, and the "Almayne Camp".
But Englishmen could still give a good account of themselves;
and Boulogne, which had fallen after a six weeks' siege to Henry
VIII., held out against Henry II. until the conclusion of peace.
No attempt was made on Calais, which was protected by
Charles V.'s guarantee; and the suppression of the peasants'
revolts disappointed the French expectations. One or two
English strongholds in Scotland fell, and on October 14 the
English garrison with its military stores was removed from
Haddington, partly on account of the plague which had
broken out in the town.

Before that date the protectorate had come to an end.
Somerset was held responsible for all the misfortunes attending
his rule, and while exercising the royal prerogative was debarred from the greatest of royal privileges, that of shifting
on to the shoulders of ministers responsibility for ill-success.
Catholics resented the treatment of Gardiner and Bonner who
had been sent to the Tower, the one in June, 1548, for refusing

[1] See Gigon, *La Révolte de la gabelle en Guyenne*, Paris, 1906.

to obey the council's injunctions, and the other in September, 1549, for resisting the new service; and some of them hoped by a change of government to secure the restoration of the Latin mass. Protestants complained of Somerset's pliancy in religion and his lukewarmness in the cause of persecution, and sometimes cast in his teeth his brother's execution. The rich aldermen of London detested his patronage of Latimer, and nearly all well-to-do people hated his social policy. A spirit of revenge was abroad for the destruction of property during the late revolts, and the protector was suspected of meditating remedial rather than penal legislation in the approaching session of parliament. The victor of Dussindale was the natural leader of this reaction, and Warwick possessed all the political arts and unprincipled craft necessary to unite these divergent factions on a common though temporary platform. His chief ally was Wriothesley, the pliant catholic who regretted the protestant reformation and his loss of the chancellorship;[1] and at Warwick's and Wriothesley's houses in London the cabal against the protector was hatched. Of similarly conservative sympathies were the Earl of Arundel and Sir Richard Southwell. Gardiner hoped for release from the Tower, and Bonner appealed against his deprivation by Cranmer. Wealthy Londoners were alarmed by fantastic reports of the protector's designs against the city; government officials had cause to resent the outbursts of anger in which he occasionally indulged at their expense; while moderate members of the council objected to his monopoly of power, and could point to its evil results. A few social reformers such as Latimer and Hales, one or two personal friends like Sir Thomas Smith, and the mass of the commons were all the support on which the protector could count. Cranmer, Paget, and Cecil, who remained with him at Hampton Court, were not noted for steadfast adherence to lost causes.

In the first week of October Somerset became aware of

---

[1] He had in Henry VIII.'s reign been a strong supporter of the imperialist alliance, and it may have been through him that Charles V. was induced to view with approbation the protector's fall. The Venetian ambassador at the imperial court wrote in February, 1550, "The news of the release of the protector was heard here with no little regret, as it will apparently be the ruin of the Earl of Warwick, with whom his Imperial Majesty has an understanding; and it has been hinted to me on authority that the arrest of the protector and these late risings in London had their root in this court," *Venetian Cal.*, v., 298.

the extent of the movement against him, and on the 5th he issued a wild appeal to the commons to rise on his, the king's, and their own behalf. On the following night he fled with Edward to Windsor, summoned the army of the west under Russell and Herbert to his support, and despatched Sir William Petre to the council in London to demand the reason for their assembly. Petre did not return ; the ten thousand peasants who are said to have responded to the protector's call were an ill-armed rabble ; the city fathers adhered to the council ; and Russell and Herbert, after pacifying northern Hampshire, which they found in an uproar, turned against the protector the balance they held in suspense. On the 7th Somerset had offered " reasonable conditions " ; on the 9th Sir Philip Hoby came from London with assurances that the protector should not suffer in lands, goods, or honour, and that his friends should retain the places they held before. On the strength of these promises Somerset surrendered ; he was formally arrested on the 10th, and sent to the Tower on the 14th. The victorious council did not deem it necessary to keep their promises made to win the victory. Smith, Cecil, and others were sent to the Tower, fined, and deprived of their offices, while Paget shortly received a peerage for his services in procuring the duke's submission.

Somerset's fate depended upon the complexion of the new government. The coalition which had overthrown the protectorate was only united in antagonism to the protector. In the early days of its rule the omens seemed to portend a catholic restoration. " Those cruel beasts, the Romanists," wrote a protestant to Bullinger, " were now beginning to triumph over the downfall of our duke, the overthrow of our gospel now at its last gasp, and the restoration of their darling the mass. . . . They had begun to revive the celebration of their abominable mass in their conventicles, to practise their ancient mummeries at funerals and other offices of that kind, and to inundate themselves with wine, as became the champions of such a religion as theirs. And their furious rage had gone so far, as to threaten . . . the faithful servants of Christ with exile, fire, and sword." [1] Wriothesley rather than Warwick appeared to rule the roost : he " is lodged with his wife and son, next the king : every man repaireth to Wriothesley, honoureth Wriothesley, saith unto

[1] *Original Letters* (Parker Soc.), ii., 464 ; *cf. ibid.*, i., 69.

Wriothesley as the Assyrians did to Haman, and all things be CHAP.
done by his advice, and who but Wriothesley?"[1] The con- II.
servative, Wotton, succeeded the protestant Smith as secretary,
and other catholics like the Earl of Arundel, Sir Thomas and
Sir John Arundell,[2] and the Southwells[3] were basking in court
favour. In England, as in Germany after 1525, catholics hoped
that the failure of the social revolution would drag down the
cause of religious reform.

Nothing, however, illustrates more vividly the essentially
middle-class character of the reformation than the fact that in
both these countries it developed most rapidly in an atmosphere of social repression. The catholic camarilla found little
support for religious reaction in the parliament which reassembled in November, 1549. But its political conservatism
touched the pitch of panic and of passion, and the classes which
it represented wreaked their revenge on the masses which had
risen against them. The ex-protector's views on liberty and
toleration were laughed to scorn, and the readiness with which
this parliament extended treasons and restrained freedom
should dispose of the idea that the milder measures of Henry
VIII. were dictated solely by his arbitrary will. It was declared high treason for twelve or more persons to meet together for the purpose of imprisoning a privy councillor—an
offence of which the council itself had been guilty towards the
protector—and the same penalty was imposed upon persons
assembling for the purpose of " altering the laws," while the
safeguards of 1547, requiring the evidence of two witnesses
and the preferment of charges of treason within a specified

---

[1] Ponet, *Treatise of Politique Power*, 1556; *Lit. Remains of Edward VI.*,
ed. J. G. Nichols, Roxburghe Club, pp. 245-46.

[2] Not to be confused with Henry Fitzalan, twelfth Earl of Arundel ; Strype
even altered a document in order to maintain the confusion, *Lit. Remains*,
ii., 246.   Sir T. Arundell of Lanherne was first cousin of Lady Catherine Grey,
the Earl of Arundel's first wife ; and his half-sister Mary (formerly Countess of
Sussex) became the Earl of Arundel's second wife. Sir Thomas had been educated
in Wolsey's household, and married Queen Catherine Howard's sister. George
Cavendish in his *Metrical Visions* makes him the chief agent of Somerset's first
fall ; he was ancestor of the Arundells of Wardour. His brother, Sir John,
married Anne, sister of the Earl of Derby, and niece of the Duke of Norfolk
then in the Tower.

[3] The two Southwells were Sir Richard and Sir Robert, who was master of
the rolls. Both were catholics ; from Sir Richard descend the catholic Lords De
Clifford, and his illegitimate son was father of the well-known Jesuit and poet
Robert Southwell.

time, were omitted.   This act was not passed until it had been read six times in the house of commons and six times in the house of lords.   Less difficulty was experienced in reversing Somerset's agrarian policy, though even here, according to Latimer, there was variance in parliament " between the gentlemen and the commons ".   In the fervour of reaction parliament went back upon the whole tenour of Tudor land legislation, and re-enacted the statute of Merton expressly permitting lords of the manor to inclose as much as they liked provided that "sufficient" commons were left for their tenants.   "Who," asked Latimer in denouncing the act, "shall judge what is sufficient?"[1]   If the lords, he thought, had only left the tenants "sufficient" in 1236, there was no more than sufficient in 1549.   The tenants were not to be consulted on the definition. The inclosures might be made "notwithstanding their gainsaying and contradiction"; and if forty of them met to break down an inclosure or enforce a right of way, they might be condemned as traitors; if twelve, the offence was felony.   It was also felony to summon such a meeting or incite to such an act, to hunt in any inclosure, or to assemble with the object of abating rents or the price of corn; but capitalists were as usual allowed full liberty to combine to raise their prices.

On questions like these the lords and gentry recognised no distinction of creed.   If catholic landlords could have risen above the interests of their class in the sixteenth century and resisted the new greed as fiercely as the new learning, the religious history of England might have been a very different tale.   But even in matters of doctrine they had as yet few settled convictions, and the first signs of opposition to the "reformed" administration are traced in the attitude of the bishops.   Somerset had secured a majority of episcopal votes for all his ecclesiastical measures.   But now the majority of bishops voted against the bill for the destruction of all servicebooks except Henry VIII.'s Primers and the Book of Common Prayer,[2] and against the bill—so often passed before but never put in execution—authorising the appointment of a commission

---

[1] *Sermons*, p. 248.

[2] 3 and 4 Edw. VI., c. 10.   A proclamation based on this act denounced the rumours current since Somerset's fall that "the old Latin service and popish superstitions were to be restored," State Papers, Dom., ix., 57.

for the reform of the canon law. Their bill for the restoration
of episcopal authority was rejected, but nine of the fourteen
bishops present approved of the act for drawing up a new
Ordinal or book of ceremonies to be used at ordinations; they
may have been conciliated by the provision that half the commissioners for this purpose should be bishops. The significance
of the session from an ecclesiastical point of view is the union
of Cranmer, Holbeach, Ridley, Ferrar, and Goodrich with
Tunstall, Heath, Thirlby, and Day against the government on
the question of the reform of canon law. The English episcopate, or at least a majority of the bishops, had favoured the
reformation so long as it meant only an attack upon their
superior the pope, or upon monasteries, many of which were
exempt from their jurisdiction, or upon abstract doctrines.
But by the end of 1549 it had come to portend an attack upon
prelacy as a whole. The bishops opposed the bill for the reform of the canon law, fearing lest reform should end episcopal
jurisdiction. They began to feel more and more that the
interests of their order were bound up with the maintenance
of the old ecclesiastical system, till the time came when reform
had to be forced upon them by parliament in the teeth of their
unanimous opposition.

The hopes which catholics had built upon Somerset's ruin
fell to the ground. Gardiner remained in the Tower and was
soon deprived, while Bonner's appeal was rejected. The
leaders of the western rebellion, who had lain in the Tower
since September, were executed in January, 1550. Wriothesley ceased to attend the council after October, 1549, was
expelled from it on February 2, 1550, and confined to his
house;[1] Sir Richard Southwell was committed to the Fleet,
the two Arundells to the Tower, and the Earl of Arundel
to his house. Their offices and those of Somerset's adherents,
together with various peerages, were distributed among Warwick's faction. Warwick himself resumed his office as lord
admiral and combined with it the presidency of the council.
St. John was created Earl of Wiltshire and lord treasurer,
Russell became Earl of Bedford, Sir William Paget a baron,
and Northampton was made lord great chamberlain of England.
The English Alcibiades, as Ponet called Warwick, had deter-

[1] *Belvoir MSS.*, i., 55; Ponet, *Treatise*, sig. iii; *Acts of the P. C.*, 1550-52
passim.

mined to play the part of a "faithful and intrepid soldier of Christ". Hooper, who hailed him thus, also called him a "most holy and fearless instrument of the word of God"; he and Suffolk were "the two most shining lights of the Church of England," and Bale compared him with Moses.[1]

It was not easy to combine the proscription of the catholic lords with that of Somerset. The protector's fall had already begun to appear as the result of a catholic plot engineered by Wriothesley and his associates; a parliamentary move had been made for his release and restoration before the end of 1549; and his liberation from the Tower on February 6, 1550, followed naturally on the fall of the catholic councillors. Two months later he was readmitted to the privy council; such of his property as had not yet been sold or given away was restored to him; and in June his daughter Anne was married to Warwick's eldest son. The two factions were expected to unite in driving England along the lines of coercion towards a protestant goal.

[1] *Original Letters* (Parker Soc.), i., 82; ii., 399.

CHAPTER III.

SOMERSET AND WARWICK.

THE new government, in which Warwick exerted an influence none the less preponderant because he was never called protector and claimed no more than a nominal equality with his colleagues, cannot be accused of extravagant pretensions in the realm of foreign policy. As soon as Warwick had secured his position by the ejection of the catholics from the council, he took steps to terminate the war with Scotland and with France. Scotland had ceased to have an independent government, and overtures were necessarily made to the French court. A foreigner, as usual, was chosen to break the ice, and Antonio Guidotti, a Florentine banker resident at Southampton, was despatched early in January, 1550, to sound the Constable of France.[1] The preliminaries were settled with unwonted celerity, and on the 20th both governments nominated four commissioners for the negotiations. Their labours, too, were expedited by the accommodating disposition of the English council, and peace was proclaimed in London on March 29. The retrocession of Boulogne for 400,000 crowns, half the sum stipulated in the treaty of 1546, was not a great surrender; but the real price which England paid for peace was the abandonment of Scotland to the French. Henry II. not only treated it as part and parcel of his dominions,[2] but looked upon it as a stepping-stone to Ireland. Monluc, the bishop of Valence, had already been there intriguing with O'Donnell, O'Neill, and other chieftains who offered to become subjects of France;

[1] Edward VI. in his *Journal* writes of Guidotti "making several errands *from* the Constable of France" as though the overture came from France; and the Privy Council (*Acts*, 1550-52, p. 5) sent two thousand crowns to Gondi "master of the French king's finances . . . because he was the first motioner and procurer of this peace". This is probably a pretence to save the national pride.

[2] Ribier, *Lettres et Memoires d'Estat*, 1666, ii., 152, 288; *cf. Acts of the P. C.*, 1552-54, pp. 113-114.

and these intrigues did not cease with the war. England was almost held in the hollow of Henry's hand; he boasted that he had absolute disposal of the English king, his subjects and resources, and that England, France, and Scotland might be reckoned as one kingdom of which he was king. "They know too well our estate," wrote Mason from Paris, "and thereby think they may ride on our backs." [1]

The peace of 1550 was not so much to blame for this ignominious position as the inertia of the government in the years which followed; for the treaty relieved the exchequer of an intolerable strain; and something was done for England's credit by the release from French galleys of the Scots—including Knox—who had been captured at St. Andrews. But the respite which the peace secured was ill-employed. Warwick depended upon the favour of partisans who could only be kept in humour by lavish grants of lands and money; and while his chief supporters were being paid thousands a year—even in the currency of that time—for maintaining bands of horse and foot, while the chantry lands were being sold and church plate confiscated or embezzled, garrisons were being dismissed, ships laid up, and fortifications dismantled. In 1552, when the Baron de la Garde brought a French fleet to St. Helen's Point, Sir Henry Dudley, the vice-admiral, had to forego the usual striking of the French flag because his forces were too weak to compel observance of the custom. Warwick dared not ask parliament for supplies; he dared not stint his friends; and the last crumbs from the table of the church were insufficient to keep up the national forces to the level required by national needs. Warwick himself wrote in 1551, with reference to the financial distress of the government, that he would rather be dead than live such a life as the council had lived the last two or three years.[2] England ceased to count in foreign affairs; even in his utmost need in 1552 Charles V. and his Flemish subjects set little store on English help; and Henry II. was meditating an attack upon Calais [3] and an invasion of England as soon as his war with Charles should be ended. That war was a godsend

---

[1] *Foreign Cal.*, 1547-53, pp. 60, 63; Melville's *Memoirs*, Bannatyne Club, p. 9; Tytler, i., 291; *Hatfield MSS.*, i., 100; *Lit. Remains of Edw. VI.*, p. 300.

[2] *Hatfield MSS.*, i., 87.

[3] *Ibid.*, i., 82; *Foreign Cal.*, 1547-53, p. 225. The French said in 1551, that the retention of Calais by England was the "only cause of war".

to Warwick; it came too late to save Scotland from French domination, but soon enough to give the earl a fairly free hand for his domestic designs in England.

The unrecorded struggle between the protestants and catholics in the council at the end of 1549, was a turning-point in English history; and its issue in favour of the protestants in January, 1550, was immediately followed by an increase in the pace of reformation. The Prayer Book of 1549 was on the whole catholic; at least it was capable of a catholic interpretation, and it probably marks no further an advance than Henry VIII. was prepared to make in the autumn of 1546. The popular protest against it was less than that against the dissolution of the monasteries, and would never have been dangerous but for the coincidence of the outbreak against inclosures. But between 1550 and 1553 measures were thrust on the nation which definitely severed the English church from medieval catholicism. For this it was not yet prepared; and the revolutionary partisanship of Warwick provoked the reactionary partisanship of Mary.

The first ecclesiastical project of the new government was the Ordinal, on the alleged imperfections of which the church of Rome has, since the exposure of the Nag's Head fable, based her denial of the validity of Anglican orders.[1] This book restricted the orders to three by making no provision for the ordination of sub-deacons, acolytes, exorcists, lectors, and janitors; it simplified the rites of the old Pontifical and swept away some which are said to have dated from a period as late as the fifteenth century. On the day (February 2) that the council nominated the commission to draw up the Ordinal, to which parliament with singular confidence in the royal supremacy had given statutory authorisation beforehand, Tunstall ceased to attend its meetings; on the 7th after four days' deliberation the council confirmed Cranmer's sentence against Bonner; and on the 8th it summoned before it Heath, bishop of Worcester, who refused to accept the Ordinal, was sent to the Fleet in March, and deprived in the following year. In June the council resolved to prosecute Gardiner under the act of uniformity; in October proceedings were instituted against Bishop Day of Chichester for "seditious preaching"; and

[1] See below, p. 216, n.

within a few months the law was set in motion against Cole, the warden of New College, Oxford ; Morwen, the president of Corpus Christi College, Oxford ; White, the warden of St. Mary's, Winchester ; Dr. Chedsey, a future president of Corpus ; Serjeant Morgan ; Sir Anthony Browne (afterwards Viscount Montague) ; and the Lady Mary's chaplains.

Gardiner's case was complicated by a divergence of opinion in the council. Somerset, who had been re-admitted a member in April, sought to moderate the policy of the new government, and to procure Gardiner's release from the Tower on condition that he observed the act of uniformity. A deputation of the council, with Somerset at its head, obtained from Gardiner an undertaking that, although he would not himself have drawn the act in its existing form, he was prepared now that it was law to observe it himself and as bishop to enforce its observation upon others. No more could legally be demanded ; but Warwick and his friends resented the duke's endeavours.[1] They felt that Gardiner would be an obstacle to the progress of reform, and wanted to fill the episcopate with more obedient agents. Warwick, who had been absent for three months in the north, re-appeared at the council early in July ; a new set of articles was presented to Gardiner by a new deputation with Warwick instead of Somerset at its head ; and these articles required an abject submission which Gardiner refused to make. He was tried by a royal commission which was appointed on December 12 and included Cranmer, Ridley, Goodrich of Ely, Holbeach of Lincoln, Sir William Petre, Sir James Hales, two civilians, and two common lawyers. The proceedings lasted two months, and a vast amount of evidence was produced with the object of incriminating Gardiner's whole career.[2] On February 14, 1551, he was sentenced to deprivation, and his appeal to the king rejected.

On October 10 Bishops Day and Heath met with a similar fate. Less of politicians than Gardiner, they based their opposition to the government more on conscientious grounds than on such constitutional arguments as the invalidity of the exercise

---

[1] Warwick to Richard Whalley, State Papers, Dom., x., 9; Tytler, ii., 21-24, prints the letter, but misdates it 1551.

[2] The records of these proceedings occupy 250 pages in Townsend's edition of Foxe, vol. vi. ; occasionally they can be corrected and supplemented by reference to the State Papers and *Acts of the Privy Council.*

of the royal supremacy by the privy council. While Heath could not in conscience accept the Ordinal, Day repudiated the re-duction of the altar to a communion-table, although he had preached against transubstantiation.[1] The sees vacated by the death of Bishop Wakeman of Gloucester in 1549 and by the deprivation of Bonner, Gardiner, Heath, and Day were filled in accordance with the protestant views now officially adopted by the government. Hooper was designated for Gloucester and Ridley for London ; Ponet succeeded Ridley at Rochester and then Gardiner at Winchester; Scory, who took Ponet's bishopric of Rochester, was within a year translated to Day's at Chichester, and Hooper added Heath's bishopric of Wor-cester to his own of Gloucester.

The first Book of Common Prayer had been a compromise patient at least of a catholic interpretation. But this interpreta-tion was now rejected, and it was with the good wishes if not at the instigation of the government that Cranmer in his *Defence of the True and Catholic Doctrine of the Sacrament*, published in 1550, set to work to prove that the protestant gloss upon the Prayer Book was the true one. Gardiner whose imprisonment was not, until his deprivation, so rigorous as to prohibit literary activity, replied in *An Explication*, to which Cranmer in 1551 rejoined in *An Answer*. He rejected both the Lutheran and the Roman doctrine of the sacrament with-out descending to the Zwinglian view that the bread and wine were mere tokens ; there was a real presence " in the godly using " of the elements, but it was spiritual and not corporal ; " corporally and really (as the papists take that word)" Christ was " only in heaven, and not in the sacrament " ; and of course there was no sacrifice. With this view Ridley and Latimer, who had hitherto been conservative in his attitude to the doctrine, concurred ; and the real presence practically ceased to divide Anglican divines until it was revived in the seven-teenth century. Divisions arose rather over questions of church government, the nature of the ministry, and the out-ward symbols of the sacerdotal office.

Hooper raised the " vestiarian " controversy in 1550. He had imbibed, in exile, the purest milk of Zwinglianism ; and now when thrust by Warwick into the see of Gloucester, he

[1] *Lit. Remains of Edward VI.*, p. 255.

objected to the vestments of a bishop and to the form of oath,
" so help me God, all saints, and the holy evangelists," prescribed
alike for deacons, priests, and bishops at their ordination.   He
persuaded the young king to put his pen through the offending oath and to write to Cranmer recommending a simpler
form of consecration,[1] and even obtained the council's approbation.   But Cranmer and Ridley resisted the concession, and
Hooper was ordered to keep to his house.   Bucer and Martyr
counselled submission, À Lasco resistance.   Hooper broke
both his confinement and his silence, rushed into print with a
confession of faith, and in January, 1551, was committed first
to Cranmer's custody and then to the Fleet.   At length " the
father of nonconformity " deigned to conform and be consecrated
on March 8.   But his conscience was justified by the result ;
for although the " Aaronic vestments " remained for occasional
use, the oath by the saints disappeared in the Prayer-book of
1552 and was not restored in any revision.[2]

Ridley, while less scrupulous than Hooper with regard to
the oath and the vestments, was not less zealous against the
Roman catholic mass.   His diocese had been enlarged by the
incorporation of Henry VIII.'s newly founded see of Westminster, the bishop of which, Thirlby, was translated to
Norwich ; but any financial advantage which might have
accrued to the Bishop of London was neutralised by his forced
alienation of various manors.   Even so he fared better than
Ponet who was compelled to surrender all the lands of the
bishopric of Winchester in return for a fixed stipend ; this
made him directly dependent on the government, while his
manors were used to win supporters for Warwick.   Ponet was
hardly the man for moral resistance ; he married, in ignorance
no doubt, a woman whose former husband was still living at
Nottingham, and was divorced from her " with shame enough,"
as the chronicler relates, after his elevation to the bench.[3]
A similar charge, brought against Archbishop Holgate of
York, was not substantiated ;[4] but such incidents discredited

---

[1] *Original Letters*, ii., 567 ; this reference seems to have escaped the notice
of Dixon who (iii., 214) refers to the incident as a " pretty story ".

[2] Vol. xii. of the Domestic State Papers of Edward VI. is composed of a discussion of Hooper's case.

[3] *Greyfriars' Chron.*, p. 70 ; Machyn's *Diary*, pp. 8, 320.

[4] *Acts of the P. C.*, 1550-52, pp. 421, 426-27, and 1552-54, p. 256 ; *cf.* State
Papers, Dom., Mary, vi., 84.

the cause of the reformation and weakened the stand which the church might have made against the greed of the ruling faction. In the early years of the relaxation of the rule against clerical marriage, such unions were popularly regarded as little more reputable than the illicit connexions common enough in the middle ages; and the character of some bishops' wives was almost enough to justify their exclusion from cathedral precincts by Queen Elizabeth. Ridley avoided the difficulty by adhering to celibacy, and his visitation of London in May, 1550, included a rigorous inquiry into the morals of his clergy.

More stir was caused by his crusade against altars and against catholic representation, or misrepresentation, of the communion service of 1549. Even after St. Barnabas' day, 1550, when the altar was taken down in response to Ridley's charge, the privy council was informed that the communion in St. Paul's " was used as a very mass ".[1] By retaining the old vestments, repeating the old manual acts, and mumbling the words of the service which harmonised ill with the old symbolism, catholic celebrants could convey the impression that the old mass remained in spite of the act of uniformity. Ridley's charge enumerated and forbade the realistic ceremonies not enjoined by the Book of Common Prayer, and exhorted churchwardens and curates to substitute a table for the altar. His example was pressed by the council on other bishops, and in November a general removal of altars throughout the country was proclaimed. There was no substance in the sacrament of the altar but bread and wine, declared the preacher at St. Paul's Cross on Trinity Sunday; this was now the official view, and the government was resolved to suppress all ritual and all symbolism which implied any other doctrine.

The comparative ease with which the new theology was imposed on a reluctant majority is capable of explanation. That majority, so far as it was lay, had never been encouraged to form opinions of their own in matters of faith; they had always been taught to obey the voice of authority, and the habit of obedience remained strong in those who rejected the right of private judgment, even when the authority was that of the state instead of the church. It is the penalty of systems not based on consent that the passive obedience, which

---

[1] *Acts of the P. C.,* 1550-52, p. 138.

they require as a normal condition, disarms the active defence they need at a crisis. The catholic laity had not been equipped to dispute theological questions, and their clerical champions had been silenced or discredited. The protestants were on principle less amenable to collective discipline and more prone to individual opinion. But even they believed in the divine ordination of the powers that be; the multitude in Tudor times paid homage to authority, and it was left to the few to debate and determine who or what that authority should be. There were a few riots against the removal of altars; but when half a dozen catholic bishops had been imprisoned, there was no one who ventured on open resistance to the government except the Lady Mary.

She had been singled out for attack by a preacher at St. Paul's Cross in August, 1550, but it was not until a year later that the council made a determined effort to reduce her to conformity. Somerset had connived at the masses celebrated in her household despite the act of uniformity, and apparently she had been promised a continuation of this privilege until Edward came of age. But in 1550 Charles V. refused to permit the English ambassador in the Netherlands to have service at the embassy according to the Book of Common Prayer. "English service in Flanders!" quoth he; "speak not of it. I will suffer none to use any doctrine or service in Flanders that is not allowed of the church;"[1] and the council thought of retaliating upon Mary and Charles's ambassador. The resort of her servants to the emperor's court was resented, especially after the French king in August informed the council of a design on the emperor's part to convey Mary to Flanders;[2] and proceedings were taken against her chaplain in December. In February, 1551, Charles reminded the council of its promise to Mary; but war had broken out between him and the Barbary corsairs, hostilities were imminent with the French in Italy, Henry was in communication with Maurice of Saxony, while a treaty of alliance between England and France was nearly concluded and the French were talking about having a national church council of their own.

[1] Wotton to the Council, June 30, 1551, *Foreign Cal.*, 1547-53, p. 138.
[2] *Foreign Cal.*, 1547-53, p. 53; *Lit. Remains of Edw. VI.*, pp. 284-85, 291; *Orig. Letters* (Parker Soc.), ii., p. 568; cf. *Acts of the P. C.*, 1550-52, p. 77.

Warwick thought it safe to repudiate the promise to Mary; CHAP.
and Wotton was sent to Flanders to tell Charles that although III.
Mary had a king for her father, a king for her brother, and was
akin to an emperor, yet in England there was but one king and
he had but one law by which to rule all his subjects.   The
whole council was summoned in August to consider the question.   Edward himself wrote a letter to Mary enjoining obedience; and Lord Chancellor Rich, Petre, and Wingfield were sent
down to argue with her in person and to arrest her household
officials.   It was ill arguing with a Tudor: "My father," she
said, "made the more part of you almost out of nothing;"
and as she read the king's letter she remarked: "Ah! good
Master Cecil took much pain here".   When Edward came of
age, she said, he would find her "ready to obey his orders in
religion," but as yet he could not judge of such things.   It was
a Tudor rather than a catholic attitude, but that made it all the
harder for the council to combat.   A privy council could not
behead or imprison a Tudor, and Mary's defiance succeeded;
her officers, Rochester, Englefield, and Waldegrave were sent
to the Fleet, but Mary herself heard mass to the end of her life.

The episode, however, was not quite fruitless for Warwick's
purposes.   Somerset had been inveigled into taking part in
these proceedings; his name stood at the head of the list of
the councillors who directed the persecution, and the deputation sent to browbeat Mary consisted of the council's least
protestant members.   "You be all of one sort therein," she
said; and the result was to cut from Somerset's feet any support he might have derived from his efforts to moderate Warwick's policy and from his imperialist sympathies in foreign
affairs.   The duke himself played into Warwick's hands by
alienating his former partisans; and as if to show that he was
now upon his good behaviour he seized and executed at the
end of August "certain that began a new conspiracy for destruction of the gentlemen at Okingham".[1]   Numerous local
risings in 1550 and 1551 showed that neither their failure in
1549 nor the drastic legislation which followed it had disposed
of the peasants' discontent.   There were commotions in Middle-

---

[1] *Lit. Remains*, p. 340. "Okingham" is now Wokingham. The initial "w"
being mute was often omitted, and Woking appears as "Oking," Woodall as
"Udall," just as the "w" in "woman" is still silent in many dialects.

sex where a mysterious "Captain Red Cap," who had escaped from the imprisonment inflicted on him for his conduct in 1549, was fêted by the commons. In Kent and Sussex they plotted to assemble at Heathfield on Whit Sunday, 1550; in Nottinghamshire "certain constables by two and two rode from parish to parish to raise the commons"; and in Essex a conspiracy of the peasants threatened to facilitate the Flemish plan for carrying off the Lady Mary. The council offered a free pardon and twenty pounds reward to each informer, and despatched the troops returning from Boulogne into Dorset, Hampshire, Sussex, Essex, Kent, and Suffolk. Bedford was once more ordered to the scene of his late exploits, and Herbert to the Welsh marches. But the "inconstant disposition of the commons" required a permanent means of repression, and measures were taken to create a standing army controlled by the county magnates. A few of the greater lords were allowed a hundred cavalry each, with five hundred pounds a quarter out of the treasury for their maintenance; others were allotted fifty and had a proportionate grant. The commissions for lieutenancy, which had long been occasionally made out for special purposes and districts, were applied to nearly all the shires for the summers of 1550 and 1551 to guard against revolts, and then became a permanent institution; and to these lords lieutenants were gradually transferred the military functions of the sheriffs.

Even so, there were risings in Leicestershire, Northamptonshire, Rutland, and Berkshire in 1551, and popular discontent was intensified by a further debasement of the coinage. Henry VIII. had raised the alloy in silver coins to two-thirds; Somerset in 1549 reduced it to one-half; but Warwick now increased it to three-quarters, and in June, 1551, it was resolved that every three ounces of silver should be mixed with nine ounces of alloy. In the following month the value of the "testoons," or debased shillings, was called down first to ninepence and then to sixpence, while a proclamation forbade the raising of prices beyond a fifth. To add to the distress the sweating sickness reappeared with unwonted virulence; one plague after another, lamented a circular letter of the council, had been sent to punish the wickedness of the people, the covetousness of the rich, and the slothfulness of the bishops. "They do take us all for damned souls," wrote Morysine from the Netherlands, where people asked in scorn: "Where is now their God?" His heart bled, said Mason, to hear men at the French court talk of the buying and selling of offices in England, the decaying of grammar schools and universities, with many other enormities which they showed one another printed in English books and set forth by English preachers. Ireland was theirs, they boasted, whenever their king should give them the signal, Calais was not a seven nights' work, and the dissensions in England were great.[1]

Popular discontent bred disunion among the ruling faction even after Warwick's purging and packing of the council. Somerset had made practically no change in its composition, but within two years of his fall twelve new members were added in Warwick's interest. Somerset, however, was not content with the secondary position to which he was now relegated, and the ill-success of the government provided him with a party and some legitimate cause for criticism. He naturally became the focus of opposition, but the function of leader of the opposition was not recognised in the sixteenth century. There was no convention by which one half of the privy council could spend its time in criticising and discrediting the other half. The whole body was part and parcel of the government, and the only arbiter of differences was the crown. To Edward VI. it was hardly possible to appeal, and an appeal to the country against the majority of the council almost amounted to treason. Faction was the inevitable result when two ambitious rivals quarrelled, and throughout 1550 and 1551 the council was distracted between the claims of Somerset and those of Warwick. Either could carry his own measures when the other was away, and Somerset utilised Warwick's occasional absences to provide for his friends and prepare for his own return to power ; but when both were present Warwick exercised the greater influence. While, however, Warwick controlled the council, Somerset counted on parliament, and a busy but indiscreet and unstable partisan named Richard Whalley mooted a scheme for Somerset's restoration to the protectorship at the next session.[2] To

---

[1] Tytler, i., 404; *Foreign Cal.*, 1547-53, pp. 58, 72, 88 ; *Hatfield MSS.*, i., 90.
[2] *Cf.* F. von Raumer, *Illustrations of History*, ii., 77, quoting MS. St. Germain, 740 : "Somerset also in conjunction with Arundel and others of the dis-

CHAP.
III.

summon or not to summon parliament accordingly became a burning question. It stood prorogued till October, 1550; in August, during Somerset's absence, the council, in spite of the lord chancellor's protests, determined to postpone the session until January, 1551. In October, while Warwick was away, the council took steps to call it earlier; but Warwick returned and frustrated the attempt,[1] and on one pretext or another parliament was kept from meeting until after Somerset's death.

The strife in which parliament was thus prevented from intervening could only end in the proscription of one or the other party. In such struggles the less scrupulous faction commonly carries the day, and Somerset was no match for the craft and subtlety of his rival. Any solution was better than the continued distraction which impressed foreign observers with a conviction of the impending ruin of England. War against England was strongly urged at the French court "on the grounds of its internal dissensions"; and in February, 1551, Mason reported that Henry was bent upon hostilities. The Guises were egging him on; their credit "passeth all others," even that of the Constable Montmorency; and their sister, Mary of Scotland, was "made a goddess". There were also English catholics, comprising the Earls of Shrewsbury and Derby, Lord Dacre, the warden of the west marches, Sir Robert Bowes, warden of the east and middle marches, and the Constables. The Lady Mary was thinking of flight to the Earl of Shrewsbury, who was threatened with the loss of his presidency of the council of the north, as was Derby with the loss of his regalia in the Isle of Man. In April Dorset was meditating a journey to the North in Warwick's interests, and Somerset a flight thither in his own; for his influence there had been strong since his services under Henry VIII. "There is chopping and changing of them of the council. The gentry are obliged to fortify themselves in their houses, except those who are obliged to go to the wars, and the common people die of hunger. . . . The end of this heavy tragedy of that realm with the ruin of

contented and envious, projected the plan of demonstrating in the next parliament that the kingdom was ill-administered and the people oppressed with fresh taxes, the king poorer than ever, and that no public servant received his just salary; that those in power governed simply after their own caprice, without observing the laws or customs of the realm" (*cf. Venetian Cal.*, v., 343).

[1] *Lit. Remains*, pp. 255, 290; *Acts of the P. C.*, 1550-52, pp. 104, 107, 141,

the king will be shortly seen."[1]   In February Whalley's plan CHAP.
had come to light, and Shrewsbury had been implicated.   Sir III.
Ralph Fane, another partisan of Somerset, offered armed resistance to Warwick's claim to Postern Park in Kent, and was
committed to the Tower.   Bishop Tunstall was imprisoned in
his house on suspicion of complicity in the catholic designs.
Others were arrested on a charge of having "practised a conspiracy tending to rebellion, especially in the city of London,"
while the lords of the council about St. George's day (April 23),
dined three days together "for to shew agreement amongst
them ".[2]

The storm blew over for the time, and Somerset was assured
by Herbert on his honour that no harm was meant him ; but
the events of these few days towards the end of April were
to furnish the indictments against him.   For more than five
months the plot, which he was accused of having hatched
against the government in April, remained unknown to its
intended victims ; and Warwick used the interval to strengthen
himself by a treaty of alliance with France and of marriage between Edward VI. and the French king's daughter Elizabeth.
Henry II. was to be father-in-law of the King of England and
of the Queen of Scotland, and a bond of union between the two
realms might be found in France.   Warwick was less concerned
about England's dependence upon France than about Edward
VI.'s dependence upon himself.   His design was to dominate
the boy-king's mind, and then release him from the trammels
of minority.   " He had raised such an opinion of himself in the
mind of the king," declares a contemporary French account,
" that the latter respected him as if he had been the Duke's [3]
subject, and did, as if of his own impulse, everything which
Northumberland desired, only to please him.   From fear of
exciting jealousy, should it be known how much he interfered
in everything, he caused all affairs in which he would not be seen
to meddle to be set going by one Gates,[4] a chamberlain, who also
brought him information of all conversation which passed about
the king.   For this Gates was always in the royal chamber, and

---

[1] *Foreign Cal.*, 1547-53, pp. 119-20.
[2] *Acts of the P. C.*, pp. 257, 262-44 ; *Lit. Remains*, pp. 315, 353.
[3] *I.e.*, Warwick, who became Duke of Northumberland in Oct., 1551.
[4] Sir John Gates (1504?-1553) had been made vice-chamberlain of the household and privy councillor in April, 1551.

was believed to be one of those who mainly instigated the king
to make a will against his sister. Northumberland used to
visit the king by night when he could not be seen and all were
asleep. In the morning, Edward entered the council, and
brought matters forward as if they proceeded from himself and
were of his own motion, to the astonishment of many." [1]

Gradually the king was made to supplant the regency
created by Henry VIII.'s will; the scheme was Warwick's
subtler and more efficient substitute for the protectorate, and
he sheltered himself behind the throne while wielding its
authority. In August, 1550, during Somerset's absence it was
resolved to dispense with the form "by the advice of the
council" in all documents signed by the king. In August,
1551, it was determined that Edward—aged thirteen— "should
come and sit at council".[2] Lord Chancellor Rich refused to
make out commissions except on warrants duly signed by the
requisite number of privy councillors; he was reprimanded by
the king who wrote pointing out that his authority did not
depend upon the number of his councillors; and in November
he was informed that for the future no councillors should
countersign royal documents.[3] With wise anticipation Rich
resigned the great seal to avoid responsibility for the acts of
Warwick's despotic puppet.

Others enjoyed the fleeting sunshine, and purchased a
transient greatness at the price of their peace of mind. On
October 11 there fell such a shower of titles and dignities as
was never seen before or after in Tudor times. The number
of dukes was doubled by the creation of Warwick as Duke of
Northumberland and Dorset as Duke of Suffolk.[4] Wiltshire
was made Marquis of Winchester and Herbert Earl of Pem-

[1] Raumer, *Illustrations*, ii., 78-79.
[2] *Acts of the P. C.*, 1550-52, pp. 110-11; *Lit. Remains*, p. 337.
[3] *Ibid.*, pp. 347-48; *Acts of the P. C.*, 1550-52, p. 416.
[4] The Tudors were chary of making dukes; only one survived Henry VII.,
and Buckingham disappeared in 1521. Two dukedoms had been revived or created
in 1514, that of Norfolk for Surrey's victory at Flodden, and that of Suffolk for
Charles Brandon; Suffolk's dukedom died out with the death of his two young
sons (by his second wife) of the plague in 1551; it was now revived in favour of
Henry Grey, Marquis of Dorset, who had married their half-sister Frances
Brandon. After the attainder of Somerset in 1551 and of Northumberland and
Suffolk in 1553, Norfolk became the only duke in England; and with the attainder
of his grandson in 1572 dukedoms died out until the 17th century,

broke: knighthoods were bestowed on Warwick's son-in-law
Henry Sidney, on his cousin Henry Dudley, on John Cheke
the king's tutor, on Henry Neville, and on Cecil, who had
deserted Somerset for Warwick and been made secretary in
succession to Wotton a year before; while Gates, Andrew
Dudley, Sir Philip Hoby, and others were appeased with the
spoils of Ponet's bishopric.[1] Warwick's was the only dukedom
conferred in Tudor times on one not connected by blood or
marriage with the royal family. No one could mistake the
signal; Warwick's faction had won, and it only remained to
deal with the vanquished. Their shrewdest adviser Paget had
already been confined to his house for having doubted the
emperor's word.

On October 7 Edward was informed that Sir Thomas Palmer,
a capable but vainglorious soldier who had once described
the protector as "the founder of his beginning and furtherer
hitherto in all his causes,"[2] had revealed to Northumberland a
conspiracy of Somerset's to invite him, Northampton, and other
lords to a banquet and cut off their heads.[3] The discovery had
been conveniently anticipated by Somerset's summons to court
to entertain M. de Jarnac, the French king's envoy. He appeared on October 4 and was sent to the Tower on the 16th.
Lord Grey de Wilton, Sir Ralph Fane, Sir Miles Partridge, Sir
Michael Stanhope, Sir Thomas Holcroft, Sir Thomas Arundell,
Whalley, and half a dozen others were arrested on the same or
the following day,[4] and a little later the Earl of Arundel and
Paget were sent to the Tower. The new *gens d'armes*, as
they were called, were mustered, and parliament which should
have met in November was once more prorogued. Various
versions of the plot were circulated to quiet the people and
satisfy foreign courts, and some of the prisoners were tortured
to provide confirmation.[5] The Constable of France suggested
that probably Charles V. and the Lady Mary were at Somerset's back, and offered troops for Northumberland's help; while
an anonymous correspondent in England informed a friend
abroad that Somerset's instigator was Christian III. of Denmark.[6]

---

[1] Royal MS., 18, C. xxiv., f. 135.   [2] *Foreign Cal.*, 1547-53, p. 308.
[3] *Lit. Remains*, p. 353.
[4] Council Warrant Book in Royal MS., 18, C. xxiv., f. 158.
[5] *Acts of the P. C.*, 1550-52, p. 407.
[6] Tytler, ii., 92; *Cal. State Papers, Domestic*, Addenda, 1547-65, p. 410.

　　　These rumours were hardly wilder than Edward's version of Palmer's tale, and the alleged plot for assassination did not find its way into the official indictments.[1] By these Somerset was charged with gathering an assembly for the purpose of imprisoning Northumberland, Northampton, and Pembroke, and with inciting the citizens of London to insurrection with drums, trumpets, and shouts of "Liberty". The former offence was treason by the act of 1550 (3 and 4 Ed. VI., c. 5) if the assembly refused to disperse at the sheriff's order; no such order having been given, Coke held that Somerset's condemnation was illegal. But he was really condemned on the second count which amounted to felony. If there had been drums, trumpets, and shouts in London "about St. George's day," they would hardly have taken five months to reach the council's ears; but "open word or deed" was enough for the act, and to that extent Somerset was probably guilty. It was, however, an act passed by his enemies after his fall in 1549; unlike Thomas Cromwell he made no bloody laws by which he himself could be condemned. His offence was that five months before, in April or May, he had made a half-hearted attempt to change the government without, he protested, intending bodily harm to his opponents; and had purposed summoning parliament to confirm the *coup d'état*.[2] He may also have tried, as Lord Strange declared, to learn the secrets of the king, to arrange a marriage between Edward and his daughter, and to influence the Lady Elizabeth against Northumberland. But the whole evidence for the plot is discredited by the character of Somerset's alleged accomplices, such as Lord Grey de Wilton and the Earl of Arundel; by the intimacy between Northumberland and Somerset's chief accuser Palmer; by the stout protestations of innocence on the scaffold on the part of the principal agents, Stanhope, Fane, and Partridge;[3] and finally by the confession of Northumberland and of Palmer themselves that the case against Somerset had been fabricated.[4]

---

[1] These are extant in the Baga de Secretis and are calendared in App. ii. (pp. 228-29) to the Fourth Report of the Deputy Keeper of the Records.

[2] Somerset's examination, Tytler, ii., 49.

[3] See my *England under Somerset*, pp. 288-305.

[4] Froude, v., 36, has printed Renard's description of Northumberland's confession to Somerset's sons that he had "procuré sa mort à tort et faulsement"; and of Palmer's confession that "l'escripture qu'il advouche et maintint contre

The trial was fixed for December 1. Winchester, whom CHAP.
Knox designates as "the crafty fox, Shebna" and describes III.
as one of Somerset's most active foes, was appointed lord high
steward to preside over the court. Of the twenty-six peers
summoned to sit, Winchester, Northumberland, Suffolk, Northampton, and Pembroke were the most conspicuous. They
were challenged as being parties to the case, but a peer was
supposed to be immune from the prejudices of ordinary
jurymen and might not legally be challenged on the score
of partiality. In the darkness of a December morning, between
five and six o'clock, Somerset was brought by water from
the Tower to Westminster Hall, and strict injunctions were
given that the people should remain indoors. The court
contained no partisan of Somerset; but even so, it could not
be persuaded to believe the charge of treason. As a compromise between acquittal and condemnation for treason, the
prisoner was pronounced guilty of felony; and Northumberland and Winchester made a merit of their mercy in withholding a penalty which they could not induce the court to inflict.
Many peers expected that the death sentence would be com-
muted for imprisonment; and the people, on seeing Somerset
taken back to the Tower, with the axe averted, cast off their
usual stony indifference, threw up their caps, and raised shouts
which rolled up Whitehall and were heard in Long Acre fields.
Some thought the duke was acquitted, others hoped for his

le feu Protecteur estoit fausse, fabricquée par le dict duc (de Northumberland) et
advoué par luy à la requeste du dict duc". He adopts it with some hesitation on
the ground that it "is strange that a foreign ambassador should be the only
authority". The absence of all reference to these confessions in contemporary
chronicles is not strange because they were privately made, and not publicly on
the scaffold. Renard was intimately acquainted with all that went on in Mary's
court; and there was no reason to fabricate such confessions : they had nothing
to do with the charges on which Northumberland and Palmer were condemned.
Moreover Renard's account is confirmed by a French narrative of which Froude
was not aware (Raumer, *Illustrations*, ii., 79-80). According to this Northumberland confessed to Gardiner, not to Somerset's sons, that "no guilt pressed so
heavily on his conscience as that of his intrigues against Somerset". It also
narrates that Palmer "before his death, repented of his conduct and declared
that he had never given evidence that Somerset was seeking the life of Northumberland; he also caused the little children of Somerset to be brought to him
and kissed them" (*ib.*, ii., 77). Unfortunately Raumer's reference to the MS.
in the Bibliothèque Nationale (Fonds St. Germain, 740) is erroneous, and my
efforts to trace the *provenance* of his quotation have failed.

pardon, and cried "God save him" all the way back to the Tower.[1]

The lords, says the chronicler, were astounded at this demonstration; and if Northumberland had ever thought of mercy, this indication of the strength of popular feeling in Somerset's favour dispelled it; he was not likely to pardon a dangerous rival. For seven weeks Somerset lay under sentence of death, consoling himself by inditing pious reflections.[2] His execution was precipitated by the necessity for summoning parliament. It was called for January 23, and would assuredly exert itself on Somerset's behalf. On the 18th Edward drew up a memorandum of business for the privy council; one of the items was "the matter for the Duke of Somerset's confederates to be considered as appertaineth to our surety and quietness of our realm, that by their punishment example may be shewed to others". Before this memorandum was submitted to the board, the wording had been altered by Edward himself or some one else so as to run, "The matter for the Duke of Somerset *and his* confederates . . . that by their punishment *and execution*," etc.[3] The first version was an instruction to the council to take measures for the trial of Fane, Partridge, Stanhope, and others who had not yet been put on their defence; the second was an order to arrange for Somerset's execution, and we shall see that by a similar alteration of Edward's words, another of Northumberland's schemes was brought to pass later on.[4]

At eight in the morning of the 22nd, "when hardly any person suspected such an event,"[5] Somerset was brought out on to the scaffold on Tower Hill; he made no confession of the crimes with which he was charged, and the crowd received with approving cries his protests of devotion to the king and com-

---

[1] Wriothesley, *Chron.*, ii., 63; *cf.* Guaras, *Accession of Queen Mary*, p. 83, "the matter being so trivial, it was held for certain in all men's esteem that the king would pardon him".

[2] Brit. Mus., Stowe MS., 1066, contains some of these.

[3] Cotton MS. Vespasian F. xiii., f. 171. The alterations are in Edward's hand or in one simulating his; in either case the author of the alterations was Northumberland, *cf. Lit. Remains*, pp. 489-90.

[4] See below, p. 84.

[5] *Orig. Letters* (Parker Soc.), ii., 731; *cf.* Guaras, p. 83, and *Foreign Cal.*, 1547-53, p. 211, where Morysine laments to Cecil in Greek that pity was banished out of the world.

monwealth. A sudden explosion interrupted his speech, and a
panic ensued; Somerset might have escaped in the confusion,
and was censured for lack of spirit in not making the attempt.

The resignation and dignity of his behaviour add to
the difficulty of summing up the protector's strangely inco-
herent character. His uniform success as a military commander is in sharp contrast with the visionary nature of his
political aims; and the greed with which he seized on the spoils
of the church seems to belie the generosity with which he
treated his tenants. The hauteur he displayed towards colleagues conflicts with the humility with which he accepted his
fate; and the obstinacy with which he championed the poor sets
off the facility with which he abandoned his brother. He had
no taste nor gift for intrigue himself, but he was pliant in
the hands of subtler schemers. Of his bravery, of his personal
morality, and of the sincerity of his religious professions there
can be no doubt, though his lack of zeal caused many protestants to compare him unfavourably with Warwick. He did
not betray his friends or shirk responsibility, and he was somewhat lost in the devious ways of the statecraft of his age.
"He was endowed and enriched with the most excellent
gifts of God both in body and in mind,"[1] wrote no friendly
critic on his execution; while another exclaimed, "And this
is the end of an ambitious heart and insatiable mind".[2]
He was greedy of wealth and grasped at authority. But he
pursued power for something more than its own sake and
private advantage. His ideas were large and generous: he
sought the union of England and Scotland, the advancement
of liberty, the destruction of social injustice. As a statesman
he was bankrupt without guile; but his quick sympathies
touched the heart of the people; and it was no slight honour
to be remembered as "the good duke" by that generation of
Machiavelli.

[1] *Orig. Letters* (Parker Soc.), ii., 733.   [2] *Foreign Cal.*, 1547-53, p. 192.

CHAPTER IV.

THE PROTESTANT REFORMATION.

SOMERSET safely removed, the way was clear for a session of parliament. An effort had been made to secure satisfactory results at the by-elections, and at the end of October, 1551, the lord chancellor was directed to inquire how many members had died since the last session "to the intent that grave and wise men might be elected to supply their places, for the avoiding of the disorder that hath been noted in sundry young men and others of small judgement". Reading, which had elected John Seymour in place of a deceased member, was ordered to choose a different representative; the sheriff of Hertfordshire was told "to use the matter in such sort as Mr. Sadler may be elected and returned"; and the sheriff of Surrey was "willed to prefer Sir Thomas Saunders".[1] Parliament met on the day after Somerset's execution, and it was soon evident that the council's interference with the elections had failed, as usual, to produce the desired effect. The legislature could not recall Somerset to life, but it could ensure that no one should be put to death by quite the same procedure; and into a treason bill which it passed there was reintroduced the clause requiring the evidence of two witnesses, with the further proviso that they must be confronted with the prisoner. Probably this was none of the council's doing; for the bill originally brought in to take the place of the expiring act of 1549 had been withdrawn, owing no doubt to opposition in the commons. The house also declined to proceed with a bill for Bishop Tunstall's attainder on a charge of misprision of treason.

The lords, however, were more amenable than the house of commons or common juries. The peers had passed the bill against Tunstall, Cranmer alone protesting, just as a court of

---

[1] *Acts of the P. C.*, 1550-52, pp. 400, 457, 459, 471.

peers had condemned Somerset. But a common jury had to CHAP.
be kept in confinement for twenty-four hours without meat or IV.
drink, candle or fire, before it would condemn his supposed
accomplice, Sir Thomas Arundell;[1] and Northumberland
feared to ask or failed to obtain from the house of commons
either a subsidy or a parliamentary confirmation of Somerset's
attainder. These exceptions to the usual readiness of parliament to sanction Tudor executions indicate a deep distrust of
Northumberland and his methods. But he could effect by
royal commission what he could not achieve through parliament; and in October, after being imprisoned for sixteen
months without trial, Tunstall was deprived of the bishopric
of Durham by a special commission of lay judges. The
pretext was his concealment of one of the numerous plots in
the north in the spring of 1551. The proof of his concealment
was discovered in December in a casket of letters belonging
to Somerset; and his real offence was that he had revealed the
plot to Somerset instead of to Northumberland.

The parliament of 1552 also showed spirit by rejecting
or refusing to consider a dozen bills drafted by the young
king himself; but its independence was not always admirable
or disinterested, and these measures were well-meant, if somewhat amateur, efforts to redress a few of the crying evils of the
time. Patrons were to be prohibited from paying to curates
and vicars only part of the revenues of their benefices, and
reserving the rest to themselves; spiritual persons were not to
hamper their successors by granting long leases of their lands;
restrictions were to be placed on the regrating of merchandise
and on the engrossing of farms; horses and bullion were not
to be exported from the realm; the growing of timber was to be
encouraged, and extravagance in wearing apparel restrained.[2]
Edward was beginning to think for himself, and he explained
his reasons for these proposals in a sensible essay. But he
could not coerce his council; and the obstruction, which his
bills encountered during their chequered career in both houses
of parliament, was probably viewed with satisfaction by his
government.

On one question, however, Edward, his council, and his

---

[1] *Lit. Remains,* pp. 393-94; Machyn, *Diary,* p. 15.
[2] *Lit. Remains,* pp. 491-95; *Lords'* and *Commons' Journals,* Feb.-April, 1552.

parliament were in general agreement. The first Book of
Common Prayer had failed for reasons similar to those
which proved fatal to Charles V.'s *Interim*. In either case
the compromise was made binding on one part only; every
Lutheran in Germany was to accept as a minimum the catholicism contained in the *Interim*, every catholic in England
the protestantism in the Prayer Book. But catholics in Germany could be as reactionary, and protestants in England
almost as revolutionary as they liked. There were indeed
limits in England; private judgment could not outrun the
royal supremacy without becoming heresy, and the faith, if
not catholic, must at any rate be national. From the point of
view of this ideal the aliens, who had fled to England as a
religious refuge, or had been imported, like Somerset's weavers
at Glastonbury, to develop English manufactures, were a difficulty.[1] The house of lords discussed a bill to protect "the
king's subjects from such heresies as might happen by strangers
dwelling among them". It was committed to some bishops
and then forgotten; but a commission "for the examination
of heresies" was appointed in October. There was "a sect
newly sprung in Kent," and Northumberland was anxious to
place Knox in Scory's see at Rochester, partly to act as whet-
stone to Cranmer and partly because "he would be a great
confounder of these Anabaptists".[2] The term was vaguely
used, but it hardly applies to the two heretics actually burnt
in Edward's reign; one Joan Bocher, or Butcher, suffered for
denying the humanity, and the other, a Dutch physician,
George van Parris, for denying the divinity, of Christ.[3]

These occasional vagaries did not distress a council, which

---

[1] See *Acts of the P. C.*, 1552-54, pp. 160-61; they refused to conform to the
second act of uniformity, and were allowed their own service for the time. They
fled on Mary's accession, but a similar licence was granted under Elizabeth and
renewed until the time of Laud.

[2] Tytler, ii., 142; *Acts of the P. C.*, 1552-54, pp. 131, 138; *cf.* Hooper in
Orig. Letters (Parker Soc.), i., 65-66.

[3] Joan, whose name is also given as Baron and Barnes, had been in trouble
for heresy in 1542, but had been protected by Cranmer (*Letters and Papers of
Henry VIII.*, 1543, pt. ii. *passim*); her opinions grew more heterodox, and she
was condemned by Cranmer in May, 1549, and burnt in May, 1550. Foxe's story
about Edward VI.'s compassion for her is probably apocryphal (see my *Cranmer*,
pp. 261-63; *Lit. Remains*, pp. 580-81). For Parris, see Cranmer's Register, f. 79,
in *Lit. Remains*, pp. 312-13, and Wriothesley, *Chron.*, ii., 47; he was burnt on
April 24, 1551.

believed with Cecil that "no state could be in safety where there was toleration of two religions,"[1] so much as the "great number of people in divers parts of the realm" who did "wilfully and damnably refuse to come to their parish churches";[2] and it resolved to cure the nation of its reluctance to accept moderate reforms by enacting more radical measures and increasing the coercion. The second act of uniformity, which passed with comparative ease in 1552, sanctioned the ecclesiastical censure and excommunication of laymen who neglected to attend common prayer on Sundays and holydays, and threatened those who attended any other than the authorised form of worship with six months' imprisonment for the first, a year's imprisonment for the second, and life-long imprisonment for the third offence. The Prayer Book thus enforced is substantially the Prayer Book of to-day without the articles. It included the Ordinal of 1550 as well as the Prayer Book of 1549, but both of them were considerably revised. Bucer supplied Cranmer with elaborate comments on the text of the earlier Prayer Book, and Peter Martyr sent advice; but the work of revision was done by the archbishop himself with Ridley's assistance, and they did not always follow the lines suggested by their correspondents. How far the views expressed in the revision were indigenous in growth, and how far due to foreign influence it is impossible to say. But it is clear that whatever foreign inspiration there may have been, was Zwinglian rather than Calvinistic, and that the point of view adopted was not exactly that of any foreign church or any foreign divine in England.

The changes were uniformly in the protestant direction indicated by Cranmer's answer to Gardiner on the mass, by Ridley's visitation charge, and by the council's proceedings against Bishops Heath and Day. The communion service was so altered and re-arranged as to exclude that Roman catholic interpretation which Gardiner and others had contrived to read into the service-book of 1549. The altar was turned into a communion-table, which was to be placed in the body of the church or in the chancel; ordinary instead of unleavened bread was to be used; the rubric enjoining the use of the alb and cope

---

[1] Peck, *Desiderata Curiosa*, 1732, i., 44. [2] Act of Uniformity, 1552.

was omitted;[1] and the sequence of the service was materially modified. Finally, when several copies of the service-book had already been printed off, the "black rubric" explaining away the significance of the kneeling posture was interpolated by order of the council in response to the objections of Knox and in spite of Cranmer's protests. Even Cranmer could not accommodate his steps to the pace of the reformation; and Bucer, more than a year before, had warned the king against "taking away by force false worship from your people without sufficient preliminary instruction. The instruments of impiety have been snatched from them by royal proclamations, and the observance of true religion has been imposed by royal command."[2] Patience, indeed, is a virtue hard for reformers to practise, and in 1552 coercion came ready to their hands. Cranmer was less willing than most men to use it, but in the incurable optimism of his soul he imagined it possible to compile codes and articles so persuasive in their perfection that all men would conform; and his last labours in Edward's reign were the *Reformatio Legum Ecclesiasticarum* and the Forty-Two articles.

The canon law sadly needed reform: its matrimonial complexities had provoked vagaries as strange as Henry VIII.'s; its authority had been shaken by the repudiation of papal jurisdiction; and the various acts of parliament empowering Henry VIII. to appoint a commission of reform had remained abortive.[3] The consequent confusion of the canonists was viewed with ill-concealed satisfaction by civilians, common-lawyers, and other laymen who had no desire to see ecclesiastical discipline re-established on a firm and lasting basis; and these influences proved fatal to the adoption of Cranmer's scheme. A commission of eight had been appointed in October, 1551, to "rough hew the canon law"; but the act of 1549, in virtue of which the commissioners had been nominated, expired, and its renewal was successfully resisted by Northumberland in the parliament of 1552. Edward himself distrusted his episcopate;

---

[1] Gasquet and Bishop, *Edward VI. and the Book of Common Prayer*, p. 294, n. 2, say that "the continued use of the alb, chasuble, and cope are [sic] expressly prohibited"; but the chasuble is not mentioned in the rubric of 1549 which says that the priest "shall put upon him the vesture appointed for that ministration, that is to say: a white Albe plain, with a vestment or cope".

[2] *Ibid.*, pp. 299-301.

[3] See above, vol. v., pp. 313, 327.

"because those bishops," he wrote, "who should execute, some CHAP.
IV.
for papistry, some for ignorance, some for age, some for their
ill name, some for all these, are men unable to execute discipline,
it is therefore a thing unmeet for these men".[1]

The strangling of the project [2] was due as much to its merits
as to its faults. The code was based upon the royal supremacy
and frankly admitted the derivation of all ecclesiastical jurisdiction from the crown, and the right of appeal to the sovereign,
even in cases of heresy, from the ecclesiastical courts; but it
contemplated the active exercise of clerical jurisdiction in its
full medieval sphere. Heresies, wills, marriages, tithes, idola-
tries, benefices, oaths, perjury, slander, forgery, and assaults on
the clergy were all to remain within the competence of clerical
judges; and the contumacious heretic was in the last resort to
be handed over to the secular arm for punishment, whatever
that might mean.[3] Here was adequate cause of offence to
a secular age; but it is curious that the hostility of the secular
power should have prevented the adoption of a code of canon
law which, while punishing adultery with forfeiture, imprisonment, or transportation for life, recognised it, desertion, "ini-
micitiae capitales," and ill-treatment as severally adequate
reasons for divorce on the part of husband or wife. Other
clauses reflected ideas of church government which ultimately
produced presbyterianism. The synodical activity of the
church was to be quickened, not in its provincial form, but in
the shape of diocesan sessions meeting once a year and com-

---

[1] *Lit. Remains*, pp. 478-79.

[2] It has been edited by Cardwell, Oxford, 1850; the original MS. with notes
by Cranmer and Foxe is Harleian MS. 426.

[3] Froude, v., 107, following Collier and Lingard, says that Cranmer "claimed
the continued privilege of sending obstinate heretics to the stake"; the document
has simply "reus, consumptis omnibus aliis remediis, ad extremum ad civiles
magistratus ablegetur puniendus," and the Harl. MS. 426 has a gloss "vel ut
in perpetuum pellatur exilium vel ad aeternas carceris deprimatur tenebras, aut
alioqui pro magistratus prudenti consideratione plectendus, ut maxime illius con-
versioni expedire videbitur," which seems to exclude burning. The gloss is,
however, said to be in Foxe's hand, and was probably suggested by the terms of
the statute of 1563, 5 Eliz. c. 23. Somerset had repealed all the heresy statutes,
but heretics like Joan Bocher could still be burned by canon or common law.
The execution was done by the state and not by the church, and it is very doubtful whether Cranmer would have excommunicated the civil magistrate who refused
to carry out the ecclesiastical sentence. See Dixon, iii., 376; Cardwell, *Reformatio*, pp. 25, 330; Hallam, *Const. Hist.*, i., 101-2.

prising laymen among their members ; and if bishops had been
induced by the adoption of Cranmer's scheme to take regular
counsel with the laity and parochial clergy of their sees, there
would have been fewer Marprelates in the reign of Elizabeth.

A statement of dogma was even more necessary than a
code for a uniform national church, and the church in England
was no sooner separated from Rome and placed on a national
basis than efforts were made to define the national faith. The
Ten articles of 1536 and the Six of 1539 were steps towards the
Forty-two of Cranmer's compilation. These were not illiberal
for the times, and only errors of the Roman church were at
all offensively specified ; free will was asserted as well as
justification by faith, and good works were wisely left unde-
fined. But only two out of the medieval seven sacraments
were retained ; "sacrifices of masses" were denounced as "fig-
ments and dangerous impostures" ; and it was declared to
be no ordinance of Christ that the Eucharist should be reserved, carried about, elevated, or adored. The articles were
published with a catechism by Bishop Ponet in June, 1553 ;
but in spite of the assertion in the preface, they had not been
authorised by convocation nor by any ecclesiastical synod other
than the six divines commissioned by the council in October,
1552, to consider Cranmer's draft.[1] Nor was sanction given
to the fifty-four articles which were prepared at this time to
secure uniformity of rites and ceremonies.[2] The real authority
by which religious changes were effected was the royal supremacy exercised by the council. Somerset, indeed, protested to
Gardiner that "we presume not to determine articles of religion
by ourself" ;[3] but after 1549 it was considered superfluous to
cloak the royal supremacy with any clerical garb.

Cranmer vainly hoped that his articles would conduce to
"concord and quietness in religion" ;[4] but the first attempt to
enforce them met with much resistance.[5] Their merits were

[1] *Acts of the P. C.*, 1552-54, pp. 148, 173. Heylyn, Collier, Cardwell, and
Hardwick, *Hist. of the Articles of Religion*, 2nd ed., 1859, have sought to prove
synodical authorisation : but against them see Burnet, ed. Pocock, iii., 368-74,
and Dixon, iii., 512-18 notes. Cranmer's admission that they were not so authorised is in Foxe, vi., 148 ; he speaks of the catechism, but the articles are included.

[2] Gasquet and Bishop, p. 304 ; they were never published, and no manuscript
copy has been discovered.

[3] Brit. Mus. Egerton MS. 2350, f. 16.   [4] *Works* (Parker Soc.), ii., 141.

[5] *Greyfriars' Chron.*, p. 77.

prejudiced by association with a corrupt and increasingly unpopular administration. There may have been need for
doctrinal change; there was certainly room for practical reformation. When Hooper visited his diocese in 1551 he
found that out of 311 clergy 171 could not repeat the Ten
Commandments (which formed no part of any service till 1552)
in English, ten could not say the Lord's Prayer, and twenty-
seven could not tell who was its author ; while sixty-two incumbents were absentees chiefly because of their pluralities.[1] There
was also the problem of how to reform the reformers : "these
men, for the most part, that the king's majesty hath of late preferred," wrote Northumberland in January, 1552, "be so sotted
of their wives and children that they forget both their poor
neighbours and all other things which to their calling appertaineth ; and so will they do, so long as his majesty shall suffer
them to have so great possessions to maintain their idle lives".[2]
Northumberland was doing his best to remedy this abuse.
The great bishopric of Durham with its palatine jurisdiction
was dismembered on Tunstall's deprivation ; two humbler sees
were to be founded at Durham and Newcastle, but the bulk
of the proceeds was designed to support Northumberland's
dignity as lieutenant-general and practically king of England
north of the Trent. The new see of Gloucester was suppressed,
like Westminster, while others were despoiled for the benefit
of Northumberland's friends ; and their appetite for church
goods, plate, and metal was at any rate one of the motives
which led them to desire a simpler ritual and to silence the
chimes of the bells of the church and peal of its organs.

The second act of uniformity rendered a vast quantity of
property inappropriate to the services of the church and applic-
able to those of the state ; and its confiscation by the government, which was no essential part of protestantism, was
rendered necessary by Northumberland's failure to obtain a
subsidy. "All such goods[3] were taken away to the king's
use ; that is to say, all the jewels of gold and silver, as crosses,
candlesticks, censers, chalices, and all other gold and silver and

---

[1] *English Hist. Review*, xix. (1904), pp. 98 ff.   [2] Tytler, ii., 153.
[3] Wriothesley, ii., 83 ; *cf. Greyfriars' Chron.*, p. 77. In Feb., 1553, the dean
and two canons of Chester were imprisoned in the Fleet for stripping their
cathedral of its lead (*Acts of the P. C.*, 1552-54, p. 218).

ready money . . . and all copes and vestments of cloth of
gold, cloth of tissue, and cloth of silver." The chantry-lands
which parliament had granted to the crown for the endowment
of education and other respectable objects, were now re-granted
or sold wholesale to private persons for inadequate sums in
cash ; for ready money was the greatest need of Northumberland's government. The king was £200,000 in debt ;[1] and
while parliament prohibited all usury whatsoever, he was paying
14 per cent. interest to the Fuggers and the Schetz.[2] The
coinage could not be further debased, and while the council
had called down the value of the testoon from a shilling to
sixpence, it threatened London with the loss of its liberties
because its citizens wilfully enhanced their prices. The expedient of a loan from the Merchant Adventurers was tried in
October, 1552, but neither the £40,000 thus raised nor the
proceeds of the chantry-lands could fill the void left gaping by
the failure to obtain a subsidy from the parliament of 1552.
It became necessary to resort once more to constitutional
machinery, and a new parliament was called for March, 1553.

Methods to some extent exceptional were employed to
make this parliament agreeable to the government ; for, when
in the following August Renard consulted Charles V. on
Mary's behalf as to her domestic policy, he asked whether she
should call a general parliament or merely an assembly of
notables after the fashion introduced by Northumberland.[3]
The exact significance of this allusion is difficult to determine.
Northumberland proposed that the eldest sons of peers should
be summoned to the upper house, and there is a phrase in a
letter from the lord treasurer to Cecil implying that parliament
when it met was not a full parliament. But the official returns
of the elections to this parliament and the journals of its sessions betray no indication that it differed essentially from any
other parliament of the time. The methods which the council
had tentatively applied to the by-elections of January, 1552,
were extended to the general election of February, 1553, and
letters were drafted to the sheriffs requiring them to admonish

---

[1] Two millions in modern currency; *Hatfield MSS.*, i., 395.

[2] *Lit. Remains*, pp. 412, 424, 460.

[3] Renard to Charles V., Aug. 16, 1553, R. O. Foreign Transcripts ; *cf.* State
Papers, Dom., Edw. VI., vol. xviii., No. 8, and *Hatfield MSS.*, i., No. 428.

the electors and to support the particular recommendations of CHAP.
the privy councillors in their various localities.[1] Fifteen can-   IV.
didates are known to have been officially recommended by the
council as a whole;[2] of these twelve were successful, but of
the twelve six had sat for the same constituencies since 1547.
Cecil recommended his father-in-law, Sir Anthony Cooke, and
the lord admiral another candidate, as burgesses for Stamford.
The electors agreed to the former proposal, though Sir Anthony's son was actually elected, but objected to the second,
and an independent local candidate was returned.[3] Similarly
the electors of Grantham informed Cecil that by reason of a
pre-engagement they could not choose the burgess he had
recommended ; and a case, in which Northumberland's own
request was refused, was recalled in parliament in 1571.[4]

The grant of parliamentary representation to six new
boroughs in the royal duchy of Cornwall, where crown influence is supposed to have been particularly strong, seems also
to imply designs against parliamentary independence.[5] But the
representatives returned by these new constituencies were anything but servile tools of government.   There were Trelawneys
and Killigrews among the Cornish members in 1553, but
hardly a court or government official ; and in Elizabeth's reign
they included the stoutest champions of parliamentary privilege
against the crown.   Nor do the names in other districts suggest
the intrusion of gentlemen about the court into strange constituencies.   The Constables—no friends of Northumberland—
were prominent among the representatives of Yorkshire ; John
Winchcombe, the famous Jack of Newbury, had local claims on
Reading which were difficult to beat ; and two Verneys sat for
Buckinghamshire.   A Musgrave, a Curwen, and an Aglionby
were returned for Cumberland ; and the Welsh representatives
were Meyricks, Griffiths, Davies, Jones, Edwards, Owens, Parrys,
Pulestons, Thelwalls, Williams, ap Hughs, and ap Howells.
Throughout the shires the local gentry, and throughout the

---

[1] Brit. Mus. Lansdowne MS. 3, art. 19.   [2] Strype, *Eccl. Mem.*, II., ii., 65.
[3] *Hatfield MSS.*, i., No. 419.
[4] Lansdowne MS. 3, art. 38 ; D'Ewes, *Journals*, p. 170.
[5] These boroughs were Bossiney, Camelford, Grampound, Looe, Michael
Borough, and Saltash ; they may have returned members in 1547, for which year
the documents are lost, so that the only comparison is with the returns of 1545
printed in the appendix to the *Official Return*, 1878.

boroughs the prosperous merchants, with a few lawyers thrown in, formed the bulk of the house of commons. The packing of parliament has always proved a difficult operation; the influence of the crown had to work in subtler ways than even Renard imagined; and the facile and shallow theory which attributes parliamentary acquiescence in Tudor rule to bribery, threats, and corruption, breaks down even as an explanation of the general election of 1553.

The choice of a Speaker was, as is still the case, arranged by the government, in order, as Northumberland wrote, "that he might have secret warning thereof . . . because he may the better prepare himself towards his preposition; otherwise he shall not be able to do it to the contentation of the hearers".[1] But the duke foresaw objections from "froward persons," especially to the financial requirements of the government. He had tried to gratify the city of London by quashing the privileges of the Stillyard[2] and by promising a bill to limit those of the Merchant Adventurers;[3] but he feared the effects of a disclosure of the extent to which the liberality of the crown to himself and his friends was responsible for its debts. A statement[4] which had been drawn up was suppressed: there was no need, he wrote to Northampton, to account to the commons for the king's "bountifulness in augmenting of his nobles or his benevolence shewed to any his good servants"; and the blame for the deficit was all laid on Somerset's shoulders.[5] Fortified with these precautions, he demanded two fifteenths and tenths and a subsidy, the payment being spread over two years. The proposal was carried with difficulty, and it was accompanied by an act for the annual audit of all collectors and receivers as a guarantee against future peculation. One or two measures suggested by Edward during the previous parliament were again brought up for discussion with similar ill-success; and bills restricting inclosures and long leases of ecclesiastical lands, together with one prohibiting the conferment of benefices on laymen, were dropped or rejected;

---

[1] Tytler, ii., 163.

[2] *Acts of the P. C.*, 1550-52, pp. 487-89; "Steelyard" is a meaningless corruption of the word. It corresponded to the English "Staple".

[3] State Papers, Dom., Edw. VI., vol. xviii., No. 13; possibly this was in return for the loan of £40,000; *cf. ibid.*, xv., 13.

[4] *Ibid.*, vol. xix.   [5] *Ibid.*, xviii., 6; Tytler, ii., 160-62.

the commons also threw out a bill for limiting the number of Merchant Adventurers. But the meagre fruits of the session provided some solace for the friends of the government. All grants made by the king—and they amounted to some £5,000,000 in modern currency—were guaranteed by act of parliament against any cavil on the ground of Edward's minority or other defects; the price of wine was fixed by statute, not in the interests of the poor consumer—for no one was to keep a cellar unless he had an income of a hundred marks a year[1] or was a peer's son—but for the benefit of the well-to-do; and the bishopric of Durham was "dissolved".[2]

One violent scene in this parliament betrayed the growing distrust between Northumberland and his best supporters, the zealous protestants. Cranmer made a last effort in the house of lords to secure legal sanction for his revision of the canon law. The duke rudely bade him stick to his clerical functions, and went on to threaten the preachers who had presumed to attack his friends. He was stung by their doubts of the zeal which he had done so much to simulate. Horne, whom he had designed for the shorn see of Durham, could not tell whether the duke was or was not a dissembler in religion; and Knox, who was meant for Rochester, proved "neither grateful nor pleasable".[3] Knox lamented in after years that he had not been more plain in his speech, but he avers that he recited the histories of Achitophel, Shebna, and Judas, and spoke of an innocent king being deceived by crafty, covetous, wicked, and ungodly councillors.[4] "As for Latimer, Lever, Bradford, and Knox," wrote Ridley, "their tongues were so sharp, they ripped in so deep in their galled backs to have purged them no doubt of that filthy matter that was festered in their hearts of insatiable covetousness, of intolerable ambition and pride, of ungodly loathsomeness to hear poor men's causes and God's words, that these men of all others, these magistrates then could never abide."[5]

The clouds were gathering for the storm. "Lewd words,"

CHAP.
IV.

---

[1] £700 in our currency.   [2] See below, p. 119.

[3] State Papers, Dom., Edw. VI., vol. xv., No. 66.

[4] *Faithful Admonition*, 1554; nevertheless Knox was recommended by the council to Cranmer on Feb. 2, 1553, for presentation to Allhallows, Bread Street, London (*Acts of the P. C.*, 1552-54, pp. 190, 212).

[5] Ridley, *Works*, p. 59; *cf.* Foxe, vii., 573.

CHAP.
IV.

" prophecies," mutterings about the succession were filling the Tower with prisoners and bringing scores of men to the pillory. Discontent was rife everywhere except in the ranks of Northumberland's immediate dependants. England, said the Venetian ambassador, Soranzo, was writhing under the domination of France in Scotland.[1] She was in no condition to fulfil her treaty obligations to Charles V. in his war with Henry II.; and Edward in reply to the emperor's demands descended to the plea that he was not bound by his father's treaties.[2] He offered instead to mediate between the two parties, and a league was suggested against the Turk; this, he ingenuously explains, " was done on intent to get some friends. The reasonings be in my desk." They were dismal enough; if England did not help the emperor, France seemed likely to secure the Netherlands, "and herein the greatness of the French king is dreadful"; he was "breaking and burning of our ships which be the old strength of this isle," and was reported to be preparing an attack on Calais and Falmouth, while Guise, with the help of the Scots, was to invade the north. Charles V., offended by England's refusal to help him, would decline to assist her; England could not keep her treaty with him because " the aid was too chargeable and almost impossible to execute," and if Charles V. died England would be left alone at war with France.

It was not Charles V. who died, but Edward VI. The age which had proved fatal to his uncle, Prince Arthur, to his half-brother, the Duke of Richmond, and to his cousin, Henry Brandon, Earl of Lincoln,[3] was also fatal to him. In his father's reign he had been described as not likely to live long; he had been attacked by measles and smallpox in April, 1552, and in the following January a cold developed into tuberculosis. He was too ill in March to go to St. Stephen's, and parliament was opened in Whitehall Palace; in April he was moved to Greenwich, and there, where all Tudor sovereigns except Henry VII. had been born, the last male Tudor died on July 6. From the fiery furnace of Mary's reign protestants looked back on Edward VI. as a saint, and his reign was long

---

[1] *Venetian Cal.*, v., 562.   [2] *Lit. Remains*, pp. 432-33, 455-57, 539-41.

[3] Edward was fifteen years, eight months, and three weeks old at his death, Arthur fifteen years and seven months, and Richmond about sixteen years.

regarded as the golden age of the protestant reformation. The gold is tarnished now, and the halo gone from Edward's head. That his abilities were above the average his journal and state-papers show; and it is not reasonable to doubt that, being a Tudor, he would have developed courage and a will of his own. But, with every allowance for the slow growth of a boy's domestic affections, the callous brevity of the terms in which he records his uncles' execution implies that he had no more heart than others of his race; while the wooden bigotry of his religious, and the obstinate absolutism of his political, views suggest the probability that the prolongation of his life and reign might ultimately have provoked an upheaval, in which the rejection of protestantism would have combined with reaction against despotism to undo the work of the Tudor monarchy.

CHAPTER V.

NORTHUMBERLAND'S CONSPIRACY.

CHAP.
V.

On October 3, 1551, two yeomen of the guard were sent to prison on a new and ominous charge; they had reported seeing "a certain strange coin" which bore the stamp of a bear and ragged staff. This was the well-known badge of one kingmaker, which had been assumed, with the title of Warwick, by another pretender to the part; and in corroboration of the rumour a citizen of Coventry averred that this coinage, which he had seen himself, issued from a mint at Dudley Castle.[1] A few weeks earlier, when Warwick was made a duke, a similar rank—the dukedom of Suffolk—was conferred upon his ally, Dorset, whose only political assets were his wife who was niece, and his daughters who were grandnieces, of Henry VIII. The Dudley coinage was a fiction, and a cautious person, who was shown the fancied ragged staff upon it, declared that he could only see a lion. But suspicion of Northumberland's designs, which bred these fancies, grew; and in August, 1552, the wife of one of his servants related at Sir William Stafford's house, at Rochford, that "my lord Guilford Dudley should marry my lord of Cumberland's daughter, and that the king's majesty should devise the marriage. *Have at the Crown with your leave*, she said with a stout gesture."[2] She was sent to the Tower, whither the Duke of Norfolk's daughter, the Countess of Sussex, and two of his servants had been despatched six months before for similar "lewd prophecies". But nothing could shut people's mouths on the subject; there were "lewd words at Eton concerning the succession";

---

[1] *Acts of the P. C.*, 1550-52, pp. 375-77; *cf. Greyfriars' Chron.*, p. 73; *Lit. Remains*, p. 374.

[2] Harleian MS. 353 f., 121. Sir William Stafford was the second husband of Mary Boleyn, Henry VIII.'s mistress; his son Sir Edward was a distinguished diplomatist in Elizabeth's reign.

"seditious ballets" were printed in London; and on one CHAP.
November day "spreaders of false rumours" were consigned V.
to the pillory at Westminster, in Kent, Essex, Yorkshire, and
Oxfordshire.[1] Throughout the realm there was a general conviction that the young king was doomed, and that Northumberland was bent on tampering with the succession.

His motives were obvious: no minister had rendered himself more odious to the nation at large; and his overbearing
temper did not endear him to his colleagues, although they
afterwards pleaded it as sufficient excuse for connivance in his
acts. Lady Jane Grey described him as being hated and
evil-spoken of by the commons,[2] and he had alienated or outraged nearly every section of the upper classes. Friends of
Mary, and friends of Somerset were in the Tower; Paget, the
most experienced and, save Cecil, the shrewdest member of the
council, had been ignominiously stripped of his Garter on the
plea that he was low-born; while Arundel and Westmorland,
the representatives of the old nobility, had been fined and suspected of disloyalty.[3] Even with Pembroke Northumberland's
relations were occasionally strained; Cecil loathed his servitude
to the duke, and rejoiced at his release;[4] and his only thorough-
going partisans were the weak-minded Suffolk and Northampton, adventurers like Sir Thomas Palmer and Sir John Gates,
or personal connexions like Sir Francis Jobson.[5] He had
spurned the old religion and sent its bishops to the Tower, and
now he was distrusted by the preachers of the new. He had
committed so many crimes and made so many enemies that
he was only safe so long as he misdirected the government
and prevented the administration of justice. His power depended upon his control of Edward VI., and Edward was
slowly dying before his eyes.

His plot to secure the throne for his family was the logical
consequence of his career; life itself depended upon his tenure

---

[1] *Acts of the P. C.*, 1552-54, pp. 12, 13, 20, 46, 69, 81, 107, 110, 120, 129,
130-31, 165, 168, 205, 211, 234, 237, 257, 263-65, 269, 273-75, 278.

[2] *Chron. of Queen Jane*, p. 25.

[3] *Acts of the P. C.*, 1552-54, pp. 90, 176, 181, 185-86, 257; *Lit. Remains*,
pp. 409, 463, 465.

[4] Lansdowne MS. 118; Tytler, ii., 103.

[5] Jobson married Northumberland's half-sister Elizabeth, daughter of Arthur
Plantagenet, Viscount Lisle, by Edmund Dudley's widow.

of despotic power, and he could only retain it through
the monarchy. Hence he must have a docile king or queen,
and the idea that Edward was growing restive may have
suggested the wild rumour that he was poisoned by Northumberland.[1] He could not trust Elizabeth in the character of
sleeping-partner to his son; still less would Mary lend herself
to his designs. No one thought of Mary Stuart; against her
there was not only Henry's will and parliamentary statute,
but her alien birth, her absence in France, and her betrothal to
the dauphin. There was next the Suffolk line; Henry VIII.'s
younger sister Mary had by her second husband Charles
Brandon, Duke of Suffolk, only two surviving daughters. Of
these the elder, Frances, married Henry Grey, Marquis of
Dorset and afterwards Duke of Suffolk, by whom she was
mother of three daughters, Jane, Catherine, and Mary. Her
younger sister Eleanor had married Henry Clifford, Earl of Cumberland; and it was for the hand of their daughter, Margaret,
that Northumberland had been negotiating in 1552, inducing
the king to write and speak on behalf of his fourth and only
unmarried son, Lord Guilford Dudley, and getting the council
to put pressure on the reluctant earl to consent, "any law,
statute, or other thing to the contrary notwithstanding".[2]
The Clifford claim was inferior to the Greys' in that the
Duchess of Suffolk was older than the Countess of Cumberland; but in one respect Margaret Clifford had the advantage
over Lady Jane Grey; her mother was not in the way, having
died in 1547. This may have suggested Northumberland's
preference; but Cumberland was cautious and perhaps a catholic. Eventually Northumberland persuaded Lady Jane's
mother to resign in her daughter's favour. Margaret Clifford
was relegated to Northumberland's brother Andrew,[3] and Lady
Jane was betrothed to Guilford Dudley.

A great deal of specious argument was required to establish
her title to the throne; and Northumberland could not, like

---

[1] "He was poisoned, as everybody says," Machyn, *Diary*, p. 35; *cf. Greyfriars' Chron.*, s.a. Protestants spread the same report; see *Orig. Letters*
(Parker Soc.), pp. 365, 684, and Scheyfne to Charles V., Aug. 6 (R. O. Transcripts).

[2] Brit. Mus. Royal MS. 18, C. xxiv., f. 236 *b*.

[3] *Ib.*, f. 364; *Hatfield MSS.*, i., 131; this "pretended marriage" was never
completed, and Margaret was married in 1555 to Lord Strange, afterwards
fourth Earl of Derby.

Henry VIII., count on parliament to cut his Gordian knots. It had been prematurely dissolved, not merely prorogued, at the end of March, 1553, having sat for barely a month; and the duke relied on his own powers of subtle intrigue to effect the plot, and on parliament to sanction the accomplished fact. Mary and Elizabeth were excluded on strictly legitimist theory; they were bastards by unrepealed acts of parliament, and the argument that if parliament could make them bastards it could also make them queens was quietly ignored. The right of a king to bequeath the crown by will was claimed for Edward as well as for Henry VIII.: the facts that parliament had granted this power to Henry and not to Edward, had confirmed and made it treason to change the succession as established by Henry's will, and that Edward was legally under age and could not make a will, were disregarded. The constitutional contention was supported on grounds of religion and policy; Mary would restore the power of Rome, marry a Hapsburg, and snare England in that net of matrimonial felicity with which the house of Austria had captured Hungary, Bohemia, the Netherlands, and Spain. Elizabeth, too, might marry abroad, and various continental suitors had been considered both for her and for her sister.[1] But the Lady Jane was safely bestowed on an English husband, who came of an older family than did Henry of Richmond, while she was nearer the throne than Margaret Beaufort. The success of Henry VII. made Northumberland's ambition plausible.

It was on religious grounds that the duke appealed to Edward VI. To the dying king religion was the main consideration, and religion meant to him the protestant faith. On this feeling Northumberland played with consummate skill; he had persuaded Edward that he was the Josiah who had put down the idolatrous priests and broken the altars of Baal. Northumberland himself seemed to Bishop Bale a second Moses, and he graced his worldliest letters with the most pious reflections. But even when he had convinced Edward of the necessity of excluding Mary and Elizabeth, there were obstacles which perhaps required forgery to remove. Henry VIII. had left the contingent remainder to the crown, not to the Duchess of Suffolk but to the heirs of her body, although Northumber-

---

[1] *Foreign Cal.*, 1547-53, pp. 17, 26, 29, 41-42, 47, 60, 120, 164, 245, 255.

6 *

CHAP.
V.

land's rejection of Henry's will barred him from pleading this clause in his own excuse. Edward's first "devise" for the succession also passed over the duchess, and bequeathed the crown to her heirs male; he seems to have adopted Edward III.'s theory of a Salic law by which women, while incapable of succeeding themselves, could transmit their title to their male descendants.[1] This at least was logical, and in its favour there could be urged the case of Henry II., who reigned while his mother, from whom he derived his claim, was alive, and that of Henry VII., who did the same. The Duchess of Suffolk, however, was only thirty-six and she might have sons, who would be fatal to the claims of Lady Jane and her heirs male. So the further condition "if she have such issue *before my death*" was inserted in the "devise"; and the succession was then limited to the Lady Jane's heirs male. That would have satisfied Northumberland, had a son been born to Lady Jane and Guilford Dudley before the death of Edward. But they were only married on Whit Sunday, May 21, and it was evident that Edward could not last.

Then Northumberland hit upon an expedient which had served its turn before.[2] By the omission of an "s" and the insertion of "and his," an order for the trial of Somerset's confederates had been converted into an order for his execution: by similarly small but significant changes Edward's bequest of the crown to Lady Jane's heirs male was changed into its bequest to the Lady Jane *and her* heirs male. The "s" is crossed out and the words "and her" are written above the line. Edward may have made these changes himself, or he may not, and there is no evidence that he ever read, or heard read, or signed, the letters patent in which his alleged intentions were officially embedded. So inconsequent were the last hurried directions of Edward's "devise," that while the alterations necessary to entail the crown on Lady Jane were made, they were not repeated for the benefit of her sisters Catherine and Mary, who remained excluded from the succession, albeit they could transmit it to their heirs male. This anomaly was removed in the letters patent, but a greater remained. The first place in the succession had been given to

---

[1] Edward's "devises" are printed and discussed in *Lit. Remains*, pp. 561-76.
[2] See above, p. 64.

the Duchess of Suffolk's sons, "being born into the world in CHAP.
our lifetime," and the male heir's claim to the throne was made V.
to depend on the accidental date of Edward's death. Thus,
the theory that women could not reign was at first asserted in
order to exclude Mary, Elizabeth, and the Duchess of Suffolk,
and then rejected in order to include Lady Jane ; and finally
the right of male succession was conditioned by a subterfuge
which, instead of concealing, only illumined the delirious
nature of Northumberland's logic and ambition.

No amount of special pleading could convince men that
the scheme was lawful, just, or practical, and Northumberland
could only win by force and fraud. Such methods, however, had
often proved successful ; and the crooked paths by which he
travelled would not make him more forgiving, if and when he
reached his goal, to those who blocked his progress. It was
treason to do what he wished ; if he won, it would be treason
to have refused. Cecil fell sick of anxiety, and after the third
week in April absented himself from the council. But the
king did not die at once, and on June 2 the guileless Cheke
was sworn secretary. Cecil was not dismissed, but the hint
was broad enough and Cecil returned to his duties on June 11.
On that day the chief justices and law officers of the crown
were summoned to court, and Noailles, the French ambassador, soon found the council more at ease. They ascribed
their satisfaction to an improvement in Edward's health, but
Noailles set it down to the fact that after many days' dissension they were at last agreed on a policy. They had succumbed
to Northumberland's pressure, and measures were being taken
to ensure the success of his plot. The city-watch was doubled ;
the gates closed earlier and opened later ; Norfolk and other
prisoners in the Tower were kept more strictly ; its guards were
increased, the ships in the Thames were being armed, and disaffected lords had been summoned with a view to their arrest.

The lawyers appeared on the 12th, and were charged by
Edward himself to draw up a will on the lines of his "devise".[1]
They told him he could not thus dispose of acts of parliament ;
but Edward would take no refusal, and they departed with the
device. On the morrow they all agreed among themselves

---

[1] See Chief Justice Montague's narrative in Fuller, *Church History*, 1656,
bk. viii., pp. 2-5.

that not only would it be treason to carry out such a scheme on Edward's death, but that even to draw it up was treason on their own and the council's part ; and they reported this answer to the council on the 13th. Trembling with anger, Northumberland called Chief Justice Montague a traitor to his face, and said he would fight in his shirt with any man in that quarrel ; and the judges departed in fear of personal violence. On the 15th they were again brought into Edward's presence. With sharp words and an angry countenance he asked why they had not obeyed his commands, while behind their backs the lords muttered "traitors" under their breath. Terrified almost out of their wits the judges cast about for excuses to justify compliance ; they reflected that it could not be treason to obey a king in his lifetime, and that, if they did nothing against Mary after Edward's death, she could not lawfully condemn them. They were promised a commission under the great seal for their action, a pardon when it was done, and a parliament to ratify the deed. Gosnold, the attorney-general, still held out, but the rest "with sorrowful hearts and weeping eyes" consented. At length, on the 21st, the instrument was completed and signed by over a hundred persons, privy councillors, peers, archbishops, bishops, judges, aldermen, and sheriffs. Only Sir James Hales, a justice of the common pleas, had the courage to refuse, though several afterwards excused their cowardice. Cecil pleaded that he signed last of the privy council, and then only as a witness.[1] Cranmer also claimed to have been the last to sign, and his contention is more credible, because he confessed to Mary in his simplicity that when he did sign he signed "unfeignedly without dissimulation"—not as a witness.

With these signatures in their possession it was no wonder that Noailles found the councillors in a gayer mood. The dynastic marriages had been arranged or carried out. Lady Jane was Guilford Dudley's wife ; Pembroke, who had shown signs of independence, was bought by the betrothal of his son, Lord Herbert, to the Lady Catherine, who stood next to Lady Jane in the succession to the throne ; Cumberland's daughter was engaged to Andrew Dudley ; and the hand of Northumber-

---

[1] Cecil of course concealed the fact that he signed the promise of the council "by our oaths and honours to observe, fully perform, and keep all and every article" of the "devise", See *Lit. Remains*, pp. 572-73 ; Cranmer, *Works*, ii., 444.

land's daughter secured Lord Hastings, who, as a descendant of CHAP.
V. the Dukes of Buckingham and of York, had distant hopes of his own.[1] Abroad, too, the signs were propitious.   Charles V. had suffered disaster at Metz ; Germany was in an uproar ; the Turks were threatening Naples.   Spanish troops were in mutiny at Cambray, the townsfolk were rising at Brussels, and the emperor himself was so ill " that some say he is already dead, others that he has lost his senses, and others that he is so feeble that his recovery is impossible ".[2]   No armed intervention threatened from that quarter ; France would not hamper a plot to exclude from the throne the emperor's cousin ; and Northumberland was perhaps receiving material as well as moral support from Henry II.   He was on intimate terms with the French ambassador, who lodged at his palace, the Charterhouse, and lavishly feasted the privy council ; and in the middle of May the French king's secretary, L'Aubespine, was despatched on a secret errand to London.[3]   Nominally he came to congratulate Edward on his reported recovery ; but he was too important a person for a merely complimentary mission, and the English ambassadors in France, from whom the secret was hidden, suspected a further design.   L'Aubespine communicated to Northumberland the measures which Charles was said to be meditating on Mary's behalf ;[4] but this did not exhaust his instructions, which were too confidential to be committed to writing.   Doubtless he conveyed an assurance of French assistance, and Scheyfne believed that France had been bribed by the promise of Ireland, where her intrigues had been persistent and active, while Guaras, a Spanish resident in London, thought that the bribe was Calais and Guisnes.[5]   French interests were too obviously on Northumberland's side for Henry II. to require much bribery.   Not that he favoured the claims of Lady Jane Grey ; it was sufficient at first to keep out Mary, and then Henry could play his best card, the Queen of Scots.   He had no use for protestant factions except as weapons of discord ; his court was thronged with English catholic refugees, and it

---

[1] See Appendix II.   [2] *Foreign Cal.*, 1547-53, pp. 275, 282-83.

[3] *Hatfield MSS.*, i., 121, 125 ; Tytler, ii., 181; *Lit. Remains*, p. 380; *Acts of the P. C.*, 1552-54, p. 266; Wiesener, *La Jeunesse d'Elisabeth*, p. 89.

[4] Lodge, *Illustrations*, i., 226.

[5] Guaras, *Accession of Queen Mary*, ed. R. Garnett, p. 86 ; Scheyfne to the emperor, May 30, R. O. Transcripts.

CHAP.
V.

was with a view to Mary Stuart's succession that he encouraged the plot to keep Mary Tudor from the throne.

Her prospects were seemingly dismal enough. Charles thought she must come to terms with the council and trust to time; and his envoys considered resistance hopeless, since help from abroad was out of the question and Northumberland could rely on France and on all the machinery of a despotic government.[1] They assumed, as others have done since, that the power of the Tudor monarchy rested upon the subservience of the people, and that the English would submit to whatever their rulers dictated. It was not a profound diagnosis of the character of a nation which had risen against half its kings since the Norman conquest, and the advice was not heroic. It was not the Tudor way to submit. Mary may have been deceived by Northumberland's smooth professions of loyalty to her claims, his daily and dutiful letters,[2] his courtesy in committing to the Tower and torturing persons charged with stealing her hawks.[3] But, when once she was undeceived, she would never yield, and would only resort to the flight, for which preparations were made, in the last extremity after testing the temper of the nation in which she trusted.

At the king's death on July 6, only the possession of Mary's person seemed lacking to ensure the duke's success. Schemes had been mooted for drawing a cordon round her residence; ships had been sent to cruise off the east coast and intercept her flight to Flanders; Windsor Castle was garrisoned with 500 men, and the lord-lieutenancies had been apportioned out among Northumberland's friends and relatives. Northampton was given almost all the east midland shires from Cambridgeshire to Surrey; Bedford nearly the whole southwest; Pembroke, Wales and Wiltshire; and Northumberland the Scottish borders; while Knox was appointed to preach in Buckinghamshire sermons different, it may be surmised, from those which he afterwards represented himself as having preached at court. Two days before Edward's death, the council summoned Mary, who was at Hunsdon in Hertfordshire, to

---

[1] *Papiers d'état du Cardinal de Granvelle*, iv., 19-20.

[2] Guaras, pp. 89, 130; *Venetian Cal.*, v., 537. Soranzo says that Mary was so deluded by Northumberland that her own friends on the council feared to give her information lest she should reveal it to the duke.

[3] *Acts of the P. C.*, 1552-54, pp. 285, 287.

his bedside; but she had now been warned of Northumberland's CHAP.
real intentions.[1] She took horse and rode for freedom and her   V.
throne. At Sawston Hall, where she spent the following night,
the people of Cambridge sallied out to attack her party, and
Mary only escaped, it is said, in disguise. She was better received at Bury St. Edmunds, but was refused admission at
Norwich; she then retired on Kenninghall, and thence to
Norfolk's castle at Framlingham in Suffolk.

On the news of her flight the council sent letters far and
wide denouncing her intention to "resist such ordinances and
decrees as the King's Majesty hath set forth and established for
the succession of the Imperial Crown of this realm". They
inveighed against the "labour and means of those which be
strangers to this realm, and would gladly have the realm so
disordered in itself that it might be a prey to foreign nations,"
but doubted not that "we shall always, as true and mere Englishmen, keep our country to be England, without putting our
heads under Spaniards' or Flemings' girdles as their slaves and
vassals".[2] Patriotism was Northumberland's last refuge, but
the appeal which woke the England of Elizabeth, was stifled in
the cloak of his ambition; and a feeble response came from a
people who believed that he had poisoned their king in order to
place his own son on the throne. Edward's death was kept
secret for three days to give the council time to complete their
plans, and if possible to secure Mary. On Sunday the 9th
Ridley declared in his sermon that the Ladies Mary and Elizabeth were bastards; and "all the people were sore annoyed
with his words, so uncharitably spoken by him in so open an
audience".[3] On the morrow Jane was brought down the river
from Northumberland's residence, Sion House near Isleworth,
and proclaimed queen amid the disapproving silence of the
people; one Gilbert Potter who ventured to suggest that Mary
had the better title, was imprisoned and lost his ears in the

---

[1] Guaras, p. 89; *Venetian Cal.*, v., 537; Scheyfne to Charles V., July 4,
R. O. Transcripts. Soranzo states that it was through his means that she was
warned. Sir Nicholas Throckmorton, who thought that the first intimation
reached her after Edward's death, claimed to have conveyed it himself (Cole MSS.,
Brit. Mus., xl., p. 272; *Chron. of Queen Jane*, p. 2; but *cf. ibid.*, p. 12).

[2] *Hatfield MSS.*, i., 93-94; Haynes, p. 117; both editors misdate these letters
"1551".

[3] *Greyfriars' Chron.*, p. 78.

CHAP.
V.

pillory.[1] Guilford Dudley claimed the crown matrimonial,
Northumberland spoke and wrote of the new "king," and the
dangers of a ruling queen were apparently to be avoided by
making a king of Northumberland's son.[2] The young queen,
however, showed a becoming sense of the dignity which had
been thrust upon her against her will,[3] and referred her husband's pretensions to the parliament which was to meet in
two months' time.

On the 11th, Queen Mary's challenge arrived, requiring the
council to proclaim her title to the throne. They replied with
defiance, but the news of the 12th was alarming. Mary had
been joined by the Earl of Bath, the eldest sons of Lords
Wharton and Mordaunt, Sir William Drury, Sir Henry Bedingfield, and scores of others; the Earl of Sussex was on his
way, and "innumerable companies of the common people".[4]
Throughout the night of the 12th-13th the lords made hasty
preparations. Northumberland, anxious to keep the council
under the terror of his eye, designed the post of danger for
the Duke of Suffolk. But Queen Jane refused to let her father
go, and the council was as anxious to be rid of Northumberland as he was to stay at home and avoid the responsibility of
bearing arms against the rival queen. He had no choice; the
council persuaded him that no one was so fit for the command,
and that his previous victory in Norfolk made him so much
feared that "none durst lift up a weapon against him".
Putting the best face on the matter, although he could only
collect 2,000 men, he addressed the councillors at a farewell
supper, appealing to their oaths to Queen Jane and to their
"fear of Papists' entrance". Arundel and others protested

---

[1] He was rewarded by Mary with various grants of land, *Chron. of Queen
Jane*, p. 115.

[2] *Papiers de Granvelle*, iv., 28; Harleian MS., 523, f. 11 *b*; Cotton MS.,
Galba B., xii., art. 63; Guaras, p. 129.

[3] The picturesque details given by Froude are derived from an authority
whom he calls "Baoardo"; by this he means the Venetian Badoaro, or Badoer
as the name is Anglicised in the *Venetian Calendar*, and he remarks that the
story "comes to us through Baoardo from Lady Jane herself". But Badoaro
was not the author of the work which Froude attributes to him; the volume
which he cites is an anonymous, mutilated, and pirated edition of Raviglio
Rosso's *Historia delle cose occorse nel regno d'Inghilterra*, published in 1558; and
Rosso in his preface of 1560 merely says that Badoaro had read the book and
approved of it, Guaras, p. 130.

[4] Wriothesley, ii., 87; *Chron. of Queen Jane*, pp. 4-5.

their fidelity, and on the morrow the duke rode out through CHAP.
Shoreditch. "The people press to see us," he remarked to Lord V.
Grey at his side, "but not one saith 'God speed'."

His back was hardly turned when intrigues began against
him. Tidings were brought that Sir Edward Hastings, Sir
Edmund Peckham, and Lord Windsor were up proclaiming
Mary in Buckinghamshire, Berkshire, and Middlesex, and Sir
John Williams in Oxfordshire; that forces were mustering at
Paget's house at Drayton to march on Westminster; and that
the ships sent to intercept Mary's flight had put in to Yarmouth
and declared against Queen Jane. Sir Peter Carew had proclaimed Mary instead of Jane in the west, and the tenants of
lords who had stolen wastes and commons refused to follow them
against the lawful heir to the throne. Northumberland was
loudly demanding reinforcements, "but a slender answer he
had again". His colleagues in the Tower were listening to
another call; protestant London was in revolt, and Northumberland's cause was clearly lost. On the 16th Winchester escaped to his house, but was brought back to the
Tower at midnight. Individual desertion was discouraged in
the interests of the council as a whole; but events soon clinched
the arguments of those who were secretly working for a change
of policy. The most active of these, according to his own
account, was Cecil; his conduct had been a miracle of evasion.
He had shifted on to Sir Nicholas Throckmorton the task of
drawing up the proclamation against Mary, on to Northumberland the drafting of the letters declaring her a bastard, and on
to his brother-in-law, Sir John Cheke, the odium of answering
her challenge. "I avoided also the writing of all the public
letters to the realm. I wrote no letter to the Lord Lawarr,
as I was commanded. I dissembled the taking of my horse,
and the rising of Lincolnshire and Northamptonshire, and
avowed the pardonable lie where it was suspected to my
danger." He now began to practise with Winchester and
Bedford to secure Windsor Castle in Queen Mary's interests;
he opened himself to Arundel "whom I found thereto disposed," and did the like to Darcy and Petre, and had horses
ready for "stealing down" to Mary.[1]

[1] This miserable apology is extant in Lansdowne MS. 102, *f.* 2; it exhibits
Cecil at his worst, but there is more excuse for it, when addressed to Mary in

Others, whose confessions, if made in writing, have disappeared, were similarly engaged; but until the 19th Suffolk kept them fast in the Tower. Their last act on Jane's behalf was a letter dated that day requiring Rich, who was arming in Essex, to remain loyal to her, a precept which the signatories promptly proceeded to break. Arundel whispered to Cecil or Petre that he liked not the air of the Tower, and the lords of the council, Suffolk being now too alarmed to resist, joined Pembroke at Baynard's Castle. The lord mayor, riding along Thames Street, met Shrewsbury and Sir John Mason who asked him to summon the recorder and suitable aldermen. Paget had joined the council, and although he had signed the letter to Rich, his advent boded no good to Northumberland, and Renard rejoiced. The question was soon decided; a message was sent to Suffolk, who told his daughter she was no longer queen, tore down the royal insignia, and went out to proclaim Queen Mary on Tower Hill. The news flew abroad, and by the time that Garter king of arms was ready with the lords of the council to make the official proclamation at the Cross in Cheapside, such a cheering crowd had gathered that his words were inaudible. Never was there a scene of greater rejoicing in London. The silenced organs in St. Paul's burst into a *Te Deum*, the bells in every parish church rang out till ten o'clock at night, and then came bonfires and banquets " through all the streets and lanes in the said city" which lasted " for the most part all night till noon next day". Throughout the 20th the bells continued to peal, and fresh *Te Deums* were sung. Some of the lords of the council, including Suffolk, Cranmer, and Goodrich, the lord chancellor, dined at the Guildhall, while others more wisely rode hard to Mary's camp to make their peace with the victor.[1]

It had fared ill with Northumberland. He spent Sunday

1553, than for the further justification which he obtained twenty years later from his servant Roger Alford printed in Strype's *Annals*, iv., 349; both documents are also printed in Tytler, ii., 171-204. Another letter from the council against Mary is endorsed by Cecil "written by Sir John Cheke," Lansdowne MS. 3, art. 25.

[1] Wriothesley, ii., 89-90; *Chron. of Queen Jane*, pp. 11-12; Guaras, pp. 96-9; Stow; Holinshed; and the despatches of Renard and Noailles. For the intense detestation felt even by protestants for Northumberland, *cf.* " The Epistle of Poor Pratte " to Gilbert Potter in *Chron. of Queen Jane*, pp. 116-21, where he is called "the ragged bear most rank," "that false duke," "the cruel bear," "with whom is neither mercy, pity, nor compassion".

the 16th at Cambridge and required the prayers of the university. Sandys, the vice-chancellor, preached; he had prayed for divine guidance in his choice of a text, and his eyes fell on the verse, "And they answered Joshua saying, All that thou commandest us we will do, and whithersoever thou sendest us we will go".[1] On Monday the duke advanced to Bury St. Edmunds; on Tuesday he was back at Cambridge. Mary's forces were reported 30,000 strong, and her camp was a mile in length. She had been accepted as queen throughout East Anglia, and the duke's rear was threatened by the attitude of Northamptonshire, where Throckmorton, who opposed her proclamation, barely escaped with his life.[2] Then came the news of the revolution in London and the council's orders to disband. The game was up; with a pitiful affectation of joy Northumberland on the 20th called a herald, threw up his cap, and proclaimed Queen Mary. Next morning Arundel arrived; he had been foremost in assuring the duke of his devotion at his departure from London, he now came with Mary's orders for his arrest. Four days later Northumberland rode a captive amid showers of curses and missiles through Bishopsgate to the Tower.[3] With him rode three of his sons and his brother Andrew, the Earl of Huntingdon and his son, Lord Hastings, Gates, Palmer, and Dr. Sandys. On the morrow Northampton, Ridley, and Lord Robert Dudley were brought in from Mary's camp, and on the 27th and 28th the Tower opened its gates to receive the two chief justices, Cholmley and Montague, the Duke of Suffolk, and Sir John Cheke. Queen Jane was still there with her husband; she had asked to go home on her release from royalty; but she was only to leave the Tower, whither she had been conveyed as queen, on her way to her trial and then to the scaffold.

[1] Foxe, viii., 570.   [2] Harleian MS., 353, p. 139.
[3] Wriothesley, ii., 90-91; Guaras, p. 99.

CHAPTER VI.

THE TRIUMPH OF MARY.

NO sooner had the gates of the Tower closed behind Nor-
thumberland than they opened to release his victims. Mary
rode into London on August 3 accompanied by the Lady
Elizabeth, Anne of Cleves, the Duchess of Norfolk, and the
Marchioness of Exeter; and set free the Duke of Norfolk,
Courtenay, the Duchess of Somerset, and Bishops Gardiner,
Bonner, Tunstall, Heath, and Day. Norfolk was restored,
Courtenay was made Earl of Devon, and the composition
of the privy council underwent a revolution. Hitherto, since
its gradual evolution from the ordinary council,[1] it had been a
comparatively small and select body. Under Henry VIII.
its numbers varied from one to two dozen ; sixteen with twelve
assistants were nominated in his will. Somerset reduced the
number, but under Warwick they rose in 1551 to thirty-three.
Mary necessarily began with a ring of personal advisers having
no connexion with the council in London, and to these she
added members of the old council as they gave in their allegiance. The result was nearly to double its size, and within
two months of her accession its members numbered well-nigh
fifty. Of these almost three-fifths had never sat at the council
board before ; one or two of them were men of moderate
abilities ; half a dozen or so had been Mary's faithful household
servants in her time of trouble ; but the majority had no claim

---

[1] The distinction between the two was familiar enough in Tudor times,
though the functions of the ordinary council were as purely formal as those of
the privy council to-day, and no records of its action have been preserved. Ambassadors, bishops, judges, and crown lawyers were generally sworn of the king's
council—our present K.C.'s are its only relic—though not as a rule members of
the privy council. Members of the star chamber, court of requests, councils of
the north and of Wales were members of the council, though not usually of the
privy council; and these courts cannot, therefore, be properly described as committees of the privy council.

to their position beyond religious sympathy and the prompti-CHAP. tude and energy with which they had espoused her cause. In their counsel there was little wisdom and in their multitude no safety.

Of the privy council, as it existed in June, 1553, a score lost their seats, including Cranmer, Cecil, Cheke, Clinton, Goodrich, Sadler, and Huntingdon, as well as the chiefs of Northumberland's faction, such as Suffolk, Northampton, and Gates; and seven who had been councillors of old but had been deprived of liberty or influence, were restored. These were all men of some mark—Norfolk, Gardiner, Thirlby, Tunstall, Southwell, Rich, and Paget; and they guided Mary's government during the first part of her reign. Twelve, who had been active to the last under Northumberland, succeeded in retaining place and power under his successor; they were the Marquis of Winchester,[1] the Earls of Bedford, Pembroke, Arundel, Shrewsbury, and Westmorland, Petre, Mason, Gage, Cheyne, Baker, and Peckham. Winchester regarded himself as permanent head of the civil service; and his retention of the lord high treasurership, in spite of Norfolk's claim to his old office, testifies at least to his address or to his repute for business-like capacity. Arundel at any rate had been in the Tower for Somerset's sake; and, although any credit for fidelity he may thus have won was forfeited by his peculiar treachery to Northumberland, no one had done more for Mary at the crisis. The other peers were perhaps retained partly for their compliance and partly for their local influence : Bedford dominated the south-west; Pembroke controlled Wales and the Welsh Marches, of the council of which he was president; Shrewsbury held similar office in the north; and Westmorland's influence counted for something on the Scottish borders. Cheyne had long been warden of the Cinque Ports, Peckham did yeoman service in July, 1553, Petre had been secretary for ten years, Baker speaker of the house of commons and chancellor of the exchequer in Henry's reign, and nearly all were tried officials of reactionary tendencies.

Nevertheless the changes in office were almost as unpre-

---

[1] Winchester and Pembroke were not retained by Mary without some hesitation ; as late as August 11 they were in confinement (*Chron. of Queen Jane*, p. 15), but on the 13th they were sworn of the privy council.

cedented as the alteration of the privy council.   Gardiner was made lord chancellor instead of Goodrich, Arundel succeeded Northumberland as lord great master of the household, Lord William Howard became lord high admiral in Clinton's place. The lord great chamberlainship of England, which, although hereditary in the Earls of Oxford,[1] had been held by Somerset, Northumberland, and Northampton, lost its political importance and relapsed into its hereditary insignificance.   But Gage succeeded Darcy as lord chamberlain of the household, and Jerningham succeeded Gates as vice-chamberlain ; all the other household officials were changed, and Sir John Bourne took Cecil's place as secretary, while the deprivation of the two chief justices, the chief baron of the exchequer, the master of the rolls, and the solicitor-general showed that judicial office was not exempt from political penalties.   Nor was their punishment merely for compliance with Northumberland's design.   Another judge, Sir James Hales, who alone had steadfastly refused to subscribe to Edward's will, lost his position for continuing after Mary's accession to enforce the unrepealed laws of Edward.[2]

The new government, however, had the goodwill of the nation ; it could afford to be merciful, and the fair promises with which it began were not at once belied.   Some of Lady Jane's supporters, such as Cecil, escaped without imprisonment or fine ; others, like Lord Willoughby, Sir Ralph Sadler, and the chief justices, Montague and Cholmley, were released after a brief confinement in private houses or the Tower ; and Mary erred on the side of lenience when, on July 30, she liberated Suffolk after two days' arrest.   But it was hardly reasonable to expect that mercy should be extended to Northumberland himself and his most active agents, Palmer and Gates.   On August 18 the duke, his eldest son the Earl of Warwick, and Northampton were brought to trial at Westminster Hall before Norfolk as lord high steward and their peers.   They were indicted upon their own confessions without

---

[1] The Earl of Oxford is said (*Dict. of Nat. Biogr.*, lviii., 242) to have been made privy councillor in Sept., 1553 ; but the register contains no mention of this fact nor record of the earl's attendance at its meetings.   He is called lord great chamberlain by Soranzo, *Venetian Cal.*, v., 552.

[2] He was imprisoned for this offence and afterwards committed suicide.

presentment by a jury ; but Northumberland, while confessing   CHAP.
to the fact, raised two legal questions : first, whether acts   VI.
authorised by the great seal of England could be treason, and
secondly, whether peers as guilty as himself could be his judges.
He had, however, in Somerset's case asserted that peers of the
realm might not be challenged as jurors, and the other plea
was overruled on the ground that the great seal under which
he acted was that of a usurper.[1]   All three prisoners were condemned to be hanged, drawn, and quartered.

Execution was expected on the 21st, but Northumberland
tried one more expedient.   He intimated his conversion to
the catholic religion, and the government was quite alive to
the effects of a recantation on the part of this Moses of the
reformation.   No promise of pardon is known to have been
made, but the duke was at liberty to hope for some reward for such signal service to the cause of religion.   On the
day he should have suffered—the forty-third anniversary, it
was believed, of his father's execution—the chief citizens of
London were summoned to the Tower "to come and hear the
conversion of the duke ".   A mass was celebrated "with elevation over the head, the pax giving, blessing, and crossing on
the crown, breathing, turning about, and all the other rites and
accidents of old time appertaining" ;[2] and before receiving the
sacrament Northumberland professed this to be "the very right
and true way, out of which true religion you and I have been
seduced these sixteen years past by the false and erroneous
preaching of the new preachers, the which is the only cause of
the great plagues and vengeance which hath lit upon the whole
realm of England ".   Then, as Somerset's sons stood by, he
knelt and asked forgiveness of all men.   More particular confessions were made in private,[3] and his general confession was
repeated at greater length upon the scaffold on the following
day, with a fervent exhortation to renounce their heresies,
which "edified the people more than if all the catholics in the
land had preached for ten years ".[4]   His conversion was a
little sudden and his unction somewhat forced.   Those who

---

[1] He did not attempt to plead the *de facto* statute of Henry VII.
[2] *Chron. of Queen Jane*, pp. 18, 19.   [3] See above, p. 63, note.
[4] Guaras, p. 109 ; *cf.* Dalby's letter in Harleian MS. 353, "there were a
great number turned with his words ".

knew him best attributed it to hopes of pardon,[1] and it is difficult to believe that Northumberland would have gratified the government had he thought his sentence would be carried out. At the last moment, as he lay stretched on the scaffold with his head on the beam, he rose again as if expectant of reprieve ; then with a gesture of despair he threw himself down once more and the axe fell on the neck of one of the most desperate political gamblers in English history. His character resembles in many respects that of another dubious champion of the reformation, Maurice of Saxony ; he was the ablest English soldier of the century, and in Elizabeth's reign men regretted that they had none like him, He lacked, not military, but moral courage, and his gallantry in the field deserted him on the scaffold. His capacity for intrigue was unchecked by scruple, and his political designs were inspired by personal ambition. The ills his failure brought on England would have been magnified by success, and he represents the second of three generations of an evil house which personified the worst aspects of the Tudor age. While his father exemplified the fiscal oppression of Henry VII., and his son Leicester the seamy side of Elizabeth's court, Northumberland is the incarnation of the hypocrisy and self-seeking which marred the reformation.

Gates and Palmer, who had been attainted the day after Northumberland, suffered with him. Palmer, who had no delusive hopes of pardon, died with almost cheerful courage after making a speech, which was published at Geneva as some set-off against the duke's. Northampton escaped with imprisonment in the Tower and the loss of all his dignities and titles. Northumberland's five sons, Lady Jane, and Cranmer were convicted of treason later in the year, but left in prison to await events. They might all have been spared except Cranmer ; for the amnesty which Mary conceded for treason was not long to hold good for heresy. The queen's mind was, she said, " stayed in matters of religion," [2] but caution was necessary until she was firmly seated on the throne. Charles

---

[1] See Lady Jane's remarks in *Chron. of Queen Jane*, p. 26, somewhat misinterpreted by R. Garnett in Guaras, p. 136. An official version of his speech was printed for circulation by the queen's printer, Cawood. The similarity of nearly all these dying speeches suggests that they were drawn up by the government.

[2] *Acts of the P. C.*, 1552-54, p. 317.

V. doubted whether the force of reaction was sufficient to restore catholicism, disbelieved altogether in Mary's ability to bring back unaided the papal jurisdiction, and sedulously kept Cardinal Pole in the background. It was obvious that Mary's triumph over the Dudleys was no test of the strength of religious parties. Guaras, the Spanish resident in England, attributed Somerset's and Northumberland's espousal of the protestant cause to popular inclination in its favour; the Venetian ambassador, Barbaro, reported in 1551 that the "detestation of the Pope was now so confirmed that no one either of the old or new religion could bear to hear him mentioned"; and his successor, Soranzo, in 1554, admitted that the "majority of the population were perhaps dissatisfied" with the restoration of catholicism.[1] Possibly they judged too much from London, but there can be little doubt that protestant opinions had permeated East Anglia, Essex, Kent, some of the midland counties, and most of the centres of industry and commerce. Even the south-west was undergoing that silent but remarkable transformation which converted it from the home of catholic revolt in 1549 to the nursery of militant protestantism in Elizabeth's reign. The north and west remained predominantly catholic, but it was not there that sixteenth century governments were made or marred.

Mary's first steps were consequently tentative, and her first proclamations disclaimed any intention of compelling or constraining men's consciences, although she expressed a hope that God's word opened to them by virtuous and learned preachers would put in their hearts a persuasion of the truth she held. She had, however, no intention of abiding by the law herself or permitting others to suffer under the act of uniformity. Cranmer was allowed to celebrate Edward's obsequies in accordance with statutory obligations and the young king's will, but for her private satisfaction Mary had a requiem mass. Everywhere her subjects were encouraged to revive the ancient services prohibited by laws which Mary thought that parliament had no right to make, and attempts to interfere with these illegal services were forcibly repressed. The interests of the government and order were at variance with the law. It was by Mary's appointment that Dr. Gilbert Bourne on

CHAP.
VI.

---

[1] Guaras, p. 81; *Venetian Cal.*, v., 346, 556.

CHAP.
VI.

Sunday, August 13, prayed at St. Paul's for the souls of the departed and denounced Bonner's imprisonment ; [1] a riot broke out which the protestant Bradford, the lord mayor, and aldermen vainly attempted to stay. A dagger was hurled at Bourne's head, and Bonner who was present barely escaped from the mob. Mary was naturally incensed, and the corporation was threatened with the loss of its liberties unless it could keep better order. At other churches priests who sought to restore the mass were roughly handled, and this opposition seems to have convinced the queen that she must strengthen her administration. Winchester, Pembroke, and others who had not yet been admitted to favour, were now sworn of the privy council and burdened with the odium of her measures of severity. They were empanelled among Northumberland's judges ; Winchester presided over the trial of Sir Andew Dudley, Gates, and Palmer ; and he, Bedford, and Pembroke were, with 200 of the guard, sent on the following Sunday to keep the peace at St. Paul's while Gardiner's chaplain denounced sedition, false preachers, and erroneous sects. On St. Bartholomew's day mass was said in five or six city churches, "not by commandment but of the people's devotion " ; and on Sunday, the 27th, the Sarum Use was restored at St. Paul's and a high altar built of brick. Becon, Bradford, Rogers, Véron, and others were sent to prison in the same month for seditious preaching, and they were soon followed by Latimer, Hooper, Coverdale, and Cranmer.

The archbishop was sent to the Tower, nominally on the two months old charge of treason, but his real offence was his maintenance of the second Book of Common Prayer ; and the sedition, with which the others were charged, consisted in the advocacy of a form of religion which was still by law established. They were the few who refused to flee from the wrath to come ; the majority hastened away with their wives and chattels to Geneva, Strassburg, Frankfort, or Basle. The foreign divines were encouraged to go, Ochino, Martyr, À Lasco and Valerand Poullain, with his French and Flemish weavers. Mary could hardly restrain these foreign subjects, and she placed few obstacles in the way of the fugitive English. Bloodshed was no part of her original design, and she preferred that protestants

---

[1] Wriothesley, ii., 97-98.

should flee or recant without compulsion. Half the bishops were exceptions to the rule, and afforded examples either of devotion to their faith or of punishment for their heresy.[1] On various grounds they were deprived; and Mary, who had conscientious objections to the royal supremacy, found it useful as a means of silencing protestant preachers [2] and restoring catholic bishops. Bonner's appeal to the council against Cranmer's sentence of 1549 was heard at last by the crown and decided in his favour. Tunstall's deprivation was ignored; and Voysey was restored to Exeter by letters patent on the ground that his resignation in 1549 had been forced and was, therefore, uncanonical. But the exercise of the same royal supremacy under Edward VI. seems to have been regarded by Mary as invalid; for Gardiner, Heath, and Day resumed their bishoprics on the assumption that both their deprivation by royal commission and the appointment of their successors by letters patent were void. In particular cases like these Mary had no hesitation in treating canon law as superior to acts of parliament; but, while she connived at wholesale infringement of Edward's legislation, she shrank from attempting to undo the work of Henry VIII. without the assistance of parliament.

The elections were held in September, and in the prevailing mood of the people Mary had less temptation than Northumberland to interfere with the constituencies. Yet Cornwall returned a third of the members who had represented it in Northumberland's parliament of March; and these included several protestants, besides Sir Thomas Smith, who had piloted the first act of uniformity through both houses of parliament, and Dr. Alexander Nowell, the compiler of the Catechism. Nowell's tenure of his seat was, however, brief. As a prebendary of Westminster his election to the house of commons was anomalous; and in October, 1553, a committee reported that Nowell, having a seat in convocation, could not have one in

---

[1] Ponet escaped, came back to take part in Wyatt's rebellion, and escaped again. Scory made a submission and recantation, but fled later. Barlow tried to escape, but was captured in the Bristol Channel and imprisoned in the Tower; being liberated after a recantation, he then fled with better success. Three sees were vacant at Mary's accession; of the remaining twenty-three bishops, four were deprived and burnt, eight deprived merely, ten conformed, and one resigned. Sodor and Man is not included, as neither the bishop's diocese nor his barony was within the realm of England.

[2] *Acts of the P. C.*, 1552-54, p. 426; *cf.* Collier, *Eccl. Hist.*, vi., 12-13.

CHAP.
VI.
the house of commons.[1] The sentiments of these Cornish boroughs were not widely reflected elsewhere ; and the fact that, side by side with some scores of protestants, most of Mary's huge privy council sat in the parliament of October, 1553, does not prove that she neglected Charles V.'s advice to allow her people wide discretion in the matter of elections.

Nor was the legislative output of this parliament by any means ideal from Mary's point of view ; it embodied the general feeling of the nation rather than Mary's personal wishes. Parliament began with a comprehensive repeal of treason laws and a repetition of the liberal sentiments of 1547 ; indeed, Mary from religious motives went further than Somerset, and abolished all penalties for *præmunire* created since 1509 and for denial of the royal supremacy. Norfolk's attainder was declared void, and the families of Somerset and his friends as well as the Courtenays and the daughters of Henry Pole, Lord Montague, were restored in blood. No difficulty was to be expected in annulling Queen Catherine's divorce and in establishing Queen Mary's legitimacy. In religious affairs the return to the conditions of Henry VIII.'s last years would meet with general acquiescence, and Edward's acts of uniformity with the rest of his ecclesiastical legislation were repealed. Tunnage and poundage were granted to the queen for life, all the more willingly because she had remitted the subsidy from the temporality granted by the previous parliament.[2] But she obtained no relief for the scruples which had induced her to dispense, where she could, with the use of the title of supreme head in official documents. Her efforts to pursuade parliament to rescind the royal supremacy were unavailing.[3] She was given to understand that no proposal for the res-

[1] *Commons' Journals*, i., 27. According to Renard eighty members voted against the restoration of the mass, and 350 for it. It is impossible to account for so many as 430 members, although in Edward VI.'s reign the privy council register speaks of nearly 400 being present on one occasion. According to the *Official Return* there should have been 372 members of parliament in 1553.

[2] She retained, however, the tenth and fifteenth, and had required a loan of £20,000 from the London merchants (Wriothesley, ii., 102 ; *Acts of the P. C.*, 1552-54, p. 337). The subsidy, which was levied on individuals, was a newer and more accurate tax than the old tenths and fifteenths, levied on communities.

[3] *Venetian Cal.*, v., 534-35. Soranzo says that a bill to this effect was rejected ; his statement is not confirmed by the Commons' Journals, but the rejection may have taken place in the Lords, whose Journals for this session are lost.

toration of abbey and chantry lands would be entertained; no penalties were attached to non-attendance at mass; and the question of papal power was merely left open for debate. Mary's legitimacy was, to Pole's intense disgust, grounded on parliamentary statute; and she was grievously annoyed when the house of commons, hearing of the negotiations for her marriage with Philip of Spain, waited on her and besought her to marry an Englishman, pointing out the detriment likely to ensue upon the course she meditated. "Not only did she reply ungraciously, but, without allowing them even to conclude their address, rebuked them for their audacity."[1]

It was the first dangerous note of discord in Mary's reign; for the "busy meddlers in matters of religion, the preachers, printers, and players," against whom proclamations had been issued in August, can only have represented a section of the people; and the petitions in Kent and agitations in Essex for the retention of protestant services were mainly local symptoms.[2] But the commons' address against the Spanish marriage was the rumble of a storm which nearly drove Queen Mary from her throne. Jealousy of foreign interference was the fiercest English passion from the "Evil May day" riots of 1517,[3] to the defeat of the Armada. It alone had enabled Henry VIII. to bid defiance to the pope and brave the displeasure of the emperor; and by an appeal to it Northumberland had hoped to cover his ambition and his crimes. While national antipathy to foreigners was the natural ally of the protestants, catholics were not by any means exempt from the feeling; Gardiner himself, whom Soranzo describes as Mary's prime minister,[4] was averse from the match, and at least a third of the privy council abetted his strenuous opposition. There were of course advantages in the alliance. To most foreign statesmen and to many timorous Englishmen England seemed fated to come within the orbit of either the Hapsburg or the Valois monarchy, and between these two the Hapsburg was the less unpopular choice. So far as the nation had any conscious predilection in foreign policy, it was attached to the traditional Burgundian alliance; and an imperial ambassador in Henry's reign had

[1] *Venetian Cal.*, v., 560.
[2] *Acts of the P. C.*, 1552-54, pp. 373, 375, 387, 389, 391, 395, 403, 426.
[3] See above, vol. v., pp. 216-19.   [4] *Venetian Cal.*, v., 559.

calculated that half the population depended directly or in-directly for subsistence upon the wool-market of the Nether-lands.[1] Englishmen were alarmed at the progress of French influence in Scotland, and at French designs on Ireland and Calais; and not a few felt that in the Hapsburg alliance lay their only protection.

The force of these arguments was, however, weakening. The development of England's manufactures was lessening her dependence on Flanders, and Philip II. was not Burgundian. Charles V. had been born a Fleming but died a Spaniard; his son was purely Spanish, and Spain did not offer the attractions of the Netherlands. While the Flemish wool-market was opened on exceptionally favourable terms to English goods, the Spanish Main was closed to English enterprise. Racial, religious, and commercial sympathy was lacking between England and Spain in a far greater degree than between England and the Netherlands. Keen as had been the desire for a male heir to the throne in Henry's reign, there was no enthusiasm now for a Spanish king-consort nor for the prospect of an heir whose blood would be three-quarters Spanish. No treaty stipu-lations for England's independence could guarantee a national policy in circumstances such as these; and the sentiment, which united most of Scotland against the proposal of an English husband for Mary Stuart, roused no small part of England against the project of a Spanish husband for Mary Tudor.

Such considerations had little weight with the queen herself. Her treatment had not been calculated to inspire her with any great affection for her English subjects; she had passionately espoused the cause of her injured Spanish mother against her English father, and theological antipathy enflamed her wounded filial piety. She scorned, Soranzo tells us, to be English, and boasted her descent from Spain.[2] She was not oppressed by any dread lest Spain should have the better of the bargain and simply use the marriage as a means for getting England's fleet. She had no eye for the coming conflict on the sea, and no sym-pathy with England's maritime aspirations. She cared only for the spiritual welfare of her people, and believed that it was safest under the tutelage of Spain and of the papacy. Even

[1] *Cf. Spanish Cal.*, Eliz., i., 113.   [2] *Venetian Cal.*, v., 560.

if she had realised the antagonism between the secular interests of her own and Philip's countries, she would have considered it entirely subordinate to the question of religion. Two English suitors were suggested, Courtenay and Cardinal Pole; but Courtenay was totally unfit to be the husband of a queen, and Pole was fifty-three. He was still only a deacon, and even the obstacle of priestly orders could have been—and was sometimes—removed by papal dispensation; but Pole thought Mary should remain unmarried,[1] felt no vocation to the married state himself, and was not qualified for the exercise of temporal authority. At length at the end of October after a remarkable scene in which Mary, Renard, and a lady-in-waiting recited the *Veni, Creator Spiritus* on their knees before the altar in Mary's room, she avowed to Renard her intention of giving her hand to Philip.[2]

Renard's joy was an index to French annoyance. Henry II. had received his first and his greatest diplomatic rebuff; and Charles was revenged for the treaty of Chambord and the loss of the three bishoprics. So highly did he prize the hand of Mary that he made Philip break off a previous engagement to the Infanta of Portugal. English armies, it is true, were worth but little, and when Philip married Mary there were only fourteen lasts of powder in the Tower and no harquebusses in the ordnance office;[3] but the navy, despite its decadence since 1547, could still command the Channel and threaten French control in Scotland. The dreams of French dominion in the British Isles became an unsubstantial fabric, and Henry's disappointment was reflected in the comments and intrigues of his ambassador. Noailles represented the English as so furious at the Spanish marriage that Philip would be murdered when he set foot in England; and he told his master that Plymouth was seeking his protection and offering to place itself at his disposal.[4] The story is too circumstantial to be mere invention, and English discontent did not depend upon Noailles' imagination or incite-

---

[1] Tytler, ii., 303.

[2] Renard to Charles V., October 31, R. O. Transcripts; Griffet, p. 47; Miss J. M. Stone, *Mary I.*, p. 265. The name of the lady-in-waiting is given by Froude as "Lady Clarence"; she was no doubt the Mistress Clarentius who attended Mary on her death-bed and related the story about Calais being found written on her heart (*Tudor Tracts*, ed. Pollard, pp. 332, 362).

[3] *Acts of the P. C.*, 1554-56, p. 4; *cf.* State Papers, Dom., Mary, i., 23.

[4] *Ambassades de MM. de Noailles*, ii., 342.

CHAP.
VI.
ments to rebellion.   When the imperial ambassadors rode through London in January, 1554, to conclude the match, the street boys pelted their suite with snowballs, and their elders hung their heads in gloomy silence.

The few short months of Mary's popularity were already past. Her easy triumph in July had been effected by a national concentration against Northumberland's attempt to substitute a Dudley for a Tudor dynasty ; but, that project once frustrated, the victorious coalition fell to pieces, and the Tudor forces were divided.   Elizabeth and her friends had been with Mary against Queen Jane, but their interests had now diverged. Such partisans as Courtenay had in Devon were against the Spanish match, and Courtenay himself became a centre and a tool of disaffection.   The government thought the malcontents might be pacified, while Noailles hoped they might be strengthened, by a marriage between Elizabeth and Courtenay. The protestant supporters of Queen Mary had been alienated by the restoration of the mass ; some of them began to fancy that Edward's death was a bad dream ;[1] while the majority of the nation, who were probably not yet offended with the length to which reaction had been carried, were displeased with the Spanish match.   When, on January 14, Gardiner read the marriage treaty before an assembly of lords and gentlemen at Westminster they were not impressed by its high-sounding promises of Burgundy and the Netherlands—and in the event of Don Carlos' death, of Spain, Sicily, Naples, and Milan—for the issue of the marriage, and of titles, honours, dignities, and dower for the queen, by its guarantees of national independence, or by its rosy prospects of peace and plenty for the people. Promises had likewise been made by Hapsburgs in Germany, the Netherlands, and Hungary, only to be belied.   Charles V. would have erected no Inquisition at Brussels had not the Duchess of Burgundy married a Hapsburg.[2]   The English could not be sure that no son would be born to Philip and Mary, and Gardiner's words were "heavily taken of sundry men, yea and thereat almost each man was abashed, looking daily for worse matters to grow shortly after ".[3]

[1] *Acts of the P. C.*, 1552-54, pp. 363, 383-84.   Rumours that Edward VI. was still alive continued until late in Elizabeth's reign ; see *English Hist. Rev.*, xxiii., 286.

[2] See P. Fredericq, *Corpus Doc. Inquisitionis Neerlandicae.*

[3] *Chron. of Queen Jane*, p. 35.

Evil tidings were already on the wing. On the day that the imperial envoys made their cheerless progress through the streets of London the council sent a summons to Sir Peter Carew ; but Carew was on his way to stir revolt in Devonshire. Similar messages were sent for the arrest of suspected persons in Essex and in Kent a few days later, and by the 22nd the council was hurriedly despatching orders throughout the country for the suppression of rebellion.[1] Sir James Crofts, late Lord-lieutenant of Ireland, had gone to raise Wales and its marches, Suffolk had fled from London to stir up the Midlands, and Wyatt was rousing the men of Kent. The plot of the Carews fell flat ; Courtenay, who was to have lent the scheme his local influence, turned coward and could not keep his secrets from the chancellor. The Carews were ill-beloved by the Devon peasants, and after a slight local tumult Sir Peter took ship for France. Crofts collected his Herefordshire tenants, but made no headway and was soon arrested. Coventry, Leicester, and the Midlands responded faintly to Suffolk's feeble efforts, and the duke, with his two brothers, Lords John and Thomas Grey, was worsted by the Earl of Huntingdon. The conspiracy had been precipitated by Courtenay's revelations ; the rising had been planned for March 18, and its chances of success may be gauged from the narrowness of the government's escape from Wyatt's premature attack.

Wyatt had not hitherto been noted for religious zeal ; he was the son of one poet and the boon companion of another, the Earl of Surrey, with whom he had been imprisoned in the Tower in 1543 for breaking windows in the City. A large family of children, not all of them legitimate, and an embarrassed patrimony, had not tamed his turbulence of temper ; he had fought with distinction in Henry VIII.'s wars, and he belonged to that high-spirited English breed of men with whom a few years later hatred of Spain did duty for religion ; and the theory that his rebellion had religion as its essence and politics only as its pretext is a little strained. There is no doubt that, had Wyatt succeeded in frustrating the Spanish marriage and removing Gardiner from the council, an attack would also have been made upon the mass. Petitions to that intent had already been

---

[1] *Acts of the P. C.*, 1552-54, pp. 383, 385, 387 ; State Papers, Dom., Mary, ii., 2-9, 11-18, 26, 27, iii., 5, 6, 10.

organised in Kent ; and Wyatt might pretend to the devout that, although the rebels talked about the Spanish marriage, the restoration of God's word was their real concern.[1] But this very resolve to put the political issue in the forefront shows that they expected it to rally more supporters to their standard than a protestant appeal. Bishop Ponet was found in Wyatt's ranks, and a future bishop of Norwich [2] was summoned before the Star Chamber for seditious preaching at Rye ; but it was fear of foreign control and not their exhortations that brought 4,000 men into Wyatt's camp.

The leaders were well connected and hoped for influential support. Wyatt himself was nephew of Lord Cobham, who had been deputy of Calais, and two of Cobham's sons were out in the rebellion. His lieutenants, the Isleys, were nephews of the wife of Sir John Mason ; the Rudstons were nephews of Mary's ablest diplomatist, Dr. Nicholas Wotton, who then represented her at Paris and was Dean of York and Canterbury ; another of Wotton's nephews was Thomas Wotton, whose imprisonment in the Fleet his uncle, warned by a dream, had procured to save him from greater ills ; and his sister had married Gawain Carew.[3] Wyatt thought he could count on Sir Robert Southwell, late master of the rolls and now sheriff of Kent, and hoped that Southwell would bring with him Lord Abergavenny. Sir Edward Hastings, Mary's master of the horse, and another privy councillor, Sir Edward Waldegrave, master of the wardrobe, had threatened to leave her service if she persisted in the Spanish marriage, and Noailles, if not Soranzo as well, gave secret assistance in money, ammunition, and arms.

Wyatt, however, learnt to his cost that there was a wide difference between antipathy and armed opposition to the policy of the queen. He summoned his friends to Allington [4] Castle on the Medway ; but while Cobham temporised and Cheyne, the Lord-warden of the Cinque Ports fell under Mary's suspicion for slackness, Southwell and Abergavenny remained

---

[1] See Proctor's contemporary *History of Wyatt's Rebellion* in *Tudor Tracts;* with it should be compared the narrative in the *Chron. of Queen Jane*, and some thirty despatches in vols. ii. and iii. of Mary's Domestic State Papers.

[2] Edmund Scambler ; *cf. Acts of the P. C.*, 1552-54, pp. 391, 395.

[3] *Foreign Cal.*, 1553-58, pp. 60, 62, 114, 117, 134, 152.

[4] Froude calls it Allingham. *Cf.* State Papers, Dom., Mary, iii., 18.

loyal and dispersed some bands of Wyatt's supporters. His
step-father, Sir Edward Warner, was arrested, with the Marquis
of Northampton, and sent to the Tower of which he had been
lieutenant ; and a force of Londoners was levied to serve under
the Duke of Norfolk in Kent. On January 25 Wyatt published his proclamations at Maidstone, Milton, and Ashford, and
on the following day at Tonbridge. The men of Tonbridge
under Sir Henry Isley and the Knyvetts marched by way of
Sevenoaks, rifling Sir Henry Sidney's house at Penshurst, towards Rochester where Wyatt had encamped ; but on the 28th
they were met at Blacksoll Field in Wrotham parish and dispersed by Abergavenny. This check was soon retrieved. Norfolk with his 600 London Whitecoats arrived on the 29th at
Strood ; but no sooner did they come in sight of Wyatt's forces
than the Londoners with their captain, Brett, went over to the
rebels crying, " We are all Englishmen," and taking with them
eight pieces of ordnance. Norfolk, Ormonde, Sir Henry Jerningham, and the yeomen of the guard threw down their arms
and fled, while Wyatt, after seizing Cobham's castle at Cooling,
arrived at Gravesend on the 30th and at Dartford on the 31st.

Never before in that century had a Tudor on the throne
been threatened with so imminent a peril. Mary did not flinch,
but she had to send her master of the horse to parley with
the rebels, and to fall back upon the late supporters of her rival
for protection. As Huntingdon disposed of Suffolk, so Pembroke, Bedford, and Clinton saved the crown from Wyatt,
while Norfolk went down to his county a broken man.
Wyatt insolently demanded the keys of the Tower, but loitered
at Greenwich and Deptford till the afternoon of Saturday,
February 3. He had missed his best chance of success. On the
1st Mary appealed in person at the Guildhall to the loyalty of
her subjects ; and when Wyatt reached Southwark he found
the gates closed on London Bridge and thousands of citizens
armed for its defence. He remained at Southwark till Tuesday
the 6th, while tidings spread of the failure of his confederates
in the Midlands, on the Welsh borders, and in Devon, and of
forces gathering in his rear at Blackheath and Greenwich under
Cheyne and Southwell. Then Mary's commanders threatened
a cannonade, and Wyatt, importuned by the people of the
Borough and alarmed for the safety of his followers, decamped

CHAP.
VI.
and marched to Kingston which he reached that night.   The
bridge had been broken down, and 200 of Mary's men kept
guard on the north bank; but Wyatt dislodged them with two
pieces of artillery and transported his forces in boats which
three or four of his men swam the Thames to seize.   Then he
pushed on to Brentford, marching with his men on foot, and
thence as far as Knightsbridge, where he halted until daylight.

Pembroke's forces were widely distributed so as to defend
Westminster, Charing Cross, and the north-western approaches
to the City.   As Wyatt advanced towards what is now St.
James's Park there was a singularly ineffective exchange of
artillery fire; Pembroke charged the rebels near Hyde Park
Corner, but his horse made little impression on Wyatt's ranks
of footmen, and his infantry did nothing.   A panic seized the
1,000 men stationed under Gage at Charing Cross and they
fled down Whitehall shouting " treason," while Wyatt pursued
his way through Temple Bar along Fleet Street to Ludgate.
In Fleet Street he was met by 300 of the lord treasurer's men,
but both forces passed without a word!   Ludgate was locked
and defended by Lord William Howard.   Wyatt was entrapped;
confident apparently that the city would not rise, Pembroke
had allowed him to advance until retreat had been cut off.   As
the rebel leader turned back towards Charing Cross he found
Pembroke's horsemen in his path at Temple Bar, and there was
a little fighting.   But Wyatt was disheartened by his cold reception in the streets, and when a herald suggested that he
might find mercy if he stopped the bloodshed, he surrendered.[1]
At five o'clock he, Thomas Cobham, Knyvett, Brett, and others
were conveyed by water to the Tower.   A further batch of
prisoners was brought in on the morrow; and on the 10th
came Suffolk and his brother.

These were not the first marked out for execution, for they
had not yet been tried.   But there were innocent victims in
the Tower for whom no more formalities were needed.   Guilford Dudley, his brothers, Cranmer, and the Lady Jane had
been condemned as traitors in November; the brothers and
Cranmer still were spared, but Guilford and his wife were

---

[1] Wriothesley's brief account (ii., 109-11) is in some respects clearer than
the more detailed narratives in Proctor and the *Chronicle of Queen Jane* (pp.
47-55); see also Underhill's narrative (*ibid.*, pp. 128-33).

doomed to suffer for the treason of their friends. They had
committed no new offence, and Suffolk himself had not ventured
to proclaim his daughter queen a second time;[1] the rebellion
of 1554, even if it had aimed at displacing Mary, would not
have resulted in Jane's enthronement.   On February 12 Guilford Dudley was brought out to the scaffold on Tower Hill;
he had begged a last interview with his wife, but she had told
him they would soon meet in another world. He died with
greater courage and dignity than his father. As he was borne
to execution he was seen by Lady Jane from the windows of
her room, and she saw his headless corpse as it was brought
away. Her scaffold was on the green within the Tower gates;
she mounted it with tearless eyes and steadfast countenance.   In
a few words she admitted the unlawfulness of her consent to
occupy the throne, but denied that she had sought or wished it.
Then she knelt: "Shall I say this psalm?" she asked Feckenham who attended her. "Yea," he answered, and she began the
Miserere mei, Deus in English. The psalm finished, she rose,
loosened her attire, and bound a handkerchief across her eyes.
"Then, feeling for the block, she said, 'What shall I do? Where
is it?' One of the standers-by guiding her thereunto, she
laid her head down upon the block and stretched forth her
body and said, 'Lord, into thy hands I commend my spirit!'
And so she ended." She was sixteen years and five months
old, an almost perfect type of youthful womanhood.   Her intellectual graces were not inferior to the modesty of her mind
or the sincerity of her character; and the fortitude with which
she bore herself upon the most affecting scene in Tudor history
was none the less impressive for being inspired by the sanity
of her convictions rather than by the exaltation of religious
martyrdom.   No queen was worthier of the crown than this
usurper, no medieval saint more saintly than the traitor-heroine
of the reformation.   Beneath the shadow of the axe her name
shines with a lustre like Sir Thomas More's; and the light
they shed upon the scaffold showed the hideous blackness of
the gulf which separated Tudor law from justice.

CHAP.
VI.

---

[1] *Chron. of Queen Jane*, App. vii.

CHAPTER VII.

THE RESTORATION OF THE CHURCH.

WYATT'S rebellion might have taught Mary a lesson like that which Henry VIII. learnt from the Pilgrimage of Grace or that which Edward VI.'s advisers failed to learn from the western rebellion. All three insurrections were suppressed; but Henry moderated the progress of reform in deference to the strength of popular opposition; and had the government of Edward VI. paid similar heed to the warning of 1549, the catholic reaction would have been less violent. In the same way Wyatt's revolt was a caution to Mary; but she was obstinate rather than prudent. She perceived immediate obstacles in her path, but not the end towards which it led; she was more impressed by the failure of the protest than by the fact that it had been made; and she was confirmed in her course by her escape from immediate shipwreck. Wyatt's resort to arms discredited the anti-Spanish and anti-papal party, of which he represented the extreme wing; for treason was always odious in the sixteenth century, and Wyatt damaged the cause of national independence as seriously as Northumberland did that of the reformation.

None of the victims except Lady Jane Grey evoked much popular sympathy. Suffolk deserved little; few men have wrought more evil by their crimes than he did by his folly. He was arraigned on February 17 and beheaded on the 23rd. Eighty-two rebels were condemned on one day at the Old Bailey, and thirty-two more at Westminster. Gallows were erected at every gate in London, besides two in Cheapside, two in Fleet Street, and others in Holborn, Leadenhall Street, Charing Cross, Bermondsey, Hyde Park Corner, and Tower Hill; on them forty-six victims were hanged on one day, while more were sent down into Kent for exemplary execution. The London prisons were so full that many rebels were confined in churches. On the other hand, over 400 were pardoned, and the citizens of London were gratified by a proclamation ordering the expulsion of alien merchants.[1]

The leaders of Wyatt's rebellion required more consideration not only on account of their rank but because of the light they might throw on the attitude of exalted persons to Mary's government ; and the examinations of Wyatt, Crofts, Throckmorton, and others betrayed the active participation of Noailles in the scheme. Other diplomatists were implicated. D'Oyssel, on his way from France to Scotland, had met several of the leaders, and suggested a Scottish diversion on the Borders and a French attack on Guisnes ;[2] and Soranzo, the Venetian ambassador, was held responsible for the transfer of artillery and ammunition from a Venetian ship in the Thames to the hands of the rebels. Soranzo was recalled in that year, and the incident closed so far as Venice was concerned. But strong protests were addressed to Noailles and Henry II. ; and Renard thought that mutual recriminations would lead to war between England and France. France, however, had no wish to add an English war to its conflict with Charles V. ; and to keep the peace was the chief desire of the councillors who supported Mary's shaken throne.

Their nerves had been upset, and the distraction of their counsels portended to Renard a civil strife from which England could only be saved by Philip's arm. Personal feeling embittered political difference ; Paget, who owed his rise in Henry VIII.'s reign to Gardiner's influence, had helped the bishop to the Tower under Edward VI., but was now his rival for Mary's confidence. He led the *politiques*—to borrow a term from French history—men who, in the words of Marshal Tavannes, " preferred the repose of the kingdom or their own homes to the salvation of their souls ; who would rather that the kingdom remained at peace without God than at war for Him ".[3] Paget, Arundel, Pembroke, Sussex, Petre, Hastings, and Lord William Howard were all for religious moderation ;

---

[1] Tytler, ii., 312 ; Wriothesley, ii., 112.

[2] The transcript of Renard's despatches in the Record Office says " Guyenne," and so Tytler prints it ; but Guisnes is obviously meant.

[3] Tavannes, *Mémoires*, ed. Buchon, p. 269.

Renard called them heretics, and with the exception of Howard and Hastings they had all served on Northumberland's privy council. Gardiner, on the other hand, was " most ardent and hot-headed in the affairs of religion " ;[1] and his partisans were Rochester, Englefield, Jerningham, Bourne, and Waldegrave, zealous catholics who, having no connexion with Edward VI.'s government, had been the first to raise Mary's standard. The unwieldy bulk of Mary's council fostered faction and cabal, and Renard favoured a proposal to reduce it to its most experienced members. These were for the most part Paget's followers, and Gardiner's party took alarm. They pointed to their own claims, based upon their fidelity to Mary and the faith, and the scheme was brought to nought.

Behind these parties loomed the figures of Charles V. and Cardinal Pole and the different policies they represented. The emperor put politics before religion, the cardinal religion before politics ; Charles saw the salvation of England in the marriage of Philip and Mary, Pole in its restoration to the bosom of the church. The emperor was never a zealous papalist ; he had more than once been threatened with excommunication, and he regarded the *Interim*, which he had established in Germany in 1548, in spite of papal censures, as an eminently satisfactory religious settlement. He was quite content with the sort of *interim* which now existed in England, and feared lest the attempt to restore the papal jurisdiction would provoke a disturbance fatal to the Spanish marriage and its fair promise for the Hapsburg fortunes. Very different were Pole's ideas ; an extreme papalist in his views of church government, he was thoroughly English in his secular politics. He thought Mary would do well, considering her age, to remain unmarried and be content with the realm which she called her first husband. He had no liking for Spain, and he wrote to his friend, Cardinal del Monte, that the Spanish marriage proposal was "even more universally odious than the cause of religion ".[2] He thought it a bar to the reconciliation of England with Rome, and in any case it appeared to him of little importance compared with that supreme consideration. His relatives, the Staffords, had been implicated in Wyatt's rebel-

---

[1] Renard to Charles V., in Tytler, ii., 346.   [2] *Venetian Cal.*, v., 464.

lion, and so indifferent was Pole thought to be to Spanish interests that he was reported to be calling himself the Duke of
York and pretending a title to the crown.[1]   Naturally Charles
put every obstacle in the way of Pole's return to England
until the marriage was completed.   Greater precipitation in
the religious reaction might have insured the success of Wyatt's
rebellion, and the ægis of Spain was an indispensable protection for the papal cause in England.   On the other hand,
Wyatt had risen rather against Spain than against Rome, the
Roman religion came back in a Spanish garb, and its consequent unpopularity justified Pole's forebodings.

Paget agreed with his fellow-politician Charles V., and
Gardiner with his fellow-churchman Pole ; but neither Paget
nor Gardiner came up to Renard's standard of severity towards
the rebels.   Lord Thomas Grey shared the fate of his brother,
the Duke of Suffolk ; William Thomas, clerk to Edward VI.'s
privy council and author of that notorious apology for Henry
VIII. called *The Pilgrim*,[2] suffered a merited death for plotting Mary's assassination ; and Wyatt was brought to the block
on April 11.   But other leaders or well-known suspects like Sir
James Crofts, Sir George Harper, Lord Cobham's nephews,
and Sir Nicholas Arnold escaped with imprisonment in the
Tower.   The council had received a warning to stay its
hand.   Sir Nicholas Throckmorton had been acquitted by a
London jury in spite of the evidence against him, and the
plaudits of the citizens greeted him on his way back to prison.
The foreman and another juror were sent to the Tower and
the rest to the Fleet, but their verdict produced its effect ;[3]
and the government did not venture to put Courtenay and
Elizabeth upon their trial.

Of Courtenay's complicity in Wyatt's designs there can be
little doubt, but Elizabeth was made of shrewder stuff.   Wyatt,
whose life had been spared for two months after his arrest in
order that he might be induced to incriminate his accomplices,
is said to have made admissions damaging to her innocence ;

---

[1] Tytler, ii., 378.   Pole was great-grandson of Richard, Duke of York.

[2] Edited by J. A. Froude in 1861.

[3] Tytler, ii., 374, 379 ; Wriothesley, ii., 115.   Mary, says Renard, was so
greatly displeased that she was ill for three days, and Throckmorton, in spite of
his acquittal, was kept in the Tower until Jan. 18, 1555, Machyn, p. 80.

CHAP.
VII.

and Elizabeth was summoned from her house at Ashridge to court.   She was indisposed and feared fatal effects from travelling; the queen sent her physicians down to look after her health, while Lord William Howard, Sir E. Hastings, and Cornwallis secured her person.   The journey of thirty-three miles was spread over five days, and Howard was the last man to inflict on his grandniece the indignities which Foxe has portrayed.[1]   Mary, however, refused to see her on her arrival at Westminster on February 23; and on March 18, in spite of her indignant protestations of innocence, she was sent down the Thames to the Tower.   She might well quail as the gates closed behind her, for few suspected traitors emerged thence except on their way to the scaffold, and Renard was moving all the powers to procure her execution.   Mary would never be safe, he urged, so long as Elizabeth lived; nor, he knew, could Philip succeed to the English throne, in spite of the pedigree which was produced before parliament showing his descent from John of Gaunt, so long as Elizabeth stood in the way.   He was playing the hand that another Spanish envoy at London had played more than fifty years before.[2]   While a rival claimant remained to the throne a Spanish spouse could not be entrusted to England's keeping.   Warwick's head had fallen in 1499 to prepare the way for Catherine of Aragon; and Mary's passionate anxiety for the coming of Philip drove her to listen to Renard's demand for a similar sacrifice.

Fortunately Mary had more heart and less power than Henry VII.   She knew her mother's remorse for Warwick's death, and must have heard her lament that her marriage was "made in blood" and punished by her divorce.[3]   Gardiner wished to deprive Elizabeth of her right to the succession, but Renard frequently complained of his remissness in proceeding against political offenders.   To shield Courtenay he boldly suppressed a despatch containing incriminatory matter; and Renard remarked that, even if the determination to save Elizabeth were against Mary's wishes, she could not help it, for Gardiner was managing the whole affair.   Her committal to the Tower was

[1] *Acts and Monuments*, viii., 606-7.
[2] See vol. v., pp. 86-87.
[3] See my *Henry VIII.*, p. 179, and the authorities there cited.   Pole also relates the story, *Venetian Cal.*, v., 257-58.

due to the refusal of the lords to be individually responsible for her safe-keeping ; and though proof of her guilt should be forthcoming, wrote Renard, "they would not dare to proceed against her for the love of the admiral, her relative, who espouses her quarrel, and has at present all the force of the kingdom in his power".[1]

That proof was not forthcoming; and without some evidence more plausible than that produced against Elizabeth, suspects were not executed in England even under Tudor sovereigns. Wyatt completely exonerated her on the scaffold, and after ten weeks' search Renard reluctantly admitted that the judges could find no matter for her condemnation.[2] Wyatt had written her a letter which he commissioned Bedford's son to deliver, but Elizabeth swore she had never received it. Her position had been canvassed by the conspirators, French and English ; and had they been successful, she might have been given the crown. But she knew well enough that it was no part of French policy to provide her with a safe seat on the throne, that Mary Stuart was the real French candidate, and that success itself would leave her a mere tenant at will of Henry II. She could bide her time for a brighter prospect. If Mary had no issue, Elizabeth could trust the English people to put no other bar between her and the crown. The very settlement in virtue of which Mary was queen placed her next in the succession, and no efforts could induce parliament to put her out; the nation was far more attached to the Tudor dynasty than to either the old or the new religion. After two months' imprisonment in the Tower, she was released on May 19 and sent to Woodstock in the keeping of Sir Henry Bedingfield. Courtenay was removed to Fotheringhay, and then in 1555 was sent abroad.

Meanwhile another parliament had been elected. Soranzo states that "through the assiduity employed no members were returned save such as were known to be of the queen's mind".[3] But no evidence survives to substantiate this sweeping statement; and though the failure of Wyatt's rebellion told in Mary's favour, the history of this, as of other Tudor parliaments,

---

[1] Tytler, ii., 375 ; *cf. ibid.*, ii., 338, 342-49, 365-67, 382-84.
[2] *Ibid.*, ii., 375 ; *cf.* Griffet, pp. 171-72, and *Venetian Cal.*, v., 538.
[3] *Venetian Cal.*, v., 561.

shows that servility to the government was not a necessary qualification for success at the elections. The usual proportion of members who had sat in the last parliament, rather more than a third, secured re-election ; and some of those who had been absent then but were now returned, were not distinguished for devotion to Mary's cause. Parliament was summoned to meet at Oxford, ever more loyal than London to old and unpopular causes, and further removed from the scene of seething discontent. Mary even thought of removing her court to York, for there the people were catholic. Such a desertion of the predominant part of the realm would have invited civil war. Renard feared that, if Mary went so far as Oxford, Elizabeth and Courtenay would be forcibly liberated from the Tower ; and the queen was well-advised to relinquish her plans for York and Oxford, and to meet parliament at Westminster.

It opened on April 2, and its course was marked by heated debates, close divisions, and government defeats. The first measure submitted to it commanded the assent of all parties, and passed with ease and rapidity. It gave once and for all a statutory quietus to the doubts, which had troubled many generations of Englishmen, whether a woman could reign in England or not, and asserted categorically that Mary's authority was every whit as great as that of any of her male predecessors. The declaration was as necessary in the interests of Elizabeth and Mary Stuart as in Mary Tudor's, and it was no less urgent in the interests of England in view of the claims which Philip II. might put forward in right of his queen or his own descent ; indeed, Gardiner's production of Philip's pedigree may not have been an entirely friendly act. Nor was there serious opposition to the terms of the treaty of marriage. Mary had promised the rebels to submit the question to parliament, but Wyatt's failure had settled the point in Mary's favour. The bill was committed in the house of lords to Bishops Tunstall and Heath and Lords Paget, Rich, Shrewsbury, and Williams ; and so far as paper guarantees could protect the realm against a Spanish king and a doting queen, the bill provided them in ample measure. Two other bills, one for changing the office of lord great master into lord steward, and the other for the restitution of Sir William Parr (formerly Marquis of Northampton) in blood but not in dignities, were passed without a division. Only Rich voted in the house of lords against a bill, which had failed in the previous session, to reconstitute the bishopric of Durham, although in the house of commons "the heretics raised such a murmur and noise about it" that Renard "looked for much disorder, to the prejudice, loss of popularity, and danger of the queen".[1]

But here the agreement between the government and the legislature ended, and on the questions of the succession to the throne, the revival of the statutes against heresy, and the extension of the treason laws Mary encountered severe rebuffs. Gardiner had no affection for the Spaniards, but his proposal that Mary should be empowered to disinherit Elizabeth [2] and bequeath the crown by will would have meant the succession of Philip II., and the scheme was not embodied in a bill in either house. The resistance to the other measures was stronger in the lords than in the commons, although in the previous parliament the opposition had relied upon the lower house and had informed Noailles that the queen and all the lords of her council counted for little when the commons were against them.[3] Two bills against heresy passed the house of commons, one reviving the Lollard statutes and the other the act of Six Articles. The lords gave the second measure two readings, but rejected it after a division on the third; the other bill was also read twice and then abandoned; and a somewhat vindictive measure to deprive the religious who had married of the pensions, to which they had been entitled on the dissolution of the monasteries, was also dropped after passing its third reading.[4] Gardiner had been too hasty in his zeal for restoration. Paget told Renard that " when the parliament began we resolved, with consent of her Majesty, that only two acts should be brought forward; the one, concerning the marriage; the other, to confirm every man in his possessions ".[5] The proposals about Elizabeth and heresy

---

[1] Renard to Charles V., April 22, R. O.; *Lords' Journals*, April 10; *Commons' Journals*, April 11 and 16. The temporalities of Durham had been confiscated in March, 1553 (see above, pp. 73, 77), and the see had been divided into two, Durham and Newcastle.

[2] Griffet, pp. 188-89; Paget to Renard, Tytler, ii., 382.

[3] Vertot, *Ambassades de MM. de Noailles*, ii., 341.

[4] *Lords' Journals*, April 16 and 19.

[5] Tytler, ii., 373, 382.

were private ventures of Gardiner and the clerical party in
violation of this resolve, and Paget, in spite of his place in
the government, led the lay opposition to them in the lords.
He was also credited with the failure of the attempt to give
Philip the protection of the treason laws; he spoke, writes
Renard, more violently against it than any one else; and although the bill was read four times in the house of lords, the
commons disagreed and dashed it. Paget's success had been
remarkable, but it was not complete; and the second of the
measures which the government had united to propose, described in the journals of the house of lords as a bill "that
no bishop shall convent any person for abbey lands," got no
farther than a second reading.[1]

Parliamentary strife like this between two parties in the
council struck at the root of the Tudor system of government,
and Mary might well complain that her father's councillors
would never have taken such liberties with him. Worse, it
was thought, would follow; the heretics, wrote Renard, were
encouraged and the catholics alarmed. Serious disturbances
took place in Suffolk and in Essex, leading to the arrest of
Dr. Rowland Taylor.[2] Throckmorton had been acquitted;
Paget was intriguing with the protestants; and he was said to
have arranged a plot with Arundel, Pembroke, Cobham, and
others for putting Gardiner in the Tower, while Gardiner was
advising the queen to imprison Paget and Arundel. The
Earls of Sussex, Huntingdon, Shrewsbury, and Derby were
also under suspicion. "The parties which divide the council,"
declared Renard, "are so many, and their disputes so public,
they are so banded the one against the other, that they forget the service of the Queen to think of their private passions
and quarrels. . . . It is the subject of religion . . . which is
the cause of these troubles." Paget agreed with this last
sentence. "For the love of God," he wrote to Charles V.'s
ambassador, "persuade the queen to dissolve the parliament
instantly . . . for the times begin to be hot, men's humours
are getting inflamed, warmed, fevered; and I see that this person [Gardiner], for his own private respects and affection, has

[1] *Lords' Journals*, April 16, 18, 21, 24, 28, and 30; *Commons' Journals*, i., 36;
Tytler, ii., 385, 392.
[2] *Ibid.*, ii., 377; *Acts of the P. C.*, 1554-56, p. 1.

resolved to hurry forward such measures as will create too much heat." [1]

Paget's view was clear enough, and he represented the most powerful section of the English laity. They were not protestants, and did not consider the protestant clergy and their conscientious followers strong enough to endanger Mary's throne. But protestantism, reinforced by the secular interests which had been built upon the ruins of the church, could raise a tumult which might shatter the Tudor monarchy. It was by the help of these secular forces that protestantism triumphed elsewhere, and Mary could not afford to offend them. Henry VIII. had effected his revolution by giving away the lands of monasteries; Mary could only undo it by confirming his grants, and the protestant conscience would thus be disarmed. It was not merely greed that dictated this policy; a complete restoration of the monastic system would destroy the lay supremacy in the house of lords, give the church control of the secular legislature, and prevent future reform by legal methods. Hence Paget's zeal for the security of the holders of abbey lands; till that was established, religious persecution must be deferred. He had, too, no more affection for the catholic than for the protestant clergy. A true Erastian, he objected not so much to persecution of the church as to persecution by the church; and he complained to Renard that Gardiner was "anxious to carry through the matter by fire and blood". He saw that Mary neither could nor would resist clerical pressure, and he hoped for a secular ally in Philip. Charles V. agreed, and Renard convinced the queen of the necessity for dissolving parliament to prevent further disputes, and for proceeding "gently in the reformation of religion".

Before the session ended on May 5 an attempt was made to heal the breach. Both houses were anxious to prove that their rejection of government bills did not proceed from disloyalty to the queen, and she was well received when she went down to dissolve parliament. Paget made some sort of apology for his conduct, and Renard reported that "the ancient penalties against heretics were assented to by all the peers".[2] Obviously, it had been pointed out for the satisfaction of the catholics that heresy was an offence at common law, and did

---

[1] Tytler, ii., 382, 398, 400.   [2] *Ibid.*, ii., 366, 379, 389.

not depend for punishment upon the statutes of Richard II., Henry IV., and Henry V., which the lords had refused to revive.   It had been possible to burn heretics before those statutes were passed; it remained possible, as Joan Bocher found to her cost, after they were repealed in 1547.   But the facts remain that these were empty consolations, and that no heretic was burnt in Mary's reign until those statutes had been revived, and until the petition[1] of the clergy, that their jurisdiction might be restored to them and the laws which impeded its operation abrogated, had been granted.

Meantime Mary had to content herself with her marriage. Parliament had removed all legal obstacles on the English side, and no difficulty was experienced in obtaining the papal dispensation which Mary and Philip desired, although it had no force by English law, removing the canonical bar of consanguinity.   But there was still some doubt, inspired by the boding fears of the imperialists, whether Philip would venture on England's forbidding shores.   Even Pole thought the match less advantageous to Philip than to Mary;[2] while Renard after Wyatt's rebellion had denounced the English as "a people without faith, without law, mixed and hazy on the question of religion, false, perfidious, inconstant, and jealous, who hated strangers and detested the authority of the government".[3] Some two or three hundred London schoolboys organised a sham fight between Wyatt and Philip, in which the Spanish champion was captured, hanged, and cut down barely in time to save his life.[4]   As late as June Renard was writing to Charles of intrigues between the lord high admiral, William Howard, the French, and the Killigrews, and of a plot on the part of Arundel, Pembroke, and Paget to marry Elizabeth to Arundel's son.   A mysterious voice in a wall prophesied ill of the Prince of Spain, and drew crowds until the imposture was detected. Numbers were pilloried in May for seditious words; on June 10 a gun was fired at the preacher in St. Paul's, and all the efforts of the authorities failed to detect the author of the outrage.   Philip was running other risks besides that of capture by the French or the English pirates in the Channel; but the fortunes of the Spanish Hapsburgs and their hold on the

---

[1] 1 & 2 Phil. and Mary, c. viii., § 31.
[2] *Venetian Cal.*, v., 491.
[3] Griffet, p. 182.
[4] Noailles, iii., 129.

Netherlands seemed to depend upon their control of the English
fleet and of English policy.

At length, after two months of feverish anxiety on Mary's
part, Philip's flotilla cast anchor on July 20 in Southampton
Water. Three days later he went on to Winchester, whither
Mary had come to meet him ; on the 24th it was announced that
Charles V. had made his son King of Naples (a title said to have
been invented for this occasion) and of Jerusalem ; and on the
morrow Philip and Mary were married in Winchester cathedral
by its bishop, Lord Chancellor Gardiner. The wedded pair became " by the grace of God, King and Queen of England, France,
Naples, Jerusalem, and Ireland, Defenders of the Faith, Princes
of Spain and Sicily, Archdukes of Austria, Dukes of Milan,
Burgundy, and Brabant, Counts of Hapsburg, Flanders, and
Tyrol ". All this might seem to the English to be well worth
a mass ; and, the marriage safely accomplished, the way was
cleared for the complete restoration of England to the fold of
the catholic church. It was still a schismatic realm, and even
those who did not believe with Boniface VIII. that no one
could be saved who was not subject to the Roman pontiff, or
with Raymond of Peñaforte that schism was heresy,[1] might yet
think that the papal jurisdiction was the best safeguard of
orthodoxy ; for Henry VIII.'s claim that the catholic faith was
safer under the royal than under the papal supremacy had
scarcely been justified.

So far religion had hardly been restored to its status in 1546.
The statute of Six Articles had not been revived, no penalties
had yet been enacted for repudiating doctrines they prescribed,
ecclesiastical jurisdiction was still in the shackles imposed by the
Submission of the Clergy, and the work of restoration had been
done in virtue of that royal supremacy, which Mary detested
and her bishops had impugned in the reign of Edward VI.
Mary's first parliament had abolished the two Books of
Common Prayer and repealed the acts requiring the administration of the sacrament in both kinds, permitting the marriage of priests, doing away with images, service-books, fast
days, processions, and holy days, reforming the methods of
ordination, and dispensing with the election of bishops.
Altars, images, and lights had been set up again ; the " scrip-

[1] F. W. Maitland in *Engl. Hist. Rev.*, xi., 465-66, xvi., 37 n.

CHAP.
VII.
tures written on rood-lofts and about the churches in London,
with the arms of England," had been washed out ; and the use
of palms, creeping to the cross on Good-Friday, "with the
sepulchre lights and the Resurrection on Easter day," had been
revived.[1]   In spite of an unrepealed act of Henry VIII., the
Litany was sung in Latin, and processions began again ; but
on Corpus Christi day, May 24, "some kept holy day and some
would not ".[2]   Secular priests who had married were deprived
of their benefices, but allowed to keep their wives ; the religious
who had married were deprived of both.

Neither seculars nor *quondam* religious were allowed to
choose between their conscience and their livings, and their
ejection was no proof of their devotion to reformed religion ;
they have therefore been refused the credit claimed for the
recusants of 1559.   The distinction is sound, but it is incompatible with the contention, with which it is often coupled, that
Mary's government was more tolerant than her sister's.   Elizabeth permitted an option which in this respect Mary denied.
At the numbers thus deprived it is difficult even to guess.
There were some 8,800 livings in England, and possibly some
2,000 ejections.   Whatever the estimate, it is certain that the
vast majority made a principle of conformity and, when they
were allowed, remained faithful to their flocks and the national
religion.   Of the bishops in possession at Edward's death, ten,
including Goodrich, Thirlby, and Oglethorpe, conformed and
retained their sees ; six vacancies were filled by the restoration
of Gardiner, Bonner, Heath, Day, Voysey, and Tunstall, but
Mary found it no easy task to provide the ten remaining bishoprics with suitable occupants.   The only prelates of any eminence
whom she raised to the bench were John White, bishop first of
Lincoln and then of Winchester, Thomas Watson who succeeded
White at Lincoln in 1557, and Cardinal Pole.

For Pole was reserved the crowning work of the catholic
reaction, the reconciliation with Rome.   It could not have
fallen into more appropriate hands ; he had never bowed the
knee to Baal nor faltered in his fealty to the papal jurisdiction.
He had not felt the doubts of papal supremacy which once
troubled Sir Thomas More, and was far removed from the
worldly considerations which had led Gardiner, Bonner, and

[1] Wriothesley, *Chron.*, ii., 113.   [2] *Greyfriars' Chron.*, p. 89.

the gentle Tunstall to serve the state under Henry VIII. and Edward VI. Royal descent, unblemished morals, theological learning, and rigid consistency had made him a traitor in England and an unsuccessful candidate for the papal chair at Rome. His virtue was somewhat oppressive. He gave most of his goods to the poor, and the commandments he had kept from his youth up. He seemed to have nothing to learn and nothing to forget. His conception of the world and of its history was as simple, clear-cut, and unpractical as a syllogism. God had ordained the papacy; all the evils of his age were due to lack of faith and to disobedience; conscience, if it coincided with the dictates of the papacy, was the voice of God; if not, it was self-will or diabolic inspiration. Dread of this self-will drove him into absolute submission to the papacy, which he held to represent the will of God, and almost deprived him of personal initiative. He lacked Luther's and Henry VIII.'s capacity for identifying the will of God with their own. As he said himself, "he always waited to be called,"[1] and he lost the papacy because he was convinced that he would get it, if it was God's will, without any effort of his own. No divided allegiance distracted his mind: the pope was his only father on earth; his king had been a cruel stepfather. The national aspirations of his age were lost on Pole; but he was the soul of papalism at its best.

With these views he had been sorely troubled by the delay in restoring the papal jurisdiction.[2] Mary's very title, he said, depended upon papal dispensation, and must be confirmed by a papal legate; acts of parliament were nothing to him, and he could see no prospect of temporal or spiritual security outside the Roman church. But Charles V., the pope, and even Mary saw the necessity of temporising. Pole was diverted by a commission to negotiate peace between the emperor and the king of France, which had no results except to ingratiate him with Henry II. By one expedient or another he was kept out of England until the marriage was completed, although Mary had illegally had recourse to him for the absolution from schism and reconciliation to Rome of six new bishops in April, 1554.[3]

[1] *Venetian Cal.*, v., 499, and *cf. ibid.*, No. 671.
[2] See *Epist. R. Poli*, iv., 162-66; *Venetian Cal.*, v., 946; and Dom Ancel, "La Réconciliation de l'Angleterre" in *Rev. d'histoire ecclesiastique*, x. (1909), 521-36, 744-98.
[3] See Pole's letter in *Venetian Cal.*, v., 495-97.

CHAP.
VII.

Even in October there were obstacles in his path ; he was still an attainted traitor, and no legate could yet be received in England. Until some guarantee had been given that the holders of abbey lands would remain undisturbed, these bars would not be removed, and they could only be removed by parliament.

The elections to Mary's third parliament were held during the latter half of October and first week of November. Dissatisfied with the composition and results of her first two parliaments, Mary now resorted to Northumberland's expedient, and sent round letters to the lord-lieutenants and sheriffs requiring them to admonish the electors to choose representatives " of their inhabitants, as the old laws require, and of the wise, grave, and catholic sort ".[1] She did not apparently suggest any names, but some of the lord-lieutenants were not so scrupulous, and a passionate oration addressed to Elizabeth at her accession speaks of Mary's denial of freedom of election, the choice of knights and burgesses by force of threats, and the extrusion of members lawfully returned.[2] This is the rhetorical exaggeration of the defeated party. An exceptionally large proportion—nearly 40 per cent.—of old members was returned to the new parliament. Renard remarks that Mary's letters were drawn up in the old form used in Henry VII.'s reign, and says that the members chosen for London were considered " fort saiges et modestes ".[3] If this indicates satisfaction on the part of the court at the result of the circulars it was easily pleased, for three of these four members had sat in the previous parliament, two of them in Northumberland's parliament of 1553, and the only new member was the chronicler, Richard Grafton, who had been deprived by Mary of his office of royal printer for protestant sympathies. Nevertheless it was from Mary's point of view the least unsatisfactory house of commons with which she had to deal.[4] Except Grafton, and Whalley who had turned the representation of Nottinghamshire almost into a freehold, hardly a protestant name occurs in the list of members. The reformation was at its lowest ebb ; Mary's

---

[1] Strype, *Eccl. Mem.*, III., i., 245 ; Pocock's *Burnet*, ii., 406, vi., 313-14.

[2] Printed in Foxe, viii., 673-79. The charge was repeated with less exaggeration in parliament in 1571, D'Ewes, p. 170.

[3] Granvelle, iv., 324.

[4] Pole at Brussels wrote on Nov. 11 to the pope of the expectations founded on " the good choice made of members of parliament," *Venetian Cal.*, v., 592.

success had succeeded in turning the heads of her people. Philip had brought a glittering array of honours for England's sovereign, the promise of light taxation and of protection from France at Spain's expense, and the prospect, over which Mary was gloating already, of a male heir to settle all disputes about the succession and to combine in one great monarchy England and her market in the Netherlands.

The session was opened by the king and queen in person on November 12, but little was done for the first week or so ; parliament had to be " entertained," as Mason suggested,[1] until Pole's business was settled. It was all to his credit as a leader of religion that his essays in diplomacy filled his friends with apprehension. The emperor urged him to be cautious, and warned him against Englishmen's intense abhorrence of " the obedience of the church," of his red hat, and of the habit of the religious ; though, as for doctrine, he said that men of this sort cared little, as they had no belief either one way or the other.[2] Renard was sent over to Brussels on behalf of Philip and Mary to make sure that Pole understood the conditions of the case, that he would not enter England as papal legate nor exercise his legatine functions without " communicating everything in the first place to their majesties," and that he possessed, and would exercise, powers not merely to treat with the holders of abbey lands but to confirm their tenure without any haggling.[3] This was the root of the matter ; the English would not admit Pole or the pope except on condition that their material gains from the reformation were placed beyond the reach of ecclesiastical jurisdiction. Pole was not required to say that the nation had done right in spoiling the church, but he was allowed no means of expressing his sense of its sin except by a fruitless appeal to its conscience. This was the true measure of England's repentance, and it cut Pole to the quick to have to grant absolution to a sinner who stipulated that he was not to suffer for his sins. He had no choice : after all there would be compensations ; and the details of the bargain, which was soon embodied in acts of parliament, were arranged before Pole started from Brussels.[4]

---

[1] Tytler, ii., 457.   [2] *Venetian Cal.*, v., 580.   [3] *Ibid.*, pp. 581-82.

[4] See his letter to Morone, Oct. 28, *Venetian Cal.*, v., pp. 588-90, and compare with it the act 1 & 2 Phil. and Mary, c. 8.

On Renard's return to London, Paget, Sir E. Hastings, and Cecil were sent on November 6 to Brussels to complete the understanding and conduct the cardinal home. A bill to repeal his attainder was rushed through both houses by the 21st, and the royal assent was given in the middle of the session, a course so unprecedented that the question was put in the house of commons whether, after such assent, parliament could proceed "without any prorogation".[1] He crossed from Calais to Dover on the 20th, and proceeded with an ever-growing escort by way of Canterbury to Gravesend, whence on the 24th he was rowed up to Whitehall with his silver cross at the prow of his barge. In the ecstasy of the moment of salutation Mary experienced the joy of the mother of John the Baptist, and *Te Deums* were ordered to celebrate the quickening of her child.[2] On the 28th the two houses were summoned to Whitehall to hear Pole's exhortation, and on the 29th a petition for reunion with Rome was passed with no dissentients in the lords and only Sir Ralph Bagnall and another in the commons.[3]   On the morrow, St. Andrew's day, the two houses gathered again in the palace at Whitehall: the petition was read by Gardiner; the king and queen made intercession for the realm, and Pole pronounced its absolution from the sin of schism and its reconciliation with the one true church.   The pious rapture of Mary, Philip, and all good catholics knew no bounds ; even the graceless Henry II. expressed his holy joy, and salvoes of artillery from the castle of St. Angelo announced the news at Rome.

And then parliament returned to business, which kept it sitting over Christmas and half-way into January.   It had to deal with three classes of proposals : bills strengthening the law against treason and sedition, and providing for the government in the case of Mary's death ; the revival of the heresy laws ; and the restoration of the papal supremacy and eccle-

---

[1] *Commons' Journals*, i., 38.

[2] Wriothesley, *Chron.*, ii., 124 ; *Descriptio Reductionis Angliæ* in *Epistolæ R. Poli*, t. v. ; *Epistolæ Tigurinæ* (Parker Soc.), p. 229 [Froude, v., 445, gives the reference as p. 169, which is the number of the epistle]; *cf.* Noailles, iv., 21-26.   The story that Pole saluted her with the *Ave Maria* is probably a fiction.

[3] The matter is not mentioned in the *Lords' Journals*, and there is only a bare reference in the *Commons'*.   Our knowledge is derived from the Italian *Descriptio Reductionis* and an English diary which Froude cites as Harleian MS., iv., 19, but is really 194.   For Sir Ralph Bagnall, see *Dict. of Nat. Biogr.*, Suppl., i., 96-97, and *Irish Cal.*, i., 152.

siastical jurisdiction.   The heresy laws occasioned little trouble ;
the three acts of Richard II., Henry IV., and Henry V. were
re-enacted by a bill which passed the commons on December
12 and the lords on the 18th, unanimously, according to the
Journals, though Renard states that objection was taken in the
upper house to the severity of the penalties and to the authorisation of clerical coercion.[1]   A proposal to make it treason
to " pray or desire " that God would shorten the queen's days [2]
naturally provoked more criticism, and it was not till January
16, 1555, that it finally passed the house of commons.   It
went farther than any of Henry VIII.'s ferocious acts ; and the
worst of these was repeated by another statute making it high
treason merely to affirm that any one else had a better title than
Mary to the throne.[3]   This latter act also gave Philip the protection of the treason laws, and appointed him regent in case
Mary at her death left issue under age.   The delay in its passage
was probably due to the efforts made to secure his coronation
and succession, or at least to give him control of the forces of
the realm.   Equally ineffective attempts had been made to
induce parliament to sanction war with France on behalf of
Charles V.   Ought not a son, inquired a peer, to help his father ?
He asked in vain, and Philip and Mary showed their displeasure by the dissolution of a parliament which might
otherwise have merely been prorogued.[4]

The most prolonged debates took place over the great act
repealing the statutes passed against Rome since 1528.   After
the bill had passed the lords, where Bonner alone had refused
to condone the secularisation of church property, the commons
devoted four whole days to discussing its second reading,[5]
and various amendments were inserted.   In its final form it

---

[1] Granvelle, iv., 347 ; *Commons' Journals*, Dec. 12 ; *Lords' Journals*, Dec.
15, 17, and 18.

[2] 1 and 2 Phil. and Mary, c. 9.   The occasion of the act was the current protestant prayer for the queen's conversion from idolatry or short life (Gairdner,
p. 347).   Sir John Mason, a good catholic, gives vent to a similar prayer with
regard to the pope, Feb. 3, 1556, *Foreign Cal.*, p. 207.   The puritan Norton cited
this act as a sound precedent in 1571, D'Ewes, p. 163 ; while the editor of
Cardinal Allen's *Letters* defends such prayers, p. xlix.

[3] 1 and 2 Phil. and Mary, c. 10.

[4] Noailles, iv., 75, 137, 149, 153-54 ; Granvelle, iv., 347-48, 357-59.

[5] *Commons' Journals*, Dec. 29, 31, Jan. 2 and 3 ; *Lords' Journals*, Dec. 20,
24, and 26, and Jan. 4.

CHAP.
VII.

was a blow to the clerical extremists who had not been satisfied with Pole's concordat, and had agitated for a restoration of the abbey lands and impropriated livings and tithes, and for a repeal of the mortmain acts.[1] The medieval strife between church and state was revived by the reconciliation with Rome ; and the demand for the repeal of the mortmain acts was compromised by their suspension for twenty years, in order to give the church at least a chance of recovering from such of the laity as were repentant some of the wealth it had lost.   But the proceeds of voluntary penance were not large, and the prospect of recoupment through the action of the ecclesiastical courts was absolutely barred.   The titles of holders of church lands were not to depend on a papal dispensation which a new pope might revoke, nor on the dubious benevolence of ecclesiastical courts, but on parliamentary statute and the courts of common law ; and the papal dispensation was, in spite of Pole's threat to go back to Rome, embedded in the act of parliament in order to give it validity and permanence.[2]   All suits relating to these lands were to be tried at common law, and any one who sought to draw them into the church courts was made liable to *præmunire*.[3]   The only appeal which Pole and the church were permitted to make was to conscience, and the conscience of the holders of abbey lands might be left to protect itself.[4] The statutes against the exaction by the clergy of excessive fees for probate and mortuary dues,[5] with which the legal reformation had begun, were not repealed ; and although the prohibition of the payment of annates and first-fruits to Rome was removed, such payment was not enjoined.

The property of the English laity was in fact ruled out of the bargain between the papacy and parliament, and the pope and clergy had to content themselves with a free hand in matters of faith and ecclesiastical government.   Every facility was afforded them in these respects ; not merely were the Lollard statutes revived, but the act prohibiting the citation of accused persons outside their dioceses[6] was repealed.   All the limitations upon ecclesiastical jurisdiction imposed by Henry VIII. were withdrawn ; appeals no longer lay to a

[1] *Cf.* Mason to Petre, Dec. 12, *Foreign Cal.*, 1553-58, p. 145.

[2] Granvelle, iv., 346.   [3] 1 and 2 Phil. and Mary, c. viii., § 31.

[4] See Pole's letter in *Venetian Cal.*, vi., 9.

[5] 21 Hen. VIII., cc. 5 and 6.   [6] 23 Henry VIII., c. 9.

secular court, and the papacy recovered its rights as absolute
sovereign of the church. Its temporal claims were also restored. Philip and Mary humbly petitioned the pope to rein-
vest them with the lordship of Ireland ; and the pope, ignoring
the act of Henry VIII., was pleased to erect it into a kingdom
and confer it on Philip and Mary.

Thus one great rent was patched in the seamless coat of
the catholic church, and men tried to believe that things were
as though the schism had never been. But only those, whose
hopes and affections distorted their vision, were deceived.
There had been no real reconversion to Rome, and the reconciliation was merely a marriage of convenience. If the church,
wrote Cecil in 1559, in advice to the Scots reformers,[1] had not
been shorn of her wealth by Henry VIII., she would have
triumphed in the struggle; and her failure to recover that
wealth in 1554 betrays the hollowness of her victory. " My
lord," said Cecil to Paget, who believed in Mary's success, " you
are therein so far deceived, that I fear rather an inundation of
the contrary part, so universal a boiling and bubbling I see." [2]
Renard's diagnosis agreed with Cecil's ; the realm was only
simulating a conversion : if Elizabeth succeeded it would again
recant, the clergy would be oppressed, and the catholics persecuted.[3] The Venetian, Suriano, who was a good catholic, remarked that the people rather from fear than from will appeared
to be Christians; and his predecessor Michiele reported that
" with the exception of a few most pious catholics, none of
whom, however, are under thirty-five years of age, all the rest
make this show of recantation, yet do not effectually resume
the catholic faith, and on the first opportunity would be more
than ever ready and determined to return to the unrestrained
life previously led by them. . . . They discharge their duty
as subjects to their prince by living as he lives, believing what
he believes, and in short doing whatever he commands, making
use of it for external show to avoid incurring his displeasure
rather than from any internal zeal; for they would do the like
by the Mahometan or Jewish creed." [4]

There is some exaggeration here, and by "the prince"

[1] *Foreign Cal.*, 1558-59, No. 1086.
[2] Harleian MS., 4992, f. 7, quoted by Birt, *Elizabethan Settlement*, p. 510.
[3] Granvelle, iv., 433.   [4] *Venetian Cal.*, vi., 1018, 1074-75.

should perhaps be understood "the state"; but substantially the passage represents the current view. " I have known long since," writes a member of parliament, " that *sola patria*, which is the prince, doth challenge to herself all duties that appertaineth to man, before kin, before friends, or any other whatsoever they be. By this rule as a moral principle agreeing with God's word I have lived. . . . The absolute authority of the prince is from the Word of God which cannot be dispensed with." [1] The political instincts of the English people were more strongly developed than their religious feelings or their moral sense; and they were profoundly impressed with the need for national unity. Elizabeth, Cecil, and others, like Pembroke and Arundel, acted consistently with this view by conforming to Mary's changes. They were known to be heretics at heart, and are commonly so called in the privacy of diplomatic correspondence. Their compliance did not deceive; they went to mass and told their beads, not because they believed, but because such was the law. It has never been considered quite decent that men of position should indulge their conscience in defiance of the law; and no gentleman went to the stake in Mary's reign, unless he were also a priest. The laity reverted to the old position that faith was not for them to determine but for the church; if they had been misled, it was by the clergy; let the clergy answer for what they had taught. Their point of view is expressed in Hobbes's *Leviathan* which, although it was written in Stuart times, is the most illuminating comment on Tudor ideas. Only those, says Hobbes, who had been called to preach should suffer for their religious opinions : the layman should bow in the house of Rimmon when required by his sovereign, for "that action is not his, but his sovereign's; nor is it he that in this case denieth Christ before men, but his governor and the law of his country ".[2]

It was an ecclesiastical issue, and the brunt of the conflict lay on the clergy, one part of whom had on their side the crown, the papacy, the tradition and *esprit de corps* of the clerical order, and the other individual faith and popular sympathies. Parliament, it is true, had revived the heresy statutes and has

---

[1] *Hatfield MSS.*, i., 530-31.
[2] *Leviathan*, caps. xxix. and xlii., and Simpson's *Campion*, 1867, p. 18.

been burdened with the whole responsibility for the persecution. But this is not an accurate statement. It was not, as
Lyndwood pointed out in the fifteenth century,[1] the province of
the state to determine the nature or extent of the penalties for
heresy, and death by burning was a punishment prescribed
by the law of the church. If the secular magistrate failed to
execute this law, he was liable to excommunication ; and the
effect of the Lollard statutes—and of their revival under Mary—
was to reinforce this spiritual sanction by a statutory obligation, and to compel sheriffs to burn heretics convicted by
the church.[2] In other words, parliament put at the disposal
of the church the executive machinery of the state. But for
the way in which that machinery was used two parties alone
were responsible — the clerical courts which condemned the
heretic, and the crown which sometimes moved the clerical
courts and always in Mary's reign carried out their verdicts.

Parliament did not compel the church to condemn heretics,
or to hand them over, when condemned, for execution, any
more than it ordered the payment of annates or the carrying
of appeals to Rome. Its legislation was permissive. No statutory penalties would have been incurred if not one heretic had
been burned. The last great persecuting act, the statute of
Six Articles, had not been put in execution for nearly a year
after its passing ; and although it was in force twice as long as
Mary's acts it claimed not a tenth of the victims. A statute
was often like a proclamation intended merely *quoad terrorem
populi.* The extent and occasions of its execution were matters
for the discretion of the executive ; and parliament, when
it revived the heresy laws, probably thought that they would
not be more rigorously applied than they had been in the
reign of Henry VIII. or the rest of the 150 years during which
they had been on the statute book. Renard urged moderation
on Philip, and expressed discontent when Bonner " had three
heretics burnt " early in February ; he at least regarded the
burning as the act of the church, and foretold that on that
ground it would exasperate the nation.[3]

---

[1] *Provinciale*, ed. 1679, p. 293 ; *Engl. Hist. Rev.*, xi., 660.

[2] " Cum ad hoc per dictum diocesanum aut commissarios ejusdem fuerint
requisiti," Stat. 2 Hen. IV., c. xv., and 1 and 2 Phil. and Mary, c. vi.

[3] Granvelle, iv., 399, 404.

It was not the fault of parliament that the untrammelled courts of Mary's church condemned ten times as many prisoners as the lay-controlled courts of Henry's. No heretic could suffer except on conviction by the clergy; no burning could take place except on a writ issued by Mary and her advisers. To describe these actions as merely official is playing with words, for no one supposes that heretics could be unofficially burnt ; and to imply thereby that the bishops and clergy were reluctant and passive instruments in the hands of parliament is to ignore the enormous discretion allowed to the executive in the sixteenth century and to conceal the fact that it was on the initiative of the church that the burning of heretics was made the normal result of its official proceedings. The " reckless baseness of the lay legislature," as it has been called, consisted in this : it protected property but not conscience from the attacks of the clerical courts. The sacrilegious harvest of the reformation was carefully sheltered ; its spiritual and moral gleanings were exposed to the furious blasts of bigotry. Once more ecclesiastical courts were freed from the shackles imposed by Henry VIII. ; and the church, whose last free act had been to dig up and burn a dead and buried heretic,[1] regained its liberty. Once more privilege, jurisdiction, and power were placed in its hands ; and upon the use made of its opportunities in the next few years would depend the answer to the question whether the experiment would ever again be repeated.

---

[1] See vol. v., p. 314, and *Dict. of Nat. Biogr.*, lvii., 140-41.

CHAPTER VIII.

THE PROTESTANT MARTYRS.

THE powers which parliament had again permitted the church to use were seized with alacrity and promptly put in force. Even before the day on which the act became law, January 20, 1555, Gardiner held a preliminary examination of some of the principal prisoners for religion; and eight days later Pole as papal legate issued a commission to various bishops and other ecclesiastics to try the accused. It was probably the general expectation that the protestant preachers would fall into line with the rest of the realm and recant with more or less mental reservation. The retractation of Northumberland on the scaffold, the welcome accorded to Mary, and the almost unanimous acquiescence of both houses of parliament in the reconciliation with Rome and restoration of the church, had confirmed Mary and Pole in their conviction that there were no better forces behind the reformation than the self-will of Henry VIII. and the greed of his courtiers, that it had been imposed on the nation by the exercise of arbitrary power, and that what had been done could be undone by the same methods. In this phantasmagoria they were quite unprepared for the strength of the spiritual forces which they encountered, and the first executions produced a shock which almost made them recoil.

The martyr "to break the ice"[1] was John Rogers, the editor of Tyndale's translations of the Old and New Testaments and the author of the first commentary on the Bible in English. There was nothing against him except his faith, for he had avoided politics even when preaching at St. Paul's Cross on the second Sunday after Edward's death; but he had been placed in confinement a few weeks later for advocating the religion which was still by law established. There he had remained

---

[1] Bradford to Cranmer, Ridley, and Latimer, Feb. 8, 1555, Bradford, *Works*, ii., 190; *cf. ibid.*, i., 410.

ever since, joining in May, 1554, with Bishops Hooper and Ferrar, Coverdale, Rowland Taylor, Philpot, Bradford, and Crome, to issue a declaration of faith which contained also a protest of loyalty to the queen and a denunciation of rebellion and sedition. Towards the end of the year the prisoners drew up another manifesto offering to defend in public the doctrines of Edward's reign. On January 28, 1555, they were brought before Gardiner and his fellow-commissioners. They all refused to recant except Crome, who followed Bishop Barlow's example. Judgment was swift : Rogers and four comrades, Hooper, Taylor, Saunders, and Bradford, were given another chance on the morrow, and then condemned. On February 4 they were degraded by Bonner, who was usually selected to perform this painful function, and in the afternoon Rogers was brought out to the stake at Smithfield. His wife and ten children were present, and the spectators were loud in expressions of sympathy ; they gave him such cheer that the occasion seemed, says Noailles, like a wedding. Before the fire was lit Rogers was offered a pardon if he would yield. He preferred torture and death, and met both with unflinching courage.

Rogers had set up a standard which most of the martyrs maintained. Hooper was sent down to suffer at Gloucester, Taylor at Hadleigh, the scene of his labours, and Laurence Saunders at Coventry. Saunders was burnt on the 8th, and on the 9th Taylor suffered at Aldham Common and Hooper at Gloucester. Hooper, too, was offered a pardon, refused it, and endured for three-quarters of an hour the agony of a slow fire. Several others were under sentence, but there was a pause either to watch the effect of severity or because the effect was far from what had been hoped. Renard was full of alarm ; people were beginning to murmur and speak strangely against the queen, and the nobles to plot against Gardiner. The protestants, instead of being terrorised, wished, some of them, to throw themselves into the fire beside their favourite pastors.[1] The execution of the martyrs had more than destroyed the effect of Mary's clemency in releasing the political prisoners, the Dudleys, Crofts, Throckmorton, Gawain Carew, and others—including Holgate, late Archbishop of York, who recanted—in January ; and for the moment Mary seemed to hesitate. Coverdale profited by the

---

[1] Granvelle, iv., 404.

distraction and was allowed to proceed to Denmark at the invitation of its king.[1]

The cold fit passed : the rising, which Renard feared, proved
abortive ;[2] and the work of the clerical courts was resumed. So
far only clerks in orders had been burnt ; in March a beginning
was made with the laity. Five were burnt that month, all of
them in Bonner's diocese, one of them at Smithfield and the
others in various parts of Essex. They were mostly humble
folk, a weaver, a butcher, a prentice boy, and two who seem to
have had some property in Essex. A priest was also burnt at
Colchester and Robert Ferrar, ex-bishop of St. David's, at Caer-
marthen. His case was an exceptionally wanton piece of
cruelty. He had been appointed bishop of St. David's by
Protector Somerset, but his patron's fall laid him open to the
annoyance of a turbulent chapter. A long list of charges, some
of them fantastic to the last degree, was brought against him.[3]
He seems in fact to have been a kindly, homely, somewhat
feckless person like many an excellent parish priest, who did
not conceal his indignation at some of Northumberland's deeds.
He was summoned to London and imprisoned on a charge of
præmunire incurred by omitting the king's authority in a commission which he had issued for the visitation of his diocese.
Sufferings on such accusations and under Northumberland
might have been expected to lead to liberation under Mary.
But Ferrar had been a monk and was married. Even so, it
is difficult to see on what legal grounds he was kept in the
Queen's Bench prison in 1553. His marriage accounts for
the loss of his bishopric in March, 1554, and his opinions for
his further punishment. He refused to submit to Rome
because he had abjured the pope under Henry and Edward,
and he was one of the few bishops who satisfied Hooper's test
of sacramental orthodoxy. After an examination by Gardiner,
he was with singular indecency sent down to Wales to be tried
by Morgan, his supplanter in the bishopric. He appealed to
Pole against Morgan's sentence ; but Pole, although he has been
credited by Foxe with a greater desire to burn dead than living heretics,[4] paid no heed, and Ferrar was burnt on March 30.

[1] Machyn, p. 80 ; *Acts of the P. C.*, 1554-56, pp. 90, 97.
[2] Granvelle, iv., 423 ; Machyn, p. 83.
[3] Foxe, vii., 4-9 ; *cf. Acts of the P. C.*, 1550-52 and 1552-54, *passim*.
[4] Foxe, vii., 91.

CHAP.
VIII.

Few of Foxe's heroes were so single-minded and consistent as Ferrar; and some of them were criminal fanatics. The violence was not all on one side; nearly a year before any protestants were burnt, a cat was found hanged in priestly garb on the gallows in Cheapside; and a new stone image of Thomas Becket over the door of the Mercers' Chapel in London was wilfully mutilated in March, 1555. A more serious outrage took place on Easter Sunday, when a quondam monk, named Branch *alias* Flower, made a murderous attack on the priest of St. Margaret's, Westminster, as he was celebrating mass. He was tried first for assault and then for heresy, and was burnt in St. Margaret's churchyard. But lest the assault should go unpunished, his hand was cut off before he was burnt.[1] Foxe calls Branch a "faithful servant of God," but he does not think that every one burnt in Mary's reign was a martyr. One of the exceptions was John Tooley, a poulterer in the City. With two others he conspired to rob a Spaniard, was caught, and condemned to death. As he stood with the halter round his neck at Charing Cross, he took the occasion to denounce the covetousness which had led him to steal, just as it led the Bishop of Rome to "sell his masses and trentals"; and he read out the petition from the litany for deliverance "from the tyranny of the Bishop of Rome and all his detestable enormities". He was hanged and buried without due consideration of this new and more heinous offence. Two days later the council informed Bonner that they thought "it not convenient that such a matter should be overpassed without some example to the world," and required him after further investigation "to proceed to the making out of such process as by the ecclesiastical laws is provided in that behalf". Others might have thought that the claims of human justice had been adequately met by hanging for a theft. But the doom of the secular judge stopped this side of the grave, while every sentence of ecclesiastical excommunication contained further pains and penalties. Tooley had not even been burnt; he had received Christian burial, and had gone to the next world with all the advantages of one who was not excommunicate. Such a miscarriage of justice would be no deterrent to heresy. So a solemn citation was served

---

[1] Machyn, p. 85; Wriothesley, ii., 127-28; *Greyfriars' Chron.*, p. 95; Foxe, vii., 68-76; *Acts of the P. C.*, 1556-58, pp. 115, 118.

on the corpse and its relatives; on May 8 Tooley's remains were dug up, depositions were taken, and judgment delivered by Bonner. The body was then handed over to the secular arm and burnt on June 4; truly an "example to the world of such process as by the ecclesiastical laws is provided".[1]

Other examples were provided at both universities after Pole had become their chancellor; he succeeded at Cambridge on Gardiner's death and at Oxford on Mason's reluctant resignation. In both cases he appointed commissions to visit and reform those seats of learning; and the visitations were chiefly remarkable for warfare waged on the dead. At Cambridge the bones of Bucer still desecrated Great St. Mary's, and the trentals, obits, and anniversaries of Sir Robert Rede's foundation were accordingly kept in the chapel at King's College; while the remains of Fagius defiled the church of St. Michael. These two heretics had not so much as been hanged like Tooley; and their posthumous punishment was solemnly considered by the university and by the visitors whom Pole had expressly charged with the duty of "damning the memory of those who were dead in heresy".[2] The proceedings lasted a fortnight; the heretics were cited to appear, and on January 26, 1557, judgment was pronounced before a large congregation of gownsmen and townsmen in St. Mary's. The coffins were exhumed, placed upright, bound to the stake with an iron chain, and burnt on Market Hill. At Oxford the only dead heretic whom the visitors deemed worthy of attention was Peter Martyr's wife, whose body was disinterred from the cathedral on Pole's order and thrown by the Dean of Christ Church on a dunghill in his stable; legal evidence of her heresy could not, however, be obtained, as the persons examined "did not understand her language". The corpse therefore escaped condemnation and burning.[3]

In these visitations the commissioners made a merit of their mercy in confining their penalties to the dead, but a similar

[1] Wriothesley, ii., 128; Machyn, pp. 86, 343; Foxe, vii., 90-97; Gairdner, pp. 360-61, who remarks that "the culprit was unhappily executed before his heresy could be brought before a spiritual tribunal".

[2] "Et expresse ad eorum qui in haeresi decesserint, memoriam damnandum"; Foxe, viii., 268-87; Bucer's *Scripta Anglica*, Basel, 1577, pp. 915-35; Machyn, p. 124; Lamb's *Cambridge Documents*, 1838, p. 217.

[3] *Dict. of Nat. Biogr.*, lviii., 255.

forbearance was not observed elsewhere. After a lull in April, 1555, when only one victim suffered, and he at Chester,[1] the burning activity began again. On May 30 John Cardmaker, *alias* Taylor, a former Observant friar and a well-known protestant preacher under Edward VI., and John Warne or Warren, a clothmaker, were burnt at Smithfield. Seven more were delivered to the executioner on June 10 to suffer in Essex and Suffolk. On July 1 was burnt at Smithfield John Bradford, one of the staunchest, ablest, and most chivalrous of the martyrs : it was he who under the influence of Latimer's sermon restored the money he had made in his unregenerate days as paymaster in Henry's camp before Montreuil ; and he had saved Gilbert Bourne from the fury of the mob when he advocated the restoration of the mass in St. Paul's in August, 1553. His career as a reformer and divine lasted barely six years ; but his enthusiasm and charm of character made a deep impression even on his jailer, who let him out one day to visit a sick friend on his promise to return at night. With him suffered a young apprentice, whom Wriothesley calls " a boy " ; and four were burnt at Canterbury on the 12th. The area of persecution gradually spread outwards from London and East Anglia ; and of the seventy victims who were burnt before the end of 1555 some suffered as far west as Wales and others in Kent and Sussex. On August 23 the first woman was burnt at Stratford ; and she was a widow bereaved in May by the execution of her husband, John Warne, the clothmaker.

The three chief reformers of the church, Cranmer, Latimer, and Ridley, were still alive. Cranmer had been condemned for treason far less serious than that of several who sat at Mary's council board. Ridley had also been arrested early in Mary's reign for his support of Lady Jane Grey ; but Latimer's imprisonment was due to his refusal to conform or to take advantage of the facilities given him for escape. Mary was too ecclesiastically-minded to execute an archbishop on a charge of treason ; but the story that Cranmer received a pardon has little foundation, and he was merely reserved to die at the stake instead of on the scaffold. In April, 1554, the three bishops were removed to Oxford and condemned as heretics after a disputation in St. Mary's. But they could not be burnt as yet,

[1] Foxe, vii., 39-68.

for the heresy statutes had not been revived ; moreover, the church in England being still dead in schism, their very condemnation was technically invalid, and the process had to be repeated after the reconciliation with Rome.

It was not till September, 1555, that their trial began ; and different methods of procedure were adopted for Cranmer and his two fellow-prisoners. Cranmer, as a metropolitan, whose appointment had been duly sanctioned by a pope, was reserved for special papal condemnation. Ridley and Latimer were accorded no such exceptional treatment. Pole, in virtue of his legatine powers, commissioned Bishops White, Brooks, and Holyman to deal with their case. They were tried on September 30 and October 1 in the Divinity School at Oxford, and as a matter of course condemned. White did his best in no unfriendly spirit to induce them to recant ; the facts that neither had married and neither had been a monk differentiated them from Ferrar and Hooper, and probably account for the delay in their condemnation. Unlike Cranmer they would have been spared on submission. But their convictions were proof against all persuasions and threats ; and on October 16 they were brought out to be burnt in the old waterless ditch outside the walls before Balliol College. The sermon was preached by Richard Smith, the first regius professor of divinity at Oxford ; he saved his own life by numerous recantations, and he chose as his text : " If I give my body to be burnt and have not charity it profiteth me nothing ". Latimer was some seventy years old, broken in health, and feeble in body ; but his courage was dauntless as ever. " Be of good comfort," he said to Ridley, " we shall this day light such a candle, by God's grace, in England, as I trust shall never be put out." He soon succumbed to the flames ; but Ridley, the younger man, endured prolonged and hideous torture before the fire reached the bag of gun-powder which his brother-in-law had been permitted to tie round the sufferer's neck.

Moloch was sated for a time, and for the seven weeks during which parliament sat, from October 21 to December 9, the government wisely held its hand. It remembered, perhaps, the inquiry which parliament threatened when Bilney was burnt in 1531 ;[1] and in any case it had trouble enough with the

---

[1] *Letters and Papers of Henry VIII.*, v., 522; vii., 171.

new house of commons without adding to the flames. The glamour of the Spanish marriage was dimmed, and the hopes it had encouraged disappointed. Symptoms, due originally either to intense desire or to physical causes,[1] had convinced Mary that she was pregnant by November, 1554 ; and for months Europe was kept in daily expectation of the birth of an heir to the English throne and the Netherlands. Endless processions and prayers were made for the happy event ; letters announcing it to crowned heads were drawn up with nothing but the date of birth to be filled in ; and envoys were appointed to bear the joyful tidings.[2] One day in April, 1555, they arrived ; the *Te Deum* was sung in St. Paul's, the bells were set ringing, and banquets arranged in the streets.[3] But the news was false, though the pretence was kept up until August in the hope, says Noailles, of assisting the negotiations for peace between France and Spain, in which England was taking part. The entire future, declared Renard to the emperor, turned on the queen's delivery. "If all goes well, the state of feeling in the country will improve. If she is in error I foresee convulsions and disturbances such as no pen can describe."[4]

The disturbances were already threatening enough. The persecution was slowly undermining Mary's popularity : "you have lost the hearts," wrote a vehement lady to Bonner, "of twenty thousand that were rank papists within this twelve months" ;[5] and Michiele bears witness to the detestation with which the burnings were regarded from the first. So great was the people's alienation from the government that they began to rejoice in its failures abroad and to sympathise with its enemies. Noailles says they were more inclined to rebel against, than to serve Philip and Mary ; and local risings, generally occasioned by some execution, in Cambridgeshire, Essex, Hertfordshire, Kent, Sussex, and Warwickshire, showed that he hardly exaggerated.[6] Frays between English and Spaniards in the streets

---

[1] See more in detail, *Venetian Cal.*, vi., 1056, 1060.

[2] See State Papers, Domestic, Mary, vol. v., Nos. 28-32 ; it was even assumed that the child would be a son.

[3] Noailles, iv., 290-91 ; Machyn, p. 86.

[4] Noailles, iv., 334. *Venetian Cal.*, vi., 1064. Granvelle, iv., 432 ; Froude, v., 525.

[5] Foxe, vii., 712.

[6] Noailles, iv., 342 ; *Venetian Cal.*, vi., 30-31, 45, 144, 147-48 ; *cf. Acts of the P. C.*, 1554-56, pp. 65, 70-71, 76, 88, 94, 105, 107, 110, 139, 141, 145, 151, 157-59, 161, 165, 168, 171-73,

of London grew frequent, and men muttered about another Sicilian Vespers.[1] A more serious, though less open, cause for anxiety arose out of Philip's designs on the English crown. But for the present his mind was set on other successions; Charles V. had determined to abdicate, and required Philip's presence in the Netherlands. Glad himself to escape from his trammels in England, he set out on September 4, leaving Mary, oppressed with grief, in the especial charge of Pole and a select privy council consisting of Gardiner, Paget, Arundel, Pembroke, Thirlby, the Marquis of Winchester, and Petre.

Philip's absence probably did the government no harm in the elections which took place in September and October; but there were reasons enough to explain that return of "many violent opposition members" which Mary lamented to Philip.[2] Michiele noted that the new house of commons consisted chiefly of suspects in religion and, "whether by accident or from design," of members of the gentry and nobility—"a thing not seen for many years in any parliament". Therefore, he thought, "it was more daring and licentious than former houses, which consisted of burgesses and plebeians, by nature timid and respectful".[3] The returns do not sustain so broad a generalisation; the proportion of old members elected was well above the average; most of the privy councillors who were not peers secured seats, and the number of gentlemen chosen by boroughs was not particularly striking. But there was some ground for the Venetian's observation: Sir Henry Radcliffe, second son of the Earl of Sussex, was returned for Maldon, a Howard and a Cobham for Rochester, Henry Carey (afterwards Lord Hunsdon) for Buckingham, a Neville for Helston, an Arundell for Michael Borough, and a Paget for Arundel. The county members were mostly chosen from the county families, and the number of them who were soon implicated in various plots against the government is remarkable.[4] Gloucestershire, where Hooper had not laboured in vain, returned his convert, Sir Anthony Kingston, and Sir Nicholas Arnold, who had just been released from the Tower; and their fellow-

---

[1] *Venetian Cal.*, vi., 126.   [2] *Ibid.*, vi., 227.   [3] *Ibid.*, vi., 251.
[4] *Cf.* the *Official Return of Members* with Machyn, p. 194, and State Papers, Dom., Mary, vii., 24, "names of noblemen and gentlemen vehemently suspected to be participators in the above conspiracy" [March 9, 1556].

conspirators, Henry Peckham, Sir Thomas and John Throckmorton, Sir William Courtenay, Sir John Pollard, Sir John Perrot, and John Appleyard (Amy Robsart's half-brother), sat in the same house of commons. Cecil, who represented Lincolnshire, can hardly be regarded as a member of the opposition; he was doing a good deal of unofficial work for the government, for some of which he was formally praised by the council; and he was even considered for reappointment to the office of secretary.[1]

The principal objects for which parliament had been summoned were to provide supplies and to remove the remaining obstacles to the completion of the restoration of the church, on which Mary had set her heart. Gardiner as chancellor dilated, in his opening speech on October 21, on the queen's necessities, on her piety in restoring the property of the church, and on her forbearance in remitting the payment of taxes granted under Edward VI. and in sparing the estates of traitors. The effort hastened his end; he was in his seat on the following day, but that was his last appearance in public. He died on November 13, and was buried in Winchester Cathedral. Pole hoped that the new chancellor would prove "less harsh and stern"[2] than the old; but the lack of Gardiner's strong hand was badly felt for the rest of the reign. His ways were rough and naturally seemed brutal to his victims. His lack of refinement, his earlier acceptance of the royal supremacy, and his advocacy of her mother's divorce prevented that sympathy between him and Mary which existed between her and Pole. But Gardiner was the ablest of Mary's advisers, and she would have done well to follow his counsel in respect to her marriage. Active, ruthless, and none too scrupulous, he was a man after Henry VIII.'s own heart. He was not ill-natured at bottom, although he resented Cranmer's promotion over his head to the see of Canterbury, and he had an honest abhorrence of heresy. He was an Englishman first and a churchman afterwards.

Meanwhile the course of parliament was not running smooth. The finance committee of twenty members, consisting as usual half of privy councillors and half of private members, suggested the grant of two fifteenths and a subsidy. Objection

---

[1] *Acts of the P. C.*, 1554-56, p. 323; Tytler, ii., 437, 476; Froude, v., 438, n.
[2] *Venetian Cal.*, vi., 246.

was raised at once: the harvest had been bad; September 29 had been marked by "the greatest rain and floods ever seen in England";[1] the fifteenths pressed upon the poor; and the proper way, it was said, to relieve the queen's necessities was to call in the vast arrears of debt which the nobility owed the crown. The queen thereupon remitted the demand for the two fifteenths, and the subsidy was granted.[2]

The question of the restitution of first-fruits and tenths proved much more troublesome. For one thing, it would increase those financial embarrassments of the crown upon which Gardiner had laid stress in asking for a subsidy; for another, the security of the abbey lands had again been called in question. The new pope, Paul IV., had issued a bill condemning the alienation of church property; and copies were sedulously forwarded to England by English exiles in Italy. It is true that a confirmation of Pole's concession, "lately received from Rome," was read before the houses to allay suspicion on October 21; but it was not the satisfactory bull from Paul IV. for which Pole was still hoping three weeks later.[3] The queen had relinquished her first-fruits and tenths, but that did not solve Pole's difficulty; for he dared not dispose of the proceeds until their surrender had been explicitly sanctioned by parliament. The bishops wished to turn Mary's voluntary sacrifice into a surrender perpetually binding on the crown, while the lay impropriators were anxious to be freed from all obligation to pay them either to the crown or to the pope. Indeed, the bill first appeared in the house of lords as a proposal "for the king and queen to give into the hands of the laity first-fruits and tenths," though on its second and third readings it was entitled a bill "for the extinguishing of first-fruits and tenths". It passed the lords, after a lecture by the queen, on November 23, and was sent down to the commons where it was entrusted to Cecil and another member "to be articled". They secured a second reading on the 26th, but the whole of the following day was occupied in discussing the bill "clause by clause," and it was then referred to a joint committee of both houses. The

---

[1] Machyn, pp. 94-95.

[2] *Venetian Cal.*, vi., 229, 238, 241, 243; *Commons' Journals*, Oct. 30, Nov. 2; Lodge, *Illustrations*, i., 255-56; Rawdon Brown in the *Venetian Calendar* makes Michiele speak of the subsidy being 8d. and 4d. in the pound instead of 8s. and 4s.

[3] *Venetian Cal.*, vi., 224, 229, 247.

measure as amended by this committee was once more laid
before the commons on December 3. The debate lasted from
daybreak until evening, and was only brought to an end by a
form of closure. The doors of the house were locked as on a
recalcitrant jury; members were not allowed to leave even for
refreshments. At length the division was taken, and there
voted for the motion 193, against 126. On the 4th the lords
passed the bill as amended without a dissentient voice, and
Pole considered it a victory equal to the reconciliation with
Rome.[1]

But it was very different from what he and the queen had
hoped. The clergy were indeed relieved from the payment of
first-fruits, and were no longer to pay their tenths to the crown
but to the legate, who was to use them to relieve the crown of
its liability for monastic pensions. But the lay impropriators
were to continue to pay their tenths to the crown, and were
left to consult their conscience as to whether they should
restore their acquisitions to the church. The queen was only
allowed to set an example by surrendering hers. The papacy
apparently got not a penny from England during Mary's reign;
even the bulls for promotions were sent free; and the church
in England only obtained what the crown relinquished of its
own free will.[2]

Such was the only victory obtained by the crown that
session, unless we reckon an act terminating without compensation at Christmas all licences to keep " houses, gardens, and
places for bowling, tennis, dicing, white and black, making
and marring, and other unlawful games," on the ground that
" many unlawful assemblies, conventicles, seditions, and conspiracies have been, and are daily secretly practised by idle and
misruled persons repairing to such places ".[3] The government was experiencing, in Pole's words, " the increasing audacity of all reprobates " ; and the opposition went so far as to
reject more than one of the measures submitted to parliament.
Two in fact were thrown out by the lords on their first read-

---

[1] *Venetian Cal.*, vi., 244, 251, 256-59, 268, 270; *Lords' Journals*, Nov. 20,
21 and 23, Dec. 4 ; *Commons' Journals*, Nov. 23, 26, 27, Dec. 3 ; Burnet, ii.,
517-18.

[2] 2 and 3 Phil. and Mary, c. 4 ; *Venetian Cal.*, vi., 260.

[3] 2 & 3 Phil. and Mary, c. 9 ; *cf. Venetian Cal.*, vi., 243 ; *Acts of the P. C.*,
1554-56, pp. 151, 334 ; 1556-58, pp. 102, 110, 119, 168 ; Lodge, *Illustr.*, i., 260-61.

ing ;[1] but less importance was attached to them than to a bill
promoted by the government against " such as departed out
of the realm without the king's special licence ".   It was aimed
especially at the religious and political exiles, whose manifestoes
against Philip and Mary caused some natural irritation.   Such
were Knox's " Godly Letter " and " Faithful Admonition," and
John Bradford's philippic against the Spaniards and their king.[2]
Sir John Cheke was suspected of writing others, and they all
found readers in England.   The government also had its eye
upon the property of wealthy refugees, particularly the Duchess
of Suffolk, whose lands it had already tried to seize.[3]   The
lords substituted the " queen's licence " for the " king's
licence," and safeguarded the heirs of refugees ; but the commons were not content with such trivial alterations, and, in
spite of the concessions made by the crown, were determined
to reject it.   The opposition feared, says Michiele, some such
practice as that by which the Speaker and court party had
brought about the passing of the bill for tenths and first-fruits ;
and to prevent its repetition Sir Anthony Kingston, supported
by the majority, obtained the keys of the house from the serjeant-
at-arms, locked the door, stood with his back to it, and secured
the rejection of the bill.   On the day after parliament was dissolved he was sent to the Tower, whither he was followed by
the serjeant-at-arms.[4]

Another member, Gabriel Pleydell, was committed to the
Tower on the same day by the star chamber, in spite of the
protest of the house of commons that the council's order binding him over to appear within twelve days of the close of the
session was a breach of privilege.   Mary was more bent on regaining control of parliament than on recognising its privileges ;
and the first bill introduced into the house of commons at the
beginning of the session was one to reclaim for the crown the
power of compelling the attendance, and the prerogative of

---

[1] *Lords' Journals*, Nov. 18 and 19 ; *cf. Venetian Cal.*, vi., 269-70.

[2] Printed in Strype, *Eccl. Mem.*, III., ii., 339-54.   This John Bradford must
be distinguished from the martyr ; he had served abroad under one of Philip's
privy council, and is probably identical with the John Bradford who landed with
Thomas Stafford in April, 1557, and was hanged, see below, p. 164.

[3] Lodge, *Illustr.*, i., 256 ; *Acts of the P. C.*, 1554-56, pp. 180, 277, 283, 294.

[4] *Lords' Journals*, Oct. 31, Nov. 12 ; *Venetian Cal.*, vi., 275, 283 ; *Acts
of the P. C.*, 1554-56, p. 202.

licensing the absence, of members of the lower house. The bill
had been introduced in 1554, and its failure to pass had been
followed by the abortive indictment in the king's bench of
thirty-nine members for unlicensed absence from the house of
commons.[1]   These claims were not disputed by the lords, and
it is doubtful whether the crown had lost the power to compel
the absence of a peer;[2] not one of them thought of being
absent without suing for a licence from the crown, and when
it was granted the crown selected the proxies to be appointed
by the absent peer.[3]   The commons were, however, more
refractory: the bill, although it reached a third reading on
October 26, was rejected or withdrawn; a new bill, which was
introduced on the 30th, proceeded no further than committee;
and a third bill, introduced on November 8, was equally unsuccessful.   Various expedients were suggested on the part of the
government to check this growing independence of the
commons; one proposal was to revive the old rule against the
election of non-resident members.   According to Michiele,
at any rate, the government thought it stood a better chance
by insisting on the choice of townsmen, who might be timorous,
instead of ambitious knights and younger sons.   The opposition countered this suggestion by adding the much more remarkable provision, " prohibiting the election of any stipendi-
ary, pensioner, or official, or of any person deriving profit in
any other way from the king and royal council, and being
dependent on them ".[4]   This first draft of the place bill of
William III.'s reign was opposed on the ground that it would
exclude ministers from the house; and the measure, thus
overloaded with clauses objectionable to both sides of the
house, was thrown out.

Audacity and discontent, wrote Michiele, were gaining
ground daily, and the government did not venture to " make
important proposals for fear of their being negatived ".[5]   Philip
was bringing pressure of every sort to bear upon Mary to
obtain parliament's consent to his coronation, which would
prolong his reign in England after Mary's death.   He was

[1] Coke, *Institutes*, iv., 17; Strype, *Eccl. Mem.*, III., i., 262-64.
[2] Cf. *Letters and Papers of Henry VIII.*, March 31, 1533.
[3] Cf. Lodge, *Illustrations*, i., 252-53.
[4] *Venetian Cal.*, vi., 252.   [5] *Ibid.*, vi., 251, 283.

accustomed, he wrote, to absolute rule in Spain ; and, anxious   CHAP.
as he was to be with the queen again, he could not return   VIII.
to his former "unbecoming" and dependent position ; and he
told her that, if parliament refused what he wished, he should
impute the blame to her.   This was a refinement of cruelty :
poor Mary would have given her crown to have him back, but
she could not fly in the face of her council, parliament, and
people ; and she wrote a piteous letter complaining that she
could not understand the arguments with which Philip's confessor, Alfonso de Castro, pestered her.[1] Philip replied by
ordering the removal of his household attendants from England, partly " to agitate the queen " and bring her into conformity with his wishes.   He then sent Luis Davila to persuade
her that she might crown him by her own authority without the sanction of parliament ; but she feared an insurrection
in such an event.   Neither in this matter nor in the declaration of war against France could Mary gratify Philip ; and the
Spaniards retorted that Philip had no reason to gratify her by
returning to England, "as she has in fact shown but little con-
jugal affection for him ".[2]

This parliament, which was dissolved on December 9, had
shown an obstructive capacity second to few, but there were
well-recognised limits to the powers of sixteenth century parliaments.   Perhaps the greatest of the constitutional achievements of the Tudor dictatorship was the permanent transference
of the initiative in legislation, which had been exercised intermittently by barons and knights of the shire from the thirteenth
to the fifteenth century, to the crown and its ministers.   It was
a necessary revolution ; for the "separation of powers" which
characterised the later middle ages, had been disastrous to the
efficiency of government and dangerous to the existence of the
state.   But the recovery of its prerogative by the crown before
the powers of the crown had been appropriated by ministers
responsible to parliament, inevitably reduced the legislature,
when it was opposed to the crown, to negative functions and
to a position of defence.   These were important enough, and

---

[1] Mary's letter is printed by Strype, *Eccl. Mem.*, III., ii., 418-19, from Cotton
MS., Tiberius B., ii., f. 124 ; it has no date, but is clearly of Oct., 1555, and
is in answer to the letter from Philip described in *Venetian Cal.*, vi., 212.
[2] *Ibid.*, vi., 227, 267, 269, 272, 281, 376.

it is a serious error to speak as though they did not exist. There was a good deal left for parliament to defend and deny in Mary's reign : it protected secularised property from the church and from the crown ; it prevented Philip's coronation, and preserved Elizabeth's claims. It often rejected measures proposed by the crown, but it did not seriously contemplate reclaiming the initiative and restricting the functions of the monarchy. Initiation was the prerogative of the crown, although in exercising this prerogative the crown, when well advised, was guided by the views expressed in parliament.

Hence, although the presence of parliament in London in the autumn of 1555 put a stop to the actual burning of heretics, no attempt was made to repeal the legislation which made such burning possible, and it was resumed as soon as parliament was dissolved. Archdeacon Philpot, a man of good birth, character, and learning, but himself an advocate of burning for heresy, suffered that penalty at Smithfield on December 18 ; and on January 22 five men and two women were burnt there between seven and eight in the morning to avoid disturbance. Four days later four women and a man were burnt at Canterbury ; in February two women suffered at Ipswich, and on March 14 three men at Salisbury. But the great martyrdom of that month was Cranmer's. He had been singled out by Philip and Mary for denunciation at Rome ; and Paul IV. had referred his case to Cardinal dal Pozzo, prefect of the Inquisition,[1] who in his turn delegated the examination and trial, but not the judgment, to Brooks, Bishop of Gloucester, Feckenham, Dean of St. Paul's, and Nicholas Harpsfield, Archdeacon of Canterbury. His previous examination and condemnation by the university were set aside as of no effect, and a fresh trial began in September, 1555. Cranmer refused to recognise the competence of this papal court, but addressed a defence alike of the royal supremacy and of himself to Drs. Martin and Story, the queen's proctors. His whole career was impugned, and besides heresy he was charged with " adultery " in marrying a second wife sixteen years after the death of his first, and with perjury. He had in fact broken his oath to the papal obedience, just as men like Tunstall and Gardiner had

---

[1] *Venetian Cal.*, vi., 188-89 ; his name appears in French as Dupuy, in Latin as de Puteo, while Cranmer calls him Cardinal of the Pit.

broken theirs first to the pope and then to the royal supremacy. In both cases acts of parliament could be pleaded annulling the oaths; but Cranmer, unlike the others, had before taking his oath to the pope explained that it was not to be considered binding if England abjured the papal jurisdiction. More simple than his contemporaries, he always blurted out his mental reservations. The records of the trial were then forwarded to Rome; and, as Cranmer admitted teaching doctrines which the Roman church regarded as heresy, the result was a foregone conclusion. The citation to Rome of a prisoner who moreover repudiated Roman jurisdiction was merely a form; and on December 4 he was deprived in consistory of the archbishopric of Canterbury, and sentenced to be handed over to the secular arm.[1]

A week later the process for his degradation was drawn up at Rome and despatched to England. Bonner was, of course, selected for this duty; and the zest which he displayed in its performance in Christ Church on February 14, 1556, shocked his gentler colleague Thirlby. Within a few days Cranmer signed four of his seven " recantations," or " submissions " as they are more accurately styled in the official version.[2] They vary from one another, but none went further than a concurrence in the national recognition of the papal claims. He had not changed his convictions, but he had moved in courts and councils dominated by those ideas which led his brother-archbishop Holgate and people like Cecil and Elizabeth to subordinate private opinions to the law of the land. He had no belief in the papal claims, but he doubted his right to resist the ordinances of the powers that be; and parliament, church, and crown had made papal jurisdiction and Roman dogma law for the English people. That law he felt bound to obey, for he had pinned his faith to the divine right of kings and not to private judgment. If national authorities had the right to repudiate Rome and enforce that repudiation upon subjects, they had also the right to restore it and enforce that restoration. It was not easy for one who had been an archbishop and had admin-

---

[1] *Venetian Cal.*, vi., 267, 273, 278-79, 286; *Foreign Cal.*, 1553-58, pp. 197-202.

[2] On Cranmer's last days see Foxe, Jenkyns' edition of Cranmer's *Works* (which is better than that of the Parker Soc.), *Bishop Cranmer's Recantacyons*, ed. by Dr. James Gairdner and privately printed by Lord Houghton in 1885, and my *Cranmer*, 1904.

istered coercive ecclesiastical jurisdiction to plead the claims of
conscience against an ecclesiastical court.   His mind, too, was
not of that dogmatic type which is so completely mastered by
one aspect of truth as to be blind to all others, and he was
too much of a scholar not to know that there were two sides
to the questions at issue.   Finally, the prospect of physical
torture made a greater impression on his than on less imaginative and less sensitive minds ; he was not blessed with that
very important element in most men's courage, an incapacity
to realise dangers unseen and pains unfelt.

But Cranmer was more conscientious than Cecil or Holgate :
he was not content to follow the logic of his political principles ;
and distracted between a logic which counselled submission and
a conscience which rebelled, he fell a victim to the craft and
assaults of those who were interested in his fall.   The object
of the government was not merely to burn Cranmer ; that was
already decided.   Every martyrdom was a duel between the
martyr and Roman catholicism, and the demeanour of every
victim was watched with the keenest anxiety.   In Cranmer's
case Mary and Pole expected an easy victory.   When Northumberland recanted on the scaffold many were turned from
their protestant faith ; in 1556, when Sir John Cheke followed
his example, thirty prospective martyrs flinched from the stake.[1]
Cranmer might even extinguish the candle which Ridley and
Latimer lit.   The peace of the catholic church, in England at
any rate, seemed to hang on the issue and to justify special
efforts.   Cranmer was plied with every sort of inducement, the
rigours of Bocardo prison, the ease of Christ Church deanery.
At length he signed a real recantation, his fifth, and then his
sixth, wherein he was made to compare himself with the thief
on the cross and to imply that like the thief he only repented
when his means to do harm had failed.

He had fulfilled his enemies' expectations.   He might now
be dismissed to the stake ; and orders were given for his execution at Oxford on March 21.   But on the previous day, or in
the night, he drew up a seventh recantation, saying nothing
about the pope.   His mind had begun to react ; the process
was completed the following day ; and the crowds, which went
out in a storm of rain on that blustering day in March to

[1] *Venetian Cal.*, vi., 769.

see a reed shaken with the wind, witnessed a different sight.
Instead of repeating, he repudiated his recantations in St.
Mary's; he reaffirmed the views on the sacraments expressed
in his books, and denounced the pope and his doctrine. Hurried off to the scene of Ridley's and Latimer's execution, he
suffered with unflinching patience and courage, holding the
right hand, with which he had signed his recantations, in the
flames that it might first be consumed. Nothing in Cranmer's
life became him like the leaving of it. His conscience found
peace at last, and his far-shining death gave lustre and strength
to the cause for which he had laboured and prayed.

Cranmer was the last of the prominent martyrs, but more
were burnt after than before him. There was a holocaust of
thirteen at Stratford on June 27, 1557, and about ninety
suffered altogether in that year; neither age nor sex was spared,
and records have survived of at least one case in which a
mother gave birth to an infant in the flames.[1] The estimates
of the total number of victims vary, but not to any great extent. Cecil late in Elizabeth's reign put the number as high
as 400,[2] but he included those who died in prison, and does
not give details. Foxe's vast martyrology, which was chained
to desks in many churches and became almost a second
Bible in Elizabeth's reign, has been subjected to minute and
searching criticism;[3] but the number of serious errors of which
he has been convicted is comparatively small, and it is not so
much his facts as his deductions from them and his animus
which need to be discounted. Nor does the number of victims
depend upon Foxe. The earliest and least accurate list was
Thomas Brice's *Register*, a catalogue in doggerel verse published in 1559.[4] His phraseology is often obscure, but his list
amounts apparently to 284. The most satisfactory statement
appears to be that printed by Strype from Cecil's papers;[5] it

---

[1] State Papers, Dom., Addenda ix., 4. These documents substantiate Foxe's
story (viii., 226-41) which was impugned by Harding in his answer to Jewel, and
has often been doubted since.

[2] Strype, *Eccl. Mem.*, III., ii., 152; Speed gives 277, and Bishop Cooper 233
for 1555-57.

[3] See especially S. R. Maitland, *Essays on the Reformation*, and Gairdner,
Lollardy and the Reformation, i., 337-62.

[4] Reprinted in my *Tudor Tracts*, 1904, pp. 260-88.

[5] *Eccl. Mem.*, III., ii., 554-56; the numbers are there wrongly added up to
288, they really come to 282. If the "index of martyrs" in Townsend's edition

puts the number at 282 ; but it does not comprise those who died in prison nor the three or four malefactors like Flower and Tooley, whose commemoration by Foxe and Brice has provoked the suggestion that many, if not most, of the martyrs were of a similar character.

It can further be tested by independent and unimpeachable authorities. For instance, in 1555 it assigns one martyr to each of the following places, Steyning, Lewes, Maningtree, Harwich, Rochester, Dartford, and Tonbridge ; the register of the privy council mentions every one of these executions.[1] In 1556 Strype's list mentions sixteen as being burnt at Smithfield : the catholic Wriothesley gives the same result, describing the burning of seven on January 27, six on April 24, and three on April 27, and he is confirmed by the equally catholic Machyn. Strype's list also states that fifteen were burnt at Stratford in the same year : Wriothesley gives thirteen on June 27 ; and Machyn, who gives the same number on that day, supplies the names and other details with regard to the remaining two who were burnt on May 15. In 1557 Strype's list gives ten martyrs for Smithfield and four for Islington : Wriothesley only mentions "divers" on April 12 and "certain" on November 13 ; but Machyn gives five at Smithfield on April 6, three on November 13, and two on December 22, thus making up the ten. For Islington he gives three on May 28 and two on June 18, which is one more than the list in Strype ; and he also mentions a burning at Staines which is not included in that list. Where it can be checked, the list printed in Strype is found to be absolutely correct. This is possible in places such as London where the greatest number suffered ; and when the list is confirmed in giving scores of martyrs, the assumption can hardly be made that it is wrong in giving units in more distant parts where tests are not available for its accuracy. It is in fact rather an under- than an over-statement, and there were cases of martyrdom which do not occur in any published list, not even Foxe's. There can be no reasonable

---

of Foxe is accurate, Foxe gives 275 as the number of those burnt, and 9 as the number of those who died in prison. It is possible that Foxe's list and Cecil's list have a common origin ; in that case they do not confirm each other, but both are confirmed by the comparisons given in the text.

[1] *Acts of the P. C.*, 1554-56, pp. 141, 147, 154.

doubt that the number of those who were burnt for religious CHAP.
opinion under Mary fell very little, if at all, short of 300.   VIII.

The geographical distribution of this persecution is remarkable.   With the exception of one victim at Chester in March,
1555, no heretic was burnt in the northern province; and with
a single exception at Exeter in 1558, not one was burnt south-
west of Salisbury.   The executions were confined almost
exclusively to London, Essex, East Anglia, the south-east
midlands, Kent, and Sussex; 112 suffered in London, Hertfordshire, and Essex.   Kent came next with fifty-four,
Sussex with forty-one, and Norfolk and Suffolk with thirty-
one between them.   Three dioceses provided seven each,
Winchester, Gloucester, and Lichfield; Salisbury provided six;
Bristol, four; Ely, Oxford, and St. Davids three apiece; Lincoln
and Peterborough two each; Chester one, and Exeter one. These
disproportionate figures may be due to absence of evidence or
to absence of heretics in some dioceses, or to individual lenience
on the part of their bishops.   There is not much doubt that
protestant opinions had secured the firmest hold in those
districts in which most of the executions took place.   But if
there were no obstinate heretics to burn in the northern and
some other dioceses, the credit for mercy which their bishops
have obtained seems hardly deserved.   The praise bestowed
on them implies a censure on their brethren, and admits the fact
that the revival of the heresy laws did not compel any bishop
to persecute.   None of these points should be pressed too far;
it is highly improbable that there were no protestants north of
the Trent or south-west of Wiltshire, and Tunstall's known
aversion from persecution had probably something to do with
the absence of executions in his diocese.   The conforming
bishops of Henry's or Edward's creation must also be credited
with a natural distaste for burning.   Capon of Salisbury was
an exception singled out for censure by Foxe; his six victims
may have owed their death partly to his desire to hold his see
against a rival, William Peto, who had been papally provided
to it in 1543.   King of Oxford was also censured as a persecuting bishop; but the only three martyrs burnt in his diocese
were Ridley, Latimer, and Cranmer, with whom King had
nothing to do.   Thirlby was also exempt from blame in respect
to two of the martyrs burnt in his diocese, though he seems to

have consented to the death of the third. On the other hand, eight of the bishops created or restored by Mary, Goldwell of St. Asaph, Bourne of Bath and Wells, Watson of Lincoln, Heath of York, Pate of Worcester, Oglethorpe of Carlisle, and Scot of Chester, appear to have been not less forbearing; and no one was burnt in Ireland or the Isle of Man. Pole commented on Gardiner's harshness as chancellor, but it is a singular fact that not a single heretic was burnt in Gardiner's diocese so long as Gardiner was alive; while Pole himself as Archbishop of Canterbury was, with Griffith of Rochester, responsible for a larger number of victims than any one except Bonner. Christopherson of Chichester and Hopton of Norwich have to answer for most of the rest.

Bonner was selected for the most savage execration; and, after making the necessary allowances, it must be admitted that he deserved the pre-eminence.[1] He was not of course so black as he was painted; on several occasions the council urged him on, and he tried to save some victims. But it cannot have been merely accident that both Henry VIII. and Mary, while excluding him from their privy council, entrusted him with the execution of the most repulsive duties; and that his colleagues shifted on to his shoulders work from which they shrank themselves. Even the children called him "bloody Bonner of London," and older protestants the "common cut-throat and slaughter-slave to all the bishops in England".[2] But Bonner did not dictate the policy which he had to execute. Nor can the pope be saddled with all the odium; Cranmer was the only victim directly condemned by Paul IV., who had enough to do without interfering with English heretics. Parliament permitted the persecution and the ecclesiastical courts carried it out. But Mary and her council must bear the chief burden of blame. The council, had it been so minded, could have prevented her from persecuting; it was not so minded, because members likely to adopt this view had been excluded by Mary from its ranks. It could not, moreover, have made her persecute against her will; and of her will to persecute there can be no more doubt than there is of her sincerity. The fact

---

[1] *Venetian Cal.*, vii., 101, "he having been the individual who, during the reign of Queen Mary, persecuted the heretics more than any one else".

[2] Foxe, vii., 712.

that the burnings ceased at once on Mary's death measures the extent of her responsibility.

Nevertheless, the number Mary burned was trifling compared with the thousands who suffered in other lands. Philip's privy councillor, Viglius van Zwickem, stated in 1556 that within eighteen months 1,300 heretics perished in the province of Holland alone;[1] and in Spain an *auto-de-fe* became almost synonymous with the burning of heretics. Hence, when Charles V. and Philip urged moderation on Mary, they did so purely from motives of policy and not of humanity. They thought that England would not tolerate a butchery which they might safely inflict on Spain and on the Netherlands. Englishmen in fact were not impressed with Mary's comparative lenity; their only standard of comparison was their own experience and the history of England, and there was nothing in either to compare with Mary's persecution. It was unique and it produced a unique impression. It stamped on the English mind a hatred, unthinking, ferocious, and almost indelible, of Rome and all its belongings; and it planted a root of bitterness which grew and cast its shadow upon many a page of English history.

[1] *Venetian Cal.*, vi., 363. Compare the account of the *auto-de-fe* on Trinity Sunday, 1559, in the presence of the Prince and Princess of Spain, *ibid.*, vii., 102-4. On March 13, 1561, Tiepolo writes: "last Sunday an *auto* of the Inquisition was performed with the usual solemnities. Four individuals were burnt," *ibid.*, p. 302. Bartolomé de Carranza, afterwards archbishop of Toledo, whom Philip left in England in 1555 as Mary's spiritual adviser, subsequently boasted that during his three years in England he had caused 30,000 heretics to be burnt, reconciled, or exiled, Lea, *Hist. of the Inquisition of Spain*, ii., 49-50.

CHAPTER IX.

PHILIP AND MARY.

" THIS day it was ordered by the Board that a note of all such matters of state as should pass from hence should be made in Latin or Spanish from henceforth." [1] So ran the first minute of the privy council after the marriage of Mary and Philip— a formal intimation of the fact that, for the first time since England had attained to national consciousness, the control of its policy had passed into the hands of a king who understood no English. Every precaution, which pen and parchment could provide, had been taken to prevent Philip from convert- ing his titular dignity to anti-national purposes. But no safe- guards could control Mary's affection for her lord, or compel her to follow the wishes of her privy council; and the Venetian ambassador declares that Philip's authority in England was as great as if he were its native king. [2] Under a constitutional system a reigning queen can discriminate between her private duty to her husband and her public duty to her country. It was not so easy under the personal monarchy of the Tudors, who regarded the crown as their private property and not as a public trust, who were not bound to act on any one's advice, and who could only be deterred by prudence or by successful rebellion. Mary, with her limited political capacity and her unlimited devotion to Philip, totally failed to distinguish be- tween her husband's and her country's interests, and to act upon the distinction.

The dim consciousness that their affairs were being adminis- tered, and their resources exploited, in Philip's interests estranged the English people from the Spaniards and from Mary's rule. Spaniards had not been unpopular in the reign of Henry VIII. ;

[1] *Acts of the P. C.*, 1554-56, p. 56.
[2] *Venetian Cal.*, vi., 1065 ; *cf.* Tytler, ii., 266-69.

and Mary herself had been almost a favourite until she committed her cause and her country to Philip's keeping. But the policy of the Spanish marriage had been based upon a profound miscalculation.   Henry VIII.'s appeal to national pride and prejudice had wakened chords which never ceased to reverberate.   However nervously ministers might watch the growth of European powers and anticipate the conquest of England, the nation was self-reliant enough to resent its patronage by Philip ; and the acceptance of the position of inferiority implied therein not only indicated a lack of trust in her people on Mary's part, but tended ever to widen the breach between them.   In vain Philip while in England schooled himself into affability ; lavished pensions upon English courtiers ; restrained Mary's persecuting zeal ; stimulated the growth of her navy ; and inflicted exemplary justice upon Spaniards who violated English laws and customs ; while he left the punishment of Englishmen to the queen and council, and reserved only to himself the prerogative of mercy and the credit for compassion.   As king of England he could do nothing right, because he was not English ; men felt that he sought to conciliate only until he could command ; and even the ships which he persuaded Mary to build were regarded as additions to the naval strength of Spain.

These suspicions were well founded.   In 1556 the government was proposing to reduce, if not to abolish altogether, England's diplomatic representation abroad,[1] on the ground that English interests could be guarded just as well by Philip II.'s ambassadors.   In case of conflict between the interests of Philip's English, and those of his other, subjects the former habitually went to the wall ; Philip at times preferred the claims of his allies, the Portuguese.   Already English sailors and merchant princes were listening to the call of new worlds, east and west, and falling foul of the Spanish and Portuguese monopoly.   Had there been any real reciprocity in the terms of Mary's marriage with Philip, her subjects would have acquired equal trading rights with his in every quarter of the globe.   It was even asserted on their behalf that Henry VII.'s commercial treaties with the house of Burgundy entitled Englishmen to trade in the Spanish Indies.   Both pretensions were repudiated ; the papal division of the new-found lands between

---

[1] *Venetian Cal.*, vi., 640.

Spain and Portugal was held to override those treaties ; and
Philip's English subjects were denied the privileges which his
other subjects enjoyed in Spanish colonies.   Under Mary they
acquiesced in this injustice, and sought some compensation by
attempting to open up a trade with the Portuguese possessions.
But Philip vetoed English expansion in this direction also.[1]
This was an ill return for the Spanish marriage and the papal
restoration.   The arctic regions, which Philip favoured as a
field for English enterprise, seemed a poor substitute for the
golden coast of Guinea and the riches of the Spanish Main ;
and bitter was the discontent with Mary's government.   " She
loves another realm," said her subjects, " better than this ; "[2]
and Suriano, no hostile witness, reported that she was bent
on nothing else than making the Spaniards masters of her
kingdom.   Mary of Hungary, the regent of the Netherlands,
was writing " well-nigh daily " letters urging her to proceed
with Philip's coronation ; and there were rumours of the
raising of Spanish troops, of a visit of Charles V., and
of the despatch of a Spanish armada to carry out the
project.[3]

The truce of Vaucelles had been concluded between Philip
and France in February, 1556 ; but Henry II. threatened to
oppose by force of arms any attempt to crown Philip against the
wishes of the English people ; and the Venetian ambassador
noted that hatred of Spain was taking the place of the old English
hatred of France.   Henry's open war against Spain was exchanged for secret support of the plots against Spanish designs
in England, which sprang up like mushrooms in the fertile soil
of popular discontent.   The Anglo-French intermediary was
the old intriguer Berteville, who had fought on the English
side at Pinkie ; Henry's court was crowded with English
refugees whose designs needed all Wotton's skill to unravel ;
and the Channel was infested with piratical craft, supplied
with French resources and manned by English sailors, who
laughed at Philip's protection of Spanish and Portuguese
shipping.   To them the Isle of Wight was a natural point of

[1] *Acts of the P. C.*, 1554-56, pp. 162, 214, 305, 322, 348 ; Kervyn de Lettenhove, *Relations Politiques des Pays-Bas et de l'Angleterre*, i., 11, 131, 144, 148,
154-55 ; *Venetian Cal.*, vi., 218, 240, 284 ; Domestic State Papers, Mary, vi., 82.
[2] *Acts of the P. C.*, 1556-58, p. 265.
[3] *Venetian Cal.*, vi., 416, 419, 623, 1065, 1147.

attack, and they found an ally in Richard Uvedale, the governor of Yarmouth Castle.   Another scheme with wider ramifications was formed in March by Sir Henry Dudley, a distant
kinsman of Northumberland,[1] to seize the exchequer, into which
half of the subsidy granted by parliament had just been paid,
to marry Courtenay to Elizabeth, and to depose Philip and
Mary.   So formidable was this plot that ministers told Suriano
they had never heard or read of the like in English history,
and it needed a comet to mark its dire import.   At least a
dozen members of the last house of commons, disgusted with
the inability of parliament to control Mary's policy, had passed
from constitutional opposition to treason ;[2] many gentlemen
of the west, who played an active part in Elizabeth's reign,
were implicated ; and disturbances broke out in Norfolk,
Suffolk, Essex, Sussex, and Dorset.   The conspirators included
a past and a future lord-deputy of Ireland, Sir James Crofts
and Sir John Perrot.   Elizabeth's cousin, Lord Thomas Howard,
and Lord Bray were imprisoned ; and suspicion fell on the
Earl of Worcester.   Henry Peckham, the son of Mary's privy
councillor, joined the plot, and Noailles was in the secret.

How much Courtenay and Elizabeth knew remains uncertain.   Courtenay's servant, Walker, was undoubtedly aware
of the design, and his master's lands were to have been sold
to defray expenses.   Elizabeth's friend, Mrs. Catherine Ashley,
was sent to the Tower, and so was her Italian master, Battista
Castiglione,[3] who had been there twice before ; but heretical
sympathies and the possession of " scandalous " books against
the king, queen, and religion, were all that could be proved
against them.   Elizabeth herself was again suspected, and
rumour credited the government with the intention of
sending her to Spain, perhaps to marry Don Carlos, while
Philip's minister, Ruy Gomez, thought the best way to deal
with Courtenay was assassination.[4]   He was in Italy, where it
could be more easily arranged than in England ; but his death

---

[1] He was son of the sixth Baron Dudley of Sutton, and must not be
confused with Northumberland's son, Lord Henry Dudley, who was killed at
Gravelines in 1557.

[2] See above, pp. 143-4.

[3] Not to be confused with Count Baldasarre Castiglione, the author of *Il
Cortegiano.*

[4] *Venetian Cal.,* vi., 294-95 ; *Foreign Cal.,* 1553-8, p. 255.

at Padua on September 18, 1556, soon relieved Philip from anxiety on that score.   Death also saved Kingston from trial and execution, and only the heads of such traitors as Stanton, Uvedale, and John Throckmorton, fell on the scaffold.   Sir Peter Carew had been induced by pardon to tell what he knew ; and Wotton's industry in Paris and a liberal application of torture in the Tower revealed more threads of the conspiracy. To Sir John Cheke was ascribed the authorship of some of the tracts which Mrs. Ashley had possessed, and obscure way-farers like Eagles, known as Trudgeover, had scattered broad-cast over the land : Cheke was entrapped, was induced to recant his heresy, and then died of remorse in the Tower.   Sir Henry Dudley and most of the western suspects escaped to carry on their schemes at the French court or pursue more active and more profitable operations in the Channel ; and fresh seeds of discord were sown between Queen Mary and the court of France.

For many months, wrote the Venetian ambassador in June, 1556, the queen had been passing from one sorrow to another.[1] The month of March, which was the mid-point of her reign, had marked the climax of her fortunes.   For the moment war had ceased between the catholic powers of Europe ; the arch-heretic Cranmer was burnt, and Cardinal Pole enthroned in his stead. Convocation had acknowledged " all the ordinances and decretal epistles of the popes and every other ecclesiastical law and tra-dition approved by the Roman church " ; and all teaching and printing of books without the licence of the ordinary had been prohibited.   The queen had been allowed to satisfy her con-science by restoring the secularised property of the crown ; Westminster Abbey was once more the home of monks ; and the knights of St. John were recalled to their pious duties. But the tide had turned, and from now till the end of the reign disappointment, disease, and disaster heaped sorrow and suffer-ing on Mary's head.   Philip still tarried abroad, shaming him-self and his queen by disgraceful debauches in Brussels ;[2] and war once more threatened with France.   But of all the troubles which, Michiele said, Mary was " intent on bearing as patiently as she could," none tried her so much as the breach between her secular husband Philip and her spiritual father the pope.

---

[1] *Venetian Cal.*, vi., 495.
[2] Raumer, *Illustrations of History*, i., 95 ; *Venetian Cal.*, vi., 303, 401.

The fault in this case was not Philip's.   Paul IV., who had CHAP.
IX. succeeded to the papal throne in 1555, was a Caraffa, a Neapolitan who viewed the dominion of Spain in Naples with as deadly a hatred as that with which he regarded every symptom of liberal theology.   In the summer of 1556 he was rejoicing at England's impatience under the Spanish yoke, while Mary lamented the encouragement which his doings afforded heretics. It was not the first nor the last time that the secular policy of the papacy led it to sympathise with the enemies of the Roman church ; and before long Paul and Philip were at open war, Philip was under sentence of excommunication and was encouraging the Lutherans, while the pope was counting on the help of the Turks.   But it was on France that Paul mainly relied ; and in January, 1557, the Italian conflict was merged in a general war between France and the papacy on one side and Spain, Savoy, and Tuscany on the other.

Mary was involved in an agonising dilemma.   Henry VIII. himself had not attacked the papacy by force of arms ; and apart from the distress it caused her to be in conflict with the vicar of Christ, there was the more mundane consideration that her subjects, even her privy council, were almost to a man opposed to war with France.   Her most trusted adviser Pole, "that accursed cardinal," as Philip's confidant Feria called him,[1] took the lead in advocating peace.   Paget alone, who, partly because he could not overcome Mary's repugnance, had staked everything upon Philip's favour, declared for war with France.[2]   In February Philip sent Ruy Gomez to London with instructions to broach the matter, not to Mary or the council, but to Paget, who was to propose a breach with France as a motion of his own and to receive as a reward the office of privy seal vacated by Bedford's death.   Even Paget's influence failed, and Philip at length determined to come himself.   He was received with ardour by Mary, who had not yet relinquished hopes of issue.   But the council still maintained its opposition to the war.   Pole appealed to Henry II. and Paul IV. to use their influence in the cause of peace.   Neither was in a pacific mood : the pope was denouncing the Spaniards as "a sewer of filth, a mixture of Jews, Moriscos, and Lutherans " ;[3] while

---

[1] Kervyn de Lettenhove, *Relations Politiques*, i., 54.
[2] *Hatfield MSS.*, i., 153-54.   [3] *Venetian Cal.*, vi., 527, 910, 923, 938, 1003.

Henry, tempted by Paul IV.'s invitation to renew the struggle with Spain for predominance in Italy, which had been interrupted by the truce of Vaucelles, and resenting the secret assistance which Mary was giving Philip, began once more to abet plots against the queen and to boast that she would have enough to do at home without attacking him.

He alluded to the last and wildest of the attempts to upset Mary's throne. Among the exiles who crowded Henry's court was Thomas Stafford, a grandson of the Duke of Buckingham who was executed in 1521 [1] and a nephew on the mother's side of Cardinal Pole. He had already in 1553 distressed his uncle and damaged his prospects by rash denunciation of the Spanish marriage, and since then had been living a quarrelsome, turbulent life in France. He now conceived the idea of asserting his own distant claims to the English throne, derived from Thomas of Woodstock, the youngest son of Edward III. The pretence was fantastic enough, but the state of feeling in England convinced the French king that Stafford might cause sufficient trouble to Mary to make it worth his while to provide the two ships with which Stafford sailed from Dieppe in April, 1557. He landed at Scarborough, seized the castle, and proclaimed his pretensions. He seems to have had no understanding with any discontented section in England, and hardly a recruit joined his standard. The Earl of Westmorland recaptured the castle a few days later, and sent Stafford up to London where he was executed.[2] His sudden failure, writes Suriano, disconcerted other schemes in England, including a design for Elizabeth's removal to France. For complicity in this the Countess of Sussex was placed in the Tower; and numerous arrests about the same time, including that of Lord Abergavenny, afforded some justification for the hopes of Henry II. and the fears of the privy council.

Stafford's rising and its flagrant assistance by France destroyed the last chance which the party of peace had against Philip's importunity. Petre resigned his secretaryship at the end of March, being succeeded by the mediocre Boxall, and Pembroke was alienated from the government. At first it was

---

[1] See above, vol. v., pp. 236 ff.
[2] *Domestic Cal.*, Addenda 1547-65, p. 449; *Foreign Cal.*, 1553-8, *passim*; *Dict. of Nat. Biogr.*, liii., 460.

given out that English support would be limited to the 10,000 CHAP.
infantry and 2,000 cavalry required by ancient treaties in case IX.
of a French invasion of the Netherlands; and that this would
not involve war with France.   But no one, says Suriano,
believed in the maintenance of peace between the two kingdoms.   On May 29 Wotton was recalled from Paris, and on
June 7 war with France was publicly proclaimed by the English
government.   It opened successfully enough for Philip.   He
crossed to Calais on July 6, and Pembroke followed him with
an English contingent of 4,000 foot, 2,000 pioneers, and 1,000
cavalry.   Siege was laid to St. Quentin, and on St. Lawrence's
day, August 10, a French relieving army was routed.   Three
thousand French infantry were slain, and 1,000 captured besides
5,000 German mercenaries.   The cavalry fared even worse,
nearly the whole of it being taken prisoners or killed.   Among
the slain was the Duc d'Enghien, and among the prisoners the
Constable Montmorency, Montpensier, Longueville, and St.
André.   On the 27th St. Quentin itself was taken by assault.

The victory was Philip's, and England won no profit from
the war.   Seldom had its government begun an enterprise amid
greater embarrassments.   Pole, who had been the instrument and
was the emblem of the reconciliation with Rome, was deprived
of his legatine authority; and Paul IV. made a merit of conferring it and the cardinal's hat on his senile and recalcitrant
successor William Peto for nothing instead of the usual 40,000
ducats.[1]   Mary prohibited Peto's acceptance of the dignities and
stopped the papal messenger; while Pole was summoned to
Rome to stand his trial for heresy, and like his confidant Priuli
was threatened with the fate of his friend Cardinal Morone,
who was vice-protector of England at the papal court.[2]   Papal
displeasure was accompanied by famine and "divers strange
and new sicknesses," which, says Wriothesley, "this summer
reigned in England";[3] and the imperialists were in no position
to repeat their gibe of 1551 and ask, "Where is now your
God?"[4]   The treasury was empty, for Mary had not called a parliament since 1555; the expenses of the government rose from

---

[1] *Foreign Cal.*, 1553-58, pp. 319-20.   [2] *Venetian Cal.*, vi., 1173, 1194.
[3] *Chron.*, ii., 139; *cf.* Strype, *Eccl. Mem.*, III., ii., 147, 156; *Hatfield
MSS.*, i., 140, 142.
[4] See above, p. 57.

£138,000 in 1554-55 to £345,000 in 1557-58; and the forced loan to which she had recourse evoked unusual resistance. Many collectors were imprisoned for defalcations or for the inadequacy of their extortions; and on one day in November as many as forty persons from Worcestershire alone were called before the council for their unwillingness to pay.[1] Seditious plays had to be prohibited, and even the house of the queen's printer was searched for disaffected literature. A deplorable lack of spirit pervaded the army and the navy; crews betrayed their ships to the French, troops deserted, and mutinies broke out.[2] Martial law was even employed to curb civilian discontent; and a citizen of Canterbury was executed on the order of the council without a civil trial, dying "blasphemously".[3] Recourse was had to German mercenaries, and Sir William Pickering was employed to secure the assistance of Count Wallerthum and 3,000 troops to defend the Scottish borders. But on their march across the Netherlands they and the money borrowed for their wages were diverted from the English service to Philip's more immediate needs.[4]

The incident was characteristic of the treatment England received at the hands of its Spanish king. Scotland, being to all intents and purposes a French province, was naturally involved in the war; and its attacks caused much anxiety on the Borders. The English privy council not unreasonably requested Philip to declare war between the Netherlands and Scotland. But the Scots were good customers of Philip's Dutch and Flemish subjects, and in their interests he refused; the fact that England had declared war on France for his sake was no reason why he should make war on Scotland for England's sake.[5] When the Venetian ambassador, who had much to say in Philip's favour, avowed that the war was waged solely in his interests, and the French asserted that it was only a pretext to facilitate his mastery of England, it is little wonder that Englishmen were suspicious, disheartened, and disloyal.[6]

---

[1] *Acts of the P. C.*, 1556-58, pp. 160, 162-63, 165, 178-81, 185, 187, 190, 193-96, 201, 203, 239.

[2] *Ibid.*, pp. 171, 212.   [3] State Papers, Dom., xii., 32, 46 (1).

[4] *Ibid.*, xii., 21; Kervyn, i., 217, 221; *cf. Foreign Cal.*, pp. 319, 388.

[5] See the arguments of Horn, Egmont, and Orange on this point in Kervyn, *Relations Politiques des Pays-Bas*, i., 93-107.

[6] *Venetian Cal.*, vi., 938, 1003.

For Mary, however, the shadows lifted in the autumn. CHAP.
Peace was made between the papacy and Spain; and the sun   IX.
of papal favour shone once more on England.   Its brief efful-
gence heralded disaster and a winter of discontent.   The chief
result of the battle of St. Quentin had been to lull the Anglo-
Hapsburg allies into a false sense of security; and while the
peace in Italy was liberating Guise for other enterprises, the
Spanish troops disbanded and English crews dispersed.   Suddenly, on December 22, Lord Grey of Wilton reported from
Guisnes news of French preparations, which had reached him
by way of Flanders.   He did not know what they portended,
but he had to confess that Guisnes had neither the men nor
victuals to resist a serious attack.   On the 26th Lord Wentworth forwarded from Calais more definite intelligence; five
French ships of war, forty other sail, vast quantities of ordnance
and provisions, and 12,000 men were concentrated at Abbeville
and Boulogne, in order, rumour said, to revictual Ardres.   On
the 27th Wentworth summoned Grey from Guisnes to a hasty
conference on the defences of the English pale.   There was
ample ground for alarm; not one of the English strongholds
was in a state to stand a siege or vigorous assault.   Six years
earlier the French had boasted that to capture Calais would only
be a week's work, and they verified their forecast to the letter.
Warnings in abundance had been sent at frequent intervals
since 1555 by Wotton, Mason, and other English representatives
abroad; and in May, 1557, the council at Calais despatched
Highfield, their master of the ordnance, to represent the facts
to the government at home.   Pembroke had vainly reinforced
their arguments in July; and, inadequate as the garrisons were
in December, they would have been even weaker, had not the
government been compelled to keep some regiments under
arms by inability to pay for their discharge.   The battle of St.
Quentin and the approach of winter had convinced Mary and
her advisers that Calais was safe.[1]

Nevertheless the French marshal, Pietro Strozzi, had secretly

---

[1] For the capture of Calais see the letters and other narratives printed
in my *Tudor Tracts*, pp. 289-332 ; *Venetian Cal.*, vi., Kervyn, *Relations
Politiques*, the *Foreign* and *Domestic Calendars* and Sandeman's *Calais under
English Rule*, 1908.   A useful contemporary map is printed in the *Chronicle of
Calais* (Camden Soc.).   For Guisnes see also *The Life of Lord Grey* (Camden
Soc.), where a contemporary sketch of Guisnes is given.

reconnoitred the defences on the night of November 11. The Venetian ambassadors in Paris knew of the impending attack by December 6; and on the 15th they reported that it was "occupying universal attention". That the English government remained in fatal ignorance is not surprising, for the sole English agent abroad was Sir Edward Carne, and he was resident at Rome. The only foreign power with which Mary considered it necessary to maintain diplomatic intercourse was the papacy; Philip had undertaken to do the rest, but his intelligence was as much at fault as Mary's. He may have given general warnings about the defenceless state of the English pale, though no trace of such occurs in his extant correspondence; but the arrival of the French at Calais was the first intimation of their design which he communicated to the English government, and this he learnt from English agents in the pale. Even then, on January 2, 1558, he wrote urging Calais to defend itself, instead of sending prompt and adequate assistance; and the Venetian ambassador asserts that before its fall five messengers had been sent from Calais to Philip in vain.

Calais, however, was taken by surprise only because the English government had temporarily thrown away its command of the sea. Mary had not neglected the navy, and it was stronger than it had been since her father's death;[1] but she did not realise that the strongest fleet is useless unless it is "in being"; and in December, 1557, there was no English fleet in being. The French had counted on this folly, and it was on the sea that Calais was lost and won. Without molestation a French flotilla transported thither men and ordnance collected in the Somme and at Boulogne, and covered troops which marched along the sand dunes of the shore. A feint was made towards Hesdin by the army under Guise; and the privy council promptly on December 31 countermanded the levies it had ordered at the first alarm. On the morrow, Sandgate, the south-west outpost of Calais on the sea, surrendered; at night, on January 2, Ruisbank, the bulwark islet opposite the town, followed suit; and the vessels sheltering under its protection fell into the enemy's hands. They could now make an attack

---

[1] This is Mr. Corbett's contention, but on May 25, 1555, Mason writes: "I would wish that our navy were looked upon in such sort as the world might at the least see we mind not to suffer it to decay" (*Foreign Cal.*, 1553-58, p. 169).

from the sea on Newnham Bridge, the fort which guarded the CHAP.
IX. road to Calais from the south across the river and the marshes; and Guise's troops poured over the lowlands, which Wentworth had delayed to inundate from fear of destroying the pasture for the cattle and contaminating the water used in brewing for the garrison. Guisnes was thus cut off from Calais; the intervening outposts offered no resistance; and from the Causeway or Cowswade, near the Flemish frontier, to Newnham Bridge, the whole pale, except Guisnes and Calais, was in French possession. Newnham Bridge itself surrendered on the morning of the 3rd, and on the 4th the bombardment of Calais began. On the 7th, the day on which Guise had promised Henry II. the delivery of Calais,[1] Wentworth capitulated; and on the 8th the French occupied the town, which had been in English hands for two hundred and eleven years.

Treachery may have supplemented the incompetence of Wentworth and the English government; as early as 1554 the French had an understanding with some of the inhabitants.[2] There was certainly discontent; the spiritual needs of Calais seem to have been as much neglected as its military defences;[3] and for good or bad reasons Mary had recently overruled its choice of a mayor and threatened it with the loss of its charter and privileges.[4] Guisnes, the last English foothold on the continent, fell less ignominiously; it had only depended indirectly on sea-power, and was not so much affected by its loss. A few Spanish troops under Mondragon were thrown in before the French closed round on January 13. Grey withstood eight assaults; and when on the 20th he capitulated to overwhelming odds, he obtained terms which permitted the departure, with their arms, of the whole garrison except himself, his son, and a third captive, who were held to ransom.

England was less humiliated by the loss of Calais than by the confessed inability of the government to make any attempt for its recovery. There were sound reasons of policy for submitting to its abandonment; and Cecil in the next reign

---

[1] *Foreign Cal.*, 1553-8, p. 358.   [2] *Ibid.*, pp. 144, 238, 267, 273, 275-76, 281.

[3] *Ibid.*, p. 158, where Cornwallis complains that Harpsfield had sent to Calais Dr. Serles—Cranmer's old enemy—"a man so rude, unlearned, and barbarous as the like was never heard in the place of a preacher".

[4] *Ibid.*, p. xv.; *Venetian Cal.*, vi., 18; *Acts of the P. C.*, 1556-58, pp. 147-48, 155-56.

doubted whether the possession of Calais was worth the cost of its maintenance. But no such grounds are alleged by Mary's council;[1] and a century later even Cromwell believed in having an English bulwark across the Channel. Sheer weakness was the cause of Mary's acquiescence, as it was of her repudiation of liability for the defence of the Channel Islands; she pleaded that they had always been neutral in wars between England and France.[2] Philip, moreover, advised her to leave Calais alone, not without some suspicion of sinister purport. At any rate, his envoy in Scotland boasted that the capture of Calais was one of the greatest strokes of good fortune that could ever have happened to Philip, for he would recover it in three months, and then could keep it for himself.[3] Possibly an inkling of some such design strengthened the council's refusal to send over an English army to Philip's assistance in 1558, though the financial distress they alleged was in itself an adequate reason.

The nation in fact appeared helpless and felt hopeless. It gleaned cold comfort from Philip's victory at Gravelines in July, to which the English fleet contributed with its artillery; and the concentration of English ships near the Straits left the French "lords of the sea" further west. For the rest England relied upon the crumbs that might fall from Philip's table at the peace negotiations, which were opened between the Spaniards and French at Lille in August and transferred to Cercamp in October. English diplomatists were asked to attend, in order, suggested Wotton, to share in the disgrace of making peace without Calais.[4] Mary's own ministers hardly troubled themselves now to conceal their hatred of Spain and their disgust at the fruits of Spanish dominion. Since the loss of Calais Philip had seized arms bought by England at Antwerp; had fixed the staple at Bruges in defiance of England's protests in favour of Middelburg; and had requisitioned English sappers to fortify Gravelines in spite of Wotton's inquiry what was the need, if Calais were restored. Alderney had been captured by the French, and an invasion of Dorset was feared; if four French ships landed their crews on English soil there would,

---

[1] See their letter in Strype, *Eccl. Mem.*, III., ii., 102-3.
[2] *Acts of the P. C.*, 1556-58, p. 287; *Foreign Cal.*, 1553-8, p. 389.
[3] Kervyn, i., 133.   [4] *Ibid.*, i., 241-45.

thought Feria, be a revolution.[1] Mary had obviously made it impossible for her successor to continue her foreign policy.

CHAP.
IX.

Fortunately for the government the news of the fall of Calais came too late to influence to any appreciable extent the elections to Mary's last parliament, which met on January 20, 1558 ; and the queen expressed herself well content with its composition. The smallest proportion on record of old members secured re-election ;[2] but considering the recalcitrance of her last parliament Mary probably did not regard that as any drawback. She had in fact taken special means to secure the return of "discreet and good catholic members," and had required the sheriffs to use their best means to procure the election of such as the council should recommend.[3] Philip, however, complained of the inadequacy of its financial grants, and urged Mary to adopt other expedients.[4] The clergy gave eight shillings in the pound, but the commons only one subsidy, one tenth and one fifteenth ; and a member for London lamented that the city had lost £300,000 since the death of King Edward.[5] Supply, inadequate though it was, occasioned some debate, and even this house of commons rejected a bill for the expulsion of French denizens by 111 to 106 votes ; while Sir Thomas Copley, a future recusant under Elizabeth, was committed to the serjeant-at-arms for expressing a fear lest the queen should abuse a proposed bill confirming letters patent, by granting the crown away from "the right inheritors".[6] The lords rejected without a division a bill compelling Frenchmen in England to contribute yearly towards the maintenance of fortifications ; and Mary was driven to adopt the other financial expedients recommended by Philip. Besides a forced loan demanded from "every shire and town in England," she imposed additional duties of 26s. 8d. on every tun of French wine imported, of 10s. on every tun of beer exported, and duties to be levied at the discretion of commissioners on the import of dry goods.[7] Some aspersions were cast on Lord

---

[1] Kervyn, i., p. 228, " si quatro naviros de Francia echan gente en este reyno, lo han de revolver " ; cf. *Foreign Cal.*, 1553-8, p. 396.

[2] About 26 per cent. [3] State Papers, Dom., Mary, xi., 61 ; xii., 2.

[4] Kervyn, i., 140. [5] Strype, *Eccl. Mem.*, III., ii., 105, 145-46.

[6] *Commons' Journals*, March 5, 1558 ; cf. *Domestic Cal.*, Addenda 1580-1625, p. 65.

[7] *Acts of the P. C.*, 1556-58, p. 305 ; Wriothesley, ii., 140-41 ; *Domestic Cal.*, 1547-80, p. 104.

CHAP.
IX.

William Howard's conduct as lord high admiral during the Calais operations, and he was punished by promotion [1] to the office of lord chamberlain, being succeeded at the admiralty by Clinton. On the whole, Mary concluded that she was not likely to secure a more amenable parliament; and a singularly barren session was closed on March 5 by a prorogation instead of a dissolution.

Sterility was the conclusive note of Mary's reign. She had more than exhausted her mandate; but constitutional theory recognised no other initiative than that of the crown; and in default of royal or ministerial leadership there could only be stagnation. Lords and commons could do no more than resist; and the statute book bears witness to the consequent deadlock. Nor was resistance limited to the houses of parliament; the whole nation malingered in divers degrees. Debarred from the paths it wished to pursue, it would not follow in Mary's wake. A blight had fallen on national faith and confidence, and Israel took to its tents. The council, wrote Feria, was distracted by faction and irresolution; and decisions reached one day were revoked the next.[2] Since the loss of Calais, he averred, not a third of those who used to attend went to church.[3] What was the use of Rome and of Spain, if they served England worse than the schismatic Henry VIII. or the heretic Edward VI.? Well might Mary exclaim that Calais would be found graven on her heart; it spelt the epitaph of all her cherished aims.

Yet, forsaken by her husband and estranged from her people, Mary went on, ploughing her cheerless furrow across a stubborn land, and reaping, as the shadows fell, her harvest of hopes deferred. She was still expecting the birth of an heir and Philip's return; both tarried, and in March Feria said that Pole was practically dead. In vain she strove to satisfy by burnt-offerings the craving of a mind diseased in a disordered frame; and only in the pursuit of heretics did the government exhibit any vigour. The fall of Calais seems to have secured them a brief respite; and it was not till the end of March that

---

[1] Kervyn, pp. 129, 134-37; *Hatfield MSS.*, i., 489.

[2] *Ibid.*, p. 135, "Todo lo que estos tratan, es confusion y passion unos con otros, y las resoluciones que toman un dia, revocan otro".

[3] *Ibid.*, p. 130, "Certifican me que, despues de perdido Cales, no va à les iglesias la tercia parte de la gente que solia".

the government recovered sufficiently to resume the executions. Some forty victims, however, were burnt in the last eight months of her reign, although it was obvious even to Mary that sacrifices were useless for her purpose. The heart of the nation was further off from Rome than ever; in London itself protestants worshipped in secret; and sheriffs had to be punished for their lenience.[1] There was little reverence for departing glory : Philip himself turned towards the rising sun; and in June Feria went down to Hatfield to secure Elizabeth's favour.

Mary's reign had been a palpable failure. The reaction against Northumberland's misgovernment and ambition and against the protestant extremes of Edward's later years was genuine enough; and, had Mary been content with restoring her father's system, she might have been successful. But the time for a real counter-reformation had not come in England, and there were few signs of catholic fervour in Mary's reign. The queen herself and Pole were the only religious enthusiasts; there was little of the missionary spirit in Bonner, Gardiner, or even Tunstall. Neither the fathers of Trent nor the disciples of Loyola had yet done their work, and the Marian reaction was no part of the counter-reformation. Pole, indeed, endeavoured to effect some reforms; but he appealed to deaf ears, and the bulk of Mary's clergy had not sufficient religious conviction to prevent them turning their coats again in 1559. Diplomatists like Renard had frequently urged that instead of burning heretics the clergy should begin by reforming themselves; but diplomatists also paid little respect to the mass which was the cornerstone of the old religion. The Venetian ambassador refers to the service as the usual opportunity for diplomatic conversations, and explains how one discussion stopped "as the mass was already at an end".[2] The reconciliation with Rome was the result not so much of popular impulse as of governmental pressure; and it stirred not a breath of spiritual fervour. From then to the end of Mary's reign no Oxford or Cambridge college bought any but servicebooks;[3] and the Stationers' Register in London is almost

---

[1] Sir Richard Pecksall, son-in-law of the Lord Treasurer Winchester, was put under constraint for releasing a heretic who recanted at the stake, Foxe, viii., 490-92; *Acts of the P. C.*, 1556-58, pp. 361, 371.

[2] *Venetian Cal.*, vi., 104-6.

[3] Thorold Rogers, *History of Agriculture and Prices*, iv., 602.

as barren of letters. Even this religious concentration produced no intellectual fruit, and Philip's confessor, de Soto,
complained in 1555 of Oxford's neglect of theology.[1] That
fervent belief in Roman catholicism is not incompatible with
the highest forms of literature and art is proved by the history
of Spain in the first half of the seventeenth century; and the
intellectual paralysis of England in Mary's reign was due, not
to its Roman catholicism, but to the insincerity of its official
religion and to the repression of its natural instincts.

The stars in their courses fought against Mary, but she deserved a better fate. The most honest of Tudor rulers, she
never consciously did what she thought to be wrong. So far
as she could, she kept her court and government uncorrupt,
and she tried to help the poor. In spite of her cruel treatment in youth, she was compassionate except when her creed
was concerned; and no other Tudor was so lenient to traitors.
Nothing could be further from the mark than the contention
that she persecuted heretics because they were traitors. It
would, indeed, have been better for her, had she hanged more
traitors and burned fewer protestants; for it was one sign of
her alienation from the England of her age that she considered
offences against the state venial compared with those against
the church. A pitiful woman by nature, she was rendered
pitiless by the inexorable logic of her creed; titled rebels taken
in the act of treason were freely pardoned, but threescore
women were burnt, many of them widows of low degree. Yet
their tortures were slight compared with the long-drawn agony
inflicted on Mary by her consciousness of failure and her
husband's conduct. The matrimonial good fortune of the Hapsburgs did not extend to their English marriages; and like her
mother, Mary was a victim of the worldly policy that sought
to bind the destinies of nations in dynastic bonds. The Spanish
strain in her blood gave her religion its fierce unbending
character, which unfitted her for dealing with the delicate problem of the English reformation; and her Spanish marriage
cast her athwart England's secular aspirations.

Her last efforts served the double purpose of salving her
conscience and harassing her successor. Between October 25
and November 10 scores, if not hundreds, of livings impropriate

---

[1] *Venetian Cal.*, vi., 226.

to the crown were granted to the bishops; many legal and CHAP.
other offices, including two judgeships, were filled with adher- IX.
ents of the old religion ; and steps were taken to supply the
vacant bishoprics.[1] It was too late. Parliament reassembled on
November 5 ; and on the 14th the commons were summoned
to confer with the lords "for weighty affairs of the realm".
Mary was dying; three weeks earlier Feria had again been
sent to England in view of this event. The council received
him, as he graphically put it, like one bringing the bulls of a
dead pope : [2] for as king of England, Philip's days were also
numbered ; and every one, wrote another Spaniard, was taking
Elizabeth for queen. On November 10, Feria visited her with
Philip's secret and verbal instructions. She took at their
proper value his protestations that her accession would be due
neither to Mary nor to the council but to Philip alone ; for she
owed her crown to the English people. Mary also sent a
message to say she was content that Elizabeth should succeed,
and to ask her to maintain religion as established and to pay
Mary's debts. Elizabeth's answer has not been preserved ; it
is said by the Venetian ambassador to have been most gracious ; [3]
and she has been accused of having bought the crown by false
pretences. But Mary had no legal nor other power to deprive
Elizabeth of the crown, nor to impose conditions on her acceptance ; and Elizabeth may be excused if, to soothe Mary's dying
hour, she said more or less than she intended to perform. Between 5 and 6 A.M. on November 17 Mary passed away ; and
"all the churches in London did ring, and at night [men] did
make bonfires and set tables in the street, and did eat and
drink, and made merry for the new queen".[4]

1 *Domestic Cal.*, 1547-80, pp. 106-13.   2 Kervyn, i., 278-79.
3 *Venetian Cal.*, vi., 1549.   4 Machyn, p. 178.

CHAPTER X.

THE NEW QUEEN AND THE NEW AGE.

As the bells of London rang out the old and rang in the new reign, Cardinal Pole breathed his last at Lambeth Palace; and, with mocking irony on the morrow, every church in the city resounded with the *Te Deum Laudamus*.[1] The old order was passing without regret; and the Spaniards were scandalised by the rejoicings at a change which meant so much for their state and church. But Mary herself had been received with similar acclamation; and it depended largely upon Elizabeth's character whether or not another five years would produce an equally striking contrast.

She was now a little more than twenty-five years of age, having been born on September 7, 1533; and in one respect she was unique among English sovereigns. Several had passed to the Tower as the result of their reign, but none had been born of a mother who died a traitor's death, or had served, before promotion to the throne, an apprenticeship behind the Traitor's Gate; none had been ushered into a world quite so contemptuous as that which smiled at the birth of a daughter to Anne Boleyn. Elizabeth, indeed, was less fortunate even than Mary, for her mother had been disgraced as well as divorced; and she has been censured for having attempted no further vindication of her mother's memory than that implied in an act of 1559, declaring that she herself was lawfully descended from the blood royal of England. But she could not clear her mother without incriminating her father, whom she proposed to imitate, and in whose prestige she trusted; for if the grounds on which their marriage was pronounced invalid were good, the offence for which Anne Boleyn was

---

[1] Machyn, p. 178, says that Pole died on the 19th, Wriothesley says the 18th, but Priuli, Pole's confidant, says 7 P.M. on the 17th, twelve hours after Mary, *Venetian Cal.*, vi., 1550.

beheaded could not have been adultery. It required all the new-found "omnicompetence" of parliament to remedy such defects; and until the act of 1544 established Elizabeth's contingent claim to the succession, she passed an insignificant childhood.

Her education, however, was not neglected; she learnt to write Greek, Latin, and Hebrew, and to speak as well as to write French, German, and Italian, though her French accent was bad;[1] and she was almost as vain of her musical attainments as she was of her dancing. After Edward VI.'s accession Thomas Seymour's intrigues brought her into unenviable prominence; and Seymour's improprieties would, had they led to secret marriage, have involved him in a charge of treason and deprived her of her right to the succession. In the trying investigations which followed, Elizabeth proved herself an adept in the feminine arts of self-defence. She was probably innocent of anything worse than a reluctant acquiescence in his coarse attentions, and a girlish admiration for his handsome face. Perhaps his tragic fate touched a deeper chord, and she certainly regarded his memory with more affection than she did his brother's children; but in 1549 she only showed resentment at the slights inflicted on herself. Fortunately she escaped the enmity and the still more dangerous favour of Northumberland; and hence in 1553 she was ranged with Mary among the duke's opponents. Her attitude towards Mary's religious changes was consistent, though not heroic. Her duty as a subject was to obey the law; the responsibility for the law was Mary's. Nevertheless, she might, after Wyatt's rebellion, have paid forfeit with her life for her nearness to the throne and for the circumstances of her birth, had not Lady Jane, who was at least as innocent, been there to blunt the edge of Mary's indignation.

After her release from the Tower Elizabeth's life passed into smoother waters, although servants of hers were often arrested, and irresponsible plotters conspired in her favour. She was Mary's only possible successor; and the English people, without distinction of creed, were determined to protect her life in order to save themselves from the certainty of civil war or Spanish rule. The theory of the divine hereditary

---

[1] De Thou, *Hist. sui Temporis*, 1621, v., 898.

right of kings was already beginning to exert its fatal fascination on the house of Stuart; and men were muttering at
Paris in 1557 that no municipal law could deprive Mary, Queen
of Scots, of her "natural right constituted by God" to the
English crown.[1] But the candidate of a foreign power at war
with England could only reach the English throne in the
train of an invading army; and neither Spain nor England
would tolerate a theory presented in that form. And so
Elizabeth passed from the mild restraint of Woodstock to the
freedom of Hatfield, where she planted trees; listened to the
lessons of Ascham and Battista Castiglione; relieved the
dulness of country life by considering proposals of marriage
made her on behalf of Don Carlos, of Philibert of Savoy, of
Eric of Sweden, of Adolf of Holstein, of one or more archdukes, of English nobles such as Westmorland and Arundel,
and eventually of Philip II. himself;[2] and waited and watched
while Mary made straight her successor's path by uprooting
whatever desire Englishmen had for catholic faith, Roman
jurisdiction, and Spanish protection.

The Venetian Michiele described her in 1557 as comely
rather than handsome, swarthy but of good complexion : "she
has fine eyes and above all a beautiful hand of which she makes
a display . . . as a linguist she excels the queen". She never
spoke anything but Italian with Italians. She was proud and
haughty, and "every lord in the kingdom was seeking to enter
her service himself, or place one of his sons or brothers in it,
such being the love and affection borne her". Philip, he says,
prevented her being declared a bastard and disinherited, or
sent out of the kingdom as Mary wished, who but for this and
the fear of insurrection "would have inflicted every sort of
punishment upon her".[3] On the eve of her accession Feria,
sketching her personal and political inclinations, said she was
full of vanity and finesse, sought to imitate her father, and would,
it was to be feared, ill-conduct herself in religious matters.
She showed much affection for the people, who were on her
side, and let it be understood that she owed her future to them
and not to Philip or to the nobility.[4]

[1] *Venetian Cal.*, vi., 1076.   [2] *Ibid.*, vi., 1078; Kervyn, i., 181, 273-75.
[3] *Venetian Cal.*, vi., 1056-64.
[4] Feria to Philip, Nov. 13 or 14, 1558, Kervyn, i., 279-80.

This was the key of her position. No English sovereign since the Danish conquest had been so purely British in blood, and her nearest foreign forebear was Catherine of France, widow of Henry V. and wife of Owen Tudor. " Mere English," she ordered her ambassadors at Cateau-Cambrésis to remember that she was, not half-Spanish like her sister; and the boast was endlessly repeated to her people. No English king or queen was more superbly insular in policy ; but "mere English" is a very inadequate description of the character of the lady whom Henry III. of France termed *la plus fine femme du monde*.[1] Like the ships of her navy, she owed much of her success to the nearness with which she could sail to the wind. She was a queen of the Renaissance, and there were points of similarity between her and Catherine de Médicis. " An Englishman Italianate," ran a current jingle, " is a devil incarnate ;" and Elizabeth was well versed in Italian scholarship, statecraft, and divinity. Veracity is hardly a diplomatic virtue, except on the assumption that it is the easiest method of deception ; but the length to which Elizabeth pushed her diplomatic artifices was almost inartistic. Scruples she had none, and she was almost as devoid of a moral sense as she was of religious temperament. So far as she can be said to have had any favourite divines—apart from bishops who were favoured as disciplinarians rather than as divines—they were Italians. She translated a sermon by Bernardino Ochino; a solemn Lutheran warned her against Peter Martyr ;[2] and she patronised and pensioned Giacomo Acontio.[3]

But Italian divines who left Rome went as a rule beyond Augsburg, Zürich, or Geneva. Ochino is apparently placed by Milton among the speculative thinkers of the infernal regions, whose wandering mazes had no end; and Acontio maintained that all dogmas were stratagems of Satan. Elizabeth told various tales about her own religion ; she hardly differed from any church with which it was expedient to agree ; but it was not expedient to publish her real opinions. The Spanish ambassador more than hinted at atheism ; and an Englishman

---

[1] *Hatfield MSS.*, ii., 462; *cf. Foreign Cal.*, 1558-59, No. 285.
[2] *Ibid.*, 1558-59, No. 297; his full name was Pietro Martire Vermigli.
[3] *Dict. of Nat. Biogr.*, i., 63. In 1575 " nearly all " the privy council spoke Italian, *Venetian Cal.*, vii., 525.

CHAP.
X.

declared in 1601 that "she was an atheist and a maintainer of atheism".[1] The dogmatic assumption implied in that word was alien to Elizabeth's mind ; but it can hardly be doubted that she was sceptical or indifferent. She kissed a Bible in the streets, and kept a crucifix in her chapel ; but both were meant for uses that were not religious. Religion is mainly a matter of feeling, and there is nothing to suggest that Elizabeth felt any religion as Mary did hers. She professed to be shocked in later years when Henry of Navarre thought Paris worth a mass ; but she herself had thought her life well worth a mass in Mary's reign. She held, in common with the ablest rulers of the age, that it was foolishness to sacrifice the security of thrones and the unity of states on the altar of disputable dogma.

Yet she was genuine enough to a certain point. A daughter of Anne Boleyn and Henry VIII. could have little regard for papal jurisdiction ; and a sceptic may honestly have disbelieved the catholic doctrine of the mass. Elizabeth might, in case of necessity, have continued after 1558 the religious observances forced upon her by the law in Mary's reign ; but even in Mary's reign her position had been understood. It was simply one of outward conformity, justified by the canons of the age and by the respect of politicians for the national religion. Every one knew that she was a heretic at heart : " she has not hitherto been a catholic" wrote Philip to Feria in 1559 ; she would, opined Michiele in 1557, in the event of her succession, " in any case" abolish the authority of the pope, and " at least" put back things to their condition during the last eight years of Henry's reign.[2] That would be a conservative measure quite in keeping with Elizabeth's cautious temperament ; and there were no political temptations to relinquish her natural dislike of Calvinism, a doctrine repugnant to princes, and, after Knox's *Blasts from the Trumpet*, especially to queens. It was not so much to Calvin's theology that Elizabeth objected as to its politico-ecclesiastical implications. The Huguenots desired, said the Cardinal of Ferrara, " to bring all to the

---

[1] *Domestic Cal.*, 1601-3, p. 23 ; *Spanish Cal.*, Eliz., i., 401 ; *cf. ibid.*, ii., 601.

[2] *Spanish Cal.*, i., 22 ; *Venetian Cal.*, vi., 1076 ; Renard had told the emperor the same in 1555: "l'hérésie sera renouvellée et la religion sera renversée," Granvelle, iv., 395, 432-33.

form of a republic, like Geneva ";[1] but when belief in pre-destination was combined, in the person of Whitgift, with a whole-hearted acceptance of the divine right of kings, Elizabeth not only made him archbishop but called him "her little black husband".

That she gave no one that title in earnest, was not for lack of suitors or of pressure from her subjects. Nor is it easy to believe that Elizabeth would willingly have deprived herself of the enormous advantage of an heir to the throne born of her body. She could not foresee in 1558 the conditions of 1603 ; nor, had she been able to pierce the veil of the future, would she have sacrificed herself to serve the ambitions of the house of Stuart. Her death at any time before 1588 would probably have been followed by civil war and the ruin of all her work ; and, egotistical as she was, resolutely as she refused to think of the possible deluge, or to contemplate a drama in which she would play no part, choice can hardly have led her to involve her kingdom in such risks. There is evidence that she had no option in the matter, and that a physical defect precluded her from hopes of issue.[2] On this supposition her conduct becomes intelligible, her irritation at parliamentary pressure on the subject pardonable, and her outburst on the news of Mary Stuart's motherhood a welcome sign of genuine feeling. Possibly there was a physical cause for Elizabeth's masculine mind and temper, and for the curious fact that no man lost his head over her as many did over Mary Queen of Scots. To judge from portraits, Elizabeth was as handsome as her rival, but she had no feminine fascination ; and even her

---

[1] *Foreign Cal.*, 1562, p. 433.

[2] The story is told with some unnecessary embroidery by Ben Jonson, *Conversations with Drummond* (Globe ed.), pp. 484-85. Jonson is not a good witness, but it is not a matter on which official documents would speak, and there is corroborative evidence. On April 29, 1559, Feria writes, " Si las espias no me mienten, que no lo creo, por la razon que de poco aca me han dado, entiendo que ella no terna hijos " (Kervyn, i., 513 ; Froude's version, vi. 197, *n.*, is not quite correct) ; and Philip II. afterwards constantly expressed his disbelief in the genuineness of Elizabeth's matrimonial negotiations. Noailles in 1559 could not believe that Elizabeth would ever marry, *Hatfield MSS.*, i. 158; Haynes, p. 215. Suriano remarks that there were " secret reasons " why Philip himself did not wish to marry Elizabeth, *Venetian Cal.*, vii., 330. De Thou has a similar story from French sources; see also Aubrey's *Lives*, ed. Clark, ii., 139. Mr. Frere has tentatively suggested the same view, but without reference to any evidence, *History of the English Church*, p. 52.

extravagant addiction to the outward trappings of her sex may
have been due to the absence or atrophy of deeper womanly
instincts.   The impossibility of marriage made her all the
freer with her flirtations, and she carried some of them to
lengths which scandalised a public unconscious of Elizabeth's
security.   She had every reason to keep the public as well as
courts and councils in the dark, and to convince the world that
she could and would marry if the provocation were sufficient.
To her and to her people, a husband would be a mere encum-
brance without children ; but for others her hand held a crown,
and it was a diplomatic asset which she could not afford to
neglect out of modest scruples.

It was with a free hand in more senses than one that Elizabeth came to the throne.   The previous reign had, it is true,
indicated certain lines of policy which she must at all costs
avoid ; but the ample discretion accorded to Tudor monarchs
gave her plenty of choice with regard to ways and means.
Mary's privy council came to an end with her life, and Elizabeth could summon whom she liked to the board.   Only three
of Mary's council, Pembroke, Clinton, and Howard, attended
the small meetings held at Hatfield before Elizabeth removed
to London ; while seven new members took their seats, Cecil,
Sadler, Sir Thomas Parry who had long been in her service,
Sir Richard Sackville her mother's cousin, Sir Ambrose Cave,
Sir Edward Rogers, and the new Earl of Bedford.   But the
absence of others was not due to design ; for at its meeting
in the Charterhouse on November 24 six more members of
Mary's council were permitted to join the board, Archbishop
Heath, the Earls of Shrewsbury and Derby, Sir Thomas
Cheyne, Sir John Mason, and Sir William Petre ; and they
were reinforced by the Marquis of Winchester on the 27th,
and by the Earl of Arundel on December 10.   When the
distribution of the great offices of state was completed, the
council contained eleven old, and seven new, members ; but
fifteen of Mary's councillors were excluded.[1]

[1] These details are from the register of the privy council.   An inaccurate list
printed by Strype (*Eccl. Mem.*, III., ii., 160) and by Father Birt (*Elizabethan Religious Settlement*, p. 12) gives among the councillors "laid aside" by Elizabeth
some who had died and others who had practically ceased to attend before the
end of Mary's reign.   Feria's information also is not always borne out by the
Register, and other correspondents often go wildly astray.   Thus Sandys writes to

A similar degree of continuity characterised the *personnel* of the administration. Elizabeth, indeed, had no option in the matter of offices conferred by patents which had been confirmed by statute towards the end of Mary's reign. Winchester was continued as lord high treasurer, Clinton as lord high admiral, Arundel as lord steward, Howard as lord chamberlain,[1] and Cheyne as treasurer of the household. On the other hand Heath, the only ecclesiastic in the council, was succeeded by Sir Nicholas Bacon, Cecil's brother-in-law, who was styled lord keeper of the great seal; Paget lost his seat on the council, while the functions of his office of lord privy seal were performed by Bacon; Cecil more than filled the two places held by Secretaries Bourne and Boxall; Parry succeeded Sir Thomas Cornwallis as comptroller, and Rogers Sir Henry Bedingfield as vice-chamberlain. A few further changes were made during the next six months; Sir John Baker and Cheyne died in December, and Heath ceased to attend in January. Northampton was restored to the council on Christmas Day; and in January Parry became treasurer of the household, Rogers comptroller, and Sir Francis Knollys vice-chamberlain. Sir Walter Mildmay succeeded Baker as chancellor of the exchequer, and Wotton was re-admitted to the council on the conclusion of his diplomatic labours at Cateau-Cambrésis; but the same favour was not extended to his colleague, Bishop Thirlby. Several of the privy councillors excluded by Elizabeth retained their administrative or judicial offices;[2] and the inevitable changes in the *personnel* and policy of the government were made gradually and with the least possible dislocation of the public service.

Elizabeth had no mind to commit her fortunes to extremists; she meant to imitate her father and so to constitute her council as to retain for herself the greatest weight in determining the issue of its deliberations. Before she had been a month on the throne Feria wrote: "She seems to me incomparably

---

Bullinger on Dec. 20, "the Queen has changed almost all her councillors," *Zurich Letters*, i., 4.

[1] In the index to the *Acts of the Privy Council* and in the *Spanish Cal.* Howard and his predecessor, Lord Hastings of Loughborough, are confused.

[2] *E.g.* Sir William Cordell remained master of the rolls, Sir Clement Heigham chief baron of the exchequer, Sir Edmund Peckham master of the mint, and Richard Weston solicitor-general.

more feared than her sister, and gives her orders and has her way as absolutely as her father did ".[1]   She was not bound to act upon the decisions of her council, even though they might be unanimous, for the function of the privy council was merely to advise; and on many occasions the council failed to persuade Elizabeth to adopt courses which it recommended, or to abandon those of which it disapproved.   Political influence, too, was not always indicated by membership of the privy council.   Lord Robert Dudley, Sir Nicholas Throckmorton, and the Earl of Sussex were not members, although they had a good deal to do with the government; and, in spite of the continuity between Mary's and Elizabeth's councils, Feria asserted that England was " entirely in the hands of young folks, heretics, and traitors," and that Elizabeth did not favour a single man whom Mary would have received.   Nevertheless, the efficiency of government could not be maintained with a council in general disagreement with the crown; Elizabeth was not as a rule impervious to remonstrance, and her selection of privy councillors conveyed a fairly accurate indication of the principles on which she meant to rule.

Her appointment of Cecil as secretary, and her steadfast reliance on him throughout forty years of her reign, prove the soundness of her judgment and the depth of the consistency which underlay the superficial fluctuations of her conduct. Cross currents and head winds compelled her to tack with a frequency and sometimes a rapidity which seem bewildering to the distant observer unfamiliar with the course; and the shifts and subterfuges to which she was driven have disgusted historians who demand in their heroes a strength of will superior to all the forces of circumstance.   But there was no variation in her purpose to free England from foreign influence and from the dread of foreign intervention, and to do it with as little risk as possible to herself.   In this she and Cecil were at one, though at times they differed as to means.   Neither was moved by the spirit that sent English seamen to girdle the globe with their ships, and English traders to compass all lands with their commerce; but both were adepts in the craft and caution required to restrain the exuberance, and to neutralise the risks, of too adventurous impulses.   Their tactics were not always Fabian,

[1] *Spanish Cal.,* i., 7.

and on occasion Elizabeth and Cecil struck swift and sudden
blows.　Indeed, they understood the need of circumspection all
the more because they were conscious that throughout the reign
their policy was fundamentally aggressive.　It was Elizabeth's
privilege to reap the fruits of public peace, while her subjects
gleaned the spoils of private war.　Heroic qualities were irrelevant to such a task, and there was little in Cecil's nature to
stir imagination.　No great conceptions sprang from his mind,
and no great heroism distinguished his conduct.　Skill in
the art of taking cover had guided him safely through the
perils of two troublesome reigns; and his keen scent for
danger enabled him to steer England through the risks of a
third.　Without being particularly sensitive about the methods
of sixteenth century statecraft, he never abetted political assassination; and, while willing to conform under Mary, he was
always at heart a protestant of real piety and upright conversation.　He took no pensions from foreign courts as Wolsey
did, and received no bribes from English suitors.　His deceits,
at any rate after 1558, were all practised in the interests of his
queen and country; and he justified the words of Elizabeth
when she said on his appointment: " This judgment I have of
you, that you will not be corrupted with any manner of gifts,
and that you will be faithful to the state ".[1]

Few others of the council counted for much in determining
Elizabeth's policy.　Winchester, Pembroke, Arundel, Clinton,
Wotton, Petre, and Mason had served Henry VIII. and
Edward VI. as well as Mary, and were officials rather than
statesmen.　Bedford was a sound protestant who exercised
almost royal authority in the south-western shires; and Northampton, though of no great ability or character, had at least
suffered more than most of Edward VI.'s councillors under
Mary.　Clinton's retention as lord high admiral is singular
considering the intimacy of his relations with Philip II. and the
Spanish pension he still drew;[2] it may be explained by the
fact that his wife—Surrey's " Fair Geraldine "—had been
equally intimate with Elizabeth.　More important was the
selection of Nicholas Bacon as lord keeper of the great seal;[3]

---

[1] State Papers, Dom., Elizabeth, i., 7.　　　[2] *Spanish Cal.*, i., 11.

[3] In April, 1559, Elizabeth issued letters patent declaring Bacon's authority
to be and have been as great as if he were lord chancellor, *Egerton Papers*,
Camden Soc., pp. 29-30; an act was passed to the same effect in 1563.

CHAP. X. his second wife was sister of Cecil's second wife, and Bacon was a stauncher protestant than Cecil. As early as 1536 Cranmer had urged his appointment as town clerk of Calais on the ground of his " towardness in the law and good judgement touching Christ's religion ".[1] But like Cecil himself he conformed during Mary's reign and even retained his attorneyship in the court of wards; this was the highest legal office he had held, when he was promoted over the heads of Cordell, Heigham, and others to be lord keeper. The law and the church had been so closely associated that until 1529 the chancellor was almost invariably an ecclesiastic; and Elizabeth's substitution of a layman for Archbishop Heath was as significant of change in the relations between church and state as Henry VIII.'s consistent appointment of laymen to that office after Wolsey's fall.

No light task confronted Elizabeth and her council. " Really," wrote the insolent Feria, " this country is more fit to be dealt with sword in hand than by cajolery : for there are neither funds, nor soldiers, nor heads, nor forces ". The financial situation was deplorable. Royal expenditure, which was about £56,000 a year at the end of Henry VIII.'s reign, had arisen to £65,000 before the end of Edward VI.'s, and during Mary's had grown to £138,000 in 1554-55, £213,000 in 1555-56, £216,000 in 1556-57, and £345,000 in 1557-58. In the last financial half-year of Mary's reign, from Easter to Michaelmas, 1558, she had spent £267,000, or at the rate of £534,000 a year, and she left a debt of nearly a quarter of a million.[2] To meet this unprecedented outlay parliament in 1558 had granted one subsidy, one tenth, and one fifteenth. The old tenth and fifteenth had, through the power of resistance possessed by the shires and towns on which it was levied, been reduced to a fixed sum of about £32,000, which, far from increasing with the wealth of the country, rapidly decreased in value with the rise in prices and decline in the purchasing power of gold and silver owing to the influx of precious metals from the New World. The subsidy, designed to meet this growing deficiency, produced at first about £120,000; but, in spite of its assessment upon the weaker individual, and of its

[1] Cranmer, *Works* (Parker Soc.), ii., 384.
[2] *Foreign Cal.*, 1559-60, p. cxv; *Domestic Cal.*, 1547-1580, p. 147.

collection by royal officials instead of by the nominees of members of parliament, the subsidy tended to diminish in produc-
tiveness. Paget in 1544 calculated that a subsidy would yield
£100,000;[1] probably it yielded less in 1558, and at the end
of Elizabeth's reign produced only £80,000. The clergy at
the same time granted eight shillings in the pound, which may
have amounted to some £35,000. The parliamentary grants of
1558 would thus have realised about £160,000, and it is little
wonder that Philip complained of their inadequacy. The
forced loan yielded £109,000,[2] the ordinary feudal dues were
worth perhaps £50,000 a year; and the customs duties, even
after the increases imposed by Mary, were farmed at only
£24,000. These would bring the revenue in 1558 up to about
£345,000; but the deficit, even when reduced by the profits
of jurisdiction and by the fines for renewal obtained through
the revocation of all grants and patents from the crown,[3] cannot
have been much less than £150,000; and Mary's expenditure
during her last year must have exceeded her revenue by nearly
40 per cent. Her predecessors, Henry VIII. and Edward VI.,
had made a fraudulent profit of something like a million by
the debasement of the coinage; but that source of revenue was
exhausted, and in 1558 Mary was with difficulty raising loans
at the ruinous interest of 14 per cent., dispensing for that
purpose with the usury laws.[4]

Yet all these financial efforts on Mary's part had produced
nothing but disaster. They did not even justify, in the government's opinion, an attempt to recover Calais; and it was
doubted whether Berwick could be held against the French who
were meditating an attack from the Scottish Borders. Its defences were said to be no better than those of Calais, and French
engineers boasted that they could make equally short work of
them. Mary's only trust was in Philip, and Philip's envoys at
Cateau-Cambrésis were declaring that they must make peace
without insisting on the restitution of Calais, unless England
could find the means for prosecuting the war with greater
vigour. Even Philip's friendship might be doubtful with

---

[1] *Letters and Papers*, Henry VIII., 1544, ii., 689.

[2] State Papers, Dom., Mary, xiii., 36; the pressure employed to produce this
sum may be estimated from Paget's calculation in 1544 that a benevolence would
yield from £50,000 to £60,000.

[3] *Ibid.*, x., 58.   [4] *Domestic Cal.*, 1547-80, p. 111.

Elizabeth as queen and heretics as her councillors; and the
French were pestering the pope with their demands to have
her declared a bastard and incapable of succeeding to the
English throne.   During the peace negotiations they even
went so far as to say that, supposing Calais were restored,
they did not know to whom they should surrender it; for the
dauphin's wife, Mary of Scotland, was rightful queen of England.   Nor had Elizabeth elsewhere to look for help than to
Philip; for such understanding as had existed in Henry
VIII.'s and Edward VI.'s reigns with the protestant princes
of Germany and Denmark had been perforce abandoned
under Mary.   England was, it seemed to some, no better than
a bone cast between two dogs;[1] and the only question was
which should carry off the prize.

These were, however, the fears of timorous souls, or the
interested calculations of enemies who wished to make a profit
out of a fictitious presentment of England's weakness.   Henry
VIII. had learnt, and taught his people to believe, that their
country could not be conquered so long as it remained united,[2]
and Elizabeth's rivals recognised that fact as fully as she did
or her ministers.   Every plan for her ruin was based on the
assumption that England was divided, and that an invading
force need only be the match to fire domestic conflagration.
Men did not dream that England could be conquered from
abroad without co-operation from within; and the English
themselves had little fear of foreigners.   The English navy, in
spite of its diminution in strength since the death of Henry
VIII., was the finest in the world.   Dejection and distrust
had for ten years characterised the court, but not the country.
The nation had no doubts about its future, if only it had
competent statesmanship to lead it in the direction in which it
wanted to go.   Feria, while emphasising Mary's poverty, agreed
with Elizabeth that " there was plenty of money in the country,
only it was difficult and dangerous to get it out of the people ".[3]
England's recent impotence arose from the fact that its
governors were bent on checking its natural impulse towards

---

[1] *Foreign Cal.*, 1559-60, p. 3.

[2] See my *Henry VIII.*, ed. 1905, p. 308; in 1557 Michiele reports that the
English forces " are capable, as is evident, to resist any invasion from abroad
provided there be union in the kingdom," *Venetian Cal.*, vi., 1049.

[3] *Spanish Cal.*, i., 30; *Venetian Cal.*, vii., 328.

new worlds and on turning its energies back into the ancient
paths; antagonism of ideals produced mutual distrust between
the rulers and the ruled, and the nation lacked the strength
which unity alone could give.

Absolute unity was not attainable by any nation in that
age of religious wars and conflicting creeds; and the best
that a government could achieve was to build its policy upon
the motives that appealed to the most vigorous or the most
numerous sections of its subjects.   It was here that Mary
failed.   However attached the mass of Englishmen may have
been to the old religion, few were enthusiastic over papal
jurisdiction, and fewer relished the shackles which a Spanish
king imposed upon national aspirations.   The strength of
religious conservatism was, moreover, shaken by the sight of
a pope excommunicating the Catholic King for secular reasons
and accusing Cardinal Pole of heresy, as well as by the fires
at Smithfield and by the loss of Calais.   But perhaps the most
potent of all the causes which estranged Englishmen from the
papacy and Spain was the bar they placed in England's path
across the sea.   A good Roman catholic could not flout the
papal award which divided the New World between Portugal
and Spain; and if the "sea-divinity," as Fuller terms it, of
Hawkins and Drake was hardly orthodox protestantism, it
was at least anti-papal.   It was no accident that those parts
of England which heard the call of new-found lands forsook
their ancient faith for one which rendered attacks upon the
papists not only a profitable pleasure, but also a religious
duty.   The most corrupt places, writes Feria, are London,
Kent, and some of the seaports.   Protestantism had come
into the east and south-east of England with the trade from
the Netherlands and Germany; it spread throughout the south-
west with the growth of enterprise across the sea; and Cornwall and Devon, which had been the scene of a catholic rising
against the Prayer Book, now provided harbours for Elizabeth's
sea-dogs and seats for puritan members of parliament.[1]

The south, the east, and the midlands were prepared to
go forward after the reaction of Mary's reign; in them were

---

[1] Peter and Paul Wentworth both sat for Cornish seats in Elizabeth's reign,
and later these constituencies elected Sir John Eliot, Hampden, Coke, Sir E.
Sandys, Holles, Hakewill, Sir R. Phelips, Sir Henry Marten, and John Rolle.

placed the centres of English manufactures, commerce, and maritime adventure.   But England north of the Humber and west of the Severn was still, in spite of the coal to which Soranzo[1] refers in 1554, mainly pastoral and sparsely populated; there the wits of men were less quickened by contact with their fellows and less receptive of new ideas; and there the feudal noble and catholic priest maintained their customary sway.   Mary had thought of removing her capital to York, and her creation of ten new parliamentary seats in Yorkshire is as significant as Elizabeth's creation of sixteen in Hampshire and twelve in Cornwall.   Frenchmen and catholic Scots dreamed that the Humber and not the Tweed might yet be the boundary between the two kingdoms; and, but for the Scottish reformation, it would have needed all the energies of the council of the north to curb the separatism of shires, which had little share in the expansion of English nationality and took little pleasure in the contraction of its catholicism.   A civil war, in which north and west should be ranged against south and east, was not impossible in the sixteenth any more than it was in the seventeenth century.   It was avoided, and England was enabled to present a united front to foreign foes, because Elizabeth and her advisers knew how to steer a middle course, which would completely alienate none but a small minority of extremists.

So far as defence was concerned, this was all she had to do; for with England united, even if only on the surface, no foreign power would care to meddle.   But the England of Elizabeth was not content with the defensive; and the real trouble of her government was to guard against the retaliation, into which other governments were provoked by the consistent aggressiveness of the English people.   It is the universal belief of the makers and owners of empires that their dominions have been secured by purely defensive measures; and no picture is more popular than that of Elizabethan England standing bravely at bay against papal plots and Spanish armadas.   In reality England was the aggressor, and few monarchs would have borne protracted provocation with Philip II.'s patience.   Long before either he or the pope struck a blow, Englishmen had been fighting and scheming to wrest

[1] *Venetian Cal.*, v., 543.

provinces from the Roman church and from the Spanish empire.
Paul IV. refused to declare the queen illegitimate on Mary
Stuart's behalf, and strove to maintain diplomatic relations
with England; it was Elizabeth who recalled her ambassador
from Rome and declined to receive a papal envoy. Philip befriended her during the first critical years of her reign, turned
a deaf ear alike to Mary Stuart and to Irish chiefs, condoned
official and unofficial assistance rendered to his rebels in the
Netherlands, and was only goaded into war by the conviction
that, if he refrained, not only the Netherlands but the New
World on which his finances depended would pass out of his
grasp for ever; while France saw its influence ruined in Scotland and its factions nourished at home by English men and
money, and never found an opening for revenge.

England, indeed, rarely missed a chance of annoying its
rivals, and used its opportunities with consummate skill.
Elizabeth's caution was mingled with the daring of her people,
and they accepted risks which she refused. She preferred, as
she expressed it herself, to wage war " underhand "; but volunteers stepped into the open breach whenever the Dutch or the
Huguenots called for help. They had to act on their own
responsibility, and could not count on Elizabeth's aid if they
failed. If a Spanish galleon were seized the queen would secretly
share the spoil; but if English sailors were caught, they might
be hanged as pirates, for Elizabeth was at peace with Philip.
She was also at peace with France, while her subjects enlisted
under Huguenot standards and took their chance of execution
as well as of death in battle; and when in 1562 Elizabeth had
signed an alliance with the Huguenots, the English troops who
were sent to their aid were, when captured by Guise, hanged
with a placard over their heads justifying their execution,
" because they had helped the Huguenots against the wish of
the English queen".

Only under two conditions was it possible thus to run with
the hare and hunt with the hounds. One arose from the in-
choate state of international law and the tacit admission that
governments could not be expected to answer for their subjects.
Two nations at peace with one another might legitimately assist
one another's enemies with men and munitions of war. Not only
William of Orange, but the Cardinal of Châtillon, could issue

letters of marque and raise troops like a sovereign prince. The other condition was the boundless enthusiasm of Englishmen for any anti-papal or anti-Spanish buccaneering enterprise. In Henry VIII.'s reign the government had forced the national pace; in Elizabeth's the nation led the way. Her policy was not one imposed upon her people by an arbitrary government, but a compromise between the froward wishes of ardent spirits and the reluctant regrets of doubting or reactionary minds. It was fashioned by her and modified so far as might be from time to time to meet the shifting needs of the diplomatic situation. But in spite of compromise, prevarication, and pretence, Elizabeth's policy constituted an aggression upon the rights of others which can only be excused on the grounds of national or religious interests. And, indeed, England, after 1558, had to be aggressive if she was to be anything more than a third-rate power, and if the protestant reformation was to hold its own in Europe and to spread into America. Resignation under the conditions, in which she found herself after the loss of Calais, might have been a moral attitude; but it held out no attractions either to the queen who redeemed her lack of faith in other things by superb assurance in herself and in her people, or to a race which had seen a vision of the future and had caught the magic inspiration of the sea.

CHAPTER XI.

THE ELIZABETHAN SETTLEMENT.

ON Wednesday, November 23, Elizabeth made her entry into London, lodging in Lord North's apartments in the Charterhouse until the 28th ; then she rode amid popular acclamations to the Tower, " to settle," in Cecil's words, " her officers and council ". On December 10 Pole's body was taken to Canterbury for burial, and three days later Queen Mary's was brought from St. James's to Westminster Abbey. Her funeral was solemnised in fitting state on the 14th at a cost which would now come to between £70,000 and £80,000 ; but no monument was raised to her memory ; and the spot where she was buried is indicated only by two black tablets at the western base of the sumptuous tomb which James I. erected over her successor. The chief mourner was her cousin, the Countess of Lennox, while Philip was represented by the Count de Feria. At the requiem mass the first lesson was read by the Abbot of Westminster, and the eight others by Archbishop Heath and seven bishops including Bonner.[1] The sermon was preached by Bishop White of Winchester on the text, " Laudavi mortuos magis quam viventes ; sed feliciorem utroque judicavi qui necdum natus est ".[2] It conveyed a bold warning against religious change ; and offence was taken at the unfortunate texts quoted by White : " A living dog is better than a dead lion," and " Mary hath chosen the better part " ; at his implied comparison of Henry VIII. with Uzziah ; and at his denunciations of the " wolves coming out of Geneva " and of the idea that Elizabeth should take the title of supreme head of the church. The bishop was summoned before the council and ordered to keep his house.

[1] See the official account printed in *Foreign Cal.*, 1559-60, pp. cxvi-xxviii.

[2] Eccl. iv. 2, 3.   The sermon is printed by Strype, *Eccl. Mem.*, III., ii., 536-50, from Cotton MS., Vespasian, D. xviii.

This was hardly the treatment the "wolves" anticipated for Mary's bishops; and loud were their complaints that such as Bonner should be left not merely at liberty, but in possession of their emoluments and jurisdictions. In 1555 Renard had prophesied retribution in the event of Elizabeth's succession; but, when Feria visited her in November, 1558, he noted that she was not revengefully inclined.[1] Even Mary's protestant prisoners were only released gradually and almost one by one. The old services still went on in the churches, and the altars stood undisturbed; and much to the regret of the French, who desired to fish in troubled waters, Elizabeth's proclamation of November 18 forbade " the breach, alteration, or changes of any order or usage presently established ". She herself continued to go to mass. The persecutions ceased, of course, with Mary's death, but such a change required no law to legalise it. Nor was Elizabeth's proclamation of December 30 illegal, enjoining the use, which had already been adopted in the queen's chapel, of English for the epistle, gospel, and litany on the following Sunday, New Year's day;[2] for Henry VIII.'s statute authorising the use of the vernacular had not been repealed, although, as Feria remarks, to say the Lord's Prayer in English was the custom of heretics.

Scrupulous legality was if possible to cloak the religious revolution; and anxiety to leave no legal loopholes to the enemy had already produced an alteration in the title of the queen. She had been proclaimed on November 18 Queen of England, France, and Ireland, Defender of the Faith, " &c. ";[3] and " &c. " stood where once had been " Supreme Head of the Church ". It was deliberately adopted after consultation between Elizabeth and Cecil on the day before, and was not a trifling matter; for a few weeks later parliament appointed a committee to decide whether the acts of Mary's later parliaments were valid, in view of the fact that they had been summoned by writs containing no mention of that supremacy, which some thought belonged by right divine to the crown and could not be abrogated by pope or parliament. Bishop

---

[1] Kervyn, i., 281.   [2] Wriothesley, ii., 142-43.

[3] F. W. Maitland in *English Hist. Rev.*, xv., 120-24. Payne Collier, who printed Lord Ellesmere's MS. copy of the proclamation (*Egerton Papers*, pp. 28-29), thought that no printed copy was extant, but there is one in Dyson's collection in the British Museum.

White had doubtless suspected this " &c.," when he preached his funeral sermon; and "supreme head" actually appeared in the original draft of Elizabeth's act of supremacy.[1] Mary, indeed, had herself employed this same " &c. " until March 26, 1554,[2] when her triumph over Wyatt emboldened her to defy the legal scruples of her chancery, and to dispense with her supremacy over the church.

Other matters claimed immediate attention. The queen's financial needs were relieved by stringent insistence upon exact accounts from the collectors of Mary's subsidy, by the cessation of the large sums which Mary was in the habit of paying Philip,[3] and by the reduction of expenses from £267,000 in the last half-year of Mary's reign to £108,000 in the first half-year of Elizabeth's. But before financial stability could be established or the religious question determined, the war must be brought to an end, and Elizabeth's relations with foreign powers defined; and for some months after her accession her gaze was anxiously fixed upon Cateau-Cambrésis, where her envoys, Arundel, Howard, Thirlby, and Wotton, had a thankless part to play. Elizabeth was burning to assert her independence of Philip, and to save the outset of her reign from such a blot as the abandonment of Calais. She upbraided her commissioners for subservience to their Spanish colleagues, and tried to emphasize her own importance by entertaining separate negotiations through various channels with the French. But she was wise enough to heed Wotton's reminder of her father's fate in 1544, and his warning that these French approaches were designed to isolate her cause from Philip's; she kept the Spanish king informed of their progress, and was careful to sign herself his " sister and perpetual confederate ". She could not afford to risk a continuance of the war without his aid; though, rather than abandon Calais, she was prepared to break off the negotiations, if Philip would do the same. Philip himself wanted peace, but he had no desire to leave England a prey to the Guises. " We must see," wrote Feria, " that the King of France does not get in or spoil the crop Your Majesty

---

[1] *English Hist. Rev.*, xviii., 525-26 n.

[2] *Athenæum*, May 2, 1908. Parliament was more legally-minded, and retained " supreme head " in its acts so long as Mary used " &c."

[3] *Foreign Cal.*, 1559-60, p. xvi.

has sown here." His appreciation of England's value led him to offer his hand to his sister-in-law. She could only refuse (February 28): apart from more private reasons, such a marriage, as she pointed out to Feria, would require a papal dispensation; and her own legitimacy depended upon a denial of the papal power to dispense with similar impediments. Her subjects, moreover, would not have tolerated a restoration of Philip's rule, and her temper would not have brooked his mastery. " They are all very glad," confessed Feria frankly to Philip, " to be free of your Majesty." The queen declined with regrets and with protestations of friendship, which necessity rendered sincere; and to soften the blow, she paraded her hopes of alliance with one of the archdukes of Austria, Philip's kindred. Philip was soon consoled by the prospect of marriage with the French king's daughter, which was really more to his mind. He had genuinely conscientious objections to wedding a heretic, and he had made it a condition that Elizabeth should become a catholic, so that it might be " manifest that he was serving God by marrying her and that she had been converted by his act".[1] It was clear by this time that Elizabeth was not to be converted: a catholic bride would help the Catholic King to play the part of catholic champion; and if the French marriage meant real peace with France, he would have no need of those English resources which had after all disappointed his expectations.

The prospect of a Franco-Spanish alliance made Elizabeth's position all the more dangerous, and Cecil's suspicions at least were aroused by Philip's delay in renewing the old treaties between England and the house of Burgundy.[2] Fortunately Scotland was bent upon peace, and England feared hostilities on the Scottish Borders more than in the Channel. Châtelherault and Lethington were already discussing an Anglo-Scottish understanding; Cecil was engaging himself to foster it; and first a truce and then a peace was concluded with Scotland early in March. France, too, wanted peace, with Philip at any rate; though Henry II. might have been glad to continue the war against England alone, and would wage it

---

[1] *Spanish Cal.*, i., 8, 15-16, 21-23; *cf.* p. 27 and p. 31, where Feria remarks that the questions of religion and marriage are really one.

[2] *Foreign Cal.*, 1558-59, No. 221.

on both rather than give up Calais. Philip, however, could not risk the chance of Elizabeth's deposition in favour of the niece of the Guises; and he used all his influence to defeat their attempts to obtain a papal pronouncement against her. Calais seemed to be the only obstacle to peace, and Elizabeth's government had to bow to the inevitable. Philip would not fight for its recovery, and neither the efforts, which Elizabeth made to revive an alliance with the German princes, nor the offers of Sweden to renew the friendship subsisting in Edward VI.'s time, were of any avail for this purpose.[1] Sweden was too weak and too distant, and the Lutheran princes would only offer 10,000 mercenaries on condition that Elizabeth accepted the Confession of Augsburg. On February 19, after considerable pressure from Philip,[2] the queen empowered her commissioners to conclude peace without the retrocession of Calais. Preliminaries containing the terms of the Anglo-French agreement were signed on March 12, and there were premature rejoicings in England; but disputes between France and Spain over Savoy caused a temporary suspension of the negotiations, and it was not till April 2 that the treaty of Cateau-Cambrésis was concluded. France abandoned to Spain the control of Italy, but consolidated her own frontiers and retained Calais, for which, provided England kept the peace, she was to pay half a million crowns in default of its restitution within eight years.[3] The wisest heads in England had adopted Cecil's doubt whether Calais was worth its cost of maintenance, and the exchequer was relieved of a heavy drain on its resources. The worst of Mary's blunders was repaired, the most perilous of Elizabeth's initial difficulties overcome, and the country entered upon the longest period of official peace it had enjoyed since the reign of Henry III.

The conclusion of peace would have smoothed the progress of Elizabeth's ecclesiastical settlement, had not the marriage alliance between Spain and France caused alarm to the protestant party. Except in the minds of those who wished to be deceived, there was little doubt as to the main lines of

---

[1] *Foreign Cal.*, 1558-59, Nos. 90, 111, 262, 269, 297, 304, 361, 394, 397, 501, 531, 541, 554, 608, 637; Ruble, *Le traité de Cateau-Cambrésis*, 1889.

[2] *Spanish Cal.*, i., 33; *Foreign Cal.*, 1558-59, Nos. 335, 340, 405.

[3] *Ibid.*, Nos. 447-48, 475.

Elizabeth's policy. They had been foreseen by catholic diplomatists in Mary's reign, and Elizabeth soon began to justify their forebodings. But all was to be done, so far as might be, decently and in order. "God save us,"[1] wrote Archbishop Parker a few months later, "from such a visitation as Knox has attempted in Scotland; the people to be orderers of things!" In England the monarchy was expected to lead the way; and it was a royal chaplain who on Sunday, November 20, sounded the first note of impending change. When Christopherson, Bishop of Chichester, retorted with a catholic sermon on the following Sunday, he was confined to his house by royal command. So, too, while the queen prohibited the preaching or practice of religious innovations, she ordered Bishop Oglethorpe to refrain from elevating the host at mass in her chapel on Christmas day, and when he refused, she walked out as soon as the gospel was finished.[2] The people followed willingly enough, and on January 2 it was reported from Paris that the majority had entirely renounced the mass, although the queen "did not prevent any of the few who attended it from continuing to do so in safety and without being outraged in any way".[3]

It was generally expected that Elizabeth would require the same omission from the celebration at her coronation, which was fixed for Sunday the 15th. For this reason Archbishop Heath and other bishops, who were present at the coronation and swore fealty to her as queen, refused to officiate at the ceremony; and Elizabeth had to fall back on the services of Oglethorpe of Carlisle, one of the three junior bishops on the bench.[4] Heath's position was identical with that adopted by Sir Thomas More in 1534; the succession to the throne was within the competence of the state to settle, the ritual and doctrine of the church were not. Feria thought likewise; he accompanied the queen to Westminster Hall, but refused to attend the mass in the Abbey, and was commended by Philip for his abstention.[5] The gorgeous pageantry of the procession

---

[1] State Papers, Dom., Eliz., vii., 32; *Parker Corresp.*, p. 105.

[2] Ellis, *Orig. Letters*, ii., ii., 262; *Venetian Cal.*, vii., 2; *Spanish Cal.*, i., 17.

[3] *Venetian Cal.*, vii., 6; cf. *Engl. Hist. Rev.*, xv., 324-30.

[4] Oglethorpe, Watson of Lincoln, and Pole of Peterborough had all been consecrated by Heath on Aug. 15, 1557.

[5] Kervyn, i., 411; this important despatch is not noticed in the *Spanish Calendar*.

through the City on the previous day had partaken of the CHAP.
nature of a protestant demonstration; Elizabeth was repre- XI.
sented as *Veritas, Temporis filia*, was exhorted in prose and
rhyme to "restore the truth in error's place" and "break
superstition's head," and was given an English Bible which
she fervently kissed and laid upon her breast.[1] The establishment of truth was not in her mind consistent with the elevation
of the host or the rejection of the vernacular in the words of
consecration. But she could not persuade, and in face of the
law she could not compel, any bishop to comply with these
conditions; and accordingly, when the mass began, Elizabeth
withdrew to her "traverse," or private room in the abbey.[2]
Some slight variations were, however, made in the ceremonial;
and these portended ecclesiastical changes to be enacted by
the parliament which had already been elected.

The official records of this election, which lasted from December 28 to January 23, are more imperfect than usual;
but the returns which exist show that about one-third
of the members who had sat in Mary's last parliament were
re-elected, and that the change in *personnel* was less than
it had been in January, 1558. Such documentary evidence as
survives to indicate crown interference on previous occasions
is entirely lacking for the first of Elizabeth's parliaments; and
the vague statements made in later years by theological
controversialists and repeated by modern historians, that this
house of commons was an assembly of crown nominees, break
down in every case in which it has been possible to test them
by reference to documentary sources.[3] It was not until
later that Elizabeth extended parliamentary representation to
six new boroughs in Cornwall and eight new boroughs in
Hampshire. Two Lancashire boroughs, Clitheroe and New-
ton, and one, Sudbury, in Suffolk, appear to have been the
only new constituencies in 1559. Feria, however, lamented
that Elizabeth had "entire disposal of the upper chamber in
a way never before seen in previous parliaments," and spoke

[1] *Tudor Tracts*, pp. 376, 380, 383, 391.
[2] The three extant accounts of the coronation are printed and discussed in the
English Hist. Rev., xxii., 650-73, xxiii., 87-91, 533-34, xxiv., 322-23, xxv., 125-26.
They are conflicting and often obscure, and doubt has been increased by omissions
and mistranslations in the *Venetian* and *Spanish Calendars*.
[3] *Engl. Hist. Rev.*, xxiii., 455-76, 643-82.

of the " great number whom she had made barons to strengthen her party ".[1]   The remark provides a useful test of his veracity in such matters; the "great number" consisted of three peers who were created, Howard of Bindon, Hunsdon, and St. John of Bletso, and two who were restored, the Marquis of Northampton and Protector Somerset's son, the Earl of Hertford.

Of the bishops, Tunstall was excused attendance on account of his age, and Goldwell, who was in the process of translation from St. Asaph to Oxford, complained of not being summoned ; on the other hand, White of Winchester was released from his easy confinement in time to take his seat in the house of lords.[2] Death and " the accursed cardinal," as Feria termed Pole, had done more than Elizabeth to thin the hostile ranks. Six (Feria says twelve) sees had been left vacant at Mary's death ; Pole himself and three other bishops (Bristol, Chichester, and Rochester) died before the year was out. The spiritual peers, who numbered twenty-eight, including the Abbot of Westminster and the prior of the Knights of St. John, were thus reduced to eighteen ; and only eleven were actually present. The use of proxies was a readier method of influencing votes in the upper house; and Mary, when licensing a peer to be absent, selected for him the proxies to whom his vote should be entrusted.[3] But Elizabeth made no improper use of this weapon, if she used it at all. At any rate, Heath was entrusted, either solely or jointly, with the proxies of all the absent bishops, and his co-trustees were Bonner, Watson, Scot, Bayne, and David Pole ; while the trimmers, Oglethorpe and Kitchin, were given none. The only proxy disallowed was that of Tresham, Prior of St. John's, whose spiritual peerage was disputed. Of temporal proxies, Bedford held fifteen, but others were held by catholics like Montague.[4]

Parliament opened on January 25 for one of the most critical sessions in its history. The ceremony was marked, like the coronation, by incidents in which the queen advertised her antipathy to catholic ritual. " Away with those torches ! " she cried, as the abbot and monks of Westminster met her in broad daylight with tapers burning: " we

---

[1] *Spanish Cal.*, i., 32.   [2] *Acts of the P. C.*, 1558-70, p. 45.
[3] Lodge, *Illustrations*, i., 252-53.   [4] D'Ewes, *Journals*, pp. 5-8.

can see well enough." [1] The litany was sung in English, and CHAP.
the host was not elevated at the mass. But a fortnight was   XI.
spent on other business before the crucial questions of ecclesiastical supremacy and uniformity were formally broached in
either house. A commons' committee reported in favour of
the validity of Mary's parliaments in spite of the omission of
the title " supreme head " from the writs of summons ; tunnage
and poundage were voted to the queen for life ; two tenths
and fifteenths were granted ; a petition that she would marry
within the realm was presented and answered to the satisfaction of the commons ; and the omnicompetence of parliament
was implicitly asserted by a bill which declared her the rightful inheritor of the throne without annulling her mother's
divorce or repealing her attainder. She was queen by act of
parliament and by her people's will.

Then, on February 9, after some preliminary discussion,[2]
a measure called "the Supremacy Bill" was introduced into
the house of commons. It was debated the whole of Monday
the 13th and Tuesday the 14th ; on Wednesday after being
committed to Sir Francis Knollys and Sir Anthony Cooke
it disappeared from view. Why it disappeared or how it
differed from the new bill introduced into the house of commons six days later, are questions upon which the extant
evidence throws no light.[3] Its fate was in all probability
linked with that of a " bill for the order of service and ministers
in the church," which was introduced on the 15th, was discussed
on the 16th as " the book for Common Prayer and ministration
of Sacraments," and then disappeared. It had apparently oc-
curred to some one that the best way to get the Book of
Common Prayer through the house of lords was to tack it
on to the royal supremacy, and that this could be done by
adding to that bill clauses, provisoes, or schedules annulling
Queen Mary's repeal of Edward VI.'s acts of uniformity.

This composite bill seemingly encountered little opposition

---

[1] *Venetian Cal.,* vii., 23.

[2] Il Schifanoya writes on Feb. 6 that there had been great talk in the lower
house about giving the queen the title of supreme head (*ibid.,* p. 26) ; probably it was in connexion with the committee on the validity of writs which
did not contain this title, as another letter says " it was debated incidentally "
(*ibid.,* p. 28).

[3] The only contemporary comment on this debate is in *Venetian Cal.,* vii.,
30-31.

in the commons. It was read a second time on the 22nd, and a third time on Saturday the 25th. On Monday it was introduced into the house of lords, and read a first time on the 28th. Then there was a fortnight's interval. The convocation of Canterbury had afforded food for thought: on the 28th it had passed, apparently without dissent, a series of articles affirming the doctrine of transubstantiation, the sacrificial character of the mass, the supremacy of Rome, and the incompetence of the laity to deal with the faith, sacraments, and discipline of the church. Bonner was president because the primacy was vacant; and he delivered this challenge to the crown and parliament of England.

In the house of lords the opposition was led by the more persuasive and acceptable person of Heath, who admitted in the second reading debate on March 13 that, were it merely a question of withdrawing obedience from Paul IV., a "very austere stern father unto us," the matter would be of comparative unimportance. But, confining himself "to the body of the act, touching the supremacy" and leaving it to others to discuss the repealing schedules, he contended that the words of the bill declaring the sovereign to be " supreme head of the church of England, immediate and next under God," involved a repudiation of the first four general councils, of canonical and ecclesiastical law, and of the "judgment of all Christian princes," as well as a breach with the unity of Christ's church.[1] The speech was brief, moderate, and effective; and the committee, to which the bill was thereupon referred, was distinctly conservative in composition. It consisted of the Marquis of Winchester, the Duke of Norfolk, the Earls of Westmorland, Shrewsbury, Rutland, Sussex, and Pembroke, Viscount Montague, the Bishops of Exeter and Carlisle, and Lords Morley, Rich, Willoughby, and North. Its proceedings, testified Bishop Scot, gave great comfort to his party; the penalties for recusants were mitigated; the clauses reviving Edward VI.'s second act of uniformity and Book of Common Prayer and legalising the marriage of priests were deleted; and the assumption of the title "supreme head" was left at Elizabeth's option.[2] "By a majority of votes," wrote

---

[1] Heath's speech is printed from the Corpus Christi Coll., Cambridge, MS. in Strype, *Annals*, I., ii., 399-407.

[2] *Ibid.*, I., ii., 408-23; Kervyn, i., 470; *Spanish Cal.*, i., 38; *Venetian Cal.*, vii., 52.

Schifanoya, "they have decided that the aforesaid things shall
be expunged from the book, and the rest of the divine offices
shall be performed as hitherto;" and the commons, alarmed at
the lords' action, pushed through in two days, March 17-18,
a bill that no one should be punished for using the Prayer Book
of 1552.   But the lords' amendments were not sweeping
enough to satisfy the bishops; and Scot's speech [1] on the third
reading on March 18 was more uncompromising than Heath's
on the second.   There were, he said, thirty-four sects in
Christendom, all disagreeing with one another and with the
catholic church; the papal supremacy was the only safeguard
of the catholic faith; and he was at pains to expose the argument that, although the queen might not be supreme head
herself, she might delegate the functions to another.   All the
spiritual peers, except Watson, who was generally absent
through ill-health, voted against the bill, and they were reinforced by Shrewsbury and Montague; it was carried apparently
by thirty-two votes to twelve, and was sent down for the
commons to agree to the lords' amendments and additions.

The commons, however, were angry; they "would consent
to nothing," [2] and their mood is indicated by the entry in the
journals, "the bill for supremacy from the lords to be reformed"
(March 18).   It was reformed by the incorporation in it of the
substance of the bill hurried through the commons on March
17-18, and of something more.   For not only did the revised
bill, which passed its three readings on March 20-22, legalise
the Prayer Book of 1552; but it revived the act of uniformity
prohibiting any other service; and probably it deprived the
queen of any option in the matter of her title.   On the
day that the bill left the commons, the Wednesday before
Easter, it was read three times by the lords, who had obviously
been impressed by the temper of the lower house; the ten
spiritual peers repeated their vote against it, but they stood
alone.   A proclamation was drawn up on the same day, in
which Elizabeth stated that in the "present last session" of
parliament she had made a statute reviving the 1552 act of
uniformity, but that its length prevented it from being printed
before Easter; she therefore by the advice of sundry of her
nobility and commons "lately" assembled in parliament de-

---

[1] Printed in Strype, *Annals*, I., ii., 408-23.   [2] *Venetian Cal.*, vii., 52.

clared Edward's act to be in force.   The English people were
to have their Easter communion in both kinds.[1]

The phraseology of the proclamation and the haste of parliament indicate a belief that the session was at an end, that
on Thursday or Good Friday the queen would dissolve parliament, and that the Elizabethan settlement of religion was to
be a simple revival of the work of Henry VIII. and Edward
VI. without any modification.   " The heretics," reported
Feria, " have made a great point of having them [the acts]
confirmed before Easter."   But at the last moment Elizabeth
hesitated.   " She had resolved," wrote Feria on Good Friday,
" to go to Parliament to-day at 1 o'clock after dinner and
there, all being assembled, to confirm what they had agreed
to in the matters they have discussed." [2]   On Thursday
the lords had met, but had been adjourned till Monday
week ; on Good Friday the commons met and were adjourned to the same date.   " I do not know why," continued Feria, " but I see that the heretics are very downcast in
the last few days."   Feria's persuasions ; caution induced by
the marriage alliance between France and Spain and the
prospect of a papal declaration of bastardy ; doubts of the
validity of an act which professed to have been passed with
the assent of the lords spiritual but against which every
spiritual lord had voted ; or the admonitions of Lever, who
" wisely put such a scruple in the queen's head that she would
not take the title of supreme head," [3] had either individually
or by their cumulative force determined the government to
seek the path of compromise.   The queen told Feria that she
would not take the title " supreme head," and Philip urged
Paul IV. to stay his hand as there was still hope of her amendment.[4]   " She seriously maintains," wrote Jewel to Bullinger,
" that this honour is due to Christ alone, and cannot belong
to any human being soever ; besides which, these titles have

[1] Maitland in *Engl. Hist. Rev.*, xviii., 527.

[2] Kervyn, i., 481 ; *Spanish Cal.*, i., 44 ; the identification of Feria's " to-day "
with March 24, which was Good Friday, rests upon an endorsement, but later on,
ibid., p. 50, Feria confirms the statement that Good Friday was the date.

[3] *Parker Corresp.*, p. 66.

[4] *Spanish Cal.*, i., 61 ; *cf. Venetian Cal.*, vii., 72-73.   It should perhaps be noted
that Il Schifanoya, *Venetian Cal.*, vii., 57, attributes the delay to a conflict of
opinion between the two houses over the terms of the royal supremacy ; but his
evidence is not exact and cannot outweigh that of the *Journals* and Feria.

been so foully contaminated by Antichrist that they can no
longer be adopted by any one without impiety." [1]

The deadlock between the official representatives of the
spirituality and the temporality constituted a situation difficult
because of its absolute novelty. There was no precedent, as
Feria pointed out to Philip,[2] in the reigns of Henry VIII. and
Edward VI.; for then a majority of the spiritual peers had
voted for reform. Now both houses of convocation had unanimously rejected the proposals of parliament, and the bishops
had declared that without their consent the nation could not
move in matters of faith. On the other hand, the protestant
clergy complained loudly that there was no one to answer in
parliament the sophistries of their opponents. They were given
their chance at the Westminster disputation; it was opened
in the abbey on Friday, March 31, and continued, in the
presence of members of both houses which adjourned for
the purpose, on April 3. The bishops were not averse from
such a trial of faiths, and Feria congratulated himself on the
arrangements he had helped to make; for differences between
protestants on the mass usually played into the hands of the
catholics. But on this occasion the lists were drawn under
Bacon's astuter guidance. The bishops had challenged the right
of parliament to pass acts of supremacy and of ecclesiastical
uniformity; they were now required, or offered, to justify the
position adopted by convocation, and to defend (1) the use of
Latin in the services of the church, (2) their denial of the
authority of a " particular church" to change rites and ceremonies, and (3) the doctrine of the propitiatory sacrifice of the
mass. Confident in the justice and strength of their cause, they
had been manœuvred into the least popular, if not the least
tenable, of their positions. Even the Emperor Ferdinand had
abandoned the first two, to which national feeling in England
also was hostile; to the third all the thirty-four sects, of which
Bishop Scot had spoken, were opposed; and the bishops were
prohibited by the conditions of the debate from carrying war
into the enemies' country and sowing dissension among them.
The upshot, when the catholic champions understood these
conditions, was an angry and undignified scene,[3] in which all

[1] *Zurich Letters,* i., 33.   [2] *Spanish Cal.,* i., 68.
[3] There is naturally some inconsistency between the catholic account given
by Il Schifanoya, *Venetian Cal.,* vii., 64-66, and the protestant account given by

of them except Abbot Feckenham refused to submit to Bacon's rulings.   Bishops Watson and White were sent to the Tower for seditious behaviour ;[1] and the most definite result was that their party lost two votes on a critical division in the house of lords.

Both houses had reassembled on April 3, and on the 10th the new bill of supremacy was ready for presentation to the commons.   The government had determined not only to drop the title "supreme head," but to treat supremacy and uni- formity as separate questions.   It was clearly more straight- forward to establish uniformity and enforce a book of common prayer by separate enactment than by means of a schedule in an act of supremacy repealing a repeal of Edward's act. But, however much Elizabeth may have eased the diplomatic situation by withholding her assent to the bills passed before Easter, she assuredly did not improve her parliamentary posi- tion.   Peers who had accepted uniformity when it was em- bedded in the royal supremacy, voted against it by itself ; and no convert to the royal supremacy, except Shrewsbury, was secured by its divorce from uniformity.   It might have been thought that the government was doubtful about the success of the uniformity bill and wanted to make sure of the royal supremacy, had not both bills passed the two houses before Easter.   The concessions may have reconciled some conserva- tive opinion outside parliament ; inside they gave the bishops an opportunity of nearly wrecking the act of uniformity.

The commons received Cecil's announcement of the gov- ernment's policy on April 10 in no good humour.   They thought they ought to be at home, and special measures were taken to deal with absentees ; and they wanted to know what Cecil meant by " coming to them every day with new proposals and objections ".[2]   But, however firmly they might believe that the royal supremacy belonged, as they told Cecil, to the crown by right divine, they could not compel the queen to assume

---

Jewel, *Zurich Letters*, i., 13-16; the official account is in State Papers, Dom., Eliz., iii., 52.

[1] *Acts of the P. C.*, 1558-70, p. 78; the other catholic disputants, Bayne, Bishop of Lichfield and Coventry, Scot, Bishop of Chester, Oglethorpe of Carlisle, and Drs. Cole, John Harpsfield, and Chedsey were also bound over in heavy recognizances.

[2] *Spanish Cal.*, i., 52 ; Kervyn, i., 497-98.

a title against her will ; and they passed the new bill creating her merely " supreme governor " in four days (April 10-13) without once dividing on the question.   In the lords, where it was introduced on the 14th, read a first time on the 15th and a second on the 17th, Heath again led the opposition ; and the bill was referred to a committee similar in composition to that of March.[1]   Its members set to work in the same spirit ; they had no clauses reviving Edward's uniformity act to strike out,[2] but they modified some of the penalties, introduced some guarantees for the protection of those who might be accused under the act, and met Heath's earlier criticism about the repudiation of the first four general councils, by acknowledging their authority in matters of faith.[3]   The bill was more than a week in committee ; on the 26th it passed its third reading, ten spiritual peers, as in March, together with Montague, voting in the minority.   Watson and White were still in the Tower, but Thirlby had come from Cambray, and Goldwell, although his translation is said never to have been completed, was allowed to vote as Bishop of Oxford.   The commons accepted the lords' amendments, but added a new proviso of their own on the 27th ; and in this form it finally passed the lords two days later.

On the 26th the lords took the first reading of the new bill of uniformity, which had passed quickly in three days (April 18-20) through the house of commons, the catholics being too weak to challenge a division at any stage.   Its course was equally rapid (April 26-28) in the lords, who dispensed with a committee.   But this speed was not due to unanimity :

[1] Norfolk, Worcester (instead of Winchester), Arundel (instead of Westmorland), Shrewsbury, Rutland, Sussex, Bedford (instead of Pembroke), Montague, Thirlby (instead of Turberville), Oglethorpe, Clinton, Howard (instead of Morley), Rich, Hastings of Loughborough (instead of Willoughby), and St. John of Bletso (instead of North).

[2] It is just possible, but very improbable, that the two lines deleted in § iv. revived the act of 1552; in that case the history of this part of the session would have to be recast.   Scot's speech (see p. 203) might be referred to April instead of March, and on this assumption the government on April 10 reintroduced the supremacy bill embodying also Edward's uniformity act ; and when this was cut out by the lords, were prepared with Elizabeth's act of uniformity, which was introduced in the commons on April 18.   This would obviate the difficulty of understanding the government's action in separating supremacy and uniformity, but it creates other serious difficulties.

[3] Maitland in *Engl. Hist. Rev.*, xviii., 519-23.

Thirlby spoke " like a good catholic and said he would die rather than consent to a change of religion ". Bishop Scot made an earnest appeal to the lords to reject the bill. " Take heed, my lords," he cried, quoting the case of Jeroboam who sinned himself and made Israel to sin, " that the like be not said by you ; if you pass this bill, you shall not only, in my judgment, err yourselves, but ye also shall be the authors and causers that the whole realm shall err after you. For the which you shall make an accompt before God." [1] Eighteen peers, nine spiritual and nine temporal, including Elizabeth's lord high treasurer, her president of the council of the north (Shrewsbury), and her warden of the marches (Wharton), voted against the bill ; twenty-one, all temporal, voted in its favour ; four spiritual peers, Watson, White, Goldwell, and Abbot Feckenham, who would certainly have turned the scale, were prevented by accident or by design from taking part in the division. By so dubious and slender a majority, it seems, did the Elizabethan settlement escape shipwreck. But the proxies, if exercised, would have increased the majority ; and, if they had failed, a conference between the two houses would probably have met the difficulty, as it did a similar deadlock in 1529.

Supremacy and uniformity, however, occupied less of the time of parliament, which was dissolved on May 8, than the scramble for episcopal lands, on which in one form or another the commons spent twenty-four days of the session. The question was mainly one of the validity of the grants and leases made by Edwardine bishops appointed on the depriva- tion of catholic predecessors. But this involved the larger issue of the legality of those deprivations and appointments ; led to lengthy discussions during which several bishops were heard in person or by counsel ; and provoked numerous legislative proposals for the confirmation of leases and grants and the restoration of bishops and incumbents deprived for heresy or for marriage under Mary. One bold catholic, or more probably an anxious lessee, introduced a bill to confirm Bonner in his bishopric.[2] This did not go further than its first reading, but parliament generally took a conservative line, except where the interests of lay grantees were concerned. The deprived

---

[1] Strype, *Annals*, I., ii., 448.   [2] *Commons' Journals*, March 2.

Edwardine bishops and clergy were not restored by statute, and the lords threw out a bill to confirm Ridley's leases; but they passed others to legalise his grants to Lords Wentworth, Darcy, and Rich, as well as those which had been made out of the lands of the bishopric of Winchester. Similar claims on the lands of Worcester and Lichfield and Coventry failed; but an act was passed enabling the queen to appropriate the temporalities of sees as they fell vacant, and to compensate the incoming bishop out of the livings which, having been restored to the church by Mary, were now regranted to Elizabeth. First-fruits and tenths were likewise bestowed again on the crown; and the religious houses and the order of St. John, re-founded by Mary, were dissolved and their lands confiscated. The taint of secularisation pervaded the Elizabethan settlement less than it did the movement under Henry VIII. and Edward VI., only because there was less left to secularise. Temporal peers who voted against the act of uniformity, voted for the confirmation of their own ecclesiastical spoils, and took care that the tests imposed on catholic priests should not extend to catholic patrons. Cecil professed to be averse from spolia-tion, but justified it on the ground that, had the church been left its wealth, it would also have retained the victory.

The victory of the state impressed contemporaries more than any other aspect of the Elizabethan settlement. It has been said that the supreme achievement of the reformation is the modern state.[1] It is characteristic of epigrams that their parts are often interchangeable, and it would be equally true to say that the reformation was the supreme achievement of the sixteenth century state. In either case it should be re-membered that the antithesis between state and church was less pronounced than now; every member of the state was a member of the church, and nothing so violent was contem-plated as the control of a church by a state whose rulers might be outside the pale of the church. It was merely an internal question whether the laity or the clergy should be the dominant force; and it would involve less misapprehension if for the state we read the laity, and for the church the clergy. On the other hand, the antithesis between laity and clergy was

---

[1] *Cambridge Mod. Hist.*, iii., 736.

sharper than at present, and it was accentuated by the fact that the clergy were organised on an œcumenical and the laity on a national basis. The medieval idea of a catholic church conflicted with the modern idea of nationality. The fundamental contention underlying the Elizabethan settlement was that a national church had the right to determine its own faith, ritual, and organisation; but inasmuch as the church in England, represented by the Marian bishops and clergy, denied this right and refused this task, they were assumed by the laity who thus asserted a novel claim to predominance.

This claim was not pressed in the English church to the extremes to which it was carried elsewhere. Spiritual powers were not derived from congregations or mixed assemblies of presbyters and elders, but from apostolical succession. Parliament did not pretend to define the faith; even coercive jurisdiction was left to a large extent in the hands of the bishops and their officials; and common law judges admitted that the court of high commission could imprison for heresy. But it did so only in virtue of a commission from the crown, and not in virtue of episcopal authority. The church retained its functions, but their limits were determined by parliament, and the old contention of Henry II. that for the sake of unity there must be some sovereign authority to settle the spheres of rival jurisdictions was asserted in various ways. The clergy could still tax themselves in convocation; but before any clerk could be made to pay, the clerical grant must be embodied in a parliamentary statute. Chapters could elect their bishops, but they must elect the royal nominees. Convocation could define new heresies,[1] but before any offender against the new definition could be punished, it must receive the sanction of parliament. The church could make new canons with the royal consent, but they were only binding *in foro conscientiae* unless they received parliamentary sanction. The Book of Common Prayer was a schedule of the act of uniformity; its use was enforced by parliament, and without parliamentary authorisation not a syllable in it could be altered.

---

[1] This is putting the case most favourably for the church. The act 1 Eliz., c. 1, sect. 20, refers to "such as hereafter shall be ordered, judged or determined to be heresy by the High Court of Parliament of this realm with the assent of the clergy in their convocation". Even in matters of faith the enacting authority is parliament, the assenting authority convocation.

Authorisation and authorship are, however, different things. Neither, as regards the Book of Common Prayer, can be attributed to the convocation of 1559.[1] After its ineffectual protest against all change it did nothing. But it would be unsafe to affirm that parliament was the author of even the few alterations made in 1559 in the Prayer Book of 1552. That book was undeniably the work of divines though not of convocation, and the only changes specifically made by the act of 1559 were " one alteration or addition of certain lessons to be used on every Sunday in the year, and the form of the litany altered and corrected, and two sentences only added in the delivery of the Sacrament to the communicants ".[2] The correction of the litany consisted in the omission of the petition to be delivered from the Bishop of Rome and all his detestable enormities. The two sentences added to the communion service enabled Elizabeth to represent it to the German princes, whose aid she was seeking, as being Lutheran rather than Zwinglian ; while no legislative action was considered necessary in order to eliminate the " black rubric " which had never received statutory authorisation. An unlucky thirteenth [3] clause provided " that such ornaments of the church and of the ministers thereof shall be retained and be in use, as was in this church of England, by authority of parliament, in the second year of the reign of King Edward the Sixth until other order shall be therein taken ". The authors of this revision may have been the seven divines convened by Sir Thomas Smith who had been a priest himself; but parliament did not consider itself precluded from meddling with such matters. During the course of its debates a member was forced to apologise for having reported that Sir Ambrose Cave disliked the book, whereas Sir Ambrose had only said that he wished it to be well considered ;[4] and John à Lasco criticised it as the outcome of " parliamentary theology ".[5]

Clear-cut definitions of the relations between church and state are, in fact, as little to be expected in English acts of parliament as declarations of the rights of man ; and the inconsistencies of the statutes of 1559 provide a fruitful field for

---

[1] *Engl. Hist. Rev.*, xvi., 376-78.   [2] 1 Eliz., c. 2, sect. 2.
[3] Not 25th, as printed in *Stat. at Large.*   [4] *Commons' Journals*, March 4.
[5] *Foreign Cal.*, 1558-59, No. 1304.

the ingenuity of theorists of various schools.   Immense trouble was taken to substitute supreme governor for supreme head in the act of supremacy; yet the same act expressly revived a statute (37 Henry VIII., c. 17) in which it was declared that the king's "most royal majesty is and hath always been, by the word of God, supreme head in earth of the Church of England, and hath full power and authority to correct, punish, and repress all manner of heresies . . . and to exercise all other manner of jurisdiction commonly called ecclesiastical jurisdiction ".   A divine right like this could not be abolished by act of parliament, and it was suspected that if Elizabeth married, her husband would have the headship from which she was debarred by her sex.[1]   Whatever title she might bear, she was undisputed sovereign over church and state alike, and Quadra ridiculed the distinction between governor and head, just as Chapuys in 1532 had gibed at the saving clause, " as far as the law of Christ permits ".[2]   A recurrence of the medieval conflicts between church and state was eliminated from the range of political possibilities, and England grasped the practical bearings of the indivisibility of sovereignty, which had been Henry VIII.'s chief contribution to the body of modern constitutional law and theory.

Fortunately Elizabeth exercised a wise discretion in her application of this theory.   She delegated ecclesiastical power so liberally to those who had wielded it of old that it almost seemed as though they exercised it in virtue of the ancient derivation.   The old order continued under somewhat changed conditions, and she no more established the English church than she did the English state.   Its reformation proceeded from other causes than her will, but the Tudor monarchy exerted a powerful influence upon the form it took.   No church would of its own motion have devised a royal supremacy, a state-controlled convocation, and a royally-nominated episcopate.   Nor did any considerable section of the English people regard the doctrinal settlement as ideal.   The anti-papal catholics of Henry's reign had either become protestants under Edward or papists under Mary.   One party would have gone

---

[1] *Spanish Cal.*, i., 69; *Letters and Papers of Henry VIII.*, v., 47.

[2] *Spanish Cal.*, i., 55; Kervyn, i., 501.   Spanish ambassadors habitually term Elizabeth " supreme head " and not " supreme governor ".

much farther than Elizabeth in 1559, the other would not willingly have moved at all. Against the clergy who were conscientious enough to refuse to abjure the papacy must be set the
protestants who were conscientious enough to go into exile under
Mary. At Strassburg, Frankfort, and Geneva they had set
up a doctrinal standard compared with which the Prayer Book
of 1552 was conservative; and even Coxe, who fought with
Knox at Frankfort, was almost a puritan. Knox himself expressed his deep repugnance to the settlement of 1559, and
denounced Cecil's carnal wisdom and worldly policy.[1] The
Zwinglian Duchess of Suffolk was as dissatisfied as the
Calvinist Knox: "how long halt ye between two opinions?"
she wrote, "Christ's plain coat without seam is fairer to the
clear-eyed than all the jaggs of Germany. This I say for that
it is also said here that certain Duchers [Germans] should
commend to us the Confession of Augsburg, as they did to
the Poles."[2] The princes of Sweden, Denmark, and Würtemberg were all sounding its praises to Elizabeth, and unwilling
testimony to its advantages was borne by catholic sovereigns.
"The emperor and the king of Spain say that since England
is not to have the religion of the pope, they do not care about
it, so long as no other doctrine than the Augsburg Confession
is introduced. If any other doctrine be adopted, these two
persons will be her chief enemies. They will help the pope
and the king of France against her. . . . On the other hand,
if she accept the Confession of Augsburg, the emperor and the
king of Spain will not make war against her on this account."[3]

Lutheranism, purged of its earlier revolutionary elements,
had at the peace of Augsburg (1555) been received into the
communion of princes; it was a legal religion in the Holy
Roman empire and practically immune from attack by the
Roman pope; thenceforth it left the burden and heat of the
struggle with Rome to sterner Calvinistic stuff. When Elizabeth was excommunicated in 1570, it was as a partaker " in the
atrocious mysteries of Calvinism". Had the fear of Rome
been before her eyes in 1559, she would have sheltered behind the Augsburg defences. Indeed she often sought that
cover, and found the modifications of Edward's religion,
whoever made them, very useful. Il Schifanoya, moreover,

---

[1] *Foreign Cal.*, 1558-59, Nos. 504, 514.   [2] *Ibid.*, No. 379.   [3] *Ibid.*, No. 297.

CHAP.
XI.

avers that the English "with regard to religion live in all respects after the Lutheran fashion".[1] But Luther had really
few disciples in England; Cranmer had passed through a
Lutheran phase only on his way towards Zwinglian Zürich;
and Bullinger, Zwingli's successor, and Calvin and Beza were
the oracles of the Elizabethan reformers. Bullinger approved of
the Elizabethan settlement and defended it before the world;
while the Jesuit Sanders called it Calvinism,[2] and the creed of
Whitgift justified the name. Its advantages, if not its merits,
did not end here; when Bishop de Quadra was in 1562 pleading
the cause of the English catholics who bowed in the house of
Rimmon, he could say that the "common prayers" contained
no impiety or false doctrine, for they consisted of Scripture and
prayers taken from the catholic church; and English diplomatists asserted that the pope, who granted the use of the cup to
the German laity, was willing to sanction Elizabeth's Prayer
Book if she would acknowledge his supremacy.[3]

But Quadra's contention must stand side by side with his
earlier complaint that in England religion had become merely
a matter of politics,[4] in which he agreed with Knox; and
Elizabeth's settlement cannot really have been Lutheran,
Zwinglian, Calvinistic, and catholic. The extreme variety of
terms applied to Elizabeth's church arises from the difficulty of
naming a new party which professes to have no new principles. Appearances, too, were useful, especially for diplomatic
purposes: during the Anjou marriage negotiations in 1570
Walsingham contended that "divine service in England did
not properly compel any man to alter his opinion in the great
matters being now in controversy in the church";[5] and compromise, enforced by a strong and skilful government, averted
civil, and postponed external, war. But the test of public
action tells its tale. All Quadra's pleas failed to move Pius
IV.: if English catholics had to choose between going to these
"catholic" common-prayers and to the gallows, they must go
for conscience' sake to the gallows; and Quadra ventured no
plea for what other catholics called the "devilish supper".[6]

---

[1] *Venetian Cal.*, vii., 94.   [2] *Engl. Hist. Rev.*, xxiii., 461, *n.* 24.
[3] *Ibid.*, xv., 531; *Foreign Cal.*, 1569-71, p. 477.
[4] *Spanish Cal.*, i., 69; Brit. Mus. Add. MS. 26056.
[5] *Foreign Cal.*, 1569-71, p. 454.   [6] *Engl. Hist. Rev.*, vii., 85, xv., 532.

Whenever the England of Elizabeth interfered with religious CHAP.
wars abroad, she did so in favour of Calvinists; whenever she XI.
meddled with religious disputes in Germany, it was to protect
the disciples of Calvin and Zwingli against those of Luther;
and Pius V., who never dared to excommunicate Lutheran
princes, would not have excommunicated Elizabeth if she had
been a catholic by general repute.

Nor was there much doubt as to the theological position
of Elizabeth's new episcopate. The Marian bishops followed
up their parliamentary protest by refusing to take the oath
of supremacy. They could not afford to be less constant
than the humble folk who had perished at the stake in Mary's
reign, or admit that that blood had been spilt without a cause.
They were thus bound to the old faith by a new bond, and it
was well for the repute of English prelates that none was
found to submit except Kitchin of Llandaff who himself had
burnt no heretics. They do not perhaps reach the moral elevation of a Campion, but they stand on a higher plane than the
bishops of the previous generation; and they had something of
the spirit of the counter-reformation which was itself not the
least admirable of the products of the reformation. They were
all deprived gradually during the summer and autumn of 1559,
and Elizabeth had to find occupants for twenty-five sees. It
was not easy to do so by legal means. The desire to prove
the validity of Anglican orders to the satisfaction of Roman
catholic critics was a later development of theological controversy;[1] and the alleged defects in Edward's VI.'s Ordinal or in
Bishop Barlow's consecration caused little uneasiness. It was
a more serious objection that that Ordinal had not been revived by the recent parliament. Defects had to be supplied
from the plenitude of royal supremacy, and Elizabeth added a
" supplentes " clause to the commission for Parker's confirmation and consecration to remove any objections that might be
raised against the four consecrators, Barlow, Scory, Coverdale,
and Hodgkins, on the grounds of their deprivation under Mary
and of the illegality of the Ordinal they followed. Parker's
election as Archbishop of Canterbury, which had taken place

[1] The literature on this subject is enormous; see for example Dixon, *Hist. of
the Church*, v., 198-248 (1902), and H. N. Birt, *Elizabethan Settlement* (1907), pp.
241-52, and the authorities there cited.

CHAP.
XI.
on August 1, was confirmed on December 9, and he was consecrated at Lambeth on the 17th.[1]

Parker had been chaplain to Henry VIII. and Anne Boleyn; but the highest preferment he had held was the deanery of Lincoln, which he lost on Mary's accession owing to his marriage and support of Lady Jane Grey.   He was not inspiring as a leader of religion; no dogma, no original theory of church government, no prayer-book, not even a tract or a hymn is associated with his name.   The fifty-six volumes published by the Parker Society contain only one by its eponymous hero, and that is a volume of correspondence.   There was nothing heroic about him; he did not care to figure at the stake, and he found means of living quietly in England throughout Mary's reign, pursuing his studies and biding his time.[2]   He was the ecclesiastical counterpart of Cecil, and he fulfilled every condition Elizabeth wanted in an archbishop except that of celibacy.   He had respected national authority even under Mary, and he could now consistently make it respected by others.   He was a disciplinarian, a scholar, a modest and moderate man of genuine piety and irreproachable morals.   He was sharply distinguished from his puritanical brethren by his love for medieval antiquities and his encouragement of historical scholarship.   His *De Antiquitate Ecclesiæ* is the fruit of an erudition better known through his editions of Asser, Matthew Paris, Walsingham, and the compiler known as Matthew of Westminster; his liturgical skill was shown in his version of the psalter and in the occasional prayers and thanksgivings which he was called upon to compose; and he left a priceless collection of manuscripts to his college at Cambridge.[3]   He reverenced monarchy, he loved decency and order, and nothing shocked him so much as violent enthusiasm.   He was not consumed by the consciousness of a mission to reform the world or the church; and it required much pressure to move him from the attitude of *nolo episcopari*

---

[1] The story of his indecent consecration at the Nag's Head tavern in Cheapside, which was first published by the Jesuit, Christopher Holywood, in his *De investiganda vera et visibili Christi ecclesia libellus*, Antwerp, 1604, has been abandoned by reputable controversialists.

[2] See his autobiographical notes in *Parker Corresp.*, pp. 481-84.

[3] See Strype's *Life of Parker;* Nasmith, *Cat. Libr. MSS. C.C. Coll., Cantabr.*, 1777; J. Bass Mullinger in *Dict. of Nat. Biogr.*, xliii., 254-64; M. R. James in *Cambr. Antiq. Soc.*, 1899; and W. M. Kennedy, *Life of Parker*, 1908.

recommended by the difficulties and dangers of an episcopal career.

With Parker seated at length in the chair of St. Augustine, it was comparatively easy to fill up the other bishoprics. Barlow was sent to Chichester, and another of Henry's bishops, Kitchin, was left in possession of Llandaff. Of Edward's bishops, Scory was given Hereford, Coverdale refused promotion, and the two suffragans, Hodgkins and Salisbury, were not apparently offered it. William May, formerly Dean of St. Paul's, was appointed to York ; and of the other new bishops, the most notable were Jewel of Salisbury, Coxe of Ely, Grindal of London, Parkhurst of Norwich, Horne of Winchester, Sandys of Worcester, and Pilkington of Durham. They were nearly all Marian exiles who had come back with a Zwinglian cast in their doctrine; they regretted the cross and candles in Elizabeth's chapel, and the relics of what they called popery in the services of the church ; and they were anxious for sterner methods than Elizabeth would permit for the eradication of catholicism in their dioceses. Their path had been prepared by a visitation, carried out mainly by laymen, to administer the oath of supremacy and enforce the Book of Common Prayer when it came into operation at midsummer, 1559. The articles and injunctions were based on those of 1547 ; but a judicious proclamation tempered the wind to the tender conscience, and whittled down almost to nothing the change against which all the bishops, supported by a unanimous convocation, had fought for three months in parliament. It was not a statesman's part to advertise the revolutionary character of a religious settlement imposed upon the clergy by the secular arm. The visitors also stretched the statutes several points, and elastic uniformity minimised dissent. Cathedral chapters were more obdurate than the parochial clergy, and more recusants were found in the north and north-west than in the east, the midlands, and the south. Against the bold assertion that Hampshire was catholic to the core [1] may be set the fact that more constituencies were created there than anywhere else in Elizabeth's reign. Camden put the total number of recusant clergy at 177 ; this errs perhaps nearly as far on one side as a modern estimate of 2,000 does on the other.[2] If we assume that one-

[1] Birt, p. 424. [2] *Ibid.*, p. 203.

eighth of the 8,000 beneficed clergy in England lost their preferments, and spread their ejection over a number of years, we shall still be puzzled to explain where they went. They certainly did not go to English prisons, and there is no evidence to suggest the presence of such a crowd of exiles in foreign parts. Even this proportion is no guide to the sentiments of the nation at large; for the clergy, and to some extent the holders of temporal offices, to whom alone the oath was administered, were the papal guard selected by Mary as the staunchest antagonists of change. We must count the returning as well as the departing exiles of 1559, and those deprived on account of the surplice as well as for the supremacy; and Elizabeth's persecution, which is said to have nearly stamped out Roman catholicism, failed to crush the puritans, who must therefore have been either more numerous or more conscientious.

The settlement was not more popular than other compromises, but it evoked less active resistance than any other great religious change, and was accompanied by less persecution. In the early years of Elizabeth's rule there was some justification for her boast that she made no windows into men's souls. There was no liberty of worship, but there was no inquisition. The deprived bishops were placed under restraint, but they were seldom sent to the Tower and never to the block; no execution for religion stained the first seventeen years of the reign. To keep Bonner alive was no slight victory for the new government over its own and its subjects' passions; and, whether Englishmen looked to their own immediate past or to the present around them, they had good reason to congratulate themselves that they lived under Elizabeth's laws, and not under those of Henry VIII. or Mary, of Philip II. of Spain or of Henry II. of France.

CHAPTER XII.

ENGLAND AND SCOTLAND.

THE ecclesiastical settlement, which had been effected by the
parliament of 1559 with little physical violence and without
forcible intervention from abroad, depended for its permanence
upon other considerations than its doctrinal orthodoxy. It
is not possible to isolate men's religious from their other
feelings, or so completely to divorce the church from the
world as to render the fortunes of the faith independent of
secular influence; and when an ecclesiastical compromise has
been moulded under the stress of political expediency, its
stability is in no slight degree involved in the strength or weakness, the competence or incompetence of the government responsible for its terms. The history of the church in England
would have been different if Mary had been as competent
as Elizabeth, or Elizabeth as incompetent as Mary; if the
political conditions of France, of the Netherlands, and of Scotland had been sound; if there had been any substantial truth
in the warnings which Feria and Quadra impressed upon the
queen, or any real ground for the fears which haunted Englishmen with the old faith in the church but without the new faith
in the nation.

The Spaniards naturally looked with jaundiced eyes upon
the revolution. Feria had been accustomed to convey the
orders of a master under the tones of a diplomatist; he was
now ignored and hoodwinked. He told Elizabeth that she
could not stand alone, while Paget prophesied that France
and Spain would "make a Piedmont" of England,[1] the
independent cockpit of their secular ambitions. The future
seemed as sombre to the Spaniard as to the Englishman:
France would assert what Feria as early as April, 1559, called

---

[1] *Hatfield MSS.*, i., 151.

the "just claims" of Mary Stuart; the pope would excommunicate and depose Elizabeth and bless the French crusade; the
majority of the English would rise in rebellion; England would
become part of a Valois-Stuart-Guise empire, stretching from
the Alps to the farthest Hebrides; and this, he wrote to Philip,
" would be the total ruin of your Majesty and all your states ".[1]
Elizabeth and Cecil played on these fears with consummate
skill.   They knew that neither France nor Spain could allow
the other to interfere in England even on behalf of the catholic
faith; and while parliament was completing the breach with
catholicism, Philip was secretly impressing upon Feria the absolute necessity of smoothing down matters as much as possible
and avoiding at all costs a rupture between the two religious
parties.   He was as anxious as the queen herself for ecclesiastical unity, if not uniformity, in England.   Neither party
was to be given the slightest excuse for appealing to France
for aid; Elizabeth was to be assured that Philip was not in the
least offended at her rejection of his hand; and a manuscript
of Pole's was to be suppressed, lest its publication should
wound her feelings.[2]

Elizabeth wisely sought more substantial guarantees for
England's security than the favour of foreign princes.   She
was not insensible to the advantages of their good-will; and
for nearly a year she dangled her hand before the eyes of the
emperor's younger son, the Archduke Charles, as an antidote
to Philip's marriage with Elizabeth of France and the dauphin's
with Mary Stuart.   But she set greater store on the goodwill of her people, on their reviving confidence, and on the
material strengthening of her realm.   Skilled Italian engineers
were employed on the decrepit defences of Berwick; a few pensions were judiciously bestowed on protestant German princes,
mainly to make them incline a willing ear to Elizabeth's requests for troops; friendly relations were developed with Sweden, Denmark, and Holstein, although Elizabeth had to decline
the various proposals of marriage which emanated thence; and
measures were taken to arm the English themselves.   Partly
owing to the disapproval of the government, which after
the rebellions of Edward's and Mary's reigns had viewed an

[1] *Spanish Cal.*, i., 51.   [2] *Ibid.*, i., 40-42.

armed people with distrust, and partly to the obsolescence of CHAP.
the favourite English weapon, the long-bow, the defensive force   XII.
of the realm had sunk to a depth which accounts for some
of the despondency of 1558. Legislative and other efforts to
revive archery and repress the use of hand-guns had failed,
and although a soldier could as late as 1596 write jeremiads
over England's preference of gun to bow,[1] the new weapons
forced their way. " Our countrymen," wrote William Harrison
in 1576, " wax skilful in sundry other points, as in shooting
in small pieces, the caliver, and handling of the pike; in
the several uses whereof they are become very expert."
Every town and village, he avers, had its convenient furniture
of armour and munition to " set forth three or four soldiers
(as one archer, one gunner, one pike, and a bill-man) at the
least"; and " seldom shall you see any of my countrymen,
above eighteen or twenty years old, to go without a dagger, at
the least, at his back or by his side ".[2] The distrust had passed
away ; and the queen in 1559 " sent a muster-master at her own
charge into every county to train the people ".[3] Instead of remaining dependent upon the Netherlands for powder, England
took to making its own ; and its ordnance factories developed
until in 1580 Roger Bodenham lamented to see "all nations
furnished with ordnance from England. We shall find the
smart of it if we brave any of them to enemies." In ship-
building England was soon supreme. The King of Denmark,
wrote a bluff English sailor in 1582, " has English ship-wrights
that build him goodly ships and galleys after the English
mould and fashion. I would they were hanged." [4]

Confidence was restored in other ways. " As for money,"
wrote Noailles at the end of 1559, " since her accession the
queen has been scraping it together from all sides, paying
nothing and giving nothing to her people, and spending
very little. She . . . has paid off large debts which Mary con-
tracted in Antwerp." The currency was gradually placed on
a sounder footing. The issue of base coin was stopped at

---

[1] Sir H. Knyvett, *Defence of the Realme*, ed. 1906.
[2] Harrison's *Description of England*, in *Tudor Tracts*, pp. 397-99; *cf. Foreign
Cal.*, 1559-60, pp. 309-10.
[3] State Papers, Dom., Addenda, ix., 91.
[4] *Foreign Cal.*, 1579-80, p. 286; 1581-82, p. 649. The commons passed a
bill in 1601 prohibiting the export of ordnance, but it went no farther.

once, and in September, 1560, it was determined to call in all
the inferior coinage minted since 1543 ; the nominal value had
been called down by proclamation to something like its real
value, and Elizabeth was actually able to make a slight profit
out of the substitution of a sound for an unsound currency.[1]
Sir Thomas Gresham, the ablest financier of the age, was sent
to retrieve England's position on the Bourse at Antwerp; and
sixteen months after Elizabeth's accession he was able to report that her honour and credit were so augmented that no
prince had the like.[2]   On the same day Throckmorton wrote
from France that she had gained such reputation that she
was more dreaded and esteemed abroad than her sister was
with all her great marriage and alliance.   She could now
borrow money at 10 instead of 14 per cent.[3]

But Scotland was the key-stone of the arch of England's
safety.   Confident as England was of her ability to hold her
own upon the sea, she shuddered at the danger of a French
attack upon her frontier on the land, where catholic and feudal
forces afforded favourable ground for an invasion.   The French
harboured designs on Hartlepool, wrote Norfolk, and "hoped
to make York the bounds of England".[4]   The state of religion
distressed Horne, the restored Dean of Durham ; and Knox, who
combined a statesman's instincts with evangelical zeal, in vain
sought permission from Elizabeth to proselytise within the
English borders.[5]   The wardens and magnates of the marches,
Wharton, Northumberland, Westmorland, and Dacres, were
all devoted to the catholic faith and to their feudal franchises ;
and Elizabeth did not at first feel strong enough to act upon
the warnings she received and remove them from their offices.
At Cateau-Cambrésis it was suspected that the French had
relinquished their designs in Italy only to concentrate their
energies upon the British Isles ; and Frenchmen themselves declared that their marriage alliance with Philip II. was designed
to lull him to sleep, while they prosecuted their enterprise
against his sister-in-law.[6]   Henry II. had not been deterred

[1] *Hatfield MSS.*, i., 151, 155 ; State Papers, Dom., xi., 6, xiii., 27, 48, etc.;
Ruding, *Annals of the Coinage*, i., 333-343.
[2] *Foreign Cal.*, 1559-60, pp. 437, 441.   [3] *Ibid.*, p. 476.
[4] *Hatfield MSS.*, i., 225.   [5] *Foreign Cal.*, 1558-59, No. 1200.
[6] *Venetian Cal.*, vii., 72.

by the failure of his efforts to procure a papal sentence against
Elizabeth; and at the jousts where he received his death-
wound on June 30, 1559, the arms of England were quartered on his son's behalf with those of France and Scotland.

His death on July 10 clouded for the moment the prospects
of the new policy. But the Guises who now came into power regarded Scotland as the corner-stone of their ambition; and
their extraordinary ability made them for half a century the
dread of England and the protestants. The head of the family
was Francis, Duke of Guise, the defender of Metz and the
captor of Calais, a daring soldier but a hesitating politician.
His brother, the Cardinal of Lorraine, was, on the other hand,
personally timid, but bold in policy; while their sister Mary,
queen-dowager and regent of Scotland, combined the better
qualities of both her brothers. Her daughter, Mary, was now
queen-regnant of Scotland, queen-consort of France, and queen-
claimant of England and Ireland. She was only seventeen,
her husband Francis II. was nearly two years younger, and
the queen-mother Catherine de Médicis was forced to acquiesce
in the domination of Mary's uncles. The constable of France,
Montmorenci, retired from the government; and the Bourbons
lost all influence at court. Mary, on her marriage, had secretly
conveyed the crown of Scotland as a free gift to France, and
had annulled the public stipulations for Scotland's independence.[1] Both she and her husband were frail in health, and
the Guises were clandestinely bent on strengthening their hold
on Scotland so that it might not pass out of their control,
should Francis and Mary die without issue. In that event
two other families would claim the Scottish throne, the Hamiltons represented by the Duke of Châtelherault and his son
the Earl of Arran, who were descended from James II.'s
daughter Mary, and the Lennox branch of the Stuarts who
had contingent claims to the throne of England as well.
Matthew Stuart, Earl of Lennox, was like Arran descended,
though in the female line, from James II.'s daughter, and his
wife was daughter of Margaret Tudor by her second husband,
the Earl of Angus; both claims were united in the person of
their son Henry, Lord Darnley.[2]

Into this web of political and family intrigue was woven

---

[1] Labanoff, *Lettres de Marie Stuart*, i., 50.   [2] See Appendix IV.

the woof of the Scottish reformation. The Bibles and proclamations which Somerset's troops scattered broadcast in the track of their blood-stained marches through the lowlands in 1547-49 may have produced some effect. But it was neutralised by the political aims and the warlike guise of the missionaries; and national spirit supported the French and the clerical factions in their resistance to an English protestant union. When Northumberland abandoned in 1550 the policy of uniting Scotland with England, Henry II. nearly effected its union with France. The infant queen had already, in 1548, been carried off to Brittany, and Mary of Guise had secured the regency in place of Arran, who received the French duchy of Châtelherault as compensation. The great seal of Scotland was entrusted to Roubay, a Frenchman; and D'Oyssel, the French ambassador, became Mary's prime minister. All the chief fortresses except Edinburgh were garrisoned with French troops; and Scotland was treated as though it were a province of France. At last a popular link was being forged between England and Scotland; French domination north, and Spanish south, of the Tweed provoked national antagonism, and gave that antagonism an anti-catholic bias. Henry forced Scotland to make war on England in the interests of France, just as Philip forced England to make war on Scotland in those of Spain; and involuntary hostilities did more than the treaties of Henry VII. and Henry VIII. to promote an alliance between the peoples.

A greater obstacle than national jealousy was soon removed. "When," wrote Maitland of Lethington to an English correspondent in January, 1560,[1] "in the days of your princes, Henry VIII. and Edward VI., means were opened of amity betwixt both realms, was not at all times the difference of religion the only stay they were not embraced? Did not the craft of our clergy and power of their adherents subvert the devices of the better sort? But now has God of His mercy removed the block forth out of the way; now is not their practice like to take place any more when we are come to a conformity and profess the same religion as you." Mary Tudor had helped this work by driving Scottish protestants, who had found favour with Edward VI., back across the Borders. Harlow, Willock,

---

[1] Cotton MS., Caligula, B., ix., 99; *Foreign Cal.*, 1559-60, p. 300.

and Knox laboured with such effect that in December, 1557,
the ancient Scottish "band" or "bond" appeared under its new religious form of "covenant". The lords who signed it called themselves the lords of the Congregation, a title as significant of the political aspect of the Scottish reformation as "supreme head" is of the English. The former movement was carried out in spite of the monarchy, the latter by its means; and this antagonism caused deep searchings of heart to the Queen of England whom circumstances forced to appear as the ally and chief support of the Scottish insurgents.

Elizabeth had been barely two months on the throne when Châtelherault and Sir Henry Percy were discussing the prospects of an Anglo-Scottish agreement.[1] The breach between the Congregation and the Guises grew apace. Release from the war with Spain, and Philip's entanglement in the French matrimonial net hardened the hearts of Scotland's rulers, while the dawning gospel light across the Borders encouraged the elect. Knox lay chafing at Dieppe, seeking in vain a passage through England; he remembered too late that Deborah was a woman, and repented of that *First Blast from the Trumpet against the monstrous Regiment of Women*, which "had blown from him all his friends in England".[2] But by May, 1559, he was in Fife "putting more life" into his hearers "than five hundred trumpets continually blustering"; and where he went, altars and images fell to the ground, and armies sprang into being. The French, wrote Kirkcaldy, would soon be expelled; would England, he asked, be friends with Scotland? and he expressed a hope that Elizabeth would not be too hasty in her marriage.[3]

Cecil was alive to the momentous issues. Somerset, it seemed, had not cast his bread upon the waters for nought; and phrases about a united Great Britain, impregnably girt by the sea,[4] which Cecil as the protector's secretary may have penned in 1548, were now on Scottish lips. But the Scots who spoke them were rebels, inspired by feudal ideas of government and by the republican creed of Geneva. To countenance such a movement would make Elizabeth a traitor to her order, place her outside the pale of monarchical society, and provoke

---

[1] *Foreign Cal.*, 1558-59, Nos. 262, 316, 350.   [2] *Ibid.*, Nos. 504, 1032.
[3] *Ibid.*, Nos. 710, 743.   [4] See above, p. 11.

a catholic crusade against which she could look for no support from Lutheran princes.   The alternative was equally perilous : if she refused her assistance, the Guises would make Scotland French, and with their legitimist and catholic arguments undermine Elizabeth's doubtful hold over Ireland and the north of England.   The rebellion of 1569 might have been anticipated with a catholic Scotland and France at its back.   " This realm neither may nor will see them ruined," wrote Cecil of the Scottish protestants ; [1] and he studied means to save them without precipitating war with France and its possible allies.   The English people had no stomach for a fight with France after their late experience ; and the interests of Elizabeth's religious settlement, of her financial situation, and of her foreign policy all counselled a period of peace for the establishment of her throne.

Fortunately the loose ideas, which governed the mutual relations of states in the sixteenth century, permitted considerable latitude of offensive action under the cloak of peace. Advice, promises of aid, and actual assistance with money and munitions were not regarded as *casus belli*, though they might be used as pretexts.   Charles V. had told Henry VIII. that even invasion by a thousand troops was " too contemptible, with such great princes, to be a cause of war " ; [2] and Elizabeth proposed to take full advantage of this laxity.   To avert Philip's hostility to the religious aspect of the enterprise, she represented her help to the Scots as being purely a measure of temporal self-defence, imposed upon her by the Guises, who would destroy England's independence and ultimately threaten Philip's own position in the Netherlands.   To the truth in this contention Philip and his representatives were keenly alive.   It was obvious that Francis II. and Mary were trying to suppress rebellion ; but it was equally clear that their success would make France supreme in Scotland and possibly in the British Isles ; and in warding off this danger Elizabeth was defending Philip's interests as well as her own.   Inasmuch as the Guises were seeking to make France the arbiter of Scotland, Elizabeth was acting on the defensive, and the real aggressor was Mary Stuart, who had become a Frenchwoman and conveyed her realm to France.

[1] *Foreign Cal.*, 1558-59, No. 953.   [2] *Letters and Papers*, 1545, ii., 875.

Yet the extirpation of French influence in Scotland involved an offensive movement against a power with which England was at peace, rebellion against a legitimate sovereign, and another rent in the catholic church.

CHAP.
XII.

Elizabeth stretched monarchical etiquette as far as she could to cover the breach made by national forces. She denied that the Scots were rebels, or that she was helping them if they were. The Guises had first offended by impugning her title to the English throne, and she threw down the gauntlet to that house in a fierce proclamation which she circulated among their rivals in France.[1] The Scots, she maintained, were merely defending their national independence, and she was only protecting England from the invasion intended by the troops which France was sending to Scotland. But she prepared more drastic measures. Arran, who had been captain of the Scots Guards in France, but had fallen under Calvin's influence, was smuggled with English help out of France to Geneva, and thence by way of Lausanne and Antwerp to Cecil's house and Hampton Court, where Knox wanted him to be "tested".[2] Henry VIII. had long ago proposed his marriage to Elizabeth, and Scottish heads were now full of the idea. He might be king of Scotland, should Mary succumb to her frequent swoons; and Elizabeth was tested as well as Arran during their secret interviews. She was saved, or saved herself, from the political and personal shipwreck in which she would have been involved by such a union; and Arran was dismissed to do some hard work in the protestant cause in Scotland, and then to live insane for forty years.

His impetuous zeal brought over his wavering father; and in October the lords of the Congregation entered Edinburgh and deposed Mary of Guise from the regency. They had abandoned their earlier scheme of "electing" Arran or Lord James Stuart, a bastard son of James V.; and Knox wrote that the authority of the French king and queen would "be received in word, until they deny the just requests of the Scots".[3]

[1] *Foreign Cal.*, 1559-60, pp. 472-73; *Venetian Cal.*, vii., 167.
[2] *Foreign Cal.*, 1558-59, Nos. 1119, 1274. Cecil gives contradictory accounts of Arran's journey, one in cipher, the other not; the former was true, the latter was meant for hostile eyes.
[3] *Ibid.*, 1559-60, p. 52.

15 *

But the Scots' power to enforce their requests was doubtful. A thousand French troops had arrived under D'Oyssel, and all the ordnance in Scotland was in the regent's hands. Only the lords and their retainers could be trusted to keep the field for more than a fortnight; and they were more accustomed to Border raids and cattle-lifting forays than to the severer ordeal of meeting a disciplined army. In November the regent recovered the capital. Bothwell seized the money which Elizabeth secretly sent to the rebels' aid; and in December, in spite of another £6,000 from England, they were driven out of Stirling, while the French overran Fife and advanced on St. Andrews. English money was not enough; there must be men and measures of statecraft. All the autumn English agents were buying munitions of war in the Netherlands and bribing the customs officials to let them pass; and English levies were advancing towards Berwick, ostensibly for the defence of the Borders. In August there had been a holocaust of images and popish gear at St. Bartholomew's fair, it was guessed in Brussels, to encourage the Scots.[1] But now candles and crosses began to deck the altar in the queen's private chapel;[2] the emperor's ambassador was discussing her marriage with the Archduke Charles; and the Cardinal of Lorraine was saying that she repented of her religious changes and would give no help to Scottish Calvinists. She liked two strings to her bow, and cloaked her advance from the eyes of the French, while she prepared for retreat to the arms of Spain.

Still she trembled on the brink of an open breach, and her council was divided in mind. Arundel was utterly opposed to the whole business; Bacon spoke against armed intervention; and he was supported by Mary's old councillors, Winchester, Petre, Mason, and Wotton. On December 20 Noailles reported that after eight days' debate the council had resolved not to meddle in Scottish affairs. It was the queen's decision rather than the council's: nine of its members held Cecil's view, and he begged her to relieve him of all responsibility in the matter, as his advice had not found favour in

---

[1] Kervyn, ii., 16-17.

[2] *Foreign Cal.*, 1559-60, pp. 76, 110; Teulet, *Relations Politiques*, i., 354; Burnet, vi., 442-47.

her sight.[1] But the winds and the waves intervened in the   CHAP.
cause of insular solidarity. Elbœuf, who had lingered at   XII.
Calais with his armament destined for Scotland, dreading the
English ships, set sail in December, only to meet with greater
destruction in the storm. Four vessels were wrecked on the
coast of Holland, from one to two thousand troops were
drowned, and the best part of the war-stores and horses were
lost. Another force under Martigues fared little better, being
driven upon the coast of Denmark. Elizabeth revised her
judgment by the light of these events. In the last days of
December Norfolk was sent north as lieutenant-general to super-
sede the disaffected wardens of the marches. Grey was to
command in the field, Sadler to advise in the council; and,
more important than all, Admiral Winter was to blockade
the Forth, prevent reinforcements, and on his own authority
pick any quarrel he could with the French.[2]

Sea power made Great as well as greater Britain, and Winter's
squadron was the decisive factor in the expulsion of the French
from Scotland; an old Scottish saw foretold great changes
when there should be two Winters in Scotland in one year.[3]
The admiral's fleet arrived in the Forth on January 22, 1560,
after encountering storms which wrecked a second French
convoy. The French were compelled to evacuate Fife and
retire on Edinburgh and Leith; determined Scots were further
emboldened, and the waverers were converted to the cause of
religion or to that of union. Huntly, a catholic, came to
terms with the Congregation, and hardly a Scot of note remained on the French side except the bishops and Bothwell.
On February 27 the treaty of Berwick was concluded between
Norfolk and the Scottish lords " for the defence of the ancient
rights and liberty of their country," the original words " for
the maintenance of Christian religion " being cut out from
the final version. Elizabeth undertook to send an army into
Scotland to drive out the French, and to hand over the places
she won to the Scots. The lords bound themselves to resist

---

[1] Bacon's speech is printed from Harleian MS., 253, f. 83 *b*, in *Foreign Cal.*,
1559-60, pp. 197-98, and Cecil's letter, *ibid.*, p. 186, from Lansdowne MS., 102,
art. 1. See also Cecil's memoranda in *Foreign Cal.*, pp. 224, 256, and *Egerton
Papers*, pp. 30-34.

[2] *Foreign Cal.*, 1559-60, pp. 199, 295, 302-3, 329-30; *Hatfield MSS.*, i., 169.

[3] *Foreign Cal.*, 1559-60, p. 355.

any closer union between Scotland and France than already existed by Mary's marriage, to assist England against France with all their forces if the French invaded it north of York, and with 2,000 foot and 1,000 horse if the invasion took place elsewhere; and Argyll promised to aid in the reduction of northern Ireland.[1] A month later, on March 30, Grey's army crossed the frontier, effected a junction with the Scots, and laid siege to Leith.

Catholic Europe marvelled at England's presumption, and prophesied swift retribution. The Spaniards in particular could not disabuse their minds of the impressions derived from Mary Tudor's reign. Margaret of Parma was at pains to find means whereby Spain could prevent the French conquest of England; Noailles thought Quadra must have secretly encouraged Cecil in order that Elizabeth's impending defeat might make her dependent on Philip. "Is it not strange," the Bishop of Arras asked Chaloner, "that ye believe the world knoweth not nor seeth not your weakness?" Chaloner himself succumbed to the bishop's dejection, and besought Cecil to consider what lessons a candid stranger might deduce from England's condition—"religion, disunion, disfurniture, miscontentment of the old sort for the change, of the new for want of liberality, the grudge of our nobles and gentlemen to see some one [Dudley] in such special favour, the little regard the Queen had to marriage". Feria roundly asserted that Elizabeth had "no friends, no council, no finances, no noblemen of conduct, no captains, no soldiers, and no reputation in the world". "We know you," he continued, "as well as you know yourselves": seeing Elizabeth "will not be advised, she must be ordered; and as for your realm, doubt you not but there will be means found to govern it better, and such councillors will be put there as shall better look to the realm".[2]

Feria, whose wife was English and catholic, had all the spleen of a refugee; but less biassed observers regarded Elizabeth and Cecil as desperate gamblers, staking their all on a turn of fortune's wheel or a throw of the dice. The metaphors were not quite exact; no one left less to chance or took fewer avoidable risks than Elizabeth and her minister. They were

---

[1] Rymer, xv., 569; Haynes, p. 253; *Foreign Cal.,* 1559-60, pp. 413-15.
[2] *Ibid.,* 1559-60, pp. 164-65, 168-70, 188, 209, 252, 594-95.

playing a sound and skilful game with very good cards in
their hands.   Their opponents ignored their own weakness or
were more probably trying to bluff.   Religion was troubling
Philip and Francis more than Elizabeth at that moment, and
their resources in men and money were farther to seek.   One
of Henry II.'s motives for the peace of Cateau-Cambrésis had
been his desire to deal with the Huguenots, who now provided
more powerful reasons against the renewal of war.   " In Paris
and other cities," wrote a Venetian on December 1, "not a
week passes without many persons being burnt alive, and a
yet greater number being imprisoned ; the contagion nevertheless does not cease, but spreads more and more daily." [1]   As
early as May, 1559, 50,000 Frenchmen were reported to have
" subscribed a form of religion akin to that of Geneva " ; [2] and
a few weeks later Cecil was noting "what is to be done in
France for maintenance of the faction ". [3]

A religious alliance with Antoine de Bourbon, King of
Navarre, was suggested, as part of a wider project, including
all princes who had rejected Rome, [4] while Sir Nicholas
Throckmorton, Elizabeth's first ambassador to France and a
good judge of conspiracy, maintained secret relations with
Huguenots high and low, and with other enemies of the
Guises.   He had arranged Arran's escape ; his agents were
busy in Brittany ; and when he came to England for three
months in the autumn on the plea that his wife was ill, he
may have brought in his train La Renaudie, who in the
following March headed the Tumult of Amboise.   Throckmorton was needed in England more for measures in France
than in Scotland ; and the Tumult, with its widespread ramifications in Normandy, Guienne, Gascony, Dauphiné, and Pro-
vence, [5] synchronised somewhat suspiciously with Elizabeth's
proclamation against the Guises and her wish to divert French
reinforcements from Scotland.   Nor were these all the troubles

---

[1] *Venetian Cal.*, 1558-70, p. 135.

[2] *Foreign Cal.*, 1558-59, No. 685 ; cf. Nos. 790, 833, and *Venetian Cal.*, p. 126.

[3] *Foreign Cal.*, 1558-9, No. 1008.   [4] *Ibid.*, No. 1197 ; *Venetian Cal.*, p. 171.

[5] *Venetian Cal.*, 1558-70, pp. 153, 158, 160-62, 172-77.   The conspirators included Germans, Swiss, Savoyards, English, Scots, " and such like," as well as
Frenchmen ; " so this has been the greatest conspiracy of which there is any record, for there was knowledge of it in England, Scotland, Germany, and almost
all over Christendom " ; it "was also fomented by the Queen of England " ; cf.
Spanish Cal., i., 125, 140 ; Cotton MS., Calig. E. v., ff. 63, 72-80, and arts. 19,
20, 33.

of France: the emperor, probably without deliberate intent, was doing his best to further his son's suit for Elizabeth's hand by choosing this moment to despatch an embassy to France with a demand for the restitution of Metz, Toul, and Verdun to the empire. The French government hardly knew which way to turn except to Philip. " For want of treasure," wrote two English envoys, " they are at present not able to do any great matter, being indebted above eighteen millions, their country poor, their nobility and gentry not recovered since the last wars, and having much to do for ordering of religion." [1]

Philip was little more happily placed. In August, 1559, much to Elizabeth's relief, he had left the Netherlands " in such confusion that words can barely describe it," never, it was acutely surmised, to see them again ; and buried himself in the heart of Spain three weeks' distance from the scene of action. Venetian diplomatists were as contemptuous of his council as Feria was of Elizabeth's.[2] In Spain he was distracted by his merciless crusade against heresy, which had contaminated even his archbishops, and by his ill-fated expedition against the corsairs of Tripoli, while his Dutch subjects made common cause with the Scots in their resistance to foreign garrisons. In case of war, wrote Gresham, Elizabeth would be more sure of friends in the Low Countries than Philip : she was immensely popular as the champion of " natural " men against aliens ; and a friar who preached against her in Antwerp had to hide in fear of his life. Philip was " clean out of money, armour, munitions, and credit, wherein the Queen has prevented him " ; and " the Estates would never consent to war ".[3] L'Aubespine, the French ambassador at Madrid, might " irritate " Philip against Elizabeth with triumphant success,[4] and Quadra might declare that Elizabeth was possessed of 100,000 devils, in spite of her yearnings to be a nun and to pass her time praying in a cell ; [5] but Philip could not carry out his ambassador's suggested invasion of Norfolk. He could only

---

[1] *Foreign Cal.*, 1559-60, p. 189.   [2] *Venetian Cal.*, vii., 118, 196.

[3] *Foreign Cal.*, 1559-60, pp. 563, 573, 582 ; 1560-61, pp. 29, 50 ; *Venetian Cal.*, p. 142.

[4] L'Aubespine, *Négociations*, 1559-60 (*Coll. de Doc. Inédits*).

[5] Kervyn, ii., 157-58, " que tiene cien mil demonios en el cuerpo, y por otra parte me dice siempre que muere por ser monja y por estarse en una celda rogando " ; *cf.* Froude, vi., 299.

indulge in vague promises to Francis and veiled threats to
Elizabeth, combined with an offer of mediation which she
promptly rejected.　The Guises were reduced to the sorry
expedients of trying to soften her heart by smooth words, and
of pretending not to perceive her proceedings, to avoid being
forced into war.　They sadly admitted to their sister, stricken
to death by disease and hemmed in by foes at Leith, that no
help could be sent till July.　Even then it depended on Philip;
and before July came, Philip's thoughts had been turned elsewhere by the defeat of his forces at Gerbes, and Mary of Guise
had passed beyond the reach of human help or of worldly
misfortunes.

She fought to the bitter end with a stout heart and watch-
ful skill; and more than three months passed after Grey had
crossed the Tweed before England secured the victory.　Brave
as a soldier, Grey was no scientific tactician: on May 7 he
sent his troops to storm Leith with scaling ladders six feet too
short, while some one had informed the regent of the manner,
hour, and plan of the assault.[1]　They were disgracefully routed
with serious loss; and amid mutual recriminations between
officers and men, the whole force, Scots and English, threatened to melt away.　Cecil had to face an exacting sovereign,
but she saw that she could not retreat.　Reinforcements were
despatched, the siege was converted into a more effective
blockade, and Cecil and Wotton were sent to complete by
diplomacy the work of hunger.[2]　The regent died on June 10,
six days before they arrived.　Monluc, Bishop of Valence,
made a good diplomatic fight, but his arguments could not
feed French troops nor baulk Cecil of his prey; and by the
treaty of Edinburgh, signed on July 6, the English and Scots
gained every substantial point for which they had fought and
intrigued.　The pride of the Guises was humbled, and the
sovereigns of Scotland were forced to concede the demands
of their rebels as conditions of peace with their rival.　All
French troops save 120 were to be sent back to France; and
no Frenchman was to hold any important office.　Till Mary
returned, the government was to be in the hands of a body of

---

[1] *Foreign Cal.*, 1560-61, p. 72.

[2] The details are given very fully in Bain's *Scottish Cal.*, the *Foreign Cal.*, and
Hatfield MSS., i., 170-248.

twelve, of whom she would choose seven and parliament five. The fortifications of Leith were to be demolished, and the use of the arms of England to be abandoned by Mary and Francis.

The English had done more than expel the French ; they had won the prayers of Knox for perpetual amity between the two realms.   They brought away no spoil nor captives, but they left behind a grateful nation.   No towns or territories were retained, and no new titles were taken ; but surer foundations than conquest were laid of an ultimate union.   To restore England to the English had been Elizabeth's first achievement ; to secure Britain for the British was her second. Spanish influence had been eliminated from the English state and Roman from the English church.   Now French and Roman jurisdiction were expelled from Scotland ; and the bones, over which foreign dogs had quarrelled, came together, moved by a common inspiration.   Yet there was some hardihood in Elizabeth's assertion that Scotland " had received the same religion that was used in Almaine," from which, she told the Lutherans, her own hardly differed.   The Scottish parliament which met in August, 1560, could not adopt the Anglican settlement, nor follow the precedent of Denmark, which Cecil recommended as a better example.   Papal jurisdiction was rejected, the mass abolished, and monasteries dissolved ; but, as the lords of the Congregation pointed out, "authority" in Denmark had favoured reform as in England, while in Scotland there could be no royal supremacy nor royally - chosen episcopate.   Monarchy in Scotland at that moment was too weak to support monarchical principles in the church, or to save for its prelates endowments on which secular peers had set their hearts.

Nor could there be any " parliamentary theology " ; for the stunted Scottish estates never ventured to assert the sovereignty claimed by the English parliament, and left effective authority to be disputed between feudal barons and a self-governed kirk.   In Scotland the reformers were ministers of religion not ministers of state ; there was no royal doctrine like " the King's Book " ; and the Confession and the first Book of Discipline were the work of Knox and his friends.   The kirk, with its hierarchy of assemblies in which laymen sat side by side with the clergy, was as much superior in influence to the Scottish estates as it was to the English convocation; and in it, when monarchy revived, was found the focus of resistance. Privilege was claimed for the Scottish pulpit rather than for the Scottish parliament, and popular protests all assumed an ecclesiastical aspect.   The reformed kirk, deprived of the wealth and privilege, recovered much of the prestige and power, of its medieval predecessor.   Melville spoke of kings in language which might have been Hildebrand's; and the new presbyter soon developed a striking resemblance to the old priest.[1]   Theocratic Scotland and Erastian England had quarrels enough in store, but they were over domestic questions, and were decided without intervention from abroad. Henceforth Great Britain was to be the arena for none but battles of its own; no Spaniard in London nor Frenchman in Edinburgh was to dictate the issues of peace and war.   The feud, which had long been fomented by alien irritants, slowly died; and gradually the Borders disappeared.

[1] Compare *Foreign Cal.*, 1569-71, p. 521: " The ministers at this parliament request that they may excommunicate those indebted to them, and not be tried by temporal judges," with the Constitutions of Clarendon.

CHAPTER XIII.

THE RIVAL QUEENS.

IN less than two years Elizabeth's government had raised England from a slough of despond to a height of almost presumptuous confidence; had made a religious settlement which was to prove unexpectedly durable; had restored the currency; and had freed Britain from foreign control. France had been challenged with impunity and success, Philip had been rebuffed; and when in July, 1560, a new pope, Pius IV., sent Parpaglia, Abbot of San Salvatore[1] in Turin, Pole's old friend, to Elizabeth with the gentlest of exhortations and the most attractive of bribes to return to the bosom of the church, she brusquely refused to look at the olive branch, and replied to the overture by putting the deprived Roman catholic prelates in prison. For a while Francis and Philip and Pius might dissemble their anger and bide their time for revenge. But the papacy, France, and Spain could not easily acquiesce in the triumph of protestant Britain: Elizabeth had yet to reckon with Mary Queen of Scots; and the rest of her reign was mainly occupied in defence of the positions she had seized by 1560. Her ministers were convinced that provision could only be made for defence by offensive measures, and that England's immunity from attack could best be secured by giving her enemies no peace at home. Pretexts for intervention abounded; there was religion in France, provincial or national liberties in Scotland and in the Netherlands, and commercial and other monopolies in the New World, based on a papal authority which England refused to recognise. But the pretexts of Elizabeth were the principles of her people; and principles made them aggressive. Spoiling the Egyptians was no

---

[1] He is usually called Abbot of San Saluto, although Camden, *Annales*, i., 72, and Fuller, *Church Hist.*, iv., 308, give his title correctly.

piracy; eradicating Antichrist was a religious, if not a moral obligation; and on occasion killing a papist was no murder.

For a few months after the treaty of Edinburgh Elizabeth and her ministers were concerned with a more domestic question. The queen was not married, and the succession was as doubtful as ever. The archduke obtained no more satisfaction than Arran; and the emperor complained that Elizabeth " never gave his proposal serious consideration, but only made use of it for her own advantage with the other powers".[1] Male susceptibilities were hurt that she should dare to rule alone and hold husbands and marriage so cheap. Queens regnant were still something strange, and a queen reigning without a predominant partner was a novelty barely compatible, men thought, with divine and human ordinance. Even the contrast between the capacity of queens like Elizabeth, Mary Stuart, and Catherine de Médicis and the incapacity of prospective consorts like Arran, Don Carlos, and Darnley hardly inured them to the idea of feminine government. They were therefore all the readier to be shocked at Elizabeth's relations with Lord Robert Dudley, the master of her horse and apparently of her heart. Companionship in misfortune had prepared the way for his advance in Elizabeth's graces, and his physical attractions betrayed her into a flirtation that seemed to portend personal crime and public disaster. Dudley had married ten years before Amy Robsart, the daughter of a Norfolk knight; but he did not bring his wife to court, and the disease from which she suffered was soon given a sinister connexion with the intimacy between Dudley and the queen. In April, 1559, Feria mentions gossip that they were only waiting for Amy's death to marry; and in November Quadra reports a rumour that Dudley had arranged to poison his wife.[2]

Nine months later, in August, 1560, Cecil was in despair. He had returned from perhaps his greatest triumph in Scotland only to find Dudley dominant at court and himself further out of favour than he had been since the reign began;[3] he was even refused the expenses of his journey, while lucrative privileges were heaped on his worthless rival. To account

---

[1] Haynes, *State Papers*, p. 407; *Hatfield MSS.*, i., 286.
[2] *Spanish Cal.*, i., 58, 112; *cf. Venetian Cal.*, vii., 81.
[3] See Winchester's letter in Haynes, p. 361.

for Elizabeth's moods passes the wit of man. Gratitude for faithful service was not to be expected from the true daughter of Henry VIII., and nothing galled Elizabeth like the sense of personal obligation. Cecil had falsified her doubts and fears about Scotland, and she resented as a slight the non-fulfilment of her evil prognostications. He had, moreover, really forced her hand over the Scottish business; he had sometimes acted without her knowledge; he had compelled her to spend money; and a good part of two years' savings had vanished. The Scots, too, were still thrusting Arran upon her attention, while the King of Sweden and the archduke continued to press their suits. Nothing was more hateful than thus to be driven into the matrimonial yoke; and Dudley was a welcome diversion, perhaps because he was agreeable as a lover, but impossible as a husband. Her nerves, too, may have been upset by Parpaglia's mission, and by the implied threat that, if he were not received, she might be excommunicated and exposed to the risks of a crusade from abroad and rebellion at home. In any case Cecil wrote to his friend Randolph in Edinburgh,[1] and spoke to Quadra at Windsor, about retiring into private life, and the Spaniard described him as already in disgrace. He was alarmed by Elizabeth's conduct; he did not think the realm would tolerate the Dudley marriage, and apparently he doubted Elizabeth's self-restraint.

A tragedy came to his help: on September 8 Dudley's wife was found at the foot of the staircase at Cumnor Place, near Oxford, with a broken neck. That she was done to death by, or in the interests of, Dudley and Elizabeth was a popular suspicion, as natural as it is incredible; and Quadra, who was in the pay of the Guises,[2] by a deft economy of dates conveys the impression, in a despatch[3] written on the 11th,

---

[1] *Foreign Cal.*, 1560-61, pp. 283, 313.   [2] *Ibid.*, 1559-60, pp. 210, 582, 598.

[3] It is printed in full by Kervyn, ii., 529-33, and translated by Dr. Gairdner in *Engl. Hist. Rev.*, xiii., 84-86. The postscript is dated September 11, and probably the whole despatch was written on that day or the 10th; the news of Amy Robsart's death reached Windsor on the 9th, and the conversations Quadra reports with Elizabeth and Cecil were probably held subsequent to its arrival. Maitland (*Cambridge Mod. Hist.*, ii., 582) is inclined to regard most of Quadra's statements as fabrications designed to provoke joint Franco-Spanish intervention in England, or at least the repudiation of the treaty of Edinburgh. Quadra certainly hints elsewhere that prompt action should be taken without waiting to consult or extract a decision from Philip. But Cecil's talk of his retirement is

that Elizabeth told him, before the event, that the victim "was dead or nearly so," and that Cecil prophesied poison. He works these details into a lurid picture of Elizabeth's prospective imprisonment and the establishment of Huntingdon on the throne by means of a French expedition, and actually represents Cecil as saying that Huntingdon was the true heir because Henry VII. usurped the kingdom from the house of York.[1] Quadra's testimony to Elizabeth's complicity in the death of Amy Robsart would have stood better alone, if it was to stand at all. But a meaner intelligence than Elizabeth's or even Dudley's would have perceived that murder would make their marriage impossible; and Dudley was soon lamenting his rustication from court, and beseeching Cecil's sympathy and advice in this " so sudden a chance" which had " bred so great a change" in his fortunes.[2] He pressed for a full inquiry at the coroner's inquest, and the verdict amounted to one of accidental death. Behind that verdict it is impossible to go. A witness spoke of Amy's " desperation"; painful disease, mental distress at her treatment, or both, might account for the act of suicide. But there were also scandals and feuds in the family; Amy had a half-brother, John Appleyard, whose mistress was Elizabeth, the sister of Anthony Foster, Dudley's steward. Rumour pointed at Anthony Foster, and Appleyard in 1567 accused Dudley of shielding the criminal from a trial for murder, but withdrew his charges after seeing the jury's verdict and reflecting in the Fleet.[3] "She brake her neck

---

established by Randolph's letters. Margaret of Parma, to whom Quadra's despatch was addressed, apparently discounted the bishop's imaginative zeal, and on October 7 urged Philip not to declare war on Elizabeth in spite of all his grievances against her (Gachard, *Correspond. de Marguerite*, i., 308). Quadra himself complained that his despatches found little credit with Philip (Kervyn, ii., 607).

[1] See Appendix II.   [2] Haynes, p. 361.

[3] *Hatfield MSS.*, i., Nos. 1131, 1136-37, 1150-55, where the chronological order is defective; No. 1137 is later than the others. Froude (vi., 430) gives Appleyard's charges, which he appears to regard as decisive against Dudley, but does not mention his recantation. The details of Amy's death are derived from Dudley's correspondence with his cousin Sir Thomas Blount, which is extant only in transcripts among the Pepys MSS. at Magdalene Coll., Cambridge, and is printed in Pettigrew's *Inquiry*, 1859. See also the bibliography in the *Dict. of Nat. Biogr.*, xvi., 121; Dr. Gairdner in *Engl. Hist. Rev.*, i., 325, xiii., 83; Bekker, *Das Ende Amy Robsarts;* and P. Sidney, *Who Killed Amy Robsart?* The author of *Leycester's Commonwealth* and Sir Walter Scott are responsible for the popular view of the episode.

down a pair of stairs," writes Killigrew on October 10, " which I protest unto you was done only by the hand of God, to my knowledge."

A heavy cloud, however, hung over Dudley, and years later Cecil was not above using the rumour to damage his prospects.[1] But tried by the old legal test of *Cui bono?* the charge would recoil on other heads than those of the queen and Dudley. Elizabeth herself appeared to regard the affair with a composure in which royal dignity blended with moral indifference. Dudley was only a pleasant plaything, useful for flouting superior people; and when the queen was thought to be dying in October, 1562, she protested that " as God was her witness, nothing improper had ever passed" between them.[2] She was not made for love or genuine friendship; but amid the isolation and formality of her public life she felt the need of some one with whom she might be familiar, and Dudley was fitted to fill the position. He was soon restored to his place as principal courtier, and continued, by " back counsels " to Elizabeth and intrigues with the Spanish ambassador, to distract her responsible advisers. Some of them were haunted by the fear that the queen would marry Dudley and purchase Philip's support by restoring catholicism;[3] she had imitated her father in matters enough to colour the suspicion that she might take a leaf from his conduct in 1539-40. But when a patent was made out for Dudley's elevation to the peerage, Elizabeth cut it across with a knife, and remarked that the Dudleys had been traitors for three generations. A year later, in December, 1561, his elder brother Ambrose was made Earl of Warwick; but it was not till the autumn of 1564 that Robert became Earl of Leicester and chancellor of the university of Oxford; and he was not admitted to the privy council before October, 1562.

The queen needed all the wisdom she could command, for the effect of the episode upon the nation was deplorable, and at the end of 1560 the long duel between her and Mary Queen of Scots really began. Francis II. died on December 5. On the surface it seemed a stroke of good fortune for England.

[1] Haynes, p. 444.   [2] *Spanish Cal.*, i., 263.
[3] *Ibid.*, i., 178-79, 200, 201, 213. Quadra can hardly be guiltless of having caused this report.

The niece of the Guises was now merely a dowager in France; a long minority was in prospect, for Charles IX. was a boy of ten; and power passed into the hands of a triumvirate consisting of Catherine de Médicis, the King of Navarre, and the Constable Montmorenci. Catherine, like Elizabeth, regarded religion as a department of politics, and bore no love towards the Scottish queen. A French attack upon England in the interests of the Guises was now out of the question, and Mary appeared as a friendless widow in France with no supporters in Scotland. In reality she was loosed from disabling bonds. She was a greater menace to Elizabeth without the arms and the crown of France. As the queen of a hostile country and the head of a foreign invasion, she would have met with united resistance from English and Scots : as the leader of native catholics, the undoubted Queen of Scotland, and the legitimate heir of England, she could unite in her support the catholics, and divide in their opposition the protestants, of both kingdoms. Her loneliness as a widow appealed to more hearts in Great Britain than her greatness as Queen of France; her wits were more potent than armies, her charms more destructive than fleets. " In communication with her," wrote Knox of his first interview, " I espied such craft as I have not found in such age." [1] Elizabeth, too, seemed to be smoothing the path of her rival; her final rejection of Arran left the Scots no choice of allegiance, and her refusal to marry any one else made the succession an apple of discord among her own subjects. If Elizabeth married a Scot, the Scots would abandon the Stuart claim to the English succession : but if they took Mary as queen they would claim the assets in return for accepting the risks ; and her right by descent to the English throne was to Scots like Maitland and Lord James worth the risk of a catholic restoration. There was already a rift in the union of forces which had driven the French out of Scotland.

Yet it was with sore regret that the widow of eighteen turned from the land of her adoption to the country whence she had been smuggled twelve years before, and where in the interval her religion had been trampled in the dust and her mother brought with sorrow to the grave. " When she comes here," wrote Randolph, " it will be a mad world. Their ex-

[1] Haynes, p. 372.

actness and singularity in religion will never concur with her judgment;"[1] and it was only after Catherine de Médicis had rejected a proposal for her marriage with Charles IX. and foiled another for the hand of Don Carlos, that Mary fell back upon Scotland. Even that forbidding shore was better than France under the control of a mother-in-law like Catherine. The catholic Gordons with Huntly at their head had already sent John Leslie, the future bishop of Ross, to bespeak her presence in the north, and to promise a triumphant march upon Edinburgh. But Mary was not yet prepared for the part of catholic champion or catholic martyr; her kingdom was worth some religious concession, and she rejected Leslie's proposals in favour of the offers brought by Lord James. She stipulated for personal freedom of worship, but was willing to respect the established religion.

To Elizabeth she thought she could afford to be less complaisant. She explained, indeed, that her assumption of Elizabeth's arms and title was the fault of Henry of France and her husband; but she refused to confirm the treaty of Edinburgh without consulting her subjects or to acknowledge explicitly Elizabeth's right to the English throne. Till she did so, Elizabeth could hardly give her a passport through England; but she refrained from acting upon the more hostile suggestion that she should intercept Mary upon the high seas;[2] and the Queen of Scots reached Holyrood in August, 1561, without greater distress than that caused by a dense fog and the psalms of her covenanting subjects. She consoled herself with her private mass, and Lord James dealt with the Master of Lindsay's truculent threat that the "idolater priest" who performed it should die. Within two months Knox was lamenting Lord James's and Maitland's backsliding, while Maitland[3] was defending Mary's refusal to ratify the treaty of Edinburgh, asserting her claim to the English succession, and maintaining that the English parliament had "gone about to prevent the Providence of God" (December, 1561). In the same month Elizabeth sent her cousin, Lord Hunsdon, and Sussex to provide for the defence of the Borders.

While on August 13 Mary lay at Calais awaiting a favour-

---

[1] *Foreign Cal.*, 1560-61, p. 583.   [2] Kervyn, ii., 604.
[3] Haynes, pp. 372-81; *Spanish Cal.*, i., 306.

able wind for her voyage, Elizabeth sent to the Tower another   CHAP.
claimant to the succession.[1] Since the execution of Lady Jane   XIII.
Grey, her sister Catherine had been the principal representative
of the Suffolk line; and as such she had from the beginning of
the reign been the object of Feria's and Quadra's perilous attentions. In March, 1559, she had promised Feria that she
would not change her religion or marry without his consent;
and a few months later there was talk of enticing her to
Flanders to be married to Don Carlos.[2] In November Quadra
was advising her marriage with the Archduke Charles, and in
September, 1560, he alluded to the fear of the English lest by
her means Philip should get control of the realm if Elizabeth
died. To guard against this and other dangers, another scheme
was formed in England after Amy Robsart's death, not, according to Quadra, without the connivance of various members
of the council including Arundel, Bedford, and Cecil himself,
as well as Bishop Jewel.[3] This was her marriage with Protector Somerset's son, the Earl of Hertford; and the pair were
to be set up—Catherine against Elizabeth and Hertford against
Dudley the son of his father's enemy—in case the queen and
her lover, overwhelmed by Amy Robsart's fate, threw themselves
on the mercy of Philip and the Roman catholic church.[4]
Cecil, says Quadra, withdrew from the project on receiving a
promise from Elizabeth that she would not marry Dudley, and
on recovering his own predominance in her councils. But the
affair of state became one of the heart to the unfortunate
couple themselves, and they were secretly married. The lady's
condition prevented concealment after July, and Hertford was
summoned from Paris to join her in the Tower.

The marriage of persons of royal blood without the royal
licence was no longer treason, as it had been from 1536 to

---

[1] Quadra (August 16) to Margaret of Parma, and to Philip in Kervyn, ii.,
604-6, 608; these are two of the numerous Spanish despatches which do not occur
in the *Spanish Calendar*, though one paragraph from Quadra's letter to Philip is
printed as a separate despatch in September, *ibid.*, i., 212; Kervyn, ii., 609.

[2] *Spanish Cal.*, i., 45; Kervyn, i., 486; *Foreign Cal.*, 1558-59, No. 1116, 1559-
60, pp. 1-2; *Hatfield MSS.*, i., 158, where "the Lady K." interpreted by the editor
as Lady Knollys is Catherine Grey.

[3] *Spanish Cal.*, i., 176, 179-80, 213; Kervyn, ii., 608, 619-21.

[4] Charles V. had profited in a similar way by the bigamy of Philip of Hesse,
Cambridge Mod. Hist., ii., 241-42.

1553;[1] but Elizabeth knew enough to suspect conspiracy, and her severity against the culprits was not unnatural. A commission, over which Archbishop Parker presided, pronounced the marriage void for lack of witnesses;[2] but Catherine gave birth to a son on September 24, and the archiepiscopal sentence would not be a very serious bar to intrigues in the infant's interest. Quadra, whose capacity for thinking evil was almost unlimited, opined that both the infant and its mother would soon perish by poison, and he discovered in her ill-health confirmation of his discernment. She recovered, however, and her detention in the Tower was sufficiently lax to permit of the birth of another son in January, 1563. For this second offence the earl was condemned, though not required, to pay an enormous fine; but Lady Catherine was removed six months later to the house of her uncle, Lord John Grey, and not again committed to prison. She died in January, 1568, and her eldest son, in spite of his doubtful legitimacy, was always called Lord Beauchamp; he got into similar trouble about his own marriage, and became father of the youth who provoked the tragedy of Arabella Stuart.[3]

This was not the only matrimonial affair that tried Elizabeth's temper. Sussex had lately explained to Cecil with a candour fit only for private communications that it did not so much matter whom Elizabeth married provided she had the desired issue.[4] He was even prepared to put up with Dudley rather than see the queen continue childless. This condition she knew she could not fulfil, and the knowledge exasperated her at the number of suitors with whom she was pestered, and at the subterranean schemes concocted to force her hand. The candidate most favoured by her subjects at this time was Eric, the new King of Sweden, who was a protestant, was reported to be enormously rich, and was considered as a possible foil to Dudley. An English merchant was sent to Sweden with Elizabeth's portrait and a strong hint that his presence in England might be advantageous; prints with his

---

[1] *Cf.* Quadra in Kervyn, ii., 625.

[2] *Hatfield MSS.*, i., 272; ii., 71-72; *Spanish Cal.*, ii., 403.

[3] Kervyn, ii., 636; *Dict. of Nat. Biogr.*, l., 296-97, 310-12; *Engl. Hist. Rev.*, xiii., 302-7; and see below, vol. vii., pp. 56-57, where, however, Lord Beauchamp should be described as the son, not the husband, of Catherine Grey.

[4] Sussex to Cecil, October 24, 1560, State Papers, Ireland, Eliz., ii., 13.

and the queen's portraits side by side were published in London; and while the Guises thought it an excellent match, Philip, whose aunt had, with her husband Christian II., been turned off the Swedish throne by Eric's father Gustavus Vasa, regarded the prospective alliance as so dangerous to the security of the Netherlands that he meditated leaving Spain to prevent it. Eric, however, was madder than Arran: he instructed his envoy in London to bribe Elizabeth's council and to procure Dudley's death; he also challenged his rival to fight a duel, and in spite of Elizabeth's unusually definite rejection of his suit he prepared to start on his quest. The queen suppressed the portraits and refused his passports; but she could not resort to force, and at times she had doubts whether it would not be better to temporise in order to frustrate the designs which Eric had also on the hand of Mary Stuart.[1] Eventually troubles nearer home diverted his attention from Great Britain, and in 1568 he was deposed.

Distractions like these were not conducive to the pursuit of a clear and simple policy, and Elizabeth relied mainly upon her talent for mystification. Intrigue became a second nature to her, and it is seldom easy to distinguish her real features from the disguises she wore. Nevertheless in 1561 she was gradually adopting a more definite attitude of hostility towards the forces of reaction. Perhaps the rumours, which she taxed Quadra with having spread, that she would seek refuge in catholic protection, drove her, out of sheer contrariety, into an opposite course. The action of the pope in filling up two Irish bishoprics and despatching a papal legate, David Wolfe, to Ireland was a more substantial grievance; it was done, she said, "to excite disaffection against her crown".[2] Circumstances also seemed to favour a further attack on Rome. In France the Guises and papalism were in retreat; l'Hôpital was chancellor, and religious toleration, or rather, perhaps, anarchy reigned. At Pontoise in July-August, 1561, the secular estates asserted that it was a crime to interfere with liberty of conscience, demanded the exclusion of churchmen from temporal office on the ground of their incompatible allegiance to the pope,

---

[1] Kervyn, ii., 628, 630-34, 639, 645, 690; *Spanish Cal.*, i., 211-13; *Foreign Cal.*, 1561-62, p. 369; Haynes, p. 368; Geijer, *Hist. of the Swedes*, ch. x., xi.

[2] *Spanish Cal.*, i., 199; see below, p. 427.

and advocated more sweeping measures of confiscation than Henry VIII. had effected.

The Guises appeared to have prophesied truly when in March, 1560, they had told their sister in Scotland that the French nobles were playing "much the same game" as the Scots;[1] and Elizabeth hoped to repeat her Scottish success on the other side of the Channel. Her methods, however, were different. She could not play the nationalist card in France, and Mary had trumped it in Scotland. She fell back on her religious suit, with just a hope that Mary would follow the lead. To the Scots she now explained that community of religion with England was their best guarantee of peace and independence; to France she sent Bedford, her stoutest protestant peer, to keep the French government from participation in the revived council of Trent; and to the meeting of princes at Naumburg in January, 1561, she despatched envoys to recommend a general protestant union. At home Cecil, on Quadra's testimony, was "ruling all";[2] and the queen flatly refused to receive Martinengo, the new papal envoy, in spite of Philip's recommendations,[3] or to accept the invitation that England should be represented at the council of Trent. Could she also be "the instrument to convert Mary to Christ and the knowledge of His true Word"?[4] Maitland hoped that she could, and was busy preparing arguments against the validity of Henry VIII.'s bequest to the Suffolk line. The indiscretion of Catherine Grey had increased Elizabeth's aversion from that house; and the obvious advantages of Mary's detachment from catholic interests induced Elizabeth to dangle the bait. An interview between the two queens was proposed for 1562, and it was pointed out that, had James V. accepted his uncle's invitation to York twenty years earlier, a world of troubles might have been saved. Mary seemed eager to fall in with the scheme; she was going to mass, it was true, but she was also taking lessons from George Buchanan, and her acknowledged ministers were Maitland and Lord James.

The news of the massacre of Vassy on March 1 broke in upon these dreams. Could Elizabeth with the blood of her slaughtered fellow-saints crying for vengeance against the CHAP.
XIII. Guises, meet the niece of those whose hands had shed it? could she trust the nursling of that brood? or would Mary use her recognised title as heir to trouble the possessor? The English, said Cecil, thinking of Mary Tudor's reign, "run after the heir to the crown more than after the present wearer"; and Elizabeth, according to Quadra, "based her security on there being no certain successor, to whom the people could turn if they tired of her rule".[1] The Countess of Lennox was nursing the catholic cause in the province of York and promoting a match between her son and Mary. "The faithful had placed all their trust" in the countess and Darnley: Quadra himself was deep in intrigues on their behalf; and the fidelity of the northern earls and the Duke of Norfolk to Elizabeth's throne was suspect.[2] The Queen of Scots herself had not relinquished her hopes of Don Carlos, and she had just told the pope that she was determined to re-establish catholicism.[3] Elizabeth doubted with reason the possibility of building the future of England on Stuart foundations; and there was not the least chance that she would have been able to induce the parliament of 1563 to repeal the succession as established by law.

Mary, however, had not yet changed patience for passion or zeal; and she still preferred the chances of peaceful diplomacy to those of religious warfare. To avow her religious designs would break her power in Scotland and shatter her hopes elsewhere. The Scottish throne was her most substantial foothold, her principal coign of vantage; and from that base she must work towards the English succession, retaining her subjects' allegiance. To them the massacre of Vassy was more hateful than it was to Elizabeth, and Mary lamented with tears her uncles' proceedings, and protested that not even for them would she sacrifice Elizabeth's friendship. She created Lord James Earl of Mar and then Earl of Moray, and in the autumn of 1562 accompanied him on the expedition to the north to crush the rebellious and catholic Gordons, who had been the first to invite her to Scotland.

[1] *Spanish Cal.*, i., 176, 221, 307.
[2] *Ibid.*, pp. 183, 220, 244-46, 250, 317; *Foreign Cal.*, 1562, pp. 13, 23.
[3] Philippson, *Marie Stuart*, ii., 33, 37.

Elizabeth was duly impressed by this sign of protestant grace, and wrote a friendly letter, to which Mary replied by saying that she hoped to come as far south next year. Moray was even expecting to bring Goodman, who had once sounded a more furious blast than Knox against the rule of women, to bless the godly union.[1] This was the nearest point of approach in their orbits. Mary's patience began to give way when she heard in November that, during Elizabeth's serious illness of the previous month, only one voice in the council had been raised in favour of her succession; and in February, 1563, she sent Maitland to press her claims on the English parliament and to threaten resort to other methods if they were not admitted.[2] Nor was it in human nature to suffer with permanent acquiescence the indignities forced on Mary in the very precincts of her palace on account of her religion;[3] and Elizabeth was now at open war with Mary's friends in France.

England's intervention in the first French war of religion was perhaps the greatest blunder of the reign; but the temptations were almost irresistible. The massacre of Vassy had turned the two religious parties into two hostile and rapidly arming camps. The old conditions, under which the disruption of France between Burgundian and Armagnac factions had tempted Henry V. into war, seemed to have reappeared in another form, and to be sufficient justification for attempting to recover Calais and helping that religion, which came to be spelt with a capital R and to mean the Huguenot cause. "It lies in her hands," wrote Killigrew, "to banish idolatry out of France." "All Picardy, Normandy, and Gascony," it was also said, "might belong to England again;" and this war, Elizabeth protested, was "not war on France but only one for religion".[4] There were stormy scenes at the council-board, but on this occasion the queen pressed for adventurous action; she is reported by Quadra to have said that, as her councillors were so afraid, she would take the risk of failure herself.[5] Her best excuses were perhaps the fact that Philip was helping the Guises and the rumour, vouched for as correct by Throck-

---

[1] *Foreign Cal.*, 1562, pp. 51, 420; Haynes, pp. 388-90, 393.
[2] Keith, ii., 177, 188-92; *Spanish Cal.*, i., 262.
[3] See, for instance, *Foreign Cal.*, 1562, p. 605.
[4] *Ibid.*, 1562, pp. 324, 344.   [5] *Spanish Cal.*, i., 260.

morton, that he was "practising to put his foot in Calais ".[1]
By the treaty of Hampton Court, concluded with Condé's
agents on September 20, she was to assist the Huguenots with
men and money and to hold Havre till Calais was restored.[2]
Here was one flaw which distinguished the French from the
Scottish enterprise; and her troops found even Huguenot
soldiers loth to deliver forts into English hands.   England
appeared as the national friend in Scotland, but as the national
foe in France.   The Huguenots lost Rouen on October 25,
and the battle of Dreux on December 19, though Guise was
shot in the back on February 18, 1563, and died six days later.[3]
Then Condé and Catherine patched up the religious compromise, embodied in the edict of Amboise, which lasted four
years; and both parties joined to expel the invaders.   They
were besieged in Havre, and surrendered on July 28, a few
hours before thirty vessels under Clinton hove in sight with
reinforcements.

In the midst of the fever of war it was thought well to have
a general election; and a plot, which was too crazy to be considered even a Guisard retort to the Tumult of Amboise, further
stimulated the passion of loyalty.   Arthur Pole, a nephew
of the cardinal, who had been housed by the malcontent Lord
Hastings of Loughborough, was encouraged by the protestant
idea of setting up his cousin Lord Huntingdon as Elizabeth's
successor to meditate on his own better claim to the throne.
He was "caressed" by some of the catholics, and Northumberland gave him his sister's hand in marriage.   But Quadra
thought him a foolish and turbulent youth; and the French
ambassador, to whom he next turned, was not inclined to
favour a rival to Mary Stuart.   He was seized in October, with
two brothers and a brother-in-law, when on the point of embarking for France; he confessed he was going to serve the
Guises in the hope that, if Mary secured the English throne,
she would reward him with the dukedom of Clarence.   The
brothers were kept prisoners in Beauchamp Tower, and their
plot was used as a diplomatic weapon against Quadra, the

[1] *Foreign Cal.*, 1561-62, p. 609; *cf.* the petition to Elizabeth from Rouen in
Hatfield MSS., i., 271; *Foreign Cal.*, 1562, p. 295.

[2] Whitehead, *Coligny*, App. i.

[3] *Foreign Cal.*, 1563, p. 399; Sir A. H. Layard, *Despatches of Marc Antonio
Barbaro* (Huguenot Soc.), pp. cii-iv.

Guises,[1] and the English Romanists, who were subjected to new penalties in the principal act of the ensuing parliamentary session.

Elizabeth's second parliament and first reformed convocation, which met on January 11, 1563, showed a good deal of protestant fervour. The usual proportion of old members, or rather more, had been chosen; and the only noticeable feature of the elections, held in December, 1562, was the return of members for seven new constituencies, Tregony, St. Germains, and St. Mawes in Cornwall, Stockbridge in Hampshire, Minehead in Somerset, Tamworth in Staffordshire, and Beverley in Yorkshire. It did not occur to the commons that this handful of members had been introduced in order to pack the house; but Henry VIII. had made his additions to the parliamentary system by statute, and it was deemed advisable to demand an explanation of their presence. Their letters patent were brought to the house for inspection and found satisfactory; and members continued to sit for these boroughs without dispute until nearly sixty years later their right was challenged by James I.[2] The house also asserted its privileges by extending immunity from arrest for debt to members' servants, and requiring the issue of various new writs in cases where members had been elected for more than one constituency; but a proposal to grant parliamentary representation to Durham failed to become law.[3]

In 1559 the trouble had been with the house of lords; but now the substitution of protestant for Roman catholic bishops gave the queen an assured majority. In the commons, although a bill against usury was rejected by 134 to 90 votes, and one respiting homage in certain cases was lost without a division, the only occasion on which there was anything like a religious party vote was when, after prolonged discussion and the withdrawal of one bill, another for increasing the severity against Roman catholics was carried by 186 to 83. This measure imposed the oath of supremacy on all present and future ecclesiastics, schoolmasters, public and private teachers of children, barristers, attorneys, notaries, officers of the law,

[1] *Spanish Cal.*, i., 119, 259-60, 262, 275, 278, 288, 292, 331; *Foreign Cal.*, 1562, pp. 423-24; *Dict. of Nat. Biogr.*, xlvi., 19.
[2] State Papers, Dom., Eliz., xvii., 23, 24; *Commons' Journals*, January 19 and 22, 1563.
[3] *Commons' Journals*, January 18, 25, 26, 28, 29, 30.

and members of the house of commons; and made the second CHAP.
refusal thereof high treason.   The occasion for it was the con-   XIII.
scientious objections which Roman catholics had developed
against taking any oaths at all : " so that," wrote the bishops
of London and Ely to the council, " it is likely that Papistry
will end in Anabaptistry ".[1]

Other measures embodied the grant of two tenths and
fifteenths ; promoted the maintenance of the navy by making
Wednesday as well as Friday " a fish-day," and thus encouraging fishermen and sailors; prohibited the import of foreign
manufactures (a proposal for free-trade in corn failed) ;[2] declared
the authority of a keeper of the great seal and a lord chancellor
to be identical ; authorised the translation of the Bible and
Book of Common Prayer into Welsh ; and made writs *de excom-
municato capiendo* returnable to the court of queen's bench.
Parliament also began the series of poor laws which culminated
in 1601 ; and regulated the conditions of labour and apprenticeship by enforcing seven years' apprenticeship in trades and
crafts and compulsory service in husbandry, by empowering
justices of the peace to settle labour disputes and fix wages,
and by imposing a minimum of twelve hours' labour in summer
and heavy fines on masters who paid, and men who received,
higher wages than the legal rate.[3]

But the questions which occupied most attention were
those of the queen's marriage and the succession.   They had
been discussed at the usual dinners which were held preparatory
to a parliamentary session, and a petition was drawn up in
the first week of the session by a committee of the house of
commons, consisting of the Speaker, the privy councillors in
the house, and twenty-four other members.   The lords concurred, and the queen " thankfully accepted" it on January

---

[1] Haynes, p. 395.   In their attitude towards oaths the anabaptists anticipated
the quakers.

[2] *Commons' Journals*, Febr. 11 and 12.   The importance of these regulations
may be gathered from Philip II.'s list of grievances against England in January,
1564, *Spanish Cal.*, i., 355.   " The first is the prohibition in England of certain
Flemish manufactures. . . .   Another is the great increase of customs, port dues,
and other charges on many kinds of goods sent from here to England.   Another
is the recent decree issued by the queen of England respecting navigation, giving
preference to English ships taking English goods to Flanders, the effect of
which is to give the English a monopoly of this trade and shut out the Flemings
altogether."

[3] Prothero, *Select Statutes*, etc., 3rd ed., pp. 41-54.

28, but deferred her answer. Repeated attempts to extract something more definite only elicited the hint that she was still young and there was plenty of time. With regard to the succession she assured them that the greatness of the question " maketh me to say and pray that I may linger here in this vale of misery for your comfort . . . and I cannot with *nunc dimittis* end my life, without I see some foundation for your surety after my gravestone ".[1] With this maternal but vague assurance parliament was prorogued on April 10.

In convocation, a set of puritan articles requiring the observance of Sundays and "the principal feasts of Christ" as holydays, and the abrogation of all others, the omission of the sign of the cross in baptism, and the removal of organs ; enabling the ordinary to dispense with kneeling at the communion ; and declaring the surplice a sufficient vestment for the ministrant, was only lost by fifty-eight votes to fifty-nine. Even this narrow victory was won by proxies ; for of those actually present forty-three voted for the articles and thirty-five against, while twenty-seven votes were not recorded.[2] Five deans, including Nowell the prolocutor, twelve archdeacons, the provost of Eton, and fourteen proctors subscribed a still more extreme memorial advocating also the entire abolition of copes and surplices and of " all curious singing" of the Psalms. The positive work of convocation consisted of the Thirty-nine articles ; substantially these were Cranmer's Forty-two revised and reduced by three. The crucial article was the twenty-ninth, on the doctrine of the Eucharist : it was omitted by the queen, before she authorised the publication, in order to avoid friction with the Lutherans, behind whose Confession she was endeavouring to shelter from a possible papal anathema ; but it was restored in 1571 when Paul V. had shot his empty bolt. As a whole the articles avoided extremes with as much success as the rest of the Elizabethan settlement. Something no doubt was due to the wisdom and comparative toleration of the bishops and clergy ; something perhaps to their mutual differences ; and not a little to an active desire for political co-operation with foreign protestants and to lingering hopes of a reformed catholic church. Eliza-

[1] *Spanish Cal.*, i., 271 ; *Commons' Journals*, Feb. 16 ; D'Ewes, pp. 75-81.
[2] Strype, *Annals*, I., i., 500-5.

beth was hand-in-glove with the Huguenots; she was ingeminating peace among dissentient German and Swiss divines; and
it was an inauspicious moment for the English church to set
an example of theological strife and severing definitions. That
might be left to the Tridentine council now drawing to its
close; with it at least there was in England no idea of compromise, and its sacrifices of masses were bluntly pronounced
blasphemous fables and dangerous deceits.[1]

The Huguenots, however, were not to be bound to the
English alliance by any theological weaving. They made
their hollow truce with Catherine de Médicis; and the expulsion of the English from Havre was followed by months of
alarm on the southern coasts and in the Channel Islands.[2]
Elizabeth loudly proclaimed that she had been deceived; and
her ambassador, Throckmorton, who had been denounced by
Catherine as "the author of all these troubles," was joined in
October, 1562, by Sir Thomas Smith, who "spoke like a
peacemaker, and so took his commission to be".[3] Elizabeth
in fact had no sooner made war than she began to talk of
peace. But she could not extinguish the fire without burning
her fingers. Both Smith and Throckmorton were confined for a
time to their houses in France; and it was not till the end
of 1563 that Smith could begin his task of laying the foundations of the great diplomatic revolution of Elizabeth's reign.
Philip had hitherto on the whole played the part of England's
friend against France; but there were indications in the
Netherlands, in the New World, and on the sea that this alliance was incompatible with the dynamics of English development; and slowly England veered towards France. It took
eight years to complete the change, and there were endless
fluctuations; but a beginning was made when on April 11,
1564, the treaty of Troyes was concluded.[4] Ostensibly little
was settled except that the war should end; but the quarrels
between Smith and Throckmorton, that disgraced the negotiations, symbolised a conflict between the old and the new
policy. It was Throckmorton who retired to England on

[1] This is the version of 1571; the articles of 1563 are in Latin, Hardwick,
Articles of Religion, p. 317.
[2] *Hatfield MSS.*, i., 277; *Spanish Cal.*, i., 321.
[3] *Foreign Cal.*, 1562, pp. 306, 309, 324, 347, 359, 404, 431, 437.
[4] *Foreign Cal.*, 1564-65, pp. 101-5.

the release of the two ambassadors, while Smith remained in France to foster the new understanding.

Its development had a great effect on Mary Stuart's fortunes. Ultimately it meant that she would be converted from the representative of France into the client of Spain. Immediately, it led to the defeat of her designs on the hand of Don Carlos. "No, no," said Elizabeth when that project was mentioned, "it will not be done as they think;"[1] and the diplomatic defeat was inflicted by the hands of Catherine de Médicis and Mary's own uncle, the Cardinal of Lorraine. The French, wrote Smith to Elizabeth in August, 1563, "marvellously fear the marriage".[2] They knew that it would make Mary a lever in Philip's hands, and that Guise influence and French interests would count for little with a pair who might possibly rule over Spain, Scotland, the Netherlands, and England. Mary was bitterly disappointed, and she found little comfort in the alternative suggestions for her marriage with the Archduke Charles, Charles IX. of France, or Robert Dudley. The archduke was favoured by the English exiles at Louvain and by Mary's uncle, the cardinal. But the Scots would not hear of him; for he was poor and brought no prospect of the English crown. The emperor, moreover, would be no party to a move against Elizabeth, although he politely poured cold water on Elizabeth's counter-revival of the idea that she should wed the archduke. The match between Mary and Charles IX. was frustrated by Guise's assassination; while the Dudley proposal would have placed the crown matrimonial of Scotland on the head of Elizabeth's minion. Maitland regarded the offer as an insult, and Mary asserted that she would never accept a husband at her rival's hands. Nevertheless, the scheme was discussed throughout 1563 and 1564, and it is said to have been with the object of furthering Dudley's suit that Elizabeth created him Earl of Leicester.

Meanwhile the failure to make any provision for her marriage and the succession during the parliament of 1563 provoked a fresh agitation of Lady Catherine's claims. Cecil himself favoured this solution; Quadra says that London was strongly

---

[1] *Spanish Cal.*, i., 305-19, 348.
[2] *Foreign Cal.*, 1563, pp. 506-7, 510, 551, 579, 590.

on the same side ;[1] and John Hales, the nephew of the opponent
of the inclosure movement, wrote a defence of the validity of
Hertford's marriage based on information gleaned from Lord
John Grey and from his niece and prisoner, the Lady Catherine.
Hales was committed to the Fleet for six months, and Elizabeth was said to have been prevented from proceeding against
his abettors only by their number and influence. But her indignation and threats could not blind Mary Stuart to the extent of protestant hostility to her claims in England. She felt
that she must rely on catholic aid; and the failure of her
schemes abroad, owing to the jealousy between her French
relatives and catholic Spain, led her to look more and more
for that assistance in Great Britain. In Scotland her staunch
adherence to the mass had secured some converts, her personal
charms had made more, and her political claims had appealed
to the nation; while in England she had come to be regarded
as the rising hope of catholic reaction. Her marriage with a
natural-born Englishman, who should also be a catholic, would
bind together sufficient elements to make a formidable party.

Her chance was provided for her by Elizabeth, with a good-
natured carelessness or a malevolent intuition [2] which seem
equally incredible. As far back as the reign of Henry VIII.
the Lennoxes had been used as English pawns against the
elder branch of the Stuart family; and to this circumstance
Henry, Lord Darnley, owed his birth in 1545 on English soil
and his English nationality. In 1554 Mary Tudor is said to
have wished to settle the succession on his mother Margaret,
Countess of Lennox, instead of on Elizabeth; and in 1559-60,
when Elizabeth was working with the Hamiltons, she kept
their rivals from interfering. In March, 1560, Quadra remarked that Darnley was the candidate of the English catholics
for the throne; and in 1561 mother and son were put in the
Tower on account of her intrigues in the northern counties.[3]
The opportunity was taken to discredit their dynastic position
by denying the legitimacy of the countess: her mother, Margaret Tudor, had in 1527 obtained a papal sentence against the

---

[1] *Spanish Cal.*, i., 314, 321.

[2] *Foreign Cal.*, 1564-65, p. 334 : "the sending of Darnley home was done of
purpose to match this Queen meanly ".

[3] *Spanish Cal.*, i., 135, 137.

validity of her marriage with the countess' father, Angus, and
had furnished her brother Henry VIII. with a precedent for
his proceedings against Catherine of Aragon ;[1] and the Scottish
estates had declared the countess a bastard.

Having thus disarmed the countess and her son, Elizabeth
invited them to court, where Darnley showed himself proficient
with the lute. The countess pretended satisfaction ; but the
attack on her own legitimacy made her all the more determined
to push the fortunes of her son. She had conceived the idea
of marrying him to Mary as soon as Francis II. was dead ;
and within a year Elizabeth was aware of the design.   In
July, 1562, Quadra thought there was an understanding on
the subject between Mary and the countess ; but Mary would
have preferred Don Carlos, and in June, 1563, Elizabeth was
petting Darnley as his rival.   In August, 1564, however, her
suspicions were aroused by the request of the earl and his
countess to be allowed to take Darnley with them into Scotland ; and she revoked the leave she had already granted his
parents.   Subsequently she allowed Lennox to go alone, and
Mary restored his long-forfeited estates.   In December it was
reported that Elizabeth had offered Mary the choice of three
English husbands, Leicester, Norfolk, Darnley, and had promised her the succession if she would marry any one of them ;
and Lennox was saying that Mary would marry his son.
Mary's instance was now added to that of Lennox ; and in
February, 1565, Darnley, in spite of Cecil's earlier doubts, and
of Randolph's present forebodings, set out with Elizabeth's
leave for Scotland.[2] He saw Mary for the first time on the
18th, and within two months it was rumoured that they were
secretly married.   But the public ceremony did not take place
until July 29, after Elizabeth had sent Throckmorton on a vain
errand to prevent it.   Love had sped the counsels of statecraft, and Mary had given her heart to the tall and handsome
youth, whom the catholics had made their choice.

Their hopes ran high in 1565.   Philip wrote that the news
of the marriage was very pleasing to him,[3] sent Mary 20,000

---

[1] *Letters and Papers of Henry VIII.*, iv., 4130-31 ; *Foreign Cal.*, 1562, pp.
12-15, 23-24 ; Haynes, p. 381.

[2] *Spanish Cal.*, i., 391, 399 ; *Foreign Cal.*, 1564-65, pp. 55, 259, 299.

[3] *Spanish Cal.*, i., 404, 432, 490-92.

crowns, and urged the pope to do the like, while France seemed
equally glad.   Philip also informed Silva, his new ambassador
in England, that the Queen of Spain was to meet her mother
of France.   He was to tell Elizabeth that it was merely a
family gathering; but Philip sent Alva to Bayonne from
other motives than affection for his mother-in-law; and other
things than domestic affairs were discussed at the famous
conference, where Mary herself was represented.[1]   Elizabeth,
too, whose ear was quick, seemed to be bowing before a coming
storm.   The coercion that had hitherto been reserved for catholics was extended to puritans ; and, when Dean Nowell was
preaching against images on Ash Wednesday, 1565, she broke
out: "To your text, Mr. Dean—leave that; we have heard
enough about that ".   Silva was further gratified by her catholic conduct on Holy Thursday, when she washed and kissed
the feet of twelve poor women and made the sign of the cross
upon them.   "We only differ from other catholics," she told
him, "in things of small importance."   "And those things," he
replied, "your Majesty will soon amend."   "And you will see
it," she said.[2]   It was Mary who seemed to be the missionary
now; and the prospect of Elizabeth being the means to "convert her to Christ" was distant.   Yet Mary's secular mission
was more successful than her religious example.   On June 19
in the following year she gave birth to the child who became
James VI. of Scotland and James I. of England.   Whatever
might be her fate in life, the future belonged to her issue.
"The Queen of Scots," moaned Elizabeth when she heard the
news, "is mother of a fair son, and I am but a barren stock." [3]

[1] *Spanish Cal.*, i., 491; *Foreign Cal.*, 1564-65, pp. 400, 401, 403; Marcks, *Die
Zusammenkunft von Bayonne*, 1889.
[2] *Spanish Cal.*, i., 405-6, 425; Strype, *Parker*, i., 318-19, iii., 94; *Parker
Corresp.*, p. 235 ; *Dict. of Nat. Biogr.*, xli., 245.
[3] Melville, *Memoirs*, ed. 1683, p. 70.

CHAPTER XIV.

THE FALL OF MARY.

THE Darnley marriage and the birth of a son to Mary seemed to have made the realisation of her ambition only a matter of patience and self-restraint. Headlong enthusiasm for a Roman catholic restoration might indeed have ruined her prospects; but Mary had ruled five years in Scotland without risking her throne in a collision with Scottish puritanism, and she was politician enough to be capable of practising a similar economy of zeal with regard to the less obnoxious church of England. Englishmen might have accepted, in spite of her religion, a sovereign whom even Knox had been constrained to tolerate; and the majority would soon have turned towards the rising sun. Political forebodings as well as pangs of envy justified Elizabeth's consternation at the fortune of her rival.

Yet James VI. was the only result of her marriage which Mary at the time could contemplate with any satisfaction; and before she died, she disinherited her son. Fraught as it was with brilliant promise, the Darnley marriage brought in its train misery, shame, and disaster. Elizabeth had faced a similar test when she entertained Arran in 1559. He stood to the Scottish throne in the same relation as Darnley did to the English; he was the chosen of the protestants in Scotland as Darnley was of the catholics in England; and his mental disqualifications were hardly more serious than Darnley's. But while Elizabeth, perhaps perforce, rejected the bait, Mary succumbed to the personal and political temptation. Passion ruled her will, or her judgment was at fault. She did not wait to gauge her suitor's character, or to fathom the depths to which such a husband could drag such a wife. Age might have tempered Darnley's follies and sated some of his vices; but if it is possible to judge a murdered youth of twenty-one,

Darnley can of all the Stuarts only be pronounced the worst. CHAP.
XIV. Physically handsome, he was intellectually imbecile; he was obstinate, quarrelsome, licentious, ill-bred, and weak. He treated his royal bride with disgusting brutality and her nobles with insufferable insolence; he betrayed her trust and her honour as a woman and as a queen; and his own fate hardly did him injustice.

Mary had warnings in time. Two months before their marriage Randolph wrote that Darnley had grown so proud that he was intolerable to all honest men, "and almost forgetful of his duty to her". "God," said the Scots, "must send him a short end, or themselves a miserable life to live under such government as this is like to be." [1] But so far from paying heed to these monitions, Mary became infected with Darnley's arrogance. She hinted openly at asserting not only her own but her husband's claims to the English throne; and the idea, instilled into her mind in youth, that she had a divine hereditary right to the English throne which no act of parliament could take away, began to warp her action under his influence. Her boundless infatuation for him was widely ascribed to magic; and Randolph, who had not long before declared that she was "strictly obeyed, perfectly served, and honoured by all," now lamented that "the fame she had gotten through virtue and worthiness was now clean fallen from her, as though neither the one nor the other had been known unto her. Her country was so evil guided that justice lay dead in all places." [2] Like Richard II. in 1397, she was seized with an apparently sudden resolve to make herself absolute; and possibly there was some psychological connexion between the loosing of her sexual and her political passions. The circumspection of her conduct since her arrival in Scotland was cast aside, and she turned with fury upon those whom she now conceived to be enemies. Moray was proclaimed a rebel for having entered into a bond with Knox to defend the religion of the Congregation; and he fled to England after a vain attempt at resistance. Elizabeth dared not show him countenance; and France threatened war if England intervened by force of arms in Scotland. Philip sent Mary money; the pope sent her a

---

[1] *Foreign Cal.*, 1564-65, pp. 372-73, 381, 436.   [2] *Ibid.*, p. 495.

legate and money; and behind them loomed the black form of a catholic league to which the conference at Bayonne was believed to have given birth.

Mary had struck hard and in season, and Knox alone did not flinch. But others, like Ruthven and Morton, "only espied their time and made fair weather until it should come to the pinch". "A stranger, a varlet" had "the whole guiding of this queen and country;" and as early as October, 1565, Randolf reported "jars" between Mary and Darnley.[1] The varlet was David Riccio; originally principal bass singer in Mary's chapel, he was in 1564 appointed her French secretary, and was possibly the real author of the Darnley marriage and of the queen's resolute catholic policy. He was abler far than Darnley; and as her husband's incompetence grew clearer to Mary, she gave Riccio the place which Darnley should have occupied. Riccio practically superseded Maitland as secretary, Moray as chief minister, Morton as chancellor, and Darnley as the most intimate friend of the queen. The innocence of their relations can only be defended by denying Mary's common-sense; and Riccio's egregious insolence almost coerced his dispossessed rivals into conspiracy. Maitland was the most dangerous, Morton the boldest of the band, while Darnley's griefs as a discarded husband were the most useful weapons in their hands. So soon had Mary thrown away her best cards: she had alienated the national feeling represented by Maitland, as well as the catholic support of the Lennox faction. The exiled lords in England, Moray, Argyle, and Glencairn, subscribed a bond to procure Darnley the crown-matrimonial in return for their own restoration and the maintenance of the Protestant religion; and Riccio was brutally murdered almost in Mary's presence on March 9, 1566.[2] Mary swore revenge, and the great catholic design was merged in a mortal feud between its leading champions: "all the wise ordinances made by the good queen with regard to religion," wrote Silva, "have been upset, and will be very difficult to establish again".[3]

The "good" queen did not possess Elizabeth's faculty for walking secure on the edge of a precipice, but she knew how to deal with Darnley. A few hours after Riccio's murder she

---

[1] *Foreign Cal.*, 1564-5, pp. 489, 495.   [2] *Hatfield MSS.*, i., 333-36.
[3] *Spanish Cal.*, i., 550.

had soothed Darnley into subjection, and wormed out the CHAP.
secrets of the conspiracy. The hostile coalition was broken XIV.
up. Moray, who appeared the day after the murder, was
received with effusion and admitted with Argyle and Glencairn
into the council; while Morton and Ruthven were outlawed,
and Darnley was left more powerless than before. A composite ministry consisting of Moray, Argyle, and Glencairn,
the catholics Huntly and Atholl, and the protestant Bothwell
—in whom, wrote Randolph in October, 1565, "is her chief
trust"[1]—pursued conciliation and peace for a period during
which James VI. was born (June 19), and a fresh effort was
made to recover Elizabeth's favour and to secure by diplomatic
argument the reversion to the English throne. Mary's case
was carefully prepared by Maitland,[2] who maintained that
Henry VIII.'s will was invalid as not being signed by his own
hand, and asserted that Paget had admitted the fact in the
house of lords in Mary's reign. This was sounder legal ground
than Mary's theories of divine hereditary right; and the anxiety
of the English parliament for the settlement of the succession
showed clearly enough that the Suffolk title was considered
extremely doubtful.

It was not in Elizabeth's power to gratify Mary, even
had she wished; for parliament, which reassembled on September 30, 1566, after various prorogations, could press
Elizabeth harder in one direction than Maitland and Mary's
ambassador, Sir James Melville, could in the other. The
members of the lower house were, wrote Silva, "nearly all
heretics and adherents of Catherine"; even the Speaker,
Onslow, was "a furious heretic".[3] The question came up as
soon as supply was mooted, many members contending that
it must be settled before a subsidy was granted; some wanted
the doors locked to precipitate a division, and the house, says
Silva, came to blows. The *Journals*, however, only record
that the usual committee of privy councillors and other members was appointed to deal with the question of supply on

---

[1] Bain, *Scottish Cal.*, ii., 221.
[2] Burnet, ed. Pocock, iv., 533-39; *Egerton Papers* (Camden Soc.), pp. 41-49.
[3] *Spanish Cal.*, i., p. 583. "Two other men were nominated, but this man
had a great majority of votes, which proves how strong the heretics are." Onslow was elected by 82 votes to 60, but he was proposed by the government,
and the division of opinion was on different grounds (see D'Ewes, pp. 120-22).

October 17, and that a motion to consider the succession was well received next day.   Elizabeth told Silva she would not allow the Suffolk claim to be discussed, and she tried to divert the house by a subterfuge.   Cecil and Sir F. Knollys were sent to say that she was " by God's special grace moved to marriage," and to advise the house to wait for the result of that motion before proceeding with their own.   Members were not satisfied, and they persuaded the lords to join them in a further petition. Elizabeth flew into a royal rage ; she called Norfolk a traitor, said Pembroke talked like a swaggering sailor, and recommended Northampton, instead of mincing words with her, to explain how he managed to marry a second wife while his first was still alive.   She talked of placing them all under arrest and dissolving parliament.   Silva advised a prorogation instead, but she replied that she could not punish members unless parliament were dissolved.[1]

Eventually cooler counsels prevailed.   The queen consented to receive a deputation on November 5.   She rated its members, bishops, peers, and commons, like schoolboys, told them she would marry, but "some one who will not please you" [a foreigner], and would not deal with the succession. This answer, when reported to the commons, was received in stony silence ; and two days later William Lambert, member for Aldborough, summoned up courage to suggest persistence. A hot debate followed, and on the 9th Knollys brought down a sharp order from the queen to stop it.   For the moment the house was silenced, but on the 11th Paul Wentworth raised the question whether this command were not against its liberties ; the debate lasted for five hours and was then adjourned.   Next morning the Speaker was summoned into the queen's presence, and told to reiterate her commands to the house.   She said to Silva that "she did not know what these devils wanted".   He replied that "what they wanted was simply liberty, and if kings did not look out for themselves, and combine together to check them, it was easy to see how the licence that these people had taken would end".[2]

These proceedings, however, were partly a comedy with a serious diplomatic purpose on Elizabeth's part.   The threat to

[1] *Spanish Cal.*, i., 591-92, 594 ; D'Ewes, pp. 107-8.
[2] *Spanish Cal.*, i., 590.

marry a foreigner would certainly deter parliament from pestering the queen about her marriage, and consequently about the succession. It was also designed to lead up to further discussion of the Archduke Charles and Anglo-Hapsburg friendship. Elizabeth was still nervous about catholic designs. Philip was believed to be coming to the Netherlands to crush their discontent; Mary was supposed to be in league with Shane O'Neill, who "is so good a Christian that he cuts off the head of anybody, even an Englishman, who enters his country and is not a catholic";[1] and a rising of English catholics was expected. Elizabeth therefore grew solicitous for Philip's happiness; she denounced his Dutch and Flemish rebels in unmeasured terms, and spoke of Philip and his queen "with the many kind words she knows so well how to employ". Silva was really affected at the picture she drew of herself and her position in the midst of heretic wolves, and he communicated his emotion to Philip—"God help her! I wish I could have more hope of her welfare".[2] The queen, however, was eminently fitted to look after herself, and as a parliamentary tactician she almost equalled her father. Her attack upon the liberties of the house of commons banished all other thoughts from members' minds, and for a fortnight public business made little progress. Then came a gracious message which threw the house into ecstasies; on November 25 she revoked her twice repeated prohibition of debate, and on the 27th she remitted one-third of the supply the commons had proposed.[3] The house was delighted with what it thought was victory, and no more was heard of marriage or the succession.

There still remained what Silva called the second of the two "principal points which the heretics thought to carry," the question of religion, which came up in two forms, the Thirty-nine articles[4] and the legal status of the bishops. On December 5 was introduced into the lower house "the bill with a little book printed 1562 [3] for the sound christian religion": it was read a second time on the 10th, a third on the 13th, and was sent up to the lords on the 14th as "the bill with the Articles". The commons obviously thought that, as parliament had passed an act of six articles in 1539, it should now pass an act of

---

[1] Silva to Philip, *Spanish Cal.*, i., 550.   [2] *Ibid.*, i., 547, 577, 581, 586.
[3] *Commons' Journals*, i., 78; D'Ewes, pp. 130-31.   [4] See above, p. 252.

thirty-nine.   The queen thought otherwise, and required Bacon
to withdraw the bill after its first reading in the house of lords.
The two archbishops, however, complained of Bacon's action,
"and went to speak to the queen on the subject.   She refused
to receive them for two days, and on the third day they tell
me she treated them in such a manner that they came out
very crestfallen ; and so the heretics remain." [1]   Silva regarded
the result as a catholic victory, won by the queen with the help
of her temporal peers, over an attempt made by a heretical
house of commons and an equally heretical episcopate to impose a statutory and heretical uniformity of dogma.   No one
appears to have had any concern for ecclesiastical autonomy ;
the bishops and commons demanded, while the queen resisted,
a doctrinal uniformity based on act of parliament.   She was
moved less by desire for toleration than by a diplomatic aversion to having her hands bound and her discretion fettered by
inflexible statutes.

The bishops' lot was most unhappy.   They could not obtain coercive machinery for their articles of religion, and they
could not secure a decently legal status.   The combined ingenuity of Bonner and the catholic lawyer Plowden had contrived to find in the anomalous position of Elizabeth's bishops
a loophole of escape from the obligation to take the oath of
supremacy.   It had to be administered by the bishop of the
diocese, who in Bonner's case was Horne of Winchester.   But
even though Horne might have been consecrated a bishop
with proper ecclesiastical ceremony, his legal claim to the
bishopric of Winchester depended upon a multitude of doubtful points ; and the government, which venerated legal forms,
stopped the proceedings against Bonner.   Only a parliamentary statute could establish the bishops in security and
comfort.   The bill for their confirmation passed the commons
without opposition, but in the lords a proviso was inserted that
it should not validate any of their acts with regard to life and
property ; and even as amended eleven temporal peers voted
against it. [2]   There were few in those days to reverence the

---

[1] *Spanish Cal.*, i., 606; *Domestic Cal.*, 1547-80, p. 284.
[2] *Spanish Cal.*, i., 596, where, of the eleven names, five are incorrectly given :
Exeter is printed for Worcester, Windsor for Mounteagle, Darcy for Dacre,
Morden for Mordaunt, and Montague is styled earl instead of viscount; see *Lords'
Journals*, Nov. 6, and D'Ewes, p. 108.

bishops of the new creation. Many protestants did not want them at all, catholics wanted the older sort, and lords and gentry wanted their lands. The queen herself, says Silva, "does not like them, although she pretends to"; and the temporary relief which the catholics obtained under this act was partly due to her dislike, partly to lay greed for the bishops' lands, and partly to popular complaints of episcopal mismanagement.

The session closed on January 2, 1567, with a two hours' address from the Speaker to the queen, and a reply by Lord Keeper Bacon, in which he rebuked the house for calling in question the queen's grants of patents or monopolies. Then Elizabeth, after assenting to thirty-four acts, thought she would say a few words herself, despite the reluctance she expressed to do so "in such open assemblies". Her words were brief and pointed enough. " I have in this assembly," she said, " found so much dissimulation, where I always professed plainness, that I marvel thereat, yea two faces under one hood, and the body rotten, being covered with two vizors, Succession and Liberty. . . . But do you think that either I am unmindful of your surety by succession, wherein is all my care, considering I know myself to be mortal? No, I warrant you. Or that I went about to break your liberties? No, it was never in my meaning, but to stay you before you fell into the ditch. . . . And therefore henceforth, whether I live to see the like assembly or no, or whoever it be, yet beware however you prove your Prince's patience, as you have now done mine."

Elizabeth felt sore not only because her prerogative had been called in question over monopolies, but also because privy councillors had moved the house to act on the question of the succession, and had voted for the bishops' bill and for the bill confirming the queen's patents. Henry VIII. had freely invoked parliamentary action to relieve himself from responsibility. But it was a different thing for parliament to imply that its sanction was necessary to validate royal grants; and the act, which was passed for that purpose, was the prelude to a long constitutional struggle. The activity of the house of commons was also vindicated by its rejection of three bills on one day, and several others during the session, often by narrow majorities, and by its delay of supply in order to force through the bishops' bill.[1] Nevertheless, Elizabeth's tactics had won the substantial victories : parliamentary authorisation had been refused to the Thirty-nine articles; the succession was still unsettled, and there was only her promise to bind her to marriage.

Mary's efforts had once more failed. The punishment of Dalton, a Cornish member, which she demanded for words spoken against her in the house of commons, and the examination of Henry VIII.'s will, which Elizabeth promised her, came to nothing.[2] But by the time that parliament was dissolved, she was thinking of other things than her claims to the English throne. There is only the word of her enemy Lennox to vouch for the truth of the story that over Riccio's grave she had vowed that "a fatter than he should lie anear him ere one twelvemonth was at an end";[3] but there is ample evidence that the thraldom of Darnley's yoke was proving intolerable to her haughty and impatient spirit. Public wrongs inflamed her private griefs. Darnley intrigued against her abroad as well as at home. He sought support from the pope and catholic sovereigns on the ground that Mary was trifling with religion : he plotted with Elizabeth's prisoners, the Poles, who bestowed on him their claims to the English throne;[4] and he schemed to secure the Scottish crown matrimonial, and to limit Mary's authority. He seemed bent on ruining her policy as well as destroying her happiness, and Mary was driven to desperation. "How to be free of him," wrote Maitland, "she sees no outgait."[5] She frequently wished she were dead, and she was near death's door from illness in October, 1566. If she wished Darnley dead and let her wish be known, others did the same. It seemed monstrous that such a wretch should be permitted to trouble the peace of Scotland; and few of its lords were entire strangers to one or other of the schemes for his removal.

Some sort of bond to this effect seems to have been signed by Moray in October; but however much he may have "looked

---

[1] *Spanish Cal.*, i., 604, 606.

[2] Bain, *Scottish Cal.*, ii., 308-9, 310 ; *Hatfield MSS.*, i., 341 ; *cf. Foreign Cal.*, 1566-68, pp. 148-49, 162, 164 ; *Domestic Cal.*, 1547-80, p. 283.

[3] Lang, *Mystery of Mary Stuart*, p. 72.

[4] *Foreign Cal.*, 1566-68, p. 165 ; Bain, ii., 293. On Mary's relations with the Papacy see Pollen, *Papal Negotiations with Mary Queen of Scots*, 1901.

[5] Lang, pp. 94, 108 ; Bain, ii., 301-2 ; *Spanish Cal.*, i., 612, 618 ; *Documentos Ineditos* lxxxix., 442.

through his fingers," he took no active part in the conference CHAP. XIV. of Craigmillar early in December, when Mary discussed methods of procedure.   Maitland suggested a divorce ; it was objected that such a measure would bastardise the young prince, and Mary said she would rather leave it to God than do anything to smirch her honour or her conscience.   Maitland besought her to leave it to her council, and assured her that their meas- ures would be good and approved by parliament.   To conspire against the husband of a queen was, however, dangerous work ; and retribution could best be avoided by making accomplices of all who might be willing or able to inflict it.   So, at the end of 1566, after James had been baptised in his father's absence, we find Moray and Maitland combining with Bothwell and Huntly to press for the pardon of the lords betrayed by Darnley and exiled for Riccio's murder, and Mary graciously granting their request.   Three weeks later the enmity between husband and wife apparently came to a sudden end ; Darnley made offers of amendment, and Mary travelled from Edinburgh on January 21, 1567, to visit her sick and penitent husband. He was at Glasgow safe in the Lennox country, but she per- suaded him to accompany her to Craigmillar for the sake of his health.   A few miles from Edinburgh they were met on the 31st by Bothwell and conveyed to a house in Kirk o' Field, where the university now stands.   Early in the morning of February 10, while Mary was absent at a marriage feast, the house was blown up by gunpowder placed in the room below Darnley's which the queen had occupied.   Darnley himself was found strangled some distance away.

Bothwell's responsibility for the murder is hardly a matter of doubt.   The vexed problem is the extent of Mary's com- plicity ; and the various actors in the tragedy spent more energy in seeking to prove others guilty than themselves innocent.   In each case it is a question of degree, to which verdicts of guilty, not guilty, or not proven are severally crude and inadequate answers.   That Mary actively plotted her husband's assassination can only be proved by the disputed "casket letters".   That she wished for his death is indubitable : whether she desired the means is more doubtful ; but it is probable that she let her wish be known to men who were prepared to adopt the means and had grounds for expecting forgiveness and favour. Such conduct on Mary's part was a breach of morals rather than of the criminal law; and to men's moral sense it was less shocking that Mary should wish for the murder of such a husband than that she should marry his murderer. Moray kept aloof from a plot of which he doubtless had suspicions; and it is a plausible though gratuitous assumption that he "looked through his fingers" rather to save his prospects than to salve his conscience. Maitland's complicity was more serious, and he was perhaps responsible for covert suggestions of the murder.

From the historical, as distinct from the biographical point of view, Mary's guilt or innocence is less important than the impression which her action produced upon public opinion. Long before the casket letters came to light, friends as well as foes, Archbishop Beaton and Morette, the ambassador of Savoy, as well as Randolph and Drury suspected her complicity; and their suspicions were confirmed by her subsequent conduct. She refused to prosecute Bothwell, and permitted him to over- awe the court which was to have heard Lennox's accusation. Lennox dared not appear, and his suit was lost by default. Bothwell then by force or cajolery induced some lords to sign a bond at a supper at Ainslie's Tavern in Edinburgh for his marriage with Mary.[1] Five days later, on April 19, he waylaid Mary and carried her off to Dunbar. "It is believed," wrote Silva, "that the whole thing has been arranged so that, if any- thing comes of the marriage, the queen may make out that she was forced into it." [2] She remained at Dunbar till May 3, while Bothwell was divorced from his wife, Lady Janet Gor- don. Returning on that day with Bothwell to Edinburgh, Mary solemnly denied before the court of session that she was act- ing under restraint; created Bothwell a duke; and then on the 15th married him according to protestant rites—a step which Du Croc was sure, before the pretended abduction, that Mary would take.[3]

Catholic Europe stood aghast at Mary's wild career. "With

---

[1] The existing copies of this bond give varying lists of signatories. That in Bain's *Scottish Calendar*, ii., 322-23, includes Moray, who was not in Scotland at the time. See Lang, *Mary Stuart*, pp. 177-78, and *Foreign Cal.*, 1569-71, p. 355.

[2] *Spanish Cal.*, i., 638.

[3] *Ibid.*, p. 635; *cf.* Kirkcaldy's letters in Bain, ii., 324-25.

this last act, so dishonourable to God and herself," wrote the papal nuncio destined for Scotland, "the propriety of sending any sort of envoy ceases. . . . One cannot as a rule expect much from people who are slaves to their desires." [1] For the moment Mary had lost all her friends in Europe and roused all her foes in Scotland. To both alike the Bothwell marriage seemed a damning comment on the Darnley murder; and almost universal horror was expressed by those who did and those who did not feel it. The Hamiltons alone, her former rivals, supported Mary out of hatred for Lennox, Moray, and the other Stuarts. At Carberry Hill on June 15, Mary was taken captive by the confederate lords and imprisoned on Loch Leven, while Bothwell fled to the north and then to Denmark. Mary refused to give up her third and only protestant husband, or "lend her authority to prosecute the murder".[2] On July 16 she was accordingly forced to sign a deed of abdication and to nominate the absent Moray as regent;[3] and on the 29th her infant son was crowned as James VI. On May 2, 1568, she escaped from Loch Leven, repudiated her abdication, and, joined by the Hamiltons, met the regent's forces at Langside. Routed in battle, she fled across the Solway, and on the 17th appealed on English soil, not for safety, but for aid to chastise her rebellious subjects.

The dilemma in which Elizabeth now found herself was largely of her own creation. While Pius V., Philip II., and Charles IX., estranged by Mary's conduct and impeded by their own affairs, had left the Queen of Scots to her fate, Elizabeth had proclaimed aloud her sympathy for her fellow-sovereign. There was always some sincerity in her partisanship of crowned heads against their subjects, and she would feel especially drawn towards a queen deserted by catholic powers. That Mary had married a protestant and had apparently destroyed her power for evil may also have tended to soothe Elizabeth. "Two special causes move her," wrote Cecil in cipher to Throckmorton, "one, that she be not thought to the world partial against the queen; the other, that by this example none of her own be encouraged." She vehemently denied

---

[1] "Che sono sottoposte ai lor piaceri," Pollen, pp. 392-3; *cf. ibid.*, Introd., pp. cxxix-cxxxi.   [2] Bain, ii., 350.

[3] Moray had obtained from Mary leave to travel abroad because he feared Bothwell's intentions, *Spanish Cal.*, i., 635.

the right of subjects to call their queen to account, and threatened to "take plain part against them to revenge their sovereign,
for example to all posterity". She refused to recognise James
VI.'s government; and she was only deterred from forcible
intervention on Mary's behalf by a strong hint from Edinburgh
that such a step would precipitate her execution and provoke
an appeal to the French, who, declared Throckmorton, "take
it not greatly to heart whether the queen live or die, be at
liberty or in prison, if they can renew their old league".[1]
Elizabeth, wrote Silva on the news of Mary's arrival in England, "has always shown goodwill to the queen of Scots; and
the council, or a majority of it, has been opposed to her and
leant to the side of the regent and his government".[2] She
had sent Mary a ring while in prison as a gage of her bene-
volent interest, and wrote an effusive letter of congratulation
on her escape; and Mary's envoys asserted that, relying on
these tokens, their sovereign had sought assistance in England
instead of appealing to France.[3]

Elizabeth's first impulse was, in fact, to treat Mary as Queen
of Scotland, and to require the regency to recognise her as
such. It needed weeks of discussion in the privy council to
convince her of the dangers of that course. Sir Francis
Knollys, who had been sent down to attend on Mary at Carlisle, was impressed by her "eloquent tongue, discreet head,
stout courage, and liberal heart," and thought she should be
given her choice between returning to Scotland or remaining
in England. But, as he watched her demeanour and her disappointment at Elizabeth's procrastination, his comments grew
more critical. "The thing that most she thirsteth after is
victory . . . so that for victory's sake pain and peril seemeth
pleasant unto her." On June 12 he described her as "being
dedicate to revenge in hope of victory by the aid of strangers";
and on the 13th he wrote: "It is great vanity (in my opinion)
to think she will be stayed by courtesy, or bridled by fear,
from bringing the French to Scotland, or employing her
money, men of war, and friendship to satisfy her bloody appe-

[1] Bain, ii., 363, 367-68, 372, 375, 377, 379, 384, 532.
[2] *Spanish Cal.*, ii., 36. In one letter from Elizabeth, Cecil went so far as
to alter an expression of dislike for "their" doings into one of dislike for "her"
[*i.e.* Mary's] doings, Bain, ii., 366.
[3] *Spanish Cal.*, ii., 42; *cf. Hatfield MSS.*, i., 356; Bain, ii., 506.

tite to shed the blood of her enemies ".[1] She was indeed at that moment appealing for aid to Alva as well as to France and the pope, protesting her fidelity to the catholic religion, and winning the hearts of the English catholic gentry who flocked to see her.[2] For a few weeks she had thought of trying to conciliate Elizabeth by religious conformity. She " had grown to good liking of our common prayer," and taken an English chaplain into her service. But she soon changed her mind, and " openly professed herself of the papists' religion more earnestly than before". " Why," she asked Knollys, " would you have me lose France and Spain and all my friends in other places by seeming to change my religion, and yet I am not assured that the queen my good sister will be my assured friend?"[3] She grasped the facts that her alienation of national sentiment in Scotland had put an end to her *rôle* as a *politique,* and that henceforth she must play the part of a champion of the catholic faith.

Cecil, as usual, drew up a statement of the perils likely to attend each of the three alternative courses open to Elizabeth, without committing to paper any definite recommendation.[4] If Mary were allowed to go to France, she would revive her claim to the English throne, relying on those who—" some for religion, some for affection to her title, others for discontentation and love of change "—favoured her cause in England ; and the old league between France and Scotland would be renewed. If Mary remained in England, she would practise with her friends there for the English crown, and then use the prospect of her succession as a bait to attract to her side all parties in Scotland. Thirdly, if she returned to her throne in Scotland, she would ruin the friends of England and rule with the help of France. The policy which commended itself to the government is tersely and accurately indicated by Silva in July : Elizabeth would keep Mary in honourable imprisonment, " the one object of these people being so to manage Scotch affairs as to keep that country friendly with them, in the belief that, whilst the two kingdoms are in accord, they have nothing to fear ; and they think this could not be the case whilst the

---

[1] Bain, ii., 416, 428-29, 431.   [2] *Spanish Cal.,* ii., 31-32, 42.
[3] Bain, ii., 466, 510.   [4] *Ibid.,* ii., 418-19.

queen remained free, because of religion and other causes ".[1]
" It is not meant," wrote Cecil in cipher to Sussex, " if the
Queen of Scots shall be proved guilty of the murder, to restore
her to Scotland, howsoever her friends may brag to the contrary ; nor yet shall there be any haste made of her delivery,
until the success of the matters of France and Flanders be
seen." [2]

The problem was how, while pursuing in secret this substantive policy of accord with the regent's government, to maintain
in view of Spain, France, and the English catholics, the correct
monarchical attitude towards rebels and the mask of friendship
with the Scottish queen. Cecil attached more importance to
the substantive policy, Elizabeth to the mask ; and this divergence produced that combination of " fair words enough and
no deeds," of which Mary complained.[3] One example must
suffice. At Mary's instance Elizabeth required both parties
in Scotland to refrain from mutual hostilities ; and Knollys
lamented that Moray's efforts to reduce south-west Scotland
to order would thereby be frustrated. He did not know that,
while this public intimation went to Scotland, Cecil sped a
private message to the regent bidding him do quickly what
he had to do.

Mary meanwhile was importuning Elizabeth for help, and
insisting that if it were not forthcoming she would be driven
to seek it in other quarters. The attraction she exerted over
the catholic gentry of the north brought home the danger to
Elizabeth's government ; and in July she was removed to
Bolton, whence escape was not so easy as from Carlisle. But
the most pressing question was Elizabeth's attitude towards
the regency in Scotland. Even if Mary had been proved
innocent, her forcible restoration to the Scottish throne was
a quixotic enterprise which no ruler in the sixteenth century
would have undertaken without powerful motives of self-interest ;
and, apart from the political considerations which were sufficiently deterrent, Elizabeth could not on moral grounds attack
the Scottish lords without some proof that they had acted
wrongly. She therefore called upon them to justify their

[1] *Spanish Cal.*, ii., 57 ; *cf.* Bain, ii., 438-39.
[2] Bain, ii., 516; *cf. ibid.*, 643 ; *Foreign Cal.*, 1569-71, p. 357.
[3] Bain, ii., 441.

proceedings. Moray and his colleagues expressed their readiness to do so, and a conference was arranged at York between commissioners representing Elizabeth, Mary, and the Scottish government.

The conference was in no sense a judicial trial of Mary for the murder of her husband. The proceedings were political, not legal : no lawyers were employed on either side ; no witnesses were heard or cross-examined ; and nothing in the form of a verdict was intended or returned. Elizabeth's representatives were authorised merely to hear and report the proofs and allegations of the two contending parties : they were a commission of inquiry and not a court of law; and their object was simply to elicit information for the guidance of their government. Mary's guilt or innocence was regarded only as a factor in determining Elizabeth's political relations with the Scottish rulers. Mary had repudiated the idea that Elizabeth had any jurisdiction over her; Elizabeth did not claim it yet; and in spite of Moray's express wish that her commissioners should have full power to pronounce Mary guilty or not guilty, Elizabeth neither gave this power nor exercised it herself. She held that sovereigns were subject to no legal tribunal; and notwithstanding the old English pretensions to suzerainty over Scotland, she hesitated to set the example of sitting in judgment on princes. But she conceived that the view she took of Mary's conduct must influence her own policy, and asserted the right to investigate it for her own information.

Her commissioners, Norfolk, Sussex, and Sir Ralph Sadler, met at York on October 3. Mary's principal representatives were Leslie, Bishop of Ross, and Lord Herries ; and Moray was accompanied by Morton and Maitland. Mary's commission was limited so as to bar any conclusion that should infringe her sovereignty or touch her in estate and honour. Moray and his colleagues refused to produce their charges or proofs, unless they were assured of Elizabeth's protection against Mary's vengeance, in case they succeeded in establishing her guilt. They had no misgivings about the conclusiveness of their evidence ; but they feared lest Elizabeth should abandon them, when they had made their breach with Mary irreparable by publishing the documents in their hands. They felt that they could not stand alone ; and if Elizabeth would not guarantee her support, they would prefer to suppress their charges and make terms with Mary in spite of her guilt. Maitland, in fact, actuated partly by patriotism and partly by Mary's denunciation of his own complicity in the murder, was in favour of compromise. But, despite her protestations, Elizabeth had no wish to see Mary restored by agreement with any one except with herself; the informal communication of the contents of the "casket" letters induced her to give assurances which were accepted as satisfactory by Moray; and he consented to lay bare the Queen of Scots' infamy. Even so, it was Elizabeth's countenance and not Mary's condemnation that he wanted. Châtelherault contended that if Mary's condemnation barred her from the throne, it also barred her son and cleared the way for his own succession. For this reason Sussex thought that Moray would not push matters to extremities. The Scots lords would not have a Hamilton as king; they much preferred a royal minority.[1]

The scene of the inquiry was now changed from York to Westminster, where a new commission met on November 25. It included the Lord-Keeper Bacon, Arundel, Leicester, Clinton, and Cecil, as well as the original three. But again the commissioners protested that they did not "mean to proceed judicially"; and their commission, like the first, was only to hear and report. On December 7 Moray produced a casket which Morton swore had been left in Edinburgh Castle by Bothwell on his flight in June, 1567. It contained letters and sonnets written in French and, it was alleged, by Mary's hand, which, if genuine, proved that she was infatuated with Bothwell months before Darnley's murder, and that she had deliberately contrived that crime. Difficult as it is to believe these evidences true, it is still more difficult to account for the diabolical ingenuity and psychological insight of an unknown hypothetical forger.[2] Maitland alone can by any flight of imagination be credited with the necessary knowledge and skill to counterfeit Mary's hand, language, and mind; and little short of certainty that Mary was not their author would justify a suspicion that Maitland forged the sonnets. An attempt

---

[1] *Foreign Cal.*, 1569-71, p. 285; Lodge, *Illustrations*, i., 458-464.

[2] *Cf.* Lady Blennerhassett, *Maria Stuart, Königin von Schottland*, 1907, p. 200 ff.; Lang, *The Mystery of Mary Stuart*, p. 309 ff.

might perhaps be made to show that these, like other sonnets of the period, were mere literary exercises without any autobiographical application.[1]　But the overwhelming weight of coincidence between the testimony of the casket letters, the independent evidence which led diplomatists and others to believe in Mary's guilt before the letters were discovered, and the depositions and confessions of accomplices who were brought to trial, has convinced the majority of scholars that, while undoubtedly there was a political conspiracy to get rid of Darnley, in which several of Mary's accusers were implicated in varying degrees, her own responsibility for the actual murder is only a question of degree.

Further documents were produced before the commissioners on December 8 and following days; and on the 14th the whole series was read out at Hampton Court in the presence of the Earls of Northumberland, Shrewsbury, Huntingdon, Westmorland, Worcester, and Warwick.　Mary made no serious effort to meet the charges.　She wrote, however, to her friends in Scotland, the Earls of Huntly and Argyle, a countercharge for them to "eke and pare" at their discretion, and then to sign and publish.　This they did on January 12, 1569, accusing Maitland principally, and Moray in a less degree, of complicity in the murder on the ground of their participation in the discussion at Craigmillar in December, 1567. But Mary relied for the most part on political weapons to counteract the political aims which Elizabeth had in view at the conferences at York and Westminster.　She appointed Châtelherault regent, and declared him heir to the throne in the event of her own and her son's decease.　She asserted that Elizabeth and Moray had formed a compact whereby Moray was to succeed on James VI.'s death, to surrender certain strongholds into Elizabeth's hands, and to hold Scotland as an English fief.　She alleged a further league between Moray and Hertford (who was to marry Cecil's daughter) for mutual support of each other's pretensions to the Scottish and English thrones; and she appealed to her loyal subjects against "the ancient and natural enemies" of her realm.[2]

---

[1] It has been suggested that the sonnets were really written to Darnley in 1565; but in that case it is strange that Bothwell should have kept them.

[2] Bain, ii., 574-75, 596-600, 608-9.

Elizabeth repudiated these designs, and pressed Mary to answer Moray's charges. In case of refusal, she threatened to publish Mary's infamy. But she offered oblivion if Mary would resign her crown to her son and consent to his education in England as heir to both the thrones. Mary would have been well-advised to accept ; and for a day or two at the end of December she seemed inclined to consider Elizabeth's terms. But Spain intervened, and Mary was swept on to her fate. "It appears," wrote Guerau de Spes, the new Spanish ambassador in London, on November 6, "as if the time was approaching when this country may be made to return to the catholic church " ;[1] and at the end of December Philip offered either to marry Mary himself, or to promote her marriage with the Archduke Charles or with Don John of Austria. "Praise God," exclaimed Mary on January 5, 1569, "our friends increase and theirs decrease daily." She did not exaggerate : "Huntly," lamented Kirkcaldy from Edinburgh, "reigns in the north, the Hamiltons seize houses and take prisoners, . . . the Hepburns in East Lothian lie in garrison. . . . Meantime for lack of heads the willing hearts hang in suspense whether to abide their fury or defend themselves." There was great appearance of war shortly between England and Spain, wrote one of Mary's friends to another ; she counted on "at least 10,000 men " from France or from Spain before the end of March ; and Elizabeth's own minister, Arundel, told her bluntly that resignation of a crown was not to be pressed by one sovereign on another. "It may be a new doctrine in Scotland, but it is not good to be taught in England." Mary's buoyant spirits rose. She sent her reply to Elizabeth's offer : she would rather die than resign, and the last word of her life should be that of a Queen of Scotland.[2]

[1] *Spanish Cal.*, ii., 83.   [2] Bain, ii., 590, 593-97, 604.

CHAPTER XV.

THE CRISIS OF ELIZABETH'S REIGN.

FOR ten years England and Elizabeth had been guided along
the path of reform by a minister who had risen to power solely
by his own capacity and the royal favour. During a period of
similar length a minister in a like position had directed affairs
under Henry VIII.: then Thomas Cromwell had fallen a victim
to the forces of political and religious reaction; and the progress of the reformation was checked. In 1569 a storm was
brewing in the same quarters, which threatened to make the
same term of years fatal to Cecil's career. He was Cromwell's
political heir, bred in the milder school of Protector Somerset.
So far no execution for treason or religion had blotted Elizabeth's reign; she had prayed, she told Silva, when she came to
the throne, "that God would give her grace to govern with
clemency, and without bloodshed, keeping her hands stainless"; [1]
and the axe stood idle in the Tower. But Cecil's design remained the same as Cromwell's, the delivery of English
sovereignty by the help of the English parliament from the competition of rival jurisdictions, secular and ecclesiastical, domestic
and foreign, and the centralisation of the state by means of
personal monarchy. In Elizabeth's as in Henry's reign this
policy encountered a threefold resistance, from catholics who
resented the nationalisation of the church, from the holders of
medieval franchises who objected to their absorption into a uniform national system, and from nobles who disliked a monarchy
served by upstarts independent of their support. These forces
all came to a head in 1569: their conjunction produced a
situation more critical than that of 1588, when attack from
abroad alone was threatened; and by its triumph in 1569 the
monarchy was enabled to face its external foes with comparative

[1] *Spanish Cal.*, ii., 51.

equanimity.   Englishmen from Henry VIII. to Shakespeare proclaimed that England was unconquerable so long as it remained united ; and the crisis of 1569 was to test the strength of English unity.

It was in England north of the Trent that reaction in all its forms was most widely spread and deeply rooted.   Feudal authority survived Henry VIII.'s establishment of the council of the north in 1537, because great nobles continued to exercise as royal officials a power which they had previously wielded as feudal lords ; and neither they nor their dependants recognised the change in their position.   Sadler complained in 1559, that the Earl of Northumberland wrote letters, " the like of which he had not seen written by any subject ".[1]   When Mary Stuart fled to England he claimed her custody in virtue of his feudal rights over Workington, where she had landed, just as an earlier rebellious Percy had claimed the custody of other Scottish prisoners in 1403 ;[2] and when it was refused, wrote Lowther, the queen's officer, " he grew into great heat and anger, and in the hearing of all men gave me great threatenings with very evil words ".[3]   On similar grounds Northumberland asserted his right to treasure which had been cast ashore within his jurisdiction ; and a more prolonged dispute arose between him and the crown over the copper which Elizabeth began to mine near Keswick.   Less selfish was his championship of the interests of crown tenants in the north against the government ; for the economic changes, which had elsewhere produced inclosures and dissension between the landlords and the peasantry, had hardly touched the pastoral uplands of the northern shires.   Constant warfare on the Borders kept alive a feudal militarism, which had rapidly died out in the more peaceful south since the Wars of the Roses.   Northern lords and gentry passed their time on their estates instead of coming to court, although pressed to do so. In this " natural refuge for lost causes "[4] " the old goodwill of the people, deep-grafted in their hearts, to their nobles and gentlemen " was still a political power.   In Yorkshire " the sheriff has small force, the liberties are so many and so great " ; and " throughout Northumberland," wrote Hunsdon, " they know

<hr>

[1] *Foreign Cal.*, 1558-59, No. 1339.
[2] See above, vol. iv., p. 180.   [3] Bain, ii., 412, 421.
[4] Miss R. R. Reid, " The Rebellion of the Earls," in *Trans. of the Royal Hist. Soc.*, N.S., xx., 176-201,

no other prince but a Percy". Collision between the Percy and the crown was therefore almost unavoidable. In 1560 Northumberland was compelled to resign his wardenship of the east and middle marches; in the same year he refused his assistance to Lord Grey during the Scottish campaign; he gave his sister in marriage to Arthur Pole; and in 1566 Mary Stuart was sending him friendly messages, while he was secretly offering his services to Philip II.[1]

Closely allied with Northumberland was Thomas, Lord Dacre, the warden of the western march, a " rank Papist" who " winked at the incursions of the Grahams," and like Northumberland, " had no desire for protestant success either in Scotland or in England ". " He sat still," wrote Sadler in 1559, " in time of war, and now in peace increases unquietness." [2] He, too, was deprived of his office on Sadler's recommendation; but he died in 1566 leaving his brother Leonard, and his widow, who became the Duke of Norfolk's third wife on January 29, 1567, to fight out his quarrel with the crown. With Norfolk was also connected Charles Neville, Earl of Westmorland, who married the duke's sister in 1564, and like Norfolk had hitherto been loyal to Elizabeth. Much, however, was hoped from Lady Dacre's marriage with the duke; for the lady was a zealous catholic, and Norfolk's household soon assumed the same religious tone.[3] But the immediate effect was to provoke family quarrels over the guardianship of Lord Dacre's children and the disposition of their lands, which Norfolk tried to win from Leonard Dacre and his brothers.

Norfolk himself had in 1560 been grieved to find "this town [Durham] and country hereabouts far out of order in matters of religion ; and the altars standing still in the churches contrary to the Queen's Majesty's proceedings ". The lapse of eight years had not reconciled the mass of the population to religious change. All classes of society, earls, gentry, commons, entirely abstained from public worship, or attended with mental reservation. " To speak plainly," writes the Bishop of Carlisle, " the noblemen's tenants in this country dare not be known to favour that way for fear of losing their farms." Two things,

---

[1] *Foreign Cal.*, 1569-71, p. 159 ; *Spanish Cal.*, ii., 260, 292, 546, 556-57, 565.
[2] *Foreign Cal.*, 1558-59, Nos. 1346, 1364, 1367-68, 1409, 1412.
[3] *Spanish Cal.*, i., 605, 614, 616, 631-32.

explained Pilkington, Bishop of Durham, were a hindrance to
religion.   One was "the Scottish priests that are fled out of
Scotland for their wickedness, and here be hired in parishes on
the Borders because they take less wages than others".   The
other was "the great number of scholars born hereabout, now
lying at Louvain without licence and sending in books and
letters".   Often the same priest read the Anglican service in
public to satisfy the law and then said mass in secret to satisfy
his conscience.   In many Richmondshire parishes there had
been no sermons since the queen's accession.   Numbers of
catholic clergy were ejected, but it was not possible to apply
the tests of 1563 to the justices and other lay officials.   "So
great dissembling, so poisonful tongues and malicious minds,"
wrote Pilkington, "I have not seen."   Ignorance and im-
morality were denounced as bitterly as papistry.   "I cannot," he
continued, "find ten able Justices of Peace of wisdom and
authority of [n]either religion;" and Horne declared that there
was such uncleanness of life "as hath not been heard of among
the heathen".[1]

Neither religious party can claim exemption from responsibility for such a state of things; and it does not in the least
follow that, because we know more of moral conditions in
the sixteenth century, they were therefore worse than in earlier
times.   It is in the nature of reformers to exaggerate the ills
they seek to reform.   It is obvious, however, that a population,
whose spiritual needs were left for the most part to the care
of Scottish priests who had escaped from Knox, of English
priests who had returned from Louvain, or of crypto-Romanists
who remained at home, would readily turn against Elizabeth's
government.   As early as 1561 a rising had been projected;
and in 1565 Mary had "trusted to find many friends in England whensoever time did serve," especially among those of
the old religion, which she meant to restore and "thereby win
the hearts of the common people".[2]   She was then intriguing
with the northern gentry including Leonard Dacre and Christopher Lascelles, who told her in 1566 that the papists in England were ready to rise when she would have them.   She said

---

[1] See Birt, c. viii., *passim; Camden Soc. Miscellany*, vol. ix.; *Domestic Cal.*,
Addenda, 1566-79, *passim;* and *Hatfield MSS.*, i., 310-11.

[2] Haynes, pp. 445-47; *Hatfield MSS.*, i., 338-39, 471.

that foreign aid had been promised her, and that she intended to stir up war in Ireland, and then march her army into
England and proclaim herself queen.

Mary's challenge would appeal to the northern catholics
all the more for being made to them through their natural
leaders and neighbours, and being emphasized by economic
distress. For this last symptom there were probably four
principal causes. In the first place, the destruction of the
monasteries and the transference of their lands, in many cases
to absentee courtiers, continued to increase unemployment and
poverty. Secondly, the decay of the Borders involved a decline
in a prosperity which depended upon horse-breeding and the
provision of other requisites for Border garrisons. Thirdly,
the council of the north now sat only at York, instead of
migrating to Newcastle and elsewhere to accommodate suitors ;
and this put all who had business before it to considerable expense in travelling.[1] Finally, the interruption of the wool
trade with the Netherlands in 1568-69, which caused local disturbances in Norfolk and Suffolk, also inflicted no little injury
upon the Northumbrian towns, where the wool from the moors
was marketed and packed for transport across the North Sea.
For these drawbacks the north derived no compensation from
the maritime adventure and commercial expansion which were
converting the south to enthusiasm for progress in politics and
religion.

Mary Stuart's arrival in England gave backbone to a resistance which might otherwise have succumbed peacefully to
the absorbing pressure of national monarchy ; and the con-
solidation of reactionary forces in the north round her cause
provided also a basis of support for the discontent with Cecil's
policy which was felt by the nobility and catholics in other
parts of England. The trend of his ideas is illustrated by a
singular passage in one of his memorials to Elizabeth : " This
conceit I have thought upon (which I submit to your farther
piercing judgment) that your majesty, in every shire, should
give strict order to some that are indeed trusty and religious
gentlemen ; that, whereas your majesty is given to understand,
that divers popish landlords do hardly use such of your people

---

[1] *Domestic Cal.*, Addenda, 1566-79, pp. 60, 65-66.

and subjects as, being their tenants, do embrace and live after
the authorised and true religion ; that therefore you do constitute and appoint them to deal both with intreaty and authority
that such tenants, paying as others do, be not thrust out of
their living, nor otherwise unreasonably molested. This would
greatly bind the commons' hearts unto you (in whom, indeed,
consisteth the power and strength of your realm), and it will
make them less, or nothing at all, depend upon their landlords."[1] This was more than Cecil's "conceit": the Earl of
Shrewsbury complained of the intervention of the crown on behalf of his "evil tenants of Glossopdale";[2] though few lords
had greater claims on Elizabeth's gratitude than the patient
warder of Mary Queen of Scots. But while it was difficult for
the lords to prevent the judicial encroachments of the crown,
they were able in the parliament of 1566 to check the legalisa-
tion of its policy. A bill for the incorporation of Hexhamshire
with Northumberland, which passed the house of commons,
was rejected by the lords ; and they refused to give statutory
sanction to the queen's claim to minerals wherever they might
be found.

The opposition to this aspect of Tudor policy was not confined to religious reactionaries ; and against Cecil, as its main-
stay, movements obscure though extensive in their ramifications,
confused though comprehensive in their aims, dangerous and
destructive in their tendencies, gradually gathered strength in
1569. Characteristically, this resistance to centralisation was
itself devoid of unity. Even among the catholic gentry and
nobles of the north local faction paralysed their efforts ; and
there was no coherence between the various sections of the
discontented. There were the nobles headed by Norfolk who
wanted to get rid of Cecil and his middle-class ideas, to exclude
the Suffolk line from the succession, and consequently to make
some terms with Mary, Queen of Scots; they were still loyal
to Elizabeth and to her ecclesiastical settlement, though anti-
puritan as a rule. The chief members of this party were Norfolk, Arundel, Lumley, and Pembroke ; while Cumberland,
Derby, Morley, Worcester, Wharton, and even Sussex, were

---

[1] Somers' *Tracts*, i., 167.

[2] Lodge, *Illustrations*, ii., 157, 165, 188 ; *Acts of the P. C.*, 1581-82, pp. 22,
204, 208, 219.

suspected of leaning in the same direction. Leicester and his henchman Throckmorton—"a heretic," says Don Guerau, "but such an enemy of Cecil's that on this account he belongs to the Queen of Scotland's party"—gave in a fitful adhesion, mainly from jealousy of Cecil; and Westmorland formed a weak link between Norfolk's faction and the northern gentry, who were distinctively catholic and pronounced in their sympathy with Mary. But they, too, were not prepared to advocate Elizabeth's deposition; they simply wanted their old religion and their ancient feudal franchises. Both of these parties were regarded by Mary as pieces in her struggle for victory; and, after what had passed, it is probable that she desired a victory as comprehensive as her passion for revenge. She could not expect security until she had wreaked vengeance on her English as well as her Scottish foes, and had re-established throughout Great Britain the Roman catholic religion. With this end in view she would welcome foreign invasion and civil war.

Meanwhile, it was necessary to devise some plan by which these various sections might be temporarily brought into line. The idea of keeping Mary in permanent confinement was not yet seriously contemplated; and it was generally thought in England that the best way of rendering her innocuous was to bridle her with an English husband devoted to Elizabeth. Knollys had in October, 1568, mentioned to Norfolk his own and Elizabeth's kinsman, George Carey, Lord Hunsdon's son, as a possible candidate for the post. But a more dangerous scheme suggested itself simultaneously to more heads than one. The Duchess of Norfolk had died in September, 1567; and Lascelles, an old partisan and correspondent of Mary, proposed to Northumberland that she should marry the duke.[1] The earl, who was now a fervent catholic and was perhaps influenced by his brother-in-law Dacre's quarrel with the duke, objected to Norfolk's protestantism, and would have preferred a match between Mary and a foreign catholic prince. Mary herself, however, was willing to entertain the proposal for what it was worth; and in October Northumberland at her instance broached the matter to the duke at York. At the

---

[1] Northumberland's confession in Sharp, *Rebellion of 1569*, pp. 193-94.

same time Maitland propounded the same idea; and Moray himself discussed it with various lords at Hampton Court in November. From his point of view it possessed two advantages. If Elizabeth refused him her support against Mary, the Norfolk marriage might be used to soothe the Queen of Scots. Or, more probably, he may have regarded the suggestion as a means for forcing Elizabeth's hand; for assuredly she would rather countenance Moray than the Norfolk marriage. On the other hand, the real authors of the scheme wished to improve its chances of success by fathering it on Moray, and to make him responsible, if it failed; and Leicester tried to persuade him that Elizabeth was not averse from the proposal.

Norfolk himself fell an easy victim to his own vanity and to the wiles of schemers who wished to exploit his wealth and his influence as the sole remaining duke in England; and, as the spring of 1569 wore on, the volume of aristocratic opinion in favour of his marriage with Mary and of the settlement of the succession on their children steadily increased. In deference to the popular anxiety expressed in the parliament of 1566, Elizabeth had despatched Sussex to Vienna to renew the negotiations for a match between her and the Archduke Charles.[1] But, as Philip II. wrote to Silva, it was " all an artifice to entertain her subjects"; and Sussex returned from a fruitless quest. This failure and the discussion of Mary's position brought the problem of the succession again to the front; and the council was hopelessly divided in mind. Cecil was the great obstacle to any recognition of Mary's claims, and Norfolk's party came to the conclusion that he must be removed. To achieve this end they sought alliances far and wide, and made promises to their allies, which, if carried out, would have undone all that Elizabeth and Cecil had yet accomplished.

An understanding between the opposition and Spain on the one hand and France on the other was facilitated, and to some extent provoked, by Cecil's audacious and aggressive foreign policy. On December 3, 1568, William Hawkins, who had heard that his brother John had been killed by the Spaniards at S. Juan de Ulua,[2] wrote to Cecil suggesting reprisals at the expense of the Spanish treasure-ships, which had been

---

[1] Cf. Von Sybel, Hist. Zeitschr., xl., 385 ff.   [2] See below, pp. 314-315.

driven into English ports by storms and Huguenot privateers.[1]
The Count Palatine had already set an example by seizing
200,000 crowns on their passage down the Rhine to Alva's
coffers ; and Cecil promptly took the hint. Sir Arthur Cham-
pernown accepted the task under the usual conditions of service
to Elizabeth : he hoped, he wrote, that "after bitter storms of
her displeasure shown at the beginning to color the fact," he
would find the calm of her favour.[2] Elizabeth had her own
grievance against Philip ; for he had expelled from Spain her
ambassador, Dr. John Man—"that dogmatising scamp," as
Philip called him—for insisting upon his right to the English
church service and making free comments on the pope. The
treasure, which amounted to £150,000,[3] had been consigned
to private Genoese merchants ; and Elizabeth pretended that
she was entitled to seize it as a loan in return for her service in saving it from the privateers. Some of the money was
used by Elizabeth to pay the troops of the German princes,
Count Casimir, the younger son of the Elector Palatine, and
the Duke of Zweibrücken, who marched to the assistance of
the Huguenots in 1569. But the results of this barefaced
attempt to make the foreigner pay for Elizabeth's foreign
adventures reached farther than France. Alva's soldiers were
clamouring for arrears of wages, and the treasure had been designed to meet their needs. Its loss compelled the duke in March
to impose the " hundredth," " twentieth" and " tenth" pennies on
the Netherlands ; and this inordinate taxation did more than
anything else to provoke their general revolt.

Nothing short of success could redeem such a stroke from
the charge of suicidal folly. But Cecil had gauged exactly
Spain's power of retaliation ; and, while Mary Stuart was encouraged by the prospect of war between England and Spain
to refuse Elizabeth's terms, Philip was forced to stomach the
insult. Alva, indeed, retorted by placing an embargo on English property in the Netherlands and prohibiting English trade.

---

[1] *Domestic Cal.*, 1547-80, p. 323 ; Kervyn, v., 194. Spinola, the Genoese
banker in England, who was apparently financially interested in Hawkins' venture,
seems to have also made the suggestion as a means of recovering his losses.

[2] Stählin, *Walsingham*, i., 213 n., 218 n.

[3] *Foreign Cal.*, 1569-71, pp. 517-18. The amount seized was 450,000 ducats,
and the single Spanish ducat was officially estimated in 1554 as being worth
6s. 8d. (*Acts of the P. C.*, 1552-54, p. 410).

But he gained, as he admitted, far less than Elizabeth when she in her turn seized all Spanish goods in England. Some discontent and local disturbances were caused by the dislocation of English commerce. But Cecil made strenuous efforts to open up rival trade routes : the Spanish ambassador wrote "the Hamburg business is turning out well for them ; and, although they feel the stoppage of trade with Flanders, this outlet prevents the people from raising a disturbance".[1] Moreover, England's strained relations with Spain excused Cecil for placing Guerau de Spes under surveillance; and he was thus enabled to watch the intrigues of Silva's inexperienced, intractable, and bigoted successor with the opposition lords.

The licence of these intrigues on the part of Norfolk's friends indicates that the Tudor dictatorship, with all its prerogatives and exceptional legislation, was barely adequate for the purpose of preventing treason and preserving national unity. Cecil's opponents were in frequent communication with Guerau, advised him as to the best means of defeating the ends of their own government, and generally behaved in such a way as to lead him to think that the golden opportunity had come for placing Mary Stuart on Elizabeth's throne. They drafted a proclamation, which was forwarded to Alva and published by him, with some modifications, restraining English trade with the Netherlands, in order that the consequent dissatisfaction might strengthen their hands against Cecil.[2] They approached La Mothe Fénelon, the French ambassador, with a similar request, thinking that if England's commerce with France were also stopped, Cecil's fate would be sealed. Through La Mothe they further urged the French government to remonstrate with Elizabeth over Cecil's policy, to claim substantial reparation on its own account as well as on Mary Stuart's, and to move the papal troops in the French service to the shores of the English Channel in order to encourage the catholics and strike terror into the hearts of the protestants.[3] They regarded every success of the English government as a blow to their cause,

---

[1] *Spanish Cal.*, ii., 190; La Mothe, *Correspondance Diplomatique*, i., 408; *Domestic Cal.*, Addenda, 1566-79, pp. 69-71. See generally on this point Ehrenberg's *Hamburg und England im Zeitalter der königin Elisabeth*, 1896.

[2] *Spanish Cal.*, ii., 109, 111-13, 136, 142, 145-47, 153.

[3] La Mothe, i., 331.

and every rebuff as a victory; and they took active steps to
prevent the one and provoke the other.

Easter, 1569, had been fixed by the privy council for the
further consideration of Mary's case.   The French catholics had
routed the Huguenots on March 13.   The Bishop of Ross,
Northumberland, Montague, and other catholic lords were
invited by Norfolk's party to assist at Cecil's downfall; and a
papal agent was concealed in London, watching developments
and striving to harmonise French and Spanish intervention.[1]
Thrice, wrote Guerau, the lords made up their minds to
arrest the secretary; and thrice their courage failed, because
Leicester told the queen.   She stood staunchly by her minister,
although, as his opponents informed La Mothe, they had, short
of actually laying hands on her, done everything to dissuade
her from his policy.   In May they resolved that, if a final
effort failed, they would one and all abandon the court and
privy council.   The strife was reflected in the growing sever-
ance of catholics and protestants throughout the country,
and Sussex wrote from York deploring the open breach
between Cecil and Norfolk.   Protestant preachers came flying
to London from the wrath of their catholic audiences in
the north, while in Suffolk, according to Guerau, "at the
instance of certain ministers, the heretics planned to kill all
the catholics".   Londoners were burning the "gods of the
Spaniards" seized in Antonio Guaras's house; protestant pulpits
resounded with exhortations to a war of vengeance for the
slaughtered saints in France; and Elizabeth thought of reas-
serting her claims to Calais.   In the council she insisted that
she would have no war; and La Mothe wrote hopefully to
his anxious government of her aversion from decided measures
and expense.   But the success of the Germans under Zweibrücken, in forcing the passage of the Loire and effecting a
junction with the Huguenots, put strong temptation in Elizabeth's way; and she was on the verge of making some attempt to profit by the civil war.[2]

Nevertheless, the quarrel between English ministers was
not so much a question of war or peace as La Mothe and
Guerau imagined.   Elizabeth, Cecil, and the majority of the

[1] La Mothe, i., 332, 369, 373; Lodge, *Illustrations*, i., 472.
[2] La Mothe, ii., 405, iii., 10, 27, 44.

nation were certainly opposed to open war with either France or Spain. Cecil would secretly support the Huguenots, and encourage a similar party in the Netherlands ; and Winter, who convoyed the merchantmen to Hamburg, comforted the Dutch fishermen he met upon the sea with Elizabeth's promises of protection. Norfolk's party, on the other hand, would have apologised and made restitution to Spain, and have abandoned the French, Scottish, and German protestants. But mainly the quarrel was one of domestic parties. Arundel complained bitterly that a peer of his lineage should be overruled in council by an upstart ; and Norfolk championed his cause. Both, moreover, were deep in debt, a common cause of oligarchic discontent. The peers charged Cecil with sowing dissension between the queen and her nobility ; and they struggled hard to break his yoke.[1]

For a time and to some extent they succeeded. Both La Mothe and Guerau reported in May that Cecil's power was curbed ; and on June 9, Sussex congratulated him on his reconciliation with Norfolk. How far he bent to the storm is uncertain ; but he was forced to admit the lords to some share in diplomatic business which he had hitherto transacted by himself or with the queen. The surrender was, however, delusive, and its results unsatisfactory. In July two sets of negotiations were in progress with Alva, one carried on by the lords through their confidant and creditor Ridolfi, the other by Cecil through Eschiata, the brother of Guido Cavalcanti. But La Mothe soon discovered that Cecil was disentangling himself from the meshes of the opposition, and that the lords were floundering in diplomatic pitfalls laid by their wily antagonist. Their efforts to establish Mary's claim to the succession were parried by Cecil's disclosure of her alleged cession of her rights to the duke of Anjou, which barred further discussion until the story could be disproved ;[2] and French support of her cause was undermined by hints of the possibility of a match between Anjou and Elizabeth, and by the embargo of an expedition destined for La Rochelle. With equal skill Cecil

---

[1] La Mothe, iii., 50-54 ; *Spanish Cal.*, ii., 146, 157-58.

[2] The real cession had been in favour of Francis II. See the documents in La Mothe, i., 423 ff. Cecil perhaps deliberately substituted Anjou for the dead legatee ; *cf.* Bain, ii., 642, 646, 649.

led Alva to believe that he had been won over to Spain by the duke's offer of bribes. Guerau was released from his confinement; and amicable discussions began, which led to the restoration of normal relations, but not to the restitution of Spanish treasure.

Cecil had resolved to deal with his foes in detail, and to pacify his foreign enemies in order to crush their domestic accomplices. The danger consisted in the possible combination of the northern earls and Mary's friends with Norfolk's faction and the catholic powers. France and Spain were disarmed partly by Cecil's diplomatic suasion, and partly by domestic troubles which unofficial Englishmen fomented; while Norfolk was lulled into reconciliation with Cecil by a bribe which broke up his alliance with the Dacres and their friends. In May the young Lord Dacre met with a fatal accident. His uncle Leonard assumed the title Lord Dacre and claimed the family estates ; but as the result of an understanding between Cecil and Norfolk and of a lawsuit between Norfolk and Dacre, the lands were awarded on July 19 to Dacre's three nieces, who were all betrothed to Norfolk's sons. Two days earlier Guerau wrote that Cecil had once more got the upper hand in the government.[1]

It was a precarious victory which merely gave him time and opportunity to prepare for further struggles. Elizabeth, who was Cecil's sole support, seemed herself to be losing her hold over her government. Convinced by this time that she would never marry, and doubting her longevity, men began to look for a successor; and Elizabeth felt some of the pangs which she had caused her sister. She knew, she told her council in August, that they were betraying her and abetting Mary Stuart. A complete and official denial of Mary's bequest to Anjou came from France on the 17th of that month ; and Leicester made himself the mouthpiece of urgent demands that Mary's claims should be recognised and her restoration effected. He wrote a letter to Mary, which was signed by Pembroke and other lords, pledging her their support; and on the 27th Guerau reported that the council had decided on Mary's liberation, provided she married an Englishman. La Mothe

---

[1] *Dict. of Nat. Biogr.*, xxviii., 69; *Domestic Cal.*, Addenda, 1566-79, pp. 255-57; *Spanish Cal.*, ii., 177.

CHAP.
XV.

thought the pressure so great that Elizabeth would not dare to resist; even Cecil was apparently swimming with the stream and pretending zeal for Mary's marriage with Norfolk.[1]   But Norfolk's success would have meant Cecil's ruin : the lords were already proposing to offer him as a scapegoat to Spain ; and he was only feigning assent to a scheme, which would have practically divided sovereignty in England between Mary and Elizabeth, and encouraged civil war.   Of Elizabeth's sentiments there was no doubt.   It was a question whether she or the majority of her council was supreme ; they were preparing to proceed with the Norfolk marriage without her consent; while she, in La Mothe's presence, threatened to cut off their heads.[2]

Cecil's temporary expedients seemed to have been exhausted.   Alva had, indeed, refused Mary's applications and had soundly rated Guerau for his meddlesomeness.   But his hesitation was due to his desire that Spain should dictate Mary's marriage and secure possession of her son; and he was willing to give such aid to the Scottish queen as Elizabeth rendered the Huguenots.   A further prohibition of English trade in the Netherlands was issued in August; and first 6,000 and then 10,000 Spanish crowns found their way into Mary's exchequer.   In September he appointed deputies to discuss an accommodation with Elizabeth in England; but one of them was Chiappino Vitelli, Marquis of Cetona, the ablest soldier in Alva's train; and in view of Guerau's assurance that all the north was ready to rise, awaiting only Mary's release, the marquis had probably been selected for purposes more in keeping with his profession.   His numerous suite included trained captains and engineer officers ; Norfolk was pressing the French government not only to support his marriage, but to despatch forces to Dumbarton before the end of October; and Maitland was doing his best to revive Mary's party in Scotland.   Moray, however, was convinced that Elizabeth would never consent to the Norfolk marriage or to Mary's restoration.   At Perth, in July, the Scottish estates refused to permit her divorce from Bothwell, or to consider proposals for her return to the throne ; and on September 3, Maitland, who was to have sought in

---

[1] La Mothe, ii., 127 ; *Hatfield MSS.*, i., 451 ; Stählin, *Walsingham*, i., 232-33.
[2] La Mothe, ii., 169, 272.   Her father had used almost identical language in 1528, *Letters and Papers*, iv., 4942.

London Elizabeth's consent to the Norfolk marriage, was arrested on a charge of complicity in Darnley's murder.

This was the first blow in the coming conflict; but the fire, wrote La Mothe on September 5, had been lit at the English court. There was a stormy interview between Elizabeth and Norfolk during her progress in Hampshire, in which the queen, assured of Moray's support, forbade the duke's marriage, and he refused to obey her orders.[1] Undismayed by the forces at his back, she challenged him to submit or to rebel. Mary's friends were rejoicing over the match and her restoration as accomplished facts; but Norfolk was daunted by Elizabeth's royal wrath. He went off without permission to consult the Earl of Arundel at Hendon and then his friends in London. In the midst of his preparations at Howard House an order to return to Windsor reached him on the 21st. He pretended illness, but promised to come in four days; and then fled to Kenninghall. He had been forced into the open, and his court intrigue went to pieces when put to the test of overt action. The queen had proved her supremacy over her council. Cecil had feigned acquiescence in Norfolk's scheme with such success that he passed among the schemers as their most earnest friend; he continued feigning in 1569, as he had in 1553, until a higher power intervened; and, according to La Mothe, he and Leicester had to beg on their knees for the queen's forgiveness; while Pembroke, Arundel, Lumley, and Throckmorton were summoned to answer for their conduct and placed under arrest. La Mothe's and Guerau's despatches were intercepted, and Alva's envoys forbidden to enter England. Hunsdon concerted measures with Moray on the Borders, and Huntingdon was sent to exercise a surer watch than Shrewsbury's over Mary. She was taken from Wingfield to Tutbury; her guards, as well as those in the Tower, were doubled, her coffers searched, and her papers seized.

Meanwhile, the northern earls, under the guise of hunting and hawking, had been debating what to do in more serious matters. Northumberland was in communication with the Spanish ambassador, and on Norfolk's flight from court he asked the duke what he intended. One of his servants boasted on September 27, that on the morrow the earl would be in the

[1] La Mothe, ii., 222, 236.

field with 20,000 men unless they were discouraged by Norfolk's action. The duke professed his determination to see the matter through; but he met with little response in Norfolk; while in the north the Dacre tenantry were denouncing him as "a greedy tyrant," the murderer of his wife and of her son, and were calling for Leonard Dacre to rule them. Dacre naturally held aloof, and Norfolk's courage failed. On the 30th he prepared, after many feints and in spite of La Mothe's dissuasions, to obey Elizabeth's summons. He sent a message to the earls telling them not to rise, for he was going to court. He hoped to resume his more peaceful intrigues. But at Uxbridge he was met on October 3, and conveyed under guard to Paul Wentworth's house at Burnham; thence on the 11th he was sent down the Thames in the royal barge to the Tower.[1] His message to the earls was received with dismay. Some of the plotters wished to persist, but Westmorland asked what their quarrel was. "For religion," they replied; and the earl refused to move. Those, he said, who rose for religion in other countries were accounted rebels, and he would not blot his house with such a stain. Father Copley was consulted; and he argued against the zealots that only excommunication published throughout the land could absolve catholics from allegiance to their anointed queen. The meeting broke up in despondency and discord; the earls went home; others prepared for flight abroad; and Dacre came to court to make his profit out of Norfolk's ruin.

Sussex, the president of the council of the North, hoped that the plot had come to nothing; and the two earls, whom he summoned to York on October 8, did their best to reassure him. They might not have risen in 1569, had they been left alone; and La Mothe was counting on Elizabeth's fear to provoke them, just as he had relied on her fear to break with Norfolk. She was therefore well advised not to let matters rest. Delay would merely have postponed rebellion to a less convenient season; and it would have been folly not to take advantage of the confusion, into which the unmasking of Norfolk had thrown all sections of the opposition. Moreover, the

[1] Not the 8th, as stated in *Dict. of Nat. Biogr.*, xxviii., 70, and Creighton, *Elizabeth*, p. 119. See *Hatfield MSS.*, i., 469, and La Mothe, ii., 278. The order is dated the 8th, Haynes, p. 540.

extremists had continued to urge Northumberland into action, representing that they had already committed themselves too deeply to be forgiven, and that it would be disgraceful to turn back having set their hands to the plough. Accordingly on October 24 Sussex was required to communicate to the earls Elizabeth's orders for their repair to London. Their conscience told them what to expect; and they refused in the hope that the arm of the government would not reach to their feudal fastnesses. They rose, in fact, because they doubted their pardon for their intended revolt in September. At Brancepeth the earls, the Nortons, the Tempests, and other catholic gentry mustered their retainers; swept in munitions of war; appealed to the catholic lords across the Scottish Borders, Buccleuch, Cessford, Herries, Maxwell, and Lochinvar; and sought aid from Alva and from the French and Spanish ambassadors. Their hopes had been raised by the great defeat of the Huguenots at Moncontour on October 3; but their fears were a stronger stimulant. Elizabeth had resolved at last to impose on them all the oath of supremacy; and to the Earl of Northumberland, as well as to thousands of humble folk who flocked to his standard, the catholic faith was a cause for which they were prepared to die.

Unhappily for them, they had been made the sport of politicians whose chief anxiety was to embarrass Elizabeth's government. Northumberland carried about with him a letter from Guerau containing specific promises of help which he repudiated at the crisis. A revolt of the Moriscos preoccupied Philip; fear of the Turks prevented him from moving his naval forces out of the Mediterranean; and Alva who thought that "the business would all end in smoke," made some preliminary success on the part of the rebels—such as the establishment of a catholic La Rochelle in the north of England—a condition of armed assistance from the Netherlands. The design of a Spanish conquest of England, and of the marriage of Mary to Don John instead of to Norfolk, which La Mothe attributed to Alva, impeded French and Spanish co-operation in support of the rebellion. La Mothe confined himself to generalities, having no commission to do more; and he, Guerau, and Mary all deprecated action which might involve an open breach. Rebellion, moreover, always drove

moderates over to the crown.   All the suspected lords except
the two northern earls gave guarantees of loyalty.   Pembroke,
Arundel, and Lumley were soon released; and Pembroke
was entrusted with a military command in the west, where
Wales afforded hopes of support to the catholics hardly less
delusive than those which La Mothe entertained of Cornwall.   Leonard Dacre, who could have raised 3,000 men,
was bought off by the Dacre estates; and Sir Henry Percy,
who was connected with Cecil by marriage, resisted his brother
Northumberland.   It was little help to the rebels that Sussex's
brother Egremont Radcliffe joined them, and that the Earl of
Southampton and Viscount Montague were only prevented by
contrary winds from seeking Alva's court.[1]

The simple souls of the rank and file rose above the nicely-
calculated lore of politics and warfare.   They were making
the last armed protest in England against the secular spirit;
and they breathed the aspirations of a bygone age.   They
wore on their coats the red cross of the crusaders; they bore
on their banners the five wounds of Christ and that homely
supplication of all peasants in revolt, "God speed the plough";
and they demanded that England should turn again to the
ancient ways of faith and governance.   The catholic religion
should be restored; the council purged of its new, and filled
with its old, noble members; Norfolk should be liberated;
Mary restored to her throne in Scotland and recognised as heir
and second person in the English realm; and all refugees from
abroad should be expelled.   On November 14 they entered
Durham Cathedral; tore to pieces the English Bible, and
trampled on the Book of Common Prayer; demolished the
communion table; and celebrated mass with its old abundance
of ritual.   On the 18th they were at Ripon, still gathering
forces, some volunteers and some pressed men: many came
from places like Richmond, of which Northumberland was
steward; and it was said that he could count on 1,200 from his
honour of Cockermouth.   They had now at least 1,200 horse

---

[1] For the northern rebellion see Sharp, *Memorials*, 1841, a collection of
documents largely from the Bowes papers at Streatlam Castle.   Much of the
English correspondence is summarised in *Domestic Cal.*, Addenda, 1566-79, while
La Mothe and Guerau give good accounts.   See also Thorpe and Bain's *Scottish
Calendars*, the confessions of prisoners in *Hatfield MSS.*, vols. i.-ii., and *Trans.
of the Royal Hist. Soc.*, N.S., xx., 170-203.

and 5,000 foot; and they hoped to capture York, which was
cut off from the south, and to liberate Mary by a raid on Tutbury.   But Shrewsbury was informed in time, and swiftly
hurried Mary off to Coventry.

Upon the release of Mary depended the rebels' one chance
of success.   Had that been accomplished, or had Scotland
been in the hands of Mary's friends, the dream of making
the Humber the frontier of the kingdoms might have come
near realisation.   But Elizabeth could congratulate herself on
having left Moray in possession of the Scottish government.
He brought a strong force to the Borders and kept the Border Scots from joining in the rebellion.   The earls were between two fires, for Elizabeth was preparing greater forces, it
was said, than had ever gathered in England to suppress a
revolt.   They were not needed.   Divided in counsel and disheartened by Mary's removal, the insurgents began their retreat on November 24.   Barnard Castle was besieged in vain
for eleven days, though Hartlepool was occupied on the 30th
in the delusive hope of help across the sea from Alva.   None
came; and when, after visiting Chester, Sussex advanced from
York on December 12th, Hartlepool and Durham were evacu-
ated on the 16th and 17th.   The rebels fled to Hexham Moor,
and then dispersed, while the earls took refuge with the Border
thieves of Liddisdale.   Westmorland escaped to live an exile
at Louvain for over thirty years; but Northumberland was
sold to the Scottish regent by Hector Armstrong, whose
treachery earned him a proverbial fame.[1]

The trouble was not yet at an end.   On January 22, 1570,
Moray was assassinated in the streets of Linlithgow by James
Hamilton of Bothwellhaugh; and, while Knox drew tears from
a congregation of 3,000 people with a sermon on the text
" Blessed are they which die in the Lord," Mary gratefully promised to pension her brother's assassin.[2]   Encouraged perhaps
by the consequent confusion and by a Scottish catholic raid on
the Borders led by Westmorland, Leonard Dacre determined to
raise once more the standard of revolt.   He had gone north
in November, 1569, with the full favour of the court to make
sure his newly won and his old estates; and he had earned the

[1] Hodgkin, *Wardens of the Northern Marches*, p. 13.
[2] Labanoff, *Lettres de Marie Stuart*, iii., 354.

CHAP.
XV.

government's commendations for the vigour with which he had fortified Greystock and Naworth against the rebels. Prosperity had, however, turned his head; and he thought he could defy Elizabeth with a success denied to Norfolk and the earls. At the end of January, 1570, he disobeyed a summons to answer at court for his loyalty; and on February 15 Hunsdon was ordered to arrest him. It proved a perilous enterprise. Dacre had collected 3,000 "rankriders of the Borders" at Naworth, while Hunsdon and his lieutenant, Sir John Foster, had only 1,500 men. Unable to capture Naworth, Hunsdon was marching towards Carlisle, when Dacre fell upon him by the banks of the Gelt. Hunsdon himself bore testimony to the vigour of Dacre's charge; but the royal troops were trained, and the rankriders soon gave way. Dacre fled, the first of his army, to Liddisdale, and thence to Brussels, where he died in 1573, and Elizabeth wrote an unusually gracious letter congratulating "my Harry," her cousin, on his victory.[1] She had no grace to spare for rebels; and she pressed their punishment with a ferocity which Moray's murder did not tend to mitigate. Not fewer than 800 suffered execution, sometimes for other reasons than their guilt. Care was taken to make at least one example in every village represented in the rebels' camp; and where only one rebel joined, he was executed. Elsewhere the proportion of victims to offenders sank as low as one in six; out of 845 rebels in Durham, 201 were put to death.[2] Sometimes a rebel's possessions barred the mercy of a necessitous government, which scouted the Bishop of Durham's plea that, in virtue of his regalia,[3] convicts' lands were forfeit to him. It was not for nothing that Elizabeth stamped out the dying embers of feudal liberty.

Now that the rebellion had been crushed, the papacy prepared to remove one of the principal difficulties which had disconcerted its leaders. They had been harassed by doubts whether they might as good catholics rebel against a sovereign who was not yet excommunicate; but the path of future rebels was to be made straight. After a process at Rome which began in December, 1569, Pius V. issued on February 25, 1570,

---

[1] *Domestic Cal.*, Addenda, 1566-79, p. 256.
[2] See the details for Durham in Sharp, pp. 250-51.
[3] *Cf.* Fuller, *Church History*, 1656, bk. ix., p. 109.

his bull *Regnans in Excelsis*, in which he excommunicated and deprived Elizabeth of her "pretended right" to the English throne. It contained some echoes of the northern earls' complaints; the queen had made her realm a harbour for the worst of doctrines; she had expelled the nobility from her council, and filled their places with obscure heretics. The burden of her crimes was theological; and pains were taken to condemn her for reasons which would give least offence to other princes; she was said to have usurped the place of supreme head of the church, and to have defiled her soul with Calvin's impious mysteries. Nevertheless the bull met with unanimous reprobation from the crowned heads of Europe; and the pope's efforts to induce Alva and Anjou to undertake its execution failed. Ridolfi imported six copies into England,[1] and an Englishman, John Felton, was found bold enough to affix one, which he obtained from Guerau's chaplain, on the Bishop of London's door in May. After being racked, he was executed for high treason on August 8.

Elizabeth's excommunication completed the breach between the Roman and Anglican churches, which had really been made irreparable in 1559 except on terms which Rome would never concede. It gave ecclesiastical encouragement to the remnants of Norfolk's party, but at the same time it destroyed their national pretensions and changed the issue from a question of domestic, into one of European, politics. Pius V. compelled catholics to choose between Elizabeth and himself; and it now became impossible to combine a catholic scheme in favour of Mary's succession and of the restoration of feudal influence in the council with any pretence of loyalty to Elizabeth. Hence, instead of a domestic party working at Elizabeth's court with foreign ambassadors as secret and subordinate accomplices, we have a European conspiracy suggested by Guerau[2] controlling an opposition which in England dwindles in numbers and in influence, is limited to extremists, and relies upon avowedly treasonable methods. The centre of interest is shifted from party struggles at the court to spheres of diplomatic and eventually military action.

These two phases of the struggle are only disentangled by

---

[1] *Hatfield MSS.*, i., 555; Kervyn, v., 652. The text of the bull is given in Camden, ii., 212-215, and in Pocock's *Burnet*, v., 579.

[2] La Mothe, iii., 29-30.

degrees; and so long as Norfolk lived, he formed a focus for internal strife, which prevented the domestic from being completely merged in the external aspect of the situation. The duke had not the wit to profit by experience; it was his misfortune that the possession of high rank and broad estates was deemed a sufficient qualification for political responsibility; and he blundered to his fate more from sheer stupidity than deliberately conscious treason. Neither he nor his colleagues, Arundel and Lumley, could bring themselves to recognise an authority directed by other minds than theirs; and, while begging the queen for restoration to office and power, they assured La Mothe that, once restored, they would use their position to enforce their old policy, and that if peaceable measures failed they would resort to violence. In spite of this attitude Arundel was reinstated in March, 1570, and in June was already taking the lead in the council against Cecil and in favour of Mary. Norfolk also was given another chance; in June a rising to secure his liberation was planned by John Throckmorton and some other friends of the duke at Harleston in Norfolk. Nevertheless, owing it appears to Cecil's instance on his behalf, the duke was released from the Tower in August; and Cecil offered him his rich sister-in-law, Lady Hoby, in marriage, to relieve the duke from the pressure of his debts and from the fatal attraction of Mary Stuart. As far back as October, 1569, he had advised Elizabeth not to talk of Norfolk's treason, but to refer to the statute of Edward III.; for he could not see that the duke's acts came within its compass.

Norfolk at once abused his liberty by making himself the tool of a foreign conspiracy which Ridolfi was hatching in Mary's interests. Pius V., Alva, and Philip were all involved in the scheme, by which, after the conquest of England by an invading army and a catholic insurrection, Mary was to marry Norfolk and ascend the English throne. Mary through the Bishop of Ross signified her approval; Norfolk signed a declaration that he was a catholic, though he averred on the scaffold that he had always been a protestant; the pope did his part by divorcing Mary from Bothwell, to whom Elizabeth wished to keep her tied; and Ridolfi composed a list of forty peers who were believed to be ready to draw their swords in the quarrel. In March, 1571, Ridolfi left London with full

powers from the conspirators to negotiate abroad for the necessary armed intervention.   He discussed the plan with Alva at
Brussels in March, with Pius V. at Rome in May, and at Madrid
in July with Philip II. whose council debated the question
whether it would not be more feasible (and less expensive) to
assassinate Elizabeth.[1]   There was a design to land 2,000 men
from Brittany in Lancashire, which, with Derbyshire, Shrop-
shire, and the neighbouring counties, was expected to rise on
Mary's behalf; 3,000 men from Flanders were to be disembarked on the south coast, and 1,000 in Scotland " to hold men
occupied ".

Before Ridolfi had been gone a month, Cecil, acting on
information obtained by Cavalcanti from Florentine diplomatists, had arrested Charles Baillie, the intermediary between
Ridolfi and the Bishop of Ross ; and by means of the rack the
secret of their ciphered correspondence was revealed.   Throughout the summer he was engaged in probing the ramifications
of the conspiracy and in keeping touch with Ridolfi's progress.
The conspirators were adepts in their profession, and it was
not till November that the tangled skein was quite unravelled.
Mary disavowed the Bishop of Ross, and he disavowed Ridolfi.
The bishop also, under the stress of examination, repudiated
Mary, whom he accused of murdering her husband.   " Lord,"
broke out Secretary Wilson to Cecil, " what people are these,
what a queen, and what an ambassador ! " [2]   The bishop apologised to Mary for having been compelled to reveal the plot ; but
comforted her with the thought that the revelation was God's
special providence designed to save her from recourse to like
methods in future.

Enough had been discovered by September to incriminate

---

[1] Murdin, *State Papers*, pp. 35-38 ; Froude, ix., 498-504.   The minutes of the
meeting of the Spanish council at which this plan was discussed were transcribed
by Froude (Brit. Mus. Add. MS., 26,056 ; *cf.* Mignet, *Marie Stuart*, ii., 428, and
Father Pollen in *The Month*, xcix., 145-46).   Naturally they do not occur in the
despatches printed in the *Documentos Ineditos*, t. xc.   Nor have they been included in the *Spanish Calendar*.

[2] Wilson to Burghley, November 8, 1571, in Murdin, p. 57.   Mary's adherents
at this period did not base her claims on her innocence ; *cf.* the Bishop of Gal-
loway's sermon at Edinburgh on July 17, 1571, " though she is an adulteress and
a murderer, so was David.   No subjects have power to depose their lawful
magistrates, although they commit whoredom, murder, incest, or any other
crime," *Foreign Cal.*, 1569-71, p. 472.

CHAP.
XV.

Norfolk; on the 7th he was conveyed again from Howard House to the Tower; and the Earls of Arundel and Southampton, Lords Lumley and Cobham, the Bishop of Ross, Sir Henry Percy, and a dozen or more minor culprits were placed under arrest. On January 16, 1572, the duke was brought to trial before the usual jury of twenty-six peers, Shrewsbury acting as lord high steward. He seemed incapable of realising the seriousness of his offences ; but only one sentence was possible, and he was condemned to death. Still Elizabeth shuddered at the responsibility for sending a duke, who was also her second cousin, to the block. An order was signed on February 11 for his execution on the morrow, but was revoked at eleven P.M. ; another was signed on the 26th for his execution on the 27th, but was revoked two hours before dawn ; a third, if not a fourth, was signed and revoked after nocturnal meditation on April 9. At length parliament came to Elizabeth's rescue. It pressed for the execution of Mary as well as of Norfolk ; and a compromise was effected. Mary was spared for the time ; but the duke was sent to the block on June 2.

The extinction of the last surviving dukedom in England marks an epoch in English history. It was a pendant to the failure of the northern rebellion, and sealed the ruin of that old nobility which was incompatible with the new monarchy. In the ill-compacted organism of the medieval state it had been possible for great feudatories to war with one another and with their nominal sovereign. In the sixteenth century the few survivors still cherished the idea that they could cabal against the monarchy and appeal for foreign aid against a government of which they disapproved. The exigence of the new exclusive loyalty to a single centralised and national monarchy seemed to them a tyranny which involved the negation and destruction of their medieval liberty ; and Elizabeth herself could sympathise with this plea for ancient liberties, when urged by Huguenot magnates or by provincial estates in the Netherlands against the centralising policy of French or Spanish kings. Luther and Machiavelli have both been claimed as parents of the modern absolutist "omnicompetence" of the state ; both were equally repugnant to conservatives and catholics ; and the fall of the old nobility of England was a necessary incident in the evolution of modern political organisation.

For thirteen years the old and the new forces had struggled for predominance at Elizabeth's court; and there was some significance in the current prophecy that she would not complete the thirteenth year of her reign, and in the extraordinary rejoicings which greeted its falsification on November 17, 1571. By that date the old influences had almost disappeared from Elizabeth's privy council. The principal lords who used to frequent her court, said Elizabeth to La Mothe in April, 1572, were dead, fugitives, or prisoners. Norfolk and Arundel were in prison; Pembroke had died in 1570, Northampton in 1571, and Winchester early in 1572. On the other hand, Cecil had been created Baron Burghley on February 25, 1571, Smith succeeded him as secretary, and Walsingham was forging to the front. The nobles in the council were all of Tudor creation; and the control of English affairs passed into the hands of new men prepared to give full play to the new forces, which were making for the expansion of England and for a revolution in its diplomatic relations. The year of Norfolk's death was also that of the foundation of the Dutch republic, and of a parliamentary agitation for the execution of a queen. In such a world medieval titles to power were out of date; and hardly one of the men who wrought the greatness of Elizabethan England was born of noble parentage.

CHAPTER XVI.

THE EXPANSION OF ENGLAND.

In the first year of her reign Elizabeth had reclaimed England, and in the second Britain, from foreign jurisdiction. Both of these achievements were necessary preliminaries to that expansion of England, which formed the third stage in the development of her policy, and occupied her people's energies throughout the rest of her lifetime. The expansive energy, which the English people manifested as soon as it had realised something like national unity, had been perverted during the Hundred Years' War into an attempt to conquer France; and the results of that blunder seemed for a time to have crushed national spirit and discouraged national endeavour. France committed a similar error, when in 1494 Charles VIII. sent troops across the Alps instead of launching ships across the Atlantic; and the lead in the expansion of Europe was left to Portugal and Spain. The part played by Spain has been attributed to the circumstance that the news of Henry VII.'s acceptance of Christopher Columbus' proposals was accidentally delayed until after they had been adopted by Ferdinand and Isabella. But England in 1492 was not prepared to cope with a new world; and it is perhaps fortunate that English energies were not taxed by colonies until Englishmen had dealt with their own domestic and religious problems; that the English government was not tempted by the possession of Mexican and Peruvian gold into the fiscal follies of Spain; and that inexhaustible riches made no Tudor and no Stuart independent of parliament.

When, a generation after Columbus, Englishmen began seriously to think of lands across the sea, they found that the most attractive had already been appropriated. Pope Alexander VI, had in 1493 drawn a line from pole to pole a

hundred leagues west of the Azores, and had allocated to CHAP.
Portugal all countries discovered to the east, and to Spain all XVI.
those discovered west, of this meridian.   In practice this division was limited to the tropics and to the southern hemisphere.
Newfoundland was discovered and claimed for England ; and
its patriotic inhabitants maintain that the colony has enjoyed a
continuous existence since 1497.   In 1527 the penniless father
of Queen Catherine Howard spoke of seeking there the miserable pittance he required for his family ; and in 1536 Armagil
Waad, who was afterwards clerk of Elizabeth's council, cheaply
earned the name of " the English Columbus " by a voyage to
Cape Breton.   But, while English fishing ships may in Henry
VIII.'s reign have occasionally visited the Bank of Newfoundland as a change upon their regular voyage to Iceland, English
enterprise was mainly parasitic.   More was won by pillage from
the fleets of others than by original and legitimate trade ; and
it is significant that no small proportion of the diplomatic correspondence between England and Spain during the last years of
Henry VIII. is occupied with disputes over robberies committed
by English pirates on Spanish merchantmen.   For the rest
there was promise but little performance.   Henry VIII. began
to take an interest in the Baltic in 1535 ; Robert Thorne, an
Englishman resident at Seville, urged him in 1527 to attempt
the north-east passage with the stout assurance that there was
" no land uninhabitable and no sea innavigable " ; and William
Hawkins and Robert Reniger made voyages to Guinea and
Brazil in 1528-30 and 1540.   But the time had not yet come
to challenge the catholic powers in the New World; and
Sebastian Cabot had transferred his services to Spain.

The council of Edward VI. was more enterprising ; and
geography was one of the things in which the young king took
the deepest interest.   Cabot returned to Bristol in 1547, and
in 1549 received a pension of 250 marks from the English
government.[1]   He revived the scheme of a north-east passage ;
procured the formation of " the mystery and company of
Merchant Venturers " to promote it ; and supervised the organisation of Chancellor and Willoughby's expedition of 1553.
Chancellor reached Archangel, and thence made his way to

[1] Hakluyt, vii., 156, says he was made " grand pilot " of England; but see
Lit. Remains of Edward VI., pp. clxxxviii-ix.

Moscow. Willoughby was cast away not far from the North
Cape : Chancellor, in a voyage of 1555-56 to search for his colleague, again visited Moscow, but was wrecked and drowned
on his return off Aberdeenshire. This was, however, enterprise
which Philip and Mary, in spite of the papal partition, had no
scruples about encouraging. The Muscovy Company was
founded in 1555 ; the Russian ambassador, who had escaped
shipwreck with Chancellor, was fêted at Mary's court ; and a
treaty of commerce was concluded.[1] In 1556 Stephen Borough
discovered the entrance to the Kara Sea, and explored the coast
of Nova Zembla ; and in 1557 Anthony Jenkinson followed in
Chancellor's wake to Archangel and up the Dwina to Moscow.
In 1558 he pushed on down the Volga and across the Caspian
Sea, penetrating into the heart of Asia at Bokhara, and returning in 1560.

Jenkinson, like every other explorer of that age, was trying
to establish a trade route to the East Indies which should not
be commanded by the Turk. He had himself been in the
Levant in 1553, and he had English predecessors looking out
for trade or adventures in the Mediterranean. Sir Richard
Shelley had visited Constantinople in 1539, and Sir Thomas
Chaloner had made a voyage to Algiers in 1541. Chancellor
and Roger Bodenham had been to Crete and Chios in 1550-51 ;
and other English travellers found their way to Rhodes, Cyprus,
and Jerusalem. But Turkish dominions were not an attractive field for English commercial enterprise, least of all under
Philip and Mary ; because secular as well as religious rivalry
set enmity between the subjects of the sultan and those of the
Catholic King. More to Englishmen's taste was the quest for
trade and gold mines on the southern and eastern shores of
the Atlantic. In Edward VI.'s reign Richard Eden had longed
to divert to the Tower of London the streams of gold which
flowed from the west into Spanish coffers ;[2] and in 1553
Captain Thomas Wyndham, who had already made two voyages to Barbary in 1551-52, broke into the Portuguese depend-
encies along the Guinea coast. In vain Philip sought to stop

---

[1] Machyn, pp. 127, 130, 132, 166-67, 173 ; Acts of the P. C., 1556-58, pp. 27,
328 ; Venetian Cal., vi., 1005 ; Domestic Cal., Addenda, 1547-65, pp. 424, 439, 442,
449 ; Hatfield MSS., i., 146 ; Lodge, Illustrations, i., 271, 276 ; Hakluyt, ii.,
224-38, 281-89, 311-12, 315-22, iii., 331-34.
[2] Ibid., x., 3.

the trespassers : the English, as Feria wrote in 1558, "deeply
resented being interfered with in this navigation" ; and while
Mary did what she could, her councillors winked at the offence.[1]
John Locke made a voyage to Guinea in 1554; William
Towerson made two more in 1555 and 1556, and others
followed in 1557 and 1558. Robert Tomson still more boldly
ventured to Mexico in 1556, and was sent to Spain a prisoner
of the Inquisition.

Meanwhile Englishmen, who would not bend to Mary's
faith, fled, if they were clergy, to Frankfort or Geneva, and if
they were laymen, took to privateering in the Channel.[2] So,
later on, Alva made sea-beggars of the Dutch, and the Guises
drove Huguenots into maritime and colonial adventures. The
catholic lords of the land made the protestants lords of the sea ;
and it was of supreme importance in the history of the world
that this took place when the sea was being made the link and
not the limit of dominions. With catholic sovereigns ruling
every land from the North Sea to Cape St. Vincent, the hands
of the Carews, the Dudleys, the Horseys, the Tremaynes, the
Killigrews,[3] and other rovers of the sea were against every
man ; and the habits thus engendered were not easily eradicated, when in 1558 the Queen of England became their
natural ally. Elizabeth might and did, like Mary, prohibit
illicit exploration, and issue repeated proclamations against
pirates ; but Mary meant her threats, and Elizabeth did not,
except as sops to irate victims of the pillage. The sea-rovers
were doing her work at their risk ; they made it possible for
La Rochelle to defy catholic France and prevent a Guise attack
upon England ; their depredations hampered Alva's finance
in the Netherlands, and prepared the way for the Dutch
republic ; and they bred a school of seamen who laid on
the waves of the ocean the stable foundations of British
dominion.

For dominion the English were said as early as 1560 to

[1] *Spanish Cal.*, Elizabeth, i., 5, 24.

[2] Piracy was no novel trade for an Englishman ; nor was it original protestant
sin. In the fifteenth century *Debate of the Heralds* the Frenchman girds at the
English boast that they were kings of the sea, and says that their only warfare
was plundering poor merchants who passed up and down the Channel.

[3] *Foreign Cal.*, 1553-58, pp. 229, 231, 237-39, 261.

be " marvellous greedy " ;[1] and their imperial ambition is described by Michael Drayton :—

> A thousand kingdoms will we seek from far
> As many nations waste with civil war . . .
> And those unchristened countries call our own
> Where scarce the name of England hath been known.

The reference to "unchristened countries" which we were not
to convert, but to " call our own," was characteristic ; and in
the medley of motives, which made for expansion, there was
little of that hunger for lost souls, which inspired Las Casas
and gilded Columbus' appeal to Spanish cupidity. Hakluyt
confesses himself at a loss to answer the critics, who maintained
that the conversion of infidels was the true test of catholicity
and asked how many the English had converted ; and he had
to make the most of the labours of the somewhat dubious characters who acted as chaplains to protestant buccaneers.   John
Davis, indeed, had faith in England's evangelical mission ; " Are
not we only," he asked, " set upon Mount Zion to give light to
all the rest of the world ? "[2]   But the chosen people had, as of
old, sterner work to do ; and the Elizabethan sea-dog, who cared
for Biblical precedents, found his choicest examplars in the Old
rather than in the New Testament.

Religion was therefore a very subordinate motive in the
expansion of England ; and it is a curious speculation what
Drake's theological opinions would have been, if Spain had
turned protestant.   Some honest souls complained bitterly
that English traders in Spain preferred their trade to their religion, and took the catholic oaths which Philip imposed on all
resident merchants.   The religious question hardly arose in
the enterprises which spread English influence over other
lands than those belonging to Spain and Portugal, partly
because the rulers of Russia, Turkey, and Persia were more
tolerant, but mainly because proselytism was not the in-
centive of English action.   The connexion between the secularisation of church property and the expansion of trade was
not religious but economic.   Mercantile interests had dominated the legislature since the accession of Henry VIII. ; and in
Elizabeth's reign the city of London became the mainspring of

---

[1] *Foreign Cal.*, 1559-60, p. 516.
[2] Raleigh, *Introduction to Hakluyt*, 1904, p. 31.

English foreign policy.[1] The amazing growth of English commercial enterprise was due to the fact that the English middle class was enabled by strong and skilful government, conducted mainly by men sprung from its ranks, to devote to this purpose the energies, resources, daring, and intelligence which were elsewhere absorbed in religious wars or in efforts to maintain despotic authority over rebellious subjects.

The desire for political dominion followed incidentally upon the desire for trade, because the exclusive principles adopted by Spain rendered trade without dominion a hazardous pursuit. "The least they demand," wrote Guerau in 1569, "is that Englishmen abroad shall enjoy their liberties. . . . They also demand that they shall be free to go with merchandise to the Indies, and that neither in Flanders nor in Spain shall they be molested in person or property for their heresies." [2] He described these as "absurd pretensions," just as Philip thought it absurd that Elizabeth's ambassador should expect to follow his own religion in Spain. The Spanish inquisition was determined to make the position of heretics intolerable in Spanish dominions; and Philip prohibited English trade in the Indies on pain of death.[3] This policy provoked the counter-resolve to make an end of Spanish dominion wherever possible. Thus commercial expansion, when brought into contact with Spain, gradually assumed a ferocity and the character of a political and religious contest which were lacking elsewhere. There was one other cause of the difference. When the Cham of the Tartars refused the English permission to transport their merchandise overland through his dominions to the Indies,[4] they acquiesced. England had no military force to deal with him as the sea-rovers did with Philip, and to threaten his political existence if he refused their liberties. Our conception of our rights varies with our power to enforce them.

The fate of Willoughby and Chancellor and the explorations of Stephen Borough practically put an end to the idea of a north-east passage to the fabulous Cathay. Arthur Pett and Charles Jackman made a fresh attempt in 1580; but Jackman never came back, and Pett brought discouraging re-

---

[1] *Hatfield MSS.*, i., 164; Corbett, *Drake*, i., 312.
[2] *Spanish Cal.*, ii., 194-95.   [3] *Ibid.*, i., 502, 504.
[4] *Foreign Cal.*, 1569-71, p. 440.

ports. This line of adventure resolved itself into the development of trade with Russia and Persia. Jenkinson had hardly returned in 1560, when he was sent in 1561 to foster commercial relations with the tsar and with the Sophi of Persia. Indirectly there resulted from this mission the tsar's licence to the Muscovy Company to trade with Russia by the Baltic. Narva was selected as its emporium, and in 1564 Bacon wrote to Cecil that this traffic would be found more profitable than voyages to Barbary and Guinea, or the earlier route to Russia by the White Sea.[1] By 1569 a regular summer trade was established with Narva, the chief drawback being the risk from the freebooters of Danzig. In 1567 Jenkinson obtained for the company a monopoly of the White Sea trade; and in 1569 Thomas Banister succeeded where Jenkinson had failed, and carried English merchandise down the Volga to Tiflis and Samarcand. He there disposed of 1,000 kerseys, although he complained that through ignorance of native taste the colours were not particularly acceptable.[2] The prospects of the company were clouded by quarrels among the merchants, by " the practices of such abjects and runagates of the English nation as are here," and by diplomatic bungling; and its privileges were suspended in 1570. But in 1571 Jenkinson again went to Russia at the tsar's request, and he secured their restoration.

Narva was the farthest port of England's Baltic trade. Commercial relations with the Scandinavian kingdoms were mainly left in Scottish hands; and the economic and political condition of Poland discouraged the efforts made by William Harborne in 1578 and Sir Christopher Perkins in 1590 to do for Poland what Jenkinson and Banister had done for Russia. Along the German coast the Hanseatic towns jealously clung to their dwindling monopoly; and English trade was confined mostly to Hamburg and Emden. When diplomatic relations with Spain grew strained in 1569, it seemed as though the vast English commerce with the Netherlands might be diverted to these two cities, which were also important as links in the communications between England and the Palatinate. But the revolt of the Netherlands drew closer than ever the ties between English and Dutch; and England's interest in

---

[1] *Foreign Cal.*, 1569-71, p. 594; La Mothe, ii., 192; Stählin, *Walsingham*, i., 196.
[2] *Foreign Cal.*, 1569-71, pp. 221, 251, 504.

the Baltic was dwarfed by the growth of her western adventures.

Herein lay England's true career. Her international value in the old world depended largely upon the fact that she lay athwart Spain's communications with the Netherlands and French communications with Scotland. Her steady rise since the discovery of America has been fostered by her situation athwart the routes between the eastern and western hemispheres. The outpost of the old world became the *entrepôt* for the new : it intercepted and controlled the trade from the mouths of the Loire, the Seine, the Rhine, and the Baltic ; and the importance of its position may best be realised by imagining the effect upon English history of a similar group of islands placed athwart the entrance to the Mediterranean. Spain had some similar geographical advantages ; but climate, soil, and physical configuration discouraged industry and commerce ; and the vast wealth of the Indies passed through Spain as through a conduit to spread its fertilising influences elsewhere. Spain, moreover, was a conglomerate kingdom with conflicting aspirations. Aragon contributed to the common stock a Mediterranean policy, a legacy of Italian ambitions, and the burden of rivalry with the Turk. The conquest of Granada brought in its train the perennial entanglement with the Moors across the Straits ; and the acquisition of the Netherlands imposed a further handicap in northern Europe. Spanish rulers were distracted between their various obligations ; while England by the happy loss of Calais was left freer to turn her back on Europe and follow her vocation on the sea.[1] Her lack of vested continental interests enabled her to break away from medieval politics, just as her lack of vested interests in Rome facilitated her breach with the papacy ; and a similar detachment made England the pioneer of that revolution in naval construction and warfare which gave her an oceanic empire.

Hitherto sea-power had been pelagic not oceanic ; its influence had been exerted in the Mediterranean and in other narrow seas ; and its weapon had been the galley and the cog,

---

[1] Cecil in 1559 had questioned the worth of Calais to England ; and in 1571 Northampton, Sussex, and Leicester during the marriage negotiations with Anjou "very honourably and wisely gave counsel to forbear that toy of Calais " (Cecil to Walsingham, Digges' *Compleat Ambassador*, p. 104).

CHAP.
XVI.

and not the "great ship" and the man-of-war.   In the Mediterranean, sea-power was a matter of oars and not of sails.
There naval actions were merely land-fights fought at sea; and
Mediterranean admirals, like the Dorias, expected of their
galleys the mobility and precision of a regiment; sailing ships
they thought were useless for fighting purposes.   Their object
was primarily to ram the enemy, *i.e.* to effect a naval cavalry
charge, and then to board him, fighting hand to hand.   The
galley was rather a vehicle than a fighting machine; it could
only fire from the bows and straight ahead; its guns were used
more to confuse the enemy with their smoke than to sink him
with their shot; and for this reason it sought the weather
gauge.   Galleys had to be formed for battle in "line-abreast,"
for fear of hitting or confusing friends in front; the "line-
ahead" formation, which developed naturally from broadside fire, was impossible.   They carried few guns but many
men; they had a low free-board, little storage, and small endurance.   Everything was sacrificed to mobility in action and
rapidity over short distances.   The galley was the ship for
land-locked seas, the naval weapon of the Phœnician, the
Greek, the Roman, the Italian, and the Turkish corsair; and it
dominated naval history in one form or another from the siege
of Troy to the battle of Lepanto.

Geographical exploration made it obsolescent in the fifteenth
and obsolete in the sixteenth century.   It was useless over
oceanic distances, where the requirements of strength and
storage necessitated a bulk and weight which could only be
propelled by superhuman force.   So oars gave place to sails,
mobility to endurance, and the long, narrow galley to the
"round" galleon with three masts and a beam not less than a
third its length.[1]   The Venetians developed this type for their
English and Atlantic coasting trade in the fourteenth and
fifteenth centuries; from them the Genoese, Portuguese, and
Spaniards borrowed it for their voyages of discovery and commerce.   But its adaptation to fighting purposes was the work
of Henry VIII.; and "of all others the year 1545 bests marks
the birth of the English naval power".[2]   The evolution of the

---

[1] The "galleass" represented an attempt to construct a type of oared war
vessel capable of delivering broadsides.
[2] Corbett, *Drake*, i., 59.

"great ship" was easier in the North Sea and the English
Channel than in the Mediterranean; for, although galleys were
in constant use by English sailors during the middle ages, they
had found the cog, which was a small and rudimentary "great
ship" manœuvred in battle like a galley, more serviceable; and
their task was simply to develop the cog for heavier seas, heavier
fighting, and longer voyages. Gradually a ship was evolved
which could keep the sea for months, could fire broadsides, and
could fight under sail. Guns were cast hardly inferior to those
with which Nelson won his victories; new principles of naval
tactics and strategy were worked out; and the ship became
the fighting unit instead of being a conveyance for soldiers.
The subsequent development of English sea-power in the Mediterranean measures the superiority of the new over the old
type even in the home of the original galley.

The transition was inevitably gradual, and other nations
than the English were engaged upon it. But England was
the first, and from 1545 to 1588 her naval predominance was
hardly called in question. Spain with her Mediterranean interests could not abandon her Mediterranean methods; her
faith in galleys was fortified by the great galley victory of
Lepanto in 1571; and a belated attack on England by means
of galleys was projected in 1599. Again, her American trade
was done in *flotas* not *armadas:* the ships were scarcely
armed at all; and she had not yet dreamt that her commerce
needed sea-power to protect it. In Mary's reign Philip relied
upon the English navy, and even after her death he trusted
to his diplomatic influence with the English government
and to the refuge of the English ports to save his commerce
from the Channel pirates. The aggressiveness of French
adventurers to Florida and of Huguenot corsairs first compelled him reluctantly to consider the necessity of creating a
naval force to protect his colonial trade and possessions; and
the great Spanish seaman Menendez was beginning to organise
this defence when the English appeared in the west as a more
formidable danger than the French.

From that time both nations continued to increase their
armament, though the increase on the English side was unofficial. The royal navy consisted of twenty-two great ships
in 1558 and of no more than twenty-nine in 1603. But these

CHAP.
XVI.

figures are no indication of England's naval strength which depended mainly upon privateers. "The whole Channel from Falmouth to the Downs," wrote Guerau in 1570, "is infested. . . . They assail every ship that passes, of whatever nation, and after capturing them equip them for their own purposes, by this means continually increasing their fleet, with the intention on the part of the queen thus to make war on his majesty through these pirates without its costing her anything, and under the specious pretence that she is not responsible since the pirates carry authority from Châtillon, Vendôme, and Orange." As the reign wore on, an amalgam was made between these pirates and the English trading and exploring ships. Their business was combined; and this gradual arming of England's merchantmen increased England's naval power and threatened the monopoly of Spain. In 1557 a combined force of English and French traders to the Gold Coast was outmatched by the Portuguese in gunnery; ten years later the tables were completely turned when Fenner beat off a Portuguese squadron seven times larger than his own. The transformation was determined by Spain's uncompromising denial of the English claim to trade with Spanish colonies and by the resolution of the English traders to enforce it. Elizabeth had early adopted the doctrine that English commerce needed the protection of English ships of war; and with this and other objects she acquired the habit of lending a royal ship to "stiffen" the professedly peaceful expeditions of Hawkins, Drake, and Frobisher. Before long these expeditions lost their peaceful guise; and they set out armed, prepared if not designed to fight.

The career of John Hawkins is more important in its bearing on this change than in its relation to the negro slave trade. Negro slaves had long been a valuable commodity in the Spanish West Indies, where they were introduced because the aborigines could not stand the labour in the mines.[1] But, partly owing to the humanitarian pleading of Las Casas and partly to financial motives, their importation had been restricted: prohibitive duties and licences rendered the trade practically a government monopoly; and enormous profits were within the grasp of any one who could evade the Spanish regulations. Several abortive attempts had been made to

[1] Haebler, *Die überseeischen Unternehmungen der Welser*, 1903, pp. 70-89.

open up this avenue to fortune before Hawkins started his
famous project in October, 1562. He had specious arguments
to justify his action.   Cecil had told Quadra in 1561 that
the pope had no right to partition the world; while Hawkins
pleaded the old commercial treaties of 1495 and 1499 which
guaranteed free intercourse between the subjects of Henry
VII. and those of the Archduke Philip, Philip II.'s paternal
grandfather.   But it is doubtful whether Spain was really
bound by treaties made between England and the house of
Burgundy before Spain had become part of the dominions of
that house.   From the fact that princes on their accession
usually confirmed treaties made by their predecessors it might
be argued that without such confirmation those treaties were
void; Elizabeth certainly in 1559 made a point of obtaining
from Philip II. confirmation of the ancient treaties, and Philip
persistently refused.[1]   In any case the treaties could hardly
exempt Englishmen from restrictions imposed upon the Spaniards themselves, and the whole point of Hawkins' scheme was
its evasion of these limitations.

Hawkins appears, however, to have convinced himself of
the justice of his claim; and he even sent some of the proceeds
of his trading from Hispaniola for sale to Spain, where they were
promptly confiscated.   This was mild retaliation for Hawkins'
doings, and for an incident which the Spanish ambassador reported in 1563 : two English ships—whether Hawkins' or not
does not appear—had attacked a Spanish vessel off Cape St.
Vincent, killing twenty men and seizing the gold they were
bringing from Puerto Rico.[2]   A second more elaborate expedition followed in 1564-65 in which Hawkins was accompanied
by his cousin Francis Drake; the queen herself, in spite of Cecil's
disapproval, was a partner in the venture.   After loading up
with negroes on the Guinea coast, Hawkins made for Tierra
Firma, the Spanish province stretching from the mouth of the
Orinoco to Darien, known in English history as the Spanish
Main.   By force he compelled the officials to grant him licence
to trade with the Spanish colonists, who were as anxious to buy
slaves as Hawkins was to sell them; and he also obtained, when

[1] *Spanish Cal.*, i., 218, ii., 636, iii., 33, 40-41 ; *Foreign Cal.*, 1558-59, Nos.
221, 1005; *Hatfield MSS.*, ii., 230, iii., 68.
[2] *Spanish Cal.*, i., 345-46.

his trading was done, certificates of good behaviour. The process was repeated at Rio de la Hacha ; and on his way back he
befriended the French colony in Florida. An English expedition to colonise that country had been fitted out in 1563 with
official countenance and support ; but its commander, the notorious adventurer Thomas Stukeley, preferred indiscriminate
piracy. His colonising project came to nothing ; and Menendez
exterminated the French settlement at St. Augustine's.[1]

Hawkins sailed on his third and most important voyage
to the Indies in October, 1567. This time Elizabeth lent two
ships of the royal navy, the *Jesus of Lubeck* and the *Minion ;*
and Drake commanded a small vessel, the *Judith*, of fifty tons.
It is not always easy to distinguish piracy from patriotism, and Hawkins' raid was a cunning blend. He went with
the goodwill of his queen and country to effect a warlike
purpose in a time of peace, to force the doctrine of the "open
door" upon a government that wished to keep it shut. The
end was doubtless patriotic ; and patriotic casuistry will hold
that it justified piratical means. He began by seizing Portuguese caravels on the Guinea coast in order to facilitate
his slave-hunting operations. In the West Indies, which were
reached in March, Drake first seized a government despatch-
boat, and then Hawkins captured Rio de la Hacha to enable
him to trade with its inhabitants ; for there could be no trade
without dominion. The castle and town of Cartagena were
then bombarded, and more "trade" was done without any
Spanish co-operation ; the English landed and carried off some
sack and malmsey, depositing in return some woollen and linen
cloth. The hurricanes of August now intervened ; and Hawkins,
in order to refit, put in on September 16 to San Juan de Ulua
or Ulloa, the roadstead of Vera Cruz. The Spanish treasure fleet
lay there defenceless, but Hawkins made a distinction between
compulsory trade and flagrant piracy ; and he harboured no
designs upon it. On the morrow, however, a squadron of
thirteen of Menendez' armed galleons approached the anchorage. Hawkins might have driven them off and risked Elizabeth's displeasure at this act of open war. He preferred to
make terms with the commander, and to proceed with his re-
pairs. Suddenly those of the English sailors, who were

[1] *Hatfield MSS.*, i., No. 891; *Dict. of Nat. Biogr.*, lv., 124-25.

fraternising with the Spaniards on shore, were attacked and massacred almost to a man, while the Spanish opened fire on the English ships. A fierce action ensued ; the *Jesus* had to be abandoned, and only the *Minion* and the *Judith* escaped. On January 20, the *Judith* made Plymouth Sound, and on the 25th the *Minion* laboured into Mount's Bay.

Their news had preceded them from Spanish sources to the ears of Spinola, who had communicated it to the government. Public opinion was inflamed by the tale of Spanish treachery, and there was talk of war. Elizabeth gratified public passion, and recouped herself by the seizure of the Spanish treasure in December, 1568.[1] Hawkins, who had already once deluded Guerau into a belief in his willingness to serve the King of Spain, persuaded him that he would hand over to Philip the squadron with which he was entrusted in 1570 in view of Stukeley's proposed invasion of Ireland ; and he secured as a preliminary reward the release of the prisoners left in Spanish hands at San Juan de Ulua. Drake sought less diplomatic compensation. After one or more voyages to reconnoitre in 1570-71, he sailed in May, 1572, to seize the treasure which it was the Spaniards' habit to convey from Peru to Panama, transport across the isthmus to Nombre de Dios, and there ship for Europe. Guerau had been expelled from England in January for his share in the Ridolfi plot ; and this filibustering expedition was practically an act of war. By extraordinary skill and daring Drake made himself master of Nombre de Dios ; but he was wounded and forced to retire before he could secure the treasure. After an unsuccessful attempt to surprise Cartagena, he encamped for some months on the Spanish Main, and in February, 1573, renewed his design on the treasure. This time, relying on the assistance of the Maroons, he tried to seize it on its passage across the isthmus ; and here he obtained his first glimpse of the Pacific. The attack on the treasure escort was foiled by a Spanish stratagem ; but after hard fighting and hairbreadth escapes on land and sea, in which Drake's original vessels were lost, he secured ample booty at Venta Cruz and Nombre de Dios, and brought it home in frigates captured by his pinnaces from the Spaniards. He reached Plymouth on Sunday, August 9 ; and the Ply-

---

[1] See above, pp. 284-5.

mouth folk streamed out of the parish church to welcome the great freebooter, leaving the preacher to moralise by himself.

Drake found the government ingeminating peace with Spain ; and nothing was said about him or his booty until the convention of Bristol in August, 1574, closed the score between the two powers and protected his ill-gotten gains. Anglo-Spanish relations entered a more peaceful phase ; in spite of schemes like that of Drake's pupil Oxenham, who was hanged at Lima in 1575, there was a reversion to the earlier type of trade and exploration ; and Frobisher eclipsed Drake in the public mind. He took up the work of Willoughby and Chancellor, and sought in his three voyages of 1576, 1577, and 1578 to discover the elusive north-west passage to Cathay. The scheme was the offspring of Sir Humphrey Gilbert, who, in his *Discourse to Prove a North-West Passage*, published in 1576, had used the difference of species between Asia and America to demonstrate the separation of the two conti-nents, and had less successfully tried to show that there must be an open waterway between them. On his first voyage Frobisher explored Frobisher Bay, or Frobisher Strait as he called it, Meta Incognita, and Cumberland Peninsula ; dis-covered the Esquimaux ; and brought back a lump of ore which the London assayers pronounced to be rich in gold.[1] Elizabeth was thus induced to embark £500 in a second ven-ture in 1577 ; but neither this nor a third voyage in 1578, when Frobisher commanded fifteen vessels, produced gold enough to pay its expenses. Geographical exploration of the arctic regions did not in itself attract Elizabethan seamen ; and a fourth voyage projected under Fenton was converted to the more lucrative pursuit of piracy in warmer climes.

Gilbert himself had meanwhile sounded that note in English enterprise which was in time to dominate all the rest. Piracy, slave-hunting, gold-seeking, war with Spain, and arctic exploration were incidents in the building of the empire ; its foundations were colonies. A French " colony " had already been established (and destroyed) in Florida ; and in 1569 Guerau had told Philip that the English " thought they were going to colonise " the same country, where, he said, Hawkins

---

[1] *Spanish Cal.*, ii., 567-69, 576, 595 ; *Hatfield MSS.*, ii., 147-48.

had left 240 men on his way from San Juan de Ulua.[1] These
"colonies" were probably intended as military outposts against
Spain.   But in his *Discourse* of 1576 Gilbert speaks of finding
in America a home for needy Englishmen, whose unemployment often led them to crime and to the gallows; and in 1578
he obtained a charter "to inhabit and possess at his choice
all remote and heathen lands not in the actual possession of
any christian prince".   Warlike spirit, however, perverted his
choice; and the expedition he took out in 1579 was beaten in
an attack on the Spanish West Indies.   A second in 1583 deserved success if it did not achieve it, and brought Gilbert
his death and undying fame.   He sailed with five ships to
plant a colony in or near Newfoundland.   His half-brother
and vice-admiral, Raleigh, was forbidden by the queen to sail,
and his vessel the *Bark Raleigh* soon deserted; another the
Swallow took to piracy; a third the *Delight*, after starting a
colony at St. John's, struck on a rock and foundered.   With
the *Golden Hind* and the *Squirrel*, Gilbert turned his face
homewards.   He sailed in the *Squirrel*, a tiny vessel of ten
tons, in which he had explored many a creek and inlet of the
coast; and in it he encountered the storm which struck them
on September 9.   " We are," he called to his comrades on the
Golden Hind as his vessel reeled under the shock, " as near to
Heaven by sea as by land."   At midnight the *Squirrel's* lights
went out, and the waters closed over the little bark and its
great-souled captain.[2]

John Davis took up the work of Frobisher, and Raleigh
promoted schemes in furtherance of Gilbert's.   In three voyages
between 1585-87, Davis pushed up the coast of Greenland and
the straits which bear his name to what was afterwards known
as Baffin's Bay.   But only codfish and fur rewarded his efforts,
and his failure to find a north-west passage was followed by
the abandonment of the scheme till another reign.   Raleigh's
armchair explorations were not more successful.   In 1584 he
despatched two vessels under Captains Amadas and Barlow to
search the American coast north of Florida for a site suitable
for a colony; and they brought back glowing accounts of the
peaceful and unsuspecting Red Indians.[3]   The queen was cap-

---

[1] *Spanish Cal.*, ii., 108.   [2] Hakluyt, viii., 74, xii., 38.
[3] *Ibid.*, viii., 305-6; *cf. Cal. of Colonial State Papers*, i., 2-4, and Addenda,
i., 10-30.

tivated by the idea of the colony, and christened it Virginia ;
and in 1585 Raleigh sent out Sir Richard Grenville and Ralph
Lane with seven ships to plant at Roanoke a permanent centre
of civilisation.   Philip Sidney was to have led the way to this
Arcadia, where men were "void of all guile and treason," and
lived "after the manner of the golden age".   But Elizabeth
would not let him go, and his life was lost at Zutphen ; while
Grenville harried the Red Indian "savages," and Lane drilled
them into gangs for his gold-seeking expeditions.   In a few
months Lane and Grenville quarrelled ; the Indians rebelled,
and were punished by massacre ; and the progress of North
America had begun.   The pioneers, however, were glad to accept the passage home offered by Drake in 1586, bringing with
them potatoes and tobacco ; and the fifteen men, whom Grenville landed three weeks after Drake's departure to keep alive
the colony, disappeared.   Raleigh made a final attempt in 1587,
sending out 150 colonists under Captain John White ; but they
too had scattered by 1590, when a relief force went to seek
them ; and seven only were found alive when a permanent
colony was at last established in 1607.[1]   Of such slender pro-
portions were the "Britains beyond the sea" at the death of
Queen Elizabeth.

Duller men and sterner motives were needed for the task.
Gold, adventure, and war, but not the prosaic toil of colonisation, attracted men like Hawkins, Grenville, and Drake ;
and adventure without the gold and the war lost its charm
after the failure of the arctic explorers to find a passage to
Cathay.   As the peaceful interlude with Spain gave place to
grimmer purposes, Drake emerged from his obscurity, and on
December 13, 1577, started on his famous voyage round the
world with the secret connivance of the war party in Elizabeth's
council.   The circumnavigation of the globe was in fact in-
cidental to the main object of breaking up the Spanish monopoly of the Pacific.   Disaster had invariably attended every
effort to follow in Magellan's wake ; the straits which bore his
name were a terror to sailors, and Tierra del Fuego was
still thought to be the end of a vast arm of land stretching
round from the eastern hemisphere.   The Spaniards did their
trade with the Pacific coast overland at Panama ; and so long

[1] See below, vol. vii., p. 49.

as they held the mainland in their grasp, and the extremities of America were thought impassable by sea, they could draw securely from Potosi the wealth on which Spanish ambition and power were based. The expeditions of Frobisher and Drake were corresponding efforts to turn the flanks of a hitherto impregnable position.

There was also a sinister motive behind, which led to tragedy. According to Drake's own statement, the queen had forbidden any revelation of the voyage to Burghley, who wished to avoid the risk of an open breach with Spain ; and Drake felt that he had been encouraged by Leicester and Walsingham in order that his aggression might frustrate Burghley's efforts for peace. He had also been induced to take with him one Thomas Doughty, a soldier of fortune who was suspected of complicity in Leicester's alleged poisoning of the Earl of Essex, and had made himself obnoxious to Leicester by indiscreet talk.[1] Doughty revealed to Burghley the secret of the expedition, and apparently from the first set himself, relying on Burghley's favour, to prevent Drake from ever reaching the Pacific. The weather seconded his intrigues, and storm after storm impeded Drake's progress during the winter and spring of 1577-78 to the mouth of the River Plate. Drake was not superior to sea-faring superstitions ; and when once Doughty's insubordination had roused his suspicions, he began to attribute his ill-luck to Doughty's witchcraft. Unaccountable fogs and tempests strained his nerves, and at St. Julian's Bay on the Patagonian coast the crisis came in June. On that spot Magellan had assassinated one mutinous captain, hanged another, and marooned two more ; in the neighbourhood many a crew had mutinied rather than attempt the passage of the straits ; and Doughty seemed likely to succeed in similarly working upon the terrors of Drake's men. Drake played the part of Magellan, and a court-martial was held on Doughty. Drake passed sentence of death, for which he had no commission ; and after judge and victim had solemnly taken the communion together, Doughty was executed [2] on a charge of treason committed in saying that the queen had been induced by bribes

---

[1] Camden, ii., 355.

[2] Mendoza says that Drake himself acted as executioner, because no one else would, *Spanish Cal.*, ii., 592.

to allow the expedition to proceed. A more grotesquely tragic
scene and a greater judicial travesty was never enacted in
English naval history.

There was another memorable scene in St. Julian's Bay
before Drake left it. He had been compelled to pass the
southern winter there; and amid its hardships the friction
between gentleman-adventurer and professional seaman, which
played havoc with Spanish naval discipline and had something
to do with Doughty's trouble, grew dangerous. Drake determined once for all to assert the claims of discipline. On
Sunday, August 11, after every man had confessed and taken
the sacrament, Drake took up his parable instead of a sermon
from the chaplain. He dwelt on the need of harmony and on
the dangers of their enterprise; and offered a ship to such as
wished to turn back. They all refused. Drake then cash-
iered every officer; he repeated his version of Doughty's
conspiracy, reprimanded some of his accomplices, but promised
that no more should die for their offence. He related the
origin of the expedition, revealed the fact that the queen was
interested in it, financially and otherwise, and explained the
importance of their success; if they failed, Spain and Portugal
would triumph over England's queen, and no one would venture
again to challenge them in the Pacific. He then restored the
officers, and on August 20 entered the Straits of Magellan.

Two days after emerging into the Pacific, Drake's ships
were struck by a series of terrific storms, during which he was
driven far south and separated from his vice-admiral, Winter,
who sailed home in the *Elizabeth*, while his third vessel the
Marigold foundered. He was now convinced that the great
southern continent, the *terra Australis incognita*, was a fiction,
though it is not quite certain that he actually discovered Cape
Horn.[1] After two months' buffeting, he passed into smoother
waters, and on December 5 appeared off Valparaiso "like a
visitation from heaven". The Spaniards were taken completely by surprise, and Drake looted the ports and shipping of
the Pacific at his pleasure. A rich treasure-ship fell into his
hands,[2] and the *Golden Hind* was literally ballasted with silver.

---

[1] *Cf.* Sir J. Laughton in *Dict. of Nat. Biogr.*, xv., 430, with Corbett, i.,
255-60.

[2] A detailed account of the booty is given in *Foreign Cal.*, 1581-82, pp. 371-74.

The voyage was now "made," and it became a question of return. Drake first attempted in the spring of 1579 to discover the fabled waterway through North America, which the Spaniards had apparently deduced from rumours about the great lake system and St. Lawrence Valley; but he encountered arctic conditions before he found a passage. He turned back to refit in Drake's Bay, a few miles north of San Francisco; and after proclaiming a sort of protectorate over the Red Indians of California, which he called New Albion, he struck across the Pacific on July 26.

The navigation was fairly well charted and known as far as the Philippines. At Ternate in the Moluccas he was magnificently received by a native ruler in revolt against the Portuguese; and upon a treaty, alleged to have been concluded on this occasion, England long based its pretensions to trade in the Spice Islands. The expedition and its fruits were, however, within an ace of being lost in the intricate and uncharted Molucca Sea in January, 1580. The *Golden Hind* ran on a sunken reef, and the crew spent twenty hours in prayer and ineffectual efforts to get her off. During that day of suspense Drake suffered the agony of feeling that his chaplain, Francis Fletcher, was the better man. Suddenly the *Golden Hind* slipped off, and Drake took his revenge: he put his chaplain in irons, "excommunicated him out of the church of God," and compelled him to wear a placard, "Francis Fletcher, the falsest knave that liveth". The rest of the voyage was comparatively uneventful. After some difficulty Drake cleared Celebes, by what channel it is not known; he did some peaceful trade with Java, sighted the Cape of Good Hope on June 15, touched at Sierra Leone on July 22, and on September 26 entered Plymouth Sound.[1]

While Drake was putting the crown on English enterprise and navigation, Richard Hakluyt was beginning to lecture at Oxford on the science of geography, and to collect materials for his famous epic of the Elizabethan age. It was a symptom of the expansion of England's consciousness, which may be set against the laments over the decay of university education.

---

[1] He was elected member of parliament at some by-election not recorded in the *Official Return*, the *Dict. of Nat. Biogr.*, or by Mr. Corbett, and he was present during the session of 1581 (D'Ewes, p. 290).

Those laments refer only to scholastic learning which had been the speciality of a professional class ; and complaint is frequent of the fact that youths now went to the universities for short periods of general culture instead of long years of technical study.[1] Education was becoming more secular and widely spread; it only decayed in a pedantic sense; and assuredly the generation, which could produce and appreciate the literature of the age of Shakespeare, was not less educated, in the real meaning of the word, than that which Erasmus and Sir Thomas More had satirised. At no period has the quickening of national intelligence been so marked as during the alleged decay of university education. The schoolmasters of England were its navigators and explorers ; and their pupils were its dramatists and poets. World-wide deeds expanded the parochial mind, and winged the flight of its imagination. "Which of the kings of this land before her Majesty," asks Hakluyt, "had their banners ever seen in the Caspian Sea? which of them hath ever dealt with the Emperor of Persia, as her Majesty hath done, and obtained for her merchants large and loving privileges? Who ever saw, before this regiment, an English Ligier in the stately porch of the Grand Signor of Constantinople? Who ever found English consuls and agents at Tripolis in Syria, at Aleppo, at Babylon, at Balsara, and, which is more, who ever heard of Englishmen at Goa before now? What English ships did heretofore ever anchor in the mighty river of Plate?"[2] In the fulness of time Elizabeth's seamen brought to birth new Englands across the sea; but it was a greater achievement to make a new England at home.

---

[1] Cf. Stählin, *Walsingham*, i., 68 ff.   [2] Hakluyt, xii., 93, 101-2.

CHAPTER XVII.

THE DIPLOMATIC REVOLUTION.

THE expansion of England was necessarily achieved for the most part at the expense of Spain and Portugal, because they possessed the trade and dominion which England most coveted; and the antagonism thus created gradually but inevitably produced a revolution in England's foreign relations. The deeper current of political tendency was hidden beneath the surface ebb and flow of diplomatic intercourse; but even before Elizabeth's reign forces were at work which ultimately made France the friend and Spain the foe of England. From time immemorial the corner-stone of England's foreign policy had been friendship with the power controlling the Netherlands, and to this day Great Britain is bound to those countries by special obligations of defence. Commercial as well as military reasons led Edward III. and Henry V. to seek their alliance; and the goodwill of Burgundy was one of the Yorkist assets which Henry VII. took most pains to secure. When Charles V. inherited the dominions of Ferdinand and Isabella as well as those of Margaret of Burgundy and Maximilian of Austria, Spain was brought into the friendly circle; and it was a fateful day in the history of England, Spain, Germany, and the Netherlands, when Charles V. detached the last from their natural allegiance to the empire of his brother, in order to bind them in unnatural bonds to the monarchy of his son. England was placed in a dilemma; commercial interests tied it to the Netherlands, while colonial rivalry dissevered it from Spain.

Political and religious developments accentuated this distraction. The Netherlands had been a useful and innocuous neighbour, because the heterogeneous character of the various provinces and the extent of their medieval liberties had prohibited their formation into a centralised, aggressive power.[1]

---

[1] Stählin, *Walsingham*, i., 185.

21 *

Philip II. set himself, after the fashion of the "new" monarchs of the time, to build up a unitary bureaucratic state on the ruins of provincial autonomy; and fear of possible attack from such a neighbour made Elizabeth the champion of Dutch and Flemish liberties. The interested friend of constitutional government in other countries than her own, she was also the patron of religious liberty—abroad; and the growing protestantism of the Netherlands created another bar between her and Philip, and another bond between her and his subjects. "I am certain," wrote Quadra on April 3, 1562, "that this queen has thought and studied nothing else since the king sailed for Spain [August, 1559] but how to oust him from the Netherlands." A year later he sounded a similar warning: "this great friendship between Cardinal Châtillon and the queen is only a plan to disturb the Netherlands jointly".[1] The first of these statements was unduly alarmist, but the second was an acute forecast of Anglo-Huguenot policy nine years later.

"Flanders," wrote Chaloner from Madrid on May 1, 1562, "travaileth, and lacketh but a midwife;"[2] and for years Elizabeth was considering how far she could with propriety assist at the birth of the Dutch republic. So long as Philip controlled the Netherlands it was necessary for commercial reasons to keep the peace. Elizabeth, moreover, could not afford to break with Spain until she was sure of the friendship or impotence of France and Scotland. In 1562 she had defied the French government, partly because she could still rely on Philip, and partly because she seems to have thought that the Huguenot was the winning cause. The result of the first war of religion opened her eyes; and thenceforth she set herself steadily to cultivate amicable relations with Catherine de Médicis. She always disavowed the secret aid she gave the Huguenots, and used them simply as a bit to bridle the Guises and their aggressive catholic policy. Open war she said she would not have. This abstention she had to enforce on her subjects in the teeth of a twofold opposition: the zealous protestants cried aloud against compromise with the persecutors of the Huguenots; and several of her councillors, including Cecil and Sussex, hankered after the old combination of England and Spain against France. It was still a saying in

---

[1] *Spanish Cal.*, i., 234, 319, 387.   [2] Haynes, p. 383.

England that only when the Ethiopian became white would CHAP.
Frenchmen love the English.[1]   XVII.

An integral part of this policy was the gradual weaning of
Scotland from its ancient dependence on France, and of France
from its inveterate affection for Scotland. The personal antipathy between Mary Stuart and Catherine de Médicis, the rise
of protestantism in Scotland, and the vagaries of the Scottish
queen all facilitated this delicate task; but it required skilful
and patient handling. Public opinion in France was tender on
the subject; brusque or overt action on Elizabeth's part would
play into the hands of the Guises and enable them to force
upon Catherine the open championship of Mary and of the
Scottish catholics; and Elizabeth was driven to subterfuges,
ambiguous words, and double dealing, which nearly drove to
despair the protestant rulers of Scotland and the English
agents whom Elizabeth sent to keep them in countenance.[2] A few English troops, they insisted, would suffice to
eradicate the remnants of Mary's party and to bind England
and Scotland firmly together; but Elizabeth dreaded lest
those few troops should break the web she was weaving with
Catherine, and bring French armies into Scotland. Slowly she
achieved her purpose. Before the inevitable breach came with
Spain, the French government was neutralised: Mary Stuart
was converted from a dependant of France into a client of
Spain; and the way was prepared for English intervention in
the Netherlands, and for the completion of the breach with
Spain towards which English expansion had steadily tended.

Next to commercial and colonial rivalry, the progress of
the revolution in the Netherlands did most to undermine the
Anglo-Spanish alliance. As early as 1564 the ferment produced by Philip's policy was having disastrous effects upon the
prosperity of the English merchant-adventurers in Antwerp;
and they were beginning to think of shifting their operations
to Emden or Hamburg. A conference at Bruges in 1565-66
did little to mend the situation; and the arrival of Alva in
1567, the erection of the "tribunal of blood," and the execution
of Egmont and Horn shook England's commercial confidence
as much as they shocked its moral sense. Elizabeth did not
seize the Spanish treasure in December, 1568, mainly to hamper

[1] *Documentos Ineditos*, lxxxix., 97.   [2] *Foreign Cal.*, 1569-71, pp. 286-89.

Alva's proceedings; but that result caused no little satisfaction. It contributed materially to his ultimate failure, and he was unable to retaliate, except by a suspension of trade which aggravated the evil. " This country," wrote an English agent from Madrid in July, 1569, "without doubt will be undone, if there be not an end made betwixt the Queen and the King ; many merchants bankrupt and many towns on the sea-coast undone if the traffic do cease. There is no trade but into the Indies. Out of Biscay and Galicia they have sent up their procurators, requesting his majesty to end this matter with England, as otherwise they will not be able to live." [1] Philip struggled hard to avoid humbling himself in the eyes of the world before the queen, as whose patron he had ostentatiously and condescendingly posed ; and it was little wonder that Alva hoped to assist the rising of the northern earls, or that Philip entered eagerly into Ridolfi's plot and encouraged rebellion in Ireland. Spain was being driven into an enmity with England which Philip had not yet the means to gratify ; but his encouragement of Elizabeth's enemies compelled her to countermine his schemes.

In this subtle work her courtships played a leading part. She never intended to marry, and she told La Mothe that she would feel compulsion in that respect more irksome than her confinement in the Tower. But Cecil was haunted by the fear of a war of succession in the event of her death ; and most of her subjects felt the force of the arguments in favour of marriage, which he embodied in many memorials. They produced no effect, because Elizabeth knew that no heir could be born of her. She guarded her secret as best she might ; and, while it must have been suspected by Cecil as it was by Philip, La Mothe, and others, English ministers were bound to bury their suspicions, lest they should ruin the pretences which Elizabeth had to employ. This necessity for dissimulation darkened counsel and deluded ministers ; and the obscurity of the mass of despatches on the subject is the measure of their skill and success. Lucidity would have been fatal ; and Elizabeth and her diplomatists were adepts in the use of language which concealed their thoughts.

Some points are clear enough. Elizabeth's hand could be

---

[1] *Foreign Cal.*, 1569-71, pp. 99, 432.

as useful to others as Mary Tudor's had been to Philip; and even abortive marriage negotiations might lead to other forms of alliance, or at least avert hostility for a time. Wherever a possible leader of a catholic crusade appeared, Elizabeth's hand interposed; and she placed the privileges of her sex at the service of her diplomacy. Her rupture with Spain in 1569, and the close of the third war of religion in France at the peace of St. Germain in 1570, induced her to simulate affection for the Duke of Anjou, the favourite and second surviving son of Catherine de Médicis. He had won great repute from Tavannes' victories over the Huguenots at Jarnac and Moncontour, and had been proposed as a husband for Mary Stuart and a champion for British catholics.[1] So Walsingham was sent to France in 1570 to frustrate the catholic design by means of a protestant alliance. Personally he was puritan in his politics, and stayed his hopes upon the Huguenots; but he was statesman enough to subordinate his views to those of his government and do his best for the marriage negotiation, with the private assurance that it was the surest guarantee for an Anglo-French-protestant attack upon Spanish catholicism.

Patiently he gathered the threads into his hands. Charles IX. and Catherine were pointedly congratulated on the peace of St. Germain, an act of royal grace so different from the blood and iron of the tyrant Alva. The close of the religious war revived the national ambition of France; but, while its revival in 1563 had resulted in the expulsion of the English from Havre, Elizabeth now hoped that it might effect the expulsion of Alva from the Netherlands. For this purpose it was necessary to liberate the French monarchy from Guise control, to reconcile it with the Huguenots, and to guarantee foreign support. Walsingham's policy anticipated that of Richelieu in 1624; and Elizabeth countenanced it for a time. "Her real aim," wrote Guerau in September, 1571, "is to bring the French gradually into the offensive and defensive league which many of the German princes and the Duke of Florence are said to have joined." Cosimo de' Medici, created Grand Duke of Tuscany by the Pope in 1569, was at issue with the Hapsburgs, who regarded the papal act as an infringement of imperial rights; his emissaries were scheming with Louis of Nassau, brother of

[1] *Foreign Cal.*, 1569-71, p. 268.

William of Orange, and with the Huguenots at La Rochelle ; and Venice, it was hoped, would assist in freeing Italy from Spanish control.[1] Catherine dreamt of reviving Angevin schemes in Naples, and Charles IX. the old French claims on the Netherlands. She wished to be rid of Guise control, while the king distrusted his brother, and spoke of a league to counteract that of which Anjou was the unacknowledged head. Montmorenci and his brothers, Damville, Méru, and Thoré, were ready to support the monarchy and their cousins, the Châtillons, against the Guises ; and the alliance was to be cemented by the marriage of the young Henry of Navarre with Charles IX.'s sister Margaret. The king was also annoyed with Philip II. for having carried off Anne of Austria, the bride on whom he had set his heart, for having caused his sister Juana to refuse Anjou, for having massacred the French in Florida, and for seeking to detach the Swiss from the French alliance. He was now thought to be friendly to " la religion " ; at least, his mistress Marie Touchet was a Huguenot. Catherine, too, pretended that her daughter Elizabeth, Philip's third wife, had been poisoned for her sympathy with Don Carlos.[2]

All this was heartrending news for the captive of Tutbury. " The French," wrote Guerau in April, 1571, "have abandoned her." In October, 1570, Charles said that " if he himself had the Queen of Scots prisoner, or were in the place of the Queen of England, he well knew what he would do " ;[3] and French diplomatic intervention in Scottish affairs was now limited to half-hearted requests for her liberty and to more sincere, but equally ineffective, efforts to establish influence over her son's government. Moray's assassination had been followed by civil war in Scotland, where Maitland and Kirkcaldy now took Mary's side and held Dumbarton and Edinburgh castles in her interest. At the crisis Elizabeth once more brought herself to the point of decisive intervention ; and in spite of French protests she secured the regency for Lennox in July, 1570, and sent reinforcements across the Borders to support his government in August. Châtelherault, Huntly, and Argyle were con-

---

[1] *Foreign Cal.*, 1569-71, pp. 276, 572, 576, 579 ; La Ferrière, *Lettres de Catherine de Médicis*, iv., Introd., p. xv ; *Spanish Cal.*, ii., 345, 349, 360.

[2] *Foreign Cal.*, 1569-71, pp. 314, 326, 396, 414, 509, 569, 587.

[3] *Ibid.*, 1569-71, pp. 365, 410.

strained to expel the English refugees, Westmorland, Leonard
Dacre, and others, and to consent to an armistice pending the
negotiations between Elizabeth, Mary, and the Scots government.[1]

These negotiations with Mary were designed to soothe the
French ; and when Cecil opposed the idea of Mary's restoration,
Elizabeth said she wished to be guided by Charles IX. and not
by Cecil's "brethren in Christ". Leicester supported the proposal, bribed perhaps by the suggestion that he should marry
Mary. There was a grim if unconscious humour in the idea of
matching Darnley's widow with the widower of Amy Robsart ;
but the plan can hardly have been serious. Nevertheless the
parleyings were viewed with dismay by the Scottish government, by Sussex, Randolph, and all Elizabeth's representatives
in the north ; while the French court required La Mothe and the
Bishop of Ross to counteract them in order to prevent an Anglo-
Scottish agreement. Mary's own adherents, moreover, were not
sincere in their dealings :[2] and she never realised that the object of her French and Spanish advisers was simply to foment
friction between the English and the Scots, not to vindicate her,
still less to make her queen of a united Great Britain. Relying
on their professions, she rejected the terms she might have
made with Elizabeth, and preferred the brilliant but doubtful
prospects held out by schemes for her marriage with Anjou or
Don John of Austria. Elizabeth had once rallied her on her
predilection for having two strings to her bow: the English
queen could afford to maintain several courtships at once, because she did not want to marry ; the Scottish queen, who was
still, despite the divorce, in friendly communication with Bothwell in Denmark,[3] would have done better with fewer suitors
than Don John, Anjou, and Norfolk.

The negotiation with Elizabeth, which she described as
practically settled in February, 1571, was interrupted by the
discovery of Ridolfi's mission. Dumbarton was captured by
Lennox in April; Argyle, Cassillis, Eglinton, and Boyd
were won over by Morton ; and Archbishop Hamilton of St.
Andrews was hanged. When, in September, Lennox was

---

[1] *Spanish Cal.*, pp. 285, 294, 298, 301, 325, 332, 336-37, 373, 502, 568.
[2] *Ibid.*, pp. 364, 372 ; La Mothe, iii., 188 ; *Spanish Cal.*, ii., 306.
[3] *Foreign Cal.*, 1569-71, p. 392.

CHAP.
XVII.

killed—"a most successful enterprise" as Guerau termed it,[1] which Randolph and Drury had repeatedly foretold—the Earl of Mar was chosen regent; behind his authority Morton rode roughshod over the relics of Mary's party in Scotland; and in December a majority of the French king's council recommended that official support should be tranferred to James VI.[2]

As France cooled towards Mary, so it was estranged from Spain; and the project of a French attack on the Netherlands loomed larger on the horizon. The peace of St. Germain-en-Laye converted the Huguenots from a force, which acted by way of repulsion, into one which acted by way of attraction upon the French government; and Coligny's remarkable personality soon exerted a powerful influence over Charles. The Guises, being only half French, naturally adopted a religious, and not a national, policy; catholicism was their principal stock-in-trade. The Huguenots, on the other hand, favoured national ambitions, because such ambitions could best be realised at Spain's expense, in Florida or in the Netherlands : a national war upon Spain would save them from religious war at home, and protect other protestants from Spanish attack. In 1571 France was on the edge of one of the most momentous decisions in its history. The Guises abandoned the court to their rivals, Coligny and the Montmorencies : and the Spanish ambassador left France, while Elizabeth expelled Guerau from England in December for his own complicity in Ridolfi's plot and the share of his steward Borghese in a plot to kill both her and Burghley.[3] On October 8 Walsingham wrote from Paris, "the marshals with the king and Monsieur have resolved upon the enterprise of Flanders". The German princes, who vehemently resented Alva's execution of their fellow-princes of the Empire, Egmont and Horn, were willing to join on condition that France should be content with Flanders and Artois, that Brabant, Guelders, and Luxemburg should be restored to the Empire, and that Elizabeth should have Zealand and the "rest of the islands" as the reward of her co-operation. In December a French agent was sent to fix with Louis of Nassau a day for the

---

[1] *Spanish Cal.*, ii., 338.
[2] *Foreign Cal.*, 1569-71, pp. 403, 427-29, 505, 523, 542, 576.
[3] *Spanish Cal.*, ii., 373-74; *Hatfield MSS.*, ii., 7-8; *Acts of the P. C.*, viii., 62-63.

execution of the enterprise.   On January 1, 1572, Sir Thomas
Smith arrived at the French court to complete the work he
had begun at Troyes in 1564; and on April 19 the defensive
treaty of Blois was concluded between England and France.[1]

As a decoy the Anjou marriage project had served its purpose.   "It is nothing but a cunning trick," wrote Philip in
August, 1571;[2] and now the whirlpool of intrigue, which had
raged round the duke's person, subsided.   The scheme had
been canvassed with as much zeal, with as extravagant hopes
and fears, as if it had been a serious design on Elizabeth's part.
The papacy, the Guises, and Spain had brought all sorts of
pressure to bear upon Anjou to dissuade him from a match
which they feared, and Burghley and Walsingham hoped, would
be the ruin of catholicism in Western Europe.   On the other
hand, Walsingham gave him a copy of the French version of
the Book of Common Prayer used in the Channel Islands, and
plied him with proofs of the excellence of Elizabeth's religion.
Charles IX. and Catherine employed their authority and political arguments on the same side.   But Elizabeth meant the
match to founder on the religious question; "she will no more
marry Anjou," wrote Feria, "than she will marry me".   Against
the persuasions of the puritanical Walsingham she refused to
promise Anjou even a private mass in England; and she, who
had supported the claims of the Huguenots, demonstrated to
the French court the danger of tolerating two religions in
England.   She might, for La Mothe's edification, gibe at the
"brethren in Christ"; but she knew better than to exasperate
her staunchest supporters with a catholic husband, or to burden
her own existence with a prince of the decadent house of Valois.[3]

No love was lost between the two peoples, and the mutual
distrust of the two courts paralysed the great design on the
Netherlands.   The accidental nature of the capture of Brille
by the sea-rover La Marck on April 1, 1572, which begot the
Dutch republic, has probably been exaggerated.   Elizabeth
had allowed Dutch freebooters the shelter of her ports, and
La Marck used Dover as a regular basis of operations; and,

---

[1] *Foreign Cal.*, 1569-71, pp. 507, 584; 1572-74, pp. 3, 86-87.

[2] *Spanish Cal.*, ii., 333.

[3] *Ibid.*, ii., 309, 325; La Mothe, iii., 187-8. She told Charles IX. "she could
take no husband who has not the goodwill of the protestants in whom her
principal strength lies ".

while she issued public proclamations against him and all other pirates, she privately granted him safe-conducts. In November, 1571, he was "being greatly caressed" by the English,[1] who, wrote Guerau on December 21, "at one blow with their practices in Flanders will plunge that country into dreadful war". Subsequently Guerau stated that he had information of the design on Brille six months before it was effected; that he had "duly advised the Duke of Alva at the time"; and that the place had been reconnoitred before he left England in January, 1572. In June Montmorenci told Elizabeth to her face that La Marck had left Dover to seize Brille with her consent and aid; and she admitted the charge. Finally William of Orange "thanked her warmly for her efficient aid to La Marck in taking and holding Brille"; and a Spaniard averred that La Marck's expulsion from Dover "was all a deceitful trick to cover the taking of Brille".[2]   It was no sooner occupied than Elizabeth prepared to profit by the occasion; and Sir Humphrey Gilbert was allowed to take 1,200 English troops across the sea, on the understanding that he was at liberty to neglect the council's orders to return, and obey only Burghley's private signal. Other detachments followed; Sluys, Flushing, and Bruges were occupied, an attack was made on Tergoes, and Sir Ralph Sadler and Sir William Pelham were secretly despatched to advise the rebels and their own government on the political and military aspects of the situation.[3]

Their mission was brief. On July 26 news reached London that 5,000 Huguenots, marching under Genlis with Charles IX.'s concurrence to the relief of Mons, had been cut to pieces by Alva's son; and four days later Sadler and Pelham were speeding back to England in obedience to Elizabeth's letters of recall. Gilbert and his French allies were plotting each other's ejection from Flushing, while each of their governments was meditating secret withdrawal. The real object of many an alliance in the sixteenth century was to leave the ally alone in the grip of the common enemy; and there was a funda-

---

[1] See *Hatfield MSS.*, ii., 40-41, which should be dated November, 1571.

[2] *Spanish Cal.*, ii., 348, 353, 360, 366, 376, 385, 396, 401, 461.

[3] *Domestic Cal.*, Addenda, 1566-79, pp. 422-23; *Foreign Cal.*, 1572-74, pp. 169, 176; *Spanish Cal.*, ii., 398, 402; La Mothe, v., 78, 153, 199. Tergoes is now called Goes, without the prefix.

mental divergence between English and French policy towards the Netherlands. Coligny avowedly wanted a war of conquest abroad to prevent a war of religion at home; and he had won Charles IX. over to this view. Elizabeth on the other hand feared French more than Spanish dominion in the Netherlands. Such a transference of power, wrote Burghley to Walsingham, would put English commerce with the Netherlands at the mercy of France, and endanger the sovereignty of the narrow seas which belonged to England.[1] His design was to free the Netherlands from all but nominal allegiance to Philip, and to prevent their falling into the hands of France.[2] Rather than see the French masters of the coast from Friesland to Bayonne, Elizabeth would have handed over the Flemish towns she occupied to Philip in return for commercial concessions and guarantees of political and religious liberties for the Netherlands. In this guarded attitude there was little hope for the Huguenots: it is doubtful whether they could have been saved even by that open breach between England and Spain which Walsingham desired; and it was not Elizabeth's business to involve her subjects in war in order to protect one French faction from another. She continued, however, to send secret reinforcements to the Netherlands until August 20; and it was Charles IX. who first declared that he could not afford an open breach with Spain. Genlis had been betrayed to Alva by the Cardinal of Lorraine;[3] Catherine was bent on peace; and the fate of the Huguenots depended upon the struggle for predominance over the mind of Charles IX., which caused French policy to fluctuate from day to day.

As far back as October 7, 1571, Don John's great victory over the Turks at Lepanto had made Catherine quail at the thought of war with Philip. "They doubt," wrote Walsing-

---

[1] La Ferrière, *Lettres de Catherine de Médicis*, vol. iv., p. l.

[2] French historians have never been able to forgive this adhesion to the principle of the old Burgundian alliance; Michelet calls it England's "original sin," and M. de la Ferrière its "traditional bad faith ". M. de la Ferrière has convinced himself that Elizabeth was at the same moment aiming at the conquest of the Netherlands and proposing to hand over Flushing to Philip II., *Lettres de Catherine*, vol. iv., pp. l-lxvii. By means of this same " bad faith " he seeks to relieve France of some of the guilt of St. Bartholomew's Day and transfer it to Elizabeth on the ground that she ruined the success of Coligny's policy, which alone could have saved the Huguenots.

[3] La Ferrière, *op. cit.*, p. lix; *Spanish Cal.*, ii., 403-4, 407.

ham, commenting on the news, "that the queen-mother who directs all here, being fearful by nature, will incline to Spain." Even before the battle she had opposed the prosecution of the Flemish enterprise without fuller assurance of Elizabeth's co-operation. The emperor, the papacy, and Venice reproved her anti-catholic policy;[1] and there was ample justification for her qualms in the attitude of the French. Probably the Huguenots did not number more than a third of the nobility and a thirtieth of the people. In towns, which were regarded as strongholds of the party, they were often a minority of powerful bur-gesses, while the lower classes were overwhelmingly catholic.[2] The *politiques* were a small, though influential party; and the monarchy could rely on no such body of opinion as in England. The so-called national policy of the Huguenots and *politiques* was in fact anathema to the vast mass of their countrymen. When on December 20, 1571, Coligny obtained the removal of a cross erected to commemorate the execution of three Hugue-nots, the mob paraded the streets, denouncing Charles IX., and shouting " Let us kill the Huguenots ". In January, 1572, in a sermon preached before the king, they were likened to lepers ; and in March sixteen of them perished in a *noyade* at Orleans, in retaliation perhaps for the hundred friars and monks, whom a Huguenot privateer captured from a Portuguese ship and drowned in October, 1571. There was substance in the secret warning conveyed in December, 1571, from the court to Coligny "to look to himself, for all is not gold that glisters " ; and ground for the suspicion with which Elizabeth received in August, 1572, Charles's exhortations to break with Philip II.[3]

The admiral hoped for salvation through the marriage of Henry of Navarre with Margaret of Valois, which had been fixed for August 18. For weeks Catherine had been prosecuting what the Venetian ambassador aptly calls her vendetta.[4] Do-minion was her ruling passion ; and she saw it threatened by the admiral. Twice she had baulked his Flemish enterprise ; twice, when her back was turned, he had reconverted the king.

---

[1] *Foreign Cal.*, 1569-71, pp. 545, 557.
[2] Armstrong, *Wars of Religion*, ed. 1903, pp. 20-21.
[3] *Foreign Cal.*, 1569-71, pp. 569, 581-82 ; 1572-74, p. 35 ; *Hatfield MSS.*, ii., 14 ; La Mothe, iv., 327 ; *Spanish Cal.*, ii., 412.
[4] La Ferrière, *Lettres*, vol. iv., p. lxxiv.

It was time to settle the account, and on the 22nd at her instigation an attempt was made on Coligny's life. The assassin
blundered ; Charles swore vengeance ; and within a few hours
the ministers of justice were close on Catherine's trail. Her
political existence was at stake ; and by a supreme effort of
serpentine [1] ingenuity and maternal influence, she mastered
the feeble mind of Charles IX., and persuaded him that
Coligny was at the head of a vast conspiracy against the
throne. She conveyed to him the infection of her own panic,
and aroused a ferocity from which she herself was free. The
massacre was speedily arranged ; and at dawn on St. Bartholomew's, the 24th, which happened to be a Sunday, the
bell of the *Palais de Justice* rang out its murderous call to arms.
For eight days "death and blood," to quote Tavannes, ran
through the streets of Paris. "While I write," says Zuñiga,
the Spanish ambassador, on the 26th, " they are casting them
out naked and dragging them through the streets, pillaging
their houses and sparing not a babe. Blessed be God who has
converted the princes of France to his purpose ! May he inspire their hearts to go on as they have begun ! " [2] The
massacres were perpetrated by the willing hands of mobs infu-
riated by the miseries of civil wars, which they attributed to
the Huguenots. Some 3,000 or 4,000, including Coligny, were
slain in Paris. In the provinces, where the butchery was spread
over six weeks, 800 were killed at Lyons, and 500 at Orleans,
while hundreds fell victims at Bordeaux and Toulouse as late
as October ; and a precedent for later times was set by the
general forcing of prisons and massacre of the inmates. The
lowest estimate of the numbers murdered throughout France
is 10,000 ; [3] and it was rumoured that the Huguenots had been
exterminated.

Protestants were convinced that the massacre was the outcome of a comprehensive conspiracy dating back to the conference at Bayonne. "I have often recalled," remarked Alva,
"what I said to the queen-mother at Bayonne, and what she
promised me ; and I see she has kept her word ; " and at

---

[1] " Madame la Serpente " was the sobriquet used of Catherine by her son,
Alençon, *Hatfield MSS.*, ii., 30 ; La Ferrière, p. cxlvii.

[2] La Ferrière, p. cxviii ; Tavannes, *Mémoires*, ed. Buchon, p. 435.

[3] Armstrong, p. 33 n. ; contemporary reports in the *Foreign Cal.* give higher
figures, *e.g.* 1,200 for Orleans.

Rome an inscription in letters of gold proclaimed that Charles had merely followed Roman counsels.   But the truth seems to be that Roman catholic potentates merely hastened to claim credit for a crime which they had not the courage or the forethought to contrive.   "Although," writes Zuñiga, "the French wish it to be understood that their king has meditated this stroke ever since the peace of St. Germain, and attribute to him stratagems which will not appear permissible even against heretics and rebels, I take it for certain that, granting the shot fired at the Admiral was a design planned some days before and authorised by the king, all the rest was inspired by circumstances." [1]

The tale was varied to suit the audience.   To protestants the massacre was represented as a regrettable incident in the Guise-Châtillon feud, to catholics as a meritorious royal design.   "Am I so bad a Christian," asked Catherine, who had received enough religious instruction to be able to quote Scripture for her own purposes, of the Spanish ambassador, "as Don Francis de Alava pretended?   Go back to your master; tell him what things you have seen and heard; how that the blind see and the lame walk; and do not forget to add 'Blessed is he, whosoever shall not be offended in me'."   She was wise in her generation.   Congratulations poured in upon her and Charles from Italy, Spain, and Savoy.   At Rome a jubilee was ordained, and a medal was struck, to commemorate the event; and Vasari was summoned to depict on the walls of the Vatican this triumph of the Roman church. [2]   Philip had never been known to laugh before; but he could not resist the joyous contagion, and his sombre countenance lit up with glee.   He ordered a *Te Deum* at once, announced that the news was one of the greatest joys of his life, and praised Charles's profound dissimulation: the Catholic and Most Christian Kings were now at one.

A different scene was enacted in England.   Elizabeth and her court were dressed in black when she received La Mothe: no one ventured to salute him except the queen, who greeted him, he says, with her customary courtesy; and his excuses and protestations were heard in a forbidding silence.

---

[1] La Ferrière, *Lettres*, pp. xxvi, cxiv-xv; *cf.* La Mothe, v., 120 ff.

[2] La Ferrière, pp. xciv, cxvi-cxix.   A reproduction of the medal is given in Bonnani, *Numismat. Pontific.*, i., 336.

He denied that premeditation and profound secrecy which
had so impressed Philip, and palliated the massacres on the
ground of sudden panic created by the discovery of the fabricated plot of the Huguenots.   This pretence had to be kept up
to save the English alliance, and soothe the German princes :
a solemn legal process against the admiral and his accomplices
was unfolded in September; and two *politiques*, Briquemault
and Cavaignes, were executed on this charge in October before
the eyes of Charles IX. himself.[1]

If the audience was a trying moment for La Mothe, the
crisis was a crucial test for the English government.   France
had had to stand by while her English ally beheaded the two
catholic leaders, Norfolk and Northumberland, who was handed
over by the Scottish government and executed at Berwick on
August 22.   But it was a severer strain on England to condone
the massacre of the Huguenots.   National indignation was
intense; and to seek some means of gratifying the resentment
would have been natural, popular, and just.   But it would not
have been statesmanship.   "Confess, sire," said the French
ambassador at Madrid to Philip, "that it is to the king my
master that you owe your Netherlands;"[2] and perhaps the
massacre of St. Bartholomew cost France the frontier of the
Rhine.   Catherine admitted that France had burnt her boats
and was embarked on Philip's voyage;[3] it was her political folly
and not her catholic zeal that evoked his solitary laugh.   The
duty of English statesmen was to disappoint his expectations;
to reconstruct, if possible, the policy which Philip thought the
massacre had killed; and to curb their passion for revenge.

[1] La Ferrière, *Lettres*, p. cxxxvii; *Hatfield MSS.*, ii., 24; La Mothe, v.,
205.   There had undoubtedly been a design to bring pressure to bear on the
government about St. Bartholomew's day: "Montmorenci, the Admiral, and
Foix write long letters to the queen and Burghley, saying what great things they
hope to do; but they cannot, they say, do them until after the wedding of Navarre,
when they think they will be able to get the king to agree to anything, as so
many of their principal friends will be collected together," *Spanish Cal.*, ii., 402.

[2] La Ferrière, p. cxix.

[3] *Ibid.*, p. 114: "à cause de ceste mutation nous sommes embarquez à courir
pareille fortune que eulx," Catherine to Saint-Gouard, August 29.   *Cf. ibid.*,
pp. 118, 120, 122, 126.

CHAPTER XVIII.

THE WOOING OF ANJOU.

ONE form of retaliation for the massacre of St. Bartholomew was seriously considered by the English government. Mary, Queen of Scots, was hand in glove with the perpetrators of the butchery in France; she seemed to be a standing incitement to its repetition in England; and the government resolved that she must go. Negotiations were begun in September for her surrender to the Regent Mar, on the understanding that she was to be brought to justice by the Scots, and that England was to safeguard them against the consequences. But Mar died on October 28, 1572,[1] before the compact was concluded; Elizabeth herself had always been averse from the idea; and before Morton was firmly seated in the regent's saddle the panic had subsided, and less violent expedients were adopted.[2] The massacre had discredited Mary's cause in Scotland: on February 23, 1573, Huntly, the Hamiltons, and practically all the queen's adherents, except the garrison of Edinburgh Castle, made their peace with Morton; and on April 18 Sir William Drury led an English force across the Borders to besiege the castle, while a fleet conveyed ordnance to Leith. The castle surrendered on May 28; Maitland died in prison on June 9, and Kirkcaldy was hanged. Protestantism was triumphant in Scotland; the country prospered under the iron rule of Morton, perhaps an abler if a harder man than Moray; and Mary was reprieved for fourteen years.

Catherine was powerless to prevent this last blow to French influence in Scotland, because Elizabeth and Philip were once more on friendly terms, and the outbreak of the fourth war of religion in France paralysed its government; no help could be

---

[1] Bain, iv., 426-9.

[2] *Hatfield MSS.*, ii., 23, 27-28; *Foreign Cal.*, 1572-74, pp. 182, 194, 196, 201-5, 207, 215; La Mothe, v., 133, 157, 176.

promised the garrison in Edinburgh Castle, until La Rochelle CHAP.
should fall.[1]   Catherine, moreover, was absorbed in her in- XVIII.
trigues to secure Anjou's election as King of Poland.   She
soon discovered that her wild stroke was a blunder as well as a
crime, and her first letter after the massacre to the French
ambassador at Madrid expressed the fear that Philip would
now be able to treat France with less respect than before.   St.
Bartholomew had obscured Alva's cruelties; and to point the
contrast between French perfidy and Spanish courtesy, the
heretics who had unsuccessfully defended Mons, were, on its
capture in September, 1572, allowed to depart uninjured—only
to be butchered by Charles IX.'s orders when they crossed
the frontier into Picardy.[2]

Philip cared more for the English than for the French alliance; and Elizabeth was naturally driven towards Spain by her
repulsion from France.   Catherine's repudiation of Coligny's
design on the Netherlands postponed all idea of armed intervention by England.   Indeed, it was suspected that the English
occupation of Flemish towns was intended from the first
merely to give Elizabeth something more to barter in her
negotiations with Philip;[3] and in April, 1573, the renewal was
proclaimed of intercourse between English and Spanish subjects, which had been interrupted since December, 1568.[4]   The
substitution of the pacific Requesens for the harsh and beaten
Alva in the following December eased Anglo-Spanish relations.
On August 21, 1574, the convention of Bristol settled the claims
and counterclaims arising out of the seizures and embargoes of
1568-69; and in 1575 Philip went so far as to order the expulsion of the English catholic refugees from Louvain, while some
trifling concessions were even obtained from the Spanish inquisition.   In spite of the excursions and alarms occasioned by
the equipping of Menendez' fleet at Santander in 1574, which,
it has been thought, might have anticipated the Spanish

---

[1] *Hatfield MSS.*, ii., 50.
[2] *Spanish Cal.*, ii., 418-21, 425, 434; La Ferrière, *Lettres*, vol. iv., pp.
cxxxi-ii; La Mothe, v., 160.
[3] *Spanish Cal.*, ii., 400, 407, 511.
[4] Froude misdates this proclamation April 30, 1572, instead of 1573; and
partly on this error M. de la Ferrière bases his exaggerated charge of duplicity
against Elizabeth, *Lettres de Catherine*, vol. iv., p. xlix.   See *Hatfield MSS.*, ii.,
49; *Foreign Cal.*, 1572-74, p. 327; La Mothe, v., 307; *Venetian Cal.*, vii., 486-87.

CHAP. Armada, Philip was bent on enduring Elizabeth a little longer,
XVIII. till he could subdue the Netherlands and break the Anglo-
French alliance. " There never was fairer weather made to the
English nation in Spain than there is at present," reported an
English agent as late as 1578.[1]

Elizabeth, however, restrained her anger sufficiently to resist the efforts of Spain to profit by the disunion between
England and France, though she told La Mothe that she could
place no trust in Charles's word, who apparently wished to
amend the ten commandments by cutting out the sixth.[2] She
accepted the invitation to stand as godmother to Charles's
daughter, who was born on the day that Briquemault and
Cavaignes were judicially murdered ; and sent the catholic earl
of Worcester to represent her at the christening. But she
permitted men and ships to aid the revolted Rochellese, and
smoothed the way for Montgomery's raid on Normandy. Her
most effective method, however, of embarrassing the French
government was her marriage negotiation with the Duke of
Alençon, Catherine's youngest son, who had been substituted
for Anjou as Elizabeth's suitor early in 1572.[3] He was not
burdened with the religious scruples of his elder brother ; and
Charles and Catherine were now fervently pressing the match
as the best means of counteracting bad impressions of France
and the blandishments of Spain.

Elizabeth perceived the possibilities of this amazing courtship, begun between a youth of eighteen [4] and a maiden of
thirty-nine, and continued for more than a decade. It was
the masterpiece of her diplomacy ; its variety was infinite, and
Elizabeth alone held the thread without which others were lost
in the maze. She knew her own mind, but believed that her
safety consisted in bewildering every one else ; and the peculiar
advantage of Alençon as a suitor lay in the ambiguity of his
position. He might be used as a link to bind England with
France in defence against Spain, or as a bridle upon the French
government's catholic tendencies ; "except he would show him-

---

[1] *Foreign Cal.*, 1572-74, pp. 543, 564, 586 ; 1575-77, pp. xx, 122 ; 1577-78, p.
485 ; *Spanish Cal.*, ii., 506 ; *Venetian Cal.*, vii., 515, 553 ; *Hatfield MSS.*, ii.,
81 ; Corbett, *Drake*, i., 195-98.

[2] La Mothe, v., 186.

[3] *Hatfield MSS.*, ii., 19, 22, 29-34 ; La Ferrière, *Lettres*, iv., pp. cxlv, clxxiv,
clxxxv.

[4] Alençon was born on March 17, 1554.

self a favourer of them of the religion," he was told, "he was CHAP.
not a meet husband for the queen's majesty ".[1]   The brothers XVIII.
of French kings were almost independent princes, and the
eldest was habitually in chronic opposition to the crown.
Now that Anjou had assumed his impotent sceptre in Poland,
Alençon stepped into his place as the leader of discontent in
France; and the anxiety of Charles and Catherine for his
marriage sprang at least as much from a desire to be rid of
the duke as from a wish to gratify Elizabeth.   For Alençon
could play better than Anjou the part of opponent to a catholic
policy.   It was whispered that he had promised the Huguenots
to avenge Coligny's death; and his agent Maisonfleur could
speak of him as "being banished from his country for not
having wished to take part in the most faithless massacre, the
most unworthy act, the most infamous tyranny, and the most
brutal and monstrous inhumanity, that has been perpetrated
since the creation of the world ".[2]

The "banishment" was an anticipatory flourish; for Alençon never reached the ship that hovered for weeks in the
autumn of 1572 off the Norman coast to convey him—and, if
possible, Navarre and Condé—in his flight from the French
court to Elizabeth's presence.   But he was now accepted as
their chief by all the malcontents, including the *politiques*, who
had begun to advocate the revival of the old French constitution
and the summoning of the estates-general as a remedy for the
evils provoked by Catherine's Italian despotism.   Her methods
of massacre had produced no results commensurate with the
chorus of congratulation with which they had been received.
The Rochellese with clandestine aid from Elizabeth [3] extorted
in July, 1573, terms almost as humiliating to the crown as
those of St. Germain; and five months later the magistrates
of Toulouse complained that the Huguenots had done more

---

[1] *Hatfield MSS.*, ii., 290.

[2] *Ibid.*, ii., 33-35; La Ferrière, *Lettres*, iv., p. cxlv.   Maisonfleur's correspondence, extant in the Record Office, has been published in La Ferrière's *Les
Valois et le xvime Siècle;* see also Harleian MSS. 260 *passim*.

[3] *Spanish Cal.*, ii., 456-57, 460, 464, 468.   The help was sent, Elizabeth told
La Mothe, not by her orders but by the bishop of London, "out of friendship
and in respect of his religion"; this was in answer to La Mothe's excuse that
French assistance had been sent to Scotland, not by Charles IX., but by the
Cardinal of Lorraine.

pillage and increased to a greater extent during the cessation of hostilities than they would have done after a signal victory.[1] The general anarchy was hardly made worse by the outbreak of the fifth war of religion in February, 1574, in which the Huguenots were more or less openly supported by Alençon, the *politiques*, and the German protestant princes. A fresh attempt of Alençon and Henry of Navarre to escape from court was frustrated; their accomplices, La Molle and Coconas, were executed; and Montgomery capitulated at Domfront, on a promise of his life on May 25. Four days later Charles IX. died, muttering "Que de sang, que de sang!" while the insatiable Catherine had Montgomery hanged.[2] The accession of Henry III. and the death of the Cardinal of Lorraine in November brought no peace, although Henry abandoned his earlier truculence, and subsided into palatial sloth. Alençon, henceforth called Anjou, escaped from court in September, 1575, and Henry of Navarre in February, 1576. Casimir of the Palatinate was paid to invade France by Elizabeth, although she had renewed, on April 30, 1575, the treaty of Blois with Henry III.; and the harrying of the country by half a dozen independent armies was only interrupted for a few months by the "Peace of Monsieur," concluded in April, 1576.

Its concessions to the Huguenots and the revival of the Netherlands policy of Coligny provoked the growth of the Catholic League, which spread with the blessings of Philip II. and the papacy until it included nearly the whole of catholic France. In January, 1577, Henry III. repudiated the peace: Anjou and Damville sided with the crown; and the sixth religious war broke out. Elizabeth once more hired the indispensable Casimir;[3] but the peace of Bergerac concluded the war in September before he got to work. The local disturbances of 1580, which are called the seventh war of religion, were the only breach of the nominal peace which reigned in France for the unwonted period of eight years. Catherine either could not, or from fear of Guise predominance would not, crush the Huguenots; while developments in the Nether-

---

[1] Ferrière, pp. clxxviii-ix, ccvii; *Venetian Cal.*, vii., 500-15.
[2] For this treachery she had the excuse that Montgomery had dealt the blow which accidentally killed her husband, Henry II.
[3] *Hatfield MSS.*, ii., 119, 173; *Venetian Cal.*, vii., 558-64.

lands and Portugal inclined her towards a strengthening of ties with England.

Requesens had been no more successful than Alva. The Spanish fleet was as badly defeated off Bergen in 1574 as it had been at Enkhuizen in 1573; the failure to capture Leyden in 1575 was a greater blow than the repulse from Alkmaar in 1573, and the surrender of the Spaniards in Middelburg in 1574 cleared them out of Zealand. They regained a footing there at Zierickzee in June, 1576; but Requesens had died in March, and during the seven months that elapsed before the arrival of his successor, Don John of Austria, the Spanish troops mutinied and spread rapine and disorder, which culminated in the sack of Antwerp on November 4. Some 7,000 persons perished in this " Spanish fury" which obliterated for the time the memory of St. Bartholomew. Its immediate result was the " Pacification of Ghent," by which the fifteen catholic provinces of the south made common political cause with Holland and Zealand. In February, 1577, Don John was forced to accept the terms dictated to him by the council of state; and in May he was received as nominal governor at Brussels, while the real power lay in the hands of William of Orange. His impatient spirit chafed at this restraint: in July he seized Namur and defied the states-general of the seventeen provinces; and for a moment the struggle in the Netherlands became a national war.

It was only for a moment. " The war which is about to begin," wrote a Flemish correspondent to the English government, " will be a war for religion." [1] William of Orange, the least bigoted of men, had been in turn a catholic, a Lutheran, and a Calvinist; and he strove long and earnestly to prevent this perversion of the war, which could only result in the dismemberment of the provinces. He tried at first to keep them united under the rule of the Archduke Matthias, who played the part of Anjou to the Austrian Hapsburgs, and came in October at the secret invitation of the catholic party to reclaim for the Empire the lands which Charles V. had torn from it to bestow on Philip II. In January, 1578, he made his formal entry into Brussels with Orange as his lieutenant-general. But the intervention of a rival Hapsburg goaded Philip into promp-

[1] *Foreign Cal.*, 1578-79, p. 397.

titude ;[1] and nationality in the disunited provinces was a sorry force to pit against religious bigotry. Philip despatched to Don John's assistance 20,000 Spanish and Italian veterans under his nephew Alexander Farnese, son of the former regent, Margaret, Duchess of Parma; and on January 31 the federal troops were routed at Gemblours. The Calvinists of Ghent expelled their catholic governor, the Duke of Aerschot, burnt monks and friars, and called in John Casimir ;[2] while Anjou crossed the French frontier in July and captured Mons.

The marriage negotiations between Elizabeth and Anjou were at once revived ; for there was always a connexion between Anjou's political importance and his courtship of Elizabeth. Her earlier affection for the duke had cooled when relations improved between England and Spain and between Anjou and Henry III., and when it became evident that the French king no longer aspired to the part of catholic champion. But now that the fate of the Netherlands hung in the balance, the merest featherweight might turn the scale ; and Elizabeth hoped that her encouragement of Anjou would increase her influence in the settlement, without increasing her expenses or her risks. She had already refused the sovereignty of Holland and Zealand in 1576, and had made a merit of the refusal to Philip. But she had warned him, quite honestly for once, that if he persisted in rejecting the rebels' demands for political and religious liberty, it would become difficult for her to resist their importunities. She urged Philip to be more accommodating with regard to their religion. "What does it matter to your majesty," she asked, "if they go to the devil their own way?" She was not, however, a free agent herself, and to a large extent her policy was forced upon her by the protestant fervour of her people and her council. Burghley was reputed by the Spaniards to be averse from war ; he was undoubtedly more cautious than Leicester, who is described by Mendoza as "the manager of affairs," than Walsingham, who was Leicester's "spirit,"[3] or than the subordinate agents with whom they filled the diplomatic service. Yet Burghley, to judge from his cor-

---

[1] Cf. Venetian Cal., vii., 566, 580-84.

[2] Cf. Hatfield MSS., ii., 301.

[3] Spanish Cal., ii., 527, 543-44, 573, 586-89, 601, 646 ; Foreign Cal., 1577-78, pp. xii, 128.

respondence, favoured a more decided policy than that adopted CHAP.
by Elizabeth ; and it would appear that the queen herself was XVIII.
the only obstacle to intervention, unless Sussex, Crofts who
was in the pay of Spain, and possibly others who were not in
the habit of committing their advice to paper, supported her.
As for private Englishmen, they determined, says Guaras, when
they could not obtain the queen's sanction, to help the Dutch
without it ; and La Mothe asserts that if she had refused, her
subjects would have compelled her to aid the Huguenots.[1]

To countenance Anjou as a suitor might be represented as
support of his Flemish enterprise, though Elizabeth tried to
persuade Philip that she was really using her influence to restrain him. Certainly one of the objects of the negotiation was
to frustrate the efforts being made to marry Anjou to one of
the infantas, and another was to curb the power which the
French might obtain in the Netherlands.[2] William of Orange
apparently believed in Anjou's prospects ; and the stubbornness
with which he advocated his claims was partly due to the idea
that Anjou would bring with him English as well as French
support.[3] In October, 1578, Don John died, and Anjou, who
had been declared "Defender of the Liberties of the Netherlands" in August, despatched his agent Simier to conduct his
courtship of Elizabeth. The hint had come from the English
queen, who felt, as she had done ten years before, the need of
some such protection against the gathering storm.

Her keenest anxiety was again caused by Scotland, where
the young king James VI. assumed the reins of government in
March, 1578. Morton, whose relations with Elizabeth had
only once been slightly disturbed by the raid of Reidswire in
1575, was overthrown ; and Edinburgh became a centre of
French and Spanish intrigue. Early in 1579 Philip was considering the despatch of troops to Scotland ;[4] and later in the
year Esmé Stuart, lord of Aubigny and a cadet of the Lennox
family, arrived from France and captivated James. Stukeley
and Sanders were planning invasions of Ireland.[5] The inter-

---

[1] *Spanish Cal.*, ii., 514 ; Ferrière, p. clxxxvi ; *cf. Hatfield MSS.*, ii., 165.

[2] *Venetian Cal.*, vii., 554, 574-76 ; *Spanish Cal.*, ii., 497, 633, 654 ; *Hatfield MSS.*, ii., 180, 390.

[3] *Spanish Cal.*, iii., 300.

[4] *Ibid.*, ii., 646-47 ; *Hatfield MSS.*, ii., 101, 109, 284, 317, 372, 376, 387, 396.

[5] See below, pp. 429-30.

CHAP.
XVIII.ference of the Inquisition with English traders in Spain, which Philip himself was powerless to check, continued to embitter the relations between the two countries;[1] and Philip's temporary quiescence was due more to his practical bankruptcy than to any real friendliness. His jealousy of Don John had led him to look askance on his half-brother's ambitious scheme for marrying Mary Stuart. He promised to recall him on Elizabeth's remonstrance; and early in 1578 renewed closer intercourse by sending Bernardino Mendoza as resident ambassador in London. But Mendoza was soon occupied, like his predecessors, in cultivating friendship with Elizabeth's enemies rather than with the queen herself. Jesuits and seminary priests were flocking into England ; the English ambassador at Paris was warning Elizabeth that the French king had joined the catholic league of princes ; and Philip was considering whether it would not be necessary to upset Elizabeth's government before he could regain the Netherlands.[2]

Against all these dangers the English people were confident that they could provide by their armaments, their money, and their men. Ten years earlier Roger Edwards, one of her minor diplomatic agents, had exhorted Elizabeth to have no fear of Spain; its strength and England's weakness were delusions born of ignorance. Philip might seem rich ; but in wisdom, power, and real resources he was much inferior to his father, in whose school he had learnt that war brought more care than gain, and that England's friendship was indispensable. The wealth of the Indies would profit him little if his trade with the Netherlands were stopped by their impoverishment through his tyranny and by war in the English Channel.[3] Elizabeth, however, put more trust in her diplomacy ; and the antagonism between the two methods provoked one of the sharpest conflicts of the reign between the queen and her people.

In February, 1579, according to Mendoza, she told her council that although Anjou might come to London "she would give them her word she would not marry him. Of that they might be sure."[4] But she pursued the negotiation with a zest which gave her subjects serious alarm. The council was

---

[1] *Spanish Cal.*, ii., 499, 519, 535-38, 541.
[2] *Ibid.*, ii., 556, 558, 624-25, 666 ; *Foreign Cal.*, 1579-80, p. 160.
[3] Stählin, *Walsingham*, i., 219.   [4] *Spanish Cal.*, ii., 644.

burdened with endless deliberations on the terms, and Burghley CHAP. indited elaborate arguments on both sides. In August Anjou XVIII. paid a visit to the queen, reaching Greenwich on the 17th and embarking for Boulogne twelve days later. In October a crisis in the courtship came; the council had never made so many objections; the queen had never been so insistent. "Though she thought it not meet to declare to them whether she would marry Monsieur or no, yet she looked from their hands that they should with one accord have made special suit to her for the same." [1] She did not, in fact, intend to marry; but she resented the arguments against the marriage as implications that she was not competent to secure its advantages and provide against its risks. She was quite prepared to sacrifice whatever gratification matrimony might afford her on the altar of her country's interests; but she wanted all the credit for the immolation. Compulsory self-denial, imposed upon her by her subjects, was intolerable, and she shed copious tears over the pressure brought to bear upon her by her council and over the distrust felt of her by the nation. "The people in general," writes Mendoza, "seem to threaten revolution about it;" councillors whispered that parliament would have something to say in the matter; and Wyatt's rebellion was not forgotten. Even a preacher at court denounced the marriage, and Elizabeth stalked out in the middle of the sermon.[2]

She sometimes expressed her irritation in less innocent ways. In September, a few weeks after Anjou's visit, John Stubbs, a puritan gentleman of Norfolk, published his *Discovery of a Gaping Gulf, wherein England is like to be swallowed up by another French marriage, if the Lord forbid not the banns by letting her see the sin and punishment thereof.*[3] A fierce proclamation issued against the book only, says Mendoza, fanned the flame of public indignation; and Stubbs had his right hand cut off, waving the bloody stump and crying "Long live the Queen". Even this heroic exhibition of loyalty did not save him from eighteen months' imprisonment in the Tower; for Elizabeth was more impressed by the failure of his cheer to evoke an echo from the crowd, and by legal criticism of his condemnation on a doubtful statute of Philip and Mary.

[1] *Hatfield MSS.*, ii., 273.   [2] *Spanish Cal.*, ii., 658-59, 693.
[3] *Letters of Eminent Literary Men* (Camden Soc.), pp. 40-44.

Another book followed on the same lines in October, and memorials poured in to the queen against the marriage. On the 7th the council, with the exception of Burghley, who was cautious, and of Sussex who really wanted the marriage—more, it was thought, to upset Leicester than with any other object— informed Elizabeth that in their opinion she ought not to marry Anjou or any other Frenchman ; but, understanding her state of mind, they offered at the same time to do their best to carry out the negotiation. A month later Elizabeth reaffirmed her determination to keep her word, which, she said, she had never broken yet. Even then, Mendoza was puzzled whether her decision was artifice or "a divine provision to reduce this country to the catholic religion and to punish it by means of an intestine war ".[1]

The artifice is less doubtful than the providential inspiration. Although the pretence was maintained for further diplomatic purposes, the council was soon engaged in devising means to smooth over the breach of promise, and to convert once more a dangerous courtship into a useful alliance. In January, 1580, Burghley's eldest son was dreading Anjou's resentment for " having been brought to be the author of troubles in his own country, drawn by her majesty's means from his late enterprise in the Low Countries, hindered by her of his contemplated marriage with the king of Spain's daughter," and then after all rejected by Elizabeth.[2] This remonstrance, addressed to the queen, was premature ; for two years longer she continued to turn the wooing to severely practical purposes ; and then the courtship cooled with no violent precipitation. In March, 1580, the Archbishop of York wrote that the negotiation, which " had been long asleep and seemed as dead, is now revived again ".[3] The seventh war of religion had broken out in France ; Anjou was gently warned that he must do something for the Huguenots, if he wished to be accepted as a suitor ; and his activity on their behalf was stimulated by Elizabeth's secret reception of Condé as a rival intermediary.[4] She seems to have extorted from Henry III. some undertak-

---

[1] *Spanish Cal.*, ii., 692, 702-4 ; Harleian MS. 180 ; Camden, ii., 378-79.

[2] *Hatfield MSS.*, ii., 308.   In the preface (p. xxxiii) the editor attributes this memorial to Burghley himself.

[3] Lodge, *Illustrations*, ii., 162, 170.

[4] *Hatfield MSS.*, ii., 281-82, 327, 329-30, 335 ; *Foreign Cal.*, 1579-80, pp. 317, 333.

ing to consult her wishes, while she in return restrained the German Calvinists from joining in the fray. Possibly the brevity of the war was partly due to her persuasions; and Guise lamented in "sour language" that Anjou's second visit to England, in 1581, had obstructed the execution of his designs in favour of Mary, Queen of Scots.

The influence of the courtship on Elizabeth's policy in the Netherlands is more obscure. Matthias and Casimir soon withdrew from the struggle, leaving a triangular duel between the protestants, the catholic malcontents, and Don John's successor, Parma. Religious bigotry on both sides speedily destroyed the political sympathy between the protestants and catholics; and in 1579 the protestant provinces organised themselves into the Union of Utrecht, and the catholic provinces into that of Arras. The latter made their peace with Parma and submitted to Philip II., receiving some political concessions in return for their undertaking to tolerate only the catholic religion. The protestant provinces abjured Philip's sovereignty in 1581, and five of them offered it to Anjou; Holland and Zealand, however, would not have Anjou, and bestowed their countship on William of Orange. Anjou accepted the offer at the treaty of Plessis-les-Tours in September, 1580, and ratified his acceptance at Bordeaux in the following January. Elizabeth thereupon wrote him a grave rebuke: "Pardon me if I tell you that for my part I see in me no right to take that which belongs to another; still less was there any reason to accept a gift from those who have no title to make it. . . . O, my God, what torment that one whom I honour above all others should have embarked on so intricate a sea of troubles, wherein I see no shadow of glory! For when all is over, the onlookers will say 'God ever helps the right'." "Few princes," observed Leicester, "have so good a conscience." She had always counselled him, she reminded Anjou, to avoid the snare; although, had she consulted her own interests, she would have sought to interpose him as a buckler between her enemies and herself. As for the marriage, she wrote, the Jesuit invasion had made it more difficult than ever, and the repugnance of parliament was insuperable.[1]

---

[1] *Hatfield MSS.*, ii., 480-81; Lodge, *Illustrations*, ii., 208; *Foreign Cal.*, 1581-82, pp. 142-43, 257.

CHAP.
XVIII.

The French alliance seemed, however, indispensable ; and in August, 1581, Walsingham was sent to Paris to conclude it.[1] Henry III., who was most anxious to get rid of Anjou, insisted on the marriage as the price of an alliance ; while both sovereigns tried to escape financial liability for the duke's adventures in the Netherlands. He once more attempted to force Elizabeth's hand by a visit to England in November, 1581. She was " an artist to the finger-tips," [2] but it is not certain that she worked upon her own design : " let me know," she wrote to Burghley in a confidential note giving the news of Anjou's landing, " what you wish me to do ".[3] She certainly embroidered Burghley's policy in colours that were somewhat loud ; she kissed the duke in the presence of her courtiers, and exchanged with him a ring. Leicester and his friends were horrified ; but she told them not to be alarmed, for the conditions upon which she had plighted her troth would never be fulfilled. Her promise, she explained, was conditional upon her ability to overcome her repugnance to the matrimonial state ; Henry III. must also break with Philip, abandon Scotland, maintain the war in the Netherlands at his own expense, and surrender Calais and Havre to England as guarantees that he would keep his word. Her real object had been to push Henry III. into war with Spain, and when he refused, to throw on him the onus of the breach with Anjou.[4]

Before the year was out, Elizabeth declared that she would sooner be decently rid of the duke than win another crown ; while Anjou was fuming over his ridiculous position. It was Elizabeth's money he really wanted ; and the breach of promise was compromised by a bond for £60,000, which was paid by gradual instalments. On February 1, 1582, after many " feigned tears and tender regrets," the duke departed with Leicester, a large English following, and a recommendation from the queen to the Dutch that they would receive him as her other self. Leicester returned before long, remarking that

[1] Most of his letters are printed *in extenso* in Digges' *Compleat Ambassador*, 1655, pp. 352-441 ; others are summarised in the *Foreign Cal.*, 1581-82 ; while many of Elizabeth's more intimate letters are calendared in *Hatfield MSS.*, vol. ii.

[2] F. W. Maitland in *Cambridge Mod. Hist.*, ii., 565.

[3] *Foreign Cal.*, 1581-82, p. 389.

[4] *Spanish Cal.*, iii., 212, 217, 226, 233, 240, 243, 252, 268, 409 ; *Venetian Cal.*, viii., 24-27.

he had left Anjou stranded like an old hulk on the sandbanks CHAP.
of the Netherlands;[1] and Elizabeth was soon apologising to XVIII.
Orange for having shot so much rubbish on his land. She
had refused to be "wedded to a war," because the discord of
marriage-bells and bugles grated on her ear;[2] but Anjou
might blow his martial trumpet unaccompanied by wedding
chimes. William of Orange thought him of some use as a
decoy for catholic malcontents; and Elizabeth's anxiety about
the divine right of kings and scruples about using Anjou as a
buckler disappeared. She had gauged to her own satisfaction
his chances of achieving a French conquest of the Netherlands,
and gave him just enough support to make him a thorn in
Philip's side. After chafing for a year under the restraint of
William and the States, he tried to arrest the prince and seize
the principal towns. On January 17, 1583, a "French fury"
at Antwerp succeeded the "Spanish fury" of 1576; and French
dominion over the Dutch provinces followed the Spanish into
the realm of visionary fabrics. Elizabeth did not even sigh as
a lover, and she surely rejoiced as a queen. Secretly she had
been working against Anjou through his own agent Simier;
she had never ceased her intrigues with John Casimir and the
Calvinists; and there were rumours that Parma's recapture of
Oudenarde and other successes in 1582 had not been achieved
without her connivance and support.[3] No sooner had Anjou
been received as Duke of Brabant than he was repudiated by
Elizabeth; and she frankly explained her reasons. He was
shrewd enough, she told him, to guess what sort of a turn she
would have done her successors, if peradventure Flanders had
changed its master and passed into French hands. She had
devoted her wiles to the purpose for which most English
battles in Europe were fought from Crecy to Waterloo.

There was yet another purpose to which her courtship with
Anjou was put. In 1579 Sir Henry Cobham, the ambassador
in France, expressed the hope that Philip would find a second

[1] *Spanish Cal.*, iii., 251-52, 280, 300, 310-12, 390, 397, 430; *Foreign Cal.*,
1581-82, p. 409; *Hatfield MSS.*, ii., 520; Lodge, ii., 203-4.
[2] *Foreign Cal.*, 1581-82, pp. 258, 260, 273-74; *Hatfield MSS.*, ii., 400: "et
tellement le mariage et trompette de bataille commenceront en ung mesme temps,
qui mesemble bien estrange ".
[3] *Foreign Cal.*, 1582, pp. viii, 245; *Spanish Cal.*, iii., 354-55, 382, 398; *Venetian Cal.*, viii., 31-34; *Hatfield MSS.*, ii., 511, 517-18.

Netherlands in Portugal;[1] and from time to time diplomatists opined that Portuguese affairs lay at the root of the negotiation.[2] King Sebastian, who had been killed at Alcazar in 1578, was succeeded by his great uncle, a childless cardinal of seventy-seven.[3] He died on January 31, 1580, leaving a host of doubtful claimants to the throne, including Catherine de Médicis, Alexander of Parma, and the Duchess of Braganza. The pope pretended that, as the last king was a cardinal, the kingdom escheated to the holy see; while Philip II. claimed it through his mother the daughter of King Emmanuel. Don Antonio, a natural son of Emmanuel's second son Luiz, was the most popular candidate, and was elected king; but Philip II. had determined to grasp the throne of Portugal and unite under one sceptre the two great colonial empires of the world. Alva defeated Antonio in two battles and rapidly overran the country, and Philip journeyed to Portugal to receive the oath of allegiance from its cortes on April 1, 1581. By one of the decisive events in history Spain had nearly doubled its resources; Brazil, Africa, and the East Indies were added to Spanish America, and Philip bestrode the world like a colossus. The harbours and fleets of Portugal lay at his disposal; at last he might claim command of the sea; and his revenues probably exceeded those of all other European sovereigns put together. Such was the imposing aspect; actually, the chief result was to involve Portugal in war with England and the Dutch, and to enable those powers to carve out of Portuguese possessions their empires in the east.

Don Antonio fled in July to France and thence to England; and many were the schemes proposed to unite England and France in his support. Anjou acquired a fresh importance; and France was further alienated from Philip. Elizabeth wanted a war "underhand" as she expressed it;[4] and Catherine would go thus far. She was in fact readier to intervene in Portugal than in the Netherlands, because help to the Portuguese involved no suspicion of heresy. On the other hand, a French conquest of Portugal was out of the question;

---

[1] *Foreign Cal.*, 1579-80, p. 188.
[2] *Spanish Cal.*, ii., 636, 658, 663, 669, 672; *Hatfield MSS.*, ii., 338, 344.
[3] *Ibid.*, ii., 199, 206; Lodge, ii., 164; *Foreign Cal.*, 1579-80, pp. 45, 57.
[4] *Ibid.*, 1581-82, pp. 212, 258; *cf. Hatfield MSS.*, ii., 408-10, 422-23.

Catherine would not move without the marriage; and both CHAP.
queens feared an open breach with their twice formidable foe.   XVIII.
Short of this, everything was done to hamper Philip. "We
think it good," wrote Elizabeth on July 22, 1581, "for the
king of Spain to be impeached both in Portugal and in his
Islands, and also in the Low Countries, whereto we shall be
ready to give such indirect assistance as shall not at once be a
cause of war."[1] Anjou went to the Netherlands, ostensibly
on his own responsibility; but English volunteers increased
in numbers. Catherine's kinsman, Filippo Strozzi, equipped a
fleet with Huguenot assistance to succour Don Antonio in his
last stronghold, the Azores; and when Drake sailed back from
his voyage round the world, Elizabeth gave a national sanction to his private war with Spain. She went down to Deptford
on April 4, 1581, and knighted on board the *Golden Hind* the
" master thief of the unknown world "; and, while she sequestered
his plunder, she ordered his ship to be laid up as a memorial
of his exploits.[2] She handed the sword to Marchaumont to give
Drake the accolade; and Marchaumont was the matrimonial
agent of Anjou. Slowly Philip prepared to accept the gage
of war. Strozzi's expedition, in which Drake refused Elizabeth's permission to serve, was routed in the Azores on
August 1, 1582;[3] a second attempt by Don Antonio in the
following year fared no better; and the victor, Santa Cruz,
wrote begging Philip for leave to turn his conquering armada
against the English shores.

[1] *Foreign Cal.*, 1581-82, p. 279.
[2] Corbett, i., 316; *Spanish Cal.*, iii., 95, 101.
[3] *Foreign Cal.*, 1581-82, pp. 499, 530; 1582, pp. 213-15; *Venetian Cal.*,
viii., 41-42, 60-64.

CHAPTER XIX.

CHURCH AND STATE.

THE familiar phrase "church and state" bears unconscious witness to the partial failure of the national reformation. It is a relic of that medieval dualism which nationalist fervour sought in the sixteenth century to fuse into organic unity. Instead of church and state, often divided in mind, there was to be one body, politic and ecclesiastic, which might be called indifferently a state-church or a church-state. The approximation to this idea, which was achieved during Elizabeth's reign, makes it impossible to speak with strict accuracy of the state controlling the church, or the church controlling the state, unless we revert to the medieval definition of the church and exclude from it every layman. Interpreted in that sense, the church was controlled absolutely by the state; not only had its wealth been taken from it, but it had been reduced to numerical insignificance. Firstly the dissolution of the monasteries, but secondly and more effectively the abolition of all orders under that of deacon had turned many thousands of ecclesiastics into laymen. As the exclusive representative of an order, convocation had lost its independence; whatever the house of commons may have been, the upper house of convocation was entirely, and the lower house largely, an assembly of royal nominees. The church owes much to Parker's moderation; but it was because Elizabeth wanted a man of Parker's moderation that she placed him in the seat of St. Augustine. So far as the law went, she might have given the chair to Knox or Bonner.

This medieval conception of the church was, however, passing away, and an Anglican layman is in common parlance called a churchman. In Elizabeth's reign the predominance of crown and parliament over convocation was facilitated by the facts that the sovereign was a semi-ecclesiastical person, and members of parliament belonged to the church as much as to

the state. The amalgamation of church and state had been CHAP.
brought about less by the act of supremacy than by the ad- XIX.
mission of the laity to the churchman's privileges and of the
clergy to the layman's. The destructive antagonism between
church and state, which had grown until Hildebrand represented
the church as the only sphere and work of God, and the state
as the sphere and work of the devil, was disarmed by the
Tudor monarchy, relying on the spirit of national unity. But
the process of assimilation has been regarded too much from
one point of view, as the secularisation of the church ; this had its
counterpart in the promotion of the state to a place in the divine
order, and in its devotion to duties once regarded as purely
ecclesiastical. The sovereign became supreme governor of the
church, and was endowed with right divine ; the state assumed
the care of the poor and an interest in education, sometimes even
in learning and letters ; civilians took the place of canonists in
the administration of canon law ; justices of the peace sat as as-
sessors with bishops to try offenders against the acts of uniformity, controlled with the priest the government of the parish,
and brought the union of church and state home to the humble
as the act of supremacy brought it home to the mighty.[1]

There was both loss and gain in a union which necessarily
partook of the nature of a compromise. Quadra glanced at the
loss when he said that religion in England had become merely
a matter of politics ; but it was some compensation that politics
became largely a matter of religion. The identification was not
so complete as in Geneva, or even in the Lowlands of Scotland,
which were more homogeneous than England. Here divergence
of development and sympathy obstructed the unity of religion,
which is essential to the complete identification of church and
state ; and Elizabeth had to construct out of diverse materials
a system which, while wonderfully lasting and serviceable,
never corresponded fully with the ideal design. Her work is
sometimes described in confusing terms, which seem to imply
that she and her father established, started, or even founded the
Church of England. But in truth the Tudors founded neither
catholicism nor protestantism ; and they only modified the
outward fabric of ecclesiastical organisation by substituting
the monarchy for the papacy. Nevertheless, they exerted a

[1] *Cf.* S. L. Ware, *The Elizabethan Parish*, Baltimore, 1908.

23 *

predominant influence in determining how much catholicism and how much protestantism should be embodied in the Anglican church ; or, to express the same fact in other terms, in deciding what was, and what was not, true catholicism ; and their peculiar merit in this respect consists in the skill with which they divined a public opinion half formed and unexpressed. It will, however, always be a matter of controversy whether the nation accepted Elizabeth's settlement because it embodied truth or because the government made it.

Upon Elizabeth also fell the duty of dealing with the materials too stubborn to be worked into the national edifice. Of these there was a varied assortment. In a surprising essay on the religious condition of England by one Carleton, which Thomas Cecil addressed to his father in 1572,[1] the writer divided Englishmen into three categories, papists, atheists, and protestants ; and of these, Carleton maintained that either of the first two denominations was more numerous than the third. It is not clear what he meant by any of these terms ; the proportional estimate would be less paradoxical if he had called the classes catholic, heterodox, and puritan ; and the classification more exhaustive, if he had found a category for Cecil's father and his queen. By ignoring whole-hearted partisans of Elizabeth's religious settlement, he indicates the problem of the government. Ecclesiastical bones had been broken in Edward VI.'s and Mary's reigns : they had been set again in 1559 ; but the fractures required skilful treatment and strong supports until the bones could grow together and the church could gain consistency.

Hence, while the external framework of uniformity was maintained, the government was anxious to cause as little friction as possible by inquisitorial methods. No windows, Elizabeth claimed, were made into men's souls ; they might think what they liked, provided that no expression incompatible with public order was given to their opinions. The powers of coercion, entrusted to the crown by parliament in 1559 and 1563, were tempered in the execution ; the oaths were not rigidly enforced ; and the fines for recusancy were not extorted. The mere rumour that they would be was accounted a principal

[1] *Domestic Calendar*, Addenda, 1566-79, p. 439.

cause of the rebellion of 1569.[1] The Marian bishops were, indeed, kept in a confinement which varied with their attitude to the government. Most of them were placed as guests in the homes of their successors; they were not required to attend Anglican services; and some enjoyed facilities for hearing mass. Heath lived unmolested in his own house at Chobham, where he was occasionally visited by Elizabeth.

The first general attempt to enforce uniformity was made at the expense of protestant nonconformists and not at that of catholic recusants, partly because protestant dissent from the established order was expressed in an active and visible form. The contention of protestant extremists was that the clerical profession involved no greater differentiation from the lay condition than the profession of medicine or other vocations, and therefore that there should be no distinctively clerical vestments. They held in especial horror the "Aaronic" garb and ornaments, which implied a sacrificial priesthood armed with superhuman powers. The feeling aroused for or against the cope, the alb, and the surplice was not more irrational than that excited by a royal crown or a national flag. Symbols appeal more directly to the mass of men than the abstractions for which they stand; and they are more effective than arguments with men who are more accustomed to using their sight than their reason. To them a king hardly seems a king unless he is depicted with a crown. A priest without his vestments was to the catholic no priest at all; with them, he was to the protestant a minister of idolatry; and round them raged a fierce religious controversy so soon as Elizabeth felt strong enough to notice the licence that had hitherto prevailed.

Ever since her accession the tide of popular feeling had set in a puritan direction;[2] " such be the humours of the commons house," remarked Cecil of the parliament of 1563, " as they think nothing sharp enough against the papists ".[3] This temper was reflected in the puritan petition which the lower house of convocation rejected by the narrowest possible majority; and the royal despotism, which has been held responsible for the re-

---

[1] *Cf. Spanish Cal.*, ii., 4-5. The bishops in their investigation of 1564 generally urged that the oath of supremacy should be tendered, but in vain, *Hatfield MSS.*, i., 306-10.

[2] *Cf. Spanish Cal* , ii., 49.   [3] Frere, p. 100.

jection of Rome, had quite as much to do with the repudiation
of Geneva. The old clerical garb was rapidly disappearing, and
the bishops' own "Interpretations" and "Further Considerations," issued in 1560, tolerated a lower vestiarian standard
than was prescribed by the rubric of 1559.[1] The puritans
probably regarded their defeat in convocation as a moral
victory, and were presuming upon it, when in 1564 Elizabeth,
chastened perhaps by her own and the Huguenot failure in the
first war of religion, resolved to stop the descent from her level
of uniformity. Humphrey, the president of Magdalen College,
Oxford, and Sampson, the dean of Christ Church, were required
to account for their refusal to wear the surplice. They contended, first, that scriptural warrant was necessary for all
matters of ecclesiastical importance, and, secondly, that the
surplice was important because of its doctrinal implications.
The gist of their view was the little weight they attached to
the authority of the church compared with the Scriptures.

Here they touched Elizabeth to the quick ; it was presumption to belittle the authority of a church of which she
was supreme governor ; and she would not have her jurisdiction hedged about by their interpretations of the Bible. On
January 25, 1565, she ordered an episcopal inquiry into the
prevailing laxity of vestiarian, eucharistic, and ceremonial
practice. The extent of the variety disclosed made her hesitate,
and the "Advertisements" which Parker issued in March,
1566, appeared without specific royal sanction.[2] They required, as a compromise, only the wearing of the surplice in
church, and of the ordinary academic gown and square cap and
a tippet as the outdoor apparel of the clergy. Thirty-seven
London incumbents, including Coverdale and Crowley, refused
compliance. Some of them were deprived ; and the ensuing
Holy Week and Eastertide in London were marked by much
religious turbulence and discontent. The nonconformists appealed to Zürich and Geneva, and began a pamphlet warfare,
in which the authority of the queen to enforce the wearing of
the vestments was denied. The authorities retaliated by re-

[1] W. M. Kennedy, *The "Interpretations" of the Bishops*, 1908 (Alcuin Club
Tracts, viii.) ; Frere, pp. 59-60.

[2] Frere, p. 118. Grindal, however, refers to them on May 21 as having "the
Queen's authority," *Domestic Cal.*, 1547-80, p. 272.

voking their licences to preach, and by ordering the leaders into prison.

This attempt to silence the dissentients provoked a widening of the breach. Hitherto an elastic interpretation of the act of uniformity had permitted them to carry on their propaganda publicly. Now they were driven to secret conventicles; and at Plumbers' Hall in 1567 they began the clandestine use of the Genevan Order instead of the Book of Common Prayer. To adopt or attend a different service from that prescribed by parliament was a far more serious infraction of the act of uniformity than mere abstention from public worship; and a score of the congregation, surprised at Plumbers' Hall, were thrown into prison. Although they were released within a year, the scope of the divergence widened. The vestments were merely the most obvious outward sign of the antagonism. Parker's *Advertisements* had required subscription to articles concerning rites, which were as distasteful to the puritans as the vestments; and the controversy gradually spread from vestments to rites, and from rites to doctrine and church government. At first, the low churchmen merely attacked certain views and aspects of episcopacy; but when bishops enforced the *Advertisements*, their victims began to impugn episcopacy itself; and eventually, when the crown supported the episcopate, they denied the royal supremacy over the church, and joined the political movement against the monarchy. This accounts for the sequence in the development of English presbyterianism; but the ultimate cause lies deeper. There was an intimate connexion between catholic dogma and catholic organisation; and, apart from the question whether episcopacy was or was not a matter of faith, an attack upon catholic dogma was bound sooner or later to lead to an attack on catholic forms of ecclesiastical government.

Episcopacy being, in the view adopted by the puritans, no essential part of the church, its repudiation involved in their minds no idea of separation from the church. They considered themselves quite as much entitled to remain churchmen in order to make the church presbyterian, as they were to remain Englishmen in order to make the monarchy constitutional. Their loyalty to the church was equal to their loyalty to the state, unless episcopacy was more essential to

CHAP.
XIX.

the church than personal monarchy to the state; and their hostility to the episcopate was widely shared for various reasons. There was an idea that, having emancipated themselves from medieval obligations, such as celibacy, the bishops were clinging to their medieval wealth and jurisdiction; and assuredly, even after the "great spoliation," poverty was not an episcopal hardship. It is true that considerable inconvenience was caused by the guile of the Marian bishops; foreseeing deprivation and hoping for restoration, they had made collusive leases and grants of episcopal lands to sympathisers who were to hold them in trust during the time of troubles.[1] But the Elizabethan bishops, who suffered most from their predecessors, could soon afford to despoil their sees themselves. Canterbury, although reduced to two-thirds of its value at Cranmer's election, was still in 1576 worth £2,816 17s. 9d. a year—at least £20,000 in modern currency; and the "tenth" which it was supposed to pay was assessed at half its proper amount.[2] Ely, at that time the richest bishopric in England, was said to be worth £3,000 a year. The bishops received far more than the lay ministers of the crown; and, with the doubtful exception of the earls, they were the wealthiest class of men in the kingdom.

Their riches excited the cupidity of the parsimonious queen and her greedy courtiers. Complaints against Bishop Coxe of Ely were, wrote his neighbour Lord North, "continually ringing in his ears"; and he thought the bishop would not wish the queen and council to learn "how extremely covetous" he was, "how great a grazier, how marvellous a dairyman, how rich a farmer, how great an owner. It will not like you that the world know of your decayed houses, of the lead and brick that you sell from them, of the leases that you pull violently from many, of

[1] *Cf.* Birt, *Elizabethan Settlement*, pp. 373-74; Frere, p. 63.
[2] *Hatfield MSS.*, ii., 259. Pilkington, Bishop of Durham, complains greatly of his poverty; but, says Fuller (*Church History*, 1656, bk v., p. 253), "I have heard that Queen Elizabeth, being informed that [he] had given £10,000 in marriage with his daughter, and being offended that a prelate's daughter should equal a princess in portion [she herself and Mary had each received £10,000 under Henry VIII.'s will], took away £1,000 a year from that bishopric, and assigned it for the better maintenance of the garrison of Berwick". Elsewhere (bk ix., p. 109) Fuller speaks of two daughters with £4,000 apiece. Father Birt (p. 374 n.) assigns the former version to "a modern writer". The confiscation of the £1,000 is at any rate correct, *Domestic Cal.*, 1547-80, p. 273.

the copyholds that you lawlessly enter into, of the free land which you wrongfully possess, of the tolls and imposts which you raise, of God's good ministers which you causelessly displace." [1] Coxe had refused two small requests preferred by Elizabeth; and North was writing to warn him against his ambition " to be a Latimer " in defence of his worldly goods, and against offending the queen, " our God in Earth ". His diatribe must therefore be discounted; but the bishop was undoubtedly grasping of wealth as well as of authority. In 1564 he had suggested that he and some select gentlemen of his diocese should be entrusted with a jurisdiction as extensive as that of the high commission; and he sympathised with the views expressed by a preacher at St. Paul's, who said, " I would five or six of the council were Aarons; I would the Lord Keeper were a bishop (not that I think justice ill ministered, but I would have the clergy in honour); I would a bishop were Master of the Rolls; I would all the six clerks in chancery were priests; this would make the order in estimation. In times past a good justice of peace durst not offend a parish or hedge priest; now every brave man in Kent Street will control bishops." [2]

Episcopal jurisdiction was almost as sore a point with the commons as papal jurisdiction had been with the monarchy. In questions of life and death the clerical courts could no longer rely on the secular arm since the repeal of Mary's acts in 1559 and the transference, in 1563, of the control of excommunicates to the court of queen's bench; [3] it was even contended that any attempt to try offences against the act of uniformity elsewhere than in the temporal courts was a breach of *praemunire*. [4] But the ecclesiastical courts retained wide powers of excommunication and jurisdiction over marriage and probate, and bishops could issue licences and dispensations. The courts were admittedly full of abuses, due largely to the lawyers who lived on the fees paid therein; and the efforts of well-meaning prelates to reform them were foiled by their own officials, and those of the parliament of 1571 by the jealousy of the queen.

Elizabeth's previous experience in the questions of her marriage and the succession had cooled her affection for her

---

[1] *Hatfield MSS.*, ii., 120-22.   [2] *Ibid.*, i., 308, ii., 63.
[3] 5 Eliz., c. 23.   [4] *Hatfield MSS.*, iii., 35-36.

faithful commons; she told La Mothe that she had held three parliaments, that they were enough for any reign, and she would have no more.[1] The need of supplies was, however, inexorable, and she also wanted further protection from papal bulls.   Parliament was accordingly summoned to meet on April 2, 1571.   Nine new constituencies returned representatives, who were admitted to the house after a committee had examined their claims; there was an interesting debate on a bill to relax the old rule requiring the election of resident members, which was rejected; and it was proposed in vain that a fine of £40 should be inflicted on every borough that elected a nobleman's nominee.   A precedent was set by the punishment of Westbury for allowing itself to be bribed by a burgess, and an abortive committee inquired into the alleged bribery of members themselves.   The two universities were incorporated; some alteration was made in the poor laws; usury was reprehended as being "to the destruction of young gentlemen," but a bill to establish "seven banks or stocks of money" passed; and the queen through the mouth of Lord-Keeper Bacon admonished the commons at the beginning of the session to "meddle with no matters of state but such as should be propounded unto them," and at the end rebuked them for "meddling with matters neither pertaining to them, nor within the capacity of their understanding".[2]

These were matters of the church rather than of state. The commons wanted to complete the reformation, to abolish pluralities, non-residence, licences, dispensations, and the admission of boys and papists to spiritual promotions, and to enact Cranmer's *Reformatio Legum Ecclesiasticarum* "without the bishops, who perhaps would be slow".   Strickland even introduced a bill for "the reformation of the Book of Common Prayer," and Norton maintained that the "principal liberty" of the church had been "a liberty to sin".   Norton escaped retribution; but Strickland was haled before the council to the indignation of the house, which was hardly deterred from an attack on the crown by the precedents cited for similar interference with its freedom of speech.   Religion was royal prerogative; and though Peter Wentworth "noted" Sir Humphrey

[1] La Mothe, ii., 355.
[2] D'Ewes, pp. 141-42, 151 ff.; *Commons' Journals*, i., 83 ff.

Gilbert's "disposition to flatter and fawn on the Prince," the CHAP.
house as a whole indicated its respect for the principle *rege* XIX.
non consulto.[1] While the penal laws against recusants were
strengthened, abuses of ecclesiastical jurisdiction were left unchecked. Elizabeth quashed a bill embodying a parliamentary
version of the Thirty-nine articles, saying that she liked them
well enough, but meant to have them executed in virtue of the
royal supremacy and not of parliamentary statute. "Surely,"
said Parker to Peter Wentworth, "you will refer yourselves
wholly to us therein." "No, by the faith I bear to God,"
retorted Wentworth, "we will pass nothing before we understand what it is ; for that were but to make you popes. Make
you popes who list, for we will make you none."[2]

An act, aimed against concealed papists, was nevertheless
passed enforcing subscription to the articles ; but the fact that
convocation modified the articles without reference to the parliamentary statute[3] seems to justify the puritan contention
that in enforcing subscription—to these modifications at any
rate—the clerical courts were acting illegally. A similar defect attached to the canon law. The *Reformatio,*[4] although
published by Foxe with Parker's sanction, received neither
parliamentary, royal, nor synodical authorisation ; and the
canons which convocation substituted for it failed to obtain
the queen's consent. But, although not legally binding, they
were enforced by the bishops with Elizabeth's connivance.
She cast her mantle over the church, and changed the offensive
alliance of crown and parliament, forged by Henry VIII.
against the church, into a league for mutual defence between
crown and church against parliament, which dominated English politics for a century and more. The royal supremacy
became a boon instead of a stumbling-block to the church ;
and Elizabeth's services have reaped a posthumous reward in
the contrast drawn by ecclesiastical historians between her
father's character and hers.

The queen called another parliament on May 8, 1572,
to relieve her of the responsibility of dealing with the Duke of
Norfolk. Bacon, in his opening speech, placed religion first
among the causes of its summons ; but when the commons

[1] D'Ewes, pp. 157, 160-80. [2] *Ibid.*, pp. 240-41.
[3] See Frere, p. 163. [4] See above, p. 71.

CHAP.
XIX.
proceeded to discuss "a bill for rites and ceremonies" to super-
sede the Book of Common Prayer, Elizabeth sent down a
message that "no bills concerning religion should thenceforth
be preferred or received into the house, unless the same had
first been considered and liked by the clergy".[1] The house
was too busy clamouring for the execution of Norfolk and
Mary to resent this prohibition; but, before the session ended
on June 30, Wilcox and Field published their *Admonition to
Parliament.*[2] The authors, two puritan clergymen, were sent
to Newgate; but their tract had a circulation which all the
government's efforts failed to suppress. It adjured parliament
to abolish advowsons, impropriations, the court of faculties,
private communions and baptisms, the lordship, pomp, and
idleness of bishops, and their exclusive claim to the power of
ordination; to restore "that old and true election which was
accustomed to be made by the congregation"; to revivify
excommunication; to "join assistance of elders"; to substitute
sitting for kneeling at the reception of the sacrament; and to
do nothing without the express warrant of the Word of God.
"Such is the passion engendered," wrote Guaras, "that, one of
these days, they will come to blows, which it is to be hoped
that God will permit, and that one set of heretics may confound
the other, and all of them go to perdition together."[3] For the
time, the warfare was only literary. Cartwright, who had
made a name as the puritan protagonist at Cambridge, took
up the cudgels for Field and Wilcox, while Whitgift, who had
led the opposition to Cartwright at the university, was inspired
by the bishops to undertake their defence.

Another future archbishop, Matthew Hutton, dissected
the movement more scientifically for Burghley's edification.[4]
"At the beginning," he wrote, "it was but a cap, a surplice,
and a tippet; now it is grown to bishops, archbishops, and
cathedral churches, to the overthrow of established order,
and to the queen's authority in causes ecclesiastical. These
reformers would take the supreme authority in ecclesiastical
matters from the prince, and give it unto themselves with the
grave seigniory in every parish. They would have every cause

[1] D'Ewes, p. 213.   [2] *Spanish Cal.*, ii., 409-10; Brook, *Puritans*, i., 319.
[3] *Spanish Cal.*, ii., 446.
[4] *Hatfield MSS.*, ii., 60; his letter is printed *in extenso* in Murdin, pp. 261-66.

debated in the congregation. If they cannot end it, by the CHAP.
ministers and seigniories of adjoining parishes ; if they cannot XIX.
determine it, by a national council ; if it cannot be ended there,
then to be referred to a general council of all the churches reformed. These men would not only have an equality of all
ministers, but also would deprive the queen of her authority
and give it to the people ; that every parish should choose its
own minister ; which if put in practice, divers parishes would
have none but a papist. . . . Calvin was a worthy and learned
man, and hath profited the church as much as ever did any
since the apostles' time ; but he thought not so well of a
kingdom as of a popular state, and so he liked best that ecclesiastical polity which agreeth better to a popular state than to a
kingdom."

The aphorisms of James I. were already in the making ; [1]
and Parker died on May 17, 1575, lamenting that "the governance" of the Puritans would "in conclusion undo the queen
and all others that depended upon her". He left a scene of
disorder, with which his successor Grindal was not the man to
deal : " there is such confusion here about their sects," writes
Guaras on the 29th, "that all last week they were arresting
people". Grindal sympathised with the victims and their
"prophesyings," which he refused to repress at Elizabeth's
dictation. He was more anxious to redress the abuses which,
as the lord keeper admitted, made men "utterly condemn all
ecclesiastical government" ; [2] for the failure of authority to
provide remedies was driving the puritans to take matters into
their own hands, and to devise principles and methods of
church polity, which were bound to conflict with the monarchical and episcopal system. In 1572 Field took part in organis-
ing at Wandsworth the earliest English presbytery ; and in 1574
Travers published his *Book of Discipline*. The presbytery was
an attempt to introduce into the church the principle of popular representation, in order to check episcopal despotism, as
parliament checked the arbitrary will of sovereigns ; while
Travers' book was a draft scheme of ecclesiastical self-government to be adopted by voluntary subscription in place of that
imposed by the royal supremacy. A further effort was made

[1] See below, vol. vii., p. 11.
[2] *Spanish Cal.*, ii., 492 ; *Hatfield MSS.*, ii., 196.

in the session of 1576 to obtain legislative sanction for this transference of ecclesiastical authority from the crown and the hierarchy to more democratic bodies; but the petition of the house of commons was met by the queen's declaration that she had required the bishops to consider the question. The house, in fact, was diverted by various questions of privilege,[1] and by Wentworth's outspoken attack upon the queen for her interference with parliamentary liberties. He was too bold for the majority, and was committed to the Tower; while many puritan members were alienated by the separatist and democratic tendency traceable in recent presbyterian developments. The commons were no more successful in 1581, although the lower house of convocation joined them in petitioning for the reform of ecclesiastical jurisdiction; and religious dissensions prevented the passing of a bill to suppress the "Family of Love".

This was one of the numerous sects already springing up to vindicate the vigour of Protestant individualism. As early as 1568 the Spanish ambassador reported the discovery of a new sect, said to number 5,000 adherents in London alone, which professed "the pure or stainless religion," practised "love-feasts," and refused to communicate in churches; but he makes no distinction between ordinary puritans and the followers of Hendrik Niclaes or Nicholas, who formed a link between the anabaptists and later nonconformists. In 1575 Guaras spoke of the presence of anabaptists "and many other sects" in London; and on July 22 two Flemish anabaptists were burnt at Smithfield. The repeal of Mary's legislation had merely hampered clerical jurisdiction; and death was not abolished as a penalty for heresy until 1677. But this was the first execution since 1558, and Foxe the martyrologist wrote a heart-felt protest against it to the queen. His urgency was unavailing: another heretic, Matthew Hamont, was burnt at Norwich in 1579; Francis Kett, a Cambridge graduate, was also burnt there in 1589; while Coppin and Thacker were hanged at Bury St. Edmunds in 1583.[2]

---

[1] *E.g.* Hall's case and that of his servant Smalley, the eligibility of the eldest sons of peers, and relations between the two houses; see D'Ewes, pp. 236-67; the *Journals* of both houses; and *Spanish Cal.*, ii., 524.

[2] *Ibid.*, ii., 492, 500; Camden, ii., 333, 405; Fuller, *Church Hist.*, bk. ix., pp. 104-5; *Dict. of Nat. Biogr.*, *s.vv.* Coppin, Kett, Hamont, and Nicholas, Henry.

The distinction of penalty followed a distinction of crime. Coppin and Thacker suffered not as heretics but as traitors in attacking the royal supremacy. This was a logical conclusion: ordinary puritans ascribed all the evils of the system to the bishops; Robert Browne and his followers saw in episcopacy merely a veil for the royal supremacy which, said the Speaker in 1571, was absolute.[1] It was a royal jurisdiction that the bishops exercised: by the queen they were appointed, and by the queen they might, like Grindal, be sequestered if they claimed the slightest independence. Such a system belonged to politics not to religion; extremes met, and Brownists suffered the same fate as Jesuits under the laws of treason. In other respects they were at opposite poles: for the royal supremacy the Jesuits substituted a centralised papal absolutism, and the Brownists, local autonomy. The papacy had proved unwieldy; the royal supremacy had failed to achieve reform; it was time, the Brownists thought, for the people to try. Each congregation was to be a church, self-sufficing and independent. Browne in conjunction with Robert Harrison set up a working model at Norwich in 1581; and ordination from outside, whether by bishops or by presbyterian synods, was repudiated. These ideas appealed to the old English affection for local self-government, and represented a reaction against Tudor centralisation; but they ran counter to the spirit of national unity, and the nation was not yet strong enough to tolerate ecclesiastical diversity.

To the catholic recusant protestantism, with its manifold vagaries, seemed at best but a half-way house to no religion at all. He saw church doors closed from Sunday afternoon to Sunday morning, public worship reduced from a daily to a weekly habit, and the mass converted to a quarterly communion.[2] The irreligion was not so great as the decline of public worship would indicate. Even the quarterly communion was more frequent than the annual delivery of the Host to the laity, of which the catholic rebels in 1549 demanded the restoration; and protestants laid greater stress on family prayer and private devotions—which indeed were the roots of the German reformation—than on public worship, because such methods of religious expression gave fuller scope to individual preference and escaped the deadening restraint of acts of

[1] D'Ewes, p. 141.　　　　[2] Frere, pp. 130, 208,

uniformity. "The law was not made," quoted Sampson,[1] "to forbid one man to do better than the law prescribed, but that no man should do worse;" and the private religious life of sectaries cannot fairly be measured by the public standards they abjured. At the same time the insistence upon the superiority of private judgment to public authority opened the door to endless forms of heterodoxy; and towards the end of the reign the adherents of Essex were denounced as a "damnable crew of heretics and atheists".[2]

Sampson's quotation reveals the protestant attitude towards Elizabeth's official religious compromise; protestants were to do as much "better" than the law as they liked, while catholics were to do no "worse". It was not, however, till Mary's arrival in England in 1568 provided a focus for intrigue, and Elizabeth's excommunication by the pope erected rebellion into a religious duty, that a serious attempt was made to exact the penalties for recusancy, and to sift the protestant wheat from the papal tares. For ten years the majority of English catholics followed the advice of Bishop Cheyne of Gloucester and bowed, like most protestants of Mary's reign, in the house of Rimmon, in spite of repeated injunctions from Rome to refrain.[3] Their action was approved, and not condemned, by public opinion; and many of them were considered none the less papists for their compliance. Some were privileged to hear mass in out-of-the-way country houses or in the chapels of Spanish, Portuguese, and French ambassadors in London; and a spot in St. Paul's where they gathered to talk politics or secular business was called "the Papists' Corner".[4] The more scrupulous of those who could afford it went into exile, like Sir Francis Englefield, Sir Anthony Hungerford, Sir Thomas Copley, Sir Richard Shelley, Dr. John Story, and Bishop Goldwell; they lived for the most part at Louvain where their numbers were largely increased by refugees, such as Westmorland, Markinfeld,

[1] From "a great prelate in this church," *Hatfield MSS.*, ii., 74.

[2] *Hist. MSS. Comm.*, 12th Rep., App., pt. iv., pp. 369-70; *Dict. of Nat. Biogr.*, xiv., 437; *cf. ib.*, xxxvi., 187-88, for references to other free-thinkers. The term "atheist," however, appears to have been applied to any one who did not go to church, *Domestic Cal.*, 1601-3, p. 45.

[3] Simpson, *Life of Campion*, 1867, pp. 18-19.

[4] *Hatfield MSS.*, ii., 222; Frere, pp. 135, 147; E. Hake, *News out of Powles Churchyard*, 1579.

and the Nortons, from the rebellion of the north. Some of
them indulged in intrigues, which the cautious attitude of
Philip II. rendered ineffective; and the most formidable products of the exiles were the literary attacks of their clerical
fellows upon the English church. The northern rebels were
fortified with these books, and Northumberland thought that
Harding and Sanders had written conclusively enough to
enable even Cecil and Leicester to "discern chalk from
cheese".[1] Harding's works are remembered for their own
merits by Romanists, and by Anglicans for having provoked
Bishop Jewel's apologetics. Nicholas Sanders, who was professor of theology at Louvain, joined in the controversy with
his *De Visibili Monarchia Ecclesiæ* and his *De Origine ac Progressu Schismatis Anglicani*, which earned him the nickname
of Dr. Slanders; but later research has shaken that calumny,
and his books are now accepted as worthy to be ranked with
those of his best antagonists. Thomas Stapleton, who likewise
attacked Jewel, was more learned than Sanders: he translated
Bede, and wrote lives of the *Tres Thomæ;* and John Martiall's
book *Of the Cross* was popular with the English catholics of the
north. Other exiles preferred active intrigue to literary propaganda: Laurence Vaux, who published a catechism at Louvain,
was sent as papal agent to England in 1566, and David Wolfe
and Sanders served as legates in Ireland. Dr. John Story, who
had been sent to the Tower by the house of commons in 1549
for his attack on Edward VI.'s government, and had actively
assisted Queen Mary and then Alva in their work of persecution, was kidnapped by English agents in the Netherlands,
brought over to England, and executed for treason in 1571.

His death and Felton's were the first fruits of the papal
bull of 1570, which declared open war between the Roman
church and England. Fugitives are almost invariably bad
judges of offensive strategy; and Pius V. was betrayed into one
of the most serious blunders in papal history by the English
exiles at Rome, who persuaded him that Elizabeth would have
to follow the example of King John. The temporal jurisdiction over princes claimed by the pope was denied by catholic
sovereigns; and it has been allowed to lapse with the common

---

[1] Northumberland's confession in Sharp's *Memorials*, p. 203; Murdin, p.
219; *Domestic Cal.*, Addenda, 1566-79, p. 407.

consent of the catholic world.   Pius could hope for no assistance from those who alone could execute his decree; and the
struggle was waged at the expense of his humbler allies in
England.   They tried to ignore their painful dilemma between
two forms of allegiance, for both of which they had deep respect.
But parliament and, with more reluctance, Elizabeth were driven
into aggressive measures.   The bull, among other things, ab-
solved the queen's subjects from their oath of allegiance, and
thus destroyed the guarantee upon which the government relied
for the loyalty of the catholics; for an oath which need not be
kept is valueless, and parliament set to work to devise other
tests.

In 1571 the law of treason was extended to include such
acts as joining, or reconciling others to, the church of Rome,
or obeying a papal bull; *praemunire* was stretched to cover
the mere possession of papal "things"; and the goods of
those who remained abroad without the royal licence were declared forfeit to the queen.[1]   Parliament wished to go much
farther, and to force the papist to communicate under pain
of fines and forfeiture.   Aglionby, member for Warwick, protested against this tyranny, in support of which Norton was
not ashamed to quote the worst precedents of Mary's reign.
He argued that "there should be no human positive law to
enforce conscience. . . . The conscience of man is eternal, invisible, and not in the power of the greatest monarchy in the
world, in any limits to be straitened, in any bounds to be contained, nor with any policy of man, if once decayed, to be again
raised.   Neither Jews nor Turk do require more than submission to the outward observance, and a convenient silence."[2]
Nevertheless the bill passed both houses; it was designed perhaps to supply the place of the oath as a test, but more probably
to make the papist pay for the luxury of a conscience and for
the risks and expense in which England was involved by the
papal bull.   Aglionby was told that the papists need not sacrifice their conscience, but only their goods.   There was always
a financial aspect to the penal laws; and in the light of that
temptation, it speaks well for Elizabeth that she placed her
veto on the bill.

The papal bull and the penal code between them produced

[1] 13 Eliz., cc. 1, 2, 3.   [2] D'Ewes, pp. 163, 177.

results which are stated in contradictory terms. On the one hand, we read of the ruin of Roman catholicism in England by the steady pressure of coercion; on the other, contemporary documents speak of the ever-increasing numbers of its adherents.[1] The pope and the puritans together provided a solvent of the catholic party, as it existed in England in 1558. The new penalties confirmed in their adhesion the great numbers who are always faithful to the national religion, whatever it may be; but they also provoked conscientious Romanists into the open. The party diminished in numbers, but individually its members were tested and refined by persecution. The Marian restoration had been no part of the counter-reformation; that movement now took hold of English Roman catholics, and filled them with fresh enthusiasm and conviction. The Marian clergy were dying out; the old bishops were kept out of touch with the new development, partly by governmental restraint and partly by personal disinclination. It was therefore inspired and directed from abroad by men who had come under the influence of the Tridentine decrees. The catholicism of English Romanists became less English and more Roman; and it tended to fall under the dominion of foreign and antinational forces.

The most effective agencies in this transformation were the seminaries and colleges created abroad for English catholic students as a natural result of their exclusion from English universities. In 1568 William Allen, formerly principal of St. Mary Hall, Oxford, established an English college at the newly founded university of Douai to train priests for the mission of reconverting England. Among its earliest members were Martiall, Richard Bristow, Stapleton, and Thomas Dorman; and in 1574 it sent forth its first little band of missionaries to England. Most of them soon fell into the hands of the adversary; but the government, as usual, was more merciful than the law, except in cases of treason. For this offence, and not for being a Jesuit, Thomas Woodhouse was hanged in 1573;[2] while several of the missionaries were released from more than one term of imprisonment. This leniency was no deterrent; and in 1577 recourse was had to severity in the case of Cuthbert Mayne, whose presence in Cornwall was connected

---

[1] *E.g. Spanish Cal.,* ii., 572, 710, iii., 38.   [2] *Ibid.,* ii., 491-92.

in the council's mind with Spanish intrigue in that duchy.[1]
After prolonged inquiry and deliberation, he was condemned to
death on September 30 for treason under the act of 1571, and
executed two months later; and two fellow-students from
Douai, Nelson and Sherwood, suffered a like fate in February,
1578. In that year, owing either to the orders of Philip II.,
who had already expelled the "Louvainists," or to the disturbed state of the Netherlands, the college was removed from
Douai to Reims; and in 1579 another was founded by Gregory
XIII. at Rome itself. A hundred priests, wrote Mendoza
on December 28, had within twelve months been ordained at
these two colleges and sent to England, where they converted
numbers to the Roman faith.

It was in the following year that the Jesuits, who had
secured control of the English college at Rome, took a hand
in the work, and despatched to England the two most famous
of the missionaries, Edmund Campion and Robert Parsons.
No two men of more divergent character were ever bound
together by a common purpose.[2] Parsons was a politician in
a priest's disguise; Campion was a single-minded zealot for his
creed. But both laboured for a Roman catholic restoration,
which could not fail to open a door for Philip II. "These
priests," wrote Mendoza to the King of Spain, "go about dis-
guised as laymen; and although they are young, their good life,
fervency, and zeal in the work are admirable. . . . Of the old
ones very few now remain, and they are imprisoned strictly.
This was a cause for the great decay of religion, as there was
no one to teach it, and none professed it, excepting those who
had special grace given them. . . . This is being remedied by
means of those who have recently come hither, who pray continually for your majesty, recognising that God has been
pleased to make you His principal instrument in this great
work."[3]

[1] *Foreign Cal.*, 1577-78, pp. xlix-l. *Cf.* Simpson, *Campion*, p. 299; and
T. G. Law in *Engl. Hist. Review*, i. (1886), 141-44.

[2] See their characters by Camden, who knew them both at Oxford, *Annales*,
ii., 349.

[3] *Spanish Cal.*, ii., 710-11; *cf. Foreign Cal.*, 1581-82, p. 660.

CHAPTER XX.

PLOT AND COUNTERPLOT.

THAT principal part in the reconversion of England, which Mendoza thought had been assigned by Providence to Philip, was certainly forced upon him against his will by developments over which he had little or no control. Like his father, Charles V., he eschewed aggression, because fortune had placed in his hands quite as much as he could hope to keep ; and he would have been more than satisfied to leave to his successor the possessions he had inherited. This conservative ambition included a determination to retain those realms in obedience to the Roman church ; for Philip was less a *politique* than any contemporary ruler, and it was on the religious question that his efforts at accommodation with the Netherlands had failed. But he had no thought of forcing his faith upon the subjects of other sovereigns, except by personal suasion and diplomatic representations. No king was less a knight-errant ; although, when he had to fight, he did not disdain the help which the semblance of a crusade rendered to his cause. Nevertheless, the retirement of other combatants left him the foremost champion of the Roman faith. The pre-eminence secured by Catherine de Médicis through the massacre of St. Bartholomew had been transient ; and France, harassed by Huguenots and by the frequent irruption of German Calvinists, was in no condition to wage religious wars beyond her borders. Nor was the emperor, whose subjects were half of them Lutherans ; and the papacy, always feeble as a temporal state, had wisely exchanged its policy of rivalry with, for one of reliance on, secular kingdoms.

On Philip fell the brunt of protestant aggression, and the obligation of catholic defence. His dominion as well as his religion was attacked at every vulnerable point ; and it was as the last resort of defence that he resolved to take

CHAP.
XX.

the offensive. Even so, he tried all the expedients of intrigue and of the "underhand" hostilities dear to Elizabeth before attempting the arbitrament of war. Against Anjou and his wooing he pitted Guise and the Catholic League; against William of Orange, Alexander of Parma; against Don Antonio, Mary Stuart; and against the protestant sea-dogs, the Jesuits and seminary priests. Mendoza superintended all these operations in the campaign of plot and counterplot which preceded the declaration of hostilities; while Sir Francis Walsingham, who became joint secretary in 1573 and sole secretary in 1581, performed similar services with greater efficiency for Elizabeth. He occupied the place which Burghley had filled earlier in the reign. The lord treasurer grew more conservative with advancing years, partly because the old catholic lords had disappeared from the council and their places had been taken by men more froward than he liked; and, instead of being depicted as a firebrand, Burghley now appears in the Spanish despatches as a restraining force. Walsingham was now the enemy; and Burghley's opposition to his zeal led the secretary to rely on Leicester, who championed a puritan policy in domestic and foreign affairs. The old rivalry between Burghley and Leicester thus continued; but the intellectual capacity and honesty of purpose, with which Walsingham strengthened Leicester's influence over the queen, sometimes made the combination more than a match for Burghley's wisdom and experience; and another check was removed by the ill-health, and then the death of Sussex in 1583. It was fortunate that Leicester was inspired by a man of Walsingham's loyalty; for his own action was always determined by personal motives; and, while the famous onslaught on him in *Leycester's Commonwealth*, fathered on Parsons and published in 1584, contains many libels, exhaustive research into the seamy side of Elizabethan diplomacy would probably reveal some foundation for many of its charges.[1]

The first step in preparing for the approaching struggle

---

[1] In 1577 a certain Battista di Trento addressed to the queen a long letter in Italian giving details of five plots in which Leicester was asserted to have engaged (*Hatfield MSS.*, ii., 165-70). The letter reads like a first draft of *Leycester's Commonwealth; cf. Domestic Cal.*, Addenda, 1580-1625, pp. 136-38. Is it possible that Leicester was useful to Elizabeth as an *agent provocateur?*

was to clear the English decks for action by marking and securing the malcontents or doubtful members of the state. Parliament met in January, 1581, in some alarm at the success of the missionary priests; and it proceeded to pass an "act to retain the queen's majesty's subjects in their due obedience".[1] The penalties for recusancy were to be rigidly enforced, and they were enormously increased. Any one saying mass was to pay 200 marks and suffer a year's imprisonment; any one hearing it was to pay half that fine, but undergo the same detention; the mere recusant was to forfeit £20 a month; any person or corporation employing a recusant schoolmaster was to pay £10 a month; and any one seeking to withdraw men from the established religion "with the intent" of withdrawing them from their allegiance was to be adjudged a traitor. The catholics were dismayed; they offered the queen 150,000 crowns to veto the bill,[2] and made strenuous efforts to prevent its progress in parliament. Nevertheless, the act did little more than fulfil the usual function of proclamations in frightening the people. The £20 fine was too heavy to be paid; and, in spite of the general order for their release on May 7, many recusants preferred to stop in prison at the government's expense. No provision was made in the act for the seizure of their lands or goods in default of payment; and the queen herself was not in earnest. Elizabeth, wrote Leicester, was slow to believe that the great increase of papists was of danger to the realm; "the Lord of His mercy open her eyes".[3]

Other expedients were not much more satisfactory. The object of the government was partly to raise money from the recusants to provide for the expense of keeping them in order, and partly to keep them from contact with foreign Romanism. The old Marian prelates had for some years been carefully segregated at Wisbech and elsewhere; but it was too costly to imprison the growing numbers of recusants; and the jails were inadequate. Imprisonment was for the most part used as a threat to extort fines from the wealthy; but the government had no wish to drive either them or their poorer brethren across the seas to become the agents of Philip or the

---

[1] 23 Eliz., c. 1.   [2] *Spanish Cal.*, iii., 97, 139.
[3] *Acts of the P. C.*, 1581-82, p. 41; *Egerton Papers*, pp. 84-85; *Domestic Cal.*, 1581-90, p. 69.

pope. A design was therefore formed to transport them to North America under the command of Sir Humphrey Gilbert and Sir Philip Sidney.[1] Mendoza was aghast at the proposal : if it were adopted, he wrote, " the seminaries abroad could not be maintained ; nor would it be possible for the priests, who come hither, to continue their propaganda, if there were no persons here to shelter and support them ".[2] He informed the catholics that they would be acting against Philip's interests, and would be slaughtered if they landed. His fears and warnings were both needless : Gilbert was drowned, Sidney was forbidden the voyage, and the realisation of the project for a catholic refuge across the Atlantic was deferred for fifty years.[3]

Better success attended the government's efforts to deal with the first two Jesuits who landed in England, Parsons on June 11 and Campion on June 25, 1580. Campion was seized at Lyford in Berkshire on July 16, 1581, with three seminary priests ;[4] and Parsons, although he escaped, was so hunted from place to place that he never again ventured into England. Parsons' political activity had, however, prejudiced Campion's case ; and in the parliamentary debates, while Campion was merely termed a " wandering vagrant," Parsons was denounced as a " lurking wolf ".[5] Both had sworn to their fellow-catholics that they came with no knowledge of, or concern with, affairs of state ; but though Campion confined himself to proselytising and literary controversy, Parsons discussed political intrigues with Mendoza in London.[6] Campion, however, was wisely put on his trial for treason by the government, not under any recent act, but under the statute of 1352, made by a catholic king and parliament ; and under it he was condemned, after torture to make him reveal his confederates, and executed with the usual barbarity at Tyburn on December 1. With him suffered two seminary priests, Sherwin and Briant ; and the roll of victims steadily grew till it numbered 187 by the end of the reign.[7] The persecution was horrible enough ;

---

[1] R. B. Merriman, " Treatment of the English Catholics," in *American Hist. Rev.*, xiii., 480-500 ; *Colonial Cal.*, Addenda, 1574-1674, pp. 10-20.

[2] *Spanish Cal.*, iii., 384-85, 471.   [3] See vol. vii., p. 379.

[4] *Tudor Tracts*, pp. 451-74 ; *Domestic Cal.*, Addenda, 1580-1625, pp. 24-25.

[5] Simpson, pp. 194-5.   [6] T. G. Law, in *Dict. of Nat. Biogr.*, xliii., 412.

[7] Simpson's *Life of Campion*, 1867 ; *Spanish Cal.*, iii., 231 ; Frere, p. 221 ; *Acts of the P. C.*, 1581-82, pp. 136, 144-45, 152-56, 163-64, 171-74, 176, 184-87, 260-61, 290, 567-68 ; Camden, ii., 379 ; *The Month*, xcix., 614-15.

but there is little likeness between it and Mary's. On the CHAP.
assumption that the Romanists were all executed for their   XX.
faith and not for treason, Elizabeth put to death for their
Romanism an average of four persons for every year of her
reign, or seven for every year from 1575, when the executions
began ; while Mary put to death for their protestantism fifty-
six persons for every year of her reign, or eighty for every year
from January, 1555, when the heresy laws came into force.

The vexed question, whether the Romanists died for treason
or for their faith, implies an antithesis which had little meaning
in that age of mingled politics and religion. Campion was
legally condemned on a charge of treason in which he was involved by his religion. While Chief Justice Wray presided
over the trial with a humanity which roused a suspicion of
Romanist leanings, the government, according to the usual
practice of the time, made charges against the prisoner which
were mainly intended to prejudice the jury ; but the gravamen
of its quarrel with Campion consisted in his active and strenuous adherence to the queen's enemies, which was treason by
the law of Edward III.   It would not have ventured to stretch
this law to cover merely spiritual enemies ; but Pius V., by
acting as a temporal sovereign, by claiming a temporal jurisdiction to depose Elizabeth, and by levying actual war on her
in Ireland, had made himself and his adherents the temporal
enemies of England.   So far as a pope could do so, he had
rendered treason a necessary part of the religious duties of
every English Romanist.   "The state of Christendom," wrote
Sanders in 1577, "dependeth upon the stout assailing of England;"[1] and to be a Christian according to the papal pattern
was to be a traitor by the law of England.   Campion, there is
reason to believe, disapproved of the papal policy, and had
laboured merely to make every Englishman a catholic ; but
his friends "wished to make every catholic a conspirator".[2]
Morally he was as innocent, legally he was as guilty, as Lady
Jane Grey : and in neither case was the victim the real culprit.
Pitiable tragedies like Campion's have only been rendered unnecessary through the abandonment by the heads of churches
of their claims to dispose of the fortunes of states.   Elizabeth
could not afford to ignore those claims, although she suspected

---

[1] *Letters of Cardinal Allen*, p. 38.   [2] Simpson, p. 342.

that the sharp weapons she used had a double edge. Whatever the law might be, even the crowd which witnessed Campion's execution, seems to have felt that he had not met with
justice ; while among enlightened minds the conviction grew—
slowly, it must be admitted—that it was unwise by shedding
the blood of martyrs to sow the seed of rival churches.

Abroad as well as at home the Jesuits and seminary priests
were causing anxiety to Elizabeth. Campion's death convinced
Allen and Parsons that it was better for them personally to remain beyond Elizabeth's reach, relying for the accomplishment
of their aims upon the secular arms of Guise and Philip II. ;
and they now embarked on that career of treason and intrigue,
which wrought more damage to their cause than Campion did
good, and involved their more self-sacrificing brethren in great
and needless suffering. Early in 1582 Allen, Parsons, and
Crichton, the Scottish Jesuit, were discussing with Guise, Mendoza, and Tassis, the Spanish ambassador in France, a scheme
for restoring Roman catholicism in Scotland, and liberating
Mary with the assistance of the pope and Philip II. Crichton
was sent to Rome, and Parsons, under the pseudonym of
Melino,[1] to Lisbon, where Philip then was, to procure the
necessary authorisation and help ; while Mary helped to direct
operations through Mendoza's hands.

Scotland had once more become the weak spot in Elizabeth's armour. She had vainly tried to protect Morton,
whose fall from power was followed by his arrest in December,
1580. He was executed on June 1, 1581, not for his treasonable dealings with Elizabeth, who had refused the armed
assistance he requested, but for his alleged complicity in Darnley's murder. D'Aubigny was created Duke of Lennox : the
Jesuits Holt and Crichton were allowed to try their persuasions
on James VI. ; and Philip II. began to consider a scheme for
marrying him to the eldest infanta, which had been urged in
1574 as "a certain means of reforming religion and obtaining
just possession of the two crowns, whilst completely routing
the French ".[2] In 1579 Mendoza thought that Mary's devo-

---

[1] In the *Spanish Cal.*, vol. iii., Melino and Parsons are treated as two different persons.

[2] *Spanish Cal.*, ii., 474 ; James VI.'s grandmother, the Countess of Lennox,
first suggested this plan, *ibid.*, ii., 546.

tion to the French connexion was her greatest difficulty, which could only be avoided by combining her English and Scottish adherents under Philip's banners; but, he warned the king, "we must work with muffled tools, as otherwise the whole affair will be ruined, and the queen's life sacrificed ".[1]

He was a better prophet than plotter; and the threads of his conspiracy were soon in Elizabeth's hands. He merely succeeded in inducing Mary to turn a deaf ear to the overtures which Elizabeth, somewhat fearful of the effects of her breach with Anjou, made to her and to Philip in 1582. "I have resolved," wrote Mary to Mendoza on July 29, "in view of the hopes I entertain of our enterprise, not to enter into any sort of agreement with this queen." [2] She was ever losing the substance in her efforts to grasp the shadow of departed glory; and less than a month after this letter was written, the foundation of her hopes was shattered by the Raid of Ruthven. James VI. again fell into the hands of protestant lords, and Lennox, after a vain attempt to recover his authority, escaped through England to France, where he died in May, 1583. Mendoza himself, with Philip's approval, opposed Mary's release or flight from England: "there is no desire," he wrote to the Spanish king, "that she should live for ever in prison; but it would be a pity to risk, by leaving it, the consummation for which I am so earnestly striving with great hope of success".[3] Indifferent to her danger, they regarded only the advantage of her presence in England, should Elizabeth be removed by invasion, insurrection, or murder.

All three methods were under consideration by Allen, Parsons, Guise, Philip, the papal nuncio in France,[4] the Cardinal of Como, and the pope. Now that Guise was more Spanish than French, more hostile to Henry III. than to Philip, the Spaniards felt little jealousy in leaving to him the command of the proposed expedition; but it was suggested that the force should be composed of various nationalities, and that Italians rather than Spaniards should predominate; and the conspirators disputed whether it should land in England or Scotland. Scotland seemed the most promising soil in which to sow dragon's teeth; but an army marching from Scotland

[1] Spanish Cal., ii., 647. [2] Ibid., iii., 393. [3] Ibid., iii., 466-70, 504-10.
[4] Giovanni Battista Castelli, Bishop of Rimini.

would rouse English catholic as well as protestant antagonism ;
and this debate encouraged Philip's inveterate procrastination.[1]
The plot to assassinate Elizabeth fared no better. The
prime movers were Guise and his brother Mayenne, who had
discovered an English catholic professedly willing to do the
deed for 100,000 francs. He was apparently William Parry,
a needy spendthrift, who after squandering the patrimony
of two successive wives, eked out a dishonest livelihood by
spying on English refugees abroad ; he then came under their
influence, and was persuaded of the lawfulness of killing
Elizabeth. The papal nuncio in France informed Como of the
plot, and Mendoza communicated it to Philip.[2] The would-be
assassin, however, was prevented by an unexpected order from
accomplishing his purpose, and repaid his bribe : " God wills,"
wrote Mendoza, " that the business shall not be done in this
way ". Parry's own account was that, being doubtful of the
lawfulness of the deed when he left Paris, he consulted some
one in England, and " was learnedly overruled and assured
that it ought not to fall into the thought of a good Christian ".
The difficulties, moreover, were " many, and in this vigilant
time, full of despair ".[3]

Mary had " refused to attend to it," wrote the papal nuncio
on May 2 ; she was busy with overtures for her liberation and
association with her son in the sovereignty of Scotland, in which
connexion Elizabeth wrote her, as she informed Mendoza on
June 5, " a very honest and gracious letter ; and up to the

[1] *Spanish Cal.*, iii., 464, 481-86, 488, 502, 504, 506-10, 517; *Venetian Cal.*,
viii., 70-71, 83.

[2] *Spanish Cal.*, iii., 479, 481-86. The other candidate for the distinction is
George Gifford, whose claims can be supported by some amount of evidence (see
Father Pollen in *The Month*, xcix., 607-13, cx., 245-46). Probably both of them
professed the same intention. According to Parsons, Mary also was an accomplice, *Letters of Cardinal Allen*, p. 388. The editor of Allen's *Letters*, Father
Knox, seems anxious to clear Mary of this charge, not very consistently in view
of his contention that the deed was justifiable, and had the approval of higher
authorities than the Scots queen. " The Archbishop of Glasgow," he writes
(p. xlix), " the Nuncio to the French court, himself a bishop, the Cardinal of
Como, the Spanish agent, J. B. Tassis, Philip II. of Spain, and perhaps the Pope
himself, when they were made aware of the project, did not express the slightest
disapprobation of it, but spoke only of the manifest advantage it would be to
religion if in some way or other the wicked woman were removed by death."
Father Knox's apology for religious assassination (pp. l-li), written in 1882, is
one of the curiosities of historical literature.

[3] *Spanish Cal.*, iii., 502; *Domestic Cal.*, Addenda, 1580-1625, p. 113.

present the commissioners have exhibited every appearance of
goodwill towards me ". The discussion had been renewed as
a consequence of a despairing letter, written by Mary to
Elizabeth on November 8, 1582, when it appeared that she
could entertain no hopes from Scotland. Robert Beale, a
clerk of the privy council, was sent down to Tutbury in April,
1583, to press Elizabeth's views ; and the council deliberated long
on the question.[1] Mary promised conditionally to "have no
dealings with papists, rebels, fugitives, Jesuits, or others who
might go about to trouble the estate of the policy and religion
now established" in England and Scotland ; but she would
not forego these practices pending a settlement. Elizabeth,
assured that James VI. had no desire to share his throne with
his mother, left the question of association to the Scottish
government ; and Mary herself came round to Mendoza's
opinion that it would be "most advantageous for her, in view of
the state of affairs here, to stay in this country ".[2]

Her captivity had its compensations : she hunted, visited
Buxton to take the waters, was served with sixteen dishes at
each meal, kept an establishment of some fifty servants, and
enjoyed a private income of 30,000 crowns from her French
property which she mostly spent in political intrigues. She
would have fared a great deal worse in Scotland ; and the
principal hardship she endured by her detention in England
was the restraint of her ambition. To a woman of her temperament this was sufficiently galling ; but in the summer of 1583
she was once more encouraged by news from Scotland. The
French had been stirred to action by the Ruthven raid and
by Elizabeth's rejection of Anjou ; and two envoys had proceeded to Scotland in the winter of 1582-83, La Mothe as the
accredited agent of Henry III., and Mainville of the Catholic
League, to retaliate on Elizabeth who had not been innocent
of complicity in the raid.[3] La Mothe was delayed in England by

---

[1] *Spanish Cal.*, iii., 463 ; Murdin, p. 781 ; Camden, ii., 387-95. Beale's
letters in Lodge's *Illustrations*, ii., 211-23, are misdated 1582.

[2] *Spanish Cal.*, iii., 475.

[3] Camden asserted her connivance in his first edition, but expunged the
words from his second, *Annales*, ed. Hearne, ii., 386. There is little doubt
about it : see Bowes, *Correspondence* (Surtees Soc.) ; *Spanish Cal.*, iii., 396, 400 ;
Thorpe's *Scottish Cal.*, i., 424-27. She spent over £10,000 in the cause in
1581-82.

her orders, and a copy of his instructions was obtained by one of Walsingham's spies. They were comparatively innocuous, and he was allowed to proceed ; but Mainville, who went by sea, laid the foundations of a plot for overthrowing the new Scots government. Scottish dislike of Elizabeth's parsimony contributed towards his success : James had demanded, besides other things, £10,000 down and £5,000 a year ; and Bowes in May, 1583, dared not guarantee " a continuance of quietness " unless his envoys brought back from London some " satisfaction ". Elizabeth granted James a pension, but it " was thought too small " ; at the end of June he emancipated himself from the protestant lords, and gave his confidence to James Stuart, who had usurped the earldom of Arran from the Hamiltons. In August, Elizabeth sent Walsingham to Edinburgh to see what he could do ; he brought back gloomy reports of the young king's ingratitude to England and inclination towards Spain, Rome, and his mother, " who is the layer of the plot ".[1] James, in fact, meant to be king ; he discoursed to Walsingham on his absolute power, and was quite ready to play off pope against presbyter. He wrote to Gregory XIII. in February, 1584, expressing a hope that he might be able to give the pope satisfaction, but hinting that it would depend upon the satisfaction he received ;[2] and, after the failure of the Gowrie plot of the protestants and the Hamiltons to recover power, the " Black Acts " of 1584 were passed recognising episcopacy and royal supremacy over the Scottish church.

Prelacy, however poisonous it might appear to the presbyterian, did not involve popery ; while royal supremacy was its negation. Elizabeth could not quarrel with James on these grounds, although she might harbour at Berwick the protestant lords and the presbyterian refugees. James, for royal reasons, did not agree with presbytery ; but he wished to agree with Elizabeth. " As for the pope," wrote Mary's secretary to her, " he abhors him utterly, and will not hear a word about him." He pardoned the Ruthven raiders, and sent a message to Walsingham that he " esteemed him the wisest man that ever he spoke with " ; and Arran professed himself a protestant.[3] This development produced a division in Elizabeth's

[1] Thorpe's *Scottish Cal.*, i., 433, 445, 449, 456.   [2] *Spanish Cal.*, iii., 518-19.
[3] Thorpe, i., 459, 461 ; *Hatfield MSS.*, iii., 53.

council.　Walsingham and Davison were convinced that James CHAP.
was merely Mary's stalking-horse; and they pressed for the XX.
support of the presbyterian ministers and the lodging of the
exiled earls, Angus, Mar, and Glamis, in Holy Island, whence
they could safely intrigue with their partisans in Scotland.
Elizabeth, Burghley, and Hunsdon, on the other hand, were
inclined to try an alliance with James.　The difference of
policy led Walsingham into courses in which his zeal outran
his discretion.　He denounced to Davison Burghley's "strange"
and Leicester's "underhand dealing"; complained that the
council generally was as well affected to Mary as to James;
said that Hunsdon would work Davison's disgrace; and went
so far as to counteract the negotiation which Hunsdon was sent,
in Davison's place, to pursue in Scotland.[1]

Elizabeth refused to surrender the refugee lords, arguing
that treaties to that effect between princes were now obsolete;[2]
but she agreed to receive as James's ambassador, Patrick, Master
of Gray, whose success Walsingham did his best to prejudice by
raking up his complicity in past designs against Elizabeth.
There was ground enough for suspicion; but Burghley, who
took charge of the negotiations with Gray, was justified in the
result.[3]　Gray revealed the secrets of Mary and Guise, whose
pay he was still receiving; and persuaded Elizabeth to restore
the exiled lords to Scotland in order that they might overthrow
Arran, who had selected Gray as ambassador.　This was effected
in 1585, when the public announcement of the Catholic League
in March led Elizabeth to send Edward Wotton to Edinburgh to
form a counter-agreement with James.[4]　It was concluded on
July 31; and Arran's ruin followed.　In October the protestant lords recrossed the border, and Arran, after a feeble

---

[1] Thorpe's *Scottish Cal.*, i., 475, 477, 479, 481-82, 485, 488; *Hatfield MSS.*,
iii., 13, 52-53, 74.　Leicester's defection was singular, except that he usually betrayed his friends.　He was at this time negotiating for a marriage between his
son and Arabella Stuart; James's jealousy was thus early aroused (Thorpe, i.,
486; *Domestic Cal.*, Addenda, 1580-1625, pp. 269-70), and Leicester was seeking
to placate him and also Mary.

[2] Thorpe, i., 472; Camden, ii., 408.

[3] Some of Gray's letters are in vol. iii. of the *Hatfield MSS.*; others have
been edited for the Bannatyne Club.

[4] For Wotton's negotiations see Cotton MSS., Caligula, C. viii.-ix.; Addit.
MS., 32,657, ff. 83-223; *Hamilton Papers*, ii., 643-708; *Border Papers*, i., Nos.
335-76; Teulet, *Papiers d'État*, ii., 728, iii., 404-6.

CHAP.
XX.

attempt at armed resistance, fled to the west, where he lived in obscurity till 1596; his fall was assisted by a charge of complicity in a Border outrage on July 27, 1585, in which Lord Russell, the Earl of Bedford's eldest son, was killed. The agreement of 1585 was expanded into the defensive alliance of July, 1586, by which Elizabeth guaranteed James £4,000 a year, and held out further prospects. It would seem, wrote Mary's agent in Paris, that Elizabeth had made James "some deceitful assurance of that crown after her".[1]

The toils, which Mary and her adherents ceaselessly wove for Elizabeth's feet, entangled her own. There was not much to choose, so far as morality went, between the methods employed by the rivals; but Elizabeth accomplished her purpose, while Mary failed. Walsingham knew how to fathom the deepest plots, and to detect the most secret instructions. The catholic nest at Paris harboured almost as many spies as conspirators; several played both parts so well that their real intentions are still obscure; and one or two members of Elizabeth's court achieved an equally dubious distinction. Lord Henry Howard, afterwards Earl of Northampton, was the chief of Mendoza's informants; but Mendoza's career as tempter to treason in England was drawing to its close. His last ineffectual essay was the plot of Francis Throckmorton, a member of that perversely prolific clan, which was ever exceeding the bounds of the law in a protestant or a catholic direction. After an uneventful career at Oxford Francis travelled abroad and fell among plotters. In Spain he discussed with Sir Francis Englefield, and in France with Thomas Morgan and Charles Arundel, projects of invasion and insurrection. Returning to England in 1583 he succumbed to Mendoza's wiles, and was seized in October in the act of writing a letter in cipher to Mary. In spite of the denials, in which he persisted even on the scaffold, his guilt is proved by Mendoza's despatches;[2] and he was executed under the statute of Edward III. on July 10, 1584. Somerville's insane design to shoot the queen, discovered in October, 1583, in which his father-in-law, Arden, was implicated, has less political importance, though it illustrates the effect of writings like Allen's on

---

[1] *Hatfield MSS.*, iii., 147; *cf. ibid.*, iii., 24.
[2] *Spanish Cal.*, iii., 510-12; Knox, pp. lx-lxi, lxx.

ill-balanced minds. The Somervilles and Ardens were War- CHAP.
wickshire families distantly connected with the Throckmortons XX.
and other conspirators; but the interest attaching to the plot
arises from the possible relationship between Arden and Shakespeare's mother. Somerville hanged himself in prison after conviction, and Arden was publicly executed.[1]

Mendoza had nothing to do with Somerville's treason; but
his complicity in Throckmorton's plot exhausted Elizabeth's
patience. In January, 1584, he was summoned before the
council, and told he must leave the country. He departed
breathing out threatenings and slaughter. As he had apparently failed, he remarked to the council, in his endeavour to
please the queen as a minister of peace, she would in future
force him to try to satisfy her in war; and to Elizabeth herself
he said: " Don Bernardino de Mendoza was born, not to disturb
countries, but to conquer them ".[2] William Waad, clerk to
the privy council, was sent to Madrid to explain Mendoza's
expulsion; but Philip refused to see him, and ordered him out
of the country with an intimation that he was fortunate to
escape so easily;[3] while Mendoza, at Mary's request, was
appointed to the embassy in Paris that he might there continue his fatal activity in her interests. She was herself transferred in September, 1584, from Shrewsbury's custody at
Sheffield to Sir Ralph Sadler's at Wingfield, and thence back
to Tutbury in January, 1585. Shrewsbury's termagant
countess, the famous "Bess of Hardwick," who founded the
fortunes of the house of Devonshire, had accused her husband
of undue intimacy with the Scottish queen; and in view of the
fact that, while the council formally cleared him of the charge,
Mary thought that she had won him over to her cause, it was
a wise precaution to entrust her to Sadler, whose seventy-six
years would be some protection against her wiles. The
countess was sent to the Tower, and Shrewsbury thanked
Elizabeth for having relieved him of two demons.[4] The

---

[1] *Domestic Cal.*, 1581-90, pp. 124-26, 128-31, 138, 154, 161, 182, 295.
[2] *Spanish Cal.*, iii., 513-14, 516.
[3] *Ibid.*, iii., 520-21, 581; Cotton MS., Caligula, C. vii., f. 392; Birch, *Memoirs*,
i., 45, 48.
[4] Teulet, *Relations Politiques*, v., 344; Lodge, *Illustrations*, ii., 239, 247-
49; Knox, pp. xlvii, 413; *Dict. of Nat. Biogr.*, lv., 309-11.

immovable Sir Amias Paulet succeeded Sadler as Mary's warder in October, 1585; and two months later she was at her own request installed in better quarters at Chartley.

No precautions seemed excessive after the murder of William of Orange on July 10, 1584. In September Elizabeth ascertained full details of Guise's and Allen's designs against herself. Father Crichton, the Scottish Jesuit, had been captured at sea; and some documents which he tore up and threw overboard were blown back on to the deck, secured, and pieced together by Waad.[1] The eighth Earl of Northumberland and Norfolk's son, the Earl of Arundel, were sent to the Tower for complicity; and there Northumberland died by his own hand on June 21, 1585, and Arundel a natural death in 1595. William Shelley, another conspirator arrested in 1584, was executed on February 12, 1586. The news of these plots roused England to fury; a voluntary Association was formed in which Englishmen of all ranks from peers downwards bound themselves " to withstand and revenge to the uttermost all such malicious actions and attempts against her majesty's most royal person ". In spite of her waywardness and occasional cruelty, the English people were passionately devoted to their queen; and a French ambassador told his Venetian colleague in 1581 that "he had often seen her on her way through London receive such blessings from the people as though she had been another Messiah". Whether the fate of religion ever depends upon political intrigue or not, it is as certain as anything can be in history that no assassination and no invasion could have reconverted England to Rome. The schemes of Allen and Parsons were so much criminal folly, which, if carried out, could only have produced bloodshed and disorder; and it is hard to say to what lengths a nation is not justified in going in order to protect itself.

The parliament that was elected amid this fever of resentment and alarm in the autumn of 1584, and met on November 23, went a considerable length. Its first bill legalised the Association; authorised the queen, if need should arise, to create a special commission with powers to condemn all parti-

---

[1] Camden, ii., 418. This is termed "a ridiculous story" in the *Dict. of Nat. Biogr.*, xiii., 93; but its veracity has been conclusively established, *ib.*, lviii., 403; T. G. Law in *Engl. Hist. Rev.*, viii., 698; Knox, pp. lxx, 425, 432.

cipants in any plot or invasion, to exclude them from the succession to the throne, and to expose them to the vengeance of private citizens ; declared every one, in whose interest the queen might be killed, incapable of inheriting the crown ; and provided for the execution of this law after her decease. The second act of the session banished all Jesuits and seminary priests who would not submit and take the oath ; prohibited their return on pain of treason ; and imposed the same penalty on all preparing to enter the order abroad, unless they returned within six months. The queen was more merciful than her parliament : seventy priests, says Camden, were released from prison and shipped to France, although some of them had already been condemned to death ; they included Jasper Haywood, John Hart, and James Bosgrave, all notable Jesuits, and Edward Rishton, the diarist and editor of Sanders.[1]

Thirty public and nineteen private acts received the royal assent at the conclusion of the session on March 29, 1585. The commons' complaints of Whitgift's arbitrary exercise of ecclesiastical jurisdiction and their demands for a puritan reformation met with the usual response. Elizabeth vetoed a bill for the "better observance of the Sabbath," and by a rarer use of the prerogative amended the clause legalising the Association so as to protect its possible victims from private vengeance.[2] A fresh bill against recusants, and another to introduce into England Gregory XIII.'s recent reform of the calendar, did not get beyond their second reading in the commons ; and Englishmen kept their ancient reckoning until the time of George II.[3] The committal to Sir Thomas Lucy, and the subsequent failure, of a bill for the preservation of game [4] have probably no connexion with the well-known tale about Shakespeare and Justice Shallow.

A more serious episode occupied the attention of parliament. Parry, who was still regarded by the government as a single-hearted spy, had secured election for Queenborough ; but in parliament he vehemently denounced the proposed legislation against the Jesuits as being " full of blood, danger,

---

[1] Camden, ii., 412 ; *Spanish Cal.*, iii., 531-33 ; *Venetian Cal.*, viii., 108.
[2] D'Ewes, pp. 322, 341.   [3] See vol. ix., p. 423.
[4] D'Ewes, p. 363 ; the Commons' Journals are missing from 1581 to the end of the reign.

despair, and terror to the English subjects of this realm, our brethren, uncles, and kinsfolk ". He appealed to the queen to veto it, but refused to give reasons for his opinion, reserving them for the royal ear; for this and for his unparliamentary language he was committed to the serjeant for contempt. On the morrow, December 18, he was released at Elizabeth's intercession; but a week or so later his relative and fellow-conspirator, Edmund Neville, who was nephew of Edward Arden on the mother's side and was connected with the Earl of Westmorland on the father's, turned queen's evidence, and denounced Parry for his designs to kill Elizabeth. He had been reconciled to the Roman church at Venice in 1583, had corresponded with the Cardinal of Como, and had discussed his plans with the papal nuncio and Mary Stuart's agent, Thomas Morgan, in Paris. A priest named Watts, however, condemned the enterprise, and his censures were confirmed after Parry's return to England by the Jesuit Crichton; but Parry was reanimated by a perusal of Allen's book, and by the receipt of letters from the Cardinal of Como and of a blessing and plenary indulgence from the pope. He never made a serious attempt to perpetrate the murder; but this abstinence, which was largely due to irresolution, did not save him from condemnation on his own confession, and he was executed on March 2.[1]

At the same time Elizabeth sent first the Earl of Derby and then Waad to demand from Henry III. the surrender of Parry's accomplice, Morgan. Henry would only consent to Morgan's detention in the Bastille, and Waad .was waylaid on his return and beaten by the Duke of Aumâle for his impertinence in coming to France to demand the surrender of a catholic. Aumâle's insolence was encouraged by the conclusion, on December 31, 1584, of a secret treaty between Philip II. and the Guises, which Elizabeth sought to counteract by

[1] Parry's plot is sometimes considered an invention of the government; but this theory offers no explanation of his execution and is difficult to reconcile with his letter to Morgan (*Domestic Cal.*, Addenda, 1581-90, p. 113). His identification with the would-be assassin of 1583 is more doubtful than his plot in 1584, but still seems probable; he appears, however, to have been rather the agent of the lay anti-Spanish Catholic conspirators than of Allen and Parsons. See Knox, pp. 388, 392, 434; *Spanish Cal.*, iii., 534-35, iv., 3-4; *Venetian Cal.*, viii., 113; Camden, ii., 426-30; D'Ewes, pp. 341, 344, 352, 355-56; *Hatfield MSS.*, v., 25, 59; and Father Pollen in *The Month*, c., 71-87, cix., 356-65.

conferring the Garter on Henry III. Anjou's death in July, 1584, and the king's lack of male issue had ranged France into two hostile camps over the question of the succession. The Catholic League and Philip were determined to exclude Henry of Navarre ; Henry III. occupied a middle position between Henry of Navarre and Henry of Guise ; and in April there broke out "the war of the three Henrys," which lasted until Guise and Henry III. had been assassinated and Henry of Navarre had made himself undisputed master of France, only to meet with a similar fate in the end. This war cleared the way for the duel between England and Spain. France no longer possessed international value ; Guise withdrew from his projected invasion of England, leaving the field to Philip ; James VI., deprived of all hope from France, made his peace with Elizabeth, while his mother made hers with Spain ; and Elizabeth, having barred her back-door, as Scotland was commonly called, by the treaty with James, was able to turn on Philip and let slip the dogs of war. Drake was the first to go ; Leicester followed to the Netherlands ; while Walsingham circumvented Mary, and minor agents undermined the diplomatic or material strength of Philip's position in every direction.

The cares of the English government had not impeded the spontaneous expansion of English energies. "They are daily building more ships," wrote Mendoza in 1580 ; "they have a monopoly of the shipping, whereby they profit by all the freights ;" and they were "almost the masters of commerce in other parts as well as" in the ports of Spain.[1] The papal prohibition of trade between catholics and the Turks threw it into the hands of the English, who at Constantinople were paid "almost its weight in gold" for lead and tin. The eyes of the Turk had been opened by English merchants to the value of commerce ; and the Porte began to dream of reviving the mercantile prosperity which Constantinople had enjoyed before the Portuguese discovered the route round the Cape. They granted the English facilities for their overland trade with India, and the Shah of Persia followed suit.[2] English factories were established at Constantinople, and in 1580 the first treaty was signed between England and Turkey. During the following

---

[1] *Spanish Cal.*, iii., 8, 72.
[2] *Ibid.*, iii., 366-67, 431-32, 456, 465 ; *Venetian Cal.*, viii., 65-66.

years Harborne's diplomacy routed his French and Venetian
rivals on the Bosphorus; the Levant Company was incorporated in 1581 ; and Elizabeth was even intriguing against
Philip with the Dey of Algiers and the Sheríf of Morocco.[1]
In 1583 Ralph Fitch, sailing in his ship *The Tiger* to Tripoli
and thence proceeding to Aleppo,[2] commenced the eight
years' journey, in which he surveyed the Persian Gulf, India,
Siam, and Malaya, and laid the foundations of the East India
Company.

The influence of England's sea-power and commercial
enterprise spread in the Baltic as well as in the Mediterranean.
In 1582 Peregrine Bertie, Lord Willoughby de Eresby, was
sent to Denmark to invest Frederick II. with the Garter, and
to seek protection for English ships and an assurance that he
would not join Philip II.; a second mission in 1585-86 obtained from him some assistance for the Netherlands.[3] John
III. of Sweden in 1583 sent an embassy to Elizabeth begging
her to mediate between him and Ivan the Terrible. Peace
was concluded; and Ivan, who had troubles of his own, requested Elizabeth to promise him an asylum, if he were driven
from Russia, and to give him the hand of her cousin, Mary
Hastings. The latter petition was declined; but the opportunity was taken to strengthen commercial relations. Sir
Jerome Bowes was despatched as ambassador, and Sir Jerome
Horsey as commercial agent, in succession to Anthony Jenkinson; and although the "time of troubles" which followed
almost annihilated trade in Russia, English prestige was still
high enough for James I. to be asked in 1617 to arrange the
peace of Stolbova.[4] Nor was Elizabeth unmindful of Germany; she had often intervened to protect Calvinists from the
hostility of Lutherans, and to stimulate their zeal on behalf of
their brethren in France and the Netherlands. She now sent
Thomas Bodley to persuade the Elector Palatine, the Dukes of

[1] *Venetian Cal.*, viii., pp. xxix ff., 50-58, 74-80, 86 ff., 227, 232, 235 ; *Hatfield MSS.*, ii., 294 ; Sir Edwin Pears in *Engl. Hist. Rev.*, July, 1893 ; Hakluyt, general index, *s.vv.* Algiers and Morocco ; Cunningham, *English Industry and Commerce*, ii., i., 74-75.
[2] Hakluyt, v., 465-505 ; *Spanish Cal.*, iii., 456. *Cf.* Shakespeare, *Macbeth*, act i., sc. 3 : "Her husband's to Aleppo gone, master of the Tiger ".
[3] *Spanish Cal.*, iii., 409, 582 ; *Foreign Cal.*, 1582, pp. 130, 217, 245, 254, 290.
[4] *Ibid.*, 1582, pp. 385, 520 ; Camden, ii., 399-401 ; Hakluyt, iii., 308-48 ; Geijer, *Hist. of the Swedes*, p. 240 ; *Dict. of Nat. Biogr.*, xxxvii., 319-20.

Saxony, Würtemberg, and Brunswick, and other German princes to join the protestant alliance against the Catholic League; and she lent financial assistance to the deprived archbishop of Cologne, Gebhard Truchsess von Waldorf.[1]

The England of 1585 was very different from that which Philip had left in 1557; but, deluded by the reports of ardent ambassadors like Mendoza and by the counsels of exiles like Sir Francis Englefield, he never appreciated the importance of the change. Nevertheless, he was under no delusion that he could conquer England by his own resources: even Mendoza had warned him that an invasion without a rebellion would be a forlorn hope; and when in May, 1585, he laid an embargo on English ships in Spanish ports, it was done less with any intention of going to war than in response to Mendoza's representations that the foundations of England's wealth could best be sapped by stopping its trade with Spain.[2] War, indeed, between Elizabeth and Philip was never declared on either side: it simply grew, and in 1585 Philip was merely repeating his action of 1569. On both occasions Elizabeth retaliated with a similar seizure; but she was now prepared to follow it up with stronger measures. Burghley himself had become convinced of the necessity for open support of the Dutch; and when on September 14, 1585, Drake sailed again out into the west, he went with a royal commission in command of a national enterprise. Frobisher was his vice-admiral; his force consisted of twenty-one ships, eight pinnaces, and 2,300 men, among whom were twelve companies of troops. After plundering "Bayona's hold," Vigo, and the Cape Verde Islands, he took his fleet across to San Domingo, where he seized and ravaged what he could; then crossing to the Spanish Main, he held its capital Cartagena to ransom, and burnt such shipping in the harbour as he could not bring away. Proceeding to Cuba, he found Havana too strong to be attacked; but he utterly destroyed the Spanish town of St. Augustine in Florida in retaliation for the similar fate inflicted by Menendez on the Huguenots, and returned to Portsmouth in July, 1586, bringing with him some £60,000 worth of booty and the

---

[1] Camden, ii., 436; *Hatfield MSS.*, iii., 98; Harleian MS., 285, art. 46.
[2] *Spanish Cal.*, iii., 8-9, 72. The presence of a large fleet of corn ships (Corbett, ii., 10-11) was the occasion rather than the cause of Philip's action.

survivors of Raleigh's colony in Virginia. It was afterwards thought that Elizabeth should have held the places which Drake had plundered; but England's resources were not equal to such an undertaking, and the idea was still to cut the roots of Philip's European power rather than to substitute English for Spanish dominion across the seas. "Drake's enterprise," wrote Morgan to Mary, "has done much for the diversion of the King of Spain's designs."[1]

While Drake was preparing to sail, Elizabeth was making up her mind to take the revolted Netherlands under her protection. As early as 1576 Guaras had reported, after a conversation with Burghley, that the English would help Orange openly if they saw him in danger of complete defeat and ruin.[2] In 1583 Elizabeth had for a second time refused the sovereignty of the Netherlands, preferring Burghley's advice to that of Leicester and Walsingham;[3] but the murder of Orange in 1584, Parma's capture of Antwerp in 1585, and the failure of Elizabeth's efforts to move Henry III., convinced the lord treasurer that the time had come for more decided intervention.[4] The insurgents appeared to be weaker than in 1576, and the majority of the provinces had been recovered for Spain; but their need was therefore greater, and England now was stronger. On August 10, 1585, a treaty was concluded; Elizabeth agreed to provide 5,000 foot and 1,000 horse, as well as garrisons for Flushing, Brille, and Rammekens, which were to be placed in her hands as guarantees for the eventual payment of her expenses. In December Leicester, with some misgivings as to the security of the queen's support, set out for Flushing. The venture was not a success, though it is to Leicester's credit that he spent on it the greater part of his private fortune. He was not the man for a task which taxed all the energies of William of Orange. He quarrelled with his English subordinates, Sir John Norris, Buckhurst, Wilkes, and Killigrew, no less bitterly than with his Dutch colleagues. He accepted the post of governor-general from the States without consulting Elizabeth; he knew nothing of the shoals and cross-currents of Dutch provincial politics; he alienated

[1] *Hatfield MSS.*, iii., 147.
[2] *Spanish Cal.*, ii., 521. [3] *Ibid.*, iii., 498.
[4] *Hatfield MSS.*, iii., 69-70; *Spanish Cal.*, iii., 542.

Barneveldt and the aristocratic party of religious toleration by CHAP.
encouraging the extreme and democratic Calvinists ; and he   XX.
helped to foster that party-warfare which dominated Dutch
history for two centuries.   He had his misfortunes as well as
his faults.   The disunited provinces needed the centralised
monarchy which Leicester sought to establish ; but to create it
was not the part of a foreigner.   Norris, brave and competent
though he was, had not Parma's genius ; and the loss of Sluys,
the treacherous surrender of Deventer and Zutphen by their
English captains, Sir William Stanley and Rowland Yorke,
could not be redeemed by Sidney's chivalry and death at the
battle of Warnsfeld.   In August, 1587, Leicester relinquished
his post, abandoning, he said, not the flock but its ungrateful
members.

Futile as his intervention had been, it was none the less an
act of war, which Spain could not treat with the same contempt
as Anjou's fleeting escapades ; and it behoved the government,
which by July, 1586, was well aware of Philip's naval prepara-
rations, to look to Mary, Queen of Scots.   She was the one
hope of peaceable Roman catholics and of papal and Spanish plotters, the only possible beacon to draw together English
insurgents and foreign invaders.   Nineteen years of confinement had helped her to live down her earlier ill-repute, and to
prepare for the crown of religious martyrdom.   " The accusations of complicity in the murder of her husband," wrote Silva
to Philip as early as 1568, "are being forgotten, and her marriage with Bothwell is now being attributed to compulsion and
fear.   This view is being spread, and friends easily persuade
themselves of the truth of what they wish to believe, especially
in this island." [1]   Spaniards, however, were not exempt from
this infirmity, and contributed their share towards the growth
of Mary's legend.   By 1574 Silva's colleague, Guaras, was convinced that she was " entirely innocent, being persecuted by
these tyrants only because she is a catholic," and even that " she
would be a saintly, chaste, and catholic princess," if only she
married Don John.[2]   Twelve years later she fulfilled the spirit
of Guaras' condition, by disinheriting her son and bequeathing
to Philip her claims to the English and Scottish crowns ; [3]

---

[1] *Spanish Cal.*, ii., 48.   [2] *Ibid.*, ii., 489.
[3] *Ibid.*, iii., 581, 587, 590, 644.   Philip naively remarked, on hearing the news,
that Mary had greatly risen in his estimation.

she became as much "the true instrument" for England's conquest by Spain as for its conversion by Rome. Allen and Parsons were in fact now primarily agents for the Spanish conquest, doubtless because they sincerely believed that only by Philip's arm could England be won for the faith; and when Sir Richard Shelley, a genuine but loyal Romanist, who lived in exile for thirty years rather than conform to the established religion, advocated an attempt "to convert Elizabeth by fair means," Allen cynically agreed to Shelley's employment in the work "as an appropriate instrument for deceiving the queen, whilst being himself deceived".[1] Mary herself was regarded less as the rightful Queen of England than as the forerunner destined to make straight the path of Philip or the infanta.[2]

There can be little doubt that by 1586 Walsingham's knowledge of the conspiracies against Elizabeth and of Philip's impending attack had convinced him, if no one else, of the necessity of removing Mary. But only Babington's plot enabled him to bring sufficient pressure to bear on Elizabeth to extort her consent to Mary's trial and condemnation; and, while he facilitated Mary's self-incrimination, he certainly did not invent the plot. Anthony Babington, a recusant with some property in Derbyshire, who had been page to Mary in the earlier days of her captivity, was in July, 1585, moved by a letter from her agent Morgan "to be more diligent in her majesty's service," for which the proximity of his house at Dethick to Mary's prison at Wingfield afforded some advantages. Some ten months later John Ballard, a priest, who had made an extensive survey of catholic England, instigated Babington and five others to conspire the death of Elizabeth "by poison or steel," and communicated the plot to Mendoza in Paris, in order that Philip might provide the troops and money necessary to complete the revolution when Elizabeth should have been despatched. Philip approved of the design, and placed 100,000 crowns at the disposal of "the priests who have been going thither". But he had misgivings from the first; and Morgan, who had recommended Mary to write with her

---

[1] *Spanish Cal.*, iv., 1; Knox, p. lxxxv.

[2] *Spanish Cal.*, iii., 660: "this Father Robert and Allen . . . say that the succession rightly belongs to your majesty by reason of the heresy of the king of Scotland, and even apart from this, through your descent from the house of Lancaster"; *cf. ibid.*, 561, 563, iv., 16, 32.

own hand to Babington, warned her against dealing with Ballard lest her complicity in his dangerous enterprise should be revealed.[1] Walsingham was early acquainted with the scheme through his spy Gilbert Gifford, who had been educated at the English College in Rome, and may have acted as *agent provocateur* to Ballard and Babington.[2]

Mendoza thought that "of all the plots they have hatched these many years past, none has been apparently so serious as this"; and Walsingham wrote to Leicester on July 9 that "if the matter be well handled, it will break the neck of all dangerous practices during her majesty's reign".[3] Much of the conspirators' correspondence passed through his hands, the letters being deciphered, copied, and then resealed by a skilful process discovered by one of his agents, and forwarded to their destination.[4] It was not until August that the government struck. Nearly all the plotters were arrested; Babington accused Ballard of being the chief instigator, and Ballard admitted the charge. Both were executed, with a dozen others on September 20 and 21, after Babington had explained the cipher used in his correspondence with Mary.

Mary's defence, based on the hypothesis that Walsingham interpolated the incriminating passages in her letters and then destroyed the originals to conceal his wickedness, has broken down under the weight of corroborative evidence provided by more recently-published documents from foreign archives. Walsingham could not have tampered with the letters which passed between Mendoza in Paris and Philip in Madrid. "I am of opinion," wrote Mendoza on September 10,[5] "that the Queen of Scotland must be well acquainted with the whole affair, to judge from the contents of a letter which she has

---

[1] *Spanish Cal.*, iii., 607; *Hatfield MSS.*, iii., 140-41, 147. Mendoza urged the conspirators to kill or seize Burghley, Walsingham, Hunsdon, Knollys, and Beal, as well as Elizabeth. Philip commented: "It does not matter so much about Cecil, although he is a great heretic, but he is very old, it was he who advised the understandings with the Prince of Parma, and he has done no harm".

[2] Father Pollen in *The Month*, cx., 247-53, 363-74; *Domestic Cal.*, Addenda, 1580-1625, pp. 223, 240, 258-59; *The Bardon Papers* (Camden Ser.), 1910.

[3] *Spanish Cal.*, iii., 607; *Leicester Corresp.* (Camden Soc.), p. 342.

[4] This of course is the reason why the government had to rely on copies in the prosecution; the permanent detention of the originals would have stopped the correspondence.

[5] *Spanish Cal.*, iii., 623-24; *cf. Venetian Cal.*, viii., 220.

written to me ; " and her farewell epistle to him, while denying
that she had made, practically admits that she had encouraged,
attempts on Elizabeth's life.   She bewails her ill-usage by
friends " who I wish had not shown so openly their fear to die
in so just a cause, or given way to their own disordered passions.   But withal, they have been able to get nothing out of
me, except that I am a free catholic princess and an obedient
daughter of the church, and that I was in duty bound to seek
my deliverance, and, since I had tried fair means unsuccessfully,
was obliged therefore to listen to other proposals made to me
with the same object.   Nau has confessed everything, Curle a
great deal, following his example ; and all is on my shoulders.
. . . I greatly fear that Nau and Pasquier have much promoted my death, as they kept papers." [1]

Her complicity was accepted almost without demur in
foreign courts ; and the representations, which they made to
Elizabeth in Mary's favour, were not based upon her innocence,
but upon grounds indicated in her letter to Mendoza and
adopted during her trial before a special commission at Fotheringhay in October.   She bore the stamp and seal of sovereignty
which all the water in the rough rude sea could not efface ; it
was no less indelible than that of peerage or of priesthood.
She was therefore subject to no tribunal on earth ; charges of
murder or conspiracy, whether true or false, were equally irrelevant, because no one but God had jurisdiction to pronounce
a sentence or to carry it out.   This was the real issue, which
troubled Elizabeth ; and on October 29 parliament met to help
her to make up her mind and to relieve her of responsibility.
A precedent set in 1542, when Catherine Howard was attainted,
was followed, and parliament was opened by royal commission
to spare the royal feelings.   It felt no hesitation ; the commons
toyed with a few bills, but the lords did nothing for weeks
except examine the question ; and on November 12 both
houses unanimously petitioned the queen for Mary's execution.
Elizabeth fell on her knees, it is said, and prayed for a quarter
of an hour, and then required them to consider whether there
were not other means for securing her life and the peace of
the kingdom.   After further discussion parliament replied that

---

[1] *Spanish Cal.*, iii., 663-64 ; *cf. Domestic Cal.*, Addenda, 1580-1625, p. 188.
Nau, Curle, and Pasquier were Mary's secretaries.

there were none. Thereupon she sent down this message : " If I should say unto you that I mean not to grant your petition, by my faith I should say unto you more than perhaps I mean. And if I should say unto you that I mean to grant your petition, I should then tell you more than is fit for you to know."[1]

Parliament was adjourned on December 2 without the warrant being signed, while Elizabeth tried to fathom the probable effects of Mary's execution on her allies, James VI. and Henry III. They agreed that Mary deserved the utmost rigour short of death ; but James's agent, the Master of Gray, was whispering the current counsel of the time, *mortui non mordent*, and the French ambassador supplied a practical illustration of the danger of keeping her alive. Châteauneuf was an adherent of the Guises, and had been cognisant of Mary's plots ; and he now instigated through his secretary an attempt by two young men Stafford and Moody to effect her release, if not to kill Elizabeth.[2] The nation grew impatient with the suspense ; the hue and cry was "hourly" being raised on false rumours of Mary's escape ;[3] and it was reported abroad that parliament would refuse supplies unless the sentence were carried out.[4] On February 1, 1587, after vainly urging Mary's jailer Sir Amyas Paulet to procure Mary's death without legal authorisation, Elizabeth signed the warrant and gave it to Davison, who had been made secretary in the previous July.[5]

But she had signed three warrants, and had vacillated for five months before Norfolk was executed, and then had cast the blame on Burghley ; and now the impression was conveyed to foreign courts that she had determined to spare Mary's life.[6] It was certain that some one would have to take the responsibility for her death and the risk of Elizabeth's

[1] *Venetian Cal.*, viii., 226; D'Ewes, p. 380.

[2] *Hatfield MSS.*, iii., 216; *Spanish Cal.*, iv., 13-14; *Venetian Cal.*, viii., 243-44, 248-49, 260 (where Châteauneuf is described as the chief cause of Mary's death); *Domestic Cal.*, Addenda, 1580-1625, pp. 190, 200-3; *Dict. of Nat. Biogr.*, liii., 462.

[3] *Hatfield MSS.*, iii., 218; *Acts of the P. C.*, 1586-87, p. 315.

[4] *Venetian Cal.*, viii., 244-45; *Spanish Cal.*, iv., 15, 26.

[5] Nicolas, *Life of Davison*, pp. 86-87, 100-1; *Sir Amyas Paulet's Letter-book*, ed. Morris, 1874.

[6] *Venetian Cal.*, viii., 238, 240; *Domestic Cal.*, Addenda, 1580-1625, p. 192. The removal of the black hangings from Mary's chamber seemed to be a confirmation of the rumour.

anger; and the council sought safety in its numbers. The day after the signature of the warrant they "did with one mind conclude that it was most necessary to use all secrecy herein, to delay no time, for fear of greater danger; and, in like sort, it was thought by us all unwell to acquaint her majesty with the form and circumstances for the time and manner of the doing thereof, presuming it for divers causes not convenient to trouble her majesty therewith ".[1] Pledging themselves not to tell the queen until the deed was done, they arranged for Mary's execution; and despatched Beal with their orders to Fotheringhay. There on the 8th the Queen of Scots was beheaded; and as Shrewsbury's son rode to London with the news, bells rang and bonfires blazed in his track.[2]

The contrast between Elizabeth, shrinking from her responsibilities, and Mary, meeting the supreme test with splendid courage, puts reason at the mercy of sentiment. Fortune heaped her gifts on Elizabeth's head, and brought Mary's to the block; but in the hour of death the Queen of Scots had no need to envy her rival. She was dying for a cause, her faith in which was darkened by no shadow of doubt. She has been claimed as a martyr to the Roman, as her grandson has to the Anglican, church; and, like him, she nothing common did or mean to impair the dramatic effect of the sacrifice. But in truth they both were victims to the right divine of kings. Mary, like Charles I., called a church to her help; but she lost her life in her efforts to show that

> "The breath of worldly men cannot depose
> The deputy elected by the Lord".

She anticipated his contentions, and parliament in 1586 established a precedent for 1649. This was Elizabeth's dilemma: Arundel had warned her in 1568 against subscription to the doctrine that princes might be deposed, and for fifteen years, in spite of the "ample cause," which Philip II. said she had for taking Mary's life,[3] she had stood almost alone between the Scottish queen and the clamour of parliament and the bishops for her execution. Like Mary, she held that

---

[1] *Hatfield MSS.*, iii., 218; *cf. ibid.*, iii., 217, 220, 223-24.
[2] *Venetian Cal.*, viii., 229, 256, 258; Ellis, *Original Letters*, I., iii., 22, II., iii., 106 ff.
[3] *Spanish Cal.*, ii., 319.

princes could do no wrong of which their subjects could take CHAP.
any cognisance; and she found it difficult to rebut Mary's plea XX.
that no municipal law could settle the issue between them.
Nor was there any recognised code of royal conduct. The
piety of Mary's death was no proof of her innocence towards
Elizabeth, and the strength of her religious convictions was
no guarantee for the morality of her conduct. Knox and
Philip II. were both religious men after their kind; yet Knox
termed Beaton's murder "a godly deed," and Philip instigated
the assassination of William of Orange: it was the common
property of all creeds that the saving of souls sometimes
required the slaying of bodies. The "natural law," which
alone in Mary's view governed her relations with Elizabeth,
was hardly distinguishable from a state of war; and war
supersedes the Ten Commandments. Plot and counterplot
alike were parts of a campaign; Mendoza called Mary the
mainspring of the war; and the arbitrament of war is barbarous.

CHAPTER XXI.

THE ARBITRAMENT OF WAR.

"ALL the catholic hopes in England," wrote the Venetian ambassador in Paris on the news of Mary's death, "are dashed." [1]
It remained to be seen what grounds they had for hope abroad.
Elizabeth fell ill when Mary's execution was announced, turned
savagely on her ministers, and, as she could not rule without
them, made Davison a scapegoat. She maintained that she
had never intended Mary's execution, and had enjoined the
secretary not to part with the warrant without express command. He was tried before the Star Chamber, deprived of his
office, and sentenced to a fine of £10,000 and imprisonment
during pleasure in the Tower. His fate was used to prove to
James VI. and Henry III. the clemency of Elizabeth's intentions towards Mary, and the private wrong she inflicted
on him smoothed her public difficulties. Both monarchs
found the matter hard to digest; at least, they had to show
disgust. James was told that a coat of armour would be the
best suit of mourning, and Morton made a raid across the
Borders. But the Scottish king was now Elizabeth's heir; a declaration of war would destroy his chances, and Morton was
disavowed. Henry III. was in no better position to proceed
against the English queen. "From the news contained in my
letter to the king about the way in which the King of France
is behaving towards the Englishwoman," writes Mendoza from
Paris to Philip's secretary, "it might be thought that they
would fall out in real earnest; but I can assure you nothing is
further from their thoughts;" [2] and Elizabeth with timely fore-
sight was alarming Henry by her approaches to Spain.

These negotiations had begun in December, 1586, with the

---

[1] *Venetian Cal.*, viii., 250; *Spanish Cal.*, iv., 26.
[2] *Spanish Cal.*, iv., 24, 29-30.

object of tempering Philip's indignation or of disconcerting CHAP.
his measures for revenge. In March, 1587, it was reported at XXI.
Madrid that he would refrain from attacking Elizabeth if she
would abandon the Dutch.[1] But, wrote the Venetian ambassador there, "all that woman's negotiations for an accord are
merely a ruse to keep the minds of the Spanish in uncertainty
and to throw them into confusion, as has happened; for the
news that Drake was preparing an armament in Plymouth had
hardly reached Spain when it was followed by the news that
he was off the coast with forty-two sail".[2] Drake had weighed
anchor on April 2 with orders to prevent the concentration of
Philip's forces. Contradictory instructions were immediately
despatched; but they do not prove that Elizabeth had changed
her mind. They were merely *pièces justificatives*, designed to
smooth her dealings with Parma and to prove her innocence of
Drake's exploits in case she were brought to book; and it was
probably with her connivance that they failed to reach Drake in
time. On April 19 he appeared before Cadiz, sank or burnt
two huge vessels of 1,500 and 1,200 tons apiece, and thirty-one
ranging between 1,000 and 200 tons, and carried off four laden
with provisions. He then seized Sagres as a basis of operations,
and reconnoitred Lisbon, where Santa Cruz was painfully fitting
out the principal Spanish squadron. He found it too strong to
force without support from land, and returned to Sagres. There
he remained till June; but the English navy was not yet sufficiently organised to anticipate the strategy of two centuries
later, and Drake was compelled to return to England, capturing
off the Azores an East Indiaman with enormous booty. "There
are many remarks current," wrote the Venetian ambassador at
Madrid, "such as that this woman has shown the world how
they can strike at the Spaniard in Flanders, in the Indies, and
in his own house; and that these injuries inflicted by Drake
will raise many considerations in the minds of other princes and
also of the king's own subjects. . . . Every one is amazed to see
how cleverly that woman manages in everything."[3]

---

[1] *Venetian Cal.*, viii., 255, 269.   [2] *Ibid.*, viii., 271.

[3] *Ibid.*, viii., 272, 273-77, 283-84; *Spanish Cal.*, iv., 74, 93, 97-98; *Domestic Cal.*, Addenda, 1580-1625, pp. 206-7; Drake and Fenner's letters quoted in *Cambridge Mod. Hist.*, iii., 304-6; *Acts of the P. C.*, 1587-88, pp. 141-43. The idea that Drake was prevented from attacking Lisbon by orders from Elizabeth is said to be without foundation, Corbett, ii., 94-95.

The lesson was not lost on James VI. and Henry III. ; the embargo which had been placed on English ships in France was raised, and diplomatic relations were resumed. But Mary's death had made up Philip's mind. James VI. was now the only claimant in the way of a Spanish successor to the English throne; and James, as Philip reminded the Pope, was debarred by heresy. Moreover, Drake's latest exploits had shown that not only Flanders and the Indies, but also Spain and Portugal, were insecure so long as England was unbridled. Sixtus V., who had succeeded Gregory XIII. in April, 1585, was reluctantly brought into Philip's plans. He could not help admiring Elizabeth: "What a valiant woman," he exclaimed, "she braves the two greatest kings by land and by sea". "If she were not a heretic," he declared, "she would be worth a whole world."[1] He would vastly have preferred her conversion by the papacy to her subjugation by Philip. But gradually he succumbed to the influence of Allen and Parsons, in whom Philip discovered the most zealous advocates of a Spanish conquest of their native land. Allen—"that great-hearted and apostolic man"[2]—designated himself as the future archbishop of Canterbury and lord high chancellor of conquered England. Parsons depicted to Sixtus the ease of the enterprise: two-thirds of England, he said, were catholic, and those the most warlike parts of the nation; various catholics had already tried and were still trying to kill the queen; 15,000 trained troops would be sufficient, as they would have nothing to overcome except an unwarlike and undisciplined mob.[3] Philip had only to go up against Ramothgilead, and the Lord would deliver it into his hands.

Sixtus doubted the spirit that spoke in the mouth of these prophets; he disliked Philip's aggrandisement on the one hand, and feared on the other that he might take papal money and then make peace with Elizabeth. Olivarez, the Spanish ambassador at Rome, fomented his apprehensions in order to stimulate his liberality. It would be easy enough, he said, for Philip to make peace with Elizabeth over the Netherlands; she was

---

[1] Albéri, *Relazioni*, 2nd ser., iv., 344; *Venetian Cal.*, viii., 345.
[2] Knox, *Allen*, pp. iv, cvi-vii.
[3] A document cited by Froude from the Simancas archives, *English Seamen*, pp. 147-56, but not mentioned in the *Spanish Calendar*.

not disinclined, and then all hope of a papal restoration in
England would vanish for ever.[1] Negotiations were, in fact,
proceeding with Alexander of Parma; and Elizabeth was
tempting him to set up an independent principality for himself,
a solution which offered her many attractions.[2] The proposed
marriage between Parma's son and Arabella Stuart was less
agreeable; and there is no reason to doubt the duke's loyalty
to Philip, who had ceased by this time to trust Elizabeth's
diplomacy. Mary's execution was an affront which neither he
nor the pope could ignore; and after tedious haggling Sixtus
promised to pay a million crowns as soon as the Spaniards
landed in England, and to confirm Philip's choice of a candidate for the English throne. To promote the enterprise he
made Allen a cardinal in August, 1587, and in the following
year he despatched a brief revoking the temporary licence to be
loyal with which Campion had comforted the English catholics
in 1580.[3] For his part Philip invited contributions from
Italian princes and wrung them from his Spanish subjects; the
pulpit and the confessional were set to work to counteract the
feeble protests of the cortes and town-councils; and a tax,
called "the millions," was levied on imported food.

Drake's raid on Cadiz had, however, postponed the sailing
of the Armada, in 1587, and a further delay was caused in
January, 1588, by the death of its appointed commander, Santa
Cruz. His successor was the Duke of Medina Sidonia, who
had never yet commanded a ship, much less a fleet. A duke
was chosen because the divisional commanders would serve
under no one of lesser rank; and a soldier was preferred to a
sailor because military art in Spain had not yet adapted itself
to the sea. The Armada carried thrice as many soldiers as
sailors; and the sailor's business was simply to bring the
soldier to hand-grips with the enemy by grappling his ship and

---

[1] Knox, pp. lxxiii-lxxxv, 251-61; *Spanish Cal.*, iii., 560-69, 593-95, 618-22,
657-60; iv., 116-18.

[2] *Hatfield MSS.*, ii., 301, a document assigned by the editor to 1579, although it contains a reference to "the late prince of Orange"; *cf.* Motley,
United Netherlands, 1904, ii., 611-13.

[3] All efforts to trace the bull, by which Sixtus V. is commonly said to have
renewed the excommunication and deposition of Elizabeth, have hitherto failed;
but on April 9, 1589, Attorney-General Popham acknowledged the receipt from
Burghley of what purported to be a copy of it, to be used in the Earl of Arundel's trial (*Domestic Cal.*, 1581-90, p. 590; *cf.* Knox, p. lviii).

turning the decks into a field of battle, commanded by castles, fore and aft. In social rank, in official dignity, and in fighting importance the sailor was subject to the soldier on the sea. Feudal traditions hampered the English service also: men were still made commanders because they were lords; and no one except a lord could be lord high admiral. Drake could not aspire to the command of England's navy, and it was a concession to new ideas when he was made vice-admiral to Lord Howard of Effingham. Howard, however, had devoted himself to the service of which he was the official head; although no genius, he was a competent seaman, and he had the good sense to act on Drake's advice.

Moreover, military caste in England was not what it was in Spain; the successful pursuit of her vocation on the sea had produced some effect; and her fleets were not commanded by soldiers. Her ships were the fighting units at sea; and their armament, their sailing qualities, the seamanship of their captains, and the gunnery of their crews were the factors upon which England relied for success. In actual tonnage there was little to choose between the rival forces; but in weight of gun metal, in accuracy of aim, and in nautical skill the English had a decisive superiority. Howard's force was the most formidable fleet that had ever sailed the sea; and its commanders had no doubt of their capacity to beat the Spaniards. "The Englishmen," wrote the Venetian ambassador at Madrid, "are of a different quality from the Spaniards, bearing a name above all the West for being expert and enterprising in all maritime affairs, and the finest fighters upon the sea. . . . They have no fear that their enemy will be able to come near the English shores."[1] Practical men took a different view from that of Parsons: in March Medina Sidonia reported to Philip that the Armada was unfit to sail; in May, when it did get to sea, it was scattered by a storm and driven to refit in Spanish harbours; and its commander urged Philip to abandon the enterprise.

The winds, however, were no kinder to the English. With infinite difficulty Drake had persuaded Howard and the government that "the surest way to meet with the Spanish fleet is upon their own coast or in any harbour of their own, and

[1] *Venetian Cal.*, viii.; Corbett, ii., 163.

there to defeat them ". Twice the English made the attempt, but were blown back by south-west gales into Plymouth Sound. A third effort with a north wind followed on July 7-9; but the favouring breeze turned to a head wind before they reached the Spanish coast.[1] The south-west gales which had kept them back, had also held up their victualling ships in the Thames and the Downs; and they were provisioned only for a few days. They had no choice but to run back to Plymouth to revictual; and the wind which carried them along brought the Armada within sight of England on the 19th.[2] No one seems to have anticipated this obvious possibility. The main object of the English had been to secure the weather-gauge, and that advantage had now fallen to the Spaniards, while Drake and Howard were bottled up in Plymouth Sound. But the Spaniards let their opportunity slip; during the night the English fleet was painfully warped out of its dangerous position; some ships stood across the Spanish front towards the south, and then tacked north-west; others got west between the Spaniards and the shore, till both detachments had regained the weather-gauge and forced the Spaniards past the entrance to the Sound.

The nine days' fighting which followed in the Channel was the first great conflict under sail; but there was little in the nature of a modern naval battle. The English commanders had won experience and fame in handling individual ships or groups; but they had not yet learnt the art of scientific fleet manœuvres, and even Drake's freebooting habits once got the better of his sense of discipline.[3] It has been contended that the English tactics were based on the " close-hauled line-ahead " formation, which was the natural corollary of broadside gunnery; but, while the confusion of the accounts renders it impossible to speak with confidence, it seems improbable that this conception ruled the tactics of the fleet as a whole. Drake may have used it in the squadron he commanded; but unity of design is hardly traceable; and " groups ahead " would appear to be the nearest approach then made to the " line ahead," while the Spaniards approximated to the new ideas to the extent of substituting " groups abreast " for the old " line abreast ".

---

[1] State Papers, Dom., ccxii., 57; Laughton, *Defeat of the Spanish Armada* (Navy Record Society), i., 263; Corbett, ii., 169-71.
[2] State Papers, Dom., ccxii., 80.   [3] *Ibid.*, ccxiv., 63, 64.

Tactics were in a transitional state; and the accounts would
have been less confused, had the English fleet acted on any
clear tactical principle. As it was, the commanders confined
their efforts to heading the Spaniards off the English shores,
and plucking their feathers, as Howard expressed it, one by
one. They pounced upon a lame duck whenever there was a
chance, but sheered off when supports arrived, because they
could not afford to close with the Spaniards who, wrote Raleigh,
had an army aboard them, while Howard had none.[1]   They
thought perhaps that they could grapple and master the English
ships; but when they found that superior English seamanship
and faster sailing vessels made this impossible, they simply
strove to join hands with Parma off Dunkirk, and sought protection in their close formation, undisturbed by storms.

Even so, they were severely handled by their nimble and
elusive enemy who could sail much nearer to the wind and
thus escape pursuit.   Two of their "capital" ships were
crippled and taken on the 21st;[2] and on the 23rd they
failed to retaliate off St. Alban's Head, when the temporary
isolation of Frobisher gave them the opportunity.   On the 25th
they were beaten off Dunnose Point, and the design which
they appear to have formed of landing on the Isle of Wight
was frustrated.[3]   Thence they ran without further molestation
to Calais roads, where they anchored on the 28th.   Howard
and Drake, whose forces had grown as they sailed up the
Channel, now effected a junction with Winter and Lord Henry
Seymour, who were guarding the Downs and the mouth of
the Thames; and after nightfall on the 28th they sent eight
fire-ships up with the tide and the wind to the Spaniards'
anchorage.   They succeeded where the fleet had failed; the
Spaniards slipped their cables in a panic, and drifted in disorder off to Gravelines.   The English chance had come at the
crisis of the struggle.   Parma was looking for the Spanish
fleet to cover his embarkation; it came seeking for the protection it had lost by its disarray.   Yet now, if ever, the Spaniards
must make a stand; they had reached their appointed goal, and
must abandon either their earlier tactics or the junction with
Parma upon which their success depended.

[1] Laughton, vol. i., p. lxvi.
[2] State Papers, Dom., ccxiii., 13, 27, 42-43, 47; ccxiv., 42; ccxv., 36.
[3] Ibid., ccxiii., 49.

Their commander made a brave attempt to bear up against the wind and the enemy ; but a third of his ships were too far away to the leeward to beat up to his assistance, and on the 29th he fought the one general action of the campaign with all the odds against him. Howard, indeed, was seduced, as Drake had been a week earlier, into hunting a prize when he should have been seeking battle ; but the rest of the English captains, led by Drake, attacked the Spaniards in force. For eight hours the conflict raged, the Spaniards striving to keep intact by close formation, and the English to isolate and disable individual ships and to thrust the windward vessels back.[1] The victory was won by superior seamanship and gunnery ; the Spanish fleet was not destroyed, but four ships were sunk and others were taken or rendered useless hulks ; and Medina Sidonia was driven from the point of dangerous contact with Parma. A west-north-west wind nearly blew him on the Zealand sandbanks ; and avoiding them, he was glad to escape northwards unmolested by the English.

Elizabeth had provided exceptional supplies, but the expenditure of powder and shot at the battle of Gravelines had been unprecedented ; and lack of ammunition, and the condition of the ships and crews, rather than rising storms, forbade the pursuit of the relics of the Armada.[2] The weather, which had favoured it until Gravelines, now completed its confusion ; nineteen ships were wrecked off Scotland or Ireland, and the crews who got to land were for the most part butchered by Irish natives or by English officials ; for thirty-five ships the Spaniards themselves could not account. The loss of life was incalculable ; the Irish secretary, Fenton, wrote to Burghley that on a five miles' walk along the coast of Sligo he had counted 1,100 Spanish corpses. Providential intervention by the winds was alleged by English writers in order to score a theological point over their defeated enemies ; and the legend *Flavit Deus et dissipati sunt*, by which the victory was commemorated on English medals, ignored the fact that the Spaniards were wrecked because they lacked seamanship, and because their vessels had been rendered less seaworthy than ever by the English guns at Gravelines.

[1] State Papers, Dom., ccxiii., 64-67, 71-73, ccxiv., 2-3, 7, 17, 22-23, 27; *Spanish Cal.*, iv., 370-72, 375-79, 382-84, 390-404, 422-24, 440-49.
[2] State Papers, Dom., ccxiv., 39, 43, 47-50, 53, 65-66, ccxv., 40-41, ccxvi., 3.

Neither the principles nor the effects of sea-power were appreciated by the government. Elizabeth wondered why so few Spaniards had been boarded and so few prizes taken ; and ten days after the Armada had been beaten in the decisive battle she went down to the camp at Tilbury to animate her hasty levies against Parma's threatening troops. They might have made as stout a fight as the Dutch burghers against the veterans of Spain ; but neither their bravery nor their military skill was put to that searching ordeal. Parma, albeit no seaman, knew that it was madness to attempt an invasion without the command of the sea ; and the Armada was hardly out of sight when he wisely returned to his task of fighting the Dutch. He could only get out at spring-tide, when the weather was fair, and when the Dutch blockade had been raised by superior naval force—three conditions, the coincidence of which had now been rendered impossible.

Nevertheless the defeat of the Spanish Armada marks the beginning and not the end of the war, which out-lasted Elizabeth's reign. Philip was as slow to acknowledge defeat as he had been to engage in war ; and he stubbornly set to work to recreate on a sounder basis his shattered naval power, and to reconstruct on saner principles his plans for Elizabeth's humiliation. The conquest of England at one great stroke was seen to be impracticable, and the war was reduced to the more normal level of hostilities between nations not unevenly matched, seeking to cripple rather than to annex their rivals. Philip would at any time have probably been content to abandon the pose of champion of the Roman catholic church and avenger of Mary Stuart, which was forced on him by catholic public opinion, in return for Elizabeth's desertion of the Dutch and abstention from attacks on the New World. He can have hoped for nothing better after 1588, and his designs on England were limited to attempts to seize some English port as a basis of operations. For his energies, which had momentarily been concentrated on England in 1588, were for the rest of his reign once more divided between England, France, and the Netherlands ; and the war became a European, rather than a national, struggle against Spain.

This change hinged upon developments in France, where Henry III. was ground to powder between the upper and nether millstones of the Guises and the Huguenots, and national independence was far more precarious than in England.   At Coutras in October, 1587, Henry of Navarre had led the Huguenots to their first victory in a pitched battle against the royal troops ; and on the " Day of Barricades," May 11, 1588, Guise and Paris between them reduced the king to impotence.   But for the defeat of the Spanish Armada he might have capitulated to Philip and the Catholic League.   As it was, he had Guise assassinated on December 23, and his brother the Cardinal executed on the 24th ; and then, to save himself from the fury of the catholics, he made his peace with Henry of Navarre in April, 1589.   Catherine de Médicis had died on January 5, and Henry fell a victim in his turn to the dagger of Jacques Clément on August 2.   Navarre was acknowledged as Henry IV. by the Huguenots and *politiques ;* but for eight years he had to fight for his crown and for the national independence of France against the Catholic League and Philip of Spain. Elizabeth could now intervene with her royal conscience clear. Philip was impugning the divine hereditary right of kings; Cardinal Bellarmine, as Filmer expressed it later, was " looking asquint" in the same direction as Calvin ;[1] and the League at Paris anticipated, in the interests of Spain and of the Roman catholic church, the political doctrines, the lawless expedients, and the sanguinary horrors of the Revolution of 1789.

Meanwhile English sailors had been impressed by the limitations rather than by the magnitude of their success. The capacity for resistance possessed by a close pack of Spanish ships had exceeded their expectations, and they had no desire to see another Armada in the Channel.   The government set itself to the task of devising preventive measures. These were of three kinds : to cut the root, which nourished Spain's ambition, by intercepting its treasure-fleets from the Indies ; to destroy the shipping in Spanish ports before it could sail ; or, as Cobham had written in 1579, to make another Netherlands of Portugal.   This last design was mooted in September, 1588, before the Armada had left British waters. Its success depended upon the accuracy of the reports which Don Antonio and other Portuguese exiles poured into Elizabeth's ears.   Probably there was little hope of Antonio's estab-

---

[1] Filmer, *De Patriarcha*, c. 1.

lishment on the throne of Portugal; but it would be enough
for England's purpose if his country were plunged in civil war,
or even if a few places could be strengthened to defy the
Spanish king; and the success of the Dutch at Brille might
become a precedent for a sixteenth century Torres Vedras.

The comparison was, however, fallacious; there was no
such national and religious antagonism between Spaniards and
Portuguese as between Spaniards and Dutch; and the expedition, which sailed in April, 1589, under the military command
of Norris and the naval command of Drake, lit no national
revolt in patient Portugal, although it carried a force stronger
by thousands than any Elizabeth had sent to the Netherlands. Cupidity also marred its purpose: it was fitted out
as a joint-stock enterprise, partly designed to recoup the adventurers for their expense in defeating ʼthe Spanish Armada;
and its first act was an attempt to plunder Coruña. "We
left there," wrote Don Antonio, "and disembarked at Peniche,
where the strong wines of the country increased the sickness
of the men; and when we arrived before Lisbon, there were
not enough men fit to attack a boat. . . . We were short of
powder and firematch, and we had no artillery battery. Drake's
fleet remained at Cascaes, and refrained from entering the
river."[1] Lisbon was vigorously defended by the Cardinal
Archduke Albert, who, said Henry IV., was a good general
though nobody would believe it; and the expedition returned
with hardly one-sixth of its men efficient.[2] An inquiry was
held on the conduct of the commanders; and Drake remained
under a cloud for nearly six years, while his ambitious plans
of naval warfare were exchanged for the more cautious policy
of preying on Spanish treasure-ships.

The Earl of Cumberland had, indeed, with one great ship,
the *Victory*, and a few privateers done more to please Elizabeth
than had Drake's elaborate force. He seized Fayal in the
Azores and held it to ransom; captured a number of prizes
at sea and cut others out from under the Spanish guns; and
maintained his position all the summer, narrowly missing the

---

[1] *Spanish Cal.*, iv., 553-54. On Drake's alleged disobedience to Elizabeth's
orders, see Corbett, ii., 308-9, and *Successors of Drake*, p. 2; State Papers,
Dom., ccxxii., 89, 90; ccxxiv., 50, 53; ccxxv., 15.

[2] *Spanish Cal.*, iv., 549; State Papers, Dom., ccxxvii., 32, 35. Drake is described as "being in disgrace" in 1590, *ibid.*, ccxxxi., 94, and ccxxxv., 23.

East and West Indian treasure.   But Hawkins and Frobisher,
who were sent out in 1590 to repeat and improve on the
earl's exploits, achieved comparatively little; and the immunity of Philip's harbours from attack during the years
which followed the Armada enabled him to build a navy
of fighting ships.   When in 1591 Lord Thomas Howard and
Sir Richard Grenville again sought the Azores, a powerful
fleet was sent to meet them.   Howard escaped without great
difficulty; but Grenville in the *Revenge* was too proud to obey
orders to retreat, and fought for fifteen hours against fifteen
Spanish men-of-war, refusing to surrender, and dying himself
of his wounds a few hours after his capture.   He was a magnificent barbarian who hunted Red Indians for amusement,
treated Spanish prisoners as slaves, and ate wineglasses out of
bravado; and his splendid bravery resulted in the loss of the
only English warship taken in Elizabeth's reign.[1]   Yet, like
Sir Edward Howard in 1513,[2] he added lustre to England's
renown by his defiance of all the rules of scientific warfare.
Equally heroic and more successful was the fight fought that
year by Robert Bradshaw in the *Centurion* and her little con-
sort the *Dolphin* against fourteen Spanish galleys; the *Dolphin*
was blown up to avoid surrender, but six Spanish captains
were condemned to death by their government in order to
embolden others.

For the next five years Elizabeth pursued a cautious policy.
Leicester had died on September 5, 1588, Sir Amias Paulet
three weeks later, Sir Walter Mildmay in 1589, and Walsingham on April 6, 1590.   All had favoured aggression, and had
championed Drake against the more conservative school of
politicians represented by Burghley.   Only two members were
admitted to the privy council in their places, Sir John Fortescue
as chancellor of the exchequer in 1589, and Sir Robert Cecil
as secretary on August 2, 1591.   The result was to give the
cautious party complete control of the government;[3] but it is
misleading to represent the issue as one between war and peace.

---

[1] Raleigh, Introduction to *Hakluyt*, pp. 68-69; *Spanish Cal.*, iv., 220; *Dict.
of Nat. Biogr.*, xxiii., 123; Corbett, ii., 359-62.

[2] See vol. v., p. 180.

[3] State Papers, Dom., Addenda, xxxi., 147 (8), xxxii., 7.   Burghley performed
the duties of secretary and "almost all other places" between Walsingham's
death and Robert Cecil's appointment.

The alternatives were rather a naval colonial and a continental
military war ; and this divergence continued to divide opinion for
more than a generation.[1] Nor can we be sure that Burghley and
the queen were wrong ; it was more essential for England that
France and the Netherlands should be saved from Spanish
control than that England should burden herself with a
colonial empire, the weight of which she was not yet strong
enough to bear.

Elizabeth liked to help those who helped themselves, and
both the Dutch and the Huguenots showed remarkable efficiency at this time. The outlook in the Netherlands seemed
darkest when the Spanish Armada relieved the pressure and
diverted Parma from his proper task. Oldenbarneveldt seized
the opportunity to organise the Dutch Republic, while William's
son, Prince Maurice, trained Dutch troops until they could
meet the Spaniard in the field, and developed a science of military engineering which baffled even Parma. Peregrine Bertie,
Lord Willoughby de Eresby, had been left in command of the
English contingent when Leicester withdrew in 1587, and he
with his lieutenants, Sir Francis Vere, Sir Roger Williams, Sir
Thomas Morgan, Sir John Norris, and others, saved Bergen-
op-Zoom against which Parma had turned on the dispersal of
the Armada. But many of the English officers and men were
required in September, 1589, to make up the 4,000 troops which
Elizabeth was sending under Willoughby to the assistance of
Henry IV.[2] They landed at Dieppe, and after accompanying
the king to his futile attempt on Paris, assisted in the reduction
of Le Mans, Alençon, Falaise, and Honfleur. They returned
home early in 1590, too soon to participate in Henry's victory
at Ivry on March 14 ; and only Williams and a handful of
English were present at the siege of Paris which was raised by
Parma in September.

Parma's diversion from the Netherlands enabled Maurice,
with the assistance of Vere, who had succeeded Willoughby,
to recover Zutphen, Deventer, Hulst, and Nimeguen in 1591.
But Philip's efforts to gain control of France alarmed Eliza-

---

[1] See vol. vii., pp. 117-18.

[2] *Domestic Cal.*, 1581-90, pp. 616-18, Addenda, 1580-1625, pp. 282-85 ; Camden, iii., 607-11 ; De Thou, ed. 1621, iv., 752 ff. ; Sully, *Mémoires*, 1822, i., 273.
Elizabeth also lent Henry £22,000.

beth.   In 1590 Blavet was surprised by the Spaniards, with CHAP.
whose support the Guise Duke of Mercoeur hoped to estab- XXI.
lish a petty sovereignty in Brittany; and in 1591 Elizabeth
undertook to send 3,000 troops against him.   They landed
under Norris at St. Malo on May 5, and won several engage-
ments with the Spaniards and troops of the League.   Two
months later, a portion of the force was transferred to the Earl
of Essex, who had been sent with 4,000 men to assist Henry
in his attempt to recover Rouen, an enterprise which Elizabeth
with an eye to her own interests had pressed upon the French
king.[1]   Once more, however, Parma intervened; he relieved
Rouen in April, 1592, and escaped the trap set for him by
Henry; and Norris had in the autumn to abandon Brittany
to Mercoeur.   This was Parma's last service, and he died at
Brussels in December, under sentence of recall by his ungrateful
sovereign.

It was clear by this time that France as a whole would
tolerate neither a Huguenot king nor the Spanish Infanta;
and, in order to secure the crown and save France from a per-
petuation of civil war, Henry in July, 1593, consented to receive instruction in the catholic faith.   Elizabeth, who had
received similar instruction during her sister's reign, was loud
in her virtuous indignation, and wrote Henry letters as lofty
in tone as those she addressed to Anjou when he accepted the
sovereignty of the Netherlands.   But she was not blind to the
Spanish danger on the other side of the Channel, and in September she once more sent Norris with an English army to expel the Spaniards from Crozon.   Henry, however, was too much
occupied in securing Paris to co-operate in Brittany; and not till
November, 1594, was Brest saved by the capture of Crozon
with the help of ten ships under Frobisher, who was wounded
in the operations and died at Plymouth early in 1595.

Henry IV. was now seated on the throne of France with a
power no French king had enjoyed since the death of Henry
II.   The League gradually dissolved, leaving only a Spanish
faction; the Jesuits were expelled in the autumn of 1594; and
in January, 1595, Henry, assured of English and Dutch support, formally declared war on Spain.   The catholic convert at

[1] See the journal of the siege printed in *Camden Miscellany*, vol. i. (1847),
and *Engl. Hist. Rev.*, xvii., 527-37.

length imposed on France Coligny's foreign policy. Elizabeth, too, resumed her naval aggression, and in 1595 those old companions in arms, Hawkins and Drake, sailed on their last crusade against the Spanish Main. Their reappearance was partly due to the rising influence of Essex, which in its turn was favoured by the change in the European situation. Essex was the political heir of Leicester, Walsingham, Knollys, and Sidney; his mother, the daughter of Sir Francis Knollys, married Leicester as her second husband, and Essex himself married Walsingham's daughter who was Sidney's widow. In 1591 it was said of him that he "was like enough, if he had a few more years, to carry Leicester's credit and sway"; and he had ventured to press for Davison's restoration to the secretary-ship against Sir Robert Cecil's claims.[1] He had succeeded Leicester as master of the horse in 1587, though only twenty-one, had been given the Garter in 1588, and made a privy councillor in 1593; and in 1594 he strengthened his hold on Elizabeth's favour by detecting an alleged plot of Dr. Lopez, her Portuguese physician, to poison the queen.[2] His wayward and passionate nature had been disciplined by no political apprenticeship; a spoilt child of fortune, he owed his rapid advancement less to his merits than to his birth and Elizabeth's favour; and it is doubtful whether his adventurous policy was suggested by political insight or merely by youthful impatience. In either case he reflected in 1595 a popular demand for more heroic warfare than the operations of the last few years; and volunteers flocked to Drake's standard when he once more received a royal commission to fly at Philip's throat.

The campaign was misconceived and mismanaged from the first. Hawkins was old, cautious, and distrustful of his impetuous and domineering colleague. Doubts about the policy of the expedition, and defects of organisation delayed it till the summer; and then in July the Spaniards raided Penzance and other Cornish townships. Elizabeth wondered whether, in view of Philip's improved navy and designs on both

---

[1] *Domestic Cal.*, Addenda, 1580-1625, p. 320.

[2] Lopez had certainly been concerned in a design against Don Antonio's life, and had long been in communication with Spanish spies (see *Spanish Cal.*, vol. iv., *passim*); but independent corroboration of his plot against Elizabeth is lacking, and his real object was possibly to make money out of Philip, see *Engl. Hist. Rev.*, ix., 440 ff.; and *Jewish Hist. Soc. Trans.*, vi. (1908), 32-55.

sides of the Channel, it was wise to send a fleet across the
Atlantic.   For Drake was not seeking to save England; he
was going for gold, and his ships were manned for raids on
shore rather than battles on sea.   He failed to perceive that the
effect of his early successes in the West Indies had been, as
Monson expressed it, "to waken rather than weaken" the
Spaniards.   Only in a surprise lay any hope of success;
and weeks were wasted in a futile attack on the Canaries.   It
was not till November 12 that he reached Puerto Rico, which
had been warned and placed in a state of defence.   Hawkins
died that afternoon; but the ill-success, attributed to the
divided command, was not repaired when Drake had sole control.   A rash attempt to fire the Spanish fleet at night under
the guns of the enemy's fort was repulsed with serious loss;
and Drake sailed off to burn Rio de la Hacha and Santa
Marta, and then to sack Nombre de Dios.   But a force he
sent across the isthmus to plunder Panama was driven back,
and for a month longer he hung about the Mosquito Gulf,
baffled by adverse winds, while his men were decimated by
dysentery.   At length he sickened himself, died on January 27,
1596, and was buried at sea off Puerto Rico.   His second in
command, Sir Thomas Baskerville, brought the remnants of the
expedition back to England, after beating off the Spaniards
near Cuba.

Drake's expedition had represented a reversion from the
admiral to the buccaneer; and the capture of Calais by the Spaniards in April, 1596, proved the futility of his campaign as a
design to divert attacks from the English Channel.   Nor had
Raleigh's voyage of discovery up the Orinoco in 1595 been suggested by naval strategy.   But the government was meditating
a serious effort to repeat Drake's soundest experiment in naval
warfare, and to paralyse Spain's activity by a blow at the heart.
Cadiz was to be seized, and if not permanently held, the shipping, docks, and stores were to be destroyed.   The Dutch were
induced to join in the scheme; Vere was summoned from
the Netherlands; and the command-in-chief was divided
between Howard and Essex, with Raleigh as their principal
lieutenant.   Cadiz was practically defenceless when the English fleet hove in sight on June 18.   The galleys escaped up
the river Guadalquivir to San Lucar; but two rich galleons

were captured, and the rest of the shipping was burnt by the
Spaniards to prevent its seizure by the English. Cadiz itself
was taken by assault and held to ransom. Essex wished to
retain possession of the city; but his colleagues feared Elizabeth's wrath if they exposed him to any risk. He refused to
yield the post of honour and of danger to any other officer;
and soldiers and sailors alike were anxious to get home
with their booty. Cadiz was therefore burnt and abandoned.
Further spoil was secured at Faro on the return, and Essex
carried off the bishop's library which is now in the Bodleian at
Oxford. The keener members of Howard's council pressed
for an attack on the Azores, which might have brought Philip
to his knees; but plunder had demoralised the expedition, and
every vessel raced for home.

The capture of Cadiz has been called the Trafalgar of
Elizabeth's contest with Philip;[1] it was certainly the last
great operation of the war. Its conduct had been disfigured
by many defects; but it proved Philip's inability, not merely
to challenge England's command of the sea, but to protect his
greatest ports from outrage. He was goaded by the disgrace
into attempting retaliation with a crazy fleet sent out in
October under the Adelantado of Castile; but a storm dispersed it before it had left Spanish waters, and Philip had to
repudiate his financial obligations. In 1597 a projected attack
by Essex on Ferrol miscarried, and in the same year the earl
was equally unsuccessful in his "Islands voyage" to the
Azores, where he missed the Spanish treasure *flota* by a few
hours. His failures were not so pitiable as Philip's; a third
Armada, destined for Ireland, had sailed while Essex was cruis-
ing in the Azores, but a north-east wind arose and it was
scattered. While Spanish fleets were ever at the mercy of the
winds and could never force an English fleet to fight unless it
wished, the invasion of England was a dream, which Philip
perceived before he died that he could never realise. He also
admitted in his last instructions to his son that sooner or later
Spain would have to grant the English that share in the commerce of the New World for which they fought with such
determination. In 1586-88 Thomas Cavendish had followed
Drake round the globe, plundering the Spaniards in the

[1] Seeley, *Growth of British Policy*, i., 235.

Pacific with even greater success ; in 1593-94 Richard Hawkins CHAP.
burnt Valparaiso, though he was captured after a stubborn XXI.
fight ; and in 1598 the Earl of Cumberland sacked Puerto
Rico which had defied Drake two years before.

Philip died on September 13, 1598. He had already
laid down part of his burden and abandoned some of his
ambitions. The Netherlands, in actual or potential possession,
were sundered from the dominions of Spain, and erected into
a separate sovereignty for the Archduke Albert and his wife
the Infanta Isabella. France was left to Henry IV., and
Calais and Blavet were restored by the peace of Vervins which
was concluded in May, 1598. Elizabeth sent Sir Robert Cecil
and Sir Thomas Wilkes to protest against this French desertion
of the common cause ; but Henry declined to listen to their
remonstrances, and France was eliminated from the struggle.
England might then, as often before, have made peace without
the Dutch, whom Vere helped to win at Turnhout their first
great victory over the Spaniards in the open field ; but in spite
of the " perfidy " which, according to French historians, characterised Elizabeth's dealings with the Netherlands, it was not
she who left them to their fate in 1598. She stood staunch at
some risk to herself ; for in that year it seemed that Spain
might find in Ireland a basis of operations which Philip II.
had signally failed to discover either in England itself or in
Scotland.

CHAPTER XXII.

THE CONQUEST OF IRELAND.

IN his occasional moods of despondency Walsingham would sometimes wish that Ireland were at the bottom of the sea; and few Tudor statesmen would have regretted this solution of the Irish question, though Burghley once recommended that country as an ideal resort for puritans of the preciser type.[1] Like Calais, it was regarded as a burden which might well be relinquished but that " Ireland hath very good timber and convenient havens, and if the Spaniard might be master of them, he would in a short space be master of the seas, which is our chiefest force ".[2] From England's point of view Ireland was a nuisance which had to be borne lest France or Spain should make it a greater nuisance; and the consequences of this attitude were deplorable both for the English government and for the Irish people. " I judge them," wrote Sir William Drury in 1577, " rather enemies than subjects;"[3] and every Irishman killed was regarded as a gain, not a loss, to the state. The responsibility for the peace and welfare of their subjects, which the Tudors accepted in England, was repudiated across St. George's Channel. The Irish were excluded from the benefits of civilised administration; and Sir John Perrot in 1590 alleged the attempt of the Earl of Sussex to poison Shane O'Neill as a justification for a similar outrage on another Irish chief.

The ultimate reason for these methods of barbarism was the inability of the Tudors to effect a real subjugation of Ireland, and to establish the proper relation between the government and the governed; and this inability was financial in its origin.

---

[1] *Domestic Cal.*, Addenda, 1566-79, p. 439.
[2] Lodge, *Illustrations*, ii., 171.   [3] *Cambridge Mod. Hist.*, iii., 597.

Judged by modern standards, Elizabeth was miserably poor in fiscal and military resources; and as generosity is a virtue which paupers cannot afford, so the good government of Ireland was a blessing which she could not provide without taxing her English subjects into discontent. In these circumstances, the only adequate plea for her Irish policy is the necessity of self-defence against enemies who, without improving the lot of the Irish people, would by intervention in Ireland have endangered the peace of England. But this justification, such as it is, does not apply to the adventurers who preyed upon what prosperity Ireland possessed. " The eagles of enterprise," it has been said, "spread their wings for the Spanish Main; the vultures swooped upon Ireland." [1] The vultures and the eagles were, however, often identical; and Gilbert, Raleigh, Grenville, in fact most of those Elizabethan privateers who were landed gentry and not professional seamen, had their ventures in Ireland as well as in Spanish colonies. The difference lay in the circumstances and in the quality of their prey. With Spain they fought on fairly equal terms; it was their aim to coerce Ireland into accepting an alien rule and civilisation.

The antagonism between English and Irish dates from the beginning of English expansion across St. George's Channel; and Giraldus Cambrensis is as full of prejudice as the poet Spenser or the philosopher Bacon, who called upon the younger Earl of Essex to recover Ireland " from more than Indian barbarism ". How much English and Normans had contributed to Irish organisation and culture is a disputable question; but it would be no less rash to assume that everything Irish in the sixteenth century was Gaelic than to assume that everything English was Anglo-Saxon. England, however, gained more by the Norman conquest than Ireland by the English, because the earlier conquest was more complete, and England was never ruled from Normandy in the interests of the duchy. Ireland, on the other hand, was held in English bonds, and governed in England's interests, so far as it was governed at all; and the pressure of English aggression was only limited by the weakness of government. When the Tudors gave England the peace which enabled its trade, its wealth, and its population to expand beyond its borders, they naturally

[1] Goldwin Smith, *Irish History and the Irish Question*, p. 58.

27 *

flowed towards Ireland as well as in other directions.   It appeared as a land to be colonised and converted, a market to be
exploited, and an enemy to be reduced.   The new adventurers
differed from the followers of Strongbow as widely as the English commercial landlord of the sixteenth century differed from
the feudal baron of the twelfth.   They sought riches rather
than sovereign power, and the desire for commercial monopoly
embittered the political antagonism engendered by the growth
of national feeling and by England's failure to Anglicise Ireland ; it became the recognised object of English governments to force upon the Irish people the choice between
extermination and subjection to English ideas.   Englishmen,
no doubt, preferred the latter alternative : they were convinced that English ideas were best for the Irish people ; and
the firmness of this conviction led them to paint in sombre
colours the defects of the civilisation they wished to destroy.
It is, however, irrational to judge sixteenth century policy
by twentieth century standards ; modern conceptions could
only develop through centuries of political education, and
could only be realised through a consciousness of strength
which the England of the Tudors did not possess.

It was not till Henry VIII. had subdued the church that
he seriously turned his attention to Ireland.   The monastic
lands, with which he bribed Irish chiefs, and the coronets
which he dangled before their eyes began their estrangement
from the people, which grew as chiefs were converted into
peers and assimilated English culture.   The ruin of the
religious houses had no consolations for the Irish peasantry ;
and the protestant faith was presented to them in Edward's
reign as yet another form of the English attack upon their Irish
customs.   It was not, however, pressed with any vigour.   No
Irish parliament met in Edward's reign ; but Poynings' laws [1]
had not yet been interpreted as prohibiting the English parliament from legislating for Ireland ; and the lord-deputy, Sir
Anthony St. Leger, was instructed to enforce the first Book of
Common Prayer, which was, however, to be translated into
Latin and into Irish for those who did not understand the
English tongue.[2]   The Irish version was delayed, but Limerick

[1] See vol. v., pp. 60-61.
[2] *Cal. of State Papers, Ireland*, i., 93, 105, 108, 110; Bagwell, *Ireland
under the Tudors*, i., 349-50, 354.

and other towns expressed their readiness to use the Latin form. St. Leger himself was a moderate man, opposed alike to the catholicism of the Primate Dowdall, who was deprived for recusancy in 1551, and to the protestantism of Archbishop Browne of Dublin and of Bishop Staples of Meath, and still more to the fanaticism of Bale, who in 1552 was made bishop of Ossory. St. Leger had been succeeded by Bellingham in 1548, but he was reappointed in 1550, and again by Mary in October, 1553, after a two years' tenure of office by Sir James Crofts. Bellingham, a competent soldier, suppressed the rebellions of the O'Conors and O'Mores of Leix and Offaly, which it was proposed to plant with English settlers; and his successors were troubled by Scottish and French intrigues and by the ravages of channel privateers, with whom, to avoid a worse fate, the Irish seaports, especially Cork and Waterford, made terms.[1] But religious dissension gave the government little trouble; there were no catholic martyrs under Edward, and no protestant martyrs under Mary.

The restoration of the old faith in the autumn of 1553 was effected without the intervention of the Irish parliament. Dowdall returned to Armagh, while Bale fled, and Browne and Staples were deprived as married men. Such matters diverted neither the Irish nor their government from raids, rebellions, and hostings. In 1556 St. Leger was succeeded by Thomas Radcliffe, who became third Earl of Sussex in 1557; and he was accompanied as vice-treasurer by Sir Henry Sidney. The pope had relinquished to Philip and Mary his sovereignty over Ireland; and an effort was now begun, which lasted throughout Elizabeth's reign, to complete its subjugation. The Irish parliament, which had not met since 1541, was called together in June, 1557, to enact for Ireland the English legislation reviving the heresy statutes, repealing those against the papacy, and recognising Mary's sovereignty. A draft bill sent over from England was also passed, confiscating Leix and Offaly, and providing for their settlement by English colonists. The districts were converted into King's County and Queen's County with chief boroughs or forts at Philipstown and Maryborough. The land was to be divided between the English and the Irish; the chief of every sept was to say "how many

[1] *Irish Cal.*, i., 79-80, 83, 85-87, 91-92, 96, 100, 103, 106-7, 115.

of his sept he will answer for"; they were to "hold their lands of the fort, answer the laws of the realm as the English do, cause their children to learn to speak English, keep open the fords, destroy the fastnesses, and cut the passes. None of them shall marry or foster with any but such as be of English blood, without licence of the deputy."[1]

The act was an epitome of English policy. "Fostering with the Irish" was treason throughout the kingdom; boroughs were only incorporated on condition that they admitted no Irish, and they were expected to be able to defend themselves against those whom the Earl of Desmond described as "poor savage people".[2] The weapons of the Roman catholic church were pressed into the service of English law and order; and the queen required Sussex to suffer the primate, "without peril of the laws, to exercise and use all manner of ecclesiastical censures against the disordered Irishry". The lord-deputy himself "imprisoned certain lawyers for withstanding their Majesties' prerogative"; and complained that the "bishops and ministers under them" made their churches throughout Ireland "liker to stables for horses and herdhouses for cattle than holy places to minister with due reverence the most blessed sacraments in". In 1558 Sidney thought that Ireland would follow Calais; even the inhabitants of the Pale "be weary and irk of us"; while the "Irish sort" would assist the French or Scots, and "said plainly that Englishmen had no right to Ireland". He begged for speedy succour or recall, "for it shall be more to the queen's honour that we be called home by order than driven out with shame".[3]

Nor was there any immediate change when Elizabeth came to the throne, except that peace with France and Scotland, the improvement of the coinage, and more efficient government relieved the danger of the situation. It was not until January, 1560, that Sussex,[4] who had called one parliament to establish

---

[1] *Irish Cal.*, i., 134; R. Dunlop, "The Plantation of Leix and Offaly" in *Engl. Hist. Rev.*, vi., 61.

[2] *Irish Cal.*, i., 83, 103, 138-39; but *cf.* Mrs. J. R. Green, *The Making of Ireland*, pp. 180-81.

[3] *Irish Cal.*, i., 135-36, 140-42, 148.

[4] In virtue of his rank and "cousinship" to Elizabeth she elevated him from the position of lord-deputy to that of lord-lieutenant. Poynings had been simply deputy to the lord-lieutenant, who in 1494 was Prince Henry, aged three years; see my *Henry VIII.*, pp. 17-18.

Roman catholicism, assembled another to destroy it. The parliamentary system could not extend to the native districts
where the queen's writ did not run; but all the ten counties
in the Pale [1] and twenty-eight boroughs sent two members
each to the Irish house of commons. In the house of lords the
bishops outnumbered the temporal peers; but Elizabeth's
legislation passed without serious difficulty. The bishops were
English nominees as much as the officials who sat in the
house of commons; and only two of them, Walsh of Meath
and Leverous of Kildare, refused to acknowledge the royal
supremacy. The English ecclesiastical settlement was re-
enacted in Ireland with two modifications : bishops were to be
appointed by the queen without the electoral veil which shrouded
royal nomination in England ; and the Book of Common Prayer
might be read in Latin where no English was understood.
Elizabeth had, however, little opportunity of imposing either
the royal supremacy or the protestant religion upon the native
Irish. A manual, containing the Catechism and some articles
of religion, was compiled in Erse by John Kearney, and printed
in 1563 ; and Kearney, assisted by Nicholas Walsh, afterwards
Bishop of Ossory, also translated the New Testament and
Book of Common Prayer. The English privy council lamented
in 1587 that this translation of the New Testament had never
been printed, " partly for want of proper characters and men of
that nation and language skilful in the mystery of printing ".
It also ordered that the Book of Common Prayer should be
printed in Erse, and that a church should be set apart in the
shire-town of every diocese, where it was to be read and a sermon preached to the common people.[2] But these excellent
intentions were frustrated by ruder forces.

The lull which followed Elizabeth's accession was not
broken by religious conflict; and in the wars that did ensue

---

[1] *Viz.*, Carlow, Dublin, Kildare, Kilkenny, Louth, Meath, Tipperary, Waterford, Westmeath, and Wexford. The towns represented outside the Pale were
Carrickfergus, Cork, Kinsale, Youghal, Galway, Athenry, Limerick, Dungarvan,
and Mullingar. An interesting letter of instructions to Sussex relative to the
calling of this parliament is misdated and misplaced under 1589 in the *Hatfield
MSS.*, iii., 459.

[2] *Acts of the P. C.*, xv., 201-2 ; *Dict. of Nat. Biogr.*, xxx., 268. Kearney,
Walsh, and Archbishop Henry Ussher were all Magdalene College, Cambridge,
men. A little later the New Testament and Book of Common Prayer were
also translated into Erse by William Daniel.

the Pale and the towns outside it, although predominately catholic, sided with the English government against the native Irish. The ferocity of the struggle and the baneful permanence of its results were largely due to its agrarian character, to the determination ultimately adopted by the English government to expropriate the Irish. But that resolve was not of malice aforethought; it was only adopted as the last expedient for reducing Ireland to law and order after a variety of causes, racial, religious, and political, had made the Irish apparently irreconcilable. Henry VIII. tried persuasion; the rebellion of the O'Conors and O'Mores suggested to Edward VI. and Mary the policy of colonisation; resentment and ambition stirred other septs to war; and they naturally sought what allies they could find. Under Edward and Mary they looked to France and Scotland, under Elizabeth to Philip and . the pope. Ties of common enmity were formed between Ireland and England's foes; and the native Irish appeared in the Englishman's eyes as traitors to his country, enemies to his faith, and barbarous cumberers of the ground he wished to occupy. The antagonism was reciprocated with greater justice by the Irish; and the distressful country afforded a promising sphere for Philip's and the pope's intrigues, and a still more grateful field for the nobler labours of the missionaries of the counter-Reformation.

In such a soil seeds inevitably sown by the conflict of English and Irish ideas grew apace. Henry VIII. had in 1542 created The O'Neill Earl of Tyrone with remainder to his supposed son Matthew, who was made Baron of Dungannon. Primogeniture was, however, contrary to the law and custom of the Irish clans, who clung to the privilege of electing their chiefs. All members of the clan had a common right in its lands; and it was held that Tyrone could not surrender them to Henry. Faction was, moreover, indigenous among the O'Neills:[1] Matthew was not Tyrone's legitimate son; and, worst of all, he was feeble compared with his eldest legitimate brother Shane, who soon began to champion his own claims and Irish customs. He levied war against his father and his brothers; by 1551 their country was reduced to famine and desolation; and in 1558 Dungannon was killed. In the

[1] See the details in the *Annals of the Four Masters* and *Annals of Loch Cé.*

supposed interests of peace and economy Elizabeth recognised   CHAP.
Shane, who had been accepted by his clan and was now more   XXII.
powerful in Ulster than any O'Neill had been before. But
Shane, while declaring that "the rude, uncivil, disobedient
people"[1] among whom he dwelt would mend their ways, was
in no mind to guarantee his own good conduct ; and in August,
1560, Elizabeth authorised his subjugation and the restitution of Dungannon's son Brian. Envoys were sent to rouse
against Shane his Irish rivals the O'Donnells of Tyrconnell,
the O'Reillys of Cavan, and the Maguires of Fermanagh, the
Scottish M'Donnells of Antrim, and the Earl of Argyle ; and
O'Reilly and O'Donnell were to be rewarded with peerages.

But some of the M'Donnells "used very evil language
against the Queen, and said that the Queen of Scots was rightful heir" ; and O'Donnell fell into Shane's hands.[2] Sussex,
while ravaging his country, failed to defeat him or to procure
his assassination ; and in August the Earl of Kildare, whose
loyalty was doubtful, patched up a treaty, by which Shane
agreed to plead his case before Elizabeth in person. He
arrived in London on January 4, 1562, and made his submission two days later. But he was detained while Elizabeth
was making up her mind ; and he employed the interval to
establish relations with Quadra, who wrote to Philip that
Shane would be "a most important instrument," and permitted
him to attend mass secretly at the embassy.[3] In his absence
Shane's cousin and tanist, or successor-elect, Turlough Luineach
O'Neill, murdered the young Brian, and sought to oust Shane ;
and the government, aware of Shane's dealings with Quadra,
thought it best to send him home, where his relations with
Turlough promised to be less dangerous to the English than

---

[1] *Irish Cal.*, i., 158.

[2] *Ibid.*, i., 158, 170-72, 176; *Hatfield MSS.*, i., 181, 188, 260; *Spanish
Cal.*, i., 91, 94, 105, 109, 114, 118, 298, 370.

[3] Bishop Quadra's veracity is illustrated by these two parallel passages from
his despatches to Philip :—

"Shane O'Neill and ten or twelve of his principal followers have received the holy sacrament in my house with the utmost secrecy, as he refused to receive the queen's communion," *Spanish Cal.*, i., 235.

[Charges against Quadra] 3. "That O'Neill had taken the sacrament in my house. *Answer.* This is not true . . . I have denied about O'Neill absolutely, and asserted that he never communi- cated in my house, in order not to injure him," *Spanish Cal.*, i., 247.

his intrigues with Quadra. He was recognised as actual chieftain of Tyrone with a reservation of the rights of Dungannon's younger son Hugh, afterwards the famous Earl of Tyrone. But the sinister calculations of the government under-estimated Shane's vigour and capacity. He defeated the O'Reillys, plundered Tyrconnell, and reduced the Maguires to extremities and Turlough to conformity with his wishes. Sussex made two vain efforts to punish him in 1563, and in September Kildare negotiated another unsatisfactory truce at Drumcree.[1]

In 1564 Shane, with the approval of the English government, attacked the M'Donnells of Antrim; but the completeness of his victory at Ballycastle in May, 1565, alarmed Elizabeth. No Irish chief had wielded such power for centuries; he could, wrote Sir Henry Sidney who succeeded Sussex in 1565, put 1,000 horse and 4,000 foot into the field; he had agents at the court of Mary Stuart, who like her uncle the Cardinal of Lorraine was scheming to trouble Ireland; he was seeking aid from Charles IX. as well as from Philip; and by arming his peasantry he had called the common people to his aid.[2] In July, 1566, he felt strong enough to defy the government and ravage the Pale; and Sidney retaliated by restoring O'Donnell's authority in Tyrconnell. Shane invaded that country in May, 1567; but he was routed and fled to the M'Donnells, who, at the instigation of Captain William Piers, hacked him to pieces on June 2 at the age of thirty-seven.[3]

Shane's ruin came none too soon for the preservation of English rule, which could not have survived a national uprising. A national movement was practically impossible for a people divided into clans owning no superior authority; but the pressure of English despotism was breaking down the barriers to co-operation. In April, 1567, Sidney had arrested the Earl of Desmond for conspiring with Shane O'Neill, protecting other rebellious clans, and burning villages and destroying churches in Munster.[4] The Fitzgeralds, of whom the Earl of Desmond

[1] *Cal. of Carew MSS.*, i., 352.

[2] Sidney said he was the first Irish chief to take this step, *Dict. of Nat. Biogr.*, xlii., 211; *Irish Cal.*, i., 289, 298-99; *Foreign Cal.*, 1564-65, p. 272; Bain's *Scottish Cal.*, vol. ii. *passim*; *Hatfield MSS.*, i., 286, 339.

[3] *Irish Cal.*, i., 335.

[4] *Ibid.*, i., 330, 335, 340; *Spanish Cal.*, i., 547, 618, 630, 642.

was chief, were not "wild Irish"; and their alliance with CHAP.
the O'Neills was of evil omen, more especially as it also XXII.
betokened the entrance of religion into the strife. Most
of the Anglo-Irish were better catholics than Shane O'Neill
who, in spite of the mass in Quadra's chapel, was described
by the papal nuncio, David Wolfe, as a cruel and impious
heretic; and Desmond himself was one of the first and most
influential recruits whom the nuncio enlisted under the papal
banner.

Wolfe had been despatched from Rome by Pius IV. in
August, 1560, to resume the task which his fellow-Jesuit
Salmeron had abandoned as hopeless in 1542. He landed at
Cork in January, 1561; and his horror at the religious disorder
of Ireland was soon dispelled by the success which attended
his labours. Leinster was closed to him by the vigilance of
the government, and Elizabeth used his mission as an excuse
for refusing to receive the papal legate, Martinengo, or to send
representatives to the Council of Trent.[1] The inhospitable reception given by Ulster to Salmeron, and Shane's ill-repute
led Wolfe at first to confine his efforts to Munster and Connaught, where numbers flocked to receive absolution; but in
1564 he made his way into Tyrone, where Shane's support
was indispensable for the establishment of the Roman catholic hierarchy designed by the pope to supplant Elizabeth's
nominees. Richard Creagh, who like Wolfe was a native of
Limerick, had been papally provided to the archbishopric of
Armagh, but was arrested and confined in the Tower. Being
liberated in April, 1565, he went abroad; he returned to
Ireland in 1566, and, although he refused to absolve Shane
for hanging a priest, he received a promise of his support.
But Shane burnt Armagh cathedral, and Creagh was arrested
in Connaught in May, 1567, and imprisoned in the Tower.
He was again released in 1570 on bail, resumed his activity in
Ireland, and was once more captured and sent to the Tower
in March, 1575, where he remained till his death in 1585.[2]
His companion on his visit to Shane, Meiler Magrath, had

---

[1] *Spanish Cal.*, i., 199, 204-6; see above, p. 246.
[2] *Irish Cal.*, vols. i. and ii. *passim; Acts of the P. C.*, vii., 198, 204-5; viii.,
351-52, 355; ix., 7, 31; x., 31, 43; *Domestic Cal.*, i., 646-47; *Spanish Cal.*, i., 661.
The *Dict. of Nat. Biogr.*, xiii., 63, says Creagh "escaped" from the Tower
twice, was "acquitted" in Dublin, and died "not without suspicion of poison".

been papally provided to the bishopric of Down and Connor in 1565; but he was made Anglican Archbishop of Cashel in 1571, and, although the pope deprived him of his bishopric in 1580, he continued to run with the hare and hunt with the hounds for more than half a century.

Temptation and adversity, which rendered the establishment of a regular hierarchy impossible, stimulated the zeal of the missionaries. They were sent out in ever-increasing numbers from Louvain, Douai, and Salamanca, where they were better trained for the work of converting and uniting the Irish race than they would have been in the Irish Roman catholic university more than once suggested at that time. By spreading religion among the clans, they weakened tribal hostility and developed a national consciousness; thus they co-operated with English oppression to produce an Ireland united against the government. Of this nascent unity the understanding between Shane O'Neill and the Desmonds was one of the earliest symptoms. But it was still a feeble tendency. The Desmond Geraldines of Munster were not as the Kildare Geraldines of the Pale: Munster was distracted between the Desmonds, the Butler Earls of Ormonde, and the O'Brien Earls of Thomond; and every clan was more or less divided against itself. At Elizabeth's accession the two leading Geraldines of Munster were Gerald, fifteenth Earl of Desmond, and his cousin James Fitzmaurice Fitzgerald; and both were at enmity with Thomas Butler, tenth Earl of Ormonde. Their hostility culminated in an encounter at Affane on the Blackwater in 1565,[1] and the two earls were summoned before Elizabeth. In 1567 Sidney decided in favour of Ormonde, and arrested Desmond. A few months later Desmond's brother and deputy, Sir John of Desmond, was entrapped by the lords-justices in Sidney's absence, and sent over to London; and the field was left clear for James Fitzmaurice, a more dangerous man than either of his cousins. He procured his election as "captain" of Desmond; hanged the garrison of Tracton; seduced Ormonde's brothers as well as the Earl of Thomond and John Burke, brother of the Earl of Clanricarde; and appealed to Roman catholic and anti-English sentiment. By July, 1569, south-west Ireland was in revolt as far as Kil-

[1] State Papers, Ireland, Eliz., xii., 28; Ormonde to Cecil, February 8, 1565.

kenny; Maurice Fitzgibbon, papal Archbishop of Cashel, had CHAP.
sailed to lay the cause of Roman catholic Ireland before the pope XXII.
and the princes of Europe; and Sidney wrote that there was
rebellion all the realm over, except in the English Pale.[1] But
he had little difficulty in checking its progress, though Fitzmaurice escaped the efforts of Humphrey Gilbert and Sir John
Perrot to capture him until February, 1573, when he was
forced to sue for pardon. Desmond was then permitted to return to Munster where he raised a feeble rebellion in 1574,
while Fitzmaurice went abroad to prosecute his intrigues in
France, in Spain, and at Rome.

It was clear that the Irish could achieve little without
organised foreign support; but the growth of Roman catholic
feeling in towns like Waterford as well as in the country
improved the prospects of an invasion. Fitzmaurice's appeal
to Catherine de Médicis was not received with the eagerness
which he probably anticipated from the author of the massacre
of St. Bartholomew; and Philip II., who had in 1564 instructed
his ambassador "gently to cut short his Irish negotiations as
they were not desirable,"[2] was still in 1576 on fairly good
terms with Elizabeth. Offers of the crown of Ireland to Henry
III. and Don John of Austria were accordingly declined; but
the submission of the Irish was accepted by Gregory XIII. on
behalf of his nephew, Giacomo Buoncampagni, and the papacy
made a belated attempt as a temporal power to try conclusions
with England.[3] The military part of the enterprise was entrusted to Sir Thomas Stukeley, a brilliant adventurer who had
already served and deluded half a dozen princes, had dallied
with Shane O'Neill, Creagh, Sanders, and Allen, and had
vainly tried to persuade Philip to provide him with forces for
an attack upon Ireland, of which he styled himself duke.[4] He
had commanded three galleys at Lepanto and secured Don
John's favour. He was equally successful with Gregory XIII.

---

[1] *Irish Cal.*, i., 401, 409, 411-12. The Archbishop of Cashel is variously
called Gibbon, Fitzgibbon, and Macgibbon; probably he was uncle to Edmund
Fitzgibbon known as the "White Knight".

[2] *Spanish Cal.*, i., 370.

[3] After the excommunication and deprivation of Elizabeth the pope became,
according to papal theory, temporal sovereign of Ireland, and the later invasions
were made in his name.

[4] *Dict. of Nat. Biogr.*, lv., 123-27; Digges, *Compleat Ambassador*, p. 36.

in spite of Archbishop Fitzgibbon's denunciations, which had undermined his credit with Philip; and in February, 1578, he sailed with 600 men from Cività Vecchia. But his ships were so unseaworthy that he had to beg fresh ones from the Portuguese king, and Sebastian induced him to divert his expedition from Ireland to Morocco. There he fell, like Sebastian himself, at the battle of Alcazar on August 4.

The scheme was revived in the following year, and this time Philip lent it his unofficial aid. He was preparing to enforce his claims upon Portugal, and an invasion of Ireland would serve to parry Elizabeth's interference. Fitzmaurice, who was appointed captain-general by the pope, was allowed to recruit a motley force in Ferrol, while Nicholas Sanders as papal legate sought to fan the flames of crusading zeal. The expedition sailed on June 17, 1579, captured two English vessels on the way, and on July 16 appeared off the coast of Kerry. On the north side of Dingle Bay a detachment entrenched itself in the Fort del Ore, while another occupied Smerwick; but two galleys which followed were seized by an English fleet under Frobisher. Fitzmaurice was soon slain by his cousin Theobald Burke on his way to pay a vow at Holy Cross monastery in Tipperary; but the Desmonds rose in revolt and sacked Youghal. Ormonde and Sir William Pelham waged a pitiless war of fire, famine, and sword against the rebels throughout the winter, and by June, 1580, Desmond was reduced to extremities. But in that month Viscount Baltinglas, a lord of the Pale, rose at the head of the Leinster Irish, and defeated the new deputy, Lord Grey de Wilton, at Glenmalure; and the long-delayed Spanish reinforcements arrived at last. The rebellion, however, spread no further, the chiefs of Connaught, except the Burkes, showing no inclination to join their fellow-countrymen in Munster; and in November Grey was able to join Ormonde before the Fort del Ore, while the English ships blockaded it by sea. Two days' battery by Grey's artillery drove the Spaniards to unconditional surrender; and the six hundred troops, disowned as they were by Philip, were put to the sword as pirates. Baltinglas escaped to Spain, Sir John of Desmond was hanged at Cork, Sanders died of starvation in the woods after months of wandering, and Desmond was captured and slain on November 11, 1583. Lastly, Dermot

O'Hurley, Fitzgibbon's successor in the see of Cashel, was taken, and after torture, hanged in Dublin Castle by martial law.

The O'Neill and the Geraldine rebellions did but focus and magnify the endemic strife, in which Irish clans were generally fighting one another when they were not fighting the government; and two methods, plantation and the establishment of "presidencies," were adopted to quell disorder. Elizabeth's second Irish parliament was called in January, 1569. James Stanyhurst, who had been Speaker in 1557 and 1559, was once more elected to that office on the government's recommendation; but the session was marked by some opposition.[1] The English members were challenged as strangers and incapable of election; and the government bills for repairing churches, " erecting free schools in every shire " at the expense of the shires, and imposing a duty of £4 (Irish) a tun on Spanish and Levant wines, and four marks on French wines imported by foreigners, were rejected.[2] On the other hand, a bill attainting Shane O'Neill and vesting his lands in the crown, which is supposed to have been the principal business of the session, was passed; and parliamentary authorisation was not needed for the establishment in that year of presidential governments in the provinces of Connaught and Munster. They were separately organised for administrative and judicial purposes under a president and council; and Sir Edward Fytton and Sir John Perrot were entrusted as presidents with the duty of reducing them to English law and order.[3]

Ulster was apparently considered to be still too much out of hand for this experiment, and the forfeiture of O'Neill's lands was worth little more than the parchment on which the Act was engrossed. Sir Thomas Smith projected an English settlement at Ards, which his illegitimate son lost his life in trying to plant in 1573; and the first Earl of Essex, to whom in the same year Elizabeth granted Clandeboye (the modern county of Antrim), failed to subdue either the O'Neills or the M'Donnells, in spite of an atrocious massacre of O'Neills whom he had invited to a banquet at Belfast in October, 1574, and of

---

[1] Irish State Papers, Eliz., xxvii., 25, 44.

[2] *Ibid.*, xxvii., 12, 14-15, 48. £4 Irish = £3 sterling, see *Irish Cal.*, i., 172.

[3] This scheme had been suggested under Henry VIII., *cf. Irish Cal.*, i., 376.

an equally horrible slaughter of Scottish women and children on
the Island of Rathlin in July, 1575.[1]   Turlough Luineach succeeded in playing Shane O'Neill's part on a less ambitious scale ;
and the government came to the conclusion that the best or
least expensive plan under the circumstances was to set up
the young Hugh O'Neill, Baron Dungannon and afterwards
Earl of Tyrone, in Armagh as a check upon Turlough's designs
and a buffer between him and the Pale.

Even there the government had its anxieties.   The events
of the parliamentary session of 1569 had shown the antagonism
between the English officials and the Anglo-Irish gentry ; and
the differences came to a head on the constitutional question
of "cess".   Cess was an Irish form of purveyance aggravated
by the circumstance that the officials claimed the right to take
as much "victual of all kinds" as was needed for the troops in
the constant wars at "the Queen's price," which was kept at
its former level in spite of the general rise in prices.   The lord-
deputy took his stand on royal prerogative, and the gentry retorted with parliamentary arguments about control of supplies.
In 1576, at the instigation of Christopher Nugent, fourteenth
baron Delvin, they sent a deputation to Elizabeth, who committed its members to the Fleet, while Sidney imprisoned in
Dublin Castle their principal supporters, including Viscount
Baltinglas, Delvin's brother William, and his uncle Nicholas
Nugent, chief justice of the common pleas.   They were soon
released ; but when Baltinglas rose in 1580, Delvin was again
imprisoned with his father-in-law, the Earl of Kildare, who,
though he served against the rebels, had promised his aid
to the papal plotters.[2]   William Nugent also rebelled, fled to
Turlough, and then escaped abroad ; while Nicholas was
executed in 1582 on charges of complicity in William's
rebellion and in a plot to assassinate his judicial colleagues
Sir Robert and Sir Lucas Dillon.   The only witness against
him was a personal enemy ; and his ruin was due partly to
the Nugents' share in the constitutional agitation, partly to
the feud between the Nugents and Dillons who between them
almost monopolised high judicial office in Ireland, and partly
to the support given by the government to the newer official

---

[1] *Dict. of Nat. Biogr.*, xiv., 445-46, and authorities there cited.
[2] Bagwell, iii., 116-17.

class against their rivals who depended upon the Anglo-Irish CHAP.
gentry of the Pale. Practically the execution amounted to the XXII.
judicial murder of a judge by his colleagues on the bench.[1]

Grey, whose success in crushing the Desmond rebellion
and Spanish invasion had been tarnished by this tragedy, was
succeeded in 1584 by Sir John Perrot, formerly president of
Munster. His first object, the establishment of an Irish university in Dublin, was foiled by Archbishop Loftus who resented Perrot's high-handed methods and the proposal to use
St. Patrick's for the purpose; and it was not till 1592 that
Trinity College, Dublin, was actually founded. He was not
more fortunate in his dealings with Elizabeth's third and last
Irish parliament, which met, after an interval of sixteen years,
in April, 1585. The counties had increased to twenty-seven,
the boroughs to thirty-six, while twenty-six spiritual, and an
equal number of temporal, peers were summoned. The native
Irish were not entirely unrepresented, for two O'Reillys sat for
Cavan, and two O'Ferrals for Longford. There was the usual
contest for the Speakership: Perrot's proposal to suspend
Poynings' Act, so as to enable the Irish parliament to amend
bills without further reference to the English privy council, was
again defeated by thirty-five votes; others to substitute regular
taxation for cess were rejected; and parliament was prorogued
with a recommendation from Perrot to the queen that the
leaders of the opposition should be punished.

Its second session in April-May, 1586, resulted in the
attainder of Desmond and Baltinglas, which by confiscating
their lands promoted the plantation of Munster. Many proposals had already been made with this object, and Sidney had
worked out some of the details. In re-establishing peace in
that province, the English and the Butlers between them had
gone far towards making it a desert. In six months of 1582,
30,000 men, women, and children had perished, chiefly of
starvation, and half a million acres were the victors' spoil.
They were now to be peopled by cadets of "gentle" families,
and farmed by "undertakers". No "mere" Irish could apply
for grants or acquire lands by sale or alienation from the
planters; heiresses who married Irish husbands were to forfeit

[1] See the articles on the Nugents in *Dict. of Nat. Biogr.*, vol. xli., and on
the Dillons in vol. ii., of the *Supplement.*

their inheritance; and obligations of defence against the natives were imposed upon the landed garrison. Few of the famous gentry—Raleighs, Grenvilles, Herberts, Norrises, and others mainly from Devon—who "undertook" to civilise Munster, cared for the arduous task. "Our pretence," wrote Sir William Herbert, "was to establish in these parts piety, justice, inhabitation, and civility, with comfort and example to the parts adjacent. Our drift now is, being here possessed of land, to extort, make the state of things turbulent, and live by prey and by pay." [1] Raleigh preferred the part of "shepherd of the ocean" which his friend Spenser attributed to him; and Spenser, who was successively secretary to Grey, clerk of chancery in Dublin, and clerk of the Munster council, found inadequate solace for his sojourn among the "savage nation" he depicted in his *State of Ireland* [2] by idealising the *Faërie Queene.*

Meanwhile Perrot had imprisoned Sir Geoffrey Fenton, his chief secretary, had challenged Sir Richard Bingham, the president of Connaught, had come to blows in the council chamber with Sir Nicholas Bagnal, the marshal of the army, and had used coarse and disparaging terms of the queen. But, when in 1588 he was superseded by Sir William Fitz-william, he left Ireland in a condition of unprecedented peace. A turbulent prototype of Strafford, he owed his fate to a haughty temper and "thorough" methods of government. Multifarious charges were brought against him by personal enemies, from Archbishop Loftus downwards; and a renegade Irish priest forged a treasonable correspondence between him and Philip II. After confinement in Burghley's house, he was sent to the Tower in 1591, and condemned in April, 1592, for high treason by special commissioners who only knew that he had jeered at Queen Elizabeth, and seduced Lord-Chancellor Hatton's daughter; the sentence was not carried out, but Perrot died in the Tower in September.

The Spanish Armada affected Ireland only through the wrecks which fisher-folk regarded as a godsend. Captain Cuellar, one of the shipwrecked Spaniards, wrote an account of the "savages" hardly more flattering than the usual English

---

[1] *Cambridge Mod. Hist.*, iii., 601.
[2] Another dialogue on the state of Ireland, written by Sir Thomas Wilson is often attributed to Spenser, see *Dict. of Nat. Biogr.*, lxii., 137.

descriptions; but the Spaniards suffered almost as much from the English soldiery, and one Irish chief, Sir Brian O'Rourke, was thanked by Philip for the humanity with which he treated the castaways. Policy perhaps stimulated O'Rourke's kindly feelings towards the Spanish troops, for he was at open enmity with Bingham, the president of Connaught, who defeated him at Dromore in 1589. He fled to Scotland, but James VI. sold him to Elizabeth, and he was executed as a traitor at Tyburn in 1591. Connaught, however, was less disturbed than any other part of Ireland outside the Pale. Its successive presidents, Sir Nicholas Malby and Bingham, were men of exceptional ability; the two earls, Clanricarde and Thomond, adhered to the English; and the composition, arranged with the native Irish by Perrot in 1585, was comparatively equitable.

Far more serious trouble threatened in Ulster, where Hugh O'Neill was slowly drifting from his anchorage of neutrality between Turlough Luineach and the English government. He had served against Desmond, had sat as Earl of Tyrone in the parliament of 1585, and had yet been elected tanist to Turlough. His position in Ulster was strengthened by his marriage with Joan the sister of Hugh Roe O'Donnell, a younger but more determined man than Tyrone; and the closing of the feud between the two clans, coupled with Hugh Roe's Irish and Roman catholic enthusiasm, drew Tyrone away from the English side; doubtless he was also aware of the designs, as yet unavowed, of treating Ulster like Munster. In 1591 Hugh Roe made himself undisputed chief of the O'Donnells, and in 1593, by the resignation of Turlough, Tyrone became supreme among the O'Neills. Both chiefs set themselves to extend the limits of their authority, and they were abetted by James O'Hely, archbishop of Tuam, and Edmund Magauran, archbishop of Armagh, who, as O'Hely expressed it to Philip II., "made great efforts both publicly and privately to unite the catholics of Ireland with the object of their taking up arms for the faith and in your majesty's service against the English heretics".[1] Ireland now became the principal hope of Spain in its warfare with England; and Spanish encouragement and aid were material factors in Irish rebellions for the rest of the reign.

[1] *Spanish Cal.*, iv., 609.

28 *

The first sign of O'Donnell's activity was the rising of Hugh Maguire who defeated Sir Henry Bagnal at Tulsk in June, 1593. This reverse was retrieved four months later at Belleek by Bagnal and Tyrone, who still wore the mask of loyalty while negotiating with Philip. His relations with Bagnal had not been improved by his elopement with Bagnal's sister Mabel, whom he married, he said, "to bring civility into my household and among the country people": the civility did not include faithfulness to his wife, who fled with her griefs to Dublin, while Bagnal refused to surrender her dowry. Before the end of 1594, when Sir William Russell succeeded Fitzwilliam as lord-deputy, Tyrone's relations with Spain were suspected by the government;[1] it determined to arrest him by guile in Dublin, and to send Norris with an army into Ulster. Tyrone anticipated the attack in 1595 by taking the fort on the Blackwater and ravaging Louth as far as Drogheda, while O'Donnell captured Longford and Sligo castles, and Maguire recovered Enniskillen. Russell and Norris, who quarrelled, accomplished little in Ulster; and in 1596 a hollow peace was concluded. Tyrone still denied his intrigues with Spain, and his temporary loyalty was strengthened by the wreck of Philip's fleet off Finisterre in October.

During the winter proof of Tyrone's treason fell into the government's hands. Russell, who had been deluded by Tyrone's professions, was superseded by Lord Burgh, and Norris by Sir Conyers Clifford; and in the summer of 1597 a vigorous campaign was planned. The Blackwater fort was recovered; but Burgh died in October, and a truce was concluded until June, 1598. As soon as it expired Tyrone invested the fort and on August 14 routed and killed Bagnal, who had marched to relieve it. This battle of the Yellow Ford was the worst disaster the English encountered in Ireland during Elizabeth's reign. Clifford also was defeated by O'Rourke's son in Connaught; Viscount Mountgarret, Ormonde's nephew, joined the O'Mores and O'Conors in Leinster; Tyrone sent a force south into Munster; and within a few weeks the planters had fled to the towns, leaving their lands at the mercy of the rebels. In Connaught and Leinster as well as in Munster rival chiefs were set up in place of those who had conformed to

[1] *Hatfield MSS.*, iv., 564-65, v., 80-81.

English rule; and for the first time in Irish history the English government had to face something like a national revolt.

Essex, the head and forefront of the war party in England, was sent with 16,000 foot and 1,300 horse to prove his mettle as a commander in Ireland. He landed at Dublin on April 15, 1599; wasted the summer on a fruitless march into Munster; and in the autumn, when at last he was ordered north, made a truce with Tyrone on September 8, and hurried to England without leave in order to justify his conduct. In January, 1600, Tyrone invaded Munster in person, but showed no capacity to organise the insurrection, and returned in March to defend Ulster against Charles Blount, Lord Mountjoy, who had succeeded Essex. Mountjoy was a soldier of a different type from Elizabeth's favourite, and he was ably seconded by Sir George Carew, the new president of Munster, and by Sir Henry Docwra, who established himself on Lough Foyle, on the site of the later Londonderry, and there repulsed all the attacks of the Irish. Carew secured Cork and harried the Munster rebels, while Mountjoy carefully restored English order in the Pale in July and August, and steadily pressed Tyrone northwards in September and October. Two Spanish vessels came to his help in November, but they were only important as harbingers. In the autumn the "sugane" or "straw-rope" Earl of Desmond—as he was derisively termed—was hunted down in Munster and sent to the Tower where he died in 1608, although the appeal of his nephew, the "queen's Earl" of Desmond, who had been brought up as a protestant in England, to Irish loyalty was a pitiable failure; and in January, 1601, the rebellious O'Byrnes of the Wicklow hills were finally suppressed. In June Mountjoy reached the scene of Bagnal's defeat on the Blackwater; he was preparing for a decisive winter campaign in Ulster when news arrived that the Spaniards had landed at Kinsale in September.

The naval war with Spain had languished since 1598. Philip III. had, indeed, projected an attack in 1599; but, although this "invisible" armada provoked a remarkable effort of mobilisation on the part of the English government, the armada resolved itself into six galleys which Spinola skilfully piloted to the help of the Spaniards at Sluys. As usual, Spain let slip the opportunity provided by the Irish crisis of 1598-

1600 ; and it was only when the back of the revolt had been broken that Juan dell' Aguila was sent with thirty-three ships, 5,000 troops, and a battery of siege-guns to establish on the south coast of Ireland a focus of resistance similar to that which he had successfully maintained for five years at Blavet. Mountjoy hastened to the south ; in October the Spaniards were invested in Kinsale, and in November Sir Richard Leveson's squadron blockaded the harbour. But Mountjoy's departure had freed Tyrone and O'Donnell who rapidly marched into Munster, O'Donnell through Connaught, and Tyrone through Leinster. The Spaniards made a successful sortie on December 2 ; and on the same day Pedro de Zubiaur, who had done good service at Blavet, brought a second Spanish fleet from Coruña into Castlehaven harbour. Once more naval skill decided the issue, and Leveson annihilated Zubiaur's force. Tyrone, however, arrived on December 21, and three days later he made his attack on Mountjoy's lines. It was a disastrous failure ; one Englishman and 2,000 Irish were slain. O'Donnell fled to Spain where he died in the following year, Tyrone retreated to Ulster, and on January 2, 1602, Aguila capitulated. Leveson retaliated in June for the Spanish invasion of Ireland by destroying Spanish galleys in Cezimbra Road and cutting out a rich carrack from under the guns of the fort.[1] In the same month Dunboy Castle, where O'Sullivan Beare still defended the cause of Ireland, Spain, and the pope, was captured. Carew gradually completed the pacification of Munster, while Mountjoy and Docwra reduced Tyrone to extremities in Ulster. At the end of March, 1603, he submitted, ignorant of Queen Elizabeth's death.

Thus was accomplished the first real conquest of Ireland. It cost Elizabeth in the last four years of her reign more than £1,255,000 ; and the mere multiplication of this figure by ten to reach its modern value gives no idea of the drain on England's resources. The total revenue for those four years was £931,810 ; so that during them Elizabeth's expenditure on Ireland alone exceeded her entire revenue by more than a third, and over five years' revenue was devoted to the conquest.[2] In

---

[1] Corbett, *Successors of Drake*, cap. xv.

[2] *Domestic Cal.*, 1601-3, pp. 244-45. These figures throw some light on the charge of parsimony, which might more justly be brought against Elizabeth's

human lives it cost more than the naval war against Spain, and CHAP.
no service was so unpopular with English soldiers. The XXII.
barbarism was not all on one side, and famine and murder
accounted for English as well as for Irish losses. Ferocious
as were the methods employed, it was not the conquest itself
so much as the use to which it was put that planted roots of
future bitterness and seeds of lasting strife. England spent
millions to settle English landlords in Ireland only in the end
to spend more millions in order to buy them out; and in its
efforts to extirpate Irish septs it created an Irish nation.

parliament than against the queen herself, though she boasted of being a good
"housewife". The following estimates made in 1603 of expenses during the reign
are of interest, *ibid.*, 1601-3, p. 304.

		£
" Leith, in Scotland, 1559		178,820
Newhaven, [Havre] 1562		246,380
Rebellion in the North, 1569		92,932
Shane O'Neill's rebellion, 1573		230,440
Desmond's rebellion, 1579		254,961
Tyrone's rebellion and Kinsale		192,400
Netherlands, 1585 to 1603		1,419,596
Aid of the French King, 1591 and later . . .		297,480
Spanish Armada, Tilbury Camp		161,185
Voyages to Cadiz and the Islands		172,260

		£
Towards which charges were :—		
Clergy subsidies		440,000
Laity subsidies and fifteenths . . .		3,079,464
Lands sold		817,359 "

CHAPTER XXIII.

THE AGE OF SHAKESPEARE.

No period of English literature has less to do with politics than that during which English letters reached their zenith ; and no English writer's attitude towards the questions, with which alone political history is concerned, is more obscure or less important than Shakespeare's. A catalogue of Elizabethan authors and their works would therefore be almost as irrelevant as an enumeration of the musicians and schoolmasters, builders and antiquaries, lawyers and mathematicians, who added lustre to their age and exemplified the activity of the English mind. For by no rational process can the whole range of human versatility be brought within the sphere of political history ; and within that range few things are so far apart as Elizabethan politics and literature. Shakespeare himself, whose genius was less circumscribed than any other's, shuns the problems of contemporary politics. The literature of his age was not political ; and its political writings, except in so far as Hooker's *Ecclesiastical Polity* was political, were not literature. English political literature, which was unrivalled in the latter part of the seventeenth and in the eighteenth centuries, had not yet developed, because politics were still the affair of kings and councils rather than of parliaments and peoples. Popular consciousness was less parochial than it had been ; and the awakening sense of nationality had produced insular pride and confidence. But the passion for national independence had not yet begotten any keen desire for self-government ; public opinion seems to have been as indifferent to parliamentary questions of privilege and prerogative as it was susceptible to the literary and dramatic impulse of the age ; and Shakespeare could write *King John* without a reference to the Great Charter.

There is no discoverable connexion between political liberty and Elizabethan literature; and its common derivation from protestantism is demonstrably false. Spain clung to Rome, and yet produced Cervantes, Calderon, and Lope de Vega; Calvinistic France had no one to rival Rabelais and Montaigne; and Lutheran Germany was in the latter half of the sixteenth century an intellectual desert. To the fine arts the Reformation gave no stimulus in England; and for our portraits of English sovereigns and statesmen we have to thank the foreigners Holbein, Antonio Moro, Zuccaro, Lucas d'Heere, and Geeraerts; though singularly enough, the greatest English school of church musicians followed upon the Edwardine destruction of church bells and organs, and at the end of the sixteenth century England's music was more famous on the Continent than its literature.[1] Erasmus doubtless laid the egg which Luther hatched, but it was only one among a varied progeny. The individualistic revolt from the control of the middle ages produced renaissance as well as reformation; and the variations which it bred were manifold. Protestantism was not the parent of Elizabethan literature, but both had affinities with the renaissance. The protestant broke the bonds which lay upon his conscience, and the poet those which bound his fancy. Full rein was given to each, and each came into conflict with authority. But whereas conscience is more dangerous to governments than imagination, the state regulated religion more strictly than it did imaginative literature; and—in spite of Shakespeare's disgust with "art made tongue-tied by authority" —individualism found freer scope in letters than it did within the church.[2]

Its riotous individualism, indeed, divorced Elizabethan literature from politics, which presuppose collective action and the subordination of ideals. Moreover, men's passions are prior to their politics; they are interested in the natural man before they are in what Aristotle calls the political animal; and English men of letters produced sonnets and dramas before political

[1] See Grove's *Dictionary of Music* and the *Dict. of Nat. Biogr.*, *s.vv.* William Byrd, John Dowland, Thomas Morley, John Redford, Thomas Tallis, and Christopher Tye.

[2] The principal occasion on which the government interfered with literature was its suppression of some pages of Holinshed's *Chronicles.* See State Papers, Domestic, Eliz., vol. ccxxiv., No. 3.

pamphlets or works on social science. In the age of Shakespeare the public were attracted by the individual rather than by the society, because politics were still remote from most Englishmen's lives. The national state was the only form of society which had impressed itself on their imagination, and patriotism is the only political passion which Shakespeare deigns to express. There is political fervour in King John's taunts against pope and cardinal, in Faulconbridge's boast that England " never did, nor never shall lie at the proud foot of a conqueror, but when it first did help to wound itself," in John of Gaunt's dying apostrophe to " this precious stone set in a silver sea," and in Henry V.'s speech before Agincourt. But for the most part Shakespeare's politics are perfunctory ; the people to him are as much a mob as they are to Homer. Even in his most political plays, *Coriolanus* and *Julius Cæsar*, the people merely serve as a foil to the leading characters, who themselves are moved by rivalry and ambition with little regard to political principle. The interest in Shakespeare's battle of Philippi does not concern the fall of the Roman republic, the feuds of his Montagues and Capulets have no political meaning, and the Wars of the Roses are merely a faction fight. Politics in fact are seldom successful on the stage, because dramatic action must be prompt and individual, while the movement of political forces, like the ebb and flow of the ocean, is determined by inert and voiceless masses. Shakespeare's plays might, if his details were facts, be good biography. But they could not be that perfect history which they have been called ; because history deals with societies, and includes such matter as constitutional and economic development and the growth of ideas, which cannot be represented on the stage.

In the sphere of national action Englishmen were still content to be led by their rulers, and in other departments of politics they were hardly conscious of definite aims. Religious questions had stirred the minds of some, but to most of these religion appealed as a matter of nationality, and the rapid changes of the century can only be explained by the indifference of the majority. In spite of the acts of uniformity, churches did not fill like theatres : " Woe is me," complains an anonymous writer towards the end of Elizabeth's reign,[1] "the

[1] Brit. Mus. Harleian MS., 286, f. 102.

playhouses are pestered when the churches are naked. At the
one it is not possible to get a place, at the other void seats are
plenty." The crowds were drawn by representations of the
elemental passions of mankind, love, ambition, jealousy, cruelty,
and revenge; and the barbaric ruthlessness of much of the
Elizabethan drama reflects the natural temper of an age not
yet incrusted with civil sobriety. Its untamed youth is more
renowned for its poetry than for its prose, and for its romance
than for its philosophy.

Half Elizabeth's reign had passed before it had given signs
of any remarkable literary development, and 1579 is commonly
adopted as the beginning of the age of Shakespeare. In that
year Drake was taking the first English crew across the Pacific
Ocean, and the outburst of English literature has been connected with the expansion of English knowledge of the world
and of national activity. Doubtless peace at home and the
sense of increased security, which promoted national growth,
encouraged national literature; and patriotic impulse produced
Warner's *Albion's England*, Daniel's *History of the Civil Wars*,
and Drayton's *Heroicall Epistles* as well as a mass of chronicle-
plays and ballads,[1] and prose like Holinshed's *Chronicles*, Stow's
Annals, and Hakluyt's *Navigations*. But the connexion between national expansion and the more imaginative forms of
literature is less essential. No national movement explains the
Italian renaissance, and there is little in common between the
pale cast of Hamlet's thought and the full-blooded action of
Elizabethan sea-dogs. England's great writers were at school
while Elizabeth, her statesmen, and her sailors were carving for
their country its national career; and the influence of political
conditions upon the intellectual atmosphere, in which Shakespeare's contemporaries were bred, is a matter for psychological
speculation. Spenser, Raleigh, and Camden first saw the light
under Northumberland's rule, Sidney was godson of Philip II.,
and Kyd, Peele, and Lodge were born about the year that Calais
fell. But they grew up in happier times, and the first fifteen
years of Elizabeth's reign produced the greatest of her men
of letters. Chapman was born about 1559, Greene about 1560,
Francis Bacon in 1561, Daniel in 1562, Drayton in 1563,
Shakespeare and Marlowe in 1564, Nash in 1567, Dekker and

[1] See Professor Firth in *Trans. of the Royal Hist. Soc.*, N.S., iii., 51 ff.

Middleton about 1570, and Jonson about 1573. A younger
generation, all of whom were under twenty-four at Elizabeth's
death, began in 1579 with the birth of Fletcher. Webster
was born about 1580, Massinger in 1583, Beaumont in 1584,
and Ford and Rowley about 1585; and the fact that they
belong to the Jacobean era discounts the dependence of the
drama upon political inspiration.

The youthful genius of the Elizabethans was trained in the
classical school of the renaissance. Roger Ascham, whose
Scholemaster was published in 1570, two years after his death,
had sought to humanise the rudeness of English prose as well
as the treatment of English schoolboys; and his fellow-peda-
gogues Mulcaster, Ocland, and John Twyne were all classical
scholars and translators. At Cambridge Gabriel Harvey, who
claimed to have invented the English hexameter, sought to
impose classical traditions upon native English poetry, and persuaded Spenser temporarily to abandon rhyme. The educational influence of Cambridge was then stronger than that of
Oxford: all Elizabeth's archbishops of Canterbury, Parker,
Grindal, and Whitgift, and of York, May, Young, Grindal,
Sandys, Hutton, with the exception of the undistinguished
Piers, were Cambridge men; so were the leading puritans like
Cartwright, and the separatists Browne and Barrow, while
Lodge and Peele were Oxford's only poets. Both the Cecils
and both the Bacons, and the secretaries Walsingham, Smith,
and Wilson, came from Cambridge; and only one, Sir
John Wolley, was produced by Oxford. They were brought
up in Cheke's classical school, and Smith and Wilson
sought by means of Greek and Latin to raise the level and
fix the canons of English prose. Smith's *De Republica
Anglorum*, which, notwithstanding its title, was written in
English, is more valuable as a constitutional text-book than as
literature; and Wilson's *Art of Rhetoric*, which Warton called
the first system of criticism in the English language, is culled
from Aristotle, Cicero, and Quintilian. It went through six
editions by 1585, and his *Art of Logic* through five; both were
more popular than his translation of Demosthenes' Olynthiacs
and Philippics, although Wilson's comparison of England with
Athens, and Spain with Macedon, has, *mutatis mutandis*, had a
long-lived vogue in English politics.

Imitation is the earliest form of mental activity, and the literature of the English renaissance was at first borrowed or translated. Most of the classical authors except the Greek dramatists were translated into English prose or verse in the sixteenth century; though the translations—of Greek authors especially—were more often from French or Italian versions than from the original, and few had the merits of Chapman's *Homer*, of Harington's *Orlando Furioso*, of Fairfax's *Jerusalem* or of North's translation of Plutarch's Lives—the source of Shakespeare's knowledge of ancient history. Nor was it only from the classics that England borrowed. Italian stories and plots were freely annexed or plagiarised; French came next in popularity, but not a little was taken from Spain. This influx of foreign ideas threatened to swamp English literature as completely as Roman law supplanted indigenous custom on the Continent. Wilson protested in Edward VI.'s reign against the "strange inkhorn terms" and the use of French and "Italianated" idioms which "counterfeited the king's English". His protest was vain, for Elizabeth's Italian propensities helped John Lyly to give his artificial style the tyranny of a court fashion. In his *Euphues* he marshals his tropes and his figures with the precise elaboration and mechanical regularity which the Italian *maestro di campo* expected from his *tertia* of infantry; and, while he enriched the English language, he almost reduced style to the level of mathematical science.

Lyly's influence was felt even by the most rebellious of English writers; but when *Euphues* was published in 1579, the educational and imitative period of Elizabethan literature was beginning to wane, and the greatest poets emancipated themselves from their schoolmasters. In that year Spenser, rejecting the classical counsels of Ascham and Harvey and the foreign models in fashion, published *The Shepheardes Calendar*, the first great English poem since Chaucer; and in it he proved that English was as capable of melody and harmony as any other tongue, provided that it was not torn and twisted to fit alien moulds and metres. The pastoral form of the poem was a loose convention which enabled the characters to talk about anything they pleased so long as they were clad in shepherds' clothing. Nor is there greater unity in the *Faërie*

Queene. Spenser says he intended to write an allegory; but its interpretation is obscure from the start, and the further he proceeded, the more the allegory was lost in the romantic poetry of Spenser's dreamland. Its wealth of imagery and musical diction led Charles Lamb to call Spenser the poets' poet; he was more praised than Shakespeare by his own generation, Jonson alone dissenting; and the Spenserian stanza, which he invented, has been used on occasion by most English poets since his day.

Spenser wrote sonnets as well as *The Shepheardes Calendar* and *The Faërie Queene,* and he published eighty-eight in 1595. Sonnetteering was, indeed, a literary epidemic; it was the commonest form of literary exercise, and fashion made it insincere. Many English sonnets are simply translations; in those which are not, the feeling is often as little original; and the personal and autobiographical element in them is a varying and disputable quantity. The elder Wyatt and the Earl of Surrey introduced the sonnet from Italy in Henry VIII.'s reign, borrowing mainly from Petrarch; but their poems were first published, with others, in *Tottel's Miscellany* in 1557. Twenty-five years later Thomas Watson issued a collection under the title of *Hekatompathia, or a Passionate Centurie of Love,* in which he naïvely gives references to the authors whence he derived his passion and his methods of expressing it. But it was Sir Philip Sidney's *Astrophel and Stella,* published in 1591, that created the marvellous vogue of the sonnet. His high connexions and his chivalrous death had something to do with the influence of his literary example and his fame as a man of letters. The nobility of his mind is more remarkable than his poetic genius; and, while he is more sincere than most of his imitators, even his passion owes much to Petrarch's stimulus. Daniel, Barnaby Barnes, Lodge, Drayton, and a host of others rapidly followed suit, and some of Shakespeare's "sugred sonnets" were circulated in manuscript before 1598, though they were not published till 1609. Their poetic value has been overlaid by barren efforts to discover in them materials for the dramatist's biography. Shakespeare was less conventional and imitative than his fellow-sonnetteers, and he Englished the sonnet as much as he did the drama; but the sonnet is not necessarily any more autobiographical

than the drama, and to attempt to identify Shakespeare with
the persons in the Sonnets is hardly more reasonable than to trace his features in Othello or Macbeth. His sonnets are as various as his dramas, and they were written at very different times : some are conventional exercises (*e.g.*, cliii.-cliv.), some are satires on the conventional sonnet (*e.g.*, cxxx.), and some are genuine expressions of poetic feeling (*e.g.*, cxvi.).

In the sonnet we see native English taste struggling not very successfully against Italian and French domination. The lyric of Elizabeth's time is a far more spontaneous product, and it can hardly be explained apart from the simultaneous development of musical sense, in which England was then supreme. Its popularity was not the forced and artificial fashion of the sonnet ; many besides professional poets sought lyrical expression for their thoughts, physicians, like Thomas Campion, courtiers like Essex, and divines like the Anglican Donne and the Jesuit Southwell ; and many of their amateur productions reach the highest poetic excellence. Those whose fame is associated with other forms of poetry, generally tried their hands on lyrics as well, and lyrics are scattered throughout the plays of Shakespeare, while some of the best are anonymous. The lyric was the natural outlet of the music in young England's soul, which even in the drama demanded the rhythmic cadence of the five-foot line. Convention is not of course absent, especially in the lyrics of Greene, Lodge, and Drayton ; but in their lyrics they are less conventional and attain a higher level than elsewhere. Greene's fame rests principally on the lyrics in which his romances abound. Drayton's

Since there's no help, come let us kiss and part :

is better than anything in his *Polyolbion* or *Heroicall Epistles ;* Spenser's *Prothalamion* appeals to more people than any stanza in the *Faërie Queene ;* Lyly's *Cupid and Campaspe* is his only production still read merely for pleasure ; and Sidney's "My true love hath my heart" is more natural than his *Arcadia*. The more Elizabethan literature deals with the elements of human nature, and the less it has to do with social and political organisation, the greater it is.

The heights were scaled by the drama when it had cast off its earlier English traditions and its subservience to clas-

sical foreign examples. Its derivation is complicated and
disputed, but it certainly came from many sources, miracle
plays, mysteries, moralities, pageants, masques, interludes,
and histories; and it owed something to the classical drama,
though more to Plautus and to Seneca, whose tragedies were
frequently printed in England before Shakespeare wrote, than
directly to the Attic theatre. Surrey first hit upon English
blank verse, and in 1561 Sackville and Norton's *Gorboduc*, the
first English tragedy in that literary form, was represented at
the Inner Temple. Nicholas Udall's *Ralph Roister Doister*,
the first English comedy, was published in 1566, though it had
been performed in 1551. Neither, however, is so free from
classical traditions as *Gammer Gurton's Needle*, an English
comedy played at Cambridge in 1566. In 1566 also were
acted two translations by George Gascoigne, *Jocasta*, from an
Italian version of Euripides, and the *Supposes*, from Ariosto ;
and thenceforward the number of adaptations from foreign
models was so great that the Elizabethan drama has often
been considered an exotic transplanted to English soil. The
" histories," however—the second of the three divisions in
which Shakespeare's plays are arranged in the First Folio—
are clearly a national growth ; and the transition from the
morality to the history can be traced through Bishop Bale's
Kyng Johan, which is a morality transformed into a history
with a political purpose. Sedition takes the form of Stephen
Langton, and King John is almost as much a hero in Bale's
eyes as Henry VIII. ; needless to say, there is no glorification
of the Great Charter. The history with its personal characters
gradually superseded the morality with its abstractions of
virtue and vice. But the history was not much more dramatic than the morality, and Bale distorted facts with a didactic
and not a dramatic object. His example was followed by
Romanists under Mary, and by protestants under Elizabeth ;
and the Spanish ambassador was scandalised by plays holding
up the pope and Philip II. to derision. The real drama was
slow in developing : Lyly's plays are little more than masques,
and even Shakespeare's *Henry VIII.* almost falls into this
category.

The drama could not, moreover, be popular or national
before theatres were built. The mechanics of stage produc-

tion were developed through the court masques and street CHAP.
pageants in which the Tudors delighted : Blackfriars Theatre XXIII.
and two others were built in 1576, and Shakespeare's famous
Globe Theatre in 1599; but until 1576 plays were produced for
eclectic audiences at the universities, the Inns of Court, royal
palaces, or nobles' houses.   Indeed, after 1576 the drama was
only popularised by companies of actors under the protection
and in the service of noblemen ; legally they were rogues and
vagabonds, and but for nobles' privilege, they might have been
treated as such.   The construction of three theatres in 1576
indicates a popular demand for dramatic representation.   Possibly it was keenest or most widely spread in classes which
shared in the general quickening of intelligence, but could not
read ; men whose ear has not been spoilt by reading are always
the best listeners.   In any case this popular demand gave a
powerful stimulus to dramatic authorship, and materially influenced dramatic writing.   The votaries of the theatre had not
the taste of audiences at courts and universities for classical
and foreign compositions; and the hearers, whom Shakespeare
and his colleagues wrote to please, wanted a native art to suit
the national tongue and temperament.   Classical metres could
only satisfy those who preferred classical languages to their
own ; and so, with the help of this popular inspiration, national
feeling prevailed in the drama as in other forms of literature, in
the law, the church, and the state.

Christopher Marlowe was the first to make adequate response to the new dramatic instinct.   The son of a shoemaker
of Canterbury, he was taught there by John Twyne, who was
addicted to drink, and at Cambridge by Francis Kett, who was
burnt for heresy.   After graduating he joined a company of
actors, formed many literary friendships in London, and in
1587, at the age of twenty-three, wrote his *Tamburlaine*.   His
three other masterpieces, *Dr. Faustus*, *The Jew of Malta*, and
Edward II., followed in the succeeding three years : and then
in 1593 Marlowe was killed in a brawl at Deptford.   He was
only twenty-nine, and he had accomplished far more than
Shakespeare at that age.   Nash sneered at him as an
" alchemist of eloquence," and Marlowe himself boasts of his
" high astounding terms ".   His sonorous rhetoric is monoton-
ous ; but he transmuted the iambic of Surrey and of the authors

CHAP.
XXIII.

of *Gorboduc* into the " mighty line " of the Shakespearean drama, and clothed verse in a form in which Elizabethan audiences never tired of hearing it declaimed.   In matter, too, he hit the popular taste, and *Tamburlaine* is instinct with the spirit of conquering imperialism :

> Give me a map ; then let me see how much
> Is left for me to conquer all the world.

Marlowe at least had been moved by the deeds of Drake, and probably had read the *Divers Voyages* which Hakluyt published in 1582.   He also gives vent to the popular delight in grotesque exaggeration and barbaric cruelty.   *Dr. Faustus* is less extravagant ; it typifies the lust of boundless knowledge, as *The Jew of Malta* does boundless avarice, and *Tamburlaine* that " marvellous greed of dominion " which a foreigner noted in Englishmen early in the reign.[1]   *The Jew of Malta* fails to anticipate Shylock owing to Marlowe's lack of restraint. *Edward II.*, the best of his plays, has been compared by Lamb with Shakespeare's *Richard II. ;* but it is a drama of violent action without any subtle development of character.

Marlowe was a pioneer whose lead was not accepted without some cavil and hesitation.   Greene and Nash attacked him vigorously both for his blank verse and for his extravagant bombast ; and older forms of drama still competed for possession of the stage.   Greene's *Friar Bacon and Friar Bungay*, produced apparently in emulation of *Dr. Faustus* in 1588, harks back to the old morality, although his appeal to English sentiment, while more domestic than Marlowe's, was quite as modern.   Peele, the one Oxford man among this group of dramatists, and Kyd caught Marlowe's vices rather than his virtues.   Peele's *Battle of Alcazar* produced in 1592 has almost as much bombast as *Tamburlaine*, and his *Edward I.* has none of the vigour of Marlowe's *Edward II.*   Kyd's *Spanish Tragedie* eclipsed *Tamburlaine* in bloodshed and popularity ; it anticipated some of the machinery of *Hamlet*, and was closely imitated by the authors of *Titus Andronicus*.

The Elizabethan drama was developed over again and perfected in the growth of Shakespeare's mind.   He had no academic training, and university graduates like Greene, Lodge, Nash, Peele, and Marlowe appear to have been some-

[1] See above, p. 306.

what disdainful of the rustic upstart who had been appren-
ticed to the actor's business. He found more profitable
occupation in adapting and re-writing plays, which before
the days of copyright were treated as the common property
of acting companies. Probably he was given a freer and
freer hand, till about 1590, some three years after he had
joined it, the Earl of Leicester's company accepted his
earliest original composition, *Love's Labour's Lost.* Lyly's influence is patent, as it is in *Venus and Adonis,* published under
Shakespeare's name in 1593, and in *Lucrece* published in 1594 ;
but Lyly never reached the truth, humour, or poetic power
of Shakespeare's most juvenile productions. The *Comedy of
Errors,* which followed in 1590 or 1591, was partly borrowed
from Plautus, and shows the influence of classical comedy ;
while the *Two Gentlemen of Verona,* which came probably a
year later, is drawn from Spanish and Italian sources. There
is a good deal of rhyme and little characterisation in these
three plays. The three parts of *Henry VI.* which followed
are seemingly adaptations of previous work by Greene, Peele,
and Marlowe.

With *Richard III.,* which dates from 1593, Shakespeare
achieved a higher level of success. Born in the same year as
Marlowe, he was less precocious, and in the year of Marlowe's
death Shakespeare stood where Marlowe stood in 1587.
Richard III. is his *Tamburlaine ;* Lyly and the foreign models
have been left behind, and rhyme abandoned for blank verse.
Marlowe's influence over Shakespeare is at its height in
Richard III. ; but in *Richard II.,* produced in 1593-94, Shakespeare improved upon his master. The crude villainy of Richard III.'s devouring ambition is replaced by the complexity
of the character of Richard II., and the patriotism of John
of Gaunt is mellower than the imperialism of Tamburlaine.
Titus Andronicus, produced in 1594, represents so marked a
reversion to the worst of Marlowe's faults that no critic thinks
it mainly Shakespeare's work. The breach with Marlowe is
complete in *Romeo and Juliet,* the *Midsummer Night's Dream,*
and the *Merchant of Venice,* which were all written about 1595.
Rhetoric gives place to humour and fancy, and a more civilised
view is taken of women, who become increasingly important ;
love is preferred to the ruder passions depicted by Marlowe,

and even Shylock is humanised by his natural sense of injury to his race. The contrast between him and the *Jew of Malta* shows how far Shakespeare had outstripped Marlowe. *King John* and the *Taming of the Shrew*, if they date from the same period, do not mark the same progress. *King John* appeals to a lower level of intellect, although Shakespeare did tone down the patriotic declamation of *The Troublesome Raigne of King John*, an anonymous play produced in 1591 on which he based his own. The *Taming of the Shrew* is a farce adapted from a play published in 1594. Shakespeare was intent on making money, and he may have found that even in his time the lower forms of literature were the better paid.

The Cadiz expedition, the Islands' Voyage, and the Irish crisis of 1598 may have inspired the patriotic epic of the two parts of *Henry IV*. and *Henry V.*, which are definitely assigned to 1596-99. But Falstaff is greater than Henry V., and is perhaps the finest creation of humour in literature. The queen herself was impressed, and is said to have uttered a wish to see Falstaff in love. The result was *The Merry Wives of Windsor ;* but whether the cause was haste or the constraint of royal authority, Falstaff in love does not add to his reputation. In the four plays which followed between 1599 and 1601, Shakespeare reached the climax of English comedy. In *As You Like It* the comedy is relieved by the irony of melancholy Jaques and Touchstone, and the sadder note re-appears in *All's Well that Ends Well ;* but it is absent from *Much Ado about Nothing* and from *Twelfth Night* which has been described as the perfection of comedy. Rosalind and Beatrice represent Shakespeare's most successful efforts to delineate the character of woman who dominates these plays.

Suddenly gaiety seemed to depart from Shakespeare's mood and he turned to the darkest themes of tragedy, even changing to a tragic end every story that he borrowed. A dramatist can write tragedies without the stimulus of private or public misfortune, and the Waverley novels betray no symptom of Scott's personal losses ; but the attribution of the change in Shakespeare's work to outward events is plausible. Ruin had overtaken his friends at court, and a blight fell on men of letters ; Essex was brought to the block, and Southampton was sent to the Tower. There is nothing definite to connect Shakespeare with Essex, though the earl was a friend and patron of letters; but his relations with Southampton were close. To him he had dedicated *Venus and Adonis* and *Lucrece;* and on the eve of Essex's rebellion in London Southampton sent a message to the players at the Globe Theatre bidding them revive *Richard II.*, in order, it is supposed, to tune the public mind for a removal of evil councillors if not a royal deposition. The Cecils had shown little interest in the drama, and the hopes of the dramatic world were centred in their rivals. Their failure cast a gloom over Elizabeth's last years which is intensified in Shakespeare's work. Art was tongue-tied by authority so far as direct allusion to Essex was concerned, and it was not until 1609 that Shakespeare portrayed in *Coriolanus* a man who, like Essex, had done good service to the state, but met a tragic end through lack of self-restraint. Of the ten tragedies belonging to this sombre epoch of Shakespeare's productivity only two, *Julius Cæsar* and *Hamlet*, fall within the Tudor period. The remaining eight, *Troilus and Cressida*, *Measure for Measure*, *Othello*, *Macbeth*, *King Lear*, *Timon of Athens*, *Anthony and Cleopatra*, and *Coriolanus*, were produced in 1603-9; and then in *Cymbeline*, *Winter's Tale*, and *The Tempest* Shakespeare recovered his equanimity and turned again to romance. The splendid aftermath of Ben Jonson, Beaumont, Fletcher, and Massinger belongs to the Jacobean decadence, though four of Jonson's plays, *Every Man in His Humour*, *Every Man out of His Humour*, *Cynthia's Revels*, and the *Poetaster* were written between 1598 and 1603; men's humours rather than men are now the theme of the drama.

Prose made no such progress as poetry during Elizabeth's reign, and the advance on Sir Thomas More is comparatively slight. English history did not become literature till Bacon in his declining days wrote his *Henry VII.*, and Raleigh in prison began his *History of the World*. Grafton and Stow were merely industrious chroniclers, though Holinshed's prose has been placed in a higher rank with his predecessor Hall's. Camden, too, had some conception of form, but he preferred to write in Latin like Polydore Vergil. Bacon published ten of his fifty-eight essays in 1597, but their shrewdness is more remarkable than their style; they are somewhat disjointed reflexions, terse it is true, but put together without any effort after artistic construction.   Elizabethan prose was at its best in its translations, particularly in North's *Plutarch* and Florio's *Montaigne ;* but the nearest approach to melody in prose is found in Hooker's *Ecclesiastical Polity,* and the raciest vigour in the Martin Marprelate tracts and in the literary controversy between Thomas Nash and Gabriel Harvey.   In literary criticism the most notable work was Sidney's *Apologie for Poetrie* or *Defense of Poesie*—it was published under both titles by two different printers in 1595.   While an epitome of Italian literary criticism, it may without much exaggeration be said to have created the art in England, and Webbe, Puttenham, and Jonson in his *Timber* followed in Sidney's wake.   His *Arcadia,* which is more like a book of chivalry than a novel in prose, superseded Lyly's *Euphues,* and out-distanced the crowd of stories in which Greene, Lodge, Nash, Peele, and others imitated Italian or Spanish models, and provided plots for the Shakespearean drama.   But few now read Elizabethan novels except for purposes of study ; and prose equally good, more direct, and less affected, is to be found in many a contemporary state-paper and parliamentary oration.

The one thread, which runs through the literature of the age of Shakespeare in all its forms and weaves it into English history, is the gradual emergence of a national element.   France which received the Roman law and clung to the Roman church was prone to classical traditions ;[1] in England national impulse fashioned them all into fresh designs.   Literature became national because there was a nation capable of responding to the men of letters ; they held up mirrors to a people instead of to a court or clique of learned men. Medieval localism died in the agony of the Wars of the Roses, while commerce built a golden bridge between the feudal classes, and letters formed a meeting-place for lords and commoners.   Growing intercourse between all parts and ranks developed public opinion and stimulated national consciousness ; England found itself, and then sought to impress its will on everything with which it came in conflict at home and

---

[1] Compare Jusserand, *A Literary History of the English People,* iii., 33-36, with Petit de Julleville, *Histoire de la Langue et de la Littérature Française,* iii., 261-316.

abroad. Hence the Tudor dictatorship and the expansion of English enterprise.

A striking illustration of this national temper is found in sixteenth century architecture. Under the Tudors inland castles fell into decay, while others were built along the coast. For one thing, the inland castle was no longer needed for protection; for another, the Tudors were determined that no one should build any walls over which the sovereign could not look. The castle was the hard kernel of the feudal franchise, a standing defiance to royal and national authority, in which the king's writ seldom ran. They were centres of local anarchy from which Englishmen sallied to fight one another; they were now replaced by the peaceful Tudor manor-house, designed for the comfort of living and not for the needs of defence. Englishmen's gaze was turned outward across the sea, and monastic masonry was used to line the southern coast with royal castles built to defend it against foreign enemies. This national castle-building stopped midway through the century, as England appropriated the sea, removed its frontiers to the lands beyond, and relied upon its mobile wooden walls for safety. These, too, gradually became national instead of private property, though privateers and armed merchantmen supplemented Elizabeth's royal navy.

A like spirit intruded into all sorts of domains, catholic as well as local, ecclesiastical as well as economic and social. Sometimes it spread destruction where it trod, and failed to make repair. National control of religion was not altogether a success; nor did the state fulfil the educational responsibility it assumed. It made more serious efforts in the economic sphere; and in a long series of measures, culminating in 1598, to which the famous poor law of 1601 added nothing material, parliament admitted and defined the obligations of the state towards the poor, and instituted an organised, national system which lasted till 1834. The threats of slavery and branding in the act of 1548 and of hanging in that of 1572 having failed to eradicate destitution and vagrancy, the state appealed to private charity; next it ordained that private charity should be stimulated, first by the moral suasion of the church and then by the sterner arguments of the justices of the peace; finding these ineffective, it authorised coercion and the levying of poor-rates to be applied in providing work for the able-bodied and relief for the impotent poor. Even more emphatic was its intervention in the question of employment : work was regarded as national service, from which only the well-to-do were exempt ; though employers were not expected to turn off their men whenever it suited their convenience. The masses were bound by the statutes of apprenticeship either to agricultural or industrial service, and its terms were strictly defined. The hours of labour and the rate of wages were fixed ; heavy penalties were imposed on masters who paid, and on men who took, more than the statutory amount ; men might not leave their masters, nor masters dismiss their men, without adequate cause ; and the duty of settling their disputes was imposed on the justices of the peace.[1]

There was no *laisser faire* in the economic practice of the Tudors : in agriculture and industry there was state-regulation mainly in the interests of employers ; external trade was regulated mainly in the interests of the consumer. Customs-duties might be suspended at the discretion of the crown ; the import of corn, duty-free, was usually licensed when the price rose above a certain level, its export was only permitted when the price fell unusually low. The elasticity of this system and the wide discretion granted to the crown, while liable to grave abuse, saved the consumer from rigid protective laws and the producer from unlimited competition. Nevertheless, the price of corn fluctuated far more violently than at present : England was normally self-sufficing ; it was therefore dependent on itself, and a bad harvest would double or even treble prices. Tudor regulation only palliated hardships arising from reliance upon restricted and uncertain food supplies.

This state-regulation of commerce, wages, and hours of labour, while consistent with the general centralising and autocratic character of Tudor rule, may seem incompatible with modern liberty. Nevertheless, the sixteenth century was an age of liberation, and it marks a stage in the transition from medieval custom and status to modern competition and free contract. National organisation took the place of local or sectional institutions, and national regulation was the less

[1] Prothero, *Select Statutes, etc.*, pp. 41-54, 67-74, 95-105; *Engl. Hist. Rev.*, xv., 447; Cunningham, II., i., 25-44.

minute and rigid of the two. The closeness of the medieval guilds and other associations had been largely due to the necessity for protection against the grasping instincts of the " overmighty subject"; but, when the overmighty subject had been himself made subject to a common law, the close formation of humbler folk could be relaxed. To achieve this liberation needed the strong arm of the Tudor monarchy, supported by a growing national consciousness. Feudal liberties had to be invaded and destroyed by the Star Chamber, by the Councils of the North and of Wales and its Marches; and, even so, there were districts in England at the end of Elizabeth's reign into which her writs did not penetrate.

National monarchy was needed for constructive as well as for destructive work. It could not pull down medieval institutions and put nothing in their place; and there was serious danger that the dissolution of old ties would lead to social anarchy. Privateering, indeed, threatened to become a national disease, and some aspects of protestantism betray its influence in the church. Piracy was one of its forms, and Irish plantation was another; but the operations of predatory individualism were not confined to the church, to aliens, and to the Irish. By the inclosure of commons and by fraudulent manufactures, which the decay of the guilds encouraged and scores of acts of parliament failed to check, Englishmen preyed on the commonwealth. Bribery in the courts of law, intimidation of juries by local magnates, defalcations by the collectors of taxes, and embezzlement in public offices were other signs of the deficient sense of social obligation with which the Tudors had to cope. They did their best to provide remedies by fostering national spirit and lengthening the arm of national government; but the chief service which autocracy can render to its subjects is to make its continuance unnecessary. The Tudors established order without which liberty is impossible, weakened the local and social barriers which impeded the growth of public opinion, eradicated foreign influence, and created a sense of national security. They thus prepared the way for a further advance towards self-government; and in the last years of her reign Elizabeth encountered in the nation a growing impatience of constraint.

CHAPTER XXIV.

THE LAST YEARS OF ELIZABETH.

THE year 1588 is perhaps more important as a landmark in England's domestic annals than in the history of its war with Spain; at any rate its significance has been as much underrated in the one case as it has been overrated in the other. It did not close the history of the war; but, so far as any one year can be said to have done so, it opened a new chapter in the political and constitutional development of England. During these last fifteen years of her reign Elizabeth seems like an actor lingering on the stage after his part has been played. She loses touch with her people; crown and parliament come into sharper conflict; the breach with puritanism widens; there is even a rebellion in London, and protestants look forward to a change of sovereign. The house of commons is girding itself for its hundred years' war with the crown, and only refrains from pushing its attack, as it told James I., out of respect for the age and sex of the queen. The Tudor period is dissolving into the Stuart.

The strife began characteristically with Martin Marprelate's onslaught on the bishops in 1588, which had been provoked by the repressive policy of Archbishop Whitgift. The successor of the mild and vacillating Grindal was one of the ablest politicians who ever occupied the chair of St. Augustine, and it was with a political problem that he had to deal. The presbyterians, Hutton had declared,[1] would deprive the queen of her authority, and give it to the people; in February, 1587, Anthony Cope introduced a bill into parliament abolishing . canon law and appointing "a new form of administration of the sacraments and ceremonies of the church";[2] and the

---

[1] See above, pp. 363-66.

[2] D'Ewes, p. 410. Cope and his supporters, Lewknor, Hurleston, and Bainbridge, were all sent to the Tower.

determination of subjects to have the religion they wanted CHAP.
was the prelude to their demand for a government and a XXIV.
policy to their liking. Under the outward show of godliness,
wrote Whitgift, they nourished "contempt of magistrates,
popularity, anabaptistry, and sundry other pernicious and pes-
tilent errors". It was the "popularity" that offended Whitgift most : he was no high churchman in the modern sense ;
his first lecture as Lady Margaret professor at Cambridge had
demonstrated the identity of pope and Antichrist, and he had
begged Cecil not to enforce the use of the surplice. When he
had been archbishop twelve years he issued his Lambeth
articles, in which he baldly asserted the Calvinistic doctrines
of election and predestination. He was divided from his victims only by the question of church-government ; he believed
in monarchy, they had been driven into democratic principles.
He was a pluralist, and he held medieval views of prelatical
dignity. " He maintained an army of retainers. He travelled
on the occasion of his triennial visitations with a princely re-
tinue. His hospitality was profuse. His stables and armoury
were better furnished than those of the richest nobleman." [1]
To Elizabeth he commended himself by his high opinion of
royal prerogative and his abstinence from matrimony.

From his mastership of Trinity College, Cambridge, and his
deanery of Lincoln, both of which he held simultaneously with
other preferments, he passed in 1577 to the bishopric of Worcester, and thence, on Grindal's death in 1583, to the archbishopric of Canterbury. He persuaded the queen to delegate practically all her powers of coercive jurisdiction in the
church to a new high commission consisting of forty-four
members, twelve of whom were bishops. Whitgift himself
was the moving spirit ; and he drew up twenty-four articles
for its guidance. This new commission was empowered to
tender an oath *ex officio mero* to any one it pleased, and the
victim was bound to take the oath on pain of imprisonment for
contempt, and to answer any questions unless he wished silence
to be accepted as confession. Similar powers to tender the
oath *ex officio* had been given to earlier commissions ; but the
vigour of their exercise by Whitgift was a novelty, and it
roused an opposition that had lain dormant while the oath

[1] *Dict. of Nat. Biogr.*, lxi., 132.

CHAP.
XXIV.

was not enforced. His forms of procedure were unknown to the common law, and his articles were founded upon the laws ecclesiastical, of which the statutory basis was uncertain. They constituted an inquisition comparable with those of Rome and Spain, though the high commission could not inflict capital punishment nor extort confession by physical torture : the articles, wrote Burghley to Whitgift, were " so full of branches and circumstances that I think the inquisitions of Spain use not so many questions to comprehend and to entrap their preys ".[1] The house of commons petitioned against the oath in 1585 and again in 1587,[2] and the majority of the privy council sympathised with their complaint. But Whitgift had the ear of the queen ; in February, 1586, owing perhaps to the influence of Sir Christopher Hatton, who had long been known to the puritans as " an enemy of the gospel," Whitgift and his two allies, Lords Cobham and Buckhurst, were sworn of the privy council, a privilege which none of Elizabeth's archbishops had yet enjoyed. In 1587 the archbishop supported Hatton's appointment as lord-chancellor,[3] and these two with Cobham were the principal advocates of ecclesiastical rigour.

Whitgift had taken the precaution of trying to muzzle the press ; in January, 1586, he procured the " Star-chamber decree," by which no manuscript was to be set up in type until it had been licensed by the archbishop himself or the bishop of London, and any printer who disobeyed was rendered liable to six months' imprisonment.[4] For a time this was effective, but in October, 1588, the first of the Martin Marprelate tracts was issued from Waldegrave's secret press at Kingston-on-Thames. In November the press was removed to Sir Richard Knightley's house at Fawsley in Northamptonshire, where a second tract was printed in that month. In January, 1589, Bishop Cooper published an official reply entitled *An Admonition to the People of England*. From John Hales's house at Coventry, whither the press was once more removed, Martin issued in February certain *Minerall and Metaphysical Schoolpoints*, and in March the most effective of his tracts, *Hay any Worke for Cooper.*[5]

---

[1] Prothero, p. 213.   [2] D'Ewes, pp. 358, 360, 413.

[3] Whitgift declined the office himself, and it was conferred on Hatton by Elizabeth while visiting the archbishop at Croydon.

[4] Arber, *Stationers' Register*, ii., 810.

[5] " Hay " = Ha'ye. See Pierce, *An Historical Introduction to the Marprelate Tracts*, 1909.

The press was then transferred to Roger Wigston's house at Wolston, and in July two more tracts, *Theses Martinianae* and *The Just Censure*, were printed. It was seized at Warrington in August while *More Work for the Cooper* was being set up; but a seventh and last tract, *The Protestatyon*, was published in September, having apparently been printed at Wolston earlier in the year. The secret of their authorship has never been fully revealed: the two men who had most to do with their production were probably John Penry, an able young Welshman who had been tried by the court of high commission for a treatise addressed to parliament in 1587, accusing the bishops of responsibility for the spiritual destitution of Wales; and Job Throckmorton, a nephew of the diplomatist Sir Nicholas, and a cousin of the conspirator Francis Throckmorton. But neither was convicted of the offence, of which many others, including John Udall and John Field, the joint-author with Wilcox of the *Admonition* of 1572, were suspected; and the trial of Knightley, Hales, and Wigston in February, 1590, failed to elucidate the mystery.

The Marprelate tracts achieved a fatal success: written in terse, vigorous English and composed mainly of scurrilous personal attacks, they made a bid for popularity which then damaged their cause irretrievably in the eyes of sober politicians. Replies quite as scurrilous and more indecent were, indeed, encouraged by Whitgift's chaplain Bancroft; and Lyly, Nash, and Harvey rushed into the fray to defend literature and the drama from the puritanical temper which half a century later succeeded in closing theatres in England. But grave puritans were shocked by Martin's licence, and it was clear that Whitgift had stung his bitterest enemies into a violence which recoiled upon themselves. In the parliament which sat from February 4 to March 29, 1589, there was hardly an echo of the puritan clamour which had filled the lower house for twenty years. A bill was introduced to check the evils of non-residence and pluralities, but it was smothered in committee after its second reading; and the queen found herself able to sanction all the sixteen public and eight private bills passed by parliament. Complaints had been raised about purveyance and abuses in the exchequer, but these she considered it her privilege to redress without parliamentary aid;

and supply consisted of the unprecedented grant of four
fifteenths and tenths and two subsidies.[1] The morrow of the
defeat of the Armada was not a convenient day for political or
ecclesiastical agitation.

Dangers, however, lay hid beneath the surface. A draft
bill, which apparently was not introduced into either house,
proposed to "suppress and dissolve all collegiate and cathedral churches now remaining in England";[2] and Sir Francis
Knollys inveighed in letters to Burghley and Walsingham
against the ambition and covetousness of the bishops. He
maintained that Whitgift, by asserting in his answer to Cartwright the divine right of the episcopate, had been guilty of
praemunire, and he urged that the matter should be brought
to trial.[3] Burghley himself warned the archbishop that the
ecclesiastical courts were incurring those penalties by adminis-
tering oaths *ex officio* against the law.[4] Nevertheless Whitgift
persisted: in 1590 Cartwright was committed to prison, in
spite of his repudiation of the Marprelatists and the Brownists;
and Udall was condemned to death under the act of 1581 for
having published "a wicked, scandalous, and seditious libel"
denouncing "the archbishops, lord-bishops, archdeacons, and
the rest of that order". The leading members of the privy
council made intercession for his life, and when Whitgift's ob-
duracy had been overcome, an order for Udall's release was
signed in June, 1592. He died a few days later.

An optimist observed in 1590: "these sharp proceedings
make that sect greatly diminish"; but in the parliament of
1593 Raleigh estimated that there were nearly 20,000 Brownists in the realm, and Sir Robert Cecil told that parliament
that it had been summoned to deal with religion.[5] But it was
to do so after Elizabeth's fashion, and the principal act of the
session was to solve a doubt raised at Udall's trial whether
puritans could be prosecuted under the act of 1581 which
had been aimed at Roman catholics. Parliament opened on
February 19 with the lord-keeper's ominous warning to the
Speaker, Sir Edward Coke, that the commons' privilege of

---

[1] Townshend, *Four last Parliaments of Elizabeth*, ed. 1680, pp. 1-28.
[2] State Papers, Dom., Eliz., ccxxii., 70; Addenda, xxxi., 32 [14].
[3] *Ibid.*, ccxxiii., 23, ccxxxiii., 62; *Hatfield MSS.*, iii., 412.
[4] State Papers, Dom., Addenda, xxxii., 7.
[5] *Ibid.*, xxxi., 154; Townshend, pp. 56, 76.

free speech was to say "Aye" or "No," and not whatsoever
they listed; and it was no idle threat.   On the 24th, Peter
Wentworth, supported by Richard Stephens, member for
Newport in Cornwall, and by Sir Henry Bromley and William
Walshe, the two knights for Worcestershire, asked leave to
introduce a bill entailing the succession to the crown.   The
council tried to treat them gently, but Elizabeth insisted on
their imprisonment.   Wentworth and Bromley were sent to
the Tower, Stephens and Walshe to the Fleet; and Wentworth
remained in the Tower till he died in 1596, as much a martyr
to parliamentary liberty as Sir John Eliot.   Two days after
the imprisonment of these four members, a fifth, James
Morrice, introduced a bill to check the arbitrary proceedings
of Whitgift's commissioners.   In spite of the sympathy of Sir
Robert Cecil and the support of Sir Francis Knollys, the
treasurer of the Queen's chamber, who repeated his warning
about *praemunire*, Morrice was committed to custody, while
the queen sent for the Speaker and ordered him to accept no
bills "touching matters of state or reformation in causes
ecclesiastical"; it was not meant, she said, that parliament
should meddle with such questions.   "From the tyranny of
the clergy of England," wrote Morrice from prison to Burghley,
"good Lord, deliver us."[1]

A motion for the release of the imprisoned members was
rejected without a division in fear of Elizabeth's anger;[2] but
the commons could still defend their privileges against the
lords.   The customary committee on supply proposed the
grant of two subsidies and four tenths and fifteenths: the lords
considered this inadequate, intimated that they would assent
to no bill granting less than three subsidies, and suggested a
conference.   Sir Robert Cecil threw some light on the liberality
of the lords: subsidies, he said, were "imposed for the most
part upon the meaner sort of her majesty's subjects"; in one
shire, he declared, no man's lands were assessed as being worth
more than £80 a year, and in London no one's income was
assessed at more than £200.[3]   His figures, so far as London
was concerned, were disputed by a member for the city; but

---

[1] *Domestic Cal.*, 1591-94, p. 322; Townshend, pp. 60-63; Lodge, *Illustrations*, ii., 443-46.

[2] D'Ewes, p. 497.   [3] *Ibid.*, pp. 483, 496.

in 1589 an apologist for the government averred that taxation in England was trifling then compared with former times, and that assessments were " marvellous easy," an income of £50 in land being rated at £5 and so forth.[1]   The result was that the grants of 1589 produced less than a quarter of a million, while the queen had spent more than four times that amount since the defeat of the Armada.   Various suggestions were made in the commons to graduate taxation and reform the methods of assessment; but it was replied that the queen " loved not such fineness of device and novel inventions,"[2] and the house reverted to its quarrel with the lords.   Bacon maintained that the offer of subsidies had always come from the commons : he agreed that the two houses might confer on the needs of the situation, but said that the lords had no right to prescribe to the commons what they should give; and by 217 to 128 votes the house adopted his view.   The general conference was, however, held; and eventually the commons, having asserted their privilege, granted with much grumbling the three subsidies and six tenths and fifteenths.

The ecclesiastical question occupied the house intermittently throughout the whole of the session, which lasted until April 10.   Morrice's misfortune did not prevent members from dealing firmly with the government's bill which aimed at extending the penalties of 1581 to every sort of nonconformist. The first two clauses were rejected as too severe, and the whole bill was so riddled with amendments that a fresh one had to be introduced.   Even this was committed and recommitted several times, and bandied to and fro between the houses.[3]   No one professed any sympathy with the Barrowists and Brownists, or quarrelled with the phraseology of a bill which assumed that all dissent was based upon the " colour " and " pretence " of religion ; but alarm was expressed that the mere abstainer from church might be condemned to the same penalties.   This scruple was satisfied in the act when, after many members had gone home, it slipped through in the last days of the session.   Only those who wilfully abstained from

---

[1] *Domestic Cal.*, Addenda, 1580-1625, pp. 272-73.
[2] D'Ewes, p. 492.
[3] *Domestic Cal.*, 1591-94, pp. 328, 338; *Hatfield MSS.*, iv., 298-99; D'Ewes, pp. 476-77, 497-98, 500, 516.

church for a month, and also actively impugned the queen's CHAP.
ecclesiastical power, or persuaded others to abstain from church, XXIV.
or attended or persuaded others to attend unlawful conventicles,
were rendered liable to imprisonment until they submitted ; if
they would not conform within three months they were to
abjure the realm for ever, and be treated as felons if they
returned.[1]

Such as it was, this concession was bought at a price.
" The day after the lower house had shown their dislike of this
bill," says a letter of April, 1593, Barrow and Greenwood
" were hanged early in the morning ".[2] They were the two
Cambridge men who took the lead of the Brownists when
Browne himself subsided into conformity. Barrow was a lawyer who had for seven years suffered arbitrary imprisonment
at Whitgift's hands ; Greenwood was a minister who had been
released in 1592 after four years' detention, only to be re-
arrested in December. They were tried on March 21, 1593,
under the act of 1581 against seditious writings. Barrow in
his examination asserted that the Book of Common Prayer
was false, superstitious, and popish, that the sacraments of the
Church of England were not true sacraments, that "public
parishes" were not the "true established churches of Christ,"
and that the queen, while " supreme governor over the whole
land, and over the church also, both bodies and goods . . .
ought not to make or impose other laws over them than Christ
hath made and left in his Testament " ;[3] and on these grounds
he has been claimed as one of the founders of independency
and congregationalism.[4] Preparations were made for their
execution on March 24 ; but Burghley secured a week's reprieve, remonstrated with Whitgift, and urged the council to
mediate with the queen. No one would support him, and
Whitgift was relentless ; on the 31st the prisoners were conveyed to Tyburn, but again reprieved on the scaffold. Their
execution on April 6, says the letter already cited, " proceeded
through malice of the bishops to the lower house ". Penry,
who had been for two years in Scotland, was arrested in
London on March 23, and tried on May 21, not for his share

---

[1] 33 Eliz., c. 1.   [2]*Domestic Cal.*, 1591-94, p. 341.
[3] *Egerton Papers*, pp. 167-69.   [4] H. M. Dexter, *Congregationalism of
the Last Three Hundred Years*, 1880, pp. 205-252.

in the Marprelate tracts, but on a charge of having at Edinburgh written words with an intent to excite rebellion in
England. The evidence was inadequate and the accusation
absurd; but he was condemned for treason and executed on
the 29th.

A legend grew up among the puritans that Elizabeth
asked Whitgift what he really thought of his victims, and that
he replied that they were the servants of God, but dangerous
to the state; whereupon she exclaimed, "Alas, shall we put
the servants of God to death?" This, it was believed, "was
the true cause why no more of them were put to death in
her days".[1] The real reason was the success of Whitgift's
policy; it was all that a short-sighted disciplinarian could desire. He had made England impossible for the separatists.
The mere puritans conformed, biding their time; the irrecon-
cilables abjured their country, went into exile at Leyden and
Amsterdam, and then crossed the Atlantic to make a new
world independent of Whitgift's church.

The act of 1593 expressly provided that no "popish recusant" should thereby be compelled to abjure his country.
But this exemption of recusants from the first act of the
session was merely due to the fact that the second dealt more
particularly with them. Those who possessed lands and could
pay fines were ordered to confine themselves within five miles
of their usual habitation; the poorer recusants, who could
not assist the finances of the government, were compelled to
abjure the country under the same penalties as the separatists.
Increased severity for puritans implied no mitigation for
Roman catholics, and priests continued to be executed until
the end of Elizabeth's reign. The best-known victim was the
Jesuit poet, Robert Southwell, whose poems had a wide
circulation at the time, though their deep religious feeling was
somewhat out of harmony with the lyrics of the period.
He was arrested in 1592 by the professional priest-hunter,
Richard Topcliffe, and many times racked before he was
hanged as a traitor in February, 1595.

There is no evidence that Southwell committed or contemplated any other treason than that of being a Jesuit resident
in England; but the active complicity of leading members of

[1] A. Young, *Chronicles of the Pilgrim Fathers*, Boston, 1841, p. 433.

the Society in political intrigues against Elizabeth afforded a plausible excuse for the rigour of the laws. Parsons, who lived in Spain from 1588 to 1597, did not content himself with establishing various English seminaries and communities in that country in order to strengthen the English mission. He continually urged Philip to renew his attack on England, and his religious activity was partly dictated by his conviction that no external attack could succeed unless it was supported by a strong domestic party. His hopes, however, were now mainly centred on Elizabeth's successor; and in 1594 he published his *Conference about the next Succession*, in which he advocated the claims of the Infanta of Spain, who was descended from John of Gaunt. This inflamed the dissensions already rife among the English catholics; some, reinforced by the Scottish catholics, had hopes of James VI. as Elizabeth's successor, while French catholics outside the League had no desire to see a Spaniard on the English throne; none but "Jesuited" catholics, as they were called, desired the infanta. The secular priests in England sided with the catholic laity against the Jesuits, and even the students at the English college at Rome joined in the attack.

Parsons quelled this last manifestation on a visit to Rome in 1597, and secured his own appointment as rector of the college. He then obtained the establishment of an archpriest, George Blackwell, to govern the secular clergy in England. Some such step was necessary now that the old catholic bishops were dead; but Blackwell was Parsons' tool, and he was instructed to consult Henry Garnet, the Jesuit superior in England. The result was that the secular clergy were soon in revolt against their archpriest, and the quarrel, which was carried to Rome and produced a bitter literary controversy, outlived Elizabeth's reign. The anger of the secular clergy against the Jesuits and their Spanish policy led them to desire an accommodation with Elizabeth's government, whereby they might secure immunity from molestation in return for guarantees of loyalty. William Watson, the most active and least responsible agent of the party, drew up in 1602 a form of oath of allegiance in conjunction with Bishop Bancroft; and on taking it he and several seculars were released from prison. He then went to Scotland to secure promises of toleration

30 *

from James VI. and the disappointment of his hopes led to
the Bye Plot of 1603.[1]

The measures of the parliament of 1593 concluded Elizabeth's ecclesiastical legislation, and during the last ten years of
her reign there was something like a respite from religious
strife. The naval and Irish wars produced stirring incidents
enough; but the dullness of domestic annals is only relieved
by court intrigues and occasional plots like those of Dr. Lopez
in 1594 and Edward Squire in 1598, too fantastic to be of
any political importance; and when the need for supplies
compelled the summons of another parliament in October,
1597, its activity, apart from finance, was devoted to various
questions of social reform. The new lord-keeper, Sir Thomas
Egerton (afterwards Lord Ellesmere) in his opening speech,
contended truly that taxation was by no means so heavy as it
had been in previous reigns, notably in that of Edward III.; and
the commons, notwithstanding their reluctance to grant three
subsidies in 1593, voted a like amount in 1597 with the expression of a pious hope that it was not to be drawn into a
precedent. The new Speaker, Serjeant Yelverton, made the
customary excuse in novel terms: a Speaker, he said, should
be "big and comely, stately and well-spoken, his voice great,
his carriage majestical, his nature haughty, and his purse
plentiful and heavy," whereas he possessed none of these
qualifications. He certainly made mistakes in ruling that the
adjournment of the lords involved an adjournment of the commons, and in preventing the house from formally reading a
bill before proceeding to any other business; and much time
was spent in deciding such questions of procedure as whether
lords' amendments should be submitted to the commons on
parchment or on paper, and when the lords should receive de-
putations from the commons sitting, and when standing. Jars
between the two houses were frequent, and each rejected bills
passed by the other; but no measure of greater importance
than one for restraining excess in apparel was sacrificed. It
fell through in the house of lords, but another, to limit ruffs,
was dropped in the house of commons, perhaps out of deference to the queen.

[1] T. G. Law, *Jesuits and Seculars*, 1890, and *The Archpriest Controversy*
(Camden Soc., 1896-98); *Dict. of Nat. Biogr.*, *s.v.* Watson, William. See
below, vol. vii., p. 7.

Bacon introduced two of the most serious proposals of the session, one to check inclosures, and the other to remedy the decay of husbandry and tillage. In language which might have been borrowed from Protector Somerset he denounced " lords that have inclosed great grounds, and pulled down even whole towns and converted them to sheep-pastures," so that " instead of a whole town full of people" there would be " nought but green fields, but a shepherd and a dog". His proposals to revive "moth-eaten laws" were subjected to lengthy discussion and probably to considerable modifications in both houses; and there emerged two acts, one amending the old enactments against the destruction of towns and houses of husbandry, and the other prohibiting the future conversion of arable land to pasture and requiring the re-conversion of all pastures made out of arable lands since 1558. But Bacon's legislative efforts in this direction were no more effective than his predecessors'; and seven years later one Francis Trigge published a book against inclosures as full of lamentations as anything written in 1549. Another act for the punishment of rogues, vagabonds, and sturdy beggars recalls the legislation of Edward VI.'s reign; but it was accompanied by two more practical measures regulating the appointment, and defining the duties of overseers of the poor, and providing for the erection of workhouses.[1] Two acts were also passed for the benefit of disbanded soldiers and sailors, one to provide charitable relief, and the other to punish those who sought it under false pretences. The long continuance of the war tended to make soldiering a profession instead of being an occasional occupation for the yeoman; and the soldier had thus no employment upon which to fall back when his time expired.

Altogether twenty-eight public and fifteen private acts were passed in a prolonged session which extended, with three weeks' interval at Christmas, from October 24, 1597, to February 9, 1598; but many bills were rejected by the commons, the lords, or the queen. She had graciously given parliament leave to reform some abuses in church and state; and the commons had thereupon proceeded to discuss remedies for abuses arising out of monopolies, benefit of clergy, episcopal marriage-licences, the lax assessment and collection

[1] See above, pp. 455-6; and Cunningham, II., i., 44 ff.

of clerical subsidies, and the excessive fees charged for probate and other business in the ecclesiastical courts. But the sole reforms which appeared upon the statute-book were two acts abolishing benefit of clergy for house-breakers in the daytime and for abductors of women. The commons only ventured a petition on the subject of monopolies; and the queen while promising redress, felt sure that they did not wish to deprive her of her privilege of granting patents and monopolies. Among the many bills rejected by the commons were proposals to regulate grammar-schools and the College of Surgeons, to provide work for the poor, to establish houses of correction, and to restrain misappropriation of their endowments by colleges at Oxford and Cambridge. But Elizabeth was more destructive still; of the ninety-one bills which passed both houses she vetoed forty-eight.[1] Her action illustrates both the power of the crown and the independence of parliament, for these rejected measures cannot have emanated from the crown, and most of the legislation of this parliament was prepared in its committees. The records do not say whether the rejected bills were public or private; but they were certainly unimportant, for practically all the measures to which parliament devoted any marked attention were either passed into law or rejected by one or other house; and the bills vetoed by the queen were apparently those dismissed by the parliamentary diarists without specification as being of little importance. Possibly most of them were like those described by Lord Hunsdon when he wrote to Burghley on October 6: "The approaching time of parliament has moved divers to rake up the cinders of their long-buried titles, claims, and demands to places of honour";[2] and no contemporary reference to the queen's exercise of her prerogative as being unusual or surprising has been traced.

As soon as parliament was dissolved, Cecil was hurried to France to dissuade Henry IV. from peace, or at least from an alliance with Spain. He returned to find his father failing in health. Burghley died on August 4, and Elizabeth, who occasionally helped to nurse him in his last illness, found no one to fill his place. The lord treasurership was given in the following May to her second cousin, Thomas Sackville, Lord Buckhurst, who was more remarkable for his literary than for his

[1] Townshend, p. 127.   [2] *Domestic Cal.*, 1595-97, p. 510.

political individuality; but the business of the state was transacted mainly by Sir Robert Cecil.   He was as cool and prudent
as his father, but even less of a courtier, and he was sorely
troubled by the rivalry of the brilliant but unstable Essex.
The earl lacked Cecil's solid qualities, but possessed the superficial graces in which the secretary was deficient; and he depended for statesmanship upon the counsels of Cecil's cousin,
Francis Bacon.   His chief supporters among the nobility were
the young Earl of Southampton, Shakespeare's patron, Roger
Manners, fifth Earl of Rutland, and the Earl of Pembroke's
son William, Lord Herbert.   Raleigh was his most dangerous
rival as a courtier; but Raleigh was also suspect as the patron
of the "school of atheism" to which Marlowe belonged.[1]
Essex coquetted with puritans and catholics alike, but no
political principle was involved in his struggle with Cecil for
power, except in so far as Essex stood for an adventurous, and
Cecil for a cautious, foreign policy.

Essex lost his chance by his hasty conduct in Ireland in
1599.   On October 1, three days after his arrival in London,
he was committed to the lord-keeper's custody for disobeying
his instructions in Ireland, making peace with Tyrone, and
deserting his post.   At Christmas prayers were offered in
London churches for his restoration to favour, but on June 5,
1600, he was condemned to the loss of all his offices and imprisonment at Essex House during pleasure.   He was, however, released on August 26, and returned to court; but he
was not restored to Elizabeth's favour, and he began to meditate schemes for recovering it by force.   James VI.'s support
was secretly enlisted, and all manner of discontented politicians
flocked to Essex House, including puritan divines as well as
Catesby, Tresham, John and Christopher Wright, and others
who were subsequently implicated in the Gunpowder Plot.   A
project was formed in January, 1601, to seize Whitehall and
compel the queen to dismiss her present advisers and summon
a parliament.   Rumours came to the ears of the government,
and Essex was summoned to appear before the council.   In
desperation a rising was hurriedly arranged for Sunday, February 8, and to rally his adherents Essex gave out that he was
to be murdered in his bed by Raleigh.   The lord-keeper and

[1] *Dict. of Nat. Biogr.*, xlvii., 192-93.

others who came to deal privately with Essex were detained, and the earl began to parade the streets with 200 followers. The people made no response ; Whitehall had been barricaded ; and Essex was forced to surrender on a promise of trial by common law.   Among the prisoners were the Earls of Rutland, Southampton, Bedford, and Sussex, Lords Sandys, Monteagle, and Cromwell, Lady Rich, and sixteen knights.[1]

Essex was brought to trial in Westminster Hall on February 19.   He unsuccessfully challenged three of his peers as personal enemies, and accused Cecil of saying that the infanta was the rightful successor to the throne.   Bacon, as one of the queen's counsel, took an unsavoury part in securing his former patron's condemnation to death.   He was beheaded on Tower Hill on the 25th, Elizabeth having revoked only one warrant for his execution, instead of the three or four she recalled in Norfolk's case.[2]   Southampton also was sentenced to death, but only suffered imprisonment in the Tower ; and the chief conspirators executed besides Essex were Sir Gelly Meyrick, Sir Christopher Blount, Sir Charles Danvers, and the earl's secretary, Henry Cuffe, who had been professor of Greek at Oxford, and had been promised the Speakership of the commons if Essex were successful.

Elizabeth's last parliament met on October 27 in no good humour, and the parliamentary diarist notes that few members exclaimed "God bless your majesty" as she left the house of lords after the opening ceremony.[3]   Their discontent was not due to sympathy with Essex ; nor did the extraordinary financial demands, which the war and the Irish crisis necessitated, rouse any opposition.   Supply was declared to be "the alpha and omega" of that parliament ; and the unprecedented grant of four subsidies and eight tenths and fifteenths passed without a dissentient vote, although Raleigh pointed out that the £3 or £4 at which men were rated in the subsidy-books might in some cases represent their real income and in others

---

[1] *Belvoir MSS.*, i., 367-73 ; *Hatfield MSS.*, xi., 44, 86-88.   The latter volume contains a number of fresh details about Essex' conspiracy, as does the last volume of the *Acts of the Privy Council.*

[2] The popular story that she had given him a ring with a promise of pardon if he sent it her when in danger, and that the Countess of Nottingham detained it, is unsupported by contemporary evidence.

[3] Townshend, p. 178.

not its hundredth part.[1] There was a dispute between the commons and the lord-keeper respecting the Speaker's right to issue warrants for by-elections to the clerk of the crown in chancery, in which the lord-keeper yielded; there were differences between the two houses, and on one occasion the fact that they were colleagues did not prevent Lord Buckhurst from denouncing on behalf of the lords a message brought by Cecil from the commons as "strange, improper, and preposterous"; and there were warm debates over contentious bills. One to enforce church-going on Sundays was only lost by 105 to 106 votes; the minority claimed that the Speaker who favoured the bill should give an ordinary and a casting vote, but it was held that he only possessed the latter. An important act was passed for the more peaceable government of Cumberland, Westmorland, Northumberland, and the bishopric of Durham; but the famous poor law of 1601 added only a few details to previous measures and passed almost without discussion. Other bills for the suppression of blasphemous swearing, and the exclusion of customers from alehouses less than two miles from their homes, were also rejected; and disorderly methods were used to secure votes and shorten speeches. Doubting burgesses were dragged by the sleeve; at times members "hummed and laughed and talked," at others they "hawked and spat".[2]

But the house was mostly agitated over monopolies, a word which one member derived from μόνος and πόλις. In 1597-98 the commons had proceeded by means of a petition embodied in the Speaker's concluding oration, and the queen had promised redress. But, beyond a belated and ineffective inquiry in the spring of 1601, nothing had been done, and new symptoms of popular feeling appeared. As a rule the commons fought for their privileges with few indications of support outside the house: boroughs were glad to get members to serve them without a fee, and often granted or sold to neighbouring magnates the nomination of one of their representatives.[3] Popular naval heroes like Drake, Grenville,

---

[1] Townshend, p. 204. [2] *Ibid.*, pp. 205, 220.

[3] Boroughs seldom relinquished the nomination of both their members; compare the amusing case of the Leicester election in 1601, Townshend, pp. 286, 295, 298-99, 329.

Gilbert, and Raleigh when they sat in the house of commons invariably defended the royal prerogative; and only a corporate spirit unimpaired by party-feeling enabled the house to withstand encroachments on its jurisdiction. Monopolies, however, stirred general indignation: petitions were presented to the queen on her walks abroad, and Cecil heard cries in the streets: " God prosper those that further the overthrow of these monopolies; God send the prerogative touch not our liberty ". Lists of them were handed about from member to member, and the greatest abuses were brought to light.

Some monopolies were genuine patents or copyrights: there were patents for printing almanacs, the Psalms in Hebrew, the works of Tacitus, Norden's *Speculum Britanniae*, songs in parts, and for making mathematical instruments, which were bare justice to the patentee rather than a grievance to the public.[1] But others were less innocuous. Raleigh enjoyed monopolies for tin, cards, and sweet-wines: he blushed when attention was called to the cards, but defended the tin on the ground that it enabled him to pay the miners four shillings a week instead of two. It was retorted that the monopoly of steel by doubling the price had thrown two thousand workers out of employment; that starch, which had been imported at 18s. a hundredweight, had been sent up to 56s. when protected by a monopoly, and the queen lost her import duties; and that glasses, which had been imported at 16d., had risen to 5s. a dozen with a similar loss of revenue, while salt had gone up from 16d. to 15s. a bushel. " Is not bread there?" interjected Hakewill as the interminable list was read: " No, but if order be not taken for these, bread will be there before the next parliament ".[2]

The question was, what order? Bolder spirits were for a bill; petition had been tried and failed. But a bill would trench on the prerogative, and Cecil said he would rather his tongue were cut out than consent to its abridgement; he warned the Speaker that it would be his duty to refuse to receive any such proposal. The house was not subdued; never, said Cecil on November 24, had he seen it in such confusion. Then Elizabeth intervened; she knew instinctively

---

[1] Townshend, pp. 243-45; *cf.* Cunningham, II., i., 58-77.
[2] Townshend, pp. 235, 238-41; *cf. Hatfield MSS.*, viii., 34.

when the house represented popular feeling, and when it did not. She had often defied both lords and commons; now she saw that she must stoop to conquer. A proclamation prevented a bill, and the prerogative was saved at the expense of the patentees. On the 25th Cecil in a vigorous speech conveyed to the house the queen's indignation with the monopolists who ground the faces of the poor, and her solicitude for her people: every patent in force should be revoked; "every man shall have salt as cheap as he can buy it or make it . . . train oil shall go the same way, oil of blubber shall march in the same rank, brushes and bottles endure the like judgement".[1] Members wept for joy ; five days later they went to Whitehall at the queen's request, and she made her own atonement. "Though God," she said, "hath raised me high, yet this I count the glory of my crown : that I have reigned with your loves. This makes me that I do not so much rejoice that God hath made me to be a queen as to be a queen over so thankful a people. . . . That my grants should be grievous to my people, and oppressions privileged under our patents, our kingly dignity shall not suffer it ; yea, when I heard it, I could give no rest unto my thoughts until I had reformed it. Should they escape unpunished that have oppressed you, and have been respectless of their duty and regardless of our honour? No, Mr. Speaker, I assure you . . . I have ever used to set the last judgement-day before my eyes as so to rule as I shall be judged to answer before a higher Judge ; to whose judgement-seat I do appeal, that never thought was cherished in my heart that tended not to my people's good. . . . To be a king and wear a crown is a thing more glorious to them that see it than it is pleasing to them that bear it. For myself, I was never so much enticed with the glorious name of a king or royal authority of a queen, as delighted that God had made me His instrument to maintain His truth and glory, and to defend this kingdom from peril, dishonour, tyranny, and oppression."[2]

Elizabeth could bend the Tudor bow because her arm was strengthened by her people and lifted in their cause. A sovereignty that would not respond to national impulse was already out of date ; some, said Cecil, "would be glad that all

[1] Townshend, p. 250.   [2] *Ibid.*, pp. 263-66.

sovereignty were converted into popularity,"[1] and Elizabeth's condescension was needed to stave off attack on her prerogative.   The parliament of 1601 was dissolved on December 19 without further dispute with the crown; but the seeds of future quarrels were already in existence.   That the royal prerogative was inviolable was held to be a fundamental principle by all Elizabeth's councillors: when Cope introduced his new bill of uniformity in 1587, "her Majesty had for divers good causes best known to herself thought fit to suppress the same without any further examination thereof"; and the puritan Knollys who communicated the fact to the house "conceived it very unfit for her Majesty to give any account of her doings".[2] The regulation of monopolies was left dependent upon royal grace and not on parliamentary statute.   Hardly a session passed without some member being sent to the Tower for speeches in the house.   Martial law was executed on civilians;[3] frequent demands for contributions, hardly distinguishable from ship-money, had been made and resisted;[4] the queen's authority to modify law by proclamations was maintained except for the infliction of new penalties; new customs were imposed; imprisonment *per speciale mandatum regis* was so common as scarcely to be irregular;[5] the dispensing power of the crown was constantly exercised, the principle *rege non consulto* admitted, and juries haled before the Star Chamber.[6]   In the house of commons itself Serjeant Hele, who held a monopoly of steel, averred that the queen had as much right to all their lands and goods as to any revenue of her crown, for all they had was hers.[7]   The house laughed him down, but it was capable, on provocation, of stronger measures: "I would," said Cecil, "have all men know this much, that it's no jesting with a court of parliament";[8] and Elizabeth bequeathed no easy problem to her successor.

[1] Townshend, p. 251. Townshend was a member of this parliament, and took down as much as he could of the speeches he heard, probably by one of the methods of shorthand already in use; on one occasion he notes that he could write no more as it was growing dark in the house, there being no artificial light.

[2] D'Ewes, p. 412.

[3] Rymer, *Foedera*, xvi., 279; Hallam, *Const. Hist.*, i., 241.

[4] *Hatfield MSS.*, vi., 534; Corbett, *Successors of Drake*, pp. 155-56.

[5] *Hatfield MSS.*, ii., 141, 154-55.

[6] D'Ewes, pp. 159-60, 175; *Acts of the P. C.*, 1581-82, p. 256.

[7] Townshend, p. 205.

[8] *Ibid.*, p. 250. Compare Wentworth's questions in D'Ewes, p. 411.

The succession was formally as unsettled as it had ever been, but events had made only one practical solution possible. The Venetian ambassador Scaramelli, who came in January, 1603, to renew the direct diplomatic relations between England and Venice, interrupted since 1558, discussed a variety of claims with somewhat inadequate knowledge. So far as parliamentary statute went, the lawful heir would have been the elder son of the Earl of Hertford and Lady Catherine Grey ; but although he was commonly styled Lord Beauchamp, his father had never succeeded in upsetting Archbishop Parker's declaration of the invalidity of his marriage, and Beauchamp was therefore technically illegitimate. His insignificant character helped to dissipate his claim, to which attention had been called in 1596 through a riot raised by his cousin, Sir John Smith, a rash but competent soldier. But Beauchamp had married in 1582 the daughter of Sir Richard Rogers, a Dorset knight ; and his son was reported in March, 1603, to be engaged to Arabella Stuart.[1]

The combination of these two claims might have been serious, for Arabella was not an alien like James VI. ; she was the daughter of Darnley's brother Charles and his wife Elizabeth Cavendish, the daughter of "Bess of Hardwick," Countess of Shrewsbury, and she was born on English soil. Many husbands had been suggested for her, including the sons of Leicester and of the Duke of Parma ; but Elizabeth had so far kept her single, and the news of the Seymour courtship, coupled with suspicions that Spain, if not France as well, would support any candidate rather than see England and Scotland united, led to guards being placed round Arabella's residence, and her chaplain committed suicide.[2] Scaramelli also hinted that Huntingdon, as a direct male descendant of Edward IV., might make a bid for the throne, but saw that any such attempt would fail. There was in fact no real doubt

[1] Scaramelli says Arabella was engaged to Thomas Seymour ; but the only Thomas in the family was a brother of Lord Beauchamp who died in 1600 leaving a widow. Anthony Rivers, the Jesuit, declares the rumour that she was married to Hertford's "grandchild" to be "most false". The grandchild might have been either Beauchamp's eldest son Edward who died in 1618, or his second son William, afterwards Marquis of Hertford and second Duke of Somerset, who married Arabella in 1610.

[2] *Venetian Cal.*, ix., 539-42, 549, 554, 564; *Domestic Cal.*, 1601-3, p. 290; *Belvoir MSS.*, i., 388.

about the succession of James VI.; the way had been prepared
by Elizabeth's policy for nearly twenty years, and upon that
understanding he had condoned his mother's execution, and
kept the peace with England during the Spanish and Irish
wars. He was generally regarded as the only possible successor to the throne: Essex, when he despaired of regaining
Elizabeth's favour, sought to secure his future by winning that
of James VI.; and Cecil in 1602 had begun a secret correspondence with the Scottish king. Cecil, says a letter of
March 9, 1603, "as yet ruleth all"; but he was statesman
enough to base his policy on national desires, and "the far
greater part of the realm are for the king of Scots".[1]

Success abroad continued to light the evening of Elizabeth's
days. After ineffective negotiations for peace with Spain at
Boulogne in May, 1600, English troops under the two Veres,
Fairfax, and Sir Edward Cecil helped the Dutch to win the
battle of Nieuport on July 2, 1600, the greatest of their victories on land over the Spaniards; and assisted in prolong-
ing the defence of Ostend, which was hardly less serviceable
to their cause, until after Elizabeth's death. English seamen
were as adventurous as of yore. John Davis, after exploring
the straits known by his name, left further arctic discovery to
Baffin and Hudson, accompanied Cavendish round the world,
and then devoted himself to the East where he was killed in
1605 in a fight off Singapore. In 1591-94 Sir James Lancaster,
preferring the sea-route round the Cape to that taken by Fitch,
sailed to India, broke into the Portuguese monopoly, and
brought back such profits that the East India Company was
formed. It received its royal charter on the last day of the
sixteenth century, and in February, 1601, Lancaster sailed
again to the Malacca Straits. Even further afield pushed
William Adams: passing through the Straits of Magellan in
1599, and across the Pacific, he landed in Japan in April,
1600. There, unwillingly at first, he made his home and married a Japanese wife; he built the first navy of Japan, and lies
buried on a hill which overlooks the harbour of Yokosuka. A
street in Yeddo bears his name, and an annual celebration is still
held in honour of the Elizabethan seaman who forged the earliest
link between the two great naval powers of the East and West.[2]

[1] Domestic Cal., 1601-3, p. 298.   [2] Dict. of Nat. Biogr., i., 104-6; Colonial Calendar, East Indies, 1513-1616, pp. 227-230.

No brilliant achievements, however, could relieve Elizabeth's loneliness. She thanked God for giving her " a heart which never yet feared foreign or home enemy " ;[1] but a queen who had outlived all her early friends and ministers, and had few relatives nearer than her distant cousin James VI., whom she had never seen, could not escape a sense of desolation. She felt none of the physical or mental weariness which makes men acquiesce in death; and her essentially secular mind did not respond to religious consolation. A splendid physique, abstemiousness, and careful habits enabled her to survive by many years the usual span of royal lives, and her health did not begin to fail till the end of 1602, when she was sixty-nine. In January, 1603, she recovered somewhat, and removed to Richmond, where she received Scaramelli in audience on Sunday, February 6.[2] Early in March she sickened again, and besides physical ailments suffered "a notable decay of judgement and memory, insomuch as she cannot abide discourses of government and state, but delighteth to hear old Canterbury tales, to which she is very attentive".[3] The death of her cousin the Countess of Nottingham preyed upon her mind; and whatever truth there may be in the story of her revelation of treachery towards Essex, Elizabeth was certainly worried by the necessity of having to pardon Tyrone, and complained that Essex had been condemned for granting no worse terms. Gradually she lost strength, refusing to take either food or physic; and on March 23 her councillors gathered round her death-bed.

The scene, as depicted by court-gossips, was as unreal as anything in Tudor history. Her advisers are represented as hanging on the movement of her lips and hands, striving to glean some indication of her wishes for the succession, and naming one claimant after another in the hope of extorting some sign of clear assent from the hardly-conscious queen. At one name she roused : " I will have no rascal's son in my seat," she exclaimed as Beauchamp was suggested, " but one worthy to be a king ". Lady Southwell, who tells the story in a narrative endorsed April 1, 1607, also says that the council

---

[1] Townshend, p. 266. [2] *Venetian Cal.*, ix., 531-34.
[3] *Domestic Cal.*, 1601-3, pp. 298-99, 301-3; *Venetian Cal.*, ix., 557-58, 564-65.

CHAP.
XXIV.

asked Elizabeth whether she wished the king of France to succeed her. Such tales reflected the natural feeling that something unusual and dramatic, some last act big with national weal or woe, must mark the death-bed of a sovereign, and especially of one who had left so deep an impress on her age as the last Tudor.[1] In reality the council had already made their arrangements for James VI.'s accession : all they could have sought from the queen was a royal assent to their resolutions, which would lighten their responsibility for an illegal decision and improve its chances of peaceful adoption. But nothing she could say would alter the course of events, and therefore she was dumb. She had no constitutional power to bequeath the crown ; nor did the efforts of her predecessors to regulate the succession encourage imitation. Henry VIII.'s legal dispositions were at that moment being ignored, Edward VI.'s had been rejected after nine days, and Mary had been unable to keep Elizabeth from the throne. The living must settle their own affairs : Elizabeth's thoughts were elsewhere ; and after the council had retired, Whitgift at her request prayed long by her bedside. Then she became unconscious, and died between two and three o'clock on the morning of Thursday, March 24.

[1] Wilbraham's Journal in *Camden Miscellany*, x., 54 ; *Venetian Cal.*, ix., 560-62 ; Nichols, *Progresses of Queen Elizabeth*, iii., 603-613 ; Lingard, *History of England*, 5th ed., vi., 645-9. *Cf.* Carey (Elizabeth's second cousin, afterwards Earl of Monmouth), *Memoirs*, ed. 1759, p. 144 : "there have beene many false lyes reported of the end and death of that good lady ".

APPENDIX I.

ON AUTHORITIES.

I. MANUSCRIPT SOURCES.

THE great development of the scope and activity of the central government, indicated by the phrase "the New Monarchy," is faithfully
reflected in the enormous increase in the materials for the history of
England in the sixteenth century.   The vigour of Tudor administration in home affairs resulted in the multiplication of domestic state
papers, and of such records as those of the privy council, the councils
of the North, and of Wales and its marches, the star chamber, the
courts of high commission, of augmentations, of first-fruits and tenths,
of wards, and of requests.   In external affairs the increasing diplomatic activity of the government produced an expanding bulk of
foreign correspondence, consequent upon the establishment of resident
ambassadors abroad, the frequency of special missions to more distant
courts, and the encouragement of private news-letters.   The rise of
naval and commercial enterprise begat other records, and the relations
of church and state developed the sources of ecclesiastical history.

(i.) *In the Record Office.*—A secretary of state, however, commonly
treated his official correspondence as his private property : most of
the Cecils' state papers are at Hatfield House ; and it was not till the
very end of this period that Sir Thomas Wilson began to insist that
state papers belonged to the state.   The documents in the Public
Record Office, therefore, only represent a fraction of the materials
extant for the history of England in the sixteenth century.   Of these
materials there are nineteen volumes of domestic state papers for the
reign of Edward VI., fourteen for Mary's, and 295 volumes for Elizabeth's, with twenty-four volumes of "Addenda" for the whole period.
Of Scottish state papers there are five volumes for Edward's reign, one
for Mary's, and seventy-nine for Elizabeth's, besides an appendix and
twenty-one volumes relating to Mary, Queen of Scots, from her flight
to England to her execution.   The Irish state papers comprise four
volumes for Edward VI.'s reign, two for Mary's, and over 200 for

APP. I. Elizabeth's. Besides state papers there are other domestic sources in the patent rolls, the records of the star chamber, the court of requests, and the court of augmentations (down to its abolition by Mary in 1554). The legal documents contain as a rule only bills and pleadings, and not the judicial decisions.

The foreign state papers are even more numerous than the domestic. Down to 1577 they are arranged chronologically in one series, comprising fifteen volumes (including three of Calais Papers) for Edward VI.'s reign, thirteen for Mary's, and 145 for the first nineteen years of Elizabeth's. From 1577 onwards this general series is divided into (*a*) general correspondence; (*b*) foreign entry-books kept by the secretary's clerks; (*c*) news-letters; (*d*) treaty-papers, and (*e*) treaties; and there are further divisions after 1603. The general correspondence is, moreover, subdivided geographically under the various foreign states. For France there are between July, 1577, and March, 1603, forty-eight volumes; for " Holland " and Flanders sixty-nine, for the Empire and German States thirteen, for Spain and Portugal ten, for Denmark three, for Italy, Poland, Russia, Sweden, Turkey, the Balkan States, and Venice one or two apiece. These states are also represented by a few volumes (in some cases only a few documents) in the divisions " entry-books," " news-letters," " treaty-papers," and treaties. The evidential value of this diplomatic correspondence varies : a diplomatist's prospects of promotion depended to some extent upon his success in conveying true impressions to his own government and false impressions to the government to which he was accredited ; and a contemporary document may be quite as misleading as a modern history. Two contradictory despatches from Cecil have been noted on p. 227 and two from Quadra on p. 425 ; and even in letters passing between a government and its own agents the meaning often depends upon secret understandings, verbally conveyed. Thus Gilbert was at liberty in 1572 to neglect the council's orders to return from Flushing (p. 332), and Drake was probably allowed a similar discretion on more than one occasion. The real purport of much of Elizabeth's correspondence must be read between the lines.

(ii.) *In Foreign Archives.*—For the purposes of English history, the despatches of English agents abroad are less important than those of foreign agents in England, upon which we depend for a great deal of our knowledge. This evidence has to be discounted by the prejudices or ignorance of the writers ; but they had seldom any interest in deceiving their own governments, and as a rule they are well informed and accurate. Despatches, however, were sometimes meant to be intercepted, and then their contents were written to

deceive; this caution rarely applies to correspondence in cipher.
This class of material exists for the most part in the archives of
Simancas, Rome, Brussels, Paris, Venice, and the Hague; but tran-
scripts of portions, the most important of them being perhaps BAS-
CHET's transcripts from the French, and BLISS's from the Roman
archives, have been made and are preserved in the Record Office.
For the most part, however, the English student has to depend upon
the printed or calendared despatches described below.

(iii.) *In the British Museum.*—The documents in the British
Museum are hardly less important than those in the Record Office;
but they are scattered throughout collections formed haphazard by
various collectors at different times. The most important are the
Cottonian, the Harleian, the Lansdowne, and the Additional MSS.
The Lansdowne MSS. contain a large number of Burghley's papers,
more in fact than are preserved at Hatfield, which owes its wealth of
documents to Sir Robert Cecil rather than to his father; they also include a number of John Foxe's MSS. Sir Robert Cotton made little
attempt to classify or arrange the documents he collected; and their
order, like that of the Additional MSS., is simply that of their date of
acquisition. But a useful attempt at classification is made in the fourth
volume of the folio index to the Harleian MSS. published in 1812.
Among the Additional MSS., the most valuable for the period dealt
with in this volume are BERGENROTH's and FROUDE's transcripts from
the Simancas archives (vols. 28595-97 and 26056) and the transcripts
of papal letters relating to England (vols. 15351-15400; 15401 contains a chronological index); and occasionally documents of great
value are to be found in the Royal, Sloane, Egerton, and Stowe MSS.,
for example the unique fragment of the privy council's warrant-book
in Royal MS. 18 C. xxiv.

(iv.) *Other Collections.*—Of collections still in private hands, the
most valuable is that at Hatfield House; but its contents only
become voluminous with the political activity of Sir Robert Cecil.
There are about 4,000 documents before 1588, while for the next
fifteen years there are something like 20,000. No other collection
can be compared with this; but there are important materials among
the Duke of Rutland's MSS. at Belvoir, the Marquis of Bath's at
Longleat, Lord Bagot's at Blithfield (the Stafford MSS.), Sir Matthew
Wilson's at Eshton Hall, Gargrave, and the Loseley MSS. at Guildford.
Many municipal corporations, cathedral chapters, and other bodies,
such as the Inns of Court and College of Arms, possess valuable
archives. At Lambeth are the Carew MSS., hardly less voluminous
than the Irish state papers in the Record Office, and Anthony Bacon's
MSS., Birch's transcripts of which fill sixteen volumes in the British

APP. I. Museum Add. MSS., 4109-4124. The Petyt MSS. in the Inner Temple have furnished the materials for several volumes published by the Camden Society; and there are valuable Roman catholic collections in the Archbishop's House at Westminster, and at Stonyhurst. There are a considerable number of sixteenth century documents in the Tanner, Rawlinson, and Carte MSS. in the Bodleian library, and some in certain College MSS. kept there. The chief official records outside the Record Office are the MS. statutes, the journals of the two houses of parliament, the register of the privy council kept at the Council Office in Whitehall, and the bishops' registers.

Of the guides to these MS. sources, the most useful is S. R. SCAR-GILL-BIRD'S *Guide to the Principal Classes of Documents in the Public Record Office*, 3rd ed., 1908. It is supplemented by the annual *Reports of the Deputy-Keeper of the Records* and by the *Lists and Indexes* published by the Record Office. The former contain reports on documents relating to English affairs in the archives of Paris (Nos. 36, 42-7), Rome (Nos. 44, 46), Venice (Nos. 33, 44-5), lists of French ambassadors in England and their despatches (Nos. 37, 39), of transcripts made for the Record Office, and of ciphers used in the Venetian correspondence (No. 30), as well as reports on various classes of domestic records. The *Lists and Indexes* include lists of domestic state papers (No. 3), of foreign state papers (No. 19), of star-chamber proceedings (No. 13), of chancery proceedings (Nos. 7, 12, 20, 24), and of proceedings in the court of requests (No. 21). The chief collections in private hands are described in the *Reports* of the Historical MSS. Commission: the first nine, published in folio between 1870 and 1884, contain a rapid survey of the material, while the appendices to the subsequent reports, published in 8vo, attempt something more like a calendar.

II. PRINTED DOCUMENTS.

(I.) STATE PAPERS AND LETTERS.

(*a*) *English.*—For the period 1547-1603 no such comprehensive *corpus* of printed sources as the *Letters and Papers of Henry VIII.* is available. The *Calendars* printed under the authority of the Master of the Rolls are rigidly limited to documents preserved in the Record Office; and the criticism of the *Calendars*, by Monsignor Baumgarten in his *Vor der Bartholomäusnacht* and other scholars, for the omission of documents preserved elsewhere is not deserved by the editors. JOSEPH STEVENSON, indeed, in his *Foreign Calendar* took the liberty, when he began, of including some documents from the British Museum, and of printing as notes illustrative passages from the despatches of foreign ambassadors; but he was checked when he got to the end of 1560, and from that date all sources outside the Record Office are ignored: if there is a rough draft in the Record Office and a completed despatch in the British Museum, the rough draft will be calendared without so much as a reference to the finished despatch or the alterations it may contain. The first volume of the *Domestic Calendar*, published by ROBERT LEMON in 1856, is little better than a catalogue; in one printed volume it deals with 179 MS. volumes of state papers, extending from 1547 to 1580. His second volume, published in 1865, marks a great advance, and covers only ten years, 1581-90; and the improvement was continued by Mrs. EVERETT GREEN, who assumed the task on LEMON's death, and took four more volumes to complete the remaining twelve years of Elizabeth's reign; the two volumes of "Addenda" which she also edited occupy more space than Lemon's original series.

The *Foreign Calendar* began on a more adequate scale, though W. B. TURNBULL, its first editor, compressed the whole of Edward VI.'s foreign correspondence into one volume, and the whole of Mary's into another. STEVENSON, however, commenced the reign of Elizabeth on the scale that has ultimately been adopted in all the calendars: his first volume extended only from November, 1558, to September, 1559, and his second from October, 1559, to April, 1560; and he and his successors, A. J. CROSBY and A. J. BUTLER, only succeeded in compressing the correspondence of the next twenty-three years into fourteen volumes of the *Calendar*; forty-seven years after STEVENSON began in 1863 the *Calendar* had only covered twenty-five years of Elizabeth's reign (1558-83). Scotland has been treated by the Record Office sometimes as a foreign country, and sometimes in separate calendars. Many Scottish papers are included in the *Foreign Calendar*; but they have also been made into a *Scottish Calendar* (1509-1603), meagerly edited in two volumes by MARKHAM JOHN THORPE (1858). A much more satisfactory edition of *State Papers relating to Scotland and Mary Queen of Scots*, including those in the British Museum and elsewhere, is in course of publication under the direction of the Deputy Clerk Register of Scotland; two volumes (1542-69) have been edited by JOSEPH BAIN, and three (1569-81) by WILLIAM K. BOYD. BAIN also edited two other Scottish series, each in two volumes: the *Hamilton Papers* (1532-90), which were purchased from Hamilton Palace by the German government in 1883, and re-purchased by the British Museum in 1889; and the *Border Papers* (1560-1603).

(*b*) *Foreign.*—Only portions of the materials in foreign archives and of the transcripts in the Record Office have been printed. The

APP. I. first volume of the *Spanish Calendar* relating to the reigns of Edward
VI. and Mary is still in the press, and no other published collection
of imperial sources deals with English history during that period
except the *Papiers d'État du Cardinal de Granvelle*, which fill nine
volumes (1841-52) in the French *Collection de Documents inédits*, and
the first of the ten volumes of KERVYN DE LETTENHOVE's *Relations
politiques des Pays-Bas et de l'Angleterre* (Brussels, 1882-91). This
series, which extends from 1556 to 1576, prints *in extenso* a vast
number of valuable documents from Brussels, Simancas, the Record
Office, the British Museum, and other collections ; and England's
relations with the Netherlands are further detailed in GACHARD's
Correspondance de Philippe II. sur les affaires des Pays-Bas (5 vols.,
Brussels, 1848-79), *Correspondance de Guillaume le Taciturne* (6 vols.,
Brussels, 1847-57), *Correspondance de Marguerite d'Autriche avec
Philippe II.*, 1554-68 (3 vols., Brussels, 1867-87), *Correspondance du
Duc d'Albe* (Brussels, 1850), and *Correspondance d'Alexandre de
Farnèse*, 1578-79 (Brussels) ; in GROEN VAN PRINSTERER's *Archives
de la Maison d'Orange-Nassau* (1st series, 9 vols., Leyden ; 2nd series,
5 vols., Utrecht, 1841-61) ; in MÜLLER and DIEDERICK's *Documents
Historiques inédits concernant les Relations entre le Duc d'Anjou et les
Pays-Bas*, 1576-83 (5 vols., Utrecht and the Hague, 1889-99) ; and
in other collections (see *Cambridge Modern History*, iii., 798-801).
The despatches of Spanish ambassadors in England from 1558 to
1584 are printed *in extenso* in FERNANDEZ DE NAVARETTE's *Coleccion de
Documentos ineditos*, tt. 87, 89-92 (Madrid, 1842, etc.) ; and papers
relating to English affairs are scattered through other volumes of
the *Coleccion* (*cf. Engl. Hist. Rev.*, xvi., 572-73). Both it and
KERVYN DE LETTENHOVE contain many documents not noticed in
the *Spanish Calendar*, 1558-1603 (4 vols., ed. M. A. S. Hume,
1892-99), which appears to be based on transcripts made by
Froude, or by or for the editor, though Froude's transcripts also
include some documents not noticed in the *Calendar*. Some notes
and transcripts from despatches now lost are contained in T. GON-
ZALES' *Apuntamientos para la Historia del Felippe II. y la Reina de
Inglaterra* (vol. vii. of the *Memorias de la R. Academia de la Historia*, Madrid, 1832 ; translated by Spencer Hall with the title *Documents from Simancas relating to the Reign of Elizabeth*, London, 1865).

The French archives are represented by the *Correspondance diplomatique d'Odet de Selve, 1546-48*, published in 1888 under the
direction of the French Foreign Office ; by RIBIER's *Lettres et Mémoires d'Estat*, covering Henry II.'s reign (2 vols., Paris, 1666) ; by
the ABBÉ VERTOT's *Mémoires de MM. de Noailles*, dealing with the
years 1553-69 (5 vols., Leyden, 1763 ; the originals are most of them

lost, but Vertot's selection represents only a fraction of the transcripts
still extant in the Bibliothéque Nationale) ; by the *Correspondance
diplomatique de B. Salignac de la Mothe-Fénelon*, 1568-75 (7 vols.,
ed. Charles Purton Cooper, Paris and London, 1838-40 ; re-edited by
A. Teulet for the Bannatyne Club, 1862), which is of the greatest
value for the crisis of 1569 ; by TEULET's *Papiers d'État relatifs à
l'Histoire de l'Écosse* (3 vols., Bannatyne Club, 1851), which were re-
edited as *Relations politiques de la France et l'Espagne avec l'Écosse*
(5 vols., Paris, 1862) ; by the *Lettres de Catherine de Médicis* (10
vols., *Collection de Documents inédits*, 1880 ff.) ; by HUBAULT's *Ambassade de M. de Castelnau en Angleterre*, 1575-85 (Paris, 1856) ; and
by the *Despatches of the Marquis de Courcelles* (Bannatyne Club, 1828).
Many other volumes of the French *Collection de Documents inédits* contain papers relating to English affairs ; and some additional information is found in the memoirs of French ambassadors to
England, *e.g.* those of Castelnau de Mauvissière (3 vols., ed. Le
Laboureur, Brussels, 1731) and the Duc de Nevers (2 vols., Paris,
1665). But the references to English affairs in most of the French
memoirs of the times, such as those of Villars, Brantôme, Tavannes,
Sully, and Guise, are often erroneous. A good bibliography of French
sources (down to 1559) is given in HENRI HAUSER's *Les Sources de
l'Histoire de France*, tome i. (Paris, 1909), and there is a useful
list in P. COURTEAULT's *Monluc* (Paris, 1908), pp. xxi-xlviii.

The archives of Venice and Rome are the only important Italian
sources. ALBÉRI's *Relazioni degli Ambasciatori Veneti al Senato
durante il secolo decimo sesto* (15 vols., Florence, 1839-63) print *in
extenso* the "Reports" of Venetian ambassadors, and volumes i.-vi.
contain those referring mainly or partly to England (they were
separately issued in an *édition de luxe* in 1852). But they do not
include the correspondence, and in this respect are inferior to the
Venetian Calendar edited (1864-1897) by RAWDON BROWN (vols. i.-vi.),
G. CAVENDISH BENTINCK (vol. vii.), and HORATIO BROWN (vols. viii.-
ix.). The *Calendar* varies in value : after Capello's recall in 1535 Venice
was represented in England only by a secretary, Zuccato, until 1544,
and then by another, Zambon, until 1547, when Bollani was appointed
ambassador ; but his despatches, as well as those of the two secretaries,
have disappeared, and the *Calendar* which covers twenty years, 1534-
1554, in one volume (v.) is largely occupied with Cardinal Pole's
correspondence, which is given more fully in QUIRINI's *Epistolae
R. Poli* (5 vols., Brescia, 1744-52). The despatches of Barbaro, who
was ambassador from 1549 to 1552, are also wanting, though his
"Report" has been preserved (v., 338-62), and there are only two
despatches and a "Report" (v., 532-64) from his successor Soranzo.

APP. I. For six months after Michiele's arrival in England his correspondence is equally scanty; but from the beginning of 1555 his despatches and those of his successor Suriano, who arrived in March, 1557, are the most important of all extant sources for Mary's reign, though Froude had no access to them; and the volume (vi.) in which they are calendared consists of three parts, each containing over 500 pages. Michiele's despatches have also been printed *in extenso* by Friedmann (Venice, 1869). With the termination of Philip II.'s rule, England lost its importance in Venetian eyes, and no Venetian ambassador resided here until January, 1603. One volume of the *Calendar* (vii.) suffices for the indirect references in the Venetian archives from 1558 to 1580; and though two (viii. and ix.) are required for 1580-1603, they contain principally despatches from Venetian ambassadors at Philip II.'s court and at Constantinople, where Harborne and his successors were undermining the commercial position of Venice in the Levant. Some Venetian documents relating to England are also printed in Ruscelli, *Lettere di Principi* (Venice, 1570), in G. TURBA's *Venetianische Depeschen vom Kaiserhofe* (vol. iii., Vienna, 1895), and in A. BASCHET'S *Les Princes de l'Europe au XVIme siècle, d'apres les Rapports des Ambassadeurs Venitiens* (Paris, 1862). No comprehensive effort has been made to print or calendar the Vatican archives; they deal, as is natural, mainly with ecclesiastical history, and most use of them has been made by ecclesiastical, and especially Roman Catholic, historians, *e.g.*, by Father POLLEN, S.J., in his *Papal Negotiations with Mary Queen of Scots*, 1561-7 (Scottish Hist. Soc., vol. xxxvii., Edinburgh, 1901), and in his articles in *The Month*, volumes xcix.-ci., cix.-cx., and by Father KNOX in his *Letters of Cardinal Allen* (London, 1882); upon them, however, is based A. O. MEYER'S *England und die katholische Kirche unter Königin Elisabeth* (Rome, 1910), the first adequate attempt to treat the subject historically. Occasional references of value are also found in the *Nuntiaturberichte aus Deutschland*, 1560-1572 (Akad. d. Wissenschaft., Vienna, 1897).

(*c*) *Miscellaneous State Papers.*—Besides these more or less regular series of documents edited from domestic or foreign archives, there are numerous selections of state papers calendared or published *in extenso*. The twelve volumes of the *Calendar of Hatfield MSS.* (1547-1602) are as important as most of the Calendars of State Papers preserved in the Record Office; but the dating and editing of the documents contained in the earlier volumes are very defective. The two selections of *Burghley State Papers* published *in extenso* by S. HAYNES in 1740 (1542-1570) and W. MURDIN in 1759 (1571-1596) are still useful; and other papers from the same collection were published by PECK in his *Desiderata Curiosa* (2 vols., London, 1732,

star chamber is given in Miss C. SCOFIELD'S *Star Chamber* (Chicago, APP. I.
1900), pp. iii-xxii; and examples are printed in I. S. LEADAM'S *Select
Cases from the Court of Star Chamber* (Selden Soc., 1904). Mr.
LEADAM has performed a similar service for its civil counterpart in his
Select Cases from the Court of Requests (Selden Soc., 1898). The
Court of High Commission is less adequately represented in J. S.
BURN'S *High Commission*, 1865. Materials for the history of the
common law courts are contained in the *Reports* of Staunford (1560),
Plowden (2 pts., 1571, 1579), Dyer (1585), Keilway (1602), Coke (13
pts., 1600-15; see also his *Institutes*, 3 pts., 1628, 1642), and Pop-
ham, 1656; and State Trials are recorded in COBBETT'S [or HOWELL'S]
State Trials (vol. i., 1809), from which a selection has been edited
by J. Willis Bund (3 vols., 1879, etc.). Trials of peers before the
lord high steward are reported in Harleian MS. 2194 (*cf.* L. W.
VERNON-HARCOURT, *The Steward and Trial of Peers*, 1907). Miss
C. A. J. SKEEL has dealt with *The Council of Wales and the Marches*
(1904), and G. T. LAPSLEY with the *County Palatine of Durham*
(1900); but there is as yet no published account of the scattered
records of the Council of the North.

III. NARRATIVES.

(I.) CONTEMPORARY DIARIES, JOURNALS, AND CHRONICLES.

HALL'S *Chronicle* was continued with less success by RICHARD
GRAFTON (1565) who found a rival and critic in JOHN STOW. Both
writers began with mere compilations and chronologies, but in 1580
STOW broke new ground with his *Chronicles*, which in the 1584 and
later editions bore the title *Annales*. STOW was born about 1525, and
a considerable part of his book, which he continued down to 1605, is
a contemporary authority, while his *Survey of London* (ed. Kingsford,
1908) is indispensable for the student of London topography and
antiquities. Stow was also employed on the second edition of
RAPHAEL HOLINSHED'S *Chronicles;* the first edition had appeared in
1578 (2 vols., folio); the second edition, continued to 1586 by JOHN
HOOKER with the assistance of Stow, Francis Thynne, Abraham
Fleming, and others, was issued in January, 1587 (3 vols., folio), and
both editions were expurgated at the instance of the government on
account of their outspoken criticism of living politicians. WILLIAM
CAMDEN, who was born in 1551, began in 1608 to write his *Annales
regnante Elizabetha*, a task urged upon him by Burghley in 1597;
the first part was published in 1615, the second at Leyden in 1625,
but the best edition is that by THOMAS HEARNE (3 vols., 1717; in
the *Dict. of Nat. Biogr.*, viii., 281-82, Sir E. MAUNDE THOMPSON

APP. I. defends Camden from the charge of having modified his MS. to please James I.) ; and in his *Britannia*, dedicated to Burghley in 1586, CAMDEN attempts to do for Great Britain what Stow had done for London. JOHN SPEED's *History of Great Britain from Julius Caesar to King James*, published in 1611, has been praised as the first attempt to write history as distinct from chronicles and annals; but, while SPEED tries to digest his materials, his critical acumen is very deficient ; he deserves, however, some recognition as a cartographer, though he is inferior to his contemporaries, John Norden and Christopher Saxton.

These are the chief general chronicles. Of those which do not go outside the personal knowledge or lifetime of their authors the most important (arranged chronologically) are : EDWARD VI.'s *Journal*, printed in BURNET's *History of the Reformation*, but better edited, with Edward's other extant writings and many illustrative documents, by JOHN GOUGH NICHOLS as *Literary Remains of Edward VI.* (2 vols., Roxburghe Club, 1857) ; ANTONIO GUARAS' *Chronicle of Henry VIII.* (to 1552 ; ed. M. A. S. Hume, 1889 ; very inaccurate), and *Accession of Queen Mary* (ed. R. Garnett, 1892) ; the *Chronicle of Queen Jane and Queen Mary* (Camden Soc., 1860) ; ROSSO's *I Successi d'Inghilterra* (Ferrara, 1560) ; MICHELANGELO FLORIO's *Historia de la Vita e de la Morte de Giovanna Graia* (1607 ; for Florio, see *Dict. of Nat. Biogr.*, xix., 336) ; PONET's *Treatise of Politique Power* (1556) ; *Narratives of the Reformation* (Camden Soc., 1859) ; *Verney Papers* (vol. i., Camden Soc., 1853) ; *Greyfriars' Chronicle* (to 1556 ; Camden Soc., 1852) ; WRIOTHESLEY's *Chronicle* (to 1559 ; 2 vols., Camden Soc., 1877) ; MACHYN's *Diary* (to 1563 ; Camden Soc., 1847 ; cf. *Engl. Hist. Rev.*, xi., 282-300) ; the *Travels and Life of Sir Thomas Hoby* (to 1564 ; *Camden Miscellany*, vol. x., 1902) ; WALSINGHAM's *Diary* (1570 to 1583 ; *Camden Miscellany*, vol. vi., 1871) ; Sir JAMES MELVILLE's *Memoirs* (first ed., 1683, best ed., Bannatyne Club, 1827) ; HENTZNER's *Itinerarium* (1598, ed. 1612 and 1797) ; MANNINGHAM's *Diary* (1601-3 ; Camden Soc., 1868) ; WILBRAHAM's *Journal* (1593 to 1648 ; *Camden Miscellany*, vol. x., 1902) ; R. CAREY's *Memoirs* (to 1603 ; ed. 1759, fourth ed., 1808) ; NAUNTON's *Fragmenta Regalia* (first ed., 1641 ; latest, 1870) ; CARLETON's *Thankful Remembrance* (1627), and HARINGTON's *Nugae Antiquae* (2 vols., 1769). Various contemporary narratives are also printed in the *Somers Tracts* (vol. i., 1809), and in my *Tudor Tracts* (1903).

(II.) LATER HISTORIES.

Except on its ecclesiastical side (see below), the reign of Edward VI. has not been the subject of much good historical work. HAY-

WARD'S *Life and Raigne of Edward VI.* (1632), is of no particular APP. I. value; and later historians added little until P. F. TYTLER printed a number of unpublished letters and papers in his *England under Edward VI. and Mary* (2 vols., 1839). Practically everything known about the young king is collected by J. G. NICHOLS in his Introduction to the *Literary Remains* (see above), pp. xxi-ccclx. Somerset's administration is described in my *England under Protector Somerset* (1900, with bibliography); but Northumberland still lacks a biographer. F. W. RUSSELL'S *Kett's Rebellion* (1859) is a valuable monograph, as is A. O. MEYER'S *Die Englische Diplomatie in Deutschland zur Zeit Eduards VI. and Mariens* (Breslau, 1900). There are lives of Lady Jane Grey by GEORGE HOWARD (1822), by Sir HARRIS NICOLAS (prefixed to his *Literary Remains of Lady Jane Grey*, 1825), by I. A. TAYLOR (1908), and by R. DAVEY (*The Nine Days' Queen*, 1909).

For Mary's reign GRIFFET'S *Nouveaux Éclaircissements* (Amsterdam, 1766) is a valuable criticism of the current views expressed by Hume; and Sir F. MADDEN in the memoir prefixed to his *Privy Purse Expenses of the Princess Mary* (1831, pp. xv-clxx) takes a similar line; but the most elaborate *apologia* for Mary is Miss J. M. STONE'S *Mary I.* (1901, a work of some research but not a balanced judgment). See also ZIMMERMANN'S *Marie die Katholische* (Freiburg i. B., 1890), and *Kardinal Pole* (Ratisbon, 1893); CLIFFORD'S *Jane Dormer, Duchess of Feria* (ed. Stevenson, 1887); WIESENER, *La Jeunesse d'Elisabeth* (Paris, 1878; Engl. transl., 2 vols., 1879); MUMBY'S *Girlhood of Queen Elizabeth* (1909; uses the Bedingfield Papers printed in *Norfolk Archæology*, vol. iv.); FORNERON'S *Philippe II.* (Paris, 2 vols., 1881); M. A. S. HUME'S *Visit of Philip II.* (1554) in *Engl. Hist. Rev.*, 1892, and *Two English Queens* (1908); R. DAVEY'S *Mary Tudor* (1897); I. S. LEADAM'S *Pursuit of English Refugees in Germany* (Trans. of the Royal Hist. Soc., 1896); and H. E. MALDEN'S *Notes on the Local Progress of Protestantism in England* (*ibid.*, N.S., ii., 61-76).

The earliest life of Queen Elizabeth is GREGORIO LETI'S *Storia di Elizabetta* (Amsterdam, 2 vols., 1693). This edition is said to have been suppressed, but a French translation appeared at Amsterdam in 1694, and the Italian version was republished there in 1703; it is a romance garnished with a number of imaginary letters. LUCY AIKIN'S *Memoirs of the Court of Elizabeth* (2 vols., 1818), and NICHOLS' *Progresses of Elizabeth* (3 vols., 1788-1805), contain many details of her court life. The life by AGNES STRICKLAND (1844) occupies vol. iii. of her *Lives of the Queens of England*. Of recent accounts the best are those by E. S. BEESLEY (Twelve English States-

APP. I. men Series, 1892) ; Bishop CREIGHTON (Goupil Series, with magnificent illustrations, 1896; cheaper ed., Longmans, 1899) ; and ERICH MARCKS (Leipzig, 1897) ; see also E. BEKKER, *Elisabeth und Leicester* (Giessen, 1890). There are lives of Burghley by NARES (3 vols., 1828-31 ; ponderous, see MACAULAY'S Essay on "Burleigh and His Times"), by M. A. S. HUME (1898 ; derived mainly from the Spanish State papers), and by A. JESSOPP (1902 ; a slight sketch) ; of Walsingham in WEBB, MILLER, and BECKWITH'S *History of Chislehurst* (1899), and by KARL STÄHLIN (Heidelberg, vol. i., 1908 ; an excellent and elaborate survey) ; of Davison (1823) and Hatton (1847), by Sir H. NICOLAS ; of Raleigh, by OLDYS (1736, 1829), BIRCH (1751), CAYLEY (1805), TYTLER (1833), EDWARDS (2 vols., 1868), ST. JOHN (1868), STEBBING (1891) and M. A. S. HUME (1897) ; of Bacon, by SPEDDING (*Life and Letters*, 7 vols., 1861-74), DEAN CHURCH (English Men of Letters Series, 1884) and ABBOTT (1885) ; of the Devereux, Earls of Essex, by Captain DEVEREUX (2 vols., 1853 ; see also ABBOTT'S *Bacon and Essex*, 1877) ; of Sir P. Sidney, by FULKE GREVILLE (1652), J. A. SYMONDS (English Men of Letters Series, 1886), H. R. FOX BOURNE (1862, new ed., 1891) and P. SIDNEY (1902) ; of Sir T. Smith, by STRYPE (1698, new ed., 1820) ; and of Sir T. Gresham, by J. W. BURGON (2 vols., 1839).

As general surveys of the whole period Lingard's and Froude's Histories have not yet been superseded, though the materials accessible since Lingard wrote have been vastly increased. Froude's later volumes have excited less controversy than those in which he dealt with Henry VIII., and on the whole they are less open to criticism. His anti-clerical prejudices are not after 1547 combined with partisanship for the government, and possibly he makes too little allowance for the difficulties which beset both Mary and Elizabeth. His industry is not open to question ; he not only consulted, but transcribed large portions of the Simancas MSS. though he sometimes misinterpreted his own transcripts ; and it would seem that the hastiness of many of his statements was partly due to the vastness of the materials with which he tried to cope without the help of calendars and other aids. As a literary artist he has few equals among historians ; his chief drawback, which he shares with most other writers, is that he went to history for proofs of preconceived opinions, and tried to interpret it by certain definite but disputable principles. The most important sources to which he had no access were the archives at Paris, Brussels, Rome, and Venice, which have now been calendared or transcribed for the Record Office. Some of these sources have been used by M. A. S. HUME in his *Year After the Armada* (1896), *Treason and Plot* (1901), and *Courtships of Queen*

Elizabeth (1896 and 1904), and in the *Cambridge Modern History*. APP. I.
The relevant chapters in the last-named work are vol. ii., c. xiv., " The
Reformation under Edward VI.," by myself; c. xv., "Philip and Mary,"
by J. BASS MULLINGER ; c. xvi., " The Anglican Settlement and the
Scottish Reformation," by F. W. MAITLAND (the vast erudition of
which is concealed from most readers by the lightness of touch and
absence of references) ; vol. iii., c. viii. " Mary Stuart," by T. G. LAW
(an admirable and dispassionate survey) ; c. ix., " The Elizabethan
Naval War with Spain," by Sir J. KNOX LAUGHTON ; and cc. x. and
xi., " The Last Years of Elizabeth " and the " Elizabethan Age of
English Literature," by SIDNEY LEE. The principal defect of the
scheme is that it makes practically no provision for the political,
constitutional, and ecclesiastical history of the greater part of Elizabeth's reign.

IV. SPECIAL SUBJECTS.

(1.) ECCLESIASTICAL HISTORY.

The chief unpublished source consists of the episcopal registers.
The records of convocation, so far as they were not destroyed by the
fire of 1666, have been published in WILKINS' *Concilia* (vol. iv.,
1737). Other documentary collections are ATTERBURY's *Rights of
an English Convocation* (2nd ed., 1701); CARDWELL's *Documentary
Annals of the Reformed Church of England* (2 vols., 1839; 2nd
ed., 1844), *The Two Books of Common Prayer* (1839), *Conferences*,
etc. (1840), *Synodalia* (2 vols., 1842), and his editions of the *Reformatio Legum Ecclesiasticarum* (1850), and of GIBSON's *Synodus Anglicana* (1854) ; HARDWICK's *Articles of Religion* (1851, 2nd ed., 1859) ;
GIBSON's *Thirty-nine Articles* (2nd ed., 1898) ; the *Bullarium
Romanum* (Luxemburg, 1727); and the *Alcuin Club Tracts*.

The three main printed sources are FOXE's *Acts and Monuments*, the
Parker Society's Publications, and STRYPE's works. FOXE's book,
based on a Latin work issued by him in 1559, was published in one
huge folio on March 20, 1563, and soon came to be popularly known
as the *Book of Martyrs ;* four more editions in 2 volumes were published in 1570, 1576, 1583, and 1596, and four in 3 volumes in
1610, 1632, 1641 and 1684. The best-known edition is that called
TOWNSEND's (8 vols., 1837-9), though S. R. CATTLEY did the
editorial work; it was severely criticised by S. R. MAITLAND in
some *Notes* (3 parts, 1841-42), and Cattley's name disappeared
from the re-issue of 1843-49. The Parker Society's Publications
(56 vols., Cambridge) include the works and correspondence of
most of the Anglican reformers, the most important volumes from

APP. I. the historical point of view being the two series of *Zurich Letters* (*i.e.* translations of the *Epistolae Tigurinae*) and *Original Letters* (2 vols. each, 1844-47), and PARKER'S *Correspondence* (1853). STRYPE'S works (originally published between 1694 and 1721 ; re-issued in a uniform edition, Oxford, 25 vols., 1812-24 ; general index, 1828, 2 pts.) comprise *Ecclesiastical Memorials* (to 1558 ; 3 vols., 6 pts.), *Annals* (4 vols., 7 pts. ; 1558-1603), and lives of *Cranmer* (2 vols. ; see also CRANMER'S *Remains*, ed. Jenkyns, 4 vols., and my *Life of Cranmer*, 1904), *Parker* (3 vols. ; see also W. M. KENNEDY'S *Life of Parker*, 1909), *Grindal*, *Whitgift* (3 vols.), *Aylmer*, *Sir John Cheke*, and *Sir T. Smith ;* and all are furnished with numerous documents, which are more valuable than Strype's own writings.

Of other ecclesiastical histories FULLER'S *Church History* was published in 1655 in one folio, and re-edited by Brewer (Oxford, 6 vols., 1845). PETER HEYLYN replied to Fuller from the Laudian point of view in his *Ecclesia Restaurata* (London, 1661, fol. ; ed. in 2 vols. by J. C. Robertson for the Eccl. Hist. Soc., Cambridge, 1849). BURNET took up the cudgels for Protestantism in his *History of the Reformation* (3 vols., 1679, 1715), which HENRY WHARTON vigorously attacked in his *Specimen of Errors*, published in 1693 under the pseudonym "Anthony Harmer" ; the best edition is Pocock's (Oxford, 7 vols., 1865), which contains much additional matter. BURNET, who adopted a view popular in his time, has unduly overshadowed JEREMY COLLIER'S *Ecclesiastical History* (2 vols. fol., 1708, 1714 ; best edition by Lathbury, 9 vols., 1852). The best recent history is R. W. DIXON'S from 1529 to 1570 (6 vols., 1877-1902) ; it is written from a high Anglican point of view, and suffers from the writer's residence at a distance from good libraries. J. GAIRDNER'S volume (1902) in Stephens and Hunt's series is a careful summary of facts (down to 1558) ; it also epitomises opinions expressed at greater length in his *Lollardy and the Reformation* (2 vols., 1908). W. H. FRERE contributes to the same series a volume extending from 1558 to 1625, which is somewhat broader in view, and is an excellent brief account based on very wide reading and careful study.

The principal contemporary controversialists have been mentioned in the text (p. 369). On the Roman Catholic side, the best history is Tierney's edition of DODD'S (*i.e.* Hugh Tootel's) *Church History* (5 vols., 1839-43, with many documents), while the best-known contemporary account is SANDERS' *De Origine ac Progressu Schismatis Anglicani* (Cologne, 1585) ; Sanders' book ii. deals with Edward VI. ; book iii., dealing with Elizabeth, is by Rishton ; Engl. transl. by Lewis, 1877. The chief martyrologies are DIEGO DE YEPES' *Historia de la Persecucion de Inglaterra* (Madrid, 1599), BRIDGEWATER'S (Aque-

pontanus) *Concertatio Ecclesiae Catholicae in Anglia* (Treves, 1594), APP. I.
CIRCIGNANO'S *Eccl. Angl. Trophaea* (Rome, 1584), CHALLONER'S
Memoirs of Missionary Priests (2 vols., 1741-42, also 1803 and 1842),
MORRIS'S *Troubles of our Catholic Forefathers* (3 vols., 1872-77), J. H.
POLLEN'S *Acts of English Martyrs* (1891), and *Unpublished Documents*
(1908). See also FOLEY'S *Records of the English Province of the Society
of Jesus* (7 vols., 1877-83); T. G. LAW'S *Jesuits and Seculars* (1889)
and *Archpriest Controversy* (2 vols., Camden Soc., 1896-98); JES-
SOPP'S *One Generation of a Norfolk House* (1878); SIMPSON'S *Life of
Campion* (1867; re-edited with a Life of Stukeley as *The School of
Shakespeare*, 2 vols., 1878); *Douai Diaries* (1878); and T. E.
BRIDGETT'S *Catholic Hierarchy* (1889).

For the puritans, see WHITTINGHAM'S *Brieff Discours of Troubles at
Frankfort* (1575); BROOK'S *Lives* (3 vols., 1813); NEAL'S *History* (5
vols., 1822); R. G. USHER'S *Presbyterian Movement, 1582-9* (Camden
Soc., 1905); W. A. SHAW in *Engl. Hist. Rev.*, iii., 655 ff.; MARSDEN'S
Early Puritans (1853); S. HOPKINS' *Puritans during the reigns of
Edward VI. and Elizabeth* (Boston, U.S.A., 1859); H. M. DEXTER'S
Congregationalism in the last 300 years (New York, 1880); JOHN
BROWNE'S *Hist. of Congregationalism and Memorials of the Churches
in Norfolk and Suffolk* (London, 1877); MASKELL'S *Marprelate Con-
troversy* (1845); PIERCE'S *Historical Introduction to the Marprelate
Tracts* (1909; bibliography, pp. 322-32); BRAGHT'S *Martyrology of
the Churches of Christ commonly called Baptist* (tr. Underhill, Hanserd
Knollys Soc., 2 vols. 1850, 1853); and articles on Barrow, Brown,
Cartwright, Field, and Wilcox, in the *Dict. of Nat. Biogr.*

On the Book of Common Prayer, see GASQUET and BISHOP,
Edward VI. and the Book of Common Prayer (1890); PROCTOR
and FRERE'S *New History of the Book of Common Prayer* (1901); and
H. GEE, *The Elizabethan Prayer Book and Ornaments* (1902). On
the Elizabethan religious settlement, see H. N. BIRT, *Elizabethan
Rel. Settlement* (1907); H. GEE, *The Elizabethan Clergy and the
Settlement of Religion* (1898); MACCOLL'S *Reformation Settlement*
(10th ed., 1901); and F. W. MAITLAND'S *Elizabethan Gleanings*, in
Engl. Hist. Rev. (xv., 120, 324, 530, 757; xviii., 517). For the constitutional position of the church, see MAKOWER'S *Constitutional
History of the Church of England* (Engl. transl., 1895), and, more
polemically, G. W. CHILD'S *Church and State under the Tudors*
(1890). The best contemporary statements of the Anglican position
are contained in JEWEL'S *Works* (Parker Soc., 1844-5) and HOOKER'S
Ecclesiastical Polity (1593-95; best ed. is Keble's, revised by Church
and Paget, 1888). For the biography of Anglican clergy see HOOK'S
Lives of the Archbishops of Canterbury (12 vols., 1860-76); WORDS-

APP. I. WORTH's *Ecclesiastical Biography* (4th ed., 1853); LE NEVE's *Fasti Eccl. Anglicanae* (ed. Hardy, 3 vols., 1854); and Stubbs' *Registrum Sacrum Anglicanum* (2nd ed., 1897).

(II.) CONSTITUTIONAL HISTORY.

Sir THOMAS SMITH's *De Republica Anglorum* (1583; ed. F. W. Maitland and L. Alston, 1906) gives a contemporary account of the constitution by one who had been secretary of state, ambassador, professor of civil law at Cambridge, provost of Eton, dean of Carlisle, master of requests, chancellor to the bishop of Ely, steward of the stannary court, clerk of the privy council, member of parliament, and chancellor of the order of the garter. Treatises on special institutions are LAMBARDE's *Eirenarcha: or of the Office of Justices of the Peace* (1581), and *Archeion: or a Commentary upon the High Courts of Justice* (completed, 1591; published, 1635); CROMPTON's *L'Authoritie et Jurisdiction des Courts* (1594); Sir JULIUS CAESAR's *Ancient State of the Court of Requests* (1597); HUDSON's *Treatise on the Star Chamber* (temp. James I.; published in *Coll. Juridica*, vol. ii., 1792); COWELL's *Interpreter* (1607); and POWELL's *Attorney's Academy* (1623). There is no adequate modern history of the constitution under the Tudors, neither Hallam nor Gneist attempting to deal with it in any detail; an excellent sketch is given in PROTHERO's introduction to his *Select Statutes*, etc. Aspects of the subject are treated in PORRITT's *Unreformed House of Commons* (2 vols., 1903; cheaper ed., 1909); DICEY's *Privy Council* (1887); and Lord EUSTACE PERCY's *Privy Council under the Tudors* (1908); DOWELL's *History of Taxation* (2nd ed., 4 vols., 1888); HUBERT HALL's *History of the Customs Revenue* (2 vols., 1885, 1892); BAILEY's *Succession to the Crown* (1879); HARBIN's *Hereditary Right* (1713); FIGGIS, *Divine Right of Kings* (1896); *Report of the Royal Commission on Ecclesiastical Courts*, 1883.

(III.) NAVAL AND MILITARY HISTORY.

For the administration of the navy see OPPENHEIM, *History of the Administration of the Royal Navy* (1509-1660, vol. i., 1896), and R. G. MARSDEN's *Select Cases from the Admiralty Courts* (Selden Soc., 1897, vol. ii., 1547-1602). For a list of unpublished MSS. see Sir J. K. LAUGHTON's bibliography in the *Cambridge Modern History* (iii., 816-17); Mr. J. S. Corbett has printed the documents relating to 1585-87, and Sir J. Laughton those relating to 1588 for the Navy Records Society (3 vols., 1894, 1898); others are calendared from the Foljambe MSS. (Hist. MSS. Comm., 15th Rep., App., pt. 5, 1897). Spanish naval documents are published in vol. xxxvi. of

NAVARETTE's *Documentos ineditos.* MONSON's *Naval Tracts,* which have been edited by Oppenheim for the Navy Records Society (1902), contain some valuable criticism. The standard English works are J. S. CORBETT's *Drake and the Tudor Navy* (2 vols., 1898; 2nd ed., 1899) and *The Successors of Drake* (1900); and the standard Spanish history is C. FERNANDEZ DURO's *Armada Española* (3 vols., Madrid, 1896-97). Some of the Spanish sources have been popular ised in FROUDE's *Spanish Story of the Armada* (1892).

Hakluyt's great collection of voyages, first completed in 3 vols. (fol., 1598-1600), has been re-edited in twelve (Glasgow, 1903-5, with an excellent introduction by W. Raleigh). The series is continued in *Hakluytus Posthumus, or Purchas, his Pilgrims* (4 vols., 1625; re-edited in 20 vols., Glasgow, 1905 ff.), and a number of other narra-tives have been printed by the Hakluyt Society. Selections have been edited by E. J. Payne (2 series, 1893-1900) and C. R. Beazley (1897). For biographies see BARROW's *Naval Worthies of Eliza-beth's Reign* (1845), and Sir J. Laughton's articles in the *Dict. of Nat. Biogr.* A considerable number of documents referring to explorers are calendared in the Colonial Calendar (vol. i., "America and the West Indies," 1574-1660; vol. ii., "East Indies, China and Japan," 1513-1616; and vol. ix., containing "Addenda" to "America and West Indies," 1574-1664). For general history, see ALEXANDER BROWN's *Genesis of the United States of America* (2 vols., 1890); WINSOR's *History of America* (8 vols., 1886-89); HUNTER's *History of British India* (2 vols., 1899-1900); M. EPSTEIN's *Early History of the Levant Company* (1908); H. G. ROSEDALE's *Queen Elizabeth and the Levant Company* (1904); J. VON HAMEL's *England and Russia* (1854); and EHRENBERG's *Hamburg und England im Zeitalter der Königin Elisabeth* (1896).

For military history, see THOMAS WHITHORNE's *Arte of Warre* (1560); RICH's *Pathway to Military Practice* (1587); Sir JOHN SMITH's *Discourses* (1590), and *Instructions, Observations, and Orders Mili-taire* (1594); Sir ROGER WILLIAMS' *Brief Discourse of War* (1590), and *Actions of the Low Countries* (1618); Sir H. KNYVETT's *Defence of the Realm* (ed. 1906); CLODE's *Military Forces of the Crown* (2 vols., 1869); GROSE's *Military Antiquities* (2 vols., 1801); MARKHAM's *Lives of Sir Francis and Sir Horace Vere* (1888); J. W. FORTESCUE's *History of the British Army* (vol. i., 1899); and J. D. COCKLE's *Bibliography of Military History* (1900).

(IV.) SOCIAL AND ECONOMIC HISTORY.

A collection of contemporary pieces is contained in *Social Tracts* (ed. from Arber's "English Garner," by Andrew Lang in 1904).

APP. I. See also CROWLEY'S *Works, Four Supplications of the Commons,* and
BRYNKELOW'S *Complaynt of Roderick Mors* (Early English Text
Soc. ; 1871, 1872, and 1874) ; *Ballads from MSS.* (ed. Furnivall,
Ballad Soc., 1868) ; LATIMER'S *Sermons* (Parker Soc.) ; LEVER'S
Sermons (ed. Arber, 1871) ; *Discourse of the Common Weal* (ed.
E. Lamond, 1893) ; T. WILSON'S *Discourse on Usury* (1572) ; P.
STUBBES' *Anatomie of Abuses* (1583 ; ed. Furnivall, 2 pts., 1877,
1882) ; F. TRIGGE'S *Humble Petition of two Sisters, the Church and
the Commonwealthe, for the restoring of their ancient Commons and
Liberties* (1604) ; and TUSSER'S *Five Hundred Points of good Husbandry* (1573 ; re-ed. 1878). Useful modern monographs are :
E. P. CHEYNEY'S *Social Changes in England in the Sixteenth Century* (1895) ; LEADAM'S *Domesday of Inclosures* (Royal Hist. Soc., 2
vols., 1897) ; R. RUDING'S *Annals of the Coinage* (3rd ed., 3 vols.,
1840) ; W. B. RYE'S *England as Seen by Foreigners* (1865 ; *cf. Trans.
Roy. Hist. Soc.,* N.S., vi., 1-68, the " Duke of Pomerania's Journey
through England in 1602 ") ; HUBERT HALL'S *Society in the Elizabethan Age* (4th ed., 1901) ; STEPHENSON'S *The Elizabethan People*
(1910) ; TOULMIN SMITH'S *The Parish* (1857), and G. UNWIN'S *Industrial Organisation in the Sixteenth and Seventeenth Centuries* (1904).
The best general histories of economic subjects are : CUNNINGHAM'S
Growth of Industry and Commerce (3rd ed., 3 vols., 1896-1903) ;
SCHANZ'S *Englische Handelspolitik* (2 vols., 1881) ; THOROLD ROGERS'
History of Agriculture and Prices in England (vols. iii. and iv. ; 1882),
and ASHLEY'S *Economic History* (vol. i., pt. ii., 1893). For education,
see ROGER ASCHAM'S *Works* (ed. Giles, 4 vols., 1864-65) ; GABRIEL
HARVEY'S *Letter Book* (Camden Soc., 1884) ; MULCASTER'S *Positions*
(1581, ed. Quick, 1888) ; C. H. COOPER'S *Annals of Cambridge* (4
vols., 1842-52), and *Athenae Cantabrigienses* (2 vols., 1858-61) ; J.
BASS MULLINGER'S *Hist. of the University of Cambridge* (vol. ii.,
1884) ; WOOD'S *Athenae Oxonienses* (ed. Bliss, 4 vols., 1813-20) ;
CARLISLE'S *Endowed Grammar Schools* (2 vols., 1818) ; A. F. LEACH'S
English Schools at the Reformation (1896) ; and FOSTER WATSON'S
English Grammar Schools to 1660 (1908).

(v.) HISTORY OF LITERATURE.

Of an almost infinite number of works on this subject the most
useful histories and biographies are perhaps COURTHOPE'S *History of
English Poetry* (5 vols., 1895-1905) ; JUSSERAND'S *Literary History
of the English People* (ed. 1909, vol. iii. " The Age of Elizabeth ") ;
SIDNEY LEE'S *Life of Shakespeare* (1898) ; SAINTSBURY'S *History of
Elizabethan Literature* (ed. 1890) ; TAINE'S *History of English
Literature* (Engl. trans., new ed., 1906) ; A. W. WARD'S *History of*

English Dramatic Literature (2nd ed., 3 vols., 1899); R. P. APP. I.
WÜLCKER's *Geschichte der Englischen Literatur* (2 vols., 1906-7);
and vol. iii. of the *Cambridge History of Literature* (1909), which
contains a fuller bibliography. SECCOMBE and ALLEN's *Age of
Shakespeare* (3rd ed., 2 vols., 1910) is a good handbook with many
bibliographical notes. See also the volumes on Bacon, Shakespeare,
Sidney, and Spenser in the " English Men of Letters " series.

(VI.) IRELAND.

The Irish state papers in the Record Office have been calendared
by H. C. HAMILTON and E. G. ATKINSON in ten volumes (1509-1601),
and the Carew MSS. at Lambeth by J. S. BREWER and W. BULLEN
in five (1515-1603); the patent and close rolls have also been calendared by JAMES MORRIN (3 vols., 1509-1630), and among the most
useful of the publications of the deputy-keeper of the records for
Ireland is the *Calendar of Fiants* (6 vols., 1547-1603). The *Statutes
of Ireland at Large* have been published (Dublin, 8 vols., 1765);
(the Journals of the Irish House of Lords and House of Commons
begin in 1634 and 1613 respectively). LASCELLES' *Liber Munerum
publicorum Hiberniae* (2 vols., 1824, fol.; index in App. iii. to 9th
Rep. of Dep. Keeper of Records, Ireland, 1877) contains full details
of official appointments. COTTON's *Fasti Ecclesiae Hiberniae* (6 vols.,
1851-78) does the same for prelates of the established church, and
BRADY's *Episcopal Succession* (Rome, 1876-77) and P. F. MORAN's
Episcopal Succession in Ireland during the Reign of Elizabeth (1866) for
the Roman Catholic. The Acts of the Irish Privy Council (1556-71)
are in private hands, and have been calendared in App. iii. to the 15th
Rep. of the Hist. MSS. Comm. See also HAYMAN's *Unpublished
Geraldine Documents* (4 pts., 1870-81); SHIRLEY's *Original Letters
and Papers* (1851); CUELLAR's *Letter to Philip II.* (ed. 1896);
and LODGE's *Desiderata Curiosa Hibernica* (2 vols., 1772).

The two chief contemporary Irish narratives are the *Annals of
the Four Masters* (7 vols., 1851), and *Annals of Loch Cé* (2 vols.,
1871). Of English accounts may be mentioned STANIHURST's *De
Rebus in Hibernia Gestis* (1584), STAFFORD's *Pacata Hibernia* (ed.
1896), WARE's *Annales* (1664), SPENSER's *View* (in *Works*, ed.
Grosart, vol. i., 1880), FYNES MORYSON's *Itinerary* (ed. 1903, bk. i.,
chap. iii.), Sir J. DAVIS's *Discoverie of the State of Ireland* (1612) and
Historical Tracts (1786), HARINGTON's *Short View of the State of
Ireland in 1605* (ed. 1879), Sir T. RYVES' *Regiminis Anglicani De-
fensio* (1624), and COX's *Hibernia Anglicana* (2 vols., 1689). For
ecclesiastical affairs see MORAN, *Spicilegium Ossoriense* (3 series, 1874-
84); MANT's *History of the Church of Ireland* (2 vols., 1840); ROTH's

APP. I.   *Analecta* (2 vols., 1617-19); A. BELLESHEIM's *Geschichte der kath. Kirche in Irland* (3 vols., Mainz, 1890-91); and J. T. BALL's *Reformed Church of Ireland* (1886). The standard modern work is BAGWELL's *Ireland under the Tudors* (3 vols., 1885-90); see also C. L. FALKINER's *Illustrations of Irish History and Topography* (1904); HILL's *Macdonnells of Antrim* (1873); INGRAM's *Critical Examination of Irish History* (2 vols., 1900); Mrs. J. R. GREEN, *The Making of Ireland and its Undoing* (2nd ed., 1909); MORITZ BONN, *Die Englische Kolonisation in Irland* (2 vols., 1906); and R. DUNLOP's articles in *Cambridge Modern Hist.*, iii., 579-616, and on Sussex, H. Sidney, Perrot, Shane O'Neill, Tyrone, and O'Donnell in *Dict. of Nat. Biogr.* For bibliography, see J. KING's *Irish Bibliography* (1903) and R. DUNLOP in *Cambridge Modern History*, iii., 852-59.

(VII.) RELATIONS WITH SCOTLAND.

In addition to the calendars of State Papers, see the *Register of the Privy Council of Scotland* (vols. i.-vi., 1545-1604, and vol. xiv., Addenda, 1545-1625), edited by JOHN HILL BURTON and DAVID MASSON; the *Exchequer Rolls of Scotland* (vols. xviii.-xxii., 1543-94), edited by JOHN STUART, GEORGE BURNETT, and ÆNEAS MACKAY; and the *Register of the Great Seal of Scotland* (vols. iv.-vi., 1546-1609), edited by Sir J. B. PAUL and J. M. THOMSON; LABANOFF, *Letters, etc., de Marie Stuart* (7 vols., 1844); *Letters, etc., relating to Patrick, Master of Gray* (Bannatyne Club, 1835); ANDERSON's *Collections relating to Mary, Queen of Scots* (4 vols., 1727-28); SEPP's *Mary Stuart's Briefwechsel mit Antony Babington* (1886); BUCHANAN's *Detectioun* (1572); HERRIES' *Memoirs* (1836); KNOX's *History* (in *Works*, ed. Laing, 1846, vols. i., ii. and vi.); LESLEY's *History* (Bannatyne Club, 1830); MOYSIE's *Memoirs* (Bannatyne Club, 1830); and NAU's *History of Mary Stuart* (ed. Stevenson, 1883). Of modern works on Mary Stuart there is a plethora; "about fifty writers," says Lord ACTON (*Lectures on Modern History*, 1906, p. 149), "have considered the original evidences sufficiently to form something like an independent conclusion". It must suffice to mention B. SEPP's five volumes on Mary's fall (Munich, 1882-1888); HOSACK's *Mary Stuart and her Accusers* (2nd ed., 2 vols., 1870-74); T. F. HENDERSON's *Casket Letters* (2nd ed., 1890) and *Mary, Queen of Scots* (2 vols., 1905); SKELTON's *Maitland of Lethington* (2 vols., 1894); PHILIPPSON's *Hist. du Règne de Marie Stuart* (3 vols., 1891-92); ANDREW LANG's *History of Scotland* (vol. ii., 1902), and *Mystery of Mary Stuart* (ed. 1904); HAY FLEMING's *Mary, Queen of Scots* (2 vols., 1897-8); LADY BLENNERHASSETT, *Maria Stuart* (Munich, 1907), and T. G. LAW in *Cambridge Modern History*, iii., 260-93.

For the general history of Scotland, see HUME BROWN's *Hist. of* APP. I. *Scotland* (vol. iii., 1902); and RAIT's *Relations between England and Scotland* (1901).

(VIII.) ENGLAND'S FOREIGN RELATIONS.

For England's general position in European politics, see DE THOU, *Historia sui Temporis* (Frankfort, 5 vols., 1614); LAVISSE's *Histoire Générale* (vols. iv.-v., 1894-95); the *Cambridge Modern History* (vols. ii.-iii., 1903-4); PHILIPPSON's *West-Europa im Zeitalter von Philipp II., Elisabeth und Heinrich IV.* (1882, in Oncken's series); KRETSCH-MAR, *Die Invasionsprojekte* (1892); and SEELEY's *Growth of British Policy* (vol. i., 1895). For relations with the papacy, see RANKE's *Römische Päpste* (9th ed., 1889, vols. i.-ii.), and *History of England* (Engl. transl., vol. i., 1875); PALLAVICINI's *Istoria del Concilio di Trento* (4 vols., 1833); SARPI's *Istoria del Conc. di Trento* (1619); HÜBNER's *Sixtus V.* (Engl. transl., 2 vols., 1872). For England's relations with Spain, see ARMSTRONG's *Charles V.* (2 vols., 1902); STIRLING-MAXWELL's *Don John* (2 vols., 1883); DURO's *Antonio Perez en Inglaterra* (Madrid, 1890); BROSCH, *Habsburgische Vermäh-lungsplane mit Elisabeth (Mitth. des Inst. für Oesterr. Geschichtsfor-schung;* Innsbruck, 1889). For relations with France, see A. L. PARIS, *Négociations du Règne de François II.* (1841); H. DE LA FERRIÈRE, *Les Valois et le xvime Siècle* (1879); AUMÂLE, *Les Princes de Condé* (2 vols., 1863-64); FORNERON, *Les Ducs de Guise* (2 vols., 1878); WHITEHEAD's *Coligny* (1904); PARADOL, *Elisabeth et Henri IV., 1595-8* (1885); and LAFLEUR DE KERMAINGANT, *L'Ambassade de France en Angleterre, 1598-1602* (2 vols., 1886). For Elizabeth's dealings with the Netherlands, see MOTLEY's *Dutch Republic* and *United Netherlands* (ed. 1903, 3 vols. and 4 vols.); KERVYN DE LETTENHOVE, *Les Huguenots et les Gueux* (6 vols., 1883-85); and J. P. BLOK, *Geschiedenis van het Nederlandsche Volk* (Engl. tr., 4 pt., 1898-1907).

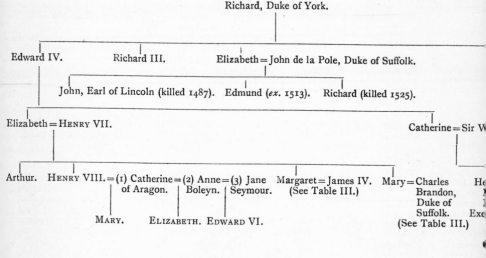

Richard, Duke of York.

Edward IV.   Richard III.   Elizabeth = John de la Pole, Duke of Suffolk.

John, Earl of Lincoln (killed 1487).   Edmund (*ex.* 1513).   Richard (killed 1525).

Elizabeth = HENRY VII.   Catherine = Sir W

Arthur.   HENRY VIII. = (1) Catherine = (2) Anne = (3) Jane   Margaret = James IV.   Mary = Charles   He
                          of Aragon.   Boleyn.   Seymour.   (See Table III.)   Brandon,
                                                                                       Duke of
                          MARY.   ELIZABETH. EDWARD VI.   Suffolk.   Exe
                                                                                      (See Table III.)

It is noticeable that Henry Stafford, 2nd Duke of Buckingham, his son the 3rd Duke, his two great
4th Duke of Norfolk, were all executed for treason, while two other great-great-grandsons, William Staff
The De la Poles, the Poles, and the Courtenays were hardly more fortunate.

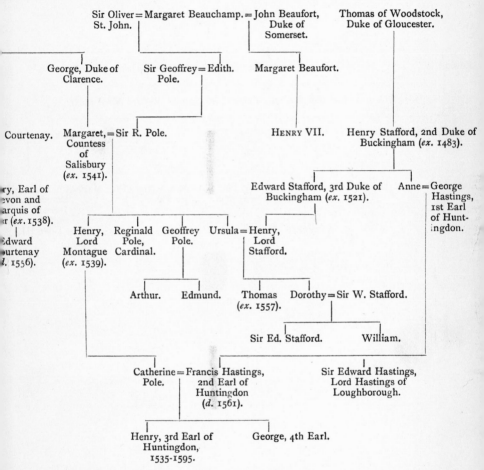

Sir Oliver = Margaret Beauchamp. = John Beaufort,
St. John.   Duke of
                       Somerset.

Thomas of Woodstock,
Duke of Gloucester.

George, Duke of   Sir Geoffrey = Edith.   Margaret Beaufort.
Clarence.   Pole.

Courtenay.   Margaret, = Sir R. Pole.   HENRY VII.   Henry Stafford, 2nd Duke of
           Countess   Buckingham (*ex.* 1483).
           of
           Salisbury
           (*ex.* 1541).

ry, Earl of   Edward Stafford, 3rd Duke of   Anne = George
evon and   Buckingham (*ex.* 1521).   Hastings,
arquis of   1st Earl
r (*ex.* 1538).   Henry,   Reginald   Geoffrey   Ursula = Henry,   of Hunt-
                Lord   Pole,   Pole.   Lord   ingdon.
Edward   Montague   Cardinal.   Stafford.
ourtenay   (*ex.* 1539).
d. 1556).

Arthur.   Edmund.   Thomas   Dorothy = Sir W. Stafford.
                             (*ex.* 1557).

Sir Ed. Stafford.   William.

Catherine = Francis Hastings,   Sir Edward Hastings,
Pole.   2nd Earl of   Lord Hastings of
         Huntingdon   Loughborough.
         (*d.* 1561).

Henry, 3rd Earl of   George, 4th Earl.
Huntingdon,
1535-1595.

grandsons, Thomas Stafford and the Earl of Surrey (see Table II.), and his great-great-grandson, the
rd and Henry Howard, and a great-great-great-grandson were imprisoned in the Tower on like charges.

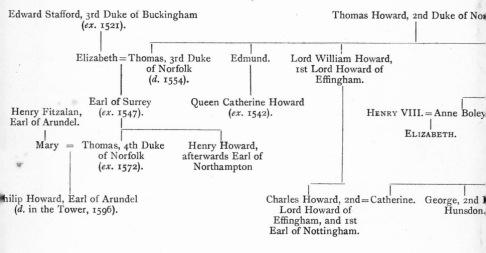

Edward Stafford, 3rd Duke of Buckingham
(*ex.* 1521).

Thomas Howard, 2nd Duke of Nor

Elizabeth = Thomas, 3rd Duke
of Norfolk
(*d.* 1554).

Edmund.

Lord William Howard,
1st Lord Howard of
Effingham.

Henry Fitzalan,
Earl of Arundel.

Earl of Surrey
(*ex.* 1547).

Queen Catherine Howard
(*ex.* 1542).

HENRY VIII. = Anne Boley

ELIZABETH.

Mary = Thomas, 4th Duke
of Norfolk
(*ex.* 1572).

Henry Howard,
afterwards Earl of
Northampton

Philip Howard, Earl of Arundel
(*d.* in the Tower, 1596).

Charles Howard, 2nd = Catherine.
Lord Howard of
Effingham, and 1st
Earl of Nottingham.

George, 2nd
Hunsdon.

KINSFOLK.

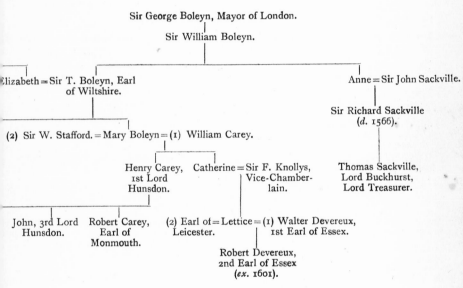

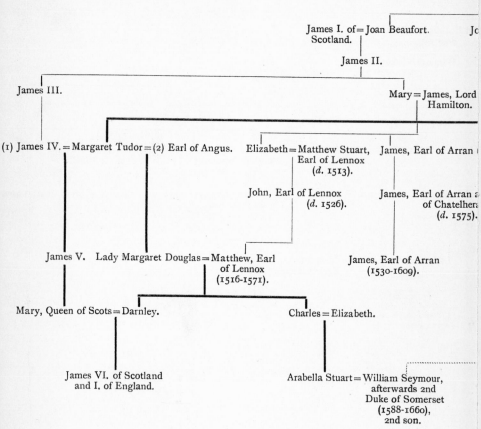

James I. of = Joan Beaufort.   Jo
Scotland.

James II.

James III.

Mary = James, Lord
Hamilton.

(1) James IV. = Margaret Tudor = (2) Earl of Angus.   Elizabeth = Matthew Stuart,   James, Earl of Arran
Earl of Lennox
(*d.* 1513).

John, Earl of Lennox   James, Earl of Arran a
(*d.* 1526).   of Chatelher;
(*d.* 1575).

James V.   Lady Margaret Douglas = Matthew, Earl   James, Earl of Arran
of Lennox   (1530-1609).
(1516-1571).

Mary, Queen of Scots = Darnley.   Charles = Elizabeth.

James VI. of Scotland   Arabella Stuart = William Seymour,
and I. of England.   afterwards 2nd
Duke of Somerset
(1588-1660),
2nd son.

The Stuart descent from Henry VII. is indica

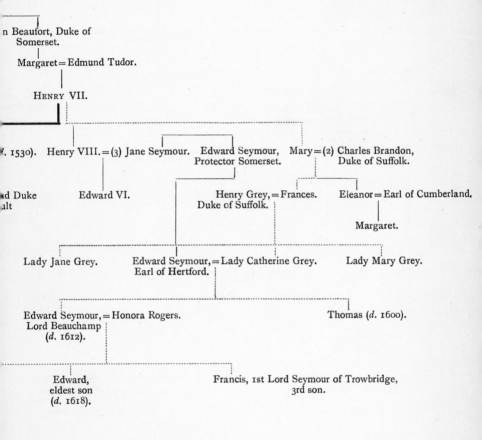

n Beaufort, Duke of
    Somerset.

    Margaret = Edmund Tudor.

      HENRY VII.

7. 1530).   Henry VIII. = (3) Jane Seymour.   Edward Seymour,   Mary = (2) Charles Brandon,
                                 Protector Somerset.   Duke of Suffolk.

d Duke   Edward VI.   Henry Grey, = Frances.   Eleanor = Earl of Cumberland.
lt   Duke of Suffolk.

                                                   Margaret.

   Lady Jane Grey.   Edward Seymour, = Lady Catherine Grey.   Lady Mary Grey.
                 Earl of Hertford.

Edward Seymour, = Honora Rogers.   Thomas (*d.* 1600).
  Lord Beauchamp
    (*d.* 1612).

        Edward,   Francis, 1st Lord Seymour of Trowbridge,
      eldest son   3rd son.
     (*d.* 1618).

ed by ———, the Suffolk descent by ·············· .

INDEX.

33 *

ABERDEEN : THE UNIVERSITY PRESS.